A HISTORY OF THE EARLY ENGLISH TEXT SOCIETY

VOLUME I

Frederick James Furnivall:
Early Life and Career, 1825–c.1864

EARLY ENGLISH TEXT SOCIETY
O.S. 364

2025

Frederick James Furnivall as a young man
© National Portrait Gallery

A HISTORY OF THE EARLY ENGLISH TEXT SOCIETY

VOLUME I

FREDERICK JAMES FURNIVALL:
EARLY LIFE AND CAREER, 1825–*c.*1864

BY

HELEN LEITH SPENCER

Published for
THE EARLY ENGLISH TEXT SOCIETY
by the
OXFORD UNIVERSITY PRESS
2025 for 2024

OXFORD
UNIVERSITY PRESS

Great Clarendon Street, Oxford, OX2 6DP,
United Kingdom

Oxford University Press is a department of the University of Oxford.
It furthers the University's objective of excellence in research, scholarship,
and education by publishing worldwide. Oxford is a registered trade mark of
Oxford University Press in the UK and in certain other countries

© Early English Text Society 2025

The moral rights of the author have been asserted

First edition published in 2025

Impression: 1

All rights reserved. No part of this publication may be reproduced, stored in
a retrieval system, or transmitted, in any form or by any means, without the prior
permission in writing of Oxford University Press, or as expressly permitted by law,
by licence, or under terms agreed with the appropriate reprographics rights
organization. Enquiries concerning reproduction outside the scope of the above
should be sent to the Rights Department, Oxford University Press, at the address
above

You must not circulate this book in any other form
and you must impose this same condition on any acquirer

British Library Cataloguing in Publication Data
Data available

ISBN 978–0–19–893408–0

Typeset by John Waś, Oxford
Printed in Great Britain
on acid-free paper by
TJ Books Ltd, Padstow, Cornwall

Links to third party websites are provided by Oxford in good faith and
for information only. Oxford disclaims any responsibility for the materials
contained in any third party website referenced in this work

PREFACE

Formal study of medieval English texts began in earnest in the nineteenth century, when the Early English Text Society (EETS) was created, though its roots lie in earlier traditions of study descending from the seventeenth- and eighteenth-century antiquarians and their successors. To this English antiquarianism were annexed, with varying amounts of enthusiasm, the methods propounded in 'scientific' study of the Germanic languages, usually by Germans. English speakers who were curious about the history of languages became excited by the developments in comparative philology associated with the names of Jakob Grimm, Franz Bopp, and the Dane Rasmus Rask. Philology was proclaimed as a 'science'—a term of huge approbation and validation in the mid-nineteenth century. Yet, though it was thrilling for lay people to observe the gymnastics that words had undergone in some obscure prehistory on which it was entertaining to speculate, few had the necessary linguistic knowledge or understanding to unravel these mysteries themselves. One of these lay people was the lawyer, long-time member and Secretary of the London Philological Society, and founder in 1864, of the EETS, Frederick James Furnivall (1825–1910).

Though it is *vieux jeu* to speak of great men, it is difficult to know how else to describe Furnivall, though rather than born great, he was one who achieved greatness, which was recognized by his contemporaries after a vast amount, and many years, of hard and patient slog. He was also larger than life. It is all too easy to be distracted from his achievements by his undoubted eccentricities, his waywardness, and his expansive and colourful personality. Like him or loathe him (and many did both), Furnivall used his influence single-mindedly throughout his life in support of his causes. As a young man, philanthropy and idealism distracted him from the comfortable middle-class life as a lawyer planned for him by his father. He became a Christian Socialist, and consequently a founding teacher at the London Working Men's College, with which he was associated all his adult life. And, as a prominent member of the London Philological Society, he was intimately involved with its great project: the all-encompassing historical dictionary, which eventually became the *Oxford English Dictionary* (*OED*), with which the EETS has enjoyed a symbiotic relationship from the start. Furnivall was general editor of the dictionary before handing over to James Murray. As if this were not enough, he founded seven publishing and literary societies, which, even in an age when such societies proliferated, was a formidable achievement. He and they were at the heart of the Victorian literary establishment, London-based, as the literary establishment has always tended to be, but outreach was part of Furnivall's agenda. He knew and corresponded with just about everybody in this world, from working men and working women—one of whom he married—to prime ministers, bishops, literary lions, and their wives—Furnivall could be as gallant as the next man.

Furnivall was involved in many of the educational and cultural movements of the second half of the nineteenth century. As a young man he became a lifelong friend and admirer of John Ruskin. Through Ruskin he also came to know the leading figures at the heart of the Gothic revival and the members of the Pre-Raphaelite Brotherhood; he shared their passion for King Arthur and their idealizing of the medieval working man, to which Ruskin contributed so greatly. Furnivall's own medieval studies blended scholarship with sentiment and patriotism to powerful effect. The medieval revival demanded access to source materials in huge quantities and at high speed. Through the EETS, which was for decades the dominant publisher of medieval English literature, Furnivall and his team of editors pioneered the printing of medieval texts on an unprecedented scale. Just as a beginning, thanks to Furnivall's enthusiasm and drive, the EETS in the nineteenth century published the majority of the Middle English Arthuriana, though even Furnivall confessed himself daunted by the *longueurs* of the romances written by the fifteenth-century hack Henry Lovelich, while still stoutly averring that they must be published. English men and women, Furnivall and his associates believed, should take ownership of their literature and language through formal and serious study of a kind which had hitherto been mostly conducted by German scholars, whose pre-eminence they ruefully acknowledged.

If we think back to 1864, when the Early English Text Society was founded, it is obvious that education and educational opportunities were very different. It would be absurd, even in the interests of promotion, to pretend that the existence of the EETS was a *cause* of change. And yet it is not preposterous to affirm that the EETS did, indeed, contribute to changes, especially in higher education in England. Furnivall was part of a circle actively concerned to widen access to education, including adult learning and education of women. He and his friends believed passionately that study of English literature and language should be an essential part of the curriculum. He wished to make English literature of all times (not just early English) available in inexpensive publications to any who could afford them, so that people could take an informed pride in their cultural heritage. And membership of the EETS has never intentionally been limited to scholars, but was open to anyone who could afford the deliberately moderate subscription. Furnivall's twentieth-century successors shared and continued these liberal principles.

Alongside Victorian giants, and some undoubted eccentrics (the two categories are not mutually exclusive), the dramatis personae of this story are largely composed of public-spirited professors, young Victorian working men and women, peers, scholars, intellectuals, amateurs, antiquaries, autodidacts, clergy, men and women of letters, and lexicographers. Even the London Ballast-Heavers played an indirect part when their grievances moved Furnivall to plunge into public life, embarking on what would now be termed cold calling, and, in the process, honing his innate brazen impudence into the fearsome soliciting tool which he needed later to get important people to co-operate in his publishing societies. Thanks to Furnivall's support for women's scholarship, which went further than the common use by men of letters of the assistance of the women with whom they shared their home, or whom they recruited, women, too, were quickly involved in his editing mission. It must be admitted, however, that, despite his enthusiasm, Victorian women editors were scarce, though Lucy Toulmin Smith was one who edited for the Society (completing her father's work). She also contributed to other EETS editions. It was commoner for women to act as transcribers and copyists, and they included Furnivall's future wife, Eleanor, as well as his young helper, Teena Rochfort Smith, with whom he was romantically involved in the early 1880s. Teena's tragic story was not only one of a young life cut short in an appalling manner, but one of a determined young scholar born before the opportunities were available to her to achieve her potential.

It has already been indicated how important Anglo-German relations have been in this story—they have by no means been always hostile. Admirably trained in the 'scientific' methods of the 'new philology' and textual criticism, German professors in the nineteenth century were apt to regard English students of the language and editors as dilettantes and amateurs—as indeed many of them were, pending reform of the universities. English scholars had much to learn. They acknowledged the superiority which it would be difficult to deny, and admired German method, though also finding it heavy going, and while also defending their own tradition of diplomatic transcription of the manuscripts. British scholars pointed out that, unlike the Germans, *they* could more easily gain access to what they saw as *their* manuscript libraries. And yet they often had German intellectual friends. Many German scholars edited for Furnivall, and he was a beacon of hospitality and kindness in an unfriendly country when they came to London. He even received the ultimate German acknowledgement of his services to its scholars and early English literature: an honorary doctorate from the University of Berlin. These intellectual ambiguities were irritated by rising political tension between Britain and the newly unified Germany in the years leading up to the First World War. Moreover, it must be stressed that, despite the unification of Germany in 1871, all Germans and German-speaking peoples were not alike, nor liked each other—it is a vast understatement to say there were many political cross-currents, and it is in many respects misleading to speak of nineteenth-century 'German' scholars in the aggregate.

Perhaps enough has been said to explain my decision to devote much of the first two volumes, especially the first, to a biography of Furnivall. Two biographies of Furnivall have previously been written, and there are biographical notices in addition to these. But there is more to say: Furnivall's interests were many, and like other busy Victorians, his correspondence was enormous. William Benzie's offers an admirably comprehensive and thorough account of what Furnivall did and when. Furnivall's friend John Munro's concise, but excellent, account gives a more personal portrait by a man who was able to discuss his biography with Furnivall himself, and who said simply: 'I knew him, and loved him.' Readers are referred to these biographies, from which I have gained much. This said, any biography of Furnivall will have its limitations: he was not simply the sum of his achievements. Like other great men of the period, much about him remains unknowable. As Evelyn Waugh said of William Holman Hunt (Waugh's distant relative):

The great men of the mid-Victorian era imposed themselves on their immediate posterity when no apparatus existed to record their words. They imposed not only their achievements but their reticence.... We know very little of their private lives, particularly of their pleasures. Some traces have been left of their early manhood... but from the moment they marry we are given only a record of professional triumphs and official honours.[1]

[1] 'The Only Pre-Raphaelite', reprinted from *The Spectator*, in Diana Holman Hunt, *My Grandfather*, 293–4.

Much of this applies to Furnivall—though we have many of his letters. We know more about his early manhood than his later life, which is largely subsumed in his literary work. And Furnivall, after his marriage, took care to keep at least some family difficulties private. But what, perhaps, could usefully be enlarged upon in the present study is the extent to which he was known to ever-widening circles of acquaintance, and what an intimate part he played in the Victorian literary and social scene, in which he was very well known. He was by no means a 'medievalist' in the narrow sense, to which current academic practice has accustomed us, but a man of letters as well as a prominent and well-known individual whom his contemporaries found impossible to regard with indifference. He was a major figure in British literary and political society. He did not compartmentalize the many parts of his life; the EETS was inextricably and organically mixed up with his other publication societies and activities, which were all reflections of his wide-ranging literary interests and large personality. I hope readers may share my view that to attempt to limit the discussion severely to the EETS in the nineteenth century would be artificial as well as impoverished.

Furnivall is deservedly becoming better known, particularly thanks to the rapidly growing interest in studying the scholars responsible for the scholarship upon which the traditions of academic pedagogy and research have been built: 'medievalism' in its recent and increasingly current sense as the study of post-medieval interest in and perceptions of the Middle Ages. The work of David Matthews and others on Furnivall and nineteenth-century scholarship has been extensive, and earlier accounts by Derek Pearsall and Derek Brewer have also drawn attention to the peculiar fascination and influence of this extraordinary man. To offer an overview of this developing discipline, though valuable, would not be appropriate in the present context. There is a danger in becoming too introspective in what is essentially a history of the EETS. David Matthews and co-workers in this subject have themselves charted the growth and origins of 'medievalism studies' in the modern sense. I refer readers to modern scholarship while also making a point of going back wherever possible to the huge reservoir of primary materials—correspondence, diaries, and other records. There has been, inevitably, a tendency for researchers to concentrate on the aspects of Furnivall's life which especially concern them, especially his literary career, but it soon becomes apparent that his activities as a young man, when he threw himself into the labour unrest of the late 1840s and early

1850s, and the consequent efforts to improve working conditions, were an essential part of his later work as a publisher and scholar of early English. The special features which distinguished the Early English Text Society from other nineteenth-century literary societies were its constitution as a co-operative and democratic association, along the lines of the Christian Socialists' experiments in backing trade associations. Co-operation and association were essential parts of Furnivall's character, fundamental to his beliefs, and he lived out his democratic visions through his antiquarian research. He firmly believed in reading the past as a commentary on the present.

One of the medieval texts which was an especially rich resource of information about fourteenth-century labourers' working conditions, their hopes and fears, was *Piers Plowman*. W. W. Skeat's editions of the three main versions of this text for the EETS are among the most important volumes which the EETS published in the nineteenth century, and one of its greatest achievements.[2] On the basis of his collected 'parallel extracts' taken from his extensive comparison of many manuscripts,[3] Skeat was the first scholar to show clearly that there were three distinct versions of the poem. He did not think he was quite the first to suspect this, but it was he who named them 'A', 'B', and 'C'. These three editions formed the essential foundation for his monumental parallel text edition, published in 1886 by Oxford University Press.[4] However, I hope it is not too outrageous to mention here the chapter on this text which I decided in the end *not* to write, though it was contemplated in the beginning. The history of editing *Piers Plowman* has already been expertly described in the detailed account by Charlotte Brewer, who enjoyed privileged access to the Skeat family's papers.[5] I did not feel that there was much that I could usefully add to its editorial history in the nineteenth century, though I do describe the broad outlines of Skeat's work. I return to the topic in the concluding volume, when *Piers Plowman* caused a crisis in the EETS's affairs at a critical period of its history, during and after the Second World War.

---

[2] *The Vision of Piers Plowman I, Text A*, EETS, OS 28 (London, 1867); *William Langland: The Vision of Piers Plowman II, Text B*, EETS, OS 38 (London, 1869); *William Langland: The Vision of Piers Plowman III, Text C*, EETS, OS 54 (London, 1873). See also *William Langland: The Vision of Piers Plowman IV, IV(ii)*, EETS, OS 67, 81 (London, 1877, 1884).

[3] *William Langland: Parallel Extracts from 45 MSS of Piers Plowman*, ed. Skeat, EETS, OS 17 (1866).

[4] *The Vision of William Concerning Piers the Plowman*, ed. Skeat.

[5] Brewer, *Editing* Piers Plowman.

Volume II will treat the history of the Early English Text Society from 1864 to 1910, and volume III from 1910 to 1984. After 1984, when Professor Norman Davis retired as Director, it becomes necessary to describe living persons known to me. Detachment becomes difficult. Meanwhile, since this is a history of the EETS, a book society which still has an ongoing history, it may be appropriate, and of interest to those who come after us, to add a note of the circumstances in which the first two volumes of this history were revised and substantially rewritten. The worldwide COVID-19 pandemic reached the UK in late January, 2020. The Coronavirus Act of the same year gave the four UK governments emergency powers which had not been used since the Second World War. Three periods of lockdown in 2020–21, during which the population was required not to travel, unless this were essential, and as far as possible to stay at home, were intermitted by brief and partial easing of the restrictions. Universities moved to online teaching and libraries closed, though I was fortunate to have access to the Bodleian Library's considerable online materials. Much historical research had to be put on hold. I, in common with other writers and researchers, was unable to visit archives, or hear—let alone get hold of—new books or check references. The effect on the present study has been to confirm its heavy dependency on contemporary nineteenth-century accounts. But, as noticed above, this is not necessarily a bad thing: I have adopted a policy of quoting extensively from primary sources. They are typically lively, impassioned, outspoken, racy—even slanderous. Furnivall, his friends, and acquaintances would be the merest shadows of themselves in paraphrase.

* * *

Although one would not wish to succumb to the frank hero-worship practised by Furnivall or some of his successors, like R. W. Chambers, it is nevertheless true that the Society has been served by just about all the best-known names of nineteenth- and twentieth-century medieval literary scholarship. It is perhaps appropriate to say something briefly here of my involvement with some of the EETS's leading scholars, and with the EETS itself. Also, how I came to write this history. It has been an honour to have been associated with these figures, either through their writings, or from personal knowledge, as an officer of the EETS's Council. When, as an undergraduate, *fer in the north*, I first purchased one of those distinctive brown volumes (the reissued Skeat B-Text of *Piers Plowman*) I felt decidedly presumptuous. But my graduate supervisor at Oxford, Dr Pamela Gradon, then the Society's Editorial Secretary, was typically no-nonsense in signing me up as a member. Professor Norman Davis interviewed and accepted me for admission to Oxford, even though I arrived at Merton College late and woebegone after a journey in which one bus was involved in an accident and the second broke down in High Wycombe (this before the coming of the M40). My youthfully presumptuous idea that I might re-edit Frances Mack's *Seinte Marherete* (OS 193)—which I soon dropped—must have amused the EETS's then Director (not that I knew he was).

Years later, while I was teaching in the English Department at Bristol, his successor as Director, Professor John Burrow, suggested that I might like to take on the post of Executive Secretary. I agreed. Respect for the EETS outweighed my well-founded doubts of my abilities in the occult art called 'balancing the books', despite the efforts of the outgoing Secretary, Mr T. F. Hoad, to initiate me into these mysteries. Soon afterwards, when the Editorial Secretary, Professor Malcolm Godden, announced his intention to step down, I boldly proposed myself to John Burrow as Malcolm's successor, telling him I thought I'd be rather more successful at dealing with editors' *amour propre* than with figures. John was amused, but took me at my word and supported me as I learned on the job. However, I defer to my predecessors in the role, especially Dr Mabel Day and Dr Robert Burchfield, who have managed both the accounts *and* the editors with aplomb. In publishing, things sometimes go wrong, usually when least expected, at the worst possible time, and needing to be sorted NOW! But, on the credit side, I have gained enormously from working with the editors, most of whom have been models of patience and courtesy, despite the rude shocks involved in preparing their intellectual offspring to meet their public. It has been a privilege. I am sorry to record that John Burrow's death, on 23 October 2017, was announced as I was first revising these remarks—I owe him much, as both medieval scholar and colleague.

'Had I wist' is a wonderful thing. I did not know when I became Editorial Secretary that, in due course, I might be asked to write the EETS's story. Opportunities to speak to people about their memories, and to secure records and photographs, passed before it could be known that they were wanted. I should have paid more attention at the time, as, for example, when Terry Hoad showed me the famous EETS cupboard, a magnificent specimen of outsize Victorian or Edwardian bespoke joinery, of which I can only remember the rows of EETS volumes in the upper shelves (a space they had long outgrown) and a fascinating series of drawers with names on them like 'C. T. Onions'. It was not suited to the nomadic life of travelling round from one new officer to the next, and went to Mallams, the Oxford auctioneers.

ACKNOWLEDGEMENTS

Missed opportunities notwithstanding, a task such as this incurs many debts, which I am glad to acknowledge. The thanks expressed here extend to the entire work, as it seems churlish to parcel out gratitude by century. I am grateful, first, to the Council of the Early English Text Society for entrusting me with the writing of this history and giving me access to the Society's early records, which have now returned to Oxford and been married up with the later, and ever-growing, archive. I also acknowledge the kindness of the archivists at King's College London, where the early records were being accommodated, appropriately so as King's also holds a rich collection of Furnivall's papers. Our archive, like the cupboard, was not suited to the nomadic life and needed a secure home.

I owe a special debt to the Leverhulme Trust for the award of a Research Fellowship in 2014–15 which made much of the writing possible, as well as two essential visits to libraries in the United States.

It will be apparent that much use has been made in the present study of the resources of genealogical research. I have used the services of the UK based website, Findmypast (created 1965).

Many libraries have allowed me access to their special collections. The librarians in charge of the Special Collections at King's College London gave invaluable assistance during my many visits. In addition to the Bodleian Library in Oxford, Cambridge University Library, and the British Library, I am pleased to record the generosity of Birmingham University Library, which holds C. T. Onions's papers, and of University College, London for access to R. W. Chambers's papers. Dr Marianne Hansen and her staff in the Special Collections, Bryn Mawr College, Pennsylvania, made me most welcome during my two weeks' stay reading through Hope Emily Allen's letters and papers, as did the Huntington Library, San Marino, California, which holds one of the two largest collections of Furnivall's papers. Dr Martin Maw and his colleagues in the archive of Oxford University Press have offered much assistance, and I acknowledge the permission of the Delegates of the Press to quote from this material. I also most gratefully acknowledge the Tolkien Estate for permission to consult and to quote from J. R. R. Tolkien's papers, deposited in the Bodleian. In addition to letters and papers, I also owe thanks to Balliol College, Exeter College,

ACKNOWLEDGEMENTS

Lady Margaret Hall, The Queen's College, and Somerville College in Oxford for their generosity in readily allowing me to consult scarce printed material. Witold Szcyglowski, Librarian of the Working Men's College, gave valuable information about the College's holdings.

I am grateful to many for sharing their memories and impressions with me, and for discussing the history. I cannot mention them all here, but silence certainly does not mean indifference. It is sad to record that the autumn and winter of 2021 saw the deaths of three members of the EETS's Council to whom I owe special thanks for their help and support in writing this history. Professor Anne Hudson, former Director, as well as long-time member of Council, believed I could write this book—indeed, the idea was hers—and she patiently listened to my disquisitions on the subject, while offering many suggestions, as well as her memories of the Society under Norman Davis. Mr Richard Hamer and Professor Derek Pearsall read and reported on the typescript of the first draft of this book on behalf of the EETS Council, as did a third, anonymous, reader. The book is stronger for all whom I approached for advice and suggestions, and for their patient attention to detail. I must apologize to the third reader that I have not adopted the recommendation to conform to the common and current practice in modern literary scholarship of conducting the discussion as a form of conversation with other scholars who have contributed to the subject. After careful consideration, I decided that this procedure was not suited to the largely biographical narratives I was attempting to write. Furthermore, as this form of discussion essentially assumes a coterie of fellow academics, it seemed inappropriate in a volume intended for publication by the EETS. Though the Society largely serves the academic community, it does not do so exclusively, and never has done. It was founded in an ardently democratic and patriotic spirit by a lawyer of staunchly liberal politics to serve anyone interested in British history and that of the English language. Furnivall's successors, though they have all been members of the academic community, have always honoured the founder's wishes. A conversation between members of an in-crowd is apt to deter others who might have an interest.

This is also the moment to acknowledge my special debt of gratitude to the unfortunate member of Council to whose lot it fell to read and report on this heavily revised and rewritten first volume: Professor Richard Beadle. I have done my best to implement his advice and recommendations, most fairly and generously made, and scrupulously considered. Our research interests overlap, and throughout my work on the history he has most generously shared with me his research on Henry Bradshaw's letters and papers, and I thank him for many other insights and discussions. He kindly agreed to read the opening chapters when I was feeling considerable anxiety on the subject, and needed some assurance that I was on the right lines. Asking him if he could decipher more than I could of F. D. Maurice's agitated letters to Furnivall—with whom Maurice was justifiably annoyed—was a lighter moment while we were all quarantined in our studies.

Other members of the Council, including Professor Janet Bately, Professor J. A. Burrow, Dr. A. I. Doyle, Professor Douglas Gray, Professor Ralph Hanna, Professor Bella Millett, Professor Thorlac Turville-Petre, and the Director, Professor Vincent Gillespie, as well as Professor Daniel Wakelin, the Executive Secretary, and Mrs Jane Watkinson, then the Membership Secretary, have all given me information and every encouragement, as has Professor Richard Dance, my successor as Editorial Secretary, and thus responsible for overseeing the production of this book. Last, but certainly not least among my obligations to the Society, I owe a huge debt to our superb production team: our copy-editor, Dr Bonnie Blackburn, and our typesetter, who have offered tremendous professional and expert scholarly support during my time as Editorial Secretary, and have saved me from many errors.

Dr Helen Brookman discussed with me her research on nineteenth-century women scholars. Mrs Elizabeth Burchfield kindly shared her memories of her husband, Robert Burchfield, as did Professor E. G. Stanley. Mr Jonathan Dent, of the *Oxford English Dictionary*, has generously shared with me his knowledge of that strange and obstinately determined scholar Carl Horstmann, as well as giving me many other tip-offs, and I am grateful also to his colleague, Dr Peter Gilliver, for discussing his work with me before and after publication of his history of the *OED*. At an early stage, Professor John Hirsh discussed his research on Hope Emily Allen with me. Professor Michael Kuczynski, now himself a member of Council, has generously shared his work on Furnivall, as well as his memories of Professor George Kane.

It would be wonderful if there were no mistakes in a long and detailed study such as this—but nothing ventured, nothing gained. I accept full responsibility for those that doubtless remain. Finally, my thanks go to Richard Franklin for moral support, encouragement, and intelligent listening. Luckily, he is interested in history—up to a point!

H.L.S.
Honorary Director, EETS
Exeter College, Oxford

CONTENTS

LIST OF ILLUSTRATIONS	xix
ABBREVIATIONS	xx
A NOTE ON TRANSCRIPTIONS	xxii

Introduction. F. J. Furnivall: Philologist and Man of Many Passions 1

I. From Tory to 'Socialist': 1825–1858

1. F. J. Furnivall, 1825–1842: Early Years 25
2. Furnivall, 1841–1848: Cambridge, and Return to London 59
3. Lincoln's Inn and the London Working Men and Women: 1846–1852 78
4. Christian Socialism and Socializing: Prelude to the Working Men's College, 1851–1853 127
5. Beginnings of the Working Men's College, 1854–1857 164
6. Slander and Strife: Disagreements within the Working Men's College 203

II. How a Lincoln's Inn Lawyer Became an 'Editor of Old Books': 1858–1864

7. Furnivall and the Philological Society of London 273
8. Furnivall's First Editions: 'Wicked Birds', Handling Sin, and 'Rose-Pink Notions' 327
9. The Philological Society and the Beginnings of the EETS 393

APPENDICES

1. Correspondence Relating to the Appearance and History of Great Fosters House — 427
2. An Account by a Schoolboy of a Visit to the Working Men's College, October 1857, with a Report of the Address Given by John Ruskin — 434

BIBLIOGRAPHY — 437

INDEX — 464

LIST OF ILLUSTRATIONS

Frederick James Furnivall as a young man
© National Portrait Gallery   *Frontispiece*

PLATES
(*between pp. 202 and 203*)

1. Frederick Denison Maurice
   © National Portrait Gallery
2. Herbert Coleridge (1863). Murray Papers, MS 31
   © Bodleian Libraries, University of Oxford
3. William Alexander Dalziel (1862). Murray Papers, MS 31
   © Bodleian Libraries, University of Oxford
4. Eleanor Nickell Dalziel, with F. J. Furnivall and Arthur Cattlin (1862). Murray Papers, MS 31
   © Bodleian Libraries, University of Oxford
5. Captain George Morris Hantler, 19th Middlesex Rifles (1863). Murray Papers, MS 31
   © Bodleian Libraries, University of Oxford
6. Hensleigh Wedgwood (1863). Murray Papers, MS 31
   © Bodleian Libraries, University of Oxford
7. Henry Benjamin Wheatley (1864). Murray Papers, MS 31
   © Bodleian Libraries, University of Oxford
8. Edmund Brock (1866). Murray Papers, MS 31
   © Bodleian Libraries, University of Oxford

ABBREVIATIONS

ACLS	American Council of Learned Societies
Bodl.	Oxford, Bodleian Libraries
Chambers Papers	Preserved in the collections of University College London
CUL	Cambridge University Library
DNB	See *ODNB*
EETS	Early English Text Society
ES	Extra Series
OS	Original Series
SS	Supplementary Series
ELH	*English Literary History*
FSA	Fellow of the Society of Antiquaries
FU	Shelfmark of items in the Huntington Library, San Marino (CA), Furnivall Papers
HEA	Hope Emily Allen papers, Bryn Mawr College
JEGP	*Journal of English and Germanic Philology*
KCL	King's College London
MÆ	*Medium Ævum*
(P)MLA(A)	(Proceedings of the) Modern Language Association (of America)
ME	Middle English
eME	early Middle English
MLR	*Modern Language Review*
MP	*Modern Philology*
Murray Papers	Letters and papers of J. A. H. Murray, Bodleian Library, Oxford
NED	*New English Dictionary*. See also *OED*
NQ	*Notes and Queries*
NS	New Series
(O)*DNB*	(*Oxford*) *Dictionary of National Biography*
OE	Old English
OED	*The Oxford English Dictionary*, first edition, ed. James A. H. Murray, Henry Bradley, William A. Craigie, and Charles T. Onions (1884–1928); *Supplement and Bibliography* (1933); *Supplement*, ed. Robert W. Burchfield (1972–6); second edition, ed. John A. Simpson and Edmund S. C. Weiner (1989); *Additions Series*, ed. John A. Simpson, Edmund S. C. Weiner, and Michael Proffitt (1993–7); third edition, *OED Online*, ed. John A. Simpson (to 2013) and Michael

	Proffitt (2013–) (Oxford: Oxford University Press, 2000–), available at ⟨https://oed.com⟩
OUP	Oxford University Press
PBA	*Proceedings of the British Academy*
RES	*Review of English Studies*
SPCK	Society for Promoting Christian Knowledge
STS	Scottish Text Society
Tolkien Papers	Bodleian Library Tolkien Papers
TPS	*Transactions of the Philological Society*
Transactions	*Transactions of the New Shakspere Society*
UCL	University College London

A NOTE ON TRANSCRIPTIONS

The present study is reliant upon manuscript source materials: correspondence and diaries. The quotations from these materials are occasionally lightly edited, where necessary for the sense, but most of the transcriptions are broad, intended for a general readership. Most of the time, one can be confident that the authors were highly literate, and when they were not, the spelling errors and other non-standard usages are preserved in order to be faithful to the spirit of the source. Original punctuation and capitalization—both largely, but not entirely, corresponding to modern usage—are preserved. Ends of pages in letters are not indicated, except in a few cases where a more diplomatic style of transcription has been used (for reasons that are explained where they occur).

The following conventions are used:

If a writer has underlined a word, or words, for emphasis, they are italicized.

| A vertical is occasionally used to indicate the end of a page or folio.

\ /   Forward and reverse primes contain superscript letters and words, marked by the writer for insertion.

[ ]   Square brackets are used to mark editorial cmendations, usually explained by a corresponding footnote.

⟨ ⟩   Angle brackets indicate an erasure by the writer. If the erasure is legible, the content is contained within the angle brackets. Dots are sometimes used to indicate the number of letters erased.

INTRODUCTION
F. J. Furnivall: Philologist and Man of Many Passions

> Once geology was all the rage; now it is theology; soon it will be architecture, or medieval antiquities, or editions and codices.
> John Henry Newman, *Loss and Gain* (1848), ch. 5

A GUINEA FOR A COLOSSUS

It currently states on the dust jackets of EETS volumes that 'The Early English Text Society was founded in 1864 by Frederick James Furnivall, with the help of Richard Morris, Walter Skeat and others'. Skeat, Morris, and the 'others' cannot long be kept out of the picture, but the EETS was above all the creation of F. J. Furnivall. Furnivall was a colossus among colossi, one of those turbo-charged Victorians who make their puny successors feel tired merely to contemplate them. 'This colossal work', as Furnivall described his ambition to print all 'early English texts' within his lifetime, needed autocratic direction. And the early *Annual Reports* speak of the 'colossal task' which the Society had set itself. The original price of a year's subscription was a guinea, and the subscriber received a colossal amount of British literary real estate in return for this modest outlay. If not exact, 'British' is appropriate because, especially in the early days, the EETS was not particular about the exact provenance of its 'early English' texts, and Scottish, Welsh, and Irish material was cheerfully included in a way which would now cause sensitive nationalist eyebrows to rise.

Guineas were a genteel currency—other Victorian literary societies, including Furnivall's other enterprises, also priced their subscription in guineas. They had not existed as coins since 1816, when they were replaced after the Napoleonic Wars by the smaller 'sovereigns', worth £1. A guinea, then, speaks of a world of solid, assured, eighteenth-century standards of wealth, still remembered while gold sovereigns jingled in gentlemen's pockets. The men whom Furnivall taught in the London Working Men's College did not have too many sovereigns to jingle (nor did Furnivall himself). Nevertheless, several of the men served the EETS ably as transcribers, if not editors. They included the rising palaeontological star Harry Govier Seeley, and Furnivall also recruited from the Working Men his future brother-in-law, W. A. Dalziel, and John Munro as officers of the EETS Council. It must be allowed that the men who attended the College were not representatives of working men as a whole: they mostly came from the level of the skilled artisans and, as another of the College's founders phrased it, 'what may be called the working man stage of the lower middle class'[1]. Yet Furnivall as a young man and his associates at Lincoln's Inn did their share of slum visiting and had witnessed poverty at first hand. Furnivall's own lack of class prejudice was remarkable, but he was not blind to the distinctions, and his EETS was inevitably a mostly middle- and upper-class and institutional society. Furnivall was a practical man, as well as an idealist, and throughout his working life he set himself to wheedle and hector those who had guineas to give them to his societies for the sake of their country's heritage. Also, a guinea was a good round number to express £1. 1s. and thus a way of making a subscription, like luxury goods, sound rather less than it really was, and squeezing a bit more juice out of the subscribers to an impoverished society.

Furnivall's EETS was only a part of his increasingly grand schemes to bring the materials of English literature within the reach of ordinary people, and in the process he was never afraid to court controversy. He was a considerable public figure and prepared to make a great deal of noise in support of his causes. His friends and associates shared the breadth of his literary interests, even if they regretted his readiness to engage in quarrels. His seven publishing societies can for convenience be separated into two groups: those of an 'ancient' or philological character (the EETS, Chaucer, Ballad, and Wyclif Societies), and those which dealt with later writers (the New Shakspere, Browning, and Shelley Societies). Yet that this divide is artificial may be seen in the case of the New Shakspere Society. A large part of the EETS's reason for being was to provide the medieval context for understanding the conundrum, which so fascinated Furnivall and his contemporaries, of Shakespeare's 'genius'. And the New Shakspere became a home for materials relating to Tudor social history which had originally been destined for the EETS.

The New Shakspere, Browning, and Shelley Societies were intimately involved in Furnivall's life—he invested them with much of his personal concerns in a way that was less true of the others; indeed, valuable evidence for Furnivall's biography comes from his writings for these

[1] [Ludlow], *John Ludlow: The Autobiography*, 273.

societies. Thus, Furnivall's societies were all expressions of his personality, his formidable energy, and endlessly enquiring mind. Accordingly, though the EETS is the focus of this study, the biography of Furnivall here gives space to his other societies also. Members of Furnivall's circle worked for more than one of them. As Furnivall's research and literary interests expanded, he would found a new society to develop them, and rope in his friends to assist. In the process Furnivall developed his understanding of what publishing societies, including the EETS, could and should do. In particular, since they were all text societies, they mutually broadened and developed his ideas about the practice of editing. Any account of Furnivall's views of editing based solely on the EETS can give only part of the picture. This is not to devalue the previous work of scholars such as Antony Singleton; I have learned much from his excellent studies of the EETS. Yet he was constrained by the strict parameters of writing a doctoral thesis and concentrated particularly on details of editorial practice and organizational history within the EETS.[2]

Accordingly, not only Furnivall, but his friends, including the expert on dialect and phonetician Alexander Ellis and Henry Wheatley, the EETS's Treasurer, worked for his New Shakspere Society as well as the EETS. Arthur Snelgrove, of the London Hospital, was the Honorary Secretary of the New Shakspere Society, the Chaucer Society, the EETS, and the Ballad Society. Editors for the EETS, like F. D. Matthew (who would become the stalwart of the Wyclif Society), A. S. Napier, or Lucy Toulmin Smith, took an active part and gave papers at the New Shakspere Society, Lucy Toulmin Smith's contribution being a paper 'On the Bond-Story in the *Merchant of Venice* and a Version of it in the *Cursor Mundi*.'[3] If we leave the EETS aside for a moment, the picture becomes still more complicated when one considers the contributors to Furnivall's other literary ventures, and those with which he was associated. For example, Eleanor Marx, daughter of Karl Marx, and friend of Furnivall, outraged James Murray by her excessive claims for time spent

[2] Singleton, 'The Early English Text Society . . . a chapter'; id., 'The Early English Text Society . . . An Organizational History'.

[3] Given at the fifteenth meeting, 9 Apr. 1875, *Transactions*, p. iv. Matthew, who chaired meetings from time to time, also audited the New Shakspere Society's accounts (with E. Bell), as acknowledged at the 85th meeting of 9 Feb. 1883. His knowledge of German (which would prove essential to the Wyclif Society's success) was useful to the New Shaksperians seeking to keep up to date with German scholarship: thus, he contributed an 'Account of the German Shaksperian Society's *Jahrbuch*, 1876', *Transactions* (1875–6), Series 1, pp. 440–4. He supplied the 'valuable' Introduction to Furnivall's edition of *Shakspere's England: William Stafford's Compendious or briefe Examination*.

on working on the *NED*'s slips; she also translated writing by another of Furnivall's German Shakespeare experts, Nicolaus Delius.[4]

Furnivall's societies regularly advertised each other's publications and notices. The names of the EETS's Committee of Management were printed at the back of the New Shakspere Society's *Transactions*. Also, Furnivall used the same printer, Charles Childs, and the same publisher, Trübner, for his societies.[5] Nicholas Trübner & Co., which specialized in language work, published the Philological Society's material, and the Wyclif Society's, as well as Furnivall's edition of Bishop Percy's Ballads.[6] Childs had taken an active interest in the New Shakspere Society, as a 'liberal helper in its undertakings' and displaying the 'warm interest of a scholar' in its success. He was also, in the interests of scholarship, prepared to extend 'tick' to the Chaucer Society—it is a good illustration of the hand-to-mouth way in which all Furnivall's societies were run:

> I have also to thank Mr. Charles Childs our printer, whose interest in the objects of the Society made him at once consent to print our 1870 work, though hardly any of his 1868 bill was paid. That there is a difference between a printer who does care for literature and one who does not, I have reason to know; for in another Society notice was sent to me early in 1869, that not a line of that year's work should be printed till the balance of the 1868 bill was paid: *business* was a printer's business, not Literature, or even waiting three months for subscriptions to come in.[7]

Stephen Austin of Hertford, who also printed EETS volumes—and was maybe the printer alluded to by Furnivall as less generous in extending credit—was likewise a New Shaksperian.[8] 'Early English' encompassed the sixteenth century to an extent that the modern EETS would not now accept. Furnivall's transactions concerning the Bard were a logical extension of the EETS. They brought him to much wider public notice

[4] Murray, *Caught in the Web of Words*, 212; *Transactions*, 29th meeting, 8 Dec. 1876, p. xxviii. She also contributed a recitation of 'The Pied Piper of Hamelin' to the Browning Society's first Annual Entertainment in 1882 (*Transactions*, 3rd Annual Meeting , 4 July 1884, p. 137*).

[5] A. J. Ellis, Richard Morris, and Walter Skeat were also Vice-Presidents of the New Shakspere Society.

[6] *Bishop Percy's Folio MS.*, ed. Furnivall and Hales (1867).

[7] *The Ellesmere MS. of Chaucer's Canterbury Tales*, ed. Furnivall, 3.

[8] Austin's membership was recorded at the 29th meeting on 8 Dec. 1876. Stephen Austin (1804–92) was the descendant, and third to bear the name, of the founder of the company of printers, still trading as 'Stephen Austin and Sons Ltd'. Furnivall recorded Childs's recent death at the following meeting on 12 Jan. 1877, *Transactions*, Series 1 (1875–6).

in his own day than the EETS ever did and brought out all that was most characteristic of the man—best and worst. As he said himself a week before his opening address in UCL's Botany Theatre, 'Well, we are getting some fun out of "The New Shakspere Society", at any rate.'[9]

Though the other societies are all considered, it is not possible to do equal justice to them here. Readers are referred to studies published elsewhere of the Chaucer Society and Wyclif Society.[10] More space will be given to the New Shakspere Society than some might consider worthwhile. It has an understandable reputation for eccentricity, and certainly Furnivall's many hobby horses were exercised at the gallop. Moreover, thanks to his literary prominence, Shakespeare mattered more than 'early English', and Furnivall's Shakespearian quarrels with fellow men of letters were accordingly ferocious, and at times unbecoming. Yet the New Shakspere's purposes were serious, and it has been pointed out that this Society in particular owed much to Furnivall's growing awareness of the value of German scholarship, and its principles were entirely consonant with German understanding of the proper ways to conduct philological enquiry.[11]

Thus, many of the controversial aspects of Furnivall's scholarship were publicized through the New Shakspere and were discussed more loudly and clearly in this forum than they were in the EETS, but they were at the heart of the early English project too. The New Shakspere was a focus for hostile criticism of what was seen as Furnivall's reliance on 'scientific', professional German scholarship by professors, and its corollary, English ownership of 'English' texts. There were also heated arguments about the emendation of texts (the quasi-sacred status of Shakespeare's writing gives these discussions particular significance). Should new readings be accepted because of a textual critic's personal authority and acumen? What weight should editors give to metrical and stylistic criteria when emending? The New Shakspere, along with the Chaucer Society, confirmed Furnivall in his strong expressed preference for diplomatic editions, adhering as faithfully as possible to the original manuscripts. Thanks largely to Shakespeare's and Chaucer's literary renown, their works deserved this exacting and demanding industry. They also confirmed Furnivall in his abiding scepticism about critical editing—the production of what he called 'doctored' texts. This

[9] Letter, *The Athenaeum*, 7 Mar. 1874, p. 326.
[10] D. C. Baker, 'Frederick James Furnivall'; Phillips, '"Texts with Trowsers"'; Matthews, 'Chaucer's American Accent'; Spencer, 'F. J. Furnivall's Six of the Best'; Spencer, 'F. J. Furnivall's Last Fling'. [11] Utz, *Chaucer*, 86.

expression glanced both at what he considered the well-meaning meddling of the scholars concerned and also at their academic credentials: Furnivall prided himself on being an amateur who encouraged other amateurs to participate in his editing mission.

But this common verdict on Furnivall as an 'amateur' should be considerably nuanced: he was university-educated, he had many friends in the academies, at home as well as abroad, and vigorously supported the teaching of early English in British universities. He enjoyed social and educational advantages which other scholars, including Richard Morris and James Murray, both schoolteachers and largely self-taught, never had. Furnivall was a gentleman, trained as a barrister by profession, albeit a lackadaisical one whose heart was not in it, and the commerce between writers, scholars, and the law was and is ancient and honourable. His professional training familiarized him with handling documents and the importance of accuracy. In due course he would himself be 'doctored', when he was given the signal honour of a doctorate from the University of Berlin.[12] Choosing texts for diplomatic transcription involved Furnivall in discussions about what were the 'best' texts to transcribe. He needed to make decisions as to how best to deal with palaeographical details in manuscripts: whether to reproduce them typographically, and, if so, how. And the diplomatic editions were meant to provide future scholars with the raw material they needed for arriving at a text's pedigree—its 'stemma codicum'—and for emendation based upon this family tree.[13] Furnivall always remained sceptical about the value of stemma-based critical editing, but he felt deeply about the value of providing the necessary facts. He was not systematic in his learning, but he acquired formidable erudition in his chosen areas, and he was a shrewd critic, even if his perception was masked by his cultivated and ostentatious informality, his prejudices, and colloquialism. He consorted with men working in the academies like Walter Skeat, Henry Sweet, and Henry Bradshaw, the Librarian of Cambridge University Library. Sweet's *Anglo-Saxon Primer*, and his *Reader*, revised by Norman Davis and Dorothy Whitelock, both of whom did much for

---

[12] On Furnivall's amateur status, which enabled him to prosecute studies more expansively and idiosyncratically than in a university setting, see the arguments of Carolyn Dinshaw, *How Soon is Now?*, 25–8. It is a broad-brush account, and the author admits that the term needs to be applied to Furnivall 'advisedly' (p. 26). It seems an exaggeration to say that Furnivall 'shunned the profession' (p. 25).

[13] 'Pedigree' was the usual term at this time; its usage in the particular sense of a diagram representing the stages of a text's transmission (especially in manuscripts) as a genealogy is first recorded in 1930 (*OED*, 'stemma', n., sense 1c).

the EETS in the twentieth century, were standard introductions until around 1980, no mean achievement for books first published in 1882 and 1876.

The systematic study of Old and Middle English texts was in its infancy.[14] For example, Skeat's early attempts to understand and classify forty-five manuscripts of Piers Plowman in the absence of modern aids to study were initially just as amateurish as Furnivall's: 'I have this morning examined the 5 MSS in the Cambridge library and find they are a poor lot. I copied out the 5 bits and when I had done so saw Wright, who told me he had done them *yesterday*; which was a sell.'[15] It could be Furnivall writing, not least because he, too, was apt to complain of things being a 'sell', that is, a slang term for a disappointment, or a take-in: a 'swizz'. But these amateurs got things done: Furnivall, Skeat, and Morris were illustrations of 'the body of enthusiastic and committed devotees ... who, whether able to involve themselves full-time, or only in their leisure hours ... formed a highly-motivated self-taught élite on familiar and friendly terms with one another and sharing a common body of knowledge'.[16] Skeat had his edition of the A-Text of *Piers Plowman*, as well as *Piers the Plowman's Creed* on his hands at the same time and had 'got together a set of jolly notes on the Crede, picked up by the biggest luck most of them'. His cheerful exhortation 'On we go and may good luck go with us', expressed the ethos of the EETS in its earliest years, when Skeat, Morris, Furnivall, and the others churned out prodigious quantities of material to realize their intention to publish the whole of early English literature as quickly as possible. They gradually understood that they would not themselves live to see the mission accomplished: 'The tide of the Society's success still flows, though not with the force needed to carry the good ship "Early English" home to its haven—its work done—during the life of the present generation.'[17]

---

[14] For some general accounts of this growing topic see Palmer, *The Rise of English Studies*; Matthews, *The Making of Middle English*, and the same author's *The Invention of Middle English*, and references there given. Further references may be found in the following chapters of the present study.

[15] KCL, Furnivall Papers 4/1/6, letter to Furnivall, 23 Jan. 1866. The comments relate to Skeat's second edition for the EETS, *William Langland: Parallel Extracts* (1866). The antiquary Thomas Wright will recur in these pages: he produced 'innumerable editions for printing societies', among other activities, though it must be said that Furnivall did not consider his work for the EETS a success. See further Levine, *The Amateur and the Professional*.

[16] Levine, *The Amateur and the Professional*, 7.

[17] KCL, Furnivall Papers, 4/1/6, letter to Furnivall, 20 Feb. 1867; *Fifth Annual Report*

THE PRIVATEER

Furnivall has been described as 'mercurial', 'a man of turbulent character, part clown, part scholar, a charlatan of fanatical integrity', a 'volatile, impulsive, meddling, cantankerous literary warmonger' (though this last commentator notes that this was only one side of a multi-faceted and complicated man).[18] It was William Paton Ker who invented the adhesive soubriquets of 'independent adventurer' and 'privateer' to describe Furnivall, who seemed from Ker's perspective as the first Quain Professor of English at UCL to be, in the best sense of the word, a gentleman amateur: a 'private' scholar as well as one bent upon seizing literary booty. The expressions are memorable, as one would expect of Ker, a man of acerbic wit, friend of still more acerbic A. E. Housman, and with a gift for the telling phrase. They have been often recalled, not least by R. W. Chambers, and in Benzie's biography of Furnivall, subtitled 'A Victorian Scholar Adventurer'.[19] 'Scholar' is the redeeming half of an oxymoron: to characterize Furnivall as an adventurer and a privateer is dashing but does not allow for his lifelong enthusiasm for adult education, or his university training at Cambridge and, briefly, at UCL before syllabuses in English language and literature became established—as has been said, in the nineteenth century, despite the usual view, 'what distinguishes the movement for popular education is its concern, not with children, but with adults'.[20] Sir Frederic Madden of the British Museum called him a 'jackanapes' who should not be allowed to edit because his taste was poor and his writing style 'disgusting'.[21] His former friend, and fellow lawyer, John Ludlow, thought him 'utterly wrong-headed', as well as full of 'overweening vanity'.[22] 'Scoundrel and mountebank' have been added to the list of opprobria, though these at least are charges from which he may be exonerated—he was too great an idealist, and, indeed, a man of 'fanatical integrity'.[23]

of the Committee, Jan. 1869. On the relations between amateur and professional scholars in the period, see Levine, *The Amateur and the Professional*, 14 *et passim*.

[18] R. W. Burchfield, preface to Murray, *Caught in the Web of Words*, p. [viii]; Sutcliffe, *The Oxford University Press*, 54; Benzie, *Dr F. J. Furnivall*, 4.

[19] Derived from Altick, *The Scholar Adventurers*.

[20] H. Hale Bellot, *University College London, 1826-1926*, 29. See further Harte, *The Admission of Women to University College London*, 6, and Bernard M. G. Reardon, '(John) Frederick Denison Maurice (1805-1872)', *ODNB*.

[21] Quoted by Dinshaw, *How Soon is Now?*, 25, from Benzie, *Dr F. J. Furnivall*, 130-1.

[22] Ludlow, *Autobiography*, 131.

[23] See Black, *Cambridge University Press, 1584-1984*, 163.

Furnivall was a man of affairs, at the heart of Victorian society. He was an indomitable optimist. He was one of the century's great networkers, whose correspondents included many of the leading men and women of arts, letters, and public affairs, including W. E. Gladstone, Robert Browning, Elizabeth Gaskell, George Meredith, John Millais, Dante Gabriel and Christina Rossetti, and their brother William Michael, John Ruskin, Alfred Tennyson, Charlotte Yonge. He was, it must be admitted, a lionizer and a name-dropper. He collected great men and women in preposterous lists of vice-presidents to lend lustre to his publishing societies. He cut out Tennyson's autograph from the poet's letters to him to give to friends and fellow admirers.

As the summary above may indicate, Furnivall was a man characterized by self-contradictions, boundless self-confidence, and zest for life. His exuberance found particular expression in quarrelling, most vehemently with Algernon Swinburne, an activity which he enjoyed immensely (Swinburne perhaps less so), if we may judge from the energy of the invective. He told James Murray, a man much more cautious than himself: 'Don't be disgusted by criticism. If you'd only had as much abuse as I you wouldn't mind it, except as giving you a chance of telling critics what geese they are.'[24] Indeed, he did relish the opportunity of calling his adversaries 'geese'—it was a favourite term of mild disapproval. Murray for his part was exasperated by Furnivall's habitual indiscretion: 'I should have thought that you would by this time have seen enough of the impolicy of quarrelling with people who are better as friends than as enemies.'[25]

Above all Furnivall was, without disparagement, an enthusiast, undeterred by obstacles, including his own relative lack of means: 'Were I rich, or were not my time triply pledgd to other work', he told Murray, he would give both in the service of the *New English Dictionary*, 'but I can do neither. All I can do is to beg from other folk.' He was unfailingly generous with what he had—or thought he might have, as when he personally pledged the EETS's funds to the Secretary and a Delegate of the Oxford University Press for the rights in their edition of Gower's *Confessio amantis*, without knowing how much money the Society had, instructing his treasurer (and brother-in-law) W. A. Dalziel after the event: 'I promised that we'd send at once £250 on acc(oun)t. if we have it ... if not, send as near to £250 as you can,

---

[24] Letter to J. A. H. Murray, 15 Nov. 1876, Bodl., Murray Papers. Quotations from Furnivall preserve his idiosyncratic reformed spellings.

[25] Letter of 25 Jan. 1882, Bodl., Murray Papers.

and tell me what goes.'[26] As a later Director of the EETS and editor of the *OED*, C. T. Onions, said, Furnivall 'never had a bean' (at least during most of his working life).[27] Beans came and went, spent in the greater cause of preserving England's literary heritage. He studied truth more than his own fortune; as his friend, and member of the EETS's Committee of Management, Major John Munro put it: 'It is probable that £500 would be a large estimate of the total sum earned by his pen in the course of his amazingly long and tireless literary career.'[28]

Furnivall's writing took the form of essays, letters, pamphlets, introductions, and 'forewords' (as he called them, disdaining the Latinate 'prefaces'). These 'forewords', commonly written in an ostentatiously colloquial and pugnacious style all his own, often treated philological or literary topics which were relatively obscure so far as the general public was concerned, though, when he turned his attention to Shakespeare and Browning, he attracted wide notice among his contemporaries. Not all of this attention was flattering, though a reviewer noted of his introduction to the edition sponsored by his New Shakspere Society, and dedicated to Prince Leopold, youngest son of Queen Victoria, that this had introduced 'one of the raciest of contemporary English writers to a wider circle than his prefaces—we beg his pardon, "forewords"— to divers out-of-the-way books are likely to have secured.' Moreover, his quirks of spelling—he was an advocate of spelling reform, as some thought to the point of affectation—also attracted disapproving notice: '"Published" he spells *publisht*, "dragged" *draggd*, "called" *calld*, "convinced" *convinct*, and so on.'[29] Others found this foible amusing:

> There are few things more pleasant than Mr Furnivall's infantine delight in his oddities of spelling, his "gract" [i.e. 'graced'], for instance, which most people will take for an unknown rhyme to "act" . . . It is delightful to read his hearty encomiums on the charming damsels, with charming names, who listen to his lectures, confide to him their ideas, and occasionally make suggestions of appalling acuteness. Nothing is grander than his sublime scorn and pity for the unlucky idiots who do not agree with him . . . But it must be remembered that Mr Furnivall is not merely an amazingly egotistical writer and a champion of a mistaken school of criticism. He is also a man who loves literature well, if not altogether wisely, one who is thoroughly familiar with his subject, and one who has discussed it with many of the foremost men of letters of the time.[30]

[26] Letter to Dalziel, 30 Jan. 1901, EETS Archive, Box 3. 21.
[27] C. T. Onions to Elizabeth Mackenzie, 6 Aug. 1952, EETS Archive, FCD-1/1, file 5.
[28] Munro, 'Biography', p. lxxxiii.
[29] 'New Books and New Editions', *The Scotsman*, 27 Apr. 1877, p. 2.
[30] *Manchester Guardian*, unsigned review, 1 Oct. 1877, p. 6.

Teena Rochfort Smith, who was the confiding 'damsel'-in-chief with a charming name alluded to here, will enter Furnivall's—and the EETS's—story in due course. She has been generally remembered for her tragic death and as one cause of the break-up of Furnivall's marriage, but this is to belittle a strong-willed young woman with powerful scholarly ambitions. That Furnivall was in his fifties at the time of his whirlwind romance with her, and she in her early twenties, may serve as a testimonial, not only to her impatience with restricting conventions, but also to what contemporaries saw as his extraordinary stamina maintained through strenuous physical exercise (principally sculling and walking) from youth into old age. News of his waterborne exploits even reached the United States, via the British papers, where it was noted that 'the bodily vigor of some of our aged politicians, especially Mr Gladstone, has been often remarked upon,' but 'one at least of our old literary men, within a few months of his threescore years, still has the use of his muscles', namely, 'Mr Furnivall, the well known founder of the Chaucer, Wycliffe, New Shakespeare, Early English Text and other societies.' His winning boat was greeted with calls of 'Well done, old 'un!' from the river bank.[31]

Furnivall, the habitué of the Thames, who enjoyed nothing so much as convivial messing about in boats laden with enormous picnic baskets, has been immortalized by Kenneth Grahame as the Water-Rat in *The Wind in the Willows* (1908) (though other friends of Grahame's also contributed to this composite literary portrait). It has also been suggested that Furnivall in old age, reposing on Canbury Island 'in his grey flannels and pink tie, under the trees there, his hair gently lifted by the summer wind', like Old Father Thames, may have furnished a hint for the novel's depiction of Pan.[32] His cheery slang, as recorded, for example, in the transactions of the Browning Society, remarkably resembles the Rat's style of discourse. Dining alone one night in Soho, Grahame had met Furnivall, whom he described as a 'huge, grey-bearded, heavily-muscled lion of about fifty', dominating the cheerfully noisy table at which he sat. Grahame chuckled at one of his anecdotes, which he could not help overhearing, and was invited to join the party. The story seems to have been a little blue—Furnivall

---

[31] Anon., 'Bodily Vigor of Aged Men', *New York Times*, 21 Oct. 1884, reported from the *Pall Mall Gazette*.

[32] Jessie Currie, in Munro (ed.), *Frederick James Furnivall*, 29–34 at 31. Peter Green, *Kenneth Grahame*, 279–80; Prince, *An Innocent in the Wild Wood*, who also detects Furnivall's presence in the character of 'Fothergill' in Grahame's short story 'A Bohemian in Exile', from *Pagan Papers* (1893).

was not squeamish. Cards were exchanged, and their shared interest in boating secured the friendship. Furnivall, who believed friends should be put to use, enlisted Grahame into both his New Shakspere Society (where he served as Honorary Secretary) and Browning Society.

When Furnivall died on 2 July 1910, at the patriarchal age of 85, his friends and associates were aware of the passing of a great if wayward man. They had already, ten years previously, assembled a Miscellany in his honour, but now got together to compile a series of personal memoirs, to which no fewer than fifty people contributed, including Munro, who composed his affectionate, as well as accomplished, biography of the man, literary quarrels and all. The contributors included many of the greatest names in medieval scholarship, as well as Furnivall's more humble friends, including girls who were members of the Sculling Club which was his great passion, and Blanche Huckle, waitress at his favourite watering hole, the A.B.C. café in New Oxford Street. There was a rather cool testimonial from James Murray, but then Murray's writings were always temperate. All the memoirs were arranged by the editors in strict alphabetical order in accordance with Furnivall's democratic and egalitarian principles. He loved incongruous mixing of his friends—he once suggested that, since Caliban had a love of natural history and geology as well as music, 'had he lived till now, he'd certainly go with Browning and Mr Morison to the Philharmonic Society'.[33] The Committee of the EETS itself, a few months after his death, proposed a memorial pamphlet and a special series of facsimiles of medieval manuscripts in his honour; neither materialized, though the Society did not forget its founder. It was agreed ten years later that his successor as Director, Sir Israel Gollancz, should prepare a facsimile in Furnivall's honour of one of the best-known of medieval English literary manuscripts, British Museum (now British Library) MS Cotton Nero A. x, containing the four poems attributed to the poet of *Sir Gawain and the Green Knight*, a fitting tribute to a man who had been fired by his enthusiasm for all things to do with King Arthur. The facsimile duly appeared, dedicated to Furnivall's 'revered memory', as 'Founder of the Early English Text Society, the indefatigable worker whose inspiration and encouragement are still potent among all the votaries of English learning'. And, as the centenary of Furnivall's birth approached on 4 February 1925, Gollancz hoped to mark the occasion 'in some special way'.[34]

[33] 24th meeting of the Browning Society, 25 Apr. 1884, p. 117*.
[34] Notes and agenda for a meeting of the Committee of 21 Oct. 1910, EETS Archive,

OF HEROES AND HEROISM

For much of the period covered by this history, the Early English Text Society was led by men, and men of distinction, though women also took an increasingly prominent part. It is fair to say that the Society's work owed a great deal to women's contribution from the beginning, though the narrative constructed by its leading men did not draw much attention to them: the men tended to see themselves as the successors to a male dynasty. It is a case where 'women's participation in public life has been severely circumscribed and unevenly remembered'.[35] It has been stated that 'the practice of feminist historiography asserts that it is not only a safe assumption but a scholarly obligation to understand women as present and participating in the earlier experiences of humanity, regardless of whether they have figured in the narratives of these experiences'.[36] The present study does not claim the status of feminist historiography, but endeavours to be fair; women's participation has been recognized where possible. That said, it would be blind to ignore the mythology of heroism with which Furnivall and some of his successors in the early twentieth century invested men they strongly admired. It is a fact, characteristic of their time, upbringing, and personal character, which governed their behaviour. Thus, if this reverence of the Society's founder by his successors sounds like hero worship, it is no accident, and Furnivall himself was animated by his profound admiration for heroes. As a young man, Furnivall had met Thomas Carlyle at John Ruskin's house, and corresponded with him. Carlyle had published his influential series of lectures, *On Heroes, Hero-Worship, and the Heroic in History*, in 1841. Furnivall, along with his contemporaries, embraced the mythology of heroism heartily (another of his favourite words), and hero-making was essential to most of his literary endeavours. His various book clubs proclaim his worship of heroes whom he identified both in history and among his contemporaries. The Early English Text Society was founded both to popularize King Arthur and his knights, and as a means of publishing authentic expressions of the pre-industrial British past.

Furnivall owed much both to Ruskin and to Carlyle's German-derived romanticism. Given his temperament, it was inevitable that he

---

Box 2. 5; Minutes of the meeting of the Committee of 5 Nov. 1920. The facsimile was published by the EETS, though the original intention had been for the property in it to remain vested in Gollancz: *Pearl, Cleanness, Patience, and Sir Gawain*, ed. Gollancz; Meeting of Committee, 11 Nov. 1924.

[35] Russell, *Women and Dictionary-Making*, 7.   [36] Ibid. 9.

would attach himself to those men whom he and his contemporaries identified as sages. Carlyle's compensation for loss of conventional Christian faith in hero-worship, his insistence that the heroic man of letters was above all manly as well as sincere, and that 'for a genuine man,' of this heroic variety, 'it is no evil to be poor; that there ought to be Literary men poor—to show whether they are genuine or not!' found a ready disciple in Furnivall, who was not well off, prized manliness, and in later life was certainly no conventional Christian. It was said of him that he 'openly scorned Jesus because, as he put it, "the fellow let himself be spat upon without at least giving the spitter a black eye."'[37]

The events of Furnivall's life brought him into contact with charismatic, talented personalities with whom, especially as a young man, he could not easily compete on equal terms. He was an ardent admirer and facilitator of their greatness (though he was not always immune from jealousy). Furnivall saw it as his task to 'trumpet' his heroes to the best of his ability. He did not set himself up as a hero—his pugnacity, waywardness, and idiosyncrasies were too conspicuous—but, by consorting with leading men of ideas and of letters, and thanks to his own extraordinary energy and vitality and the sheer amount of his achievement, he came in time to seem like a colossus himself to his successors.[38] The development of Furnivall's public persona can easily be seen in the difference between the photograph of a rather pushy and, some thought, foolish young man taken for the Working Men's College when Furnivall was in his early twenties (and see the frontispiece to the present volume), and the fine portrait in extreme old age of 'Dr. Furnivall' made by C. W. Carey, which shows him at his most dignified and patriarchal.[39] And when we look back after the cataclysm of the Great War and all that has happened since, Furnivall's life and times seem like a past seen through the wrong end of a telescope, remote and ever retreating. His son, Percy, Furnivall's only direct descendant to bear his name, died in 1938, just before the next catastrophe.[40]

Thus, in old age Furnivall even *looked* like a patriarch, or secular

[37] Carlyle, *On Heroes*, 105. On Carlyle's notions of ideal heroism, perceived by him in terms of chivalry, see Girouard, *The Return to Camelot*, 130–1. Furnivall's irreverence was noted by G. B. Shaw: Partington, *Thomas J. Wise in the Original Cloth*, 315.

[38] Cf. *Browning's Trumpeter*, ed. Peterson. The title is taken from a comment of Browning's, 'There can be no doubt of his exceeding desire to be of use to my poetry, and I must attribute a very great part indeed of the increase of care about it to his energetic trumpet-blowing' (p. xxi).

[39] It was reproduced, full page, in *The Graphic*, 9 July 1910, five days after his death, where he was described as 'one of the wonders of English life'.

[40] He died on 3 May; and see obituary in the *Western Times*, 6 May 1938.

Santa, who favoured baggy trousers, flannels, and coloured, especially pink, or red, neckties. And neither comparison was lost upon his contemporaries—as he overheard himself being discussed by two Suffolk countrymen: 'Who's that, Bill?' 'Dunno, looks like the prophet Jeremiah.'[41] And, although the subject of facial hair may seem trivial, Furnivall's was so conspicuous that something should be said about it. No one studying Furnivall's portraits can overlook the growth of their most prominent feature. Beards in Furnivall's day were an easy way to proclaim one's manliness: they were class-free and egalitarian. In his case, his beard's appearance coincided with a major upheaval in his political and social values and marked a wish to assert his independence from his father; his abandonment of shaving as a young man proclaimed him to be a revolutionary weirdo. For Furnivall the decision not to shave was a self-conscious statement about himself, not the simple time-saving practicality he claimed it to be when he said: 'Shaving is one of the bits of foolery that this age is now getting out of; but any one who, as a young man, left off the absurdity some three years before his neighbours, as I did, will recollect the delightfully cool way in which he was set down as a coxcomb and a fool, for following his own sense instead of other persons' remorseless customs.'[42] He was in advance of the fashion: from the 1860s men looked to history to find exemplars of the values befitting imperial Britain: it was the bearded Anglo-Saxons, as distinct from the clean-shaven Normans, who loved freedom.[43] It is not surprising that the new fashion should appeal to professional men and men of letters, especially ones with Furnivall's tastes. James Murray, himself extravagantly bearded, present at a meeting of the Philological Society, of which Furnivall was the lifelong Secretary, did not initially know many of the other men. Alexander Ellis, who was at this time writing the first two of his five volumes on early English pronunciation, gave a guide to the owners of the other beards present: 'The little man with spectacles . . . was Joseph Payne author of the paper on the Norman element in English dialect. The man with the full brown beard was our Treasurer, [Danby] Fry. Dr Benjamin Davies of the

---

[41] He also dressed as Father Christmas to distribute toys to children; Munro (ed.), *Frederick James Furnivall*, 201, 204 (J. H. Wylie), and see also p. 33 (Jessie Currie).

[42] Borde, *The Fyrst Boke of the Introduction of Knowledge made by Andrew Borde*, 26. He told his clean-shaven friend, Henry Bradshaw, 'I hope you've come back with a beard'; CUL, MS Add 8916/A65/25, letter of 11 Mar. 1865. Bradshaw had just returned from Paris.

[43] Middleton, 'Bearded Patriarchs'.

Regent's Park College came in late and had a full grey beard. Furnivall you know.'[44]

Furnivall belonged to a society in which it was the custom to have studio photographs of oneself taken to distribute as postcards. Most of the photographs and portraits show Furnivall in old age, with high domed forehead and silver comb-over, in addition to his prodigious facial ornaments, and, in the nature of things, this tended to be how he was remembered after his death by those who had known him. The portrait by Carey embodies this image of the grand old man, full of literary honours, and with sparkling eyes (on which his contemporaries often remarked), full of life and keen interest on what was going on around him. He loved to surround himself with young people, and younger men like John Munro. 'Jack Munro', about 25 when the memoir was compiled, who had encountered Furnivall through the Working Men's College and became a member of his Sculling Club, inevitably remembered him as an old man, but with all the gaiety of youth and remarkable stamina, who, when the time came, met death with stoic fortitude.[45] The simple arithmetic of years ensured that this was how his memory was passed on. Forty or so years after his death, Beatrice White, twice editor for the EETS, and of the journal *The Year's Work in English Studies*, planning a memoir of Furnivall, contacted the Society's Secretary, Mabel Day, to enquire about records which the EETS might hold. Dr Day put her in touch with Major Munro, then in his seventies. As Beatrice White said, 'Those people now alive, and they are not many, who knew Furnivall, call to mind most vividly the dignity with which he calmly announced in 1910 the certainty of his approaching death.'[46] Turned 90, George Bernard Shaw (died 2 November 1950) was also able to supply some personal information about Furnivall's theatrical ventures and the Browning Society.

When young, Furnivall had seen the Duke of Wellington driving through Egham. He had heard Chopin play and had worshipped Jenny Lind. He had seen Wordsworth coming out of Macmillan's the publisher, in Cambridge. His father had known Shelley and had attended Mary Shelley's confinement in 1817.[47] He had been to the Great Exhibition of 1851. It is not surprising that, even by 1910, he seemed to belong

[44] Letter of 7 Dec. 1868, Bodl., Murray Papers.
[45] See Furnivall's 'foreword' to the 1906 reissue of *The Book of the Knight of La Tour-Landry*, to which Munro contributed the list of contents and additional notes.
[46] 'Frederick James Furnivall', 75.
[47] The death of his father, G. F. Furnivall, in 1865, was reported on 27 July in *The Scotsman*: 'One who had often seen the young face of the poet and heard him speak.'

to a former age. He quickly assumed a place at the head of a genealogy of other men of letters, with whom we shall have to do in subsequent volumes. One was W. P. Ker, the Quain Professor at UCL, a huge influence in the lives and careers of three of the EETS's later Directors. Ker was another larger-than-life scholar who had known Furnivall at the end of his life and contributed to his memorial volume. He did not feel he had anything of substance to add to the other testimonials but wanted 'a place among those who remember him'.

As already said, Furnivall's successors in the early years of the twentieth century were inveterate identifiers of heroes among their predecessors and contemporaries. Ker's own literary stature, dominant personality, and the influence of his writing, especially in this context *Epic and Romance*,[48] and not least the manner of his death walking in the high Alps, of which he was a devotee, ensured that he too was identified as a literary hero, especially in the domain of University College London, then a much smaller and more compact community, in which such a personality easily towered. Ker's student, and successor to the Quain chair,[49] Raymond Wilson Chambers, fifth Director of the EETS, was addicted to hero-worship, to the point of suspending critical judgement of even some of Ker's unkinder witticisms. And it was said of Robin Flower, the sixth Director, that he 'had an admiration hardly this side of idolatry' for Ker.[50] Chambers's passionate and influential, as well as highly personal, study of his literary heroes in *Man's Unconquerable Mind*, written at the outbreak of the Second World War, 'in time of danger' when men draw comfort from their great writers, annexed Furnivall, through his work for the Philological Society, to the inspiriting tradition of great men connected with his own deeply loved college, UCL.[51] Of course Chambers subscribed to, and passionately promoted, a mythology of the creation of his subject and his institution which must be seen in retrospect with detachment. But mythology cannot be ignored as an aspect of historical study.

UCL must feature prominently in any account of Furnivall and the EETS. Thanks to his own connection with it as a student, it provided a home, not just for the Philological Society, but also for the New Shakspere Society, Browning, and Shelley Societies. As he acknowledged: 'It

---

[48] Ker, *Epic and Romance: Essays on Medieval Literature*.
[49] Richard Quain (1800–87), professor of anatomy at UCL, endowed four chairs, to commemorate his brother, John Richard Quain, as well as himself.
[50] Bell, 'Robin Ernest William Flower, 1881–1946', 363.
[51] R. W. Chambers, *Man's Unconquerable Mind*, 15.

was a great boon to have the use of the College rooms. It was a very substantial help to poor literary societies, and the Council of University College was always glad to help science and literature in that way.'[52] The foundation of a School of English at Oxford, and the teaching of early English as part of academic syllabuses everywhere, were causes which Furnivall ardently supported, and one of the aims of the EETS was to encourage, and even make possible, the study of Early English texts at universities and at grammar schools. Chambers, like all the Directors of the EETS down to 1942, all of whom had known Furnivall personally, saw him in Herculean terms, a giant of a former age, his undoubted peccadilloes no more than any hero's right. Chambers, himself a President of the Philological Society, personally remembered Furnivall facing death with courage at his last attendance at the Society three weeks before he died—a spectacle which, Chambers said, 'Those of us who were present at that meeting of the Society will not easily forget.'[53] Murray, who was also present, was said to have had tears in his eyes for the lovable old menace. In the circumstances, it is not surprising that one of the leading characteristics of the EETS in the first half of the twentieth century, especially under Chambers's influence, was to see itself as formed by a procession of great men, headed by the grand old man himself, each passing on office to the next in something like an apostolic succession. The word 'men' has been used advisedly: women took their place on the Committee under the second Director, Sir Israel Gollancz, but were long outnumbered by the men. The Directors have all been men until the election in 2006 of Professor Anne Hudson.

Perhaps those of Carlyle's lectures on heroism which spoke most immediately to men like Furnivall whose weapons were pens and the printing press were his remarks upon 'The Hero as Poet' (the third lecture, delivered on 12 May 1840), and 'The Hero as Man of Letters' (the fifth lecture, 19 May). In lieu of Goethe, whom Carlyle regarded as the supreme exponent of heroism as man of letters, but unfamiliar to an anglophone audience, he used Samuel Johnson as one of the exemplars of this variety. There has been an understandable tendency to invest Johnson's lexicographical successors, the editors of the *OED*, especially Murray and William Craigie, with something of the same pioneering glamour. Both were knighted; there were those who thought that C. T. Onions, the third editor, should have been so also.[54] All three were pro-

[52] *Transactions of the Browning Society*, Annual Meeting, 7 July 1882, p. 43*.
[53] Chambers, *Man's Unconquerable Mind*, 352.
[54] But see Russell, *Women and Dictionary-Making* for qualification of this ideology.

minent figures in the EETS's Committee, and Onions was one of its most distinguished Directors, who did much to revive the Society's ailing fortunes after the Second World War. Onions was very conscious of Furnivall's legacy—everyone who worked for the Society down to about 1960 did so under Furnivall's shadow. His spelling peculiarities were piously preserved by his successors in the EETS until, after the Second World War, the Society finally abandoned its practice of issuing its titles with Furnivall's accompanying instructions and admonitions.[55]

Carlyle's poet-hero par excellence, shining down even Dante, was, of course, Shakespeare. Both were 'Saints of Poetry; really, if we will think of it, *canonized*, so that it is impiety to meddle with them'.[56] But Shakespeare was 'ours', and compelled even 'Europe at large' to recognize him as 'the chief of all Poets hitherto'. The fulsomeness continued: 'On the whole, I know not such a power of vision, such a faculty of thought, if we take all the characters of it, in any other man. Such a calmness of depth; placid joyous strength; all things imaged in that great soul of his so true and clear, as in a tranquil unfathomable sea!'[57] Furnivall embraced the prevailing bardolatry with all the enthusiasm of which he was capable—which is to say a great deal. He insisted on spelling his hero's name 'Shakspere' after this usage was ceasing to be common, on the grounds that this is how Shakespeare signed himself.[58]

Accordingly, one cannot understand Furnivall or the EETS without seeing them in relation to the Victorian adulation of Shakespeare. Furnivall thought it was an Englishman's patriotic duty to study him: 'Although we have the greatest author of the world belonging to our nation, yet of the ordinary educated Englishmen you speak to (as a Captain in the army said to me the other day), not one in 20—or shall

---

[55] As late as 1946, the Society's then Honorary Secretary, Mabel Day, wondered whether the EETS could finally abandon the instruction that cheques should be 'crost': 'It has always been spelt so and I take it to be a relic of Dr. Furnivall. Can we keep it?' Letter to C. T. Onions, n.d. with reference to *The Letters and Poems of Charles of Orleans*, ed. Steele and Day, vol. ii,. EETS Archive, Box 1.

[56] Carlyle, *On Heroes*, Lecture III, 55.

[57] Ibid. 66.

[58] The Keeper of Manuscripts at the British Museum, Sir Frederic Madden, had argued for the adoption of this spelling in a paper read to the Society of Antiquaries in 1837, printed as a pamphlet, *Observations on an Autograph of Shakspere and the Orthography of his Name*, with an additional note by Madden of 11 Apr. 1838. The controversy, for and against, which this stirred up, was conducted in numbers of *The Gentleman's Magazine* in correspondence of 1837–8. See further Robert W. Ackerman and Gretchen P. Ackerman, *Sir Frederic Madden: A Biographical Sketch and Bibliography*, 18, 56. The usage was also favoured by Furnivall's close associate, and fellow member of the Philological Society, Herbert Coleridge: e.g. 'On the word "Gallow" as used by Shakspere'.

we say 20,000?—has any real notion of Shakspere.'[59] An important reason for studying early English texts, all of them, but especially pre-Shakespearian drama, was to arrive at a better understanding of the national poet through appreciation of the literature which preceded him: 'To every play-goer and every student of the drama, all the old Mysteries have an interest independent of their literary merit. They show him the stores and scenes in which his forefathers before and up to Shakspere's time were content to find edification and amusement.'[60]

Shakespeare could be understood in the context of medieval drama, but this did not account for a prodigy. As a man of the nineteenth century Furnivall invoked science, but even science (or quasi science) failed to give an adequate explanation of the phenomenon that was Shakespeare. Furnivall, with his associate, Munro, subscribed to the view that the sixteenth century 'shows a truly marvellous uplifting' of English 'genius'. He illustrated his thesis by a graph, which showed the steep rise in 'numbers of individuals of genius and eminent ability' in the sixteenth century after they had bounced gently on the bottom of the graph during the preceding centuries, from 1101. The number rose still further to its peak in the first half of the nineteenth century: 'From the Norman Conquest to the middle of the fifteenth century, genius and conspicuous ability were rare exceptions', although Chaucer's times saw the beginning of 'the Humanism and the Renascence, which were to lift the minds of men'. The graph was constructed from statistics derived from Havelock Ellis's 'valuable' *Study of British Genius* (1904), and Ellis had derived his conclusions from a thorough study of the *Dictionary of National Biography*.[61] The graph is a striking illustration of widely held views at the time, given an appearance of scientific substance by the use of data from the *DNB*. Munro acknowledged that the graph took no account of demographic fluctuations and conceded that this was desirable 'where possible'. Munro and Furnivall had studied medieval and early Tudor drama and were very knowledgeable about it, but neither of them probably would have taken such keen interest, had this material not, as they saw it, provided the soil out of which Shakespeare grew. Indeed, all the Directors of the EETS, from Furnivall to C. T.

---

[59] From Furnivall's opening address to the first meeting of the New Shakspere Society on 13 Mar. 1874, *Transactions*, Part I, Series 1 (1874), p. vi; *Transactions*, Series 1 (1877–9), p. v. [60] *The Digby Mysteries*, ed. Furnivall.

[61] Furnivall and Munro, *Shakespeare: Life and Work*, 57–8, diagram facing, on p. 59 (originally published as the introduction to the 'Leopold Shakespeare' (1877)). The comments appeared under Munro's name, but he and Furnivall worked closely together on the volume; some parts assigned to Munro contain Furnivall's characteristic spellings.

Onions, as well as leading members of their Committees, notably R. B. McKerrow and W. W. Greg, were at least as interested (if not more so) in Shakespeare and his contemporaries as they were in medieval material, which they considered as significant for the light it shed on Shakespeare's culture and writing.

When Munro and Furnivall published this account of progress in literary genius, Furnivall was in his eighties. For all that he constructed himself as 'Victorian', Furnivall's tastes were in part a response to what is now called the 'long eighteenth century' in which he grew up. He was after all 12 when Queen Victoria came to the throne, and his foundation of the Shelley Society was prompted in the first instance by memory of his father. For all the immense first-hand knowledge he had accrued of 'early' English writings, his sense of the progress of English literary history still reflected the view he had as a young man of how fortunate he was to be living as a Victorian, surrounded by literary and intellectual figures, women as well as men, of extraordinary ability, many of whom he knew. He was, indeed, a prime exponent of the paradox which consisted of Victorians' 'simultaneous adulation of their own age and their reverent fascination for the past'.[62]

Furnivall's own experience tended to confirm his belief in the broadly held myth of intellectual progress which had reached a high point in the nineteenth century. When, in the 1850s, he first started teaching medieval English literature and the history of the language at the London Working Men's College, he used a popular textbook by William Spalding, aimed at schools and colleges, and prepared in the 'wish to see the systematic study of English literature occupying a wider space in the course of a liberal education'.[63] The key here is 'systematic'— if one wishes to understand English properly, one must begin at the beginning. Thus, in this spirit, the book begins with the Romans, continues to the 'Age of Printing', which offered 'a means of enlightenment about the beginning of the sixteenth century', and ends with the first half of the nineteenth century. Spalding noted: 'We do not look with much hope for literary cultivation among the Anglo-Saxons', while the language of later medieval literature was 'rude and stammering'.[64] Nevertheless it was of historical and picturesque value because it called

---

[62] Levine, *The Amateur and the Professional*, 1.

[63] Spalding, *The History of English Literature*, 1. On Spalding, see J. M. Rigg, revd. Elizabeth Baigent, 'Spalding, William (1809–1859)', *ODNB*. Spalding was Professor of Logic, Rhetoric, and Metaphysics in the University of St Andrews.

[64] Spalding, *History of English Literature*, 19, 21.

up, 'by an innocent necromancy, the perished world in which our forefathers lived, a world which was the seed-bed of our knowledge, whose tempestuous energy cleared the foundations for our social regularity and refinement'.[65]

These were the views with which Furnivall began his literary career, and which he continued to express, especially (and this is hardly surprising) when he wished to propitiate his readers. They expressed his own basic beliefs—but, after they had been duly acknowledged, they left a young man who admired (and embodied) 'tempestuous energy' rather more than 'social regularity and refinement', free to enjoy the portrayal of 'scenes which fancy loves to beautify', including 'the feudal castle blazing with knightly pomp'.[66] Though Furnivall began the EETS under Tennyson's influence, he eventually tired of idylls and carried on with the early English. But the paradox remains that the EETS was created and developed by scholars who generally believed that, though there was good stuff to be found, it anticipated the superior things which came later.

Finally, whatever he was, Furnivall was rarely solemn—this was one of the criticisms levelled at him by his critics. This is not to say that he did not take things seriously. He was a man of passionate convictions, often expressed with great indignation. But he did not often take himself very seriously. Personal seriousness was a quality with overtones of religious associations and pomposity—one had to be an individual of considerable grandeur to carry it off successfully. He and his circle evidently regarded the admission that literature might touch them emotionally as indecorous—it was unmanly to admit to feeling 'throbs'. Ruskin could, and did, write lyrically, but Furnivall considered there was something feminine about him. Furnivall admitted to Tennysonian rhapsodies over the Holy Grail, but only to debunk them. He found an outlet for his own lack of philological seriousness in a quest for 'fun' and little essays in the pastoral style, which too often seemed like pastiche, about the delights of the Thames or (after he moved on to Shakespeare) the Avon. The EETS, a society which was formed to assist philological enquiry, was founded by a man who was not really a philologist himself and sympathized with those subscribers who wished for 'romance and adventure, social life and fun'.[67]

[65] Ibid. 21. [66] Ibid.
[67] Anon., 'Be Domes Dæge'.

PART I

From Tory to 'Socialist': 1825–1858

1
F. J. Furnivall, 1825–1842: Early Years

> He devoutly believed in fairies, whom he called pixies; and held
> that they changed babies.
>
> Charles Kingsley, *Westward Ho!* (1855), ch. 1

WHEN FURNIVALL WAS A BOY

Frederick James Furnivall was born on 4 February 1825, in the small town of Egham, Surrey.[1] Egham and its environs, to which Frederick returned in adult life for vacations and to visit his relations, combined an idyllic pastoral setting—as Frederick would later lyrically describe it— with romantic historical connections, and convenient access by road and rail to London.[2] His father, George Frederick Furnivall, was a surgeon, living in the High Street, who married Sophia Hughes Barwell— Frederick would testify warmly to his mother's essential place in the family.[3] He was the eldest son, and second child, of a family of nine children.[4] There were four daughters: Mary Sophia (b. 1824), who married a solicitor, William Davenport, Selina (b. 1826), Louisa Elizabeth (b. 1830), who married Lt. Col. Edward John Watson, and went out with him to India, and the youngest of the nine, Frances Ann (b. 1836), who married the Revd Charles J. Waterhouse.[5] There were five sons. Charles

---

[1] A photograph of his birthplace is included in Munro, 'Biography', facing p. 192.

[2] In 1861, the population of Egham was 3,466; the parish was bounded by the Thames and Windsor Park. It included Runnymede, 'the historic ground where the Barons received from King John the charters of the liberties of England'. The town was 'a decent, quiet place, stretching along the high road; once a place of great traffic and bustle, with eighty or ninety stage-coaches passing through it daily'; *Black's Guide to the History, Antiquities, and Topography of the County of Surrey*, 411. In Furnivall's day, the stagecoaches were replaced by the railway station at Staines, two miles away, courtesy of the Richmond and Windsor Railway. Foster House, or Great Foster's, a 'quaint Elizabethan mansion', is noticed on p. 410.

[3] Letter to Bradshaw, condoling on the death of his mother, 17 Dec. 1870: 'All your family will feel the loss of their centre. Our mother acts as that to us, and she'd be a great loss to us all'; CUL, MS Add. 8916/A70/70. Miniature portraits of Furnivall's parents are reproduced in Munro, 'Biography', facing p. xvi.

[4] See *Browning's Trumpeter*, ed. Peterson, figure facing p. xxiii, for the family tree. I refer to Furnivall in these early years as 'Frederick' *tout court* to distinguish him from his father and siblings.

[5] By the 1871 Census, Louisa was living with her sister, Selina, in Egham, presumably as a widow.

(b. 1827), two years younger than Frederick, became a farmer.[6] Edward Thomas (b. 1834) became a doctor. William and Henry George (b. 1831) were twins; William became a vet; Henry's occupation is unknown.[7] Frederick and his older siblings, Mary, Selina, and Charles, were a close group, and Charles, as a boy who could share his older brother's outdoor interests, was his nearest companion, whom Frederick also mentored when the pair were being educated in London. As the eldest, Frederick was expected to set an example to his brothers, and, when he was at home, to assist in teaching the younger ones Latin and trigonometry. He was also expected to keep an eye on them when they, too, went to be schooled. There was a sufficient distance between Frederick, aged 18, and 'Willie', aged 12, for Frederick, home from Cambridge, to keep his young brother in and whip him for 'being very obstinate' in his Latin lesson.[8] But he was also clearly fond of 'the little ones', Willie, Hen, and Teddy (or Ted), with whom he also played, and on occasion put to bed.

Looking back, Furnivall wrote a popular account for children, *When Shakespeare was a Boy*, in which he compared his nineteenth-century experience of childhood with Shakespeare's, wondering if he speculated 'as we did, where the babies came from, and looked under the gooseberry-bushes for them: or did he, later on, consult with his brothers and sisters how the youngest baby could most conveniently be made away with?'[9] Three of the sons, Edward, William, and Frederick himself, would cause some public scandal in their adult lives. Indeed, both Edward—'Ted'—and William misbehaved while still at Eton. Ted was idle, and apparently not very bright; William may have favoured more grown-up diversions: Frederick's friend, William Johnson, master at Eton, informed him that 'The prostitutes in Windsor have been using freely in their cups the name of *Furnivall*.'[10] As a young lawyer,

---

[6] By the 1881 Census Charles was a widower and retired from farming, living in his mother's former house in Guildford, Surrey.

[7] The 1871 Census shows him living in Ash, Surrey, with his wife, Sophia F., and two stepdaughters and daughters. The youngest of his two daughters, Annie L. C., was born in South Africa (1870).

[8] Diary, Saturday 7 Jan. 1843, 'but [I] made him do all that I told him to', Bodl. MS Eng. d. 2104, f. 74ʳ.

[9] Furnivall and Munro, *Shakespeare: Life and Work*, 15. Furnivall, *Shakespeare Tales for Boys and Girls, and When Shakespeare was a Boy*. This volume overlaps on Tuck's children's list with Nesbit's *Children's Stories from Shakespeare*, to which 'The Late' Dr. F. J. Furnivall's remarks on 'When Shakespeare was a boy' were also prefaced (Furnivall died in 1910; Edith Nesbit in 1924).

[10] Letter of 3 Apr. 1851, Furnivall Papers, KCL, FU 233: Edward fell under suspicion because of his surname, but 'Ted knows nothing of it, I believe him ... he says your brother William went away three months ago. I spoke to him about it on Sunday, to give him a

Frederick also had to clear himself to his father of a piece of gossip that he was about to marry a prostitute.[11] Perhaps none of the sons turned out quite as well as their father might have hoped, but it was not for want of his trying. And the greatest weight of expectation fell on Frederick.

He was called 'Fred' by his close family, and later by his wife. He himself said of his distinctive surname that 'A friend of mine explains Furnivall as Ferny-vale, but I've no idea what it means'.[12] This was disingenuous, since he knew perfectly well that it was French—these origins rankled with some of his German scholar acquaintances in later life. Munro agreed that it was a French name, of a family which had migrated from Normandy with William the Conqueror and later settled as yeoman-farmers in Sandbach, Cheshire.[13] Such Norman ancestry might be distinctive in a negative as well as a positive way. Nineteenth-century commentators in radical quarters continued the tradition of attacking the aristocracy as descendants of opportunist French thieves and freebooters. Two of Furnivall's friends as a young man, Thomas Hughes (author of *Tom Brown's Schooldays* (1857)), and Charles Kingsley, each wrote popular historical novels in defence of Saxon freedom fighters oppressed by the Normans: Hughes's *Alfred the Great* (1869) and Kingsley's *Hereward the Wake* (1866), and both had Walter Scott's enormously influential *Ivanhoe* (1819) behind them.[14] For both Hughes and Kingsley, their Saxon heroes had been inspiring leaders, who fought to defend a society based on values of mutual responsibility and respect between classes who valued traditional freedoms, unlike the competitive money-based economy introduced by the Norman overlords. The novels were expressions of their Christian Socialism, which Frederick Furnivall also actively supported as a

---

chance of clearing himself from a charge which is now, I find, received against him with full belief . . . You see, it is an uncommon name—our informants are respectable people living close to the brothel at the foot of Clewer Lane, who overheard the women in their drunken noises. It ought to be cleared before I write to your father.'

[11] Diary, entries for 20 and 27 Feb. 1851, Bodl. MS Eng. e. 2316, ff. 16^r, 17^r. Furnivall explained it as confusion with another Frederick.

[12] Furnivall and Munro, *Shakespeare: Life and Work*, 10 n.

[13] Munro, 'Biography', p. vii. Munro accepted the suggestion of a namesake, Joseph Furnivall, of Sandbach, who wrote to Frederick to say that their families were probably connected. Munro reported that Frederick Furnivall's grandfather had moved from the area to Hemel Hempstead, having offended his father by his marriage, 'and set up a straw-plaiting industry', but it is difficult to trace the connection more securely: see Peter Havercan, 'The Furnivalls of Sandbach', http://roots.havercan.net/furnivall, accessed 30 July 2019.

[14] See further, Parker, 'Anglo-Saxonism and the Victorian Novel', ch. 6, 'Literature'.

young man, but without apparently troubling himself with any guilt about the 'Norman yoke'. As he remarked on the subject of heraldry: 'No doubt one's namesakes with the Conqueror and Coeur de Lion thought much of their arms, if they had any.'[15]

His own historical imagination when he began his literary career was fired by chivalric romances and texts which illustrated his ideas of social life in the medieval and Tudor past. Naturally, he especially relished those moments in which literary romance and adventure resonated with his own family's history. In later life, while editing Francis Thynne's sixteenth-century *Emblemes and Epigrames*, he recalled: 'To me, an Egham man, the "Galloping" poem on p. 80 is interesting from its mention of Hounslow Heath, which I've so often driven over, and where my father, riding many years ago, was accosted one evening by a highwayman, who was shot a few minutes after, by Lord Stowell.'[16] In 1858 Furnivall made a pilgrimage to Normandy with a group from the Working Men's College to visit Fourneville, near Honfleur.[17] The barrister, and fellow Christian Socialist, John Malcolm Ludlow remembered that Furnivall told 'an amusing story of how he narrowly escaped being marched to the *corps de garde* for having gone in search of an out-of-the-way place called Fourniville in Normandy, which he supposes his ancestors to have come from'.[18]

His immediate family was a staunchly medical one. Frederick's father George Frederick Furnivall had been house-surgeon to John ('the great') Abernethy, assistant surgeon at St Bartholomew's Hospital, London and, in 1805, became Assistant Surgeon in the West Yorkshire Regiment (Prince of Wales's Own) (14th Foot). He retired as an army surgeon, at his mother's urging, in favour of civil practice in Egham. He had enjoyed army life, 'in spite of the enforced carousings', and regretted leaving. 'But why did you then?', asked Frederick; 'In those days . . . children obeyed their parents.'[19]

Frederick's brother Edward also trained as a surgeon, as did his nephew, and as his own son, Percy, would also do in due course.

---
[15] *Queene Elizabethes Achademy*, ed. Furnivall, p. xvi. See Chibnall, *The Debate on the Norman Conquest*, 55–68; also the useful short overview of Victorian historiography by Asa Briggs, written as a contribution to the commemoration of the Conquest in 1966, *Saxons, Normans and Victorians*.

[16] *Emblemes and Epigrames*, ed. Furnivall, p. vi, foreword dated Good Friday, 14 Apr. 1876. Lord Stowell was perhaps the judge and politician Sir William Scott, Baron Stowell (1745–1836).   [17] Benzie, *Dr F. J. Furnivall*, 54.

[18] *John Ludlow: The Autobiography*, ed. Murray, 205. Furnivall was a suspicious character because he was unable to 'prove that he was a commercial traveller, the only class of stranger ever known to go there'.   [19] Munro, 'Biography', pp. vii–viii.

His cousin John worked in the Egham surgery. It seems likely that his father wished that his eldest son would also follow him into the profession, and he seems at least to have tried Frederick out. At home during vacations he helped his father and cousin John in the surgery; he dispensed and made up medicines; he read his father's copies of the *Medical Gazette* and *Medical Lexicon*.[20] On one occasion, after a particularly severe accident at a building site, 'Papa & John drove up to Sunning-Dale & I rode after them with some splints &c; found 1 boy of 17 with a compound fracture of the leg & one simple of the thigh; another man with his thigh broken, & another very much cut & bruised, by the falling of a heavy portico, supported by only 4 *slight* brick pillars at Mr Stewart's new house'.[21] While visiting his father's and family friend Dr Edward Harman Maul, a well-known and respected family doctor in Southampton, he was again expected to help out in the surgery, where he browsed Carswell's 'Pathological Anatomy' and 'called on some poor people with Harman'.[22] Maul was a local philanthropist who did much for the poor of the town—there were many stories of his kindness. Frederick (whose interest in 'poor people' was as yet more abstract and less personal than it later became) was clearly inquisitive, both about medical science and what was wrong with his neighbours, and he took an interest in grisly textbooks. Though law was to be his profession, Frederick would later describe simple doctoring and some familiarity with surgery as part of the accomplishments which made up a model gentleman in Elizabethan times, and which had formed part of his own education.[23] Frederick was proud of his father, while in some awe of 'papa's' authority. In 1869, after George's death in 1865, he presented his Day Book for 1816–21 to Cambridge University Library, probably at least in large part because George had known the Shelleys when they were living in Marlow, and had attended Mary Shelley as accoucheur on the birth of her third child, Clara, on 3 September 1817.[24] Despite what one would imagine to be their incompatibilities,

[20] e.g. diary entries for Tuesday, 28 Dec, 1841; Monday, 13 June 1842; Monday, 17 Oct,, 1842; Saturday, 21 Jan. 1843. Bodl. MS Eng. d. 2104, ff. 10^r, 32^r, 55^r, 77^v.

[21] Bodl. MS Eng. d. 2104, f. 123^v, entry for 8 Sept. 1843.

[22] Bodl. MS Eng. d. 2104, ff. 72^v–73^r, entries for 31 Dec. 1842, 1 Jan. 1843; Sir Carswell, *Pathological Anatomy*, with coloured plates. See further http://sotonpedia.wikidot.com/page-browse:maul-edward-harman, accessed 18 Oct. 2019.

[23] Forewords to *Queene Elizabethes Achademy*, p. x.

[24] 'My father knew Shelley, attended his wife in 1816, and often told us about him'; *Bibliography of Robert Browning, from 1833 to 1881*, compiled by Frederick J. Furnivall, 3rd edn., Browning Society Papers, 1 (1881), 3 (volume includes Browning's essay, 'Shelley as Man and Poet').

Shelley would walk, or row, the sixteen miles or so down to Egham to visit George Frederick, in whom he had 'great confidence'. The surgeon liked his 'exceeding good nature', but disapproved of Mary Shelley's too great freedom in ordering her husband about, to which Shelley submitted with 'the docility of a child'.[25] George Frederick was master in his own house. He also, as a physician and master of an asylum, responded to what he must have seen as Shelley's morbid melancholy with robust common sense and a surgeon's grim humour. Arriving at Shelley's house one evening, after he had just attended a post mortem examination, George Frederick found him with Leigh Hunt, both 'talking rather big about the expediency and attractions of suicide'. Furnivall *sen.* 'proffered his case of surgical instruments for immediate use—but without result'.[26] Frederick made much of these family stories when he later founded his Shelley Society, and thanks to his son's trumpeting, George Frederick Furnivall posthumously acquired modest comic fame in London literary circles.[27]

George practised as a general family doctor and surgeon. Yet much of his income derived from a private lunatic asylum (as it was then called), licensed in 1774, but established around 1767, at Foster House (as Furnivall called it), also known as Great Foster House, in Thorpe, adjoining Egham. It is now a country-house hotel, 'Great Fosters', frequented by royalty in the twentieth century. George Frederick acquired a share in the Foster House asylum, running it as part of a consortium of local surgeons licensed on 11 January 1814.[28] Probably because of its proxi-

[25] Information given by F. J. Furnivall to W. M. Rossetti and included in the latter's 'Memoir of Shelley (with a fresh preface)', 2nd edn., Shelley Society, Series IV, Miscellaneous no. 2 (London 1886), 68, 75.

[26] Rossetti, 'Memoir of Shelley', 68. 'Talking big' sounds like Frederick Furnivall's way of telling the story—though he may well have modelled himself on his father's down-to-earth style.

[27] CUL, MS Add. 6184. Presented in 1869 (see unpublished handwritten description in the Manuscript Room). I am grateful to Richard Beadle for this reference. When his father died in 1865 Furnivall had previously offered his father's Shelley papers to the British Museum, but the gift had been declined by the Keeper of Manuscripts, Sir Frederic Madden, in a letter of 12 June 1865, FU 540: 'I am obliged to you for the copy of the personal document and letters to Mr Shelley, but had rather decline accepting it as a gift to the Trustees. I can however, if you think proper, address a letter to the Principal Librarian on the subject.'

[28] *Great Foster House Lunatic Asylum*, 19, 'Licence granted to John Chapman, George Furnival and Charles Summers, Surgeons for Great Foster House, Thorpe, recognizances of £100 each, and also from Thos. Baker, 103 Newgate St., and Edward Winstanley, Poultry'. George Furnivall had previously certified a patient sent to the asylum on 9 Feb. 1804 (p. 14). Sir John Chapman practised in Windsor; Frederick visited the Winstanleys and Summers families socially in London, e.g. Bodl. MS Eng. d. 2104, ff. 54^r, 75^v,

mity to Windsor Castle, it has been believed that George III may have spent some time there during his final period of insanity, 1811–20. This cannot be confirmed, but entries show that the Castle made use of the asylum for its staff, and that a patient was sent to Great Fosters from 'Dr Willis's Madhouse' in 1802 and certified by him—probably one of the Willis family which had attended the King.[29] Furnivall's brother Edward later assisted his father as part proprietor of the asylum.[30] Another of the licensees, Thomas Phillips, was the resident physician.[31]

George Furnivall's business prospered: there was good money to be made from private asylums and the mad trade. Munro reported that, thanks to his medical practice, and the income from the asylum, he left a considerable fortune of some £200,000 at his death.[32] Foster House provided the Furnivalls with a background of considerable grandeur, though they did not actually live there, but in the High Street in Egham. Frederick Furnivall described it as a fine Tudor house—it was built c.1550—which had given him a connoisseur's taste for antique oak panelling, and perhaps also contributed to his broader antiquarian interests as well as encouraging him to compare his boyhood with Shakespeare's.[33] Frederick showed it off to visitors; set in spacious grounds on the edge of Windsor Forest and Great Park, it is now a Grade 1 listed building described in Pevsner as 'in its severe yet serene way one of the most impressive Tudor houses in England'.[34] In adult life, Furnivall would take a more informed antiquarian interest in the house, ironically after the family had sold it to its new owner, Colonel Halkett, after George Furnivall's death and the crisis in the family fortunes. It was also known in the nineteenth century as 'Forsters'; as

entries for 12 May 1842, 11 Jan. 1843. See also Roberts, 'The Lunacy Commission', http://studymore.org.uk/4asylums.htm, accessed 30 July 2019. The business was sold to Furnivall, Chapman, and Summers in 1816. They formed a limited company and employed resident medical officers to run it. I am grateful to Jane Thomas and Joyce Sampson, of the West Surrey Family History Society, for assistance with enquiries about Great Foster House.

[29] *Great Foster House Lunatic Asylum*, 13, entry for 28 July 1802. See also p. 17, entry for 24 July 1810.

[30] *Morning Post*, 14 Dec. 1867. Edward Furnivall was called as a witness in the case against Dr Shaw, who was keeping a patient discharged from Great Fosters in his own private asylum without a licence.

[31] Census 1841: George Frederick was living there with his wife and six of his children (Frederick was studying at UCL). [32] Munro, 'Biography', p. viii.

[33] Letter in *The Athenaeum*, 22 Sept. 1888, p. 390, prompted by refurbishment taking place at Haddon Hall, Derbyshire.

[34] Nairn and Pevsner, *The Buildings of England, Surrey*, 38. A detailed architectural description is given on pp. 265–6.

the adult Furnivall would point out 'the name of the place I suppose to be derived from the forester or "forster" (to spell it as Chaucer does) who may have lived there'. By this time, he had become familiar with the manuscripts in the British Museum: 'In Norden's Map of Windsor Forest, Harl. MS 3749, a house is marked which is probably meant for "Forsters". It was certainly in Egham Walks of the forest, where red deer were in Norden's time.'[35] The house had tantalizing, but elusive, royal and aristocratic connections in its past. Furnivall described

the royal arms on the Elizabethan porch (which is supposed to be later than the house), with the date of 1578. The date on the drawing-room ceiling is 1602; and that on one of the leaden spouts of the house is 1598. One tradition is that the princess Elizabeth was confined in the house during Queen Mary's reign; and another is that the place was one of Elizabeth's hunting-lodges; but the first fact about it recorded (so far as we now know) is, that Sir John Dodderidge died there in 1628 . . . it was no doubt his family residence near London and Windsor, though he bought estates and built a mansion in Devonshire.[36]

Yet, that, however gentlemanly the setting, Furnivall had been raised on the proceeds and in the vicinity of a lunatic asylum would no doubt have seemed all too appropriate to some of his later literary associates: even without this knowledge, the Regius Professor of History at Oxford (probably Edward Augustus Freeman—an old sparring partner in the pages of the *Saturday Review*) would tell James Murray: 'Put Furnivall in an asylum and I will join the Early English Text Society at once!'[37] However, although he assisted his father in some of his medical work, Frederick and his brothers and sisters were not directly involved with the inmates of the asylum, though Frederick met some of them, and knew the matron, Mrs Mary Ann Gwillim, and her daughter, and visited her socially.[38] The house seems to have been well regulated—it satisfied

---

[35] Quotations from Furnivall [F.J.F.], 'Mr. Albert Way's letter on Great Forsters', near Egham and Thorp, Surrey'. Reference is to the cartographer John Norden's 'Description of the Honour of Windesour' (1607).

[36] 'Mr. Albert Way's letter on Great Forsters', 504. Doddridge (1555–1628), lawyer, was appointed Justice of the King's Bench in 1612. The correspondence between Way and Furnivall, and Furnivall's letter to *Notes and Queries* is printed in full in Appendix 1.

[37] Quoted by Colloms, *Victorian Visionaries*, note to p. 242 (p. 273, n. 2); also by Murray, *Caught in the Web of Words*, 90. Freeman, who held the Regius Professorship, 1884–92, and Furnivall were literary adversaries, and Freeman's adverse reviews of Furnivall's works for the EETS were notably combative. By his will, George Frederick Furnivall, d. 7 June 1865, left his medical business to his son Edward Thomas, 'and I give him the first option of purchasing the goodwill of my business at Great Foster House Lunatic Asylum (or any share thereof to which I shall not have admitted him before my death'; will proved 24 June 1865, Furnivall Papers 1/1. See further Munro, 'Biography', pp. xli–xlii.

[38] e.g. diary entry for Tuesday, 18 July 1843, 'walked over to Foster House; had some

the inspectors at the annual visitation, and only one of the inmates was reported to be under restraint on account of violence: a poor woman, Charlotte Moss, whose parish, Wokingham, had failed to provide her with adequate clothing, 'and would be in a state of total nakedness but for Mrs Radcliffe, the Superintendent's wife, who has supplied her with the "common necessities"'. In 1844 a 'gentleman' was brought to the house in 'a state of violent excitement'. Instead of physical restraints, two attendants stayed with him, though after a week of sleeplessness all round, 'muffs' were put on him 'and he soon after fell asleep'.[39] Another inmate, the Revd Nathaniel Stackhouse, performed a church service and read a sermon on Sundays.[40] At the beginning of 1829, George Furnivall and the other licensees applied to the General Quarter Session to expand the number of lunatics to thirty-three, four of whom should be pauper patients. The 1841 Census (coinciding with the beginning of Frederick Furnivall's first diary) reported that the medical superintendent, B. Lloyd, was living there with eighteen male patients and four female under his charge, and that of the matron, Mary Ann Gwillion [sic]. Most of the men are described as 'gentlemen'; the inmates included two clergymen, one draper, a butcher, a gentleman's gardener, and an agricultural labourer. In addition, there were seven male servants and nine female.[41] In adult life Furnivall, too, seems to have followed the family tradition of looking after the insane. A younger cousin, William Douglas Furnivall, lived in his house for many years, said to be living off his own means, and a lunatic.[42] As Furnivall put it, describing to a friend his bachelor existence at 3 St George's Square,

strawberries, chatted to Mrs & Miss Gwillim, and then to Revell, Badcock, &c.' Bodl. MS. Eng. d. 2104, f. 115ʳ. Thomas Backhouse Revell and Jonathan Neale Badcock were patients. Revell was a Cambridge student, discharged 8 Sept. 1846, convalescent; Badcock had come from Exeter Asylum; *Great Foster House Lunatic Asylum*, 33.

[39] Roberts, 'Part of the Asylums Index', 6.

[40] *Great Foster House Lunatic Asylum*, 30, 9 Aug. 1832, pp. 25–6, 7 Mar. 1829.

[41] Roberts, 'Part of the Asylums Index', 6; 'Gwillion' seems to be an error for 'Gwillim'. *Great Foster House Lunatic Asylum*, 31–6, gives the Admissions Register, with the names and occupations of those admitted.

[42] Census, 1871, 1881, 1891, 1901. He was Furnivall's second cousin. His name is variously recorded as William Douglas, William Furnivall, William Douglas Furnivall. He is described as a lunatic in the 1901 Census, where it is recorded that he was born in 1841, in Malta. On Douglas, and his lexicographical work, see Ogilvie, *The Dictionary People*, 144–57, who gives further biographical information, interspersed with a racy summary of Frederick Furnivall's life. The work, which is arranged thematically, and is searchable via its general index, should also be consulted for thumbnail sketches of others who worked and edited for Furnivall and his associates, e.g. Thomas Austin, jr., Henry Hucks Gibbs, Fitzedward Hall, Edward Peacock, as well as the usual suspects.

after he had separated from his wife, 'My non compos cousin and I live here, and have a maid to look after us'.[43] Douglas was by this time working as a reader for the Philological Society's new *Dictionary*.

On the strength of his family connections, Furnivall would continue to take a quasi-professional interest in the health, especially the mental health, of his friends and associates. He relished medical jargon. Aged 17, and precociously flourishing a rare word likely to have come from one of his father's medical textbooks, he observed that one of the sons of the family's dentist had returned from a cruise 'very poorly, from the effects of Lues Venerea, & had a great many blotches on his face'.[44] In 1892, Furnivall wrote a begging letter for £20 to A. S. Napier, the Merton Professor of English Language and Literature at Oxford, on behalf of their mutual friend (and associate in the Philological Society) Henry Bradley, who was to succeed James Murray as the general editor of the *OED*, but who was at this time suffering a breakdown, exacerbated by money troubles. Furnivall's nephew, Dr Waterhouse, who had examined Bradley along with his 'nerve-specialist' friend Dr Isaac Taylor, gave it as his opinion that unless Bradley stopped work and went away, 'he'd either lose his mind, sink into melancholia, or get paralysis of the brain'.[45] 'Every little helps. It's a distressing case. Poor B. looks very bad.' Everyone agreed that Furnivall, who spent much of his life writing begging letters, had a warm heart. Ten years earlier Sidney Herrtage, assistant to James Murray on the dictionary, EETS editor, and Furnivall's protégé, was thought to have been stealing books from Murray. He was dismissed. Furnivall pleaded for clemency on the grounds that 'I *do* believe in partial insanity in him, a kind of kleptomania for books like the dipsomania after sunstroke'.[46] 'Kleptomania' was a relatively recent

---

[43] Letter of 3 Mar. 1885 to C. H. Pearson, Bodl. Pearson MSS, MS Eng. lett. d. 187.

[44] Entry for Friday, 3 June 1842, Bodl. MS Eng. d. 2104, f. 30^v. See *OED*, 'lues' n. (entry first published 1903, not yet fully updated). First recorded 1637; also *Medical and Physical Journal* (1803).

[45] Son of Furnivall's sister, Frances (Fanny), who married the Revd Charles J. Waterhouse. Bodl. MS Eng. lett. d. 79, f. 43, dated 18 May 1892, Taylor was willing to take on Bradley's case until Whitsun, 'then I want him to have a sea-trip up and down the Norway fiords, from L(iver)pool on June 1. In this, 20*L*.'ll be necessary. Bradley has *nothing* saved. Gibbs and Is. Taylor have promised me 5*L*. and 2/2/- respectively'. Bodl. MS. Eng. lett. d. 79, f. 43. dated 18 May 1892. Bradley testified warmly to Furnivall's kindness during this period of ill-health in Munro (ed.), *Frederick James Furnivall*, 4–9 (p. 7). Five years after this breakdown, Furnivall wrote to Murray about what he considered to be his shabby treatment of Bradley: letter of 12 Oct. 1897, Murray Papers. I am grateful to Peter Gilliver for this reference; see further Gilliver, *Making of the OED*, 198, 225–6.

[46] Letter to Murray, 12 June 1882 (Murray Papers). Furnivall had also experienced Herrtage's infirmity: 'H. has work in hand and I feel bound to help him as much as I can. He

coinage, though it had found its way into *Middlemarch* (1872)—George Eliot thought it a polite way of describing gentlemanly theft. 'Dipsomania' had not strayed beyond medical textbooks and journals.[47] In the same spirit, Furnivall approached Sidney Lee to assist John Stephen Farmer, a prolific writer on slang and editor for the Early English Drama Society. After a bout of insanity, Farmer's wife separated from him, and, because he failed to keep up with the payments of 30s. a week which he had agreed, her solicitor put him in Holloway Prison for two months (something which Farmer was understandably keeping quiet), 'So he couldn't do a stroke of work or earn 1d. He is just out, and needs a little help. Pray help F. if you can, for he's a real worker, and a kindhearted fellow.'[48]

Furnivall began school at Englefield Green in 1831, where, as 'a little boy in a private school in Surrey', he later recalled with indignation seeing 'the first class of a dozen boys birched twice on their bare skins in one hour because none of them could translate two words in a Virgil lesson', and received his share of 'warming' himself.[49] He retained his indignation about the 'time wasted, almost, in Latin and Greek by so many middle-class boys', like himself—though the qualifier, 'almost', indicates that the classics had some use, especially Latin, for his future work as a lawyer and gentleman scholar. But 'it would have been a good thing for England' if the time spent on them at school 'had been given to Milton and Shakspere, Chaucer and Langland, with a fit amount of natural science, we should have been a nobler nation now than we

has a lot of my books still. We must take him off EETS Committee.' Herrtage's wife 'promist that she would quietly get the key, and search' for the more valuable of his suspected thefts (Furnivall to Murray, 7 Aug. 1882). Furnivall stuck to his diagnosis of 'that tendency to insanity which at times is seen, more or less, in both H(errtage) brothers'. 'I of course told H(errtage) what you said at the Phil. Soc.—not the words exactly but the purpose—in order to explain the new position which the Phil Soc and EEText Societies would have to take to him now. While officially and personally I condemn certain acts of his, he is a man with two sides to his character, and to one of these I hope to hold' (letter to Murray of 9 Mar. 1883). See further Murray, *Caught in the Web of Words*, 218; Gilliver, *Making of OED*, 110–11, 146–7. Their account is disputed by Janet Bately (Herrtage's direct descendant). I am most grateful to Professor Bately for discussion of this episode and for letting me see her reply, 'A Reputation Besmirched? S. J. H. Herrtage's Role in the Birth of the Oxford English Dictionary', in advance of publication. See further Ogilvie, *Dictionary People*, 127–30.

[47] George Eliot, *Middlemarch*, II. iii. xxiii: 'When a youthful nobleman steals jewellery we call the act kleptomania.' First recorded in *OED* in 1830 (in the form *cleptomania*); *dipsomania* first recorded 1843–4. See also letters of 26 and 31 Jan. 1882, Bodl. MS Don. D. 109/2, ff. 349, 351.
[48] Letter to S. Lee, 5 Feb. 1900, Bodl. MS Eng. misc. d. 177, f. 124.
[49] 'When Shakespeare was a Boy', in *Shakespeare Tales for Boys and Girls*, 13.

are'.⁵⁰ Afterwards he was sent to school at Turnham Green before going to Hanwell College, where Munro reported that he followed 'a thorough course of studies', including Latin and geography, and where he showed particular aptitude for languages, science, divinity, and dancing.⁵¹ Hanwell College, the 'celebrated school for young gentlemen of position',⁵² was started in 1832 and closed fifty years later. It was a private boarding school, kept by the Revd J. A. Emerton, and specialized in educating boys who were to enter the army.⁵³ Its 'thorough' curriculum, including science, with, in addition, what we might call 'life skills' like dancing, probably commended it. George Furnivall, a medical man with an army background, had no wish for at least his elder sons to be narrowly educated in the classics.⁵⁴ Frederick was followed to Hanwell by Charles. Yet their father sent his younger sons, Edward and William, to the local school, Eton—perhaps because he thought that, though they did not go on to university, the school would provide the gentlemanly polish and background which would get them through most situations in life.

Frederick reminisced later about the weekly 'Resurrection Pie' served up in Hanwell, 'in which we declared old left bits reappeared'. But he was fond of the school, which he revisited during his time at UCL, partly to keep an eye on Charles, but partly also to stay in touch and go to parties, with fireworks and dancing.⁵⁵ Munro said that the boys' progress was recorded in a coloured chart, with good boys in the white section, bad ones in the red, and the rest in the blue; Frederick 'seldom occupied the blue department'. After he left, 'Mr E[merton]. gave me 16 guineas to be spent in books as a prize for having passed the Matriculation Examination in the First Division'.⁵⁶

George Furnivall was thus anxious to form and educate Frederick as a gentleman, but with practical skills, and a grounding in science, in

⁵⁰ Preface to *Caxton's Book of Curtesye*, EETS, ES 3 (1868), p. ix.
⁵¹ 'Frederick James Furnivall', p. ix.
⁵² Mary Howitt, *An Autobiography*, ed. Margaret Howitt (London, 1889), 9.
⁵³ British History Online http://www.british-history.ac.uk/vch/middx/vol4/pp235-236 [accessed 12 Nov. 2019].
⁵⁴ George Furnivall may also have had medical contacts with the Hanwell Insane Asylum, opened in 1831.
⁵⁵ Entry for Thursday, 10 Feb. 1842 (Furnivall travelled first class by the half past seven train from Paddington), Bodl. MS. Eng. d. 2104, f. 16ʳ; *Queene Elizabethes Achademy*, p. xxii. See e.g. diary entry, 'down to Hanwell by the ½ 10 o' clock train; took Charles some trousers, paper &c . . . chatted with the masters & boys, had supper with Miss Emerton and the masters'; Saturday, 30 Oct. 1841, Bodl. MS Eng. d. 2104, f. 5ʳ.
⁵⁶ Munro, 'Biography', p. ix; diary entry for Wednesday, 27 July 1842. Bodl. MS. Eng. d. 2104, f. 37ᵛ.

addition to the traditional classical instruction. He should have a broad range of knowledge, be well informed in current affairs, as well as have good manners, and be at ease in polite society, confident and able to make his way by meeting and knowing the right people. And these plans suited Frederick: 'Furnivall and his father agreed very well', despite his father's stern admonishments, and Frederick's 'love of those pursuits which appeared subsidiary to his army-trained parent'.[57] Later, when he was editing Sir Humphrey Gilbert's treatise on a gentleman's education in 'Queene Elizabethes Achademy' for the EETS he expressed his thorough approval of a scheme designed to compensate for 'the laziness and viciousness of those who did go to Universities ... and the crying evil of the education of those only places of training ... an evil of which they are not yet free—their narrowness'. Gilbert's emphasis on 'the study and use of *English*' 'will come especially home to the hearts of our own Members'. The training of a gentleman in the sixteenth century followed a scheme which Victorian young men would do well to follow: 'Sir Humphrey would have his boys "muscular Christians," would teach them riding, shooting, and marching, navigating and the parts of a ship, simple doctoring and Natural Philosophy ... The Physitian should also teach surgery.' Law should be taught, along with modern languages, and self-defence. Heraldry was useful, but 'not the nonsense clinging round its origin'. In short, 'The plan of the Achademy is in fact one for the establishment of a great London University for the education of youths in the art of political, social, and practical life—a kind of prototype of the London University so wisely pleaded for of late years by Professor Seeley, which should gather into itself the whole range of modern London teachers and studies.'[58] And London University, though not open to all, was free from the taint of elitism, unlike Oxford and Cambridge in the sixteenth century, where 'rich men's sons had not only pressed into the Universities, but were scrooging poor men's sons out of the endowments meant only for the poor'.[59]

Yet not everything about Elizabethan schooling was admirable—

[57] 'Munro, 'Biography', p. xv.
[58] *Queene Elizabethes Achademy*, pp. x–xi. Sir John Robert Seeley (1834–95), historian and political essayist, professor in Latin at UCL from 1863.
[59] 'Learning the lessons that Mr Whiston so well shows our Cathedral dignitaries have carried out with the stipends of their choristers, boys and men'; *The Babees Book*, ed. Furnivall, pp. xxxvi–xxxvii. Furnivall refers to a question raised in the House of Commons on 11 July 1851 concerning the complaint made by the Revd Mr Whiston, headmaster of the Rochester Cathedral Grammar School, against the Dean and Chapter of the Cathedral; Hansard 1803–2005, https://api.parliament.uk, accessed 14 Nov. 2019. 'Scrooge' is a variant of *OED*, 'scrouge', v. to crush or squeeze, used figuratively.

Furnivall believed in progress. His excursions in the imaginative reconstruction of what it was like to be the young Shakespeare owed much, not only to tracing the similarities with his own childhood, but also to the historian and essayist James Anthony Froude's vivid reconstructions.[60] Yet he rejected Froude's pessimistic conclusion that the English had deteriorated since the times of Sir Walter Raleigh and Sir Humphrey Gilbert: 'Brave we may still be, and strong perhaps as they, but the high moral grace which made bravery and strength so beautiful is departed from us for ever.' 'I don't believe Mr Froude's conclusion a bit', retorted Furnivall; 'The Victorian gentleman mayn't have so much devil in him, or break out into such humours, as the Elizabethan; but in moral grace he is far ahead of him. Self-restraint and moral grace have grown in the latter days'.[61]

Frederick Furnivall's diaries which describe his own time at UCL, Cambridge, and as a young barrister, begin when he was 16, just after he had left Hanwell, and after he was living on his own for the first time in London. The entries follow a regular pattern, beginning with the time when he got up, his activities during the day, which lectures he attended, what he read, his correspondence, the money he spent, and on what, his amusements, his mealtimes, and ending with going to bed and a regular note of the weather. They do not usually say much about his thoughts and feelings. The rather priggish note which they sometimes strike, and the thoroughness of each day's account of what he did and at what time, and the inclusion of details of his health and personal hygiene, his laundry, and his religious duties, perhaps even the notes on the day's weather with which each entry ends, make it seem likely that they were written as a duty, in part for himself, but perhaps more for his parents to see, especially his father, so they could have some assurance that he was not running wild and wasting his time while away from home. Yet there is no evidence that he resented the discipline or the chore; at this stage in his life Frederick fully acquiesced in the principles of his father's regime, wanted to advance himself (though not clear how) and probably was, as the eldest son of a large, well-to-do, and pious Victorian household, sometimes self-righteous. The diaries, though discontinued, established an enduring pattern: as Munro observed, 'The reader will recognise Furnivall's habit of record-

---

[60] 'England's Forgotten Worthies', 29–32. *Short Studies on Great Subjects* (London, 1867), both cited in *Queeene Elizabethes Achademye*, pp. ii, vii. Froude's essay also inspired John Everett Millais's 'The Boyhood of Raleigh', 1870, exhibited at the Royal Academy, 1871. [61] *Queene Elizabethes Achademye*, p. vii.

ing the minutiae noticeable in his literary work'.[62] So Frederick reports, he 'had an effervescing powder . . . read my Bible & prayers, & said my prayers as I have always done morning and evening, since June 1841.[63] Staying up late over tea, with a friend, Joe Bompas, they 'chatted about 'the evil effects of bad' women; talked on Politics & our different points of Dissent from the Church of England &c till 12 o'clock'.[64] The insertion says much. Sometimes he admitted that he overslept and forgot lectures.[65]

The diaries give much detail of his family life and amusements when he returned to Egham for the vacations. They are full of the details of everyday life, manners, and social customs which were at the heart of his scholarly interests, as well as giving much information about the early life of this significant Victorian literary man: Munro, who discussed his friend's early life with him, used them extensively in his biography, and they were presented to the Bodleian Library in 1990 by his granddaughters, Ruth Davies and Jean Gordon.[66] Furnivall had a rural upbringing, and the diaries show that, as he grew up, he continued to follow the usual boys' country pursuits of rabbit and bird shooting, following the hunt, fishing, breaking in and riding their ponies, bathes in the river, and much messing about in boats.[67] Brought up on a farm, he was not sentimental about animals, though it was evidently a rite of passage into adult responsibility after he had gone to Cambridge when he 'got some shot out for Field, & saw him shoot our old grey horse which Papa 'bought' ⟨had⟩ of Sir Fredk Bathurst, soon after Charles was born'.[68] The diaries are terse and matter of fact—he was expected to comport himself in a 'manly' fashion, as traditionally understood.[69]

[62] Munro, 'Biography', p. x.
[63] Bodl. MS Eng. d. 2104, f. 40ᵛ, entry for Wednesday, 17 Aug. 1842.
[64] Ibid., f. 17ʳ, entry for Thursday, 17 Feb. 1842.
[65] Ibid., entry for Wednesday, 8 Dec. 1841 (f. 7ᵛ).
[66] Bodleian Library, Special Collections, catalogue.
[67] Bodl. MS Eng. d. 2104. E.g., out of many entries, those for Saturday, 1 Jan. 1842 'with Charles and Henry on our ponies, rode across the Green & all over the park to Hardiman's Gate & back, leaping all the ditches we could find' (f. 10ᵛ); Monday, 18 July 1842, 'rowed to the willows past Ritchings; had a very nice bathe but the water was rather cold (f. 36ʳ); Thursday, 26 Jan. 1843, 'met Prince Albert's harriers, followed them to Cumberland Lodge, & saw them fed' (f. 78ᵛ). On Saturday, 1 Oct. 1842, 'shot at a hen, Charles touched her in the tail the 1st shot, I hit her very hard the 2nd & Charles finished her the 3rd; shot a shilling at 15 paces, & 'each of us' put 2 shot in it . . . went to the Farm with Charles, rode the ponies into the yard, helped with the cows, brought up the milk, helped feed the pigs as the boy 'man' Smith had gone to his club', f. 51ᵛ.
[68] Bodl. MS Eng. d. 2104, f. 118ᵛ, Thursday, 10 Aug. 1843.
[69] As in OED, 'manly', adj., sense 2(a), and examples of usage.

Frederick thought boys, like himself (and the young Shakespeare), should be high-spirited and ripe for escapades, like 'the larking schoolboy' who in times past 'robbed orchards, played truant, and generally raised the devil in his early days'. The enjoyment of larkishness 'retained in later years many of the qualities that draw to a man the boy's bright heart'.[70] Yet the diaries show that he and Charles, whilst active, could scarcely be said to have raised the devil. They jumped their ponies over ditches and made 'toffy'; Frederick ate copious amounts of fruit wandering about the garden, but with permission, not scrumped, he drove the pony chaise and the family carriage. He also had a turn in Windsor Park driving a novelty horseless four-wheeled carriage for one person, called a 'Corncrake' from 'the machinery making a noise like the bird'. It was operated by 'treddles' worked by the legs.[71] His curiosity about modern inventions, and eagerness to try them out, continued throughout his life. As well as his medical duties, his father farmed the Foster House estate, and Frederick and his brothers were expected to muck in and assist the farmhands, even while the distinction between them and the labourers was maintained.[72] He saw the Royal family when they were at Windsor, as on 13 June 1842, 'walked up to the quadrangle in the Castle to see the Etonians present an address to the Queen; saw the Queen & Prince Albert, (looking very well) start for Slough to go to town by the railroad, the first time that the Queen had ever been by it; the Eton boys ran all the way to the College, round the Queen's carriage hurrahing'.[73]

A 'YOUNG MAN FROM HOME':
UNIVERSITY COLLEGE, LONDON

After leaving Hanwell in 1841, Frederick Furnivall went for a year to study at UCL. The choice of the new University of London (charter

---

[70] *Caxton's Book of Curtesye*, p. ix.

[71] Entry for Tuesday, 23 Aug. 1842, f. 42^r, noticed in Munro, 'Biography', p. xii, with Munro's comment, '*Oxford Dictionary*, please note'. Sense still not recorded in *OED*.

[72] Entry for Saturday, 1 Oct. 1842, f. 51^v; also Wednesday, 28 June 1843, 'raked and rowed in the hay... went to the farm, got on the rick, & took the hay from 2 unloaders... hacked the hay in... helped load the waggon'; f. 111^v.

[73] Bodl. MS Eng. d. 2104, f. 31^v; also Monday, 16 Jan. 1843, f. 76^r; Saturday, 12 Aug., f. 119^r. Also Wednesday, 28 June 1843, f. 111^v, 'Rode down to "Cap's Close" in the cart, raked and rowed in the hay till 12½ ; asked Mr Davenport for his waggon, fetched it from Boyle's, trotted down to the fields, drove about while it was loading... went to the farm (after lunch) got on the rick, and took the hay from 2 unloaders; rode Shirley to the house... went to ⟨chalk⟩ 'the race course,' and hacked the hay in'.

granted in 1836), rather than either of the older universities, probably expressed George Furnivall's wish, as a professional medical man, that his son should learn practical subjects, rather than receive a narrow classical education; also, at 16, Frederick was still young to be a student. But his father, who sent his two eldest sons to Hanwell, but two of his younger sons to Eton, was willing to take advantage of the traditional routes to social acceptance in the polite world, though he apparently grumbled when it later proved advisable to send Frederick to Cambridge if he were to be a barrister. Yet, 'It was not uncommon for men who had reached degree level at University College London... to enrol at Oxford or Cambridge'. Charles Kingsley, for example, used KCL as a 'cramming establishment' to prepare him for Cambridge.[74] This does not seem to have been George Furnivall's original plan for his son, but was, in effect, how Frederick, too, was prepared for the older university.

The foundation of the University of London had been controversial, especially as it was a 'University without religion': that is, without either religious tests or compulsory attendance at chapel. 'The Academic pulpits have resounded against it', wrote Thomas Babington Macaulay in a spirited defence of the ungodly new institution, though he gave many reasons why this shocking allegation was based in misunderstanding of the new university's different purposes, which were no threat to the ancient privileges of either Oxford or Cambridge. 'There was to be no melodramatic pageantry, no ancient ceremonial, no silver mace, no gowns either black or red... Nobody thought of emulating the cloisters, the organs, the painted glass, the withered mummies, the busts of great men, and the pictures of naked women, which attract visitors to every part of the Island to the banks of Isis and Cam'. As Macaulay continued, 'The persons whose advantage was chiefly in view belonged to a class of which very few ever find their way to the old colleges'.[75] Frederick Furnivall was the first of his family to go to university (twice), he had the good fortune to experience both the old and the new, and he benefited from what each had to offer.

The comparison between the two styles of education had also been forcefully made by Frederick's tutor in Greek at UCL, Henry Malden, in a dissertation, *On the Origin of Universities*, which he wrote in support of the University of London's petition for a charter. Frederick Furnivall

---

[74] Bristed, *An American in Victorian Cambridge*, p. xx. Kingsley studied at KCL in 1836-8: *Charles Kingsley*, ed. F. E. Kingsley, 10; Chitty, *The Beast and the Monk*, 49.

[75] 'Thoughts on the Advancement of Academical Education', 315-16. See further Palmer, *The Rise of English Studies*, 15-40.

read it twice, the first time at the end of his tuition at UCL, and again, returning home for Christmas after his first term at Cambridge.[76] Malden's book not only reinforced the sense of contrast, but gave him the materials to understand the historical context and the principles involved. Furnivall enjoyed himself at Cambridge—Munro calls this time 'exceedingly happy'.[77] But his later views of education favoured broadening access and a syllabus much more like that of London. Malden himself had been a graduate and fellow of Trinity College, Cambridge, and thus knew both systems, but he was critical of the ancient universities. He took the view that moving away from the original principles of a university, as established across Europe from medieval times, was a sign of decadence. The Oxford and Cambridge universities and colleges had moved far from their founders' and legislators' wishes and intentions and had 'settled . . . into an arrangement very different from their original form'. 'Within a comparatively short period they have departed from those bodies of statutes which were intended to perpetuate their legitimate constitution', so that 'they have become unlike every other institution in Europe which bears the same name'. By contrast, the new University of London conformed to 'the most ancient universities in their early stage'.[78] Malden drew attention to the ancient English universities' exclusion of dissenters and deplored the obligation to subscribe to the Thirty-Nine Articles of the Church of England. And—a matter closer to Frederick Furnivall's concerns and experience as a student in 1842—Malden was heavily critical of the reliance of Oxford and Cambridge on tutors in the students' own colleges, or hired in from other colleges, to give the essential instruction to students, rather than the professors in their public lectures which were central to the teaching given in the University of London. Tutors were appointed by the heads of the college: 'It is true that the masters generally appoint the most able members of their college; but this has not always been the case, and private partiality or prejudice may operate without public question; and besides the field of choice is limited.' Also 'the attendance . . . is not sufficiently numerous to produce upon the pupils the stirring effect of a public lecture'.[79]

Leaving his parents' home for London was a major rite of passage, even though in practice Frederick's father took care that he lived and socialized with family friends and acquaintances who could keep an

---

[76] Friday, 16 Dec. 1842, Bodl. MS Eng. d. 2104, f. 69ᵛ; Malden, *On the Origin of Universities*.
[77] Munro, 'Biography', p. xiii.
[78] *On the Origin of Universities*, 109, 143.
[79] Ibid. 135 (see also pp. 70–88).

UNIVERSITY COLLEGE, LONDON 43

eye on him, and his university studies provided him with a disciplined and clear daily routine. Macaulay noted sarcastically that concern that students would be led astray in London had been voiced by the new University's critics: 'It is said, "Would it not be shocking to expose the morals of young men to the contaminating influence of a great city?" Shocking, indeed, we grant, if it were possible to send them all to Oxford and Cambridge, those blessed spots, where . . . we know, all the men are philosophers and all the women vestals.' Macaulay conceded that 'The temptations of London may be greater', but 'If the student live with his family, he will be under the influence of restraints more powerful, and we will add, infinitely more salutary and respectable, than those which the best disciplined colleges can impose'.[80] Frederick boarded with Dr Walshe, a physician, elected professor of morbid anatomy at UCL in 1841, and likely to have been one of George Furnivall's acquaintances.[81] In addition to George Furnivall's extensive connections, Frederick's married sister, Mary, lived in London, and he often visited her. And Egham was not very far away.

Thus, every care was taken to prevent Frederick imitating the Prodigal Son in the metropolis, which was the natural fear of parents seeing their sons set out to carve their place in the world. One of the books which it is likely that his parents gave him to read at this time (he was certainly reading it early in his stay at London) was the religious tract by John Angell James, *The Young Man from Home* (with the telling epigraph 'Thou, God, seest me' (Gen. 16: 13)), along with Sherman's *Plea for the Sabbath*.[82] Though James's tract was aimed at young men of a lower class than Frederick Furnivall, principally apprentices and others looking for work, he described the apprehension and the excitement of the adventure clearly: 'The first year or two after quitting his father's house is the most eventful period of all a young man's history, and what he is at the expiration of the second or third year after leaving the parental abode, that in all probability he will be . . . You cannot quit so many restraints, so much inspection and guardianship and come into such new circumstances at an age when the heart is so susceptible.'[83]

[80] 'Thoughts on the Advancement of Academical Education', 322.
[81] Norman Moore, revd. Michael Bevan, 'Walshe, Walter Hayle (1812–92), *ODNB*. Furnivall did not enjoy his time at Walshe's: his landlord refused to let him have a fire (Bodl. MS Eng. d. 2104, f. 26ʳ, Sunday, 24 Apr. 1842), the dinners were poor (f. 29ᵛ, 27 May 1842), and, on 30 Sept. 1842, he 'pd. Mr Walshe £25 for 1 year's board . . . and left Walshe for good' (f. 51ʳ).
[82] James, *The Young Man from Home*; Sherman, *A Plea for the Lord's Day*. Furnivall gives the common form of the title. [83] *Young Man from Home*, 12.

James appealed to a young man's homesickness for 'the sweet fellowship of domestic bliss' left behind (and Frederick was fond of his home and family, though George Furnivall's gruff sententiousness was rather less sentimental than that of the father imagined in the tract).[84] Yet overdependence on home would result in effeminacy—a young man had to leave if he was to 'acquire a manliness of character'.[85] This played upon the youth's sense of excitement on embarking on this critical adventure: 'You have a part to play in the great drama of life, and must leave home to prepare and act it well.'[86] The virtuous young man was also canny: he could expect rewards in the here and now as well as the hereafter. James devoted a chapter to 'Religion viewed as a means of promoting the temporal interest of the possessor'.[87] To this end, a young man should avoid 'the entanglements of love and the rash formation of attachments'—Frederick Furnivall's diaries show him at this age to have been careful in this regard, though he saw much of the respectable female society, which Macaulay had considered one of the benefits of a London education.[88] Lesser evils could lead to greater: 'the first *cigar* a young man takes within his lips may become ... his first step on the career of vice. A cigar is with young persons the symbol of foppery.'[89] Frederick Furnivall did not smoke, and even his enemies never called him a fop. And his evangelical reading and upbringing fervently commended the teetotalism that he practised throughout his adult life.

At UCL he studied German, chemistry, mathematics, Greek, history, and English (for which Furnivall's textbook was Alexander Crombie's *Etymology and Syntax of the English Language*).[90] Frederick's range of studies at UCL, with the strong emphasis on science, mathematics, and modern languages, as well as Greek and Roman history, poised between the classics suited to a gentleman and practical subjects, suggest that, though he and his father were socially ambitious, Frederick had not yet decided what direction that ambition should take. Munro reported that, on 30 December 1841 (thus early in his time at UCL), he had signed indentures of apprenticeship, co-signed by George Furnivall, his cousin

[84] Ibid. 7.   [85] Ibid. 82–3.
[86] Ibid. 9.   [87] Ibid. 118.
[88] Ibid. 87; Macaulay, 'Thoughts on the Advancement of Academical Education', 323.
[89] James, *Young Man from Home*, 27.
[90] Crombie, *The Etymology and Syntax of the English Language*. The third edition was revised after a request by Thomas Dale (first professor of English at UCL, and first professor of English in England) that it should be 'one of the text books for the class of English literature in the University of London', preface, p. vi. Lionel Alexander Ritchie, 'Crombie, Alexander (1760–1840)', *ODNB*; Arthur Burns, 'Dale, Thomas (1797–1870)', *ODNB*.

John, and a Mr Harvey, but whatever the profession was (one guesses some form of medicine), the plan came to nothing.⁹¹ Accordingly, the object of his year in London was to look around him, and decide what he wanted to do. Meanwhile he should broaden his education for a year, as well as improve his knowledge of the world, become cultured in art, music, and politics, see famous people, as well as acquire some town polish and self-sufficiency, while not letting himself run loose without supervision and discipline. He was very much in the condition of the young man described by Charles Kingsley in *Yeast*:

He . . . was now reading hard at physical science; and on the whole, trying to become a great man, without any very clear notion of what a great man ought to be . . . he had gone to college with a large stock of general information, and a particular mania for dried plants, fossils, butterflies, and sketching, and some such creed as this:-
That he was very clever.
That he ought to make his fortune.
That a great many things were very pleasant—beautiful things among the rest.
That it was a fine thing to be 'superior', gentleman-like, generous and courageous.
That a man ought to be religious.⁹²

Furnivall came to know Kingsley well, and be associated closely with his, and the other Christian Socialists', mission and beliefs about education; he also read *Yeast* when first published. And his diaries also faithfully recorded the weather, a practice which Kingsley ridiculed as a 'soul-almanack'—though Frederick Furnivall did not comment on the weather's influence on his mood.

Medicine in some form had probably not yet been entirely ruled out, at least by his father: George Furnivall was understandably concerned that, with nine children to equip for adult life, his eldest son could not waste his time: 'Remember that to whom much is given from him much is expected. If you had followed my Steps now you might have been earning honourably your own Subsistence; now, perhaps, for 8 or 10 years to come you will not be able to do so.'⁹³ Thus the lectures given by Thomas Graham on chemistry to which he went, and in which he was examined, were mainly attended by medical

---

⁹¹ Munro, 'Biography', p. xii.
⁹² *Yeast, A Problem*. Furnivall also collected botanical specimens and drew.
⁹³ Quoted in Munro, 'Biography', p. xiv (reference to Luke 12: 48).

students.[94] The Natural Philosophy curriculum, taught by Professor Richard Potter (also trained as a doctor), was the 'experimental course'.[95] The Mathematics course which he took under Augustus De Morgan largely consisted of trigonometry and algebra, both with many practical applications. Frederick would continue to study trigonometry with a private tutor at Cambridge, and to coach his younger brothers in the subject.[96] Even after he left for Cambridge, he was still expected to help out in the surgery during vacations. And the contacts which Frederick made in London included his father's friends and acquaintances, medical and army.[97] Family friends included the Oswins, father and son, Fred, practising in Gower Street, who were also the Furnivalls' dentists. Frederick had much trouble with toothache, had fillings, and already some false teeth 'pivoted' onto filed down stumps, all without benefit of anaesthetic or palliative, apart from spirits of camphor. The bad teeth may have owed something to 'toffy', but 'Mr O took out the false tooth that he had put in, as he had broken it when giving me a boxing lesson; Fred fitted another one 'to' the stump, but could not make it do well'. His sister Mary also had false front teeth fitted.[98]

The study of natural philosophy gave opportunities to satisfy Frederick's curiosity to see improving sights, rather than please examiners. He went to the Polytechnic, where he 'heard a lecture on Astronomy & the Microscope; saw some Panoramic Fading Views & went down in the diving bell, bought Graham's Outlines of Botany,

---

[94] See Michael Stanley, 'Graham, Thomas (1805–69)', *ODNB*; appointed professor of chemistry at UCL in 1837.

[95] Monday, 25 Oct. 1841, Bodl. MS Eng. d. 2104, f. 2ᵛ. See Geoffrey Cantor, 'Potter, Richard (1799–1886)', *ODNB*, licenciate of the Royal College of Physicians, but did not practise; appointed professor of natural philosophy and astronomy at UCL, 1841.

[96] Leslie Stephen, revd. I. Grattan-Guinness, 'De Morgan, Augustus (1806–71)', *ODNB*.

[97] They included 'Tom Graham', 'Papa's hospital chum' (Wednesday, 31 Aug. 1842; Bodl. MS Eng. d. 2104, f. 44ʳ), perhaps Thomas J. Graham, MD of the Royal College of Surgeons, and author of the popular *Modern Domestic Medicine*, 2nd edn. (London, 1827, first published 1827). There was also John Sutton, 'an old hospital chum of Papa' (Tuesday, 26 July 1842; f. 37ʳ). Also Col. Dowse, 'an old friend of Papa's' whom Furnivall visited at the Arsenal, Tuesday, 27 Sept. 1842, Bodl. MS Eng. d. 2104, f. 50ʳ. 'walked to the Watermen's Pier at 11, went to the Hungerford Pier and then by a steamer to London Bridge; waited there till 12; went by a steamer to Woolwich; walked up to the Barracks, and then to the Arsenal'. After this journey, Furnivall found that the Colonel 'had just started for town'.

[98] Bodl. MS Eng. d. 2104, Thursday 11 Aug. 1842, f. 39ᵛ, Saturday, 14 May 1842 (having spent the night dancing quadrilles, country dances and Sir Roger de Coverley). Saturday, 14 May 1842, f. 28ᵛ, 'walked to Oswin's ... Mr Oswin ⟨cut⟩'sawed' off one of my decayed teeth, pivoted a new one on. Fred filed my teeth ... bought some camphorated spirits and cotton for my teeth.'

came away at ½ past ten and was very pleased with it'. He also went to see the wax models at Mme. Tussaud's.[99] The Royal Polytechnic Institution, which for a 'small price of admission' which 'renders this institution accessible to every one who wishes to improve his mind and enlarge his understanding', comprised indeed 'a world of wonders in art and science', with models of steam engines, 'the much admired dissolving views; the extraordinary exhibition of the microscope', along with the diving bell, the lectures on astronomy, 'and other invaluable sciences'.[100] It was a popular attraction: cheap, entertaining, and edifying—Frederick went there twice to see the dissolving views and the 'diver and his bell'. The second time, he 'weighed myself & was 9 stone & a half; was measured, & was 5 feet 8 ½ inches high with my boots on'. He also took the opportunity to see the Colosseum, the 'Artificial Ice & the Swiss Cottage'.[101] Thanks to his familial interest in medicine he took advantage of UCL's association with the hospital, and twice visited the Dissecting Room with a medical student, C. Tomkins, who also took him to the Zoological Gardens.[102] He may also at least have looked at the catalogue of the anatomical wax models in the Hunterian Museum.[103] Tomkins took him to hear a sermon to medical students by the chaplain to University College Hospital, 'but I did not like it'.[104] At the University, he went 'to the Chemistry Lecture Room for an hour to see the students take nitrous oxide or laughing gas'.[105] In the course of Natural Philosophy, he was shown the Solar Microscope.[106] On Wednesday, 18 May, he 'attended Dr Lindley's

[99] Thursday, 4 Nov. 1841, f. 4ʳ. Reference to the Royal Polytechnic Institution, founded 1838. Graham, *Outlines of Botany*, published by the Institute and based on lectures given there. Saturday, 19 Feb. 1842, Bodl. MS Eng. d. 2104, f. 17ᵛ.
[100] Review of *Outlines of Botany*, *New Monthly Magazine*, 63 (Nov. 1841), 413–15, at 415.
[101] Monday 15 Aug. 1842, Bodl. MS Eng. d. 2104, f. 40ᵛ. In the mid-19th c. the Swiss Cottage was 'a dairy, with long thatched roof and quaint little windows', as reported by Flora Masson in her memoir (daughter of David Masson, Professor of English at UCL), *Victorians All*, 34.
[102] Saturday, 23 Oct. 1841, Monday, 24 Feb. 1842, Thursday, 9 June 1842, Bodl. MS Eng. d. 2104, ff. 2ᵛ, 17ᵛ, 31ʳ.
[103] Saturday, 9 Feb. 1842, Bodl. MS Eng. d. 2104, f. 34ʳ, 'walked home looked over the list and description of the wax models'.
[104] Sunday, 7 Nov. 1841, Bodl. MS Eng. d. 2104, f. 7ᵛ. Preached by Henry Stebbing (called 'Stebbings' by Furnivall), the alternate morning preacher at St James's Chapel, Hampstead Road, St Pancras, as well as a literary figure. Furnivall's dislike may have been to his churchmanship (evangelical, but tolerant of both the Tractarians and other Protestant groups), or to his habit of preaching extempore. See further Arthur Burns, 'Stebbing, Henry (1799–1883)' (*ODNB*).
[105] Tuesday, 16 Nov. 1841, Bodl. MS Eng. d. 2104, f. 5ʳ.
[106] Saturday, 23 Apr. 1842, Bodl. MS Eng. d. 2104, f. 50ᵛ.

lecture on Vegetable Impregnation.[107] Amidst all these curiosities and wonders, the lecture which seems to have impressed him particularly, and perhaps points to his developing intellectual tastes, was Prof. Creasy's lecture On the Personal Influence of the Lives of Great Men, on the Fate of Nations'. He commented that the lecture was '*very eloquent*' (twice underlined).[108]

As things would turn out, UCL proved to be an excellent introduction to Frederick's later life for reasons neither father nor son could have anticipated. He attended Wilhelm Wittich's German lectures and bought his new grammar.[109] And this was his first opportunity to become acquainted with teachers who had been influenced by the 'new' study of comparative philology, which was developing in the wake of the discoveries of the Germans Jakob Grimm and Franz Bopp and the Dane Rasmus Rask in the 1820s. As yet, Frederick's instruction was practical rather than philological. He attended Thomas Key's 'Introductory lecture' on the Latin demonstrative pronouns.[110] And he was taught Greek by Henry Malden.[111] Malden was a disciple of Friedrich Rosen. Rosen had himself studied under Bopp, before taking up the post of Professor of Oriental Languages at UCL in 1828, the year of the College's foundation. He and Key shared the headmastership of UCL's school, which Frederick's brother, Charles, attended after leaving Hanwell. Frederick's first duty on returning to town after the Christmas break was to call upon Malden and consult him 'about the masters with whom Papa ought to place Charles'.[112] It seems likely that Frederick's favourable reports of his time at UCL influenced this decision. And, by the time he completed his studies, Malden was pleased with Frederick, too: though Frederick did not win a prize, he 'said he was very much gratified with

---

[107] Wednesday, 18 May 1842, Bodl. MS Eng. d. 2104, f. 26^r. Richard Drayton, 'Lindley, John (1799–1865)', *ODNB*; he had assisted Joseph Banks and became the first professor of botany in the University of London (1829–60). At this time Furnivall was collecting his own botanical specimen book, Wednesday, 18 May 1842, Bodl. MS Eng. d. 2104, f. 28^v.

[108] Wed. 13 Apr. 1842, Bodl. MS Eng. d. 2104, f. 24^v(see further H. C. G. Matthew, 'Creasy, Sir Edward Shepherd (1812–1878)', *ODNB*). Appointed professor of modern and ancient history in the University of London, 1840.

[109] *A German Grammar*. On one occasion he 'quite forgot Mr. Wittich's lecture', Bodl. MS Eng., d. 2104, f. 4^r, 6 Nov. 1841.

[110] Bodl. MS Eng. d. 2104, f. 1^v, Friday, 15 Oct. 1841. Key was appointed professor of Roman language, literature, and antiquities at the University of London, 1828. See Christopher Stray, 'Key, Thomas Hewitt (1799–1875)', *ODNB*.

[111] W. W. Wroth, revd. Richard Smail, 'Malden, Henry (1800–1876)', *ODNB*. Malden was professor of Greek from 1831 until his death.

[112] Monday, 3 Jan. 1842, Bodl. MS Eng. d. 2104, f. 11^r.

my progress in Greek'.[113] Prizes for the Faculty of Arts at the conclusion of his studies were given in the ceremony held in the Botanical Theatre. Lord John Russell presided, but did not, in Furnivall's opinion, give a very good speech.[114] Frederick was still expected to keep an eye on Charles at UCL school, and felt he had to speak to him 'about some vulgar drawings &c.' which he had in his drawer'.[115]

Equipped with *Leigh's New Picture of London*, Frederick made the most of his time.[116] He worked hard and played hard. He explored the city and its new achievements in civil engineering, including the Brunels' Thames Tunnel then nearing completion, the first known tunnel to be built under a navigable river. Having walked to the college, hoping, but failing, to get 'Tredgold on the Steam Engine' from the library, he 'walked to the Watermen's Pier, started by the ¼ to 11 boat, went to the Tunnel Pier; crossed over the river; walked to Mr Hague; called on Bob Dixon, & he took me over Mr Hague's iron works'. He then 'walked to the Stairs, ferried across the Thames; went to the Thames Tunnel, was very much pleased with it, but could not get quite through it as they were sinking the tower for the entrance of foot-passengers on the Rotherhithe side; walked to the Tunnel Pier at 1 ½ ; went to the London Bridge by the Locomotive Steamer.[117] He went to concerts. Once his cousin George sent him a ticket for Hullah's concert at Exeter Hall, where he 'heard 1600 vocal performers sing several pieces till 10 o' clock; the most magnificent concert I ever heard; the Queen Dowager, Duke of Wellington & many other distinguished persons were there'.[118] He briefly noted that he visited the spring exhibition of watercolours by members of the Society of Painters in Water Colours, and also the Royal Academy, at which he saw his sister Selina and her friend rather than the

[113] Friday, 1 July 1842, Bodl. MS Eng. d. 2104, f. 34ʳ. Frederick 'got the 5th Certificate in the Higher Junior Class of Mathematics, and the 5th in the Senior German'.

[114] Bodl. MS Eng. d. 2104, f. 34ʳ. Russell served as Home Secretary in Melbourne's second government, and subsequently became Prime Minister, 1846–52.

[115] Friday, 24 June 1842, Bodl. MS Eng. d. 2104, f. 33ʳ.

[116] Leigh, *Leigh's New Picture of London*. Wednesday, 13 July 1842, Bodl. MS Eng. d. 2104, f. 35ᵛ. Frederick was excused class because Mr Key's father had died that day at Andover.

[117] Tuesday, 30 Aug. 1842, Bodl. MS Eng. d. 2104, f. 43ᵛ. The Thames Tunnel, opened in 1843, connected Rotherhithe and Wapping. Intended for use by carriages, it instead became a tourist attraction for pedestrians. Hague and Grant, engineers and iron founders at Wapping Wall, declared bankrupt, 1842. T. Tredgold, *The Steam Engine*.

[118] Saturday, 4 June 1842, Bodl. MS Eng. d. 2104, f. 30ᵛ. John Pyke Hullah (1812–84), composer. Lord Wharncliffe, Lord President of the Council (1841–5), gave a speech. Furnivall mistakenly calls it the Council of Education. The Queen Dowager was Queen Adelaide, widow of William IV.

pictures, which he did not mention, though they included five oil paintings by Turner, including the controversial 'Snow Storm. Steam-Boat off a Harbour's Mouth'. Two years later Ruskin would describe it as 'one of the very grandest statements of sea-motion, mist and light that has ever been put on canvas, even by Turner'.[119] Its grandeur left the 17-year old Frederick Furnivall unmoved. Ruskin himself was not present—he had returned to Oxford to take Schools.[120] They would meet some nine years later.

At this age Frederick was more enthusiastic about parties than paintings, and he went to many. They were usually dances organized by his family's circle and their friends, though he got out of this natural habitat when he went to a Mr Besell's, where 'I did not dance much as the company were not the most genteel ever assembled; came away at 2; walked home'.[121] A week later, after he finished hemming his neck-kerchief, he was at the Grahames, where he quadrilled and waltzed. Two days later, visiting Hanwell, he danced quadrilles, waltzes, gallopades, '&c' for two nights running. He went to bed at around four in the morning, and was up at half past seven, in time to attend lectures later in the day. Saturday was a teaching day at UCL.[122]

As a young gentleman in London and representing his family's credit (and his own), Frederick was expected to turn himself out smartly as befitted his social position: there are many references in the diaries to his ordering new clothes and boots for himself. Kid gloves, fragile and easily marked, were a distinctive marker of the 'swell', as distinct from a working man—on one occasion he took five pairs to be cleaned.[123] After he 'talked with Papa about Cambridge', as well as no doubt receiving much good advice, he was measured for a new coat, pair of trousers, and a waistcoat.[124] At the end of his time in London he received a gold watch: a familiar rite of passage into adulthood and to mark achievement—

---

[119] Tuesday, 26 Apr. 1842, Wednesday, 1 June 1842, Bodl. MS Eng. d. 2104, ff. 26^r, 30^r. 'On Water as Painted by Turner', *Modern Painters*, i, Pt. 2, Sec. 5, Ch. 3, from *The Genius of John Ruskin*, ed. Rosenberg, 40.

[120] *Modern Painters*, i. 381. Hilton, *John Ruskin*, i. 69. 'Schools': the final examinations for the degree of Bachelor of Arts at the University of Oxford.

[121] Tuesday, 1 Feb. 1842, Bodl. MS Eng. d. 2104, f. 14^v.

[122] Tuesday, 8 Feb.; Thursday, 10 Feb., Friday, 11 Feb., Bodl. MS Eng. d. 2104, ff. 15^v-16^r. On Thursday evening of 10 Feb. 1842, continuing into the early morning of Friday 11 Feb., at Hanwell, 'had a very pleasant ball, but the rooms were crowded as there were 165 persons there, beautiful waltzing, Blagrove's brother at the piano & a cornet à piston from the life guards band', Bodl. MS Eng. d. 2104, f. 16^r.

[123] Monday, 8 Aug. 1842, Bodl. MS Eng.d. 2104, f. 39^r.

[124] Tuesday, 4 Oct. 1842, Bodl. MS Eng. d. 2104, f. 52^r.

though his father only paid the difference between the cost of his old watch and the new one.[125] He was expected to mend his clothes and other belongings, including horse harness, himself. He was evidently deft with his hands, sewing on buttons, covering and binding books, preparing paper and pens, as well as fishing nets and rods.[126] He had to keep regular accounts of his expenditure. One of his hobbies was painting maps, and he collected botanical specimens. He also collected stories for his 'Anecdote Book' and his book with 'Remarks on Friends'; these have not survived but anticipate his notorious later lack of tact in recording gossip, as well as his sense, strongly conveyed in his diaries, that he lived in interesting times and knew interesting people.[127] More sedately, he also made and kept a sermon-book, with notes on preaching that he heard. Remembering and reporting the gist of sermons was a well-known way of improving the memory and concentration, perhaps especially suitable for young men bent on self-improvement. It was not necessarily just to impress his parents.[128]

Indeed, attending church and hearing sermons during his time in London enabled Frederick to combine devotion with sightseeing and high-quality musical performances in the most unexceptionable way. It is notable that he never recorded going to the theatre—liable to 'destroy a right balance of character' by raising 'the passions beyond their proper tone'—leave alone tea-gardens and steamboats, 'those alluring baits for Sabbath-breaking'.[129] Frederick's taste for opera developed after his return to London after Cambridge. Collecting material for his sermon-book, he became something of a preaching connoisseur. On his very first Sunday in town, he 'went to St Paul in the morning but wasn't there in time as the service begins at ¼ to 10; heard the communion & a sermon at St Clement's Church near Temple Bar; attended the afternoon service at Westminster Abbey at 3; went to Trinity Church in

---

[125] Saturday, 16 July 1842, 'went to Douglas' & got two watches, one gold & one silver, either of which I was to have instead of my old one, Papa paying the difference; chose the gold one'. Bodl. MS Eng. d. 2104, f. 36^r. The occasion coincided with the confirmation of Charles and Selina Furnivall.

[126] He evidently had some elementary tailoring skill, e.g. 'came to my room for a coat & waistcoat; unpicked the waistcoat & got Mama to alter it; cut out some trousers for the little boys [his younger brothers]'; Friday, 14 July 1843, MS Bodl. Eng. d. 2104, f. 114^v.

[127] e.g. Monday, 25 July 1842, 'wrote in my books of Anecdotes & Remarks on friends; sharpened my knives', Bodl. MS Eng. d. 2104, f. 37^r.

[128] Monday, 21 Feb. 1842, Bodl. MS Eng. d. 2104, f. 17^v. For some other near-contemporary accounts of the practice see Martineau, *Autobiography*, i. 33. 93.

[129] *Young Man from Home*, 22, 28.

the evening'.¹³⁰ He also went to 'see' mass performed in 'a Catholic chapel' in rather less smart Soho, at Our Lady of the Assumption and St Gregory, Warwick Street. Apart from curiosity—Newman, as a boy, was also taken there by his father to see it—the attraction is likely to have been the music, for which the church was well known. He 'paid a shilling to get a good seat in the gallery, but got a very bad one'. Later that day he went to hear the Liberal M.P., Sir William Dunbar, preach at the Percy Chapel, Charlotte St, in Camden, before he 'had tea and read "Self Culture"'.¹³¹

Frederick's Sunday excursions took him from Mayfair to Clapham. He heard an 'excellent sermon' at a Curzon Street chapel, 'some very nice music' at Hanover Chapel, Regent Street (now Regent House), and had to wait half an hour before the doors were opened at fashionable St George's Hanover Square.¹³² One evening he went to the chapel of the fashionable charity the Foundling Hospital, where entry was again one shilling, and he 'heard Mr Bailey preach, took notes, a beautiful anthem was sung, "Sing O heaven & rejoice O Earth"'.¹³³ 'Beautiful singing' was also to be had at St Marylebone, where he also 'had a *most excellent* sermon from Mr Coghlan for the Society for the Propagation of the Gospel in Foreign Parts'.¹³⁴ However, Mr Hamilton, who preached at Holy Trinity Church, Marylebone, was 'rather a Puseyite'.¹³⁵ Yet Frederick did not object to the preaching he heard from the Tractarian William Dodsworth, who was at this time putting E. B. Pusey's ideals into practice at Christ Church, Albany Street. Perhaps, as a charity sermon for the newly appointed Bishop of New Zealand, G. A. Selwyn, it was uncontroversial. Frederick was interested because the new bishop had been the local curate at Windsor before his elevation.¹³⁶

¹³⁰ 17 Oct. 1841, Bodl. MS Eng. d. 2104, f. 1ᵛ.
¹³¹ Sunday, 19 Dec. 1841, Bodl. MS Eng. d. 2104, f. 9ʳ. The Catholic church was formerly the chapel of the Bavarian Embassy. John MacQueen, 'Dunbar, Sir William, seventh baronet', *ODNB*. There are several candidates for 'Self Culture'; perhaps William Ellery Channing, 'Self-Culture. An Address introductory to the Franklin Lectures', given in Boston, Sept. 1838.
¹³² Sunday, 5 Dec. 1841, Sunday, 7 Nov. 1841; Bodl. MS Eng. d. 2104, ff. 7ᵛ, 4ʳ, 9ʳ; Sunday, 14 Nov. 1841, f. 5ʳ.
¹³³ Sunday, 20 Feb. 1842, Bodl. MS Eng. d. 2104, f. 17ᵛ (see also f. 4ʳ). The anthem was composed by William Boyce (text from Isa. 49: 13).
¹³⁴ Sunday, 7 Nov. 1841. Sunday, 8 May 1842, Bodl. MS Eng. d. 2104, ff. 4ʳ, 7ᵛ, 27ᵛ.
¹³⁵ Sunday, 27 Feb. 1842, Bodl. MS Eng. d. 2104, f. 18ᵛ.
¹³⁶ Sunday, 14 Nov. 1841, Bodl. MS Eng. d. 2104, f. 5ʳ. Dodsworth joined the Catholic Church in 1851. See further S. E. Young, 'Dodsworth, William (1798–1861)', *ODNB*; also Andrew Porter, 'Selwyn, George Augustus (1809–1878)', *ODNB*; spelled 'Selwin' by Furnivall.

He went to St Stephen Walbrook by the Mansion House because it was 'said to be the master-piece of Sir Christopher Wren & the picture over the Altar showing St Stephen to be the master-piece of Sir Benjamin West'. But he was disappointed: 'the service was most irrevalently [sic] performed by Dr Crowley who did it all in 55 minutes'.[137] On Sunday, 29 May 1842, he noted the 'Anniversary of the Restoration of King Charles the 2nd in 1660'; he still accepted his father's Tory principles.[138]

The family's churchmanship was broadly, but not severely, Evangelical. At home in Egham Frederick went to church at least twice on Sundays, and, after he went to Cambridge, he took a class at Sunday school (highly recommended by John Angell James).[139] He read the Bible with 'Mama'. He prepared carefully to receive the sacrament at Easter. When his brother and sister were to be confirmed he 'bought two books on Confirmation &c Companion to the Altar for Charles; walked to Cullen's talked to Charles about confirmation &c'. He made sure that Charles knew his Catechism, and he 'bought Bickersteth's "Companion to the Communion" for Selina'.[140] But he also played at backgammon and whist with his father (he usually lost), as well as card games with his sisters, and dancing was a social accomplishment. Perhaps more surprisingly, vingt-et-un was played as a genteel pastime in houses where the Furnivalls visited, as well as at Cambridge, 'though for the lowest possible (sixpenny) points'.[141] There are no references to drinking wine or spirits; the family may have abstained (perhaps on medical as well as religious grounds), as Frederick did himself.

Reading on Sundays had to be serious, and no novels were allowed. Apart from Bickersteth, the Prayer Book, and the Bible, the titles speak for themselves. In addition to *Self-Culture* and *The Young Man from Home*, and Sherman's *Plea for the Sabbath*,[142] he read the newly published *My Life by an Ex-Dissenter*, which exhorted the clergy (and laity) of the Church of England 'at this present eventful period', 'more zealously than ever to vindicate her rights and maintain her supremacy'. This reading kept him from straying at least in one direction (it is

---

[137] Sunday, 20 Mar., 1842, Bodl. MS Eng. d. 2104, f. 21^v. Called by Furnivall 'a chapel at Walbrook'. [138] Bodl. MS Eng. d. 2105, f. 30^r.

[139] *Young Man from Home*, 124.

[140] Monday, 6 June, Thursday, 9 June, Friday, 1 July 1842, Bodl. MS Eng. d. 2104, ff. 31^r, 34^r. He bought '2 prayer-books in Oxford Street for Teddy and Henry', Thursday, 1 Sept. 1842, Bodl. MS Eng. d. 2104, f. 44^v. Bickersteth, *A Companion to the Holy Communion*.

[141] Diaries: Thursday, 8 Sept. 1842, Bodl. MS Eng. d. 2104, f. 45^v, Monday, 28 July 1851, Bodl. MS Eng. e 2316, f. 38^v, Bristed, *American in Victorian Cambridge*, 297.

[142] James, *The Young Man from Home*; Sherman, *A Plea for the Lord's Day*. Furnivall gives the common form of the title.

extremely unlikely that Frederick was ever drawn to the 'Puseyites').[143] Thomas Whytehead's *Poems* had local and topical interest: Whytehead was appointed as chaplain to the newly appointed Bishop of New Zealand, Selwyn (formerly of Windsor).[144] These titles suggest that, though Frederick was a dutiful reader of this class of literature, he was not sanctimoniously enthusiastic, if we may judge from the 'religious book' (unspecified) which he read on a summer Sunday 'in the arbour' at Egham.[145] In preparation for his time at Cambridge, he read William Paley's *Evidences of Christianity*, where it was a prescribed text, along with the Greek New Testament.[146] Thus Henry Malden, observed that the Previous Examination for the B.A. at Cambridge required 'a very moderate amount of classical knowledge, an acquaintance with one of the historical books of the New Testament in the original language, and with Paley's Evidences of Christianity'.[147]

Frederick's diaries carefully record his day-to-day reading. The *Young Man from Home* is emphatic on the importance of parental oversight of their sons' books as well as their entertainments: 'If you brought home a book it was examined. If you stayed out at night later than usual, you saw a mother's anxious eye travel upon you, and heard a father's voice, saying "My son, why so late; where have you been?"' Again, Frederick's diaries, as well as his frequent letters to his parents, provide by proxy the 'ever present inspection' to which he was subject at home: 'Wise is that young man who allows the restraints of home to follow him abroad.'[148] Although he rarely commented on what he thought of the contents, the titles nonetheless tell us much about his interests, tastes, and concerns as a young man. When at leisure Frederick read copiously on weekdays, but apart from fitful efforts to improve himself by reading the English classics, and forays into the *Medical Lexicon* and the *Medical Gazette*, he cannot be called a swot. The *Penny Cyclopaedia* was a great source of information.[149] He read Shakespeare (without further specification) and *Paradise Lost*, alongside *Punch*. The very popular *Old Humphrey's Addresses*, another publication by the Religious Tract Society, which

[143] [Rawston], *My Life by an Ex-Dissenter*, dedication.
[144] Whytehead, *Poems*. Rosemary Scott, 'Whytehead, Thomas (1815–1843)', *ODNB*..
[145] Sunday, 17 July 1842, Bodl. MS Eng. D. 2104, f. 36^r.
[146] *Evidences of Christianity Epitomized* (1835); first published as *A View of the Evidences of Christianity* (1794). James E. Crimmins, 'Paley, William (1743–1805)', *ODNB*.
[147] *On the Origin of Universities*, 132.
[148] *Young Man from Home*, 16. Ibid. 81: 'Keep up a constant correspondence with home by letters; an additional motive to which you now possess in cheap postage.'
[149] Issued in 27 slim volumes, each priced 9*d*. between 1833–43, ed. George Long.

Frederick read shortly before leaving for Cambridge, is a varied collection of shrewd, but kindly, observations from daily life from which morals are drawn.[150]

Apart from factual books on subjects that interested him, like Thomas Graham's *Outlines of Botany* (1841), Izaak Walton's *Compleat Angler*, or J. A. W. Herschel's *Astronomy* (1833), Frederick read large quantities of popular fiction, often historical and with a notable bias towards American authors and exciting action. James Fenimore Cooper's *Mercedes of Castile* (1840) concerned Columbus's expedition to the New World; his *The Red Rover* (1827) was a story of piracy. John P. Kennedy's *Horseshoe Robinson, a Tale of the Tory Ascendency* (1835) was a historical romance set in the American Revolution; Robert Montgomery Bird's *Nick of the Woods* (1837) was a best-seller set in Kentucky in the 1780s. Bird's novel in particular is now considered controversial for its savage treatment of native Americans, but it is likely that Frederick read these stories for the adventures, as he read the entertaining stories by the Irish writer Charles James Lever: *Charles O'Malley the Irish Dragoon* (1841), *The Confessions of Harry Lorrequer* (London, 1839), *Tom Burke of 'Ours'* (1857), and *Jack Hinton The Guardsman* (1857). As the dates of the last two show, he often read novels published serially in periodicals before publication in volumes. George Stephen's *The Adventures of a Gentleman in Search of a Horse* (1835) is in the same vein.

Other reading, though engaged in casually at this time, points more directly towards Frederick's future interests and concerns, though, as elsewhere, he merely notes the titles without comment. It was at this time that he read *Ivanhoe* (1819) and Scott's *Anne of Geierstein* (1829). He read William Harrison Ainsworth's story of Lady Jane Grey, *The Tower of London* (published serially, 1840). Shortly after arriving in London, he 'had tea read Chemistry and Tales of Chivalry'.[151] This sounds promising; however, these were probably not medieval romances, but narrative poems by the Canadian George Longmore, in respectful imitation of Scott and Byron, published anonymously. Frederick also read *Martin Chuzzlewit* (published serially between 1842 and 1844) and *Nicholas Nickleby* (1838-9).

At the end of his time in London, Frederick had to decide his future career. If he were not to be a doctor, law was the obvious choice (apart

---

[150] [Mogridge], *Old Humphrey's Addresses*; Monday, 10 Oct. 1842, Bodl. MS Eng. d. 2104, f. 53^v.

[151] Saturday, 18 Dec. 1841, Bodl. MS Eng. d. 2104, f. 9^r. Perhaps *Tales of Chivalry and Romance* (1826).

from holy orders) for a respectable young gentleman who wanted to do well for himself. It was not always embarked upon with a sense of vocation. Frederick Furnivall trod the same well-worn path as Pip in *Great Expectations* (1861), Richard Carstone in *Bleak House* (1852-3), or the unenthusiastic Mortimer Lightwood and Eugene Wrayburn in *Our Mutual Friend* (1864-5). The choice would allow him to live independently in rooms in London and consort with a coterie of like-minded male friends. In the summer of 1842 he was taken by a family friend, Mr Grahame, to the House of Lords to hear the divorce petition from Mr Jackson, whose wife, Georgiana, had been caught by her husband with a lover, Mr Bromehead. The unhappily married couple were beneficiaries of the increasing popularity among the middle classes in the early nineteenth century of seeking private divorce bills from Parliament as 'a remedy for the evils attendant on matrimony . . . by all who can command the pecuniary means'.[152] The interest of the case was not merely prurient: William Jackson was the editor of the *Medical Review* and likely to have been known to George Furnivall and his medical friends.[153] Apparently, Frederick was now considered sufficiently grown up to learn about such things and, no doubt, take warning (he did not). Possibly the spectacle in the House of Lords may have whetted his appetite for the legal profession.

Shortly after passing his exams at UCL, Frederick began reading *Law and Lawyers*.[154] This was not a dry account of how to become a lawyer, though its first chapter advises on the education and skills a young man seeking to enter the profession should have, but a survey of its history and leading personalities. A later edition (1858) describes it in the subtitle as *A Sketch Book of Legal Biography, Gossip and Anecdote*, which sounds like the best approach to attract Frederick Furnivall. It has an entire chapter on 'Legal Eccentricity'. 'Sketch' belies its seriousness: the two volumes give much useful information in an accessible form. Its opening stresses the importance of a modern young lawyer having a wide breadth of knowledge outside the law, that is 'science' in its older sense: they should prepare for this profession by consorting with men

[152] Stephen Lushington, MP, judge, member of Doctors' Commons, Dean of the Court of Arches, quoted by Stone, *The Road to Divorce*, 327.
[153] Tuesday, 12 July 1842, Bodl. MS Eng. d. 2104, f. 35^{r-v}. Furnivall mistook the name of the co-respondent, Joseph Crawford Bromehead, correcting 'Brownett' to 'Brownhead'. William Oliver Jackson married Georgiana Maria Jane Johnson at St Martin-in-the-Fields in 1835. Georgiana was fortunate: following the divorce, she married Bromehead in 1843; technically a divorced wife was forbidden to marry her lover, but, by this time, it was standard practice for the Lords to strike out this clause before voting on the bill (Stone, *Divorce*, 339).   [154] Polson, *Law and Lawyers*.

of letters, and 'by climbing up to the *vantage ground* . . . of science, instead of grovelling all their lives below in mean, but gainful, application to all the little arts of chicane'.¹⁵⁵ Law was not as dry as its reputation alleged, but the practitioner needed to work hard and read widely to avoid being tripped up in court. The amount of general information recommended is daunting, but would have sounded congenial to the Furnivalls, *père et fils*: the lawyer should fill his leisure hours with 'the study of anatomy, physiology, pathology, surgery, chemistry, medical jurisprudence and police'. A sense of English history, with, above all, knowledge of the Bible was also urged.¹⁵⁶ The work strongly reinforced the advice given to Frederick by the barrister, and conveyancer, Bellenden Ker, of Lincoln's Inn, that he should go to Cambridge: 'The bar is composed, for the most part of gentlemen. That sort and extent of information usually found amongst gentlemen, will, consequently be expected from any one who enters the profession. An acquaintance with the classics . . . usually forms a part of the education of every English gentleman; for this reason a classical education is desirable to all who intend to become members of the bar.'¹⁵⁷ Accordingly 'we beg to record our conviction that no student comes to the bar more qualified for success, than he whose general education has been completed at Oxford or Cambridge'.¹⁵⁸ The point was reinforced by anecdotes of barristers who had made fools of themselves in court with poor Latin. However, Frederick Furnivall was intending to become a property lawyer, and, in the early nineteenth century, Serjeant Hill, of Lincoln's Inn, 'was probably the last barrister who united the functions of the conveyancer with those of the advocate'.¹⁵⁹ Frederick continued reading *Law and Lawyers* throughout the rest of June, in between enjoying himself on the river and fishing.

Bellenden Ker, described by Munro as Frederick's father's friend, is likely to have recommended the summer reading of *Law and Lawyers*.¹⁶⁰ Frederick visited Ker for a short chat on 7 June, then in late June and early July he returned from Egham for more substantial discussions, and to get his exam results. On the same day that they were posted in Somerset House, and he attended the divorce proceedings, Ker

[155] Ibid., i. 4 (quoting Lord Bolingbroke).
[156] Ibid., i. 10, 'the Bible is the 'properest and most scientific book for an honest lawyer, as there you will find the foundation of all law and morality', 11 (quoting Macklin).
[157] Ibid., i. 5. At the date of writing, 'The law lectures at the London University . . . have not . . . proved of much service to the cause of law education' (p. 28).
[158] Ibid., i. 32. [159] Ibid., i. 83.
[160] Munro, 'Biography', pp. xi–xii.

decided that study at Cambridge was a necessary next step to Frederick's becoming a barrister, and he recommended Trinity Hall, which was 'more especially the Law College as a natural preparation for the Bar'.[161] The Master, Dr Le Blanc, was Ker's friend.[162] Ker also wrote to Henry Malden asking him to find Frederick a tutor to read for Trinity Hall. He was tutored for five weeks in trigonometry by Mr Effingham Lawrence of Henrietta Street, at a cost of £12. 10s.[163] On Wednesday, 19 October, Frederick

wished all at home good bye, went up to town by the Egham Omnibus . . . took a cab to the George & Blue Boar, Holborn, waited there; Papa came & gave me 50£ for my expenses at Cambridge; started from there at 11 ½ 'by the fly-coach' came very slowly through the city, bought a newspaper & read it through; travelled inside; dined near Bishop Stortford, got into Cambridge at 6 ¼ ; left my luggage at the Red Lion; came down to Trinity Hall'.[164]

[161] Maurice, *The Life of Frederick Denison Maurice*, , i. 59.

[162] Tuesday, 12 July, Bodl. MS Eng. d. 2104, f. 35^r; Munro, 'Biography', p. xii. Thomas Le Blanc, Master, 1815–43 (when he died), Judge of the King's Bench, 1799.

[163] Wednesday, 27 July, 1842 Wednesday, 3 Aug. Friday, 20 Sept., Bodl. MS Eng. d. 2104, ff. 37^v, 38^v, 51^r.

[164] Bodl. MS Eng. d. 2104, f. 55^r.

2

Furnivall, 1841–1848: Cambridge, and Return to London

> No doubt every study requires to be tempered and balanced with something out of itself, if it be only to prevent the mind from becoming 'einseitig' or pedantic.
> Thomas Arnold, Letter to Dr Greenhill, 31 October 1836; Stanley, *Life and Correspondence* (1864), ii. 60

FIRST IMPRESSIONS

Frederick Furnivall always took care to give details of how he got from one place to another—his diaries can be combed for useful information about transport in a time of change, as well as for other insights into social history. He got round London on foot or horse-drawn omnibus: soon after arriving there he describes seeing a horse falling down from exhaustion.[1] He went to Egham by Mr Planner's coach but, visiting Charles at school, he 'went to the new Road and by a bus to the Railway Station at Paddington & down to Hanwell by the ½ past 10 o' clock train.'[2] As seen at the end of the last chapter, the beginning of this new stage in his life was heralded by full details of the journey. Munro noted that in later life Furnivall often compared his first journey to Cambridge by coach with later railway journeys which got him there in just an hour and a quarter and 'enabled him to begin work on his beloved Chaucer in the University Library before 10 a.m.'[3] The EETS in the nineteenth century owed a great deal to the developments of the railways. Manuscript research became much easier with the advances in transport. Furnivall also 'favoured the railways because they were democratic', and he would argue with Ruskin who disliked the spoiling of the countryside—while still taking the train to his house in the Lake District.[4]

Though George Furnivall accepted Bellenden Ker's view on the desirability of sending his eldest son to Cambridge, he had mixed feelings. In hindsight, he would be proved right, though not because his son got into dissolute company or debt. Indeed, the opposite: Frederick

---

[1] Tuesday, 12 Oct. 1841, Bodl. MS Eng. d. 2104, f. 1^r.
[2] Saturday, 30 Oct. 1841, Bodl. MS Eng. d. 2104, f. 5^r.
[3] Munro, 'Biography', p. xii.   [4] Ibid., pp. xii–xiii.

began mixing with a serious and intellectual set whose liberal ideas and politics would change him radically and set him at odds with his father. A few days before he went up, Frederick noted that he 'talked to Papa about Cambridge':[5] 'talk' in his terms meant serious admonitions, distinct from 'chat'. And certainly, it took him a while in the beginning to adjust to a very different kind of instruction and pattern of living after the bustle of London.

At Cambridge, Furnivall found that the tutorial system within his college allowed the authorities to monitor academic discipline quite strictly, though he had much more leisure time.[6] He studied classics and mathematics. The Rev. William Marsh, Fellow and tutor at Trinity Hall, lectured on both (and Mr Power on mathematics).[7] He dutifully attended Mr Marsh's lectures on trigonometry, but after a while 'determined not to attend any more of them'. Marsh however politely 'asked me to attend . . . so I went to one.'[8] In London Furnivall may have missed Wilhelm Wittich's German lecture with impunity, but when he decided to bunk off his Cambridge tutor's lectures on trigonometry he was noticed—and bread-and-butter trigonometry lectures were not intended to have a 'stirring effect'.

The early entries in Furnivall's Cambridge diary convey the novelty of the experience very well in their laconic manner:

Thursday, 20 October
... walked about the garden of Trinity Hall; Mr Swan's clerk came with the valuation of the furniture in my rooms; rejected some of it, & bought some other things; called on Mr Marsh, the tutor, at 11 ½, but, as he was engaged, he came to my rooms shortly afterwards, then took me back to his, to tell me about a private tutor &c., had some apples and pears for luncheon, walked out into the town & ordered a cap & gown, & some carpet, called at the office for my crate, but it had not arrived, walked about; came home & ticketed my keys; had my gown and cap sent at ¼ to 4; went up into Mr Marsh's rooms & met ⟨Mr⟩ Badger (a freshman) and Mr Abdy, chatted, went into hall to dinner, saw Dr Le. Blanc

[5] Tuesday, 4 Oct. 1842, Bodl. MS Eng. d. 2104, f. 52^r.

[6] Bristed also commented on the freedom experienced by freshmen after leaving school and coming to Cambridge: 'only about two hours and a half of their daily time being demanded by the college authorities'; *An American in Victorian Cambridge*, 29.

[7] Marsh was a Fellow and tutor from 1840 to 1856, by which time he had become Senior Tutor. See Crawley, *Trinity Hall*, 164; there were usually two tutors and one or two assistants. After leaving the College, Marsh lived for 33 years more as vicar of the College living of Wethersfield, Essex.

[8] Tuesday, 16 May, Saturday 20 May 1843, Bodl. MS Eng. d. 2104, ff. 103^v, 104^r. On the role of college tutors at Cambridge, see Bristed, *An American in Victorian Cambridge*, 12–13.

& chatted to him; had a very nice dinner, refused to wine with Abdy, came to my rooms, put my drawer to rights, walked up to the cap-maker's and back, lay down on the sofa; lighted my candles; at 6 ¼; wrote out catalogue of things, and altered those of books and clothes; cap-maker came to try on the skeleton of a cap, which fitted very well...

Friday 21, October
... Dr Le Blanc (the master of Trinity Hall, & Mr Ker's friend) called on me... went out & bought a tea-tray: &c &c, walked about... the sempstress came & put up my muslin ½-blinds... |

Sat 22 Oct
... read the Cambridge Guide & wrote Remarks on Friends... went to the Van offices but my crate had not come; paid 7/6^d for one quarter's subscription to Stevenson's Mathematical & Circulating Library... went to Chapel at 20^m to 6 in a white surplice...

Sun 23 Oct
... attended Chapel at 8, Mr Power read the Prayers, Mr P. & Mr Marsh the Communion service, & one of the scholars the lessons... read the Greek Testament... went to Great St Mary's (or University) Church, Mr Scholefield read a short prayer and preached a sermon... the Hulsean Professor, 'Alford of Trin(ity) Coll., prayed, & preached, went to St Michael's Church... Mr Thos. Dale preached a sermon for 'The Cambridge Refuge (for Harlots)'.[9]

It is one of life's more humorous examples of imitating literature that Furnivall—a model for Kenneth Grahame's Water Rat—should meet Mr Badger at college. Though, like him, a freshman, Thomas Badger was four years older than Furnivall. They would continue friends throughout their time at Cambridge, and they continued to meet in London where both qualified as barristers at Lincoln's Inn.[10] Another friend from Trinity Hall was a South African, John William van Rees Hoets, a year older than Furnivall, who also stayed in contact with him after Cambridge.[11] He would later translate from the German, both for Bernhard ten Brink, and for the economist, Lujo Brentano, parts

[9] Bodl. MS Eng. d. 2104, ff. 55^v–56^v. Swan's were auctioneers. Bristed noted that one of a freshman's first jobs was to provide himself with a tea set and other necessities; *An American in Victorian Cambridge*, 15.
[10] Thomas Smith Badger (of Eastwood), (1821–66), born in Rotherham, called to the Bar in 1847, incorporated at Lincoln's Inn, 1850. Like Furnivall, he specialized in conveyancing. He died young, in 1866 (*Alumni Cantabrigienses*, Part 2)
[11] John William Van Rees Hoets (1824–1907) died at Hampstead. Badger and Hoets wrote to Furnivall during their stay in Frankfurt in 1843; the letter conveys something of their undergraduate style: 'Hoets has granted me his most gracious permission to insert one of my elegant effusions in his envelope.' Letter of 26 Feb. 1843, KCL, Furnivall Pa-

of whose essay 'On the History and Development of Gilds,' he translated for inclusion in Joshua and Lucy Toulmin Smith's EETS volume, *English Gilds*, for which Furnivall commissioned it.[12] As may perhaps be inferred from Hoets's work on this text (the medieval trade guilds were seen by Furnivall as the forerunners of trade unions and cooperatives) this friendship was a leading influence towards Furnivall's change of political outlooks. Hoets and Badger also kept up their friendship with each other after college. And, though Badger seems from Furnivall's diary to be mostly a Tory boating chum, he, too, would later help Furnivall to raise money for striking workmen. Both Badger and Hoets actively supported Furnivall in his later Christian Socialist activities and interests in London.

There is thus probably more to these friendships than Furnivall was letting on, and it seems likely—it is certainly not surprising—that, at least from 1843, he was prudently keeping things back in his diary that he did not wish his parents to know. In the latter part of his Cambridge career, after he came to know the Macmillans, the booksellers and publishers, he was absorbing liberal ideas which would not be well received at home. It was not that there was anything to be ashamed of in these friendships—far from it. Hoets, indeed, was later described as 'an exceedingly handsome man, generous and noble as any Englishman could be.'[13]

Furnivall soon settled into the new pattern. Morning chapel and lectures left plenty of time in the afternoons before dinner, and in the evenings. By the following Wednesday, he had found his way to the boat-houses: Munro remarked that 'Furnivall's enthusiasm for the river knew no bounds... and it is to be feared that aquatic exercises, velocipedes, walking, and running, proved some impediment to his more serious pursuits.'[14] Munro, whose account of Furnivall is grounded in

pers, FU 13; see also Hoets's letter to Furnivall of 22 June 1843, FU 388. See also letter to Furnivall from Bernhard ten Brink, 2 Oct. 1870, FU 66.

[12] *English Gilds*, ed. Toulmin Smith, EETS, OS 40, pp. xlix–clxv, acknowledgement, p. liv. Hoets was born at the Cape and came to Europe, aged around 16; he graduated in 1846 as 15th senior optime. In 1848 he would be ordained, after which he returned to South Africa. Later he returned to England and engaged in business as a shipbroker: Graves, *Life and Letters of Alexander Macmillan*, 41. He died in 1907.

[13] The description is Alexander Macmillan's, writing in 1864; *Life and Letters of Alexander Macmillan*, 41.

[14] Munro, 'Biography', p. xiii. The velocipedes were hired for himself and Charles, when his family visited in Apr. 1843. Bristed noted the importance attached to the hours of exercise between 2 and 4 in the afternoon by students; *The American in Victorian Cambridge*, 20. Trinity Hall's reputation as a rowing college was growing at this time: 'It must be re-

his own conversations with him, as well as in the diaries of his youth, makes it clear how dominant his enthusiasm for rowing became at this time. After finishing his studies, Furnivall spent the Long Vacation of 1845 up at Cambridge building himself a sculling boat and experimenting with its design.[15] He also played cricket in summer. When it froze, he borrowed skates.[16] He was clearly proud of keeping himself fit, noting, for instance that he 'went up to the Gog Magog hills 4 ½ `miles' ran a mile in 6 ¾^m', then, after Chapel, 'did nothing for ¼ hour.'[17] In his second year he gave the waterman 2s./6d. to name a new 'funny' (a narrow clinker-built boat for two scullers) after his sister, Selina.[18] At this time, probably under instruction from his medical father, he began faithfully to note the incidence of his visits to the 'locus'. The sense is not recorded in the *OED*, but the meaning is clear—it was a university euphemism—like the *partes posteriores* in which his friend Badger was inconveniently afflicted.[19]

SELF-CULTURE

Furnivall was still a serious—indeed, priggish—young man in religious and moral concerns, though he spent much time chatting and walking about the town. He disapproved of insobriety, refusing wine from another fresher, Abdy,[20] at his first dinner in College. Later, when three

---

membered that rowing was not at that time . . . a conventional or mindless activity, but was often . . . the favourite recreation (not the religion) of intellectually strenuous men'; Crawley, *Trinity Hall*, 145. Crawley was perhaps exaggerating Furnivall's strenuous intellect, which did not make itself very apparent until perhaps towards the end of his time at Cambridge, and then in circles outside the college. See also p. 158: in 1902 Furnivall was elected by the college to an honorary fellowship, in recognition of his scholarship in English literature.

[15] Munro, 'Biography', p. xv.

[16] Friday, 17 Feb. 1843, 'Read the Greek `& Italian' Testaments . . . went up to Badger, & borrowed his skates, bored some holes in my boots . . . walked to a piece of pretty good ice near Grantchester . . . skated till 10^m to 4" Bodl. MS Eng. d. 2105, f. 83^v.

[17] Wednesday, 23 Nov. 1842, Bodl. MS Eng. d. 2104, f. 64^r.

[18] Wednesday, 3 Jan. 1844, Bodl. MS Eng. d. 2104, f. 132^v. Other funnies were named from light reading, 'The Red Rover' and 'La Dama del Lago', Monday, 31 July 1843, f. 117^r. *OED*, 'funny', n. James Fenimore Cooper's sea novel *The Red Rover* was published in 1827 in London; there were three Italian translations of Walter Scott's *Lady of the Lake* (the first two in 1821, the third, in prose, in 1829. See further Ambrose, '"La donna del lago"'.

[19] 'Locus' first occurs in inverted commas (Thursday, 8 Dec. 1842), but not thereafter; Badger's complaint was noteworthy because it prevented them from taking out the boat. (Wednesday, 10 Jan. 1844), Bodl. MS Eng. d. 2104, ff. 67^v, 133^v.

[20] John Thomas Abdy, admitted to Trinity Hall in 1841, became a Fellow in 1850, and Regius Professor of Civil Law in 1854, *Alumni Cantabrigienses*, Part 2.

64 CAMBRIDGE, AND RETURN TO LONDON

drunken undergraduates broke open his door at 20 to 6 in the morning, one of them dressed up as a ghost, he 'bolstered him & pushed him out' before going back to bed.'[21] He followed James's advice that the young man from home 'should judiciously and affectionately warn your associates, who are seeking the pleasures of sin, of their danger.'[22] In his brothers' absence, he lectured his fellow students on good behaviour, in particular mentoring Henson of Corpus who 'gave me *his word of honour* to reform.'[23] Two days later he followed this up with a visit, when he 'chatted to him, & he promised to give up all his wild companions, & be a hard-reading & serious man for the future.'[24] Furnivall was still just seventeen: he noted a couple of months later on his birthday, Saturday, 4 February, 1843, that 'I am eighteen years old to-day.' Later in the day he engaged his private tutor, Mr Tozer, of Gonville and Caius College, for two terms to teach him mathematics, and he read the newly published *Anecdotes of Napoleon Bonaparte* and *Pickwick Abroad* (1839), a bestselling plagiarism of Dickens by G. W. M. Reynolds.[25] He had not yet finished with Henson, whom he coached in Virgil and Paley's *Evidences*, before noting that he managed to pass his Little-go (Responsions).[26]

Furnivall was once gated for returning to College late, but since this was because he had been attending Mr Carne's Missionary Meeting, it was to be regarded as a technical misdemeanour committed in a good cause.[27] He had heard sermons preached at Egham on behalf of the Church Missionary Society, and John Carne, author of, among other writings, the *Lives of Eminent Missionaries* (London, 1833–5), was widely travelled in the Near East. He was a good talker and teller of stories: this, along with the cause, is probably what attracted Furnivall to hear him.[28] As a result of the meeting, Furnivall was drawn into the

---

[21] Thursday, 9 Feb. 1843, passage marked with asterisk in violet ink, perhaps by Munro, who recounts the episode ('Biography', pp. xiii–xiv; the three were Matcham, E. Cook, and W. Cook. See also Thursday, 20 Oct. 1841, Bodl. MS Eng. d. 2104, ff. 81^v, 55^v.

[22] *Young Man from Home*, 151.

[23] Saturday 10 Dec. 1842, Bodl. MS Eng. d. 2104, f. 68^r. This was Francis Henson, admitted to Corpus in 1841, and who took his B.A. in 1845. It may be significant that, as a cleric, he does not seem to have held any cure for some years after ordination. *Alumni Cantabrigienses*, Part 2.   [24] Monday, 12 Dec. Bodl. MS Eng. d. 2104, f. 69^r.

[25] Bodl. MS Eng. d. 2104, f. 80^v. Cunningham, *Anecdotes of Napoleon Bonaparte*. *Pickwick Abroad* was first published in America (Philadelphia, 1838); Furnivall is more likely to have read the later English version (London, 1839). Furnivall paid Tozer £7 for a term's coaching, Saturday, 16 Dec. 1843, Bodl. MS Eng. d. 2104, f. 130^v.

[26] Thursday, 30 Mar. 1843, also Friday, 3 Mar. and Thursday, 9 Mar.; Bodl. MS Eng. d. 2104, ff. 93^v, 87^r, 88^v.

[27] Monday 20 Mar. 1843, Bodl. MS Eng. d. 2104, f. 91^v.

[28] G. C. Boase, 'Carne, John (1789–1844), *ODNB*: 'he often captivated audiences by his

Cambridge Missionary Association and agreed to become a collector. He left the Association's papers in other students' rooms and solicited contributions for the missionaries—it was perhaps his first venture into collecting money for a cause. He was persistent, but met with refusals; nevertheless, he still managed to raise £5 from members of Trinity Hall. After persuading a fellow student, Smith, to part with half a sovereign for the missions, he went to Swan's the auctioneer, & bought 'a very nice picture of "Family Devotion—Morning" in a maple frame, 25 in. by 30 ½ 'for 2s' . . . hung it up above my sofa.'[29] A contemporary observed that 'Some first-rate engravings are almost a necessary part of the University man's furniture.'[30] 'Family Devotion' evidently reminded Furnivall of home, and it was joined a month later by a picture of the Duke of Wellington, which Badger gave him, and another of Robert Peel.[31] Two Tory prime ministers and 'Family Devotion' proclaimed young Furnivall's tastes and views at this time clearly enough to his visitors, though strong conservative views were common among Cambridge students at this time.[32] During the Christmas holidays the family was visited by Mr Edgell with a memorial, addresssed to Sir James Graham, Peel's Home Secretary, 'against the atheist publications now issuing from the press, which Papa signed'.[33]

Apart from occasionally missing chapel, he continued to attend church regularly, and comment on the sermons he heard. He enjoyed the singing at King's College Chapel. Reading on Sundays continued to be serious, but on weekdays (and now also occasionally on Sundays) he read novels, among them the latest instalments of the picaresque *Martin Chuzzlewit* (being serialised 1842-4), which included at this time the notorious anti-American chapters. The adventure stories, often about military life by the Irish novelist and raconteur, Charles

tales'. On Sunday, 28 May, 1843 Furnivall 'attended Mr Carns' lecture at Trinity College on the agency of the Holy Spirit, &c.', Bodl. MS Eng. d. 2104, f. 106ʳ.

[29] The association of the two events might suggest that Furnivall used the money to buy the print, but this is surely an unfortunate impression created by his terse diary style. Friday, 28 Apr. 1843, Bodl. MS Eng. d. 2104, f. 99ᵛ. Perhaps a mid-19th-c. print, 'Family Devotion—Morning', 8×12¼▨, showing parents seated at a table in front of a fireplace, with their daughter, and a baby on the mother's lap, the father reading the Bible.

[30] Bristed, *An American in Victorian Cambridge*, 298. Portraits of great men and religious subjects were popular choices.

[31] Saturday, 27 May 1843, Bodl. MS Eng. d. 2104, f. 105ᵛ

[32] Bristed, *An American in Victorian Cambridge*, 41: 'I could not help contrasting the jacobitism (Toryism is not a strong enough term for it) then prevalent among the students.'

[33] Sunday, 15 Jan. 1843, Bodl. MS Eng. d. 2104, f. 76ʳ. See Jonathan Parry, 'Graham, Sir James Robert George, second baronet (1792-1861), *ODNB*, described as 'staunchly Anglican'.

Lever, were particular favourites, carried over from home, especially at this time *Tom Burke of Ours* (1844).[34] Furnivall also read Lever's *Charles O'Malley* (1841),[35] and *The Confessions of Harry Lorrequer* (1842).[36] Samuel Warren's *Ten Thousand A-Year* (1841) was another popular comic novel, whose pusillanimous anti-hero, a shop assistant and would-be gentleman, Tittlebat Titmouse, expresses anxieties about social climbing while also showing that the outward and visible signs of a gentlemen were very difficult for the outsider to ape. It was one of several satirical portraits of lower middle-class men which appeared in the 1840s—the young Furnivall certainly did not want to look and behave like *them*. Its author noted that, though amusing, the story was meant to be an illustration of principles, 'of character and of conduct'. The only sure route to a fortune was by earning it, behaving oneself, and going to church on Sundays. The story thus, in a light-hearted way, consorted with Frederick's reading about a young man's self-culture, and, as it concerned laws of inheritance, it had a legal interest, too.[37]

Novels were joined on Valentine's Day by a duty letter to Bellenden Ker, 'Shakespeare for ¼ of an hour',[38] and *Rasselas*.[39] Macaulay's *Lays of Ancient Rome* offered semi-edifying entertainment, as did other reading in an eclectic mix of recent publications, perhaps vaguely intended to enlarge the general knowledge of the world proper to a gentleman and a lawyer.[40] *The Wars of Europe* anticipated his later interest in the details of military engagements during the Franco-Prussian War, while the *Dictionary of Arts and Sciences* and the *Penny Cyclopaedia* also enlarged his general knowledge.[41] F. Bond Head's observations during an expedition to Argentina to report on mines offered a medley of unmethodical geography, history, and personal anecdote.[42] Throughout his life Furnivall drank copious amounts of tea—tea and chat were his

---

[34] Picked up at various times during 1843 for relaxation: Saturday, 4 Mar., Saturday, 1 Apr., Friday, 2 June, Thursday, 10 Aug. Bodl. MS Eng. d. 2104, ff. 87^v, 94^r, 107^r, 118^v. Lever, who had trained in medicine at Trinity College, Dublin, sung ballads in the streets, and had adventures in the backwoods of Canada, where he was affiliated to a Native American tribe, borrowed material for his novels from his own adventurous life. It is easy to see why his stories appealed to Furnivall.

[35] Friday, 10 June 1842, Bodl. MS Eng. d. 2104, f. 31^v.

[36] Thursday, 6 Jan. 1842, Bodl. MS Eng. d. 2104, f. 11^v.

[37] *Ten Thousand A-Year*, Preface, p. vii.

[38] Tuesday, 14 Feb. 1843, Bodl. MS Eng. d. 2104, f. 83^r.

[39] Saturday, 18 Feb. 1843, Bodl. MS Eng. d. 2104, f. 84^r.

[40] Macaulay, *Lays of Ancient Rome*.

[41] *The Wars of Europe* ed. By a Distinguished Officer.

[42] Bond Head, *Rough Notes Taken during Some Rapid Journeys*.

favourite forms of relaxation, and Sigmond, *On Tea: Its Effects, Medicinal and Moral* informed him about the beverage, which Dr. Sigmond assured him was 'the most agreeable and the most salutary diluent that has yet been introduced into Europe.' At breakfast, if not too strong, tea 'is much to be recommended,' and 'after exercise, such as dancing, warm tea is most grateful.'[43] 'The social tea-table is, like the fireside of our country, a national delight'. The book was topical and patriotic: tea-plants had been recently discovered growing wild over large portions of Upper Assam, thus breaking China's monopoly of the tea-trade. This unsuspected source would assist 'our mighty empire in the East . . . our maritime superiority, and . . . our progressive advancement in the arts and sciences.'[44] These were all causes of which Frederick Furnivall approved. As for other subjects, 'Power on Railway Accidents' may have been written by his mathematics tutor in Trinity Hall; ironically his other tutor, William Marsh served on the Cambridge and Oxford Railway Committee, investigating the proposed rail link between the two university towns.[45]

Some of Furnivall's other reading, like the *Ingoldsby Legends*, might be considered to look forward, albeit obliquely, to his later historical and antiquarian pursuits.[46] Pierce Egan's *Wat Tyler*[47] (originally intended to be a story about Oliver Cromwell) offered stirring medieval adventures. Anna Maria Porter's *The Hungarian Brothers* was another historical romance set in Central Europe in the French Revolutionary wars.[48] *The Student Life of Germany* supplemented Malden's historical account of the development of universities with a positive eye-witness account of German higher education and the training it offered. The writer, William Howitt, offered from his first-hand observation, a corrective to the uninformed partial view of German students as addicted to duelling and drinking. 'Shall I advise them to imitate the students of Cambridge?' he demanded, and 'practise the vice and the mockeries which are practised there?'[49] The Germans were, in his

---

[43] Sigmond, *Tea: Its Effects, Medicinal and Moral*, 130, 110, 116.
[44] Ibid. 66, 2–3.
[45] *Railway Chronicle*, 26 Apr. 1845, p. 488; entry for Monday, 10 Apr. 1843; Bodl. MS Eng. d. 2104, f. 96^r.
[46] 'Thomas Ingoldsby' [R. H. Barham], *The Ingoldsby Legends*, first published in book form (1840 and 1842); 2nd edn.1843.
[47] Pierce Egan the Younger, *Wat Tyler*.
[48] Anna Maria Porter, *The Hungarian Brothers*, written in 1807; Furnivall probably saw the later edition, printed London, 1839.
[49] *The Student Life of Germany, from the Unpublished MS. of Dr. Cornelius*, Preface

experience, 'amongst the most accomplished, gentlemanly, temperate, correctly-mannered, and intellectual men that European society possesses'.[50] Frederick Furnivall would have ample evidence to bear out this observation once German scholars started arriving in London in significant numbers after 1871. When he was a student, they were evidently regarded as something exotic, thanks to the notoriety of the nationalistic, anti-French, student fraternities, the *Burschenschaften*, which Howitt defended as relatively harmless, compared with English students' 'guzzlings'.[51] Yet the author recognized that the book's appeal lay in his account of strange and picturesque customs and the fraternities' mysteries. The book includes the text and score of forty student drinking songs.

The Student Life of Germany thus offered the mix of personal observation and out-of-the-way facts, all enlivened with illustrations, anecdotes, and novelties, which Frederick Furnivall liked, and allowed him to compare his own experience as a freshman with the German one. Howitt's information about the vices practised by upper-class young gentlemen in Cambridge was drawn from recent discussion in the anti-Establishment *Westminster Review*, which cannot have reassured George Furnivall if he saw it. However, his son did not mix in such circles, behaved himself, and passed his exams (written and viva voce) in the Second Class, on Virgil's *Aeneid*, Book VI, in which he 'did very tolerably',[52] the Greek New Testament, Xenophon's *Hellenica*, Book I, algebra, Euclid, and trigonometry. Maybe the demands of these examinations could be met, as an unimpressed observer has said, 'in a few weeks of cramming during the ten terms of residence required by statute', leaving time for many other pastimes, though Frederick Furnivall's were no more heinous than the river, 'and the traditional diversion of long walks in the dismal flatlands of Cambridgeshire'.[53] Although the classics, as Kingsley noted, had plenty to say about the attractions of women, Furnivall had clearly paid heed to the warnings by the authors of the religious tracts and sermons, and probably of his father, too, against not just harlots but forming serious attachments to women: 'all conversation on the subject of love had been prudishly

---

(dated Heidelberg, 6 Apr. 1841), p. viii. Charles Lever also wrote about student life in Germany and collected student drinking songs.

[50] Ibid., p. x.   [51] Ibid., p. viii.
[52] Bodl. MS Eng. d. 2104, ff. 92^v, 106^v; entry for Wednesday, 22 Mar. 1843, Thursday, 23 Mar. 1843, and Wednesday, 31 Mar. 1843.
[53] Allen, *The Cambridge Apostles*, 12

SELF-CULTURE   69

avoided, as usual, by his parents and teacher', as Charles Kingsley observed of young college men at this time.⁵⁴ Furnivall shared this prudishness. Others found out about the subject, as Kingsley said, by reading Byron's poetry in secret. *The Young Man from Home* also strenuously warned against Byron, whose writing led not merely to lasciviousness, but also infidelity in religion.⁵⁵ Furnivall did not read *Don Juan* until after leaving Cambridge for Lincoln's Inn, when he was 'much disgusted by it'.⁵⁶ Meanwhile, pornographic material and bawdy conversation inevitably circulated among students, as well as schoolboys like Furnivall's younger brothers.

DISSATISFACTION

At Cambridge, Furnivall, at least so far as his diaries allowed anyone reading them to perceive, balanced work, devotion, and play appropriately, with very few hints of larkishness. He worked conscientiously for his examinations. And Malden testified that examinations in Cambridge were 'careful, strict, and perfectly impartial; and they are conducted in a very judicious manner'.⁵⁷ His family came to see him in London after his exams and before returning to Egham for the summer—among other excursions, after a visit to the dentist, they walked to Grange's in Piccadilly, Furnivall had an ice, then walked up Regent Street, and 'saw the "Industrious Flea"'.⁵⁸ The Cambridge diary ends on 13 January 1844, but Furnivall achieved his degree without incident in 1847, after obtaining a place among the Junior Optimes in the Mathematical Tripos of 1846.⁵⁹ Furnivall's university career was unexceptionable, but not notably distinguished. Thus, he left Cambridge with a pass degree, gentlemanly credentials, and an invaluable network of social connections. In this he resembled most of his contemporaries. As Kingsley described it, a man left college 'with a good smattering of classics and mathematics, picked up in the intervals of boat-racing'.⁶⁰ And Furnivall's lifelong obsession with sculling would be as important to him and more than his literary concerns. Munro's biography gives fuller information about his competitive rowing than appears in the diaries

⁵⁴ *Yeast*, 4.
⁵⁵ *Young Man from Home*, 58.
⁵⁶ Saturday, 2 Aug. 1851, Bodl. MS Eng. e. 2316, f. 39ʳ.
⁵⁷ *On the Origin of Universities*, 132.
⁵⁸ Saturday, 24 June 1843, Bodl. MS Eng. d. 2104, f. 111ʳ·
⁵⁹ Sidgwick, 'Frederick James Furnivall', 556.   ⁶⁰ *Yeast*, 4.

and was derived almost certainly from first-hand conversation with his subject: when he left Cambridge for London, Furnivall took his boats with him, and used them daily.[61] He spent the Long Vacation of 1845 building himself an experimental wager-boat—as its name indicates, a lightweight high-performance racing boat for single scullers for winning wagers.[62] That he did not go home as usual is probably a further sign of his growing independence from his father's views.[63] But it is also likely that he was sulking—it was at this time, as will shortly be seen, that his father thwarted his hopes for his future.

For in his later time at Cambridge, Furnivall's outlook on life was changing, and the smooth path towards equipping himself to earn a living as a gentlemanly young lawyer no longer satisfied him. He left Cambridge, not merely with a degree, but with a confirmed taste for solid reading and an interest in pressing matters of social concern. This is something that cannot be appreciated from his accounts of his lighter reading and self-improvement in his diaries, though the diary of his first two years records many visits to bookshops and Stevenson's Mathematical & Circulating Library. Things changed in the autumn of 1843, when the young bookseller, and soon-to-be publisher, Daniel Macmillan, opened his first Cambridge bookshop, in Trinity Street, in time for the beginning of the University year in Michaelmas Term.[64] Previously Macmillan had worked for Johnson, another Cambridge bookseller, where he had made useful contacts with senior members of the University and had read widely. He had exalted ideals of what a bookseller should be, and he had now returned to Cambridge from London 'to test how far that early dream of a high vocation could be realised'.[65] Macmillan, serious, deeply religious, and largely self-educated, with his younger brother, Alexander, soon became a powerful influence on the undergraduates, including Furnivall—and this part of his Cambridge experience was not even hinted at in his diary.

For their part, the Macmillans found Furnivall engagingly full of himself, ignorant, enthusiastic, and easily carried away. Alexander Macmillan, in conversation with his son George about his memories of these

---

[61] Munro, 'Biography', pp. xv–xvi.

[62] See *OED*, 'wager', n², compounds, c². The compound was first recorded in 1844, just a year previously: Albert Smith, *The Adventures of Mr Ledbury* (1844).

[63] Munro, 'Biography', pp. xv–xvi.

[64] Daniel Macmillan (1813–57). See further Rosemary Van Arsdel, 'Macmillan Family', *ODNB*.

[65] Hughes, *Memoir of Daniel Macmillan*, 208. See also Morgan, *The House of Macmillan*, 16–18, 24–6.

times, 'laughingly used to say, Furnivall was a modest young man'—meaning, of course, that he was nothing of the kind. George's further comment was 'That Furnivall's zeal then, as later, sometimes outran his discretion, and led him both to say and do things which did not always please his associates, may well be supposed'.[66] Later Alexander found Furnivall's indiscretion annoying: 'it must have been some such differences which, after those early days, created a certain coolness between my father and Furnivall, though they remained at bottom good friends'.[67] Another of Furnivall's contemporaries at Cambridge also recalled the powerful influence on the young men which the Macmillans exercised:

We undergraduates felt that with men hardly older than ourselves there was opened to us a new sphere of interest. They were the first booksellers whom I, for my own part, had ever known to take an enthusiastic interest in their business and to have a literary insight below the binding of their books . . . He [Daniel] was fond of talking, especially on books, and soon groups of men would gather round him in the shop and listen to criticisms full of humour and knowledge on books and authors. It was he who first told us of a young writer 'who looked like a lion', showing us Kingsley's *Village Sermons* and the *Saint's Tragedy*, and introduced many of us to Hare's *Victory of Faith*, and *Guesses at Truth*, and to Trench's poems and other works, and to Coleridge's *Aid to Reflection*. There was a little snuggery at the top of the house, in which in the evenings many of us first learnt to appreciate little-known Scotch songs and ballads.[68]

It is easy to account for the ferment that these topical new works created in students who, like Furnivall, were becoming impatient of an

[66] Memoir of George A. Macmillan, in Munro (ed.), *Frederick James Furnivall*, 104–5.
[67] Ibid. 105.
[68] Hughes, *Memoir of Daniel Macmillan*, 211–12, quoting an anonymous informant, 'one of the earliest of their customers'. Kingsley, *Twenty-five Village Sermons*; 'The Saint's Tragedy', included in the collected edition of the *Poems* (London, 1875). Julius Charles Hare, *The Victory of Faith*, 2nd edn. published by Macmillan (Cambridge, 1847), based on University sermons preached in 1839, and 'desirous of assisting my youthful hearers, and rebutting Newman's *Lectures on Justification* (1838). J. C. and Augustus William Hare, *Guesses at Truth*. Furnivall had already read S. T. Coleridge's *Aids to Reflection* (first published, 1825), which was given to him during his 1843 visit to Southampton (Diary, Thursday, 5 Jan., Bodl. MS Eng. d. 2104, f. 74^r, *passim*). The version referred to here is probably the 6th edn., enlarged (London, 1848). The Hare brothers' *Guesses at Truth*, which went through twenty editions, brought them friendship with the Macmillans, whose business was founded on a loan from Julius, and they kept his books in print: N. Merrill Distad, 'Hare, Julius Charles (1795–1855)', *ODNB*; see also *Life and Letters of Alexander Macmillan*, 24–5, for the influence of the Hare brothers and Maurice on the Macmillans, and their move from London to Cambridge; also Morgan, *House of Macmillan*, 22–30.

academic treadmill. The Hare brothers counselled intellectual patience, 'So long as we continue under magisterial discipline and guidance, we are apt to regard our studies as a mechanical and often irksome taskwork. Our growing presumption is loth to acknowledge that we are unable to walk alone, that our minds need leadingstrings so much longer than our bodies.'[69] But their description of the ecstasy of the young scholar released from leading strings and flitting joyously and at will from one book to another is so much more exciting. The work was explicitly *not* addressed to readers who expected to be told what to think.

Furnivall fell most willingly under the Macmillan's spell, and forty years later, he, too, paid tribute to their formative influence on him as a young man. He was prompted by writing a review of Thomas Hughes's *Memoir of Daniel Macmillan*, and, as a Cambridge man, he was indignant that the assignment had been given to Hughes, who had been to Oxford and had not known his subject at this period of his life, unlike himself. Furnivall reckoned that he and other students owed to Macmillan 'the best teaching that they got at the university. For many of us our tutors did nothing but give us a little mathematical and classical cram. The man who taught us to think, and opened our boating minds, was Daniel Macmillan, along with our college friends.'[70] Furnivall was among the undergraduates, as well as senior members of the University, who assembled after four o' clock Hall in the Macmillans' upstairs drawing room.[71] In the *Memoir*, Hughes's anonymous informant described a book enthusiast (unnamed), who if not Furnivall himself, as seems likely, remarkably resembled him, and was also a boating man, at around 1843–6. The story describes Furnivall, or his look-alike, as a gauche young book collector, just up from Cambridge, who judged books by their covers:

The confidence of undergraduate readers and purchasers of books grew rapidly, as they recognized that here was a man who showed not only insight but conscientiousness in his dealings with them. One such I remember bringing an admirably selected library to his rooms in Lincoln's Inn, which he had collected at Cambridge. He had a great fancy for good binding, and used to relate how when he first began to collect, he had fixed his affections on the eight

---

[69] Hare, *Guesses at Truth*, 7–8.

[70] Review of Thomas Hughes, *Memoir of Daniel Macmillan*, in *The Academy*, 22 Aug. 1882, p. 112. 'Cram' was glossed by Bristed as 'All miscellaneous information about Ancient History, Geography, Antiquities, Law &c.; all Classical matter not included under the heads of Translation and Composition.' *An American in Victorian Cambridge*, 25.

[71] *Life and Letters of Alexander Macmillan*, 27. See also Morgan, *House of Macmillan*, 30–2.

DISSATISFACTION

volume edition of Mitford's *Greece*, beautifully bound, which he discovered on the shelves in Trinity Street. The price, having regard to the cost of such binding, he knew to be exceedingly moderate. He had accordingly ordered the books to be sent to his rooms, but on mentioning the purchase to Daniel, and admitting that it was the binding which had decided him, he was advised that the contents rather than the backs of books was the point to be studied; and that as he wanted the best history of Greece, this would not be his proper investment. He exchanged it, after further talk, for the edition of Thirlwall in cloth, became a steady customer, and always attributed the absence of rubbish on his shelves to the good advice which he got on this and subsequent occasions.[72]

Furnivall's new sense of restlessness at the end of his university career, and his dissatisfaction with himself, and perhaps his university work, too, can be detected in the final entry in his Cambridge diary for Sunday, 31 December, 1843, with its telling insertion at the end summing up the past year:

Myers of Trinity . . . preached the last Sermon of his Advent Course on the future state, shewing that we shall dwell on this earth when renewed 'by fusion' having our souls purified, & our occupation being perhaps to find the density of stars & carry out to the fullest extent our present worldly knowledge. Water was the first purifying agent in the deluge, & fire will be the last at the judgement day . . . read Wheatley on Com(mon) Prayer . . . read Pearson on the Creed, about Christ's Descent into Hell, which is to be taken as the abode of tormented Spirits; Christ's immortal soul descended into it, but suffered no pain. Very fine day. 'Have lost all my time since June, ½ year gone.'[73]

Classical and mathematical 'cram' apparently did not seem to be worth much *sub specie aeternitatis*. This would not be the last of such self-critical vows of amendment. And the cessation of the Cambridge diary before the end of his time there was itself a minor declaration of independence.

It was not usual, or intended, that the first degree should be a preparation for formal academic research: 'in every faculty the course of real study terminates with the first degree'.[74] Formally and socially Furnivall had achieved what was expected of him at Cambridge: no more, no less. In his last year it had remained to Macmillan to open

---

[72] Hughes, *Memoir of Macmillan*, 212–13. Furnivall had also 'bought Mitford' *History of Greece* (8 vols.) . . . for 12*s*., though from a fellow undergraduate, and another rowing man, Goode, rather than from a bookseller; Diary, Tuesday, 1 Nov. 1843, Bodl. MS Eng. d. 2104, f. 58ᵛ. Connop Thirlwall's *A History of Greece*, 8 vols. (London, 1835–44) had recently been completed. See further, John Connop Thirlwall, Jr., *Connop Thirlwall: Historian and Theologian*, 96–107. [73] Bodl. MS Eng. d. 2104, f. [133]ʳ (unnumbered).
[74] Malden, *Origin of Universities*, 131.

his 'boating mind'. The introduction of Furnivall to the Macmillans, if one were needed, could easily have come from his college friend John Hoets, who was certainly a fan and lodged with them. The attraction of Daniel and Alexander Macmillan's shop and conversation did not merely rest on their own brilliance, but on their easy familiarity with some of the greatest and most influential Cambridge graduates of their day: intellectuals, writers, and theologians. Cambridge was well known for the club formed in 1820 for serious-minded discussion and debate, the Conversazione Society, more familiar by its nickname, the 'Cambridge Apostles', so called perhaps because its members were limited to twelve at any one time. Julius Hare, Archdeacon of Lewes, had been one. Furnivall was never invited to become an Apostle, and the meetings seem unlikely to have attracted him. But Daniel Macmillan, whose shop Furnivall frequented after 1843, was intimate with some of the most influential Apostles, especially Frederick Denison Maurice (a founding member), also Richard Chenevix Trench 'and others of the liberal school of Churchmen and social reformers'. It was said of these men by another Cambridge observer that their 'cant was inveighing against cant . . . they all affected much earnestness and a hearty dislike of sham and formula'—characteristics which Furnivall also shared.[75] And Macmillan also knew Charles Kingsley (who had graduated from Magdalene College in 1842), though Kingsley was not an Apostle.[76] Even if these influential writers were not known to him personally, he sold—and read—their books. The Apostles, especially those of the slightly older generation in the 1830s, included many who had distinguished and influential lives after they left Cambridge. The group 'became a powerful coterie of considerable importance in the development of Victorian culture, allied to the Establishment, yet persistently liberal in their views'.[77] Others in the circle included John Mitchell Kemble and Alfred Tennyson. Another, William Johnson, writer and Eton schoolmaster, was Furnivall's close friend.[78] But three, in particular—Frederick Denison Maurice, Richard Chenevix Trench,

[75] Bristed, *An American in Victorian Cambridge*, 114.
[76] Hughes, *Memoir of Macmillan*, 208.
[77] Allen, *Cambridge Apostles*, 10. 'Liberal' and 'socialist' views were expressed in these men's active concern with the welfare of the working class: see e.g. Alexander Macmillan's letter of 8 Aug. 1850 to the theologian and biblical scholar Fenton Hort, *Life and Letters of Alexander Macmillan*, 44.
[78] Allen, *Cambridge Apostles*, list of members, 219–24, also 6, 177. They included James Furnival (1820–7), a clergyman, not apparently a near relation of F. J. Furnivall. Johnson later changed his surname to Cory, after he resigned from Eton in 1872; Tim Card,

and Connop Thirlwall, scholar and bishop of St David's—would shortly become known personally to Furnivall, after he moved to London, as, among other things, members of the Philological Society.[79] Of these, Maurice and Trench, in very different ways, would have a profound influence on Furnivall's life, activities, and views. Trench, associate of Hare, Kemble, and Thirlwall, long-time friend of Maurice, whom he had known since Cambridge, and future Archbishop of Dublin, would become the President of the Philological Society, and originator of the Society's Dictionary.[80] As for Maurice, it is hard to overestimate his influence on impressionable young men. Daniel Macmillan raved about him:

> I really don't believe that Maurice has any *second* in our time. He towers far above all others, and yet he is the most profoundly humble man I ever knew... Truly his mind is lofty and lowly, like the Master whom he serves; and just because he is so lofty and so lowly he keeps clear of all narrowness and one-sidedness: and looks honestly at the principles of all parties, and recognises and appropriates the truth which lies in them. Art, science, literature, everything that is a development of the good, the beautiful, and the true, is dear to him. No man is so free from all pedantry, all pretence. He only seems to care for what is living and real—what has to do with man's life. He is what Carlyle calls 'a true truth-loving man'.[81]

This charismatic figure and intellectual leader was, by the time Furnivall left Cambridge, Professor of English literature (1840) and Professor of theology (1846) at KCL. Before taking up this appointment, Maurice, like so many of the other Apostles, including Tennyson—a lifelong friend—had entered Trinity College, Cambridge (in 1823), where he attended Julius Hare's Greek lectures. He transferred in 1825 to Furnivall's college, Trinity Hall, to read law.[82] After a period in London studying for the bar, he returned to Cambridge, where he achieved a first class in civil law. In a change of career, he then moved to

'Cory, William Johnson (1823–1892), *ODNB*. Also Mackenzie, *William Cory*. See further Michael J. Sullivan, 'Tennyson at Trinity', 12–13.

[79] See further Gilliver, *Making of the OED*, 8, 11; also John Connop Thirlwall's biography of his ancestor, *Connop Thirlwall*. Furnivall read Thirlwall's *History of Rome* (1828) as well as, in all likelihood, his *History of Greece*; see Benzie, *Dr F. J. Furnivall*, 13.

[80] The standard biography of Trench is by J. Bromley, *The Man of Ten Talents: A Portrait of Richard Chenevix Trench 1807–86, Philologist, Poet, Theologian, Archbishop* (London, 1959).

[81] Letter to his fiancée, Frances Orridge, 19 June 1850, quoted in Hughes, *Memoir of Macmillan*, 181–2. For a photograph of Maurice as a young man, see Colloms, *Victorian Visionaries*, 17.

[82] See the biographical account in Crawley, *Trinity Hall*, 134–6.

Oxford to study theology at Exeter College, and was ordained in 1831. Most importantly, so far as Furnivall was concerned, he was also appointed in 1846 as chaplain to Lincoln's Inn, where Furnivall was destined to train for the bar. Maurice's Lincoln's Inn sermons would be a powerful draw. And Hughes, Kingsley, Ludlow, and, through Ludlow, Furnivall, would all become disciples in his Christian Socialist movement.[83]

Thus, by the time he left Cambridge, Furnivall, thanks largely to Daniel Macmillan and his circle, was learning to think more independently, and was ripe to benefit from these new liberal influences. It was a case of 'cometh the hour, cometh the man'. As Hughes observed of Macmillan: 'The time was singularly fortunate for a man of his peculiar experience and wide sympathies to start as a bookseller in a University town. England has seldom been in a more electric state, intellectually and morally. The Anti-Corn Law agitation was stirring the nation to its depths . . . the great movement of the working-class was already making itself felt, in Chartism, and half blind attempts at association.' And Macmillan's thoughts and sympathies 'were fermenting in the minds of all the best men who were growing into manhood. And here at Cambridge he had in his hand as it were on the pulse of the reading public.'[84]

No doubt Furnivall's comment about the narrowness of the official university syllabus—its 'cram'—was coloured by the wisdom of hindsight and his later views. But he was already beginning to rebel against the pressure to become a lawyer, a profession about which he had probably never been very enthusiastic. And in 1845, when he spent his Long Vacation hanging round Cambridge building a boat rather than going home, another opportunity had presented itself. Daniel Macmillan was seeking to purchase the business of 'the ablest of the older Cambridge booksellers', Stevenson, who was retiring because of ill health. It was a big risk, as the valuation was upwards of £6,000, and obliged the Macmillan brothers, Daniel and Alexander, to look for other partners who could put up some of the capital to develop the publishing side of their business.[85] Until as late as 1855, the Macmillans were seriously

---

[83] For the salient facts of Maurice's biography, see Bernard M. G. Reardon, 'Maurice, (John) Frederick Denison (1805–1872), *ODNB*. The standard full-length biography was written by his son, Frederick Maurice, *The Life of Frederick Denison Maurice*. Julius Hare married Maurice's younger sister, Esther (1844), and, in 1849, Maurice would take as his second wife Georgina Hare-Naylor, Hare's half-sister.

[84] Hughes, *Memoir of Macmillan*, 208.

[85] Ibid., 221; Morgan, *House of Macmillan*, 29–30.

DISSATISFACTION

hampered by their failure to find partners who, even if willing to provide some limited capital, lacked the necessary 'flair' about books necessary for their business.[86] Furnivall found it an exciting prospect: 'Here was a mine, hitherto almost unworked, of the best book-producing power of the nation, especially for educational works. There was a great want of these, and in every generation of undergraduates were men specially fitted for writing or editing them.'[87] Indeed, Furnivall had been so impressed 'that, when I took my degree in 1846, I wrote to my father begging for a few thousand pounds to go into partnership with the Macmillans instead of to the Bar; and grievously was I disappointed when the money was refused, and I sent up to London to grind at conveyancing precedents.' It was unlikely that George Furnivall would have agreed to finance such a venture when he considered that, after all this education, his eldest son needed a safe profession: 'Make then what Knowledge, what little Wisdom you can attain to, subservient to your future Necessities and Wants, and learn to support yourself, if not your Family hereafter.' As Munro summarized this 'serious admonishment', 'with nine children to tender, he will stand no foolery'.[88]

In hindsight Frederick Furnivall himself admitted that the Macmillan brothers might have been better off in worldly, though not idealistic, terms without him: 'I'm sure I should have done the firm much good, and prevented it getting so rich as it has become.'[89] This was an honest self-assessment. He had abundance of 'flair'—if by this is meant imaginative energy or 'get up and go', but, if we may judge from his swashbuckling way of conducting the EETS's finances, the Macmillans' business would certainly not have prospered.

[86] *Life and Letters of Alexander Macmillan*, 30.
[87] Hughes, *Memoir of Macmillan*, 221.
[88] Quoted by Munro, 'Biography', pp. xiv–xv. The date of this letter is not given, and it is said to be one of many giving 'constant admonishments' (p. xiv).
[89] Review, *Daniel Macmillan*, p. 112. George Furnivall's refusal is noted, e.g. by Benzie, *Dr F. J. Furnivall*, 13. See further Van Arsdel, 'Macmillan Family'.

3

Lincoln's Inn and the London Working Men and Women: 1846–1852

> Liberalism . . . now . . . is nothing else than that deep, plausible scepticism, of which I spoke above, as being the development of human reason, as practically exercised by the natural man.
>
> John Henry Newman, *Apologia pro Vita Sua*, 'General Answer to Mr. Kingsley', 26 May 1864

LINCOLN'S INN

Accordingly, on 26 January 1846, nine days short of his twenty-first birthday, Furnivall was admitted to Lincoln's Inn.[1] As he summed up his legal training, 'Entered at Lincoln's Inn on the 26 January 1846. Kept exercises in the Trin(ity). & Mich(aelma)s Terms of 1847 & the Hilary Term of 1848. Called at Gray's Inn on the 30th of January, 1849.'[2] Furnivall took his place in the pupil room in a set of chambers on the first floor of No. 8, Old Square, belonging to the reforming Whig conveyancer Bellenden Ker. Ker was a highly distinguished lawyer, who, in the opinion of his pupil John Malcolm Ludlow, 'ought to have reached much higher than he did . . . He was in fact one of the three or four cleverest men I ever met with; for quickness of thought I don't think I ever knew his equal.'[3] The book Furnivall read on leaving UCL, Polson's *Law and Lawyers*, described—and even celebrated—the legal intricacy attending on the transfer of real property by this time, after its simple origins: 'There is no branch of our jurisprudence which tasks in a greater degree the learning and ingenuity of the practitioner than conveyancing.' In addition to ingenuity and an immense quantity of knowledge,

---

[1] *Registers of Admissions by the Honourable Society of Lincoln's Inn*, ii (1800–93), https://www.lincolnsinn.org.uk/libraryarchives/digitisedrecords, accessed 14 Dec. 2018; also Benzie, *Dr F. J. Furnivall*, 14.

[2] As he noted under 'Occasional Memoranda' in his 1848 diary, Bodl. MS Eng. e. 2315, f. 60ᵛ.

[3] On Ker, see W. R. Cornish and David J. A. Cairns, 'Ker, (Charles) Henry Bellenden [*formerly*] Charles Henry Gawler (c.1785–1871), *ODNB*; also Ludlow, *Autobiography*, esp. 40–7 (p. 44). Ker's father's name had been Gawler, but he took the name Bellenden Ker by royal licence at around the time when he became a claimant for the Duchy of Roxburgh (Ludlow, *Autobiography*, 44).

the conveyancer needed 'patient labour, untiring research prosecuted in the retirement of the closet' away from the excitement and publicity of the courts.[4]

A conveyancer's highly specialized activities were a result of 'the complicated and ramifying system of our commerce—the highly artificial state of society', and the consequent multiplication of property interests. Property lawyers needed to advise clients 'not only what is *legal*, that is, in conformity with law, but also what, under the circumstances of the case, is most prudent and desirable, and often most *fair*', that is, equity. Such advice required the conveyancing lawyer to absorb useful information of all kinds, not merely to have knowledge of business transactions.[5] Conveyancers were historically barristers, but by Furnivall's time 'a great deal of conveyancing is now transacted in solicitors' offices, the superior education of that branch of the profession rendering them better qualified than formerly for this line of practice'.[6] Dickens's Mr Tulkinghorn (*Bleak House* (1853)) is an example of this superior kind of family solicitor. As a result, conveyancing barristers could expect to be less well paid; also, to the writer's regret, solicitors had introduced 'a less prolix and verbose style of conveyancing', which 'has been the source of much undeserved injury to the profession'— though the writer conceded that the length of a document should not be the sole measure of the work put into it. But, thanks to 'the increase of commerce, and consequently of litigation, which has been so remarkable in our time', there was still plenty of work to go around.[7] Ludlow noted that, in the 1830s and 1840s, 'with a well-filled pupil-room at 100 guineas a year each, a conveyancer's income . . . might often amount to £2,000 a year'. Ker expected his former pupils to work for him even after they had qualified, but, thanks to his wide range of activities and connections, his patronage was valuable. According to Ludlow's reckoning, Ker had between eight and ten pupils during the time he was there, 'though the number latterly fell off'.[8] Clearly Furnivall, young, impetuous, and energetic, did not have a vocation for this kind of patient, undemonstrative, confidential work, though he could 'grind', and there would be compensations. Not at least among them were the conviviality and the Long Vacations. Charles Kingsley, a friend of Ludlow,

[4] Polson, *Law and Lawyers*, ii. 236.
[5] Ibid., ii. 236–7.
[6] Ibid., ii. 243.
[7] Ibid. Ludlow also described the changing nature of conveyancing, thanks to simplification of the law, shorter deeds, and the increased role of better-educated solicitors; *Autobiography*, 40.   [8] Ludlow, *Autobiography*, 40.

and well known to Furnivall too, described in a poem, 'The Invitation to Tom Hughes' (1856), the anticipated pleasure of an evening spent at the Inn:

> Then to chat till midnight
> O'er this babbling world—
> Of the Workmen's College.[9]

Kingsley also described the pleasures of the Long Vacations spent in the vale of Windsor, after the Inns of Court had emptied. Furnivall's vacations at nearby Egham gave him plenty of time to develop his growing antiquarian and medieval interests. As Dickens remarked at about this time: 'How England can get on through four long summer months without its bar ... is beside the question.'[10] England managed without Furnivall, at least.

Bleak House (1853), Dickens's satire on Chancery, and the property lawyers of Lincoln's Inn, portrays the Inn and its environs in considerable detail at the time when Furnivall knew them, though Dickens heightened some features for satirical effect. He described the mud in the streets, the Inn's seclusion, the peace in its gardens and Lincoln Inns' Fields away from the jostling small streets and courts nearby, with small businesses dependent in various ways upon the legal profession. And in the Inn itself, 'in dirty upper casements, here and there, hazy little patches of candle-light reveal where some wise draughtsman and conveyancer yet toils for the entanglement of real estate in meshes of sheepskin, in the average ratio of about a dozen of sheep to an acre of land'.[11] Familiarity with parchment proved invaluable in later life: the Austrian scholar Alois Brandl commented in his memorial that Furnivall 'owed to his legal studies an intimate acquaintance not only with old customs and notions of law, but with the archives and the ways of scribes and copyists, which stood him in good stead later on'.[12] His training in inheritance law, which familiarized him with the intricacies of pedigrees as represented in a family tree, is likely to have assisted in his understanding of arguments concerning the 'pedigrees'

---

[9] Quoted in *A Lincoln's Inn Commonplace Book*, 276. Hughes was another Lincoln's Inn lawyer. For images of Kingsley and Ludlow at around this time, see Colloms, *Victorian Visionaries*, 133, 208 (the photograph of Ludlow is in the archive of the Working Men's College). See also the striking photograph of Kingsley included by Girouard in *Return to Camelot*, 129.

[10] *Bleak House* (1853), ed. Nicola Bradbury (Harmondsworth, 1996), 300.

[11] Ibid. 504.

[12] In Munro (ed.), *Frederick James Furnivall*, 11.

of texts, and their representation in a *stemma codicum*.[13] Such genealogical tables had an arcane significance, understood primarily by noble families and their confidential lawyers, not outsiders.[14] But Furnivall's late-night toils should not be exaggerated. He did 'work at night for Mr. Ker' before he was called to the Bar at Gray's Inn on 20 January 1849, after which he set up his own practice at 11 New Square.[15] But this was not usual, and he increasingly spent time at the office reading, chatting to visitors, and correcting proofs of the *Christian Socialist*.

Furnivall received minimal formal training in his duties. Ludlow was scathing about the perfunctory 'exercises' which, for a fee, allowed a man the right to 'share in the privileges of practising at the bar'. Law students received 'absolutely no legal instruction' However, Ludlow noted that 'Ker's chambers were a place where one was expected to learn without being taught, but where nevertheless one could learn a good deal by finding out how'. It was no use asking Ker, who 'would tell you sharply that it was your business to find out'. Yet, if the pupil was prepared to listen, not ask questions, Ker was a rich source of information. Otherwise, his pupils read textbooks at home. In chambers 'you were set down to copy out in a book of your own the Ms. [manuscript]. precedents used in chambers'—as Furnivall also experienced. After a while 'a draft was given you to draw, or an abstract to read and make marginal notes on in pencil, without the slightest explanation'.[16]

Lincoln's Inn and its surroundings provided a sense of belonging to a place closely implicated in English history, with historic buildings which were also undergoing considerable development and change in Victorian times, among them Furnival's Inn, a medieval building, which was demolished and rebuilt in the early nineteenth century, but which had previously been affiliated to Lincoln's Inn, and where Dickens had rented rooms. Furnivall's own chambers in New Square (built 1682–93). were admirably located, not just for his work, but for his developing literary and social interests. He lived a short walk from the

[13] The original meaning of a 'stemma' was a 'genealogical tree'; the specialized sense of a diagram representing 'a reconstruction . . . of the position of the surviving witnesses in the tradition of the transmission of a text' is not recorded in the OED until 1930 (and then in inverted commas); see 'stemma', n. 1(b) and 1(c).

[14] As in Samuel, *Ten Thousand A-Year* (1841); the novel's protagonist does not understand the marks indicating the ramifications of a pedigree on a paper in his lawyers' office, which purports to represent his descent from a noble family, thinking it must be 'a sort of conjuring paper' (i. 40). His failure to understand these conventions indicates his status as an outsider.

[15] Wednesday, 2 Aug., Friday, 4 Aug. 1848, Bodl. MS Eng. e. 2315, f. 38^{v}. Foster, *Register of Admissions to Gray's Inn*, 472.   [16] Ludlow, *Autobiography*, 39–42.

British Museum and the Strand, Somerset House, UCL, and KCL, the College of Surgeons, Temple Bar, and other places commemorated by Dickens: Bell Yard and Cook's Court were all nearby—the Union Workhouse was also not far away.[17] The novel's portrait of an area of sharp contrasts between the poor and well-to-do was still evident by the time of Charles Booth's 1889 maps of London poverty, showing streets of the 'lowest class, vicious, semi-criminal' close by the neighbourhood of the well-to-do middle class, with a sprinkling of 'mixed' housing: 'some comfortable, others poor'.[18] Lincoln's Inn lawyers who had a social conscience could not easily ignore the world just outside their gated walls, perhaps especially when Dickens represented their home ground so particularly. Furnivall's associate, Ludlow, was one who engaged in visiting the poor in what he described as 'the foully vicious neighbourhood around the Inns of Court'.[19]

Bellenden Ker bore little resemblance to the enigmatic Mr Tulkinghorn. He was a grandee with a colourful family history, who had thought at one time he would inherit the duchy of Roxburgh. He was an old friend of the statesman Lord Brougham, and intimate with 'the highest figures in government circles'.[20] Ludlow, who had entered Lincoln's Inn and pupillage with Ker ten years before, in 1838, and continued to 'devil' for him for many years afterwards, described him as 'short, rotund, rubicund, quick, talkative, irascible', also 'outspoken, (and) coarse in his language'. On the positive side, 'There was a great deal of kindliness in him in his better days, and in his way, of high purpose, though latterly I am afraid he became a good deal of a jobber.' Yet, when in a good humour, he was pleasant company, 'his mind stored with anecdote, flashing both with wit and humour', and his stories were as likely to be against himself as others.[21]

Ludlow was the favourite pupil; to Furnivall, Ker was a somewhat remote presence who commanded respectful attention even when he unbent, but who was subject to gout and consequently irritable.[22] Conversations with him, his travels to the Mediterranean and Paris, and

---

[17] Stanford, *Stanford's Library Map of London*, Sheet 10. For descriptions of the area and its history in 1861 see Blanchard, *Bradshaw's Guide through London*, 59, 125–6.

[18] Booth, *Booth's Maps of London Poverty*, west sheet (the first group marked in black; the second in red).

[19] Quoted by Masterman, in *John Malcolm Ludlow*, 46 (see further 47–9, and for Ludlow's relations with Ker, 34–8).

[20] Masterman, *Ludlow*, 34; Ludlow, *Autobiography*, 47.

[21] Ludlow, *Autobiography*, 41, 46, 45.

[22] Monday, 7 Aug., Monday, 4 Sept. 1848, Bodl. MS Eng. e. 2315, ff. 39^v, 43^v.

a two-day visit to his 'charming country place' in Cheshunt (Herts.)[23] (a mark of favour bestowed on Furnivall after he had qualified, and at the end of which he was driven to the station in Ker's own carriage), were all recorded in Furnivall's diaries, which were now evidently being written up for his own interest, rather than his father's—he was moving in remarkable circles and encountering celebrities among the many notables. One of the Cheshunt circle was the writer and social theorist Harriet Martineau, whom Ludlow also met there, 'so persuaded of her personal immortality that she had fixed on the particular star which she was certain to inhabit after death'. He reported that she was pleasant company, 'but her oracular utterances were sometimes astounding.'[24] She spent much time ruralizing at Ker's 'Swiss Cottage', which 'was a sort of home to me'.[25] Probably under Ludlow's influence (though her fame also preceded her), Furnivall was prepared to find her an eccentric, as well as a literary celebrity, though he clearly respected her writings on political and economic affairs. Ker had brought her to Furnivall's attention one day in chambers, when he showed him a 'very happy note' from her. Furnivall recorded: 'She is founding a cottage-building Society for the poor, lecturing them (in crowds) on sanitary reform—publishing "Household Education" & the "30 Years Peace". The sale of "Eastern Life" going on well, the garden, cow &c. &c.—it does one good to | hear of such a woman'.[26] Thanks to Ker, Furnivall met her in person when he dined at Cheshunt in August, 1851, and found her 'fat & well'. He 'had a long chat with H(arriet) M(artineau) about 'Dearbrook &c' Carlyle, Sterling, E(rasmus) Darwin, mesmerism, &c. till 11. H. M. tried to mesmerise me, but couldn't & nearly mesmerised herself.'[27]

[23] Ludlow, *Autobiography*, 46.
[24] Ibid. 50.
[25] Martineau, *Autobiography*, i. 375.
[26] Monday, 4 Dec. 1848, Bodl. MS Eng. e. 2135, f. 56^v; 'hear of' substituted for 'see her' (cancelled). See Warren, 'Harriet Martineau and the Concept of Community'. See also R. K. Webb, 'Martineau, Harriet (1802–1876)', *ODNB*. *Household Education* (1848); *Eastern Life: Present and Past* (1848) was based on her travels in Egypt and the Near East, 1846–7; *The History of the Thirty Years' Peace* first appeared 1849–50, covering 1815–45; her novel *Deerbrook* (1839), misspelled here by Furnivall, was her most sustained piece of fiction; Thomas Carlyle's *Life of John Sterling* (1851) had just been published; Erasmus Alvey Darwin (1804–81) was the elder brother of Charles, and Harriet Martineau's close friend; the enthusiasm for mesmerism was at its height in the early 1840s, and she claimed she had been relieved by it of the symptoms of serious illness. For her memories of Carlyle (whom she knew well) and Sterling, see her *Autobiography*, i. 377–87.
[27] Monday, 18 Aug. 1851, Bodl. MS Eng. e. 2316, f. 41^v(narrative continued, Tuesday, 19 Aug., when Furnivall heard more about her views on socialism, her schools, and lectures). Ker's wife had been her confidante during the writing of *Deerbrook*; Martineau, *Autobiography*, i. 375.

After Cambridge, Furnivall's diary begins again in 1848. It is no longer hand-made, but a commercial product: 'The Universal Diary for 1848, Price one shilling', bound in dark green, and containing, among other useful facts, details of the Royal Family of Great Britain, the Ministry of England, the Law Terms, the penalties under the Stamp Act, the eclipses and phases of the moon (important information for horse-drawn travellers). And there is a marked change in the content. The first substantial entry is an extended piece of musical appreciation: of Chopin's playing style, and an appraisal of the respective merits of Mozart and Beethoven, followed by opinions of the leading opera sopranos, Giulia Grisi and Jenny Lind. Jenny Lind had made her London debut in 1847; Furnivall made the most of his opportunities to see her before she left in 1849. The entry seems to be Furnivall's note, set out below, of a conversation among the group of supporters of F. D. Maurice, who was soon to become a decisive influence on his life and ideas. Scott is the Revd Alexander Scott, Maurice's particular friend, and much admired by Ludlow: 'His thoughts seemed to flow naturally into the most telling language. He had a most wide range of sympathy. No branch of learning seemed foreign to him; he was an admirable critic both of art and music.'[28] The conversation which Furnivall recorded may have taken place in the big room over the shop in the Strand owned by the publisher John William Parker, where Ludlow recalled meeting these men and discussing art and music—indeed he met Chopin there on one occasion.[29] The tone, which shifts from literary grandstanding to the colloquial, reflects Furnivall's fascination with the biography and foibles of geniuses, as well as his willingness at this stage of his life to absorb impressions from cultivated men who knew much more than he did. Furnivall records the others' views, and soaks up their sayings and manner of speech, and does not obtrude his opinions, at least on the music. He was out of his depth but strove not to appear so. He defers (with some of the others) to the authority of the senior men, Scott and Ludlow, who had spent much time in Paris, where Ludlow frequented the opera. These two speakers, Scott and Ludlow, had both known Chopin personally and heard him play. The conversation took place after Scott, Ludlow, and a third person, 'C', or

[28] *Autobiography*, 133; Ludlow, *Autobiography*, endorsed the opinion of Charles Mansfield that Scott 'charms you by giving you back your Highest thoughts in the most beautiful language' (p. 134). See further J. Philip Newell, 'Scott, Alexander John [Sandy] (1805–1866)', ODNB. Scott was appointed professor of English language and literature at UCL in 1848, and in 1849 was one of the founders of Bedford College; in 1850 he became the first Principal of Owens College, Manchester. [29] *Autobiography*, 133.

'Ch',³⁰ had attended a concert over the weekend and were describing it to Furnivall before comparing the two singers:

[Ludlow?]: Chopin. Playing is not a 'subject' expressed musically, it is a 'thought, & only a thought' so expressed. Mozart excites the same emotions in men as Raphael, every thing is perfect, finished; all in perfect harmony 'all perfect music'—you cannot displace a note without injury. 'Every beginning must have the very middle & end he has given it, & every end the same middle & beginning; his is the right & only right; another's touching spoils the whole. Beethoven not as perfect as Mozart, who is a lofty pinnacle.

Scott: Had not B(eethoven) feelings to express that M(ozart) never had?

'C.': Perhaps so, that accounts for his ⟨failure⟩ defects—he had something in him to say & could not say it in music, musically, tho' he tried—& these faulty parts his imitators copy, & ruin music.

Ludlow: M(ozart) was a pinnacle, high & in true, but yet you could follow him up & see where he stopped. Beethoven had no end, he was lost in the infinite.

S(cott): Music is sculpture in its purest form.

L(udlow) & Ch: No—Architecture.

S(cott): True.

Ch: Jenny Lind's singing is moonlight calm—Grisi's hot angry sun.

S(cott): J(enny) L(ind)'s (the) Blue (of heaven); Grisi's (Red) of storm.³¹

Furnivall, having heard Chopin for himself at a concert on Saturday, 26 July 1848, felt able to contribute his own impressions—a characteristic mix of biographical facts, with a glance at gossip, a description of the genius's personal appearance, and his own efforts to keep up with the connoisseurship:

[Furnivall]: Chopin is ½ Sclavonian ½ French, has fought for Poland. Lived 2 years in the same house as George Sand. 'G' described in her residence in Majorca. Morals not corrupted but is high minded and good 'so Scott, but he lived regularly with G(eorge) S(and) many years'³²—shrinks from political rows now.

---

³⁰ 'C' may refer to another of Parker's visitors, the architect Archibald ('Archie') Mansfield Campbell, cousin of Charles Mansfield, also members of Ludlow's circle; 'Ch's' identity is not known; 'C' and 'Ch' may be the same person.

³¹ Bodl. MS Eng. e. 2315, ff. 8ᵛ–9ʳ. Furnivall's account does not relate to the dates in January where it appears, occupying the space allocated for several days: he used blank sheets at the beginning of the diary for this extended report. The concerts described relate to performances in July and August (see below). The note is written in sections, largely corresponding to each speaker's contribution, set out as continuous prose but separated out here to indicate the different speakers. Ludlow had met Chopin: *Autobiography*, 133.

³² A significant later revision by Furnivall (added in a different ink) expressing his own down-to-earth dissent from Scott's more high-flown view.

Is a little man with high shoulders—very pale, light hair & bold nose; seems consumed with the fire within. Chief peculiarity in playing is the delicious murmur he brings out of the piano, sweeps over the keys like a breath 'inconceivably' rapid & light.[33]

L(udlow): Meyerbeer has no melody, strings ½ a doz. notes properly & then begins to fiddle with them. Has not taken & is incapable of taking the highest conception of the *Huguenots*, but has carried 'out' the music of each character wonderfully, makes them all speak differently all the way through.[34]

This was the beginning of a hectic couple of musical seasons for Furnivall, when leading international composers and performers were present in London and at the height of their careers. Jenny Lind would retire from opera the following year, aged just 29. Chopin came to Britain in April 1848, after quitting Paris for a time in 1848, during that year of European revolutions, but he was already gravely ill, and died in Paris in the following year. Furnivall 'heard Chopin play' on 26 July, and compared notes with Arthur Penrhyn Stanley, whom he chanced to meet. They 'talked about Jenny Lind. Tom Arnold's Biblical Criticism &c. He cannot appreciate music, only understands J. L's eyes & smile'.[35] At the concert Chopin probably performed Ballade no. 2, Op. 38, 'La gracieuse'. Furnivall did not comment, but was evidently impressed, noting the next day that he must acquire the score, probably for his sisters.[36] On 26 August, as well as hearing Jenny Lind, he heard another virtuoso piano player, Sigismond Thalberg, whom he considered

---

[33] Bodl. MS Eng. e. 2315, f. 9^{r-v}, spaces for Saturday, 8 Jan. 1848, carried over to Monday, 10 Jan. (actual date 26 July 1848; see below). I have interpreted the description of Chopin's appearance and manner of life as Furnivall's own mixture of precis and opinion: the insertion, 'so Scott . . . now' is added by Furnivall in a different ink (he revised the account lightly). The same description is quoted by Munro, 'Biography', p. xxiv, with the further comment that Chopin was 'a little thin man'. Munro is likely to have augmented the diary entry after discussing it with Furnivall, who was reminiscing in old age. At the time when he wrote them, Furnivall himself clearly considered these accounts of Jenny Lind as prime pieces of eyewitness description by the Lincoln's Inn music aficionados as well as himself—he gave them a special place out of sequence in his diary and revised them (he did not otherwise go back over his diary entries and touch them up).

[34] Entry for Wednesday, 12 Jan. 1848, Bodl. MS Eng. e. 2315, f. 9^v (not the actual date of performance). Giacomo Meyerbeer's *Les Huguenots* premiered in Paris, 1836.

[35] Wednesday, 26 July 1848, Bodl. MS Eng. 2315, f. 37^v. Stanley (1815–81), Dean of Westminster, was author of the influential *Life and Correspondence of Thomas Arnold*, and thus familiar with both Arnold's son Thomas and Thomas Hughes, who portrayed him as 'George Arthur' in *Tom Brown's Schooldays* (1857).

[36] Thursday, 27 July 1848, Bodl. MS Eng. 2315, f. 38^r: 'Order Chopin's Ballad, no. 38, 'La Gracieuse, op.' '38' corr. from '138']. He also wished to buy the set of three mazurkas (Op. 50), written in 1842.

LINCOLN'S INN

'very brilliant but did not care for him'.[37] Furnivall got his chance to hear Giulia Grisi, whose performance he thought 'very pretty'.[38] But, under Ludlow's guidance, Furnivall was already Jenny Lind's devoted admirer: he heard her in Donizetti's *Lucia di Lammermoor*. In Bellini's *I Puritani* she was 'better than ever', and 'very beautiful' when he took his sister, Selina, two days later to hear her.[39] He reported that, in *I Puritani*, her voice was remarkably expressive: 'seems as if she had 3, one for joy, one for grief, & one for ordinary purposes. Queen there—came up from Osborne.'[40] He also saw Grisi in *I Puritani*: 'her voice is failing very much—acts with no energy, does not enter into the character or make 1/3 of what Jenny Lind does of it'.[41] He also had the good fortune to see Jenny Lind several times in her showcase role as Amina in Bellini's *La Sonnambula*: 'house crammed—"Ah non giunge" called on 3 times. She has brought out the first part more than before—like it better if possible every time.'[42]

Being Furnivall, as well as a true admirer, he went to look at the house in London where Jenny Lind was staying.[43] He called on her, 'but was refused admittance', so he wrote to her suggesting that she should give a concert at Exeter Hall.[44] It was probably just coincidence that he heard a week later from his friends the Wedgwoods that she had agreed to sing there in the premiere of Mendelssohn's *Elijah*. The failed visit was perhaps one of Furnivall's first attempts at courting lions, but in this case he was doubtless one of many turned away from her door, though Munro said, and he is likely to be right, that Furnivall later got to know the diva.[45] The Exeter Hall was used for concerts of sacred music, where Furnivall had previously, when studying in UCL, heard a massed choir of 1,600 sing (though the hall could accommodate 3,000 singers), and had been greatly impressed. Jenny Lind's agreement to sing there was a

---

[37] Saturday, 26 Aug. 1848, Bodl. MS Eng. e. 2315, f. 42^r: 'Jenny Lind at the concert. The trio with the 2 flutes very wonderful—the last Swedish melody most beautiful—the echoes marvellously done.'

[38] Saturday, 22 July 1848, Bodl. MS Eng. e.2315, f. 37^r.

[39] Thursday, 3, Saturday 5 Aug. 1848, Bodl. MS Eng. e. 2315, f. 39^r.

[40] Tuesday 15 Aug. 1848, Bodl. MS Eng. e. 2315, f. 40^v.

[41] Thursday, 17 Aug. 1848, Bodl. MS Eng. e. 2315, f. 41^r.

[42] Thursday, 10 Aug. 1848: concluding aria, 'Ah non giunge uman pensiero'. Also Saturday, 12 Aug.: 'Jenny Lind in "La Figlia" made more of the 2nd part than before, called on 5 times, bouquets &c. Wonderfully good.' Bodl. MS Eng. e. 2315, f. 40^r. Donizetti, *La Figlia del reggimento*.

[43] 'Saw Jenny Lind's house'; Sunday, 23 Aug. 1848, Bodl. MS Eng. e. 2315, f. 40^v.

[44] Wednesday, 16 Aug. 1848, Bodl. MS. Eng. e. 2315, f. 40^v.

[45] Munro, 'Biography', p. xxiv.

coup for the Exeter Hall, for London, and for Furnivall (though maybe not for his powers of persuasion). It would be her first appearance in oratorio, and the last time she would perform in London. Jenny Lind had been Mendelssohn's close friend, but, after he died prematurely, had felt unable to sing the soprano part which he had written for her. She finally agreed to give a single performance, which took place on 15 December.[46]

CATCHING THE SPIRIT OF THE TIME: THE YEAR OF REVOLUTION, 1848

The evangelical tract which Furnivall was given on leaving home advised the model young man reading it that he 'catches the spirit of the time, and is a man *of* the age, and *for* the age'.[47] Furnivall took at least this advice to heart: he revelled in the sense of living at an important time, and the late 1840s and early 1850s gave him ample opportunities to show himself both *of* and *for* the age. This was the time when the character of his adult life and his personal character were formed, and by this is meant his inner character, or personality, not just his public character, or reputation. As the *Young Man from Home* had advised, 'there is such a thing as the formation of character, or fixed habits of action, arising out of fixed principles'.[48]

In the beginning of his London career, Furnivall's character seemed unformed. As his junior, he was impressed by Ludlow's authority, taste, and *savoir faire*. As Munro later said: 'For Furnivall, this was the beginning of his acquaintance with the man who exercised the most formative influence over his character at this stage of his life'.[49] But Ludlow's first impressions of the Furnivall 'of those days' were more nondescript: merely of a 'very pleasant companion'. He described 'A pleasant looking young man', who 'called on me one day at my chambers, to express his sympathy with what we were doing, and his admiration for Mr. Maurice. I offered to introduce him to the latter, but so great were then his diffidence and humility that he shrank from accepting the offer at first.' He was persuaded, however, and accepted an invitation to tea. Ludlow thought him a 'most desirable recruit' to his causes, though he

---

[46] Wednesday, 16 Aug.; Friday, 15 Dec. 1848, Bodl. MS Eng. e. 2315, ff. 40^v, 58^r (however, in the entry for 15 Dec., the note 'Jenny Lind in the Elijah at Exeter Hall' is struck through).
[47] James, *Young Man from Home*, 124.
[48] Ibid. 8.
[49] Munro, 'Biography', p. xvii. Munro evidently expressed Furnivall's own opinion.

THE YEAR OF REVOLUTION, 1848

would soon modify this good opinion.[50] At the time, Ludlow noted Furnivall was full of zeal for recruiting others to the new cause of Christian socialism, though Ludlow soon realized that zeal was closely allied to pugnacity. Thus, when the Christian Socialists' first paper, *Politics for the People*, appeared in 1848, Ludlow contributed a paper, 'Universal Suffrage not Universal Representation', expressing his scepticism about the Chartists' belief in universal suffrage as a panacea for working-class discontent. One of them, William Lovett, sent in an address, to the middle classes, on the suffrage question, in which he seems to have attacked Ludlow, who had to deter Furnivall from taking up the cudgels in his defence: 'Mind,—there is no returning of evil for evil. It is fair that I should be justified, but bullying or abusing Mr Lovett won't do it.'[51]

Despite the tedium of copying conveyancing precedents, Furnivall's time at Lincoln's Inn was a formative one. It was an exciting time to be there. 1848, the year of Furnivall's first Lincoln's Inn diary, was, to say the least, eventful. As Ludlow said: 'The wave of revolution which had swelled and burst in France was now sweeping over the rest of Europe. In our own country, it gave a great impetus to the Chartist movement.'[52] The 'Hungry Forties', as Munro reminded his readers, were stirring times, witnessing the working-class radicalism expressed in the agitation leading up to the repeal of the Corn Laws in 1846, the opening of the first Co-operative Stores at Toad Lane, Rochdale, in 1844 and, in 1848, Chartist riots in London. 1848, the year of revolution in Europe, affecting France, Germany, Italy, and Austria among others, saw the publication of Marx's Communist Manifesto, and there was much fear of a socialist revolution in Britain. Furnivall, who up to this point had unthinkingly adopted his father's Toryism, had his eyes opened to the sufferings of the London poor through his friendship with Ludlow, along with Frederick Denison Maurice, Charles Kingsley, and Thomas Hughes. As the chaplain of Lincoln's Inn, Maurice, as Ludlow said, had inspired by 'the nobility—I would rather call it the grandeur—of his character' a group of young men, mostly young barristers and law

---

[50] Ludlow, *Autobiography*, 131.

[51] Letter to Furnivall, [1848], FU 512. Ludlow's (unsigned) article appeared in the first number of *Politics for the People*: see nos. 1–17, for 1848 (facs. repr., New York, 1971), 13–14. Lovett's address (not included in the paper) was reviewed by F. D. Maurice, in no. 6 (p. 110). See also Raven, *Christian Socialism*, 111.

[52] *Autobiography*, 120. See also Matthew Arnold's account of events in Paris, quoted by his niece, Mary Ward, *A Writer's Recollections*, 49–51. The secondary literature is large, but see e.g. Evans and Pogge von Strandman (eds.), *The Revolutions in Europe, 1848–1849*; also Postgate, *The Story of a Year, 1848*.

students, to become involved with his projects to improve the conditions of the working poor.[53] Furnivall was 'initiated by Ludlow, in 1848, into a world where drink, disease, and hunger held their terrible sway'.[54] This world was drastically at odds with social visits and opera-going.

1848 was the year when 'the Chartists announced their intention of holding a monster meeting on what was then Kennington Common [now Kennington Park], and proceeding from thence to Westminster to present the People's Charter to Parliament'.[55] In this manifesto they petitioned for parliamentary reform, calling for universal suffrage for men, the secret ballot, annual general elections, electoral boroughs of equal size, and the abolition of property qualifications for MPs, thus in principle allowing working men to stand for election. J. S. Mill described 'the democratic movement among the operative classes, commonly known as Chartism', as 'the first open separation of interest, feeling, and opinion between the labouring portion of the commonwealth and all above them'.[56] Although the mass demonstration on 10 April fizzled out in pouring rain, and the crowds melted away after the police refused to let them cross Westminster Bridge, it had caused such alarm that the Duke of Wellington, aged nearly 80, was called on to take charge, and had positioned cavalry and infantry troops out of sight to avoid provocation. The British Museum had prepared for a three-day siege; firearms were provided for those members of staff able to use them, and stones were ordered to be taken up to the roof to throw on the rioters in case the crowd got past the outer defences.[57] But, instead of an intimidating mass descent on the Houses of Parliament, the leader, Feargus O'Connor, was allowed across the bridge to deliver the petition in three hansom cabs. In addition to the army, 170,000 citizens were sworn in as special constables, each issued with a truncheon and white arm band.

Among them were many members of Lincoln's Inn who had prepared themselves to defend the Inn and to assist in preventing a riot.[58] J. M. Ludlow was not one of them. He had no great expectations of the event: 'having, I may say, seen two revolutions, I felt perfectly satisfied that I

[53] Litchfield, 'The Beginnings of the Working Men's College', 3, 10.
[54] Munro, 'Biography', p. xviii. See further Briggs, *Chartism* and references there given; Chase, *Chartism, a New History*; Thompson, *The Chartists*.
[55] Ludlow, *Autobiography*, 120–1.
[56] 'The Claims of Labour', in *Dissertations and Discussions*, ii. 181–217 at 188. Originally published in the *Edinburgh Review*, Apr. 1845.
[57] Miller, *Prince of Librarians*, 165.
[58] *A Lincoln's Inn Commonplace Book*, 283–4.

was not going to see another one now'. He felt no sympathy with either side, or perhaps, more accurately, had some sympathy with each: 'For myself, advanced Radical as I was for those days, I had long ceased to look for any substantial results from merely political reform . . . I fully recognise and admire the wonderful demonstration in favour of law and order by the people of London . . . But I had no wish to break any Chartist's head.'[59] But, going about his normal business with unimpaired *sangfroid*, he gave a lively account of what he saw. Unfortunately, Furnivall's diary has a gap between entries for January and late June, and we do not know what part, if any, he took. But, given his fondness for sightseeing and witnessing history happen, it seems unlikely that he meekly stayed at home. And, in any case, the Chartists' demonstration on 10 April led directly to the establishment of the movement known as Christian Socialism, and indirectly to Furnivall's involvement in it.[60]

On that day Ludlow set out as usual for his chambers in Chancery Lane, though he expected no business waiting for him, and there was none. But 'towards 12 o'clock . . . my clerk told me that a gentleman wished to see me. There entered a tall young clergyman with strongly marked features . . . who, stuttering something about M-M-Maurice, presented me with a note from the latter.'[61] This was Charles Kingsley, anxious about the meeting on Kennington Common, who had come up to London from his rectory at Eversley 'to see what could be done to prevent a collision'. He was determined to go 'and see what he could do'. Ludlow went with him, but they discovered before they even got to Waterloo Bridge that the crowd had already dispersed without Kingsley's help.[62] The pair went to call upon Maurice, and all three agreed that the Church must accept responsibility for the bad relations between the labouring classes and those whom Mill called 'all above them' which had

[59] *Autobiography*, 120–1. The sense that political reform would not give the men what they wanted was shared by Kingsley: F. E. Kingsley (ed.), *Charles Kingsley*, 65–7 (extract from 'Parson Lot's Letters to Chartists').
[60] For the influence of both chivalry and Carlyle on the leading Christian Socialists, J. M. Ludlow, F. D. Maurice, Charles Kingsley, Thomas Hughes, and E. V. Neale; see further Girouard, *Return to Camelot*, 132–44: 'Not only did they come to the support of the underdog in causes which brought them no worldly rewards, gave them considerable unpopularity amongst most of their class, and in some cases lost them a great deal of money or actively harmed them in their careers; in addition most of them were alive to the concept of chivalry and regularly used its metaphors' (p. 132).
[61] *Autobiography*, 121–2.
[62] For a personal account (in hindsight) of Kingsley, and his contribution to Christian Socialism, see Thomas Hughes's 'Prefatory Memoir' to Kingsley's *Alton Locke*. Kingsley's own account of the Chartist meeting (as reported in a letter to his wife) is on pp. xiv–xv; see also F. E. Kingsley (ed.), *Kingsley, Letters and Memories*, 62–4.

led to the unrest. Maurice, Ludlow, and Kingsley agreed to establish some sort of Christian journal—or perhaps tracts—to discuss political and social questions, raise consciences, and perhaps go some way to bridge the divide. It would be followed by other ventures: schools, a newspaper—*The Christian Socialist*—co-operative associations, and the Working Men's College.[63] Hughes commented in retrospect: 'We were all full of enthusiasm and hope in our work and of propagandist zeal: anxious to bring in all the recruits we could. I cannot even now think of my own state of mind at the time without wonder and amusement.'[64]

The enterprise thus began in 1848 with a journal, *Politics for the People*, which ran from 6 May to July, issued weekly and priced 1*d*. The authors assured their readers that they did not mean to 'put forth readymade theories . . . or vehement opinions upon one side or the other', but to *consider* questions of the day. At least this was the intention: Kingsley, for one, was not always able to restrain the savagery of his indignation.[65] Maurice and Ludlow offered themselves as middle-men: 'Never mind who we are . . . We who have started this Paper are not idlers in the land . . . But we do not work with our hands; we are not suffering hardships like many of you . . . We do not, properly speaking, belong to your body.' They offered sympathy to working men but assured them it 'will be strongest if it is least maudlin. The poor man wishes to be treated as a brother, not to be praised as an angel.'[66] They were, like others, addressing the 'condition of England question' (the phrase coined by Carlyle a few years earlier), and seeking to bridge the gap between what Disraeli called the 'two nations', Furnivall reread the numbers three years later; by this time he was deeply committed to Ludlow's and Maurice's social concerns.[67]

'CHRISTIAN SOCIALISM'

The name of this movement, 'Christian socialism' was not ready-made, but evolved. The 'Christian' emphasis of Ludlow's and Maurice's social concerns is evident in the very beginning of *Politics for the People*, in

---

[63] Ludlow, *Autobiography*, 122 (and for Ludlow's description of Kingsley, see 123–9). See further Morris (ed.), *To Build Christ's Kingdom*, 15. See further Acland and Jones, *Working Men Co-operators*.　　[64] Hughes, *Memoir of a Brother*, 110–11.

[65] Hughes, 'Prefatory Memoir', pp. xv–xix.

[66] Carlyle, *Chartism*; Benjamin Disraeli, *Sybil, or The Two Nations* (London, 1845); *Politics for the People*, no. 1, 6 May 1848, pp. 1–2, Prospectus. Furnivall read Carlyle's *Chartism* on Monday, 24 Mar. 1851, along with Byron and Burns: Bodl. MS e. 2316, f. 20ᵛ.

[67] Diary entry for Thursday, 20 Mar. 1851, Bodl. MS Eng. e. 2316, f. 20ʳ.

which Ludlow appropriated the revolutionary slogan of 'Fraternity' to express his ambition 'to hold converse with our readers of all classes, as fellow-men and fellow-workmen, by labouring strenuously in God's strength, that we may realize the true Fraternity of which this age has dreamed, and without which we believe it cannot be satisfied'.[68] 'Socialism' was, of course, a provocative label: Furnivall had been warned against the evils of socialism, or 'devilism', in no uncertain terms by the tract *The Young Man from Home*.[69] Hughes commented that the choice of name for the movement had been unwise. It caused confusion among people who were otherwise supportive, and was later quietly dropped.[70] A factory inspector writing in 1840 was only saying what he expected his readers to agree with when he warned that 'The two great demons in morals and politics, Socialism and Chartism, are stalking through the land'.[71] Friedrich Engels's account of the 'Condition of the Working Class in England' had been published in 1845, following his visit, with Karl Marx, to London and Manchester; their *Communist Manifesto* in 1848. Accordingly, 'to the general public in England all proposals for co-operation came branded with the stigma of anti Christian Revolutionary Communism'.[72] For the *soi disant* Christian Socialists, the emphasis was on the 'Christian', and had little to do with Marx. 'Communism' was an ancient Christian principle in the Church, though not the state. As Maurice said: 'Our great desire is to christianise Socialism.'[73] And he told Ludlow, defending the title of their proposed series of tracts on Christian socialism: 'It is a great thing not to leave people to poke out our object and proclaim it with infinite triumph, "Why, you are Socialists in disguise!" "In disguise; not a bit of it. There it is staring you in the face on the title page" . . . This is fair play, which English people like.'[74]

Maurice's idea of socialism was very different from other people's common understanding of the word: 'Christian socialism is, to my mind, the assertion of God's order. Every attempt to hide it under a

[68] *Politics for the People*, no. 1, 'Fraternity', 2–5 at 5. Most of the contributions are unsigned, but the 1971 reprint includes an appendix of authors, compiled by G. J. Gray, from the marked-up copy belonging to the publisher, John W. Parker.
[69] James, *Young Man from Home*, 45–6 (directed especially against Robert Owen).
[70] *Memoir of a Brother*, 114.
[71] Horner, 'On the Employment of Children in Factorie', 180.
[72] Frederick Maurice (son of F. D. Maurice), *Life of Maurice*, ii. 6. As pointed out by Girouard, it was considered that gentlemen who sought to combine 'socialism' with 'Christian' 'must be traitors to their class'; *Return to Camelot*, 132.
[73] Letter to Daniel Macmillan, 7 Feb. 1850, *Life of F. D. Maurice*, ii. 36.
[74] Letter of 1850 to Ludlow, text in *Life of F. D. Maurice*, ii. 35.

great machinery, call it organisation of labour, or what you like, I must protest against as hindering the gradual development of . . . a divine purpose.' He would have agreed with Kingsley that 'a true democracy, such as you and I should wish to see, is impossible without a Church, and a Queen, and, as I believe without a gentry'. As Woodworth observed, this was 'not a very revolutionary attitude, even for a clergyman in the middle of the century'.[75] Maurice was 'socially conservative, suspicious of democracy, but equally committed to resisting tyranny, and to defending moral and religious freedom . . . It was an attempt to make the national vocation of the Church of England just that—a faith that would seek to renew and transform all classes.'[76] The movement sought to alleviate the condition of working people by offering religious and voluntary solutions to problems, rather than political ones. Ludlow, though less conservative than Maurice, was sceptical of merely political reform: 'Social reform alone was worth living for, and if need were, dying for.'[77]

The difficulty, as Maurice and Ludlow recognized, was distinguishing what they stood for from the efforts being made by other sincere and socially conscious members of the gentry and clergy, do-gooders who left the poor feeling deprived of their rights. Mill had commented scathingly that 'the newly-awakened interest in the condition of the labouring people' was often little more than a new fad which 'adds to the more ephemeral attractions of the latest new fashion'. The problem was not excess of zeal among the ruling classes, but in applying this energy to raising the condition of labouring people 'by raising the class itself in physical well-being and estimation'.[78] As Kingsley described the poor, 'They'll take their alms, but they'll hardly take their schooling, and their advice they won't take at all . . . the poor have got in their heads . . . a strange confused fancy, maybe, but still a deep and fierce one, that they haven't got what they call their rights'. The words are spoken by a fictional character, but a wise and virtuous poor man used by Kingsley to act as an interpreter of lower-class discontent to a well-disposed member of the gentry who, like the Christian Socialists themselves, wants to understand, as well as to help: 'The question with them, sir, believe me, is not so much, How shall we get better fed and better housed, but whom

---

[75] Woodworth, *Christian Socialism in England*, 38–9. Woodworth made an independent study, at the end of the 19th c., based on the original sources, and which benefited from Ludlow's criticism.

[76] J. Morris, *F. D. Maurice and the Crisis of Christian Authority*, 15.

[77] *Autobiography*, p. 120.

[78] J. S. Mill, 'Claims of Labour', in *Dissertations and Discussions*, 181–3.

'CHRISTIAN SOCIALISM' 95

shall we depend upon for our food and for our house? Why should we depend on the will and fancy of any man for our rights?'[79] Garnering information about the labouring classes fuelled the sense of urgency that something needed to be done but left what that was profoundly unclear. There were tensions within the group of men who allied themselves with Maurice in this work. It is not surprising that 'Christian socialism' is difficult to define. Furnivall said simply: 'We had taken the name of Christian Socialists, because we adopted the trade-organization proposed by the Socialists, but we were Christians, and our object was "to apply the principle of Christianity to trade and industry".'[80]

The unifying principle behind the Christian socialists was admiration for Frederick Denison Maurice. As Maurice himself said to Ludlow:

When you first spoke to me it was as the Chaplain of Lincoln's Inn. You wished that I could do something there to unite such young men as would be disposed to join in working for the poor in that locality . . . Lincoln's Inn is a very powerful body of cultivated men in the midst of as bad a neighbourhood for health and probably education as most in London. If a small body of us could unite to do something for that place our bond would be surely a quasi-sacramental one.[81]

The trio of Ludlow, Maurice, and Kingsley was an odd, but successful, alliance to steer the movement, in which, metaphorically, 'Ludlow stood at the helm, Kingsley flew the flags and sounded the horns, Maurice poked round the engine-room to see that the engines were of authentic Christian manufacture'.[82] Maurice's sermons at Lincoln's Inn were proving a great draw to its young men. As Ludlow noted, 'That little upstairs chapel, with its horrible window . . . became ere long the spiritual centre of our beginning movement. "Bring him to hear Maurice," came to be the usual counsel when a possible recruit was spoken of.'[83] Furnivall, too, noted the effectiveness of Maurice's Lincoln's Inn preaching, in particular a *very striking* sermon on the Fall', part of a series on Genesis.[84] He, too, 'became zealous in beating up recruits and generally promoting what was already beginning to be felt as a social movement'.[85] Always enthusiastic, Furnivall was discovering his life's work as an organizer,

[79] Kingsley, *Yeast*, 233–4.
[80] *Working Men's College Magazine*, 2. 145. 'The blanket of Christian Socialism . . . sheltered a variety of political opinions'; Girouard, *Return to Camelot*, 133, *et seq.*
[81] Letter to J. M. Ludlow, 24 Nov. 1849, *Life of F. D. Maurice*, ii. 26.
[82] Chadwick, *The Victorian Church*, i. 151. [83] *Autobiography*, 129.
[84] Sunday, 23 Feb. 1851, MS Eng. e. 2316, f. 16ʳ.
[85] Ludlow, *Autobiography*, 131.

recruiter to causes, and promoter. Yet, when Tom Hughes called on Maurice to offer his services, and Maurice proposed him to the group, the suggestion was laughed at, by Furnivall among the rest—Hughes was known as a sporting hearty and cricketer.[86] And Furnivall, who might perhaps, as a rowing man, have been expected to sympathize, 'pooh-poohed the idea of getting any good from him', though Hughes was to prove one of the most valuable members of the group.[87] As Ludlow noted, Furnivall's natural assertiveness soon overcame his initial bashfulness in this new company.

Most of the members of the movement attended Lincoln's Inn chapel on Sunday afternoons—Furnivall among them. As Ludlow discovered, they did not all have a good grounding in Christian faith. On his suggestion, Maurice agreed, in late 1848, to hold regular Bible readings on Monday evenings at his house—Furnivall was also a regular visitor on these occasions from at least July 1848.[88] Maurice's Monday meetings were 'in a real sense the sacrament, the effective symbol, of their unity'.[89] He would himself trace the origins of the Working Men's College back to these meetings.[90]

Maurice was a deeply spiritual and charismatic man, behind a reserved manner. Ludlow considered him 'by far the greatest man I have ever known . . . I think I have met as good men as Mr. Maurice, but the combination of greatness and goodness in him was absolutely unique.'[91] Victor Aimé Huber, who met Maurice, remembered his 'striking union of severe earnestness of purpose with irresistible kindliness', and, though he shunned oratory, 'there were times when the intensity of his feeling, the outpouring of his spirit under conditions which powerfully wrought upon him, produced an impression on an audience that hardly any oratory could have done'.[92]

After *Politics for the People* folded, the group of young men who clustered round Maurice, and which included Furnivall, met to address the question 'what practical work could be done by us in common for our fellow-men'. The first idea 'was the taking in hand some black spot in London', with the intention 'to moralise and christianise it'. The local

---

[86] Raven, *Christian Socialism*, 130.   [87] Ludlow, *Autobiography*, 135.
[88] Monday, 24 July 1848, *et passim*, Bodl. MS Eng. e. 2315, f. 37ᵛ.
[89] Raven, *Christian Socialism*, 134.
[90] J. F. C. Harrison, *A History of the Working Men's College*, 16.
[91] *Autobiography*, 114–15.
[92] *Life of F. D. Maurice*, ii. 2–3. Huber, Professor of the University of Berlin, and keenly interested in co-operation, visited England from Germany in the 1850s: see Raven, *Christian Socialism*, pp. 382–3.

clergyman, the Revd William Short, proposed, if they were looking for a black spot, that they should 'try to civilise the inhabitants of Little Ormond Yard', leading from Great Ormond Street, 'within a stone's throw, so to speak, of Mr Maurice's house in Queen Square'.[93] It was so rough that at that time neither clergy nor police dared to enter. The real poverty and hardship suffered by people living there is suggested by the Connor family, whom Furnivall came to know through the school which Maurice's disciples founded and visited. He found Mrs Connor with her baby lying dead. Connor had left his work 'as too hard for him'.[94] It is very close to the world described in *Bleak House*.

The means chosen of 'civilising' this neighbourhood was the establishment of a ragged school. A house was taken, a housekeeper, Mrs Troubridge (spelled by Furnivall 'Trowbridge'), was engaged, and a free school established, with classes for both adults and children (it was originally intended to be a night school for men). Ludlow considered Mrs Troubridge, a former national schoolmistress, 'rather behind the requirements of the age, but an excellent creature'. She taught a class for girls.[95] Furnivall wrote to his father asking for money to equip the school and spent the £10 he received on desks and furniture. George Furnivall's reaction shows the considerable degree of overlap between a traditional Tory gentleman's full acknowledgement of his duty to show charity to the poor, and the Christian Socialists, whose truculence tended to put off those who would otherwise support their general principles—he had had no objection to Frederick's teaching in Sunday schools at home.[96] With the money came a stern admonition:

You ought to know much more of Latin than I do, but tho' your learning that Language cost 50 times more than mine did, you appear to have forgotten the Adage of ne sutor ultra crepidam.[97] Your business is Law; mine is Physic. Neither you nor I have any business with Teachers or Ragged Schools. I am sure there are 100's of rich, lazy, and independent people who have nothing else to do than devote their Time and their Passion for Praise to such useful Employment

[93] Ludlow, *Autobiography*, 135; Raven, *Christian Socialism*, 128.
[94] Monday, 10 Mar. 1851 (the baby had been born without arms), Wednesday, 13 Sept. 1851. Bodl. MS Eng. e. 2316, ff. 18ᵛ, 44ᵛ.
[95] *Autobiography*, 136, and see Ludlow's extended description of the school, 135–8.
[96] Hughes, *Memoir of a Brother*, 113. See also the evangelical James, *Young Man From Home*, 24: the model young man teaches in a Sunday school, associates with a Tract Society, 'and visits the habitations of the poor with the admirable compounds of Bible truth', he supports missionaries, and other societies, and 'gives his time, his wisdom, and his labour to the committees that direct their affairs', 124. Furnivall's activities, though taken too far in his father's view, can easily be assimilated to this teaching.
[97] 'The shoemaker should stick to his last.'

as instructing their indigent, uninformed Brethren and Children. Leave these things to them; it is yours to do your Duty in that State of Life in which it has pleased God to place you ... With ragged Schools, Socialism, or any other ism, you have really no business at all ... Lawism ... ought to be your End and Aim, your Duty, your Pleasure, and Pursuit. Don't play at Law and work at School teaching.[98]

His son was undeterred: the opening of this school, on 21 September, was the great event of 1848 for Furnivall, if we may judge by the heading at the very beginning of his diary.[99] On the day itself, he recorded: 'Bought texts &c. Opened the school in Little Ormond Yard. Clark the curate said a few verses from Eccles(iastes) & prayed. Penrose, Campbell, Ludlow, Parker & I there, taught reading, writing & arithmetic, read in the Bible after it.'[100] Gradually the school was equipped with forms, desks, and books, including hymn books and catechisms, as well as a lending library. Short took an active interest in the school, and the place was eventually sufficiently orderly for him to conduct weekly evening prayer-meetings.[101]

Furnivall's first impressions of the pupils were 'Saul G. a dreadful swearer, passionate to the nth. Girls larkish.' Or, as he later described them, 'Ragged, merry, and mischievous, the young urchins were'.[102] Ludlow noted that some of the boys were 'very nice young chaps', but the girls' class gave rise to complaints that the boys were being neglected: there was only one room and the boys had to be taught with the men.[103] Furnivall taught there regularly—the classes were held in the evenings, which enabled labouring men to attend. Eventually the difficulties in securing regular teaching by volunteers proved too great and John Self, described in Maurice's *Life* as a scripture reader,[104] took on all the teaching, though Furnivall stood in on at least one occasion when he was away.[105] However, this first, direct experience of teaching working people gave Furnivall and the other volunteers invaluable knowledge of

[98] Munro, 'Biography', pp. xix–xx.
[99] On flyleaf 'Opened Little Ormond Yard School, 21 September, 1848.'
[100] Bodl. MS e. 2315, f. 46ʳ. John William Parker was the group's publisher, with a shop in the Strand. F. C. Penrose, Campbell's fellow-lodger, Surveyor of St Paul's Cathedral and President of the Society of Architects (Ludlow, *Autobiography*, 131–3).
[101] Furnivall, diary, entry for Monday, 24 Nov. 1851, MS Bodl. Eng. e 2316, f. 55ᵛ. Furnivall consulted Short regularly about the school and met the Shorts socially.
[102] Sunday, 24 Sept. 1848, Bodl. MS e. 2315, f. 46ʳ. *Working Men's College Magazine*, II. 144.   [103] *Autobiography*, 137.
[104] *Life of F. D. Maurice*, ii. 27.
[105] Ludlow, *Autobiography*, 138; Diary, Wednesday, 16 July 1851, 'took the (8) boys till 9.50, talked to Mrs Trowbridge'. Bodl. MS Eng. e 2316, f. 36ᵛ.

what was needed. It laid the foundation for the Working Men's College. And, as with the College, the volunteers realized the need for their pupils to get out into the fresh air, as well as to study. It was a great day when the first of these outings was arranged, on 27 June 1849, when vans carried them all for an excursion to Epping Forest.[106] Furnivall's experience anticipated his later disputes with Maurice over the value to the working men of Sunday excursions into the countryside.

The better-off public was being bombarded with information about the state of the poor. It was at this time (1849–50) that Henry Mayhew was publishing his hugely popular series of articles on 'Labour and the Poor' in the *Morning Chronicle*, which would later become his *London Labour and the London Poor*.[107] Furnivall read them, as did Dickens.[108] Kingsley was annoyed that Mayhew's work had trumped his own descriptions of the hardships of the rural poor: he could not give details, 'for if I did the reviewers would declare as usual, one and all, that I copied it out of the *Morning Chronicle*'. But he acknowledged its 'invaluable investigations'.[109] Maurice, too, recognized the importance of Mayhew's work, as offering more complete and detailed evidence than had been given before.[110] Hughes commented that the articles were a wake-up call after the alarm created by the Chartists had subsided, and 'startled the well-to-do classes out of their jubilant and scornful attitude, and disclosed a state of things which made all fair minded people wonder, not that there had been violent speaking and some rioting, but that the metropolis had escaped the scenes which had lately been enacted in Paris, Vienna, Berlin, and other Continental capitals'.[111] On 25 September, one of the *Morning Chronicle* articles gave such an appalling account of the conditions in Bermondsey around Jacob's Island, where the ditch had become an open sewer, that sanitary reform temporarily eclipsed other attempts at improvement. Cholera cases were reported.[112] In his preface to the 'cheap' edition of *Oliver Twist* (1850),

---

[106] Raven, *Christian Socialism*, 129; Ludlow, *Autobiography*, 137 (his experience with the school made him realize the importance of hop-picking as a holiday for the London poor).

[107] *London Labour and the London Poor*. 'All England was stirred by the results of an enquiry, set going by the *Morning Chronicle* newspaper, into the conditions of London operatives'; Litchfield, 'The Beginnings of the Working Men's College', 2.

[108] Furnivall stayed up until 2.40 a.m. reading *London Labour*, Friday, 11 Apr. 1851, Bodl. MS Eng. e. 2316, f. 23ʳ. On the same evening, at the Philological Society, 'Key read a paper on the Verb, very interesting.' [109] *Yeast*, 132.

[110] *Life of F. D. Maurice*, ii. 13. [111] 'Prefatory Memoir', pp. xiii–xiv.

[112] Maurice, *Life of F. D. Maurice*, ii. 13; Ludlow, *Autobiography*, p. 154. Maurice was opposed to the group's plan of forming a Health League but approved their practical work

Dickens pointed out that the place really did exist, and was not a fiction.[113] The Christian Socialist doctors Charles Blanchford Mansfield and Charles Robert Walsh, both known to Furnivall, worked together in Bermondsey during the outbreak, and were, like Ludlow, disappointed when Maurice considered the movement should concentrate on co-operative and educative initiatives, rather than health. Mayhew's reports, based on his extensive interviews with working people, and visits to see them at work, are detailed, colourful, and often distressing. Facts and figures are brought to life by first-hand observation, reported speech, and by his vigorous indignation. It was exactly the material to engage Furnivall's sympathy. His later antiquarian researches were based in the same warm engagement with the details of everyday life in the past.

Politics for the People had more success in reaching working men than the Christian Socialist group realized. Ludlow had given copies to the teacher at the Little Ormond Yard school, John Self, who lent them to his acquaintances, among them a tailor, Walter Cooper, 'a professed chartist and infidel', and too proud to accept relief when out of work, whose mistrust of the paper's aims had been defused by its failure. Cooper introduced the group to others and he himself became a regular attender at Maurice's Sunday sermons.[114] Fortnightly meetings at the Cranbourne Tavern, near Leicester Square, were established between the gentlemen and the working men.[115] Ludlow remarked of these experiments in crossing the class barrier that 'I never recollect any meetings so interesting... As a rule, the tone of the working men who spoke was courteous as well as manly, though now and then there was an insolent fellow.' At the end of the meeting, Maurice would invite everyone back to his house for tea.[116] Maurice's presence and spiritual power at these meetings became increasingly impressive, though, when Kingsley first spoke; his stammer, which was mistaken by the critic David Masson for drunkenness, caused unholy stifled laughter. The

---

in Bermondsey. Kingsley visited Bermondsey with Mansfield and Walsh and gave a grim account of what he saw to his wife; F. E. Kingsley (ed.), *Charles Kingsley: His Letters and Memories*, 86-7. For an image of Jacob's Island c.1810, see Chitty, *The Beast and The Monk*, facing p. 224.

[113] Litchfield, 'Beginnings of the Working Men's College', 4.

[114] Ludlow, *Autobiography*, 144-5. Later Cooper would prove dishonest: Raven, *Christian Socialism*, 142.

[115] See further Maurice's letters to Ludlow (Apr. 1849), to his future wife, Georgina Hare (23 and 24 Apr. 1849), and to Kingsley (29 Apr. 1849); *Life of Maurice*, i. 536-9.

[116] Ludlow, *Autobiography*, 146-7.

laughter was also a welcome release of tension, as the meeting seemed likely to get out of control before Kingsley stood up and declared 'I am a Church of England parson... and a Chartist'.[117] The group discussed setting up co-operative workshops for individual trades, which Maurice saw as a better way of improving working conditions than strikes.

Probably because the initiative had begun with the tailor Walter Cooper, and Lloyd Jones, a tailor working in Oxford Street and an ex-Owenite lecturer, two men who were good organizers and highly articulate, the Christian Socialists agreed at a dinner at Ludlow's house to begin enacting the principle of co-operation by setting up tailoring workshops. Prompted by Kingsley's pamphlet describing the poor conditions in the clothing trade, *Cheap Clothes and Nasty*, which appeared at the beginning of 1850, Maurice proposed they begin with the Working Tailors' Association, a co-operative workshop. It was started in 34 Castle Street East (off Oxford Street), with Walter Cooper as manager, and was followed by a Needlewomen's Association in Red Lion Square.[118] Ludlow considered that, 'of all the publications in connection with our movement' *Cheap Clothes and Nasty* 'was unquestionably the most telling'. It was followed by Thomas Hughes's account of the formation of the co-operative after it was beginning to establish itself, and he was able to rejoice 'to see men of high birth and station going even the length of Regent Street out of their way to lend a hand to their struggling fellow-countrymen'.[119]

Yet, despite this evidence of support, the pamphlet and Kingsley's 1850 novel about the tailoring trade, *Alton Locke*, also attracted violent criticism from middle-class reviewers and commentators. Among

---

[117] Ibid. 149, and see this passage for its biographical sketches of the other persons present; Hughes, 'Prefatory Memoir' to Kingsley's *Alton Locke*, p. xix. Also, F. E. Kingsley, *Kingsley, Letters and Memories*, 67.

[118] Ludlow, *Autobiography*, 161. Letter to Kingsley, 2 Jan. 1850, *Life of F. D. Maurice*, 31–3. Kingsley, *Cheap Clothes and Nasty*, published under the pseudonym 'Parson Lot' as an independent tract, reprinted as one of the *Tracts by Christian Socialists*, priced 1d. For the origin of this pen-name see Hughes, 'Prefatory Memoir' (to Kingsley), p. xii. Richard Graham Maul (friend of the Furnivall family, and supporter of the trade associations), wrote to Furnivall to express his support for the tailors, though he regretted the poor quality of the work: 'Those tailors have made me a miserable waistcoat—the buttons are so far apart the white shirt shows thro! & I wish they hadn't altered my coat for now it is too tight! Nevertheless I shan't give them up.' Letter of 26 Mar. [1850], FU 564. Maul mentioned Johnson's support for the Christian Socialists: 'Johnson is but poorly, his digestion & circulation are all wrong: but he is most valuable and profitable for all that.'

[119] Ludlow, *Autobiography*, 159. *History of the Working Tailors' Association, Castle Street*, Tracts on Christian Socialism No. II (London [1850?]), 6 (published anonymously).

them was Anne March, who attended Kingsley's lecture on the subject, and expressed her disapproval to Furnivall in a torrent of scorn and heavy sarcasm, extending over thirteen pages:

> The socialist paper containing a resumé of the lecture has been sent me by somebody—but the principles to which I object here being much softened down in the report. Mr K's eloquence is such that one does not easily forget what he has said—& I heard what I heard—if I am mistaken as to its object I should be glad to be enlightened but others may be mistaken too—& such mistakes are dangerous. As to mutual co-operation—there is nothing very new in that—the system of benefit clubs is a testimony which I should think—& if trade can be carried on without the middlemen . . . for goodness sake let it be done—but why set class against class & strike at the foundation of society?[120]

Nevertheless, Kingsley's words were warmly received by the working men themselves. It is worth quoting Walter Cooper's artless, but heartfelt, appreciation in full. The letter was sent to Ludlow, who evidently circulated it among other leading members of the movement. Furnivall copied it and kept it among the correspondence which he particularly valued (the collection now in the Huntington Library) as a testimony to the reciprocal warmth of feeling at this time between the Christian Socialists and the men, who were losing their distrust of their gentlemen supporters:

> I trust you will excuse me writing you but the truth is I am anxious to know how you are what you are doing in the Council and tell me if our dear friends Hughes, and father Maurice have returned to London oh how I thank you for Alton Locke god Bless its noble author I felt while reading it as I never felt before I laught 'and' then Burst in to tears my full heart was ready to break 'and' start [do] not now think me a Hypocrite I only found relief in exclaiming our father who art in heaven verily there is a God and I my soul I believe we are doing his work 'and' that too frequently when in our Blindness we know it not I am working every night some times on Committee at other times lecturing I find the face of father Maurice and Christian / Socialism has extended all over the land I went to Bury in Lancashire to meet as I supposed some two or three delegates of the Town trades but to my astonishment I found five hundred men waiting to receive me These are the Bravest men I ever meet with one of the delegates read a letter he had received from parson Lot and of which he was not a little proud they are getting up a general labour fund to assist men of all trades and men of no trades no more strikes what they want to establish is self employment Leading to Brotherhood and fraternity next week we intend to hold a labour Conference in the Town of Manchester Councilor Heywood will take

[120] FU 549, dated [c.1855?]; Anne March is otherwise not known.

the Chair we will have the Managers and delegates from all the Cooperative Stores and associations in Lancashire and Yorkshire and by God's help we will do something for labour that will / not soon be forgotten. Thousands of working men with throbbing hearts and streaming eyes are looking to Christian Socialism for help will you be kind enough to give me some programme to lay before the Conference excuse the freedom I take I always forget rank and Class when I write to you.[121]

'ASSOCIATION A NECESSARY PART OF CHRISTIANITY'

This was the title of Furnivall's first publication.[122] Because his surviving diaries do not cover the years 1849–50, it has been necessary to establish the chronological narrative of the Christian Socialists' founding activities during this interval.[123] When Furnivall's own accounts resume in 1851, it is clear from the passing nature of the references that he had been taking a full part in these activities and continued to do so. His diary for 1851 charts his growing up from pleasant young man to committed social activist and educationalist. His association with the Christian Socialists affected him profoundly, and, although Maurice's greatness impressed him, and had started him on this journey, he was to be more attracted, as one might expect, to the group's activism, and the powerful sense of camaraderie, than to the spirituality. He was closer to Ludlow, of whom Furnivall noted with characteristic oversimplification, 'J. M. Ludlow was 'the true mainspring of our Christian Socialist movement. Maurice and the rest knew nothing about Socialism.' Ludlow, 'educated in Paris, knew all. He got us round Maurice and really led us.' Ludlow, for his part, observed that 'one of his habitual misrepresentations has been to exalt my share in the Christian Socialist movement as against that of Mr. Maurice'.[124]

---

[121] Letter of 2 Aug. 1850, FU 200. Furnivall's transcription (presented here) preserves the original lack of punctuation and the capitals, and Cooper's spelling is retained.

[122] Furnivall's first publication, a pamphlet (London, 1850). William E. A. Axon, 'F.J.F', *The Bookman*, 41 (Oct. 1911), 42–3 at 43.

[123] There was originally one other diary, at least, covering 1850, from which Furnivall quoted: 'Under Tuesday, Jan. 8, 1850, in my diary, I find the entry, "Little Ormond Yard School, from 7.30 till 9.15; meeting at Maurice's about starting an Association of Tailors—about twenty there—talked till 12; appointed a Committee, etc.; £300 wanted."' *Working Men's College Magazine*, 2, p. 145.

[124] Handwritten note on the flyleaf of his copy of the *Tracts on Christian Socialism*, now in the British Library. Quoted by Raven, *Christian Socialism*, 55. Raven notes that Furnivall made the same claim for Ludlow's leadership in founding the Working Men's College, but with less justice; Ludlow protested vehemently against the 'preposterous over-praise'; *Autobiography*, 133–4.

Other associations followed the Working Tailors. It soon proved necessary, despite Maurice's profound aversion to managerial systems and organizations, to set up a Council of Promoters, consisting of the organizers (with Ludlow and Kingsley among the rest) and a Central Board, on which the managers of the trades associations and a delegate from each of them sat. These governed what became the Society for Promoting Working Men's Associations. Fresh recruits were joining, including men with whom Furnivall worked closely, among them Edward Vansittart Neale (a member of the Vansittart family), Jules Lechevalier, the French refugee, and Paris correspondent of the *New York Tribune*,[125] and Charles Sully, the paid secretary of the Council, bookbinder, former Chartist, and socialist with a colourful past, as well as present.[126] Another was the then Lord Goderich, son of the Earl of Ripon, a representative of the higher ranks of society which were beginning to take an interest in the Christian Socialists' ideas.[127] He did good work for the movement, but Ludlow was wary of him 'as I always have shunned through life persons much above me in position'.[128] They were all high-minded and men of strong principle, but they had different emphases and concerns within the movement. Maurice respected Sully but found him difficult. Neale would come to see the diversion of the group's resources into educational initiatives a distraction. Ludlow distrusted Lechevalier as an intriguer, charming and able though he was. Furnivall became increasingly absorbed in Maurice's Working Men's College. But before this, he became involved in the heady excitement of industrial unrest leading up to the great iron trades strike of 1852.

The beginning of 1851 found Furnivall still much involved with the school in Little Ormond Yard, and in the thick of co-operation and the Christian Socialists, which included his friend William Johnson, the Eton schoolmaster:

Wednesday, 1 January, 1851
Johnson up.... to chambers, Ker's; wrote letters. Johnson in at 3.20, talked.

[125] Photograph of Neale: Colloms, *Victorian Visionaries*, 251. See further Girouard, *Return to Camelot*, 133.
[126] See Ludlow, *Autobiography*, 157, 162–3, 171; Maurice, *Life of Maurice*, ii. 33, 35, 42–5, 75; Edward Norman, *The Victorian Christian Socialists* (Cambridge, 1987), 2–5.
[127] Colloms, *Victorian Visionaries*, 117; also Anthony F. Denholm, 'Robinson, George Frederick Samuel, first marquess of Ripon (1827–1909)', *ODNB*. Goderich, the son of the caretaker prime minister of 1827–8, was born in 10 Downing Street, and was first elected to Parliament in 1852. On his retirement from politics in 1908, he said: 'I was considered to be a very dangerous young man. I am a Radical still ... but I am afraid that I am much more respectable.' [128] Ludlow, *Autobiography*, 166.

Bezer in; corrected Lambert's copying, translated a little; read 'Christian Socialist' no. 10; dined at the Whittington; read the papers—to Cooperative Store and Central Office—Johnson's lodgings, chatted, tea.[129]

John James Bezer was, as Thomas Hughes described him, 'the one-eyed Chartist costermonger whom we—Heaven save the mark!—had set up as our publisher!'[130] He had been imprisoned between 1848 and 1850 for sedition, and, after his release, opened a radical bookshop in Fleet Street. Furnivall, who had undertaken to act as sub-editor of the *Christian Socialist* and correct proofs, saw him regularly and chatted. He also read Bezer's *Autobiography of One of the Chartist Rebels of 1848*, which was appearing in serial form in the *Christian Socialist*—'a really remarkable thing', as Ludlow described it.[131] As its title suggests, the *Autobiography* was published anonymously. Furnivall's mention of it confirms the authorship, for which the evidence is otherwise indirect. Bezer's life had been hard, and the account is as speech-based (though clearly tidied up for publication), racy, irreverent, and colourful as one might expect. Bezer's views did not conform to those of his middle-class sponsors, but it is likely that his quick wits, highly articulate slang, and rough and readiness appealed to Furnivall. As Bezer described 'sincerity': '"He can't be wrong whose life is in the right." But that's not orthodoxy—Well it's my doxy, and I am writing my auto, if you please.'[132]

The Whittington Club, in Arundel Street, convenient for the Inns of Court, was another kind of co-operative enterprise, intended to bring the conveniences of a gentlemen's club from the West End to the lower middle-class clerks and shop assistants. It was open to women as well as men (Harriet Martineau was a member). Upstairs, there were a library and reading rooms where newspapers were taken. It also promoted self-improvement through classes and lectures—its name, the Whittington, described the acme of upward social mobility available to

---

[129] Bodl. MS Eng. e. 2316, f. 8ᵛ. Furnivall also noted that a scheduled meeting of the Conference had been adjourned.

[130] Letter to Frederic Maurice Jr. [c.1872], *Life of Maurice*, ii. 126. Bezer had lost an eye through smallpox.

[131] Tuesday, 14 Jan. 1851, Bodl. MS Eng. e. 2316, f. 10ᵛ; Bezer's *Autobiography* is included by David Vincent in *Testaments of Radicalism: Memoirs of Working Class Politicians, 1790–1855* (London, 1977), 153–87. It appeared in twelve issues of the *Christian Socialist*, from 6 Sept. to 13 Dec. 1851. For Ludlow's estimate of Bezer, see Ludlow, *Autobiography*, 190.

[132] *Testaments of Radicalism*, 170: 'When I commenced this history, I determined it should be a *genuine* one, and that I would put down my thoughts without reserve' (p. 157).

Londoners.[133] It provided good, inexpensive meals, and on Fridays it held a Vegetarian Dinner when Furnivall often dined there—it seems to have been his introduction to vegetarianism, which was gaining a following among the classes of people which the Whittington served, especially those with a radical or dissenting background.[134] He also, while there, had his pocket picked and had an old silk handkerchief stolen.[135]

WILLIAM (CORY) JOHNSON

Furnivall often visited William Johnson at Eton, where he taught his brothers, especially Ted. The friendship might seem on the face of it an unlikely one; however, it was based not only on the family connection and Eton's closeness to Egham, but also their many shared friends, interests, and acquaintances. They were close in age. Both had been to Cambridge and had many mutual Cambridge friends and acquaintances, who had led both to engage in questions of social justice and politics. Johnson was, with Furnivall, one of the Promoters in the Society for Promoting Working Men's Associations.[136] They were also both members of the Philological Society: indeed, philology tended to be popular among the Christian Socialists, particularly those who had studied at Cambridge and their circle.[137] Moreover, the friendship with Johnson did much to foster Furnivall's developing interests in education and the teaching of English, as well as books and painting—Johnson was much the more cultivated and better informed of the two, and had the sharper mind. Johnson, though only two years older, also had the knack of freely criticizing without giving offence—thus he advised 'I recommend you to try going to Lincoln's Inn Chapel every morning at 9 before breakfast. You should also get some sensible man to read

[133] See further Christopher Kent, 'The Whittington Club: A Bohemian Experiment in Middle Class Social Reform', *Victorian Studies*, 18 (1974), 31–55.

[134] E.g. Friday, 3 Jan. 1851, Bodl. MS Eng. 2316, f. 9ʳ *et passim*. 'Vegetarian' was a recent word: OED, 'vegetarian', A. n. 1a (1842), B. adj. 1 a (1843). See further James Gregory, *Of Victorians and Vegetarians: The Vegetarian Movement in Nineteenth-Century Britain* (London, 2007). See further Ogilvie, *Dictionary People*, 286–7.

[135] Monday, 24 Feb. 1851, Bodl. MS Eng. e. 2316, f. 16ᵛ.

[136] Raven, *Christian Socialism*, 251.

[137] For example, Maurice, who, taught social history by tracing the development of families of words (as noted by Colloms, *Victorian Visionaries*, 191), and Richard Chenevix Trench, whose *On the Study of Words*, a lecture series addressed to the pupils at the Diocesan Training School, Winchester, appeared in 1851, and he joined the Philological Society in 1857. See further Kenneth Milne, 'Trench, Richard Chenevix (1807–1886)', ODNB.

law with at fixed hours.'[138] Johnson soon noticed that Furnivall's law work, hours, and attendance at chambers had become increasingly irregular, as can be seen as his diary progresses. Comparisons between Eton and the Little Ormond Yard school were inevitable: 'It is good for me', Johnson noted, 'now & then to think of ragged schools &c that I may with more content bear the silliness of my division & of my pupils.' Ted was proving tiresome: 'I am half sick of him. Only I bethink me of your ragged ones & take heart.'[139] Furnivall also acted as Johnson's go-between with London publishers and booksellers when Johnson was unable to come to town himself and catch up with new exhibitions of paintings at the Royal Academy, or William Mulready's show.[140]

Their correspondence belongs mainly between 1848 and 1856, and covers many topics, though Ted's lack of aptitude as a pupil is a recurrent theme: Johnson found him 'very gauche and unlucky'.[141] Unable to write out Latin verses because he had hurt his arm, he blundered through a recitation of the St Crispian's day speech from *Henry V*: 'I suppose it is his first acquaintance with Shakspere—he repeats his lessons very clownishly.'[142] 'Ted must be pushed through Hecuba in the holidays . . . Goad him, flap him, make him get up early.'[143] Ted told tales of the other boys' cheating to his brother, Frederick, to Johnson's disgust: 'What *Ted* told you about other boys verses is gross slander—Don't encourage him to talk about other boys—particularly my pupils.'[144] Ted's poor rendition of Wordsworth reminded Johnson to tell Furnivall that he was considering the publication of an inexpensive anthology of English poetry for use in schools, perhaps to be published by Bohn (or Parker), though 'I am rather afraid of Bohn'. 'I propose to take what is really *pleasant* reading—stuff that has some tune in it—'that' will scan and construe pretty easily . . . no extracts that are not intelligible by themselves.' Incidentally, it may be noted that the spelling, 'Shakspere', which Furnivall used throughout his life, and which came to be seen as one of his distinctive foibles, was widely used in the first half of the nineteenth century. Not only Johnson, but others who influenced him as a young man, including F. D. Maurice and Harriet Martineau, employed the spelling as a matter of course: Furnivall is likely to have clung to it as a habit

---

[138] Letter to Furnivall, 16 Jan. 1849, FU 216.
[139] Letter to Furnivall, 23 Apr. 1850, FU 230.
[140] Letter to Furnivall, 10 July [1848], FU 205.
[141] Letter to Furnivall, 20 Feb. [1849], FU 218
[142] *Henry V*, Act IV, Sc. iii, 18–67; letter to Furnivall, 25 Oct. 1848, FU 211.
[143] Letter to Furnivall [?1849], FU 228.   [144] Letter of 19 Oct. 1849, FU 222.

formed in youth, as well as on principle.[145] Although Johnson was a member of the Philological Society, he was not interested in showing the historical development of English poetry in his collection: 'Probably I shall have no Spenser, Milton, Dryden, Cowper as I do not mean to give historically specimens of all styles of English poetry.' But he was keen to include ballads.[146] And he asked Furnivall to consult Alexander Scott, 'if you know him well enough', or one of the founding members of the Philological Society, either Thomas Key or Hensleigh Wedgwood, on how best to teach the English language:

1) Is it necessary that a boy who is constantly translating both ways & studying Greek & Latin Grammar, should ostensibly study English? Is he not studying English incidentally & unavoidably?
2) If English Etymology is to be taught methodically, what book is fit for the middle classes of a public School?
3) If the arrangement of English sentences is to be taught, what exercise-book or Grammar is to be used—or what method?
4) If *rhetoric* is to be taught is there anything better than Blair & Campbell?

He added: 'These questions concern not me & my work only, but still more they bear upon the education of women who do not as a general rule write themes, read Euclid, or practise translation.'[147]

In addition to their mutual friends and interests, the friendship between Johnson and Furnivall owed much to the more intangible attractions of personalities which were dissimilar as well as alike. Johnson had the flair and brilliance which Furnivall lacked. Johnson was mercurial and charming, a clever and fluent articulator of his ideas, as well as an admirable, unconventional teacher, though a poor disciplinarian, scrupulously fair, at least in intention, if not always in practice. While serious and thoughtful about his work of education, he enjoyed a lark—as did Furnivall—but Johnson as a young man was far more quirky than Furnivall. Johnson's pamphlet, *Hints for Eton Schoolmas-*

---

[145] See Harriet Martineau's discussion of the point, writing in 1855, but describing her schooling as a girl of 15 in 1818: 'A school-fellow spelled Shakspere as I spell it here. Mr. Perry [the schoolmaster] put in an *a*, observing that the name was never spelt in print without an *a*. I ventured to doubt this; but he repeated his assertion. At afternoon school, I showed him a volume of the edition we had at home, which proved him wrong.' *Autobiography*, i. 88.

[146] Letter to Furnivall, 20 Oct. 1848, FU 210.

[147] Letter to Furnivall, 21 Feb. 1849, FU 217. Hensleigh Wedgwood's *Dictionary of English Etymology* would be published in 1857; as one of the founders of Bedford College (1850), addressing such questions to Scott about the education of women was highly topical. Johnson also noted that 'You should have better topics at the Philological.' Letter to Furnivall, 28 Apr. 1849, FU 221.

ters, written in hindsight, and published posthumously, is obscurely confessional.[148] While full of practical wisdom about teaching and boys' psychology, conveyed with a light hand, it is also wryly—but unapologetically—self-deprecating: the best teacher is 'free, and I wish I were too from caprice'. But caprice should 'be protected from harsh censure in so far as it is connected with that susceptibility to *ennui* which besets people gifted with some imagination'.[149] He did his best 'to deliver the poor lads from the weariness of their dead language lessons' by drawing parallels from English literature and history—though 'I am quite aware that, if they came into school to read *Othello*, or *Tom Jones*, or Southey's *Life of Nelson*, they would be equally bored when the novelty was over'.[150]

This is probably the point to engage with another source of attraction between the two—a sensitive one. Johnson emphasized that the 'man who speaks to the young must guard all that is in him that is feminine', by which he meant that he should not become so hardened that he lose 'the sensitiveness of a good woman'.[151] Johnson was fonder of boys than was wise, and, although he probably did not engage in impropriety, he would suddenly, and without explanation, resign from his position at Eton in 1872. He was not the only close male friend to whom Furnivall at this stage in his life was drawn because he admired the friend's greater knowledge, especially in matters of taste and literature, in which he showed his appreciation and sensitivity. In a controversial word, he was drawn to their 'feminine' qualities. Furnivall's friendship with Johnson was a rehearsal for his friendship with John Ruskin, whom he would soon meet—Johnson also admired Ruskin, going to London especially to see his drawings.[152] Ruskin's sexuality was (and is) a matter of speculation, and his contemporaries commented on his 'feminine' nature. Ludlow, among others, described him as having had 'a woman's soul in a man's body'. Hence in Ludlow's view, Ruskin's extraordinary fascination by 'that essentially male genius, Carlyle'.[153] Furnivall also, as we shall see, recognized Ruskin's 'feminine' qualities.

[148] *Hints for Eton Masters* by W. J. [William Johnson] (London, 1898).
[149] Ibid. 18. [150] Ibid. 8.
[151] Ibid. 31.
[152] 'I heard from Blakeley of an interesting exhibition of small bits of paintings, drawing, engraving, modelling &c. &c. by many artists, including *Ruskin* at the North London School of Design, St Mary's Terrace, Camden Town | It closes tomorrow.' Letter to Furnivall, 9 Jan. 1851, FU 231 (Blakeley was taking Johnson's portrait).
[153] *Autobiography*, 144.

Ruskin's extraordinary powers of expression as an art critic had been taking society by storm since the appearance of the first volume of *Modern Painters* in 1843. His achievement was to convey his aesthetic opinions in an opinionated and forceful way which depended both on his fascinating personality and his formidable powers as a stylist. There was an element of deferring to an older brother in both these friendships. As Furnivall's comments on opera and singing show, he wished, as a man of the world, to seem a moderately well-informed connoisseur, but, modesty aside, he was not comfortable himself in discoursing in a way which might seem to compromise the manliness which he and his society so prized. His own later comments on the literary quality of texts tend to be either awkward or no-nonsense. As Ludlow's comment shows, such attractions between the 'male' and 'female' in respectable male friendships were admitted in a society where social intimacy between young men and women of Furnivall's class was strictly monitored.[154]

THE CHRISTIAN SOCIALIST: FURNIVALL AS ACTIVIST

Johnson was a supporter of the Christian Socialists, but a critical one, and commented on what he saw as their errors: 'Cooperation is a good thing—but (is) not the opposite of competition.'[155] He thought the extravagance and stridency of some of the movement's adherents showed poor taste, as when he objected to some of Kingsley's especially turbulent expressions in print.[156] He noticed the essential divide between its founding members, and preferred the more practical approach of Ludlow, whom he admired. Maurice (and Kingsley) he thought guilty of 'unbusiness-like paradoxical Rousseau-like writing';[157] indeed, Maurice was referred to by Ludlow and their associates as 'the Prophet'. Johnson read their newspapers, *Politics for the People* and *The Christian Socialist*, as well as their other publications: 'The last number

[154] For another view (more radical than the one expressed here) of this question of Furnivall's participation in Victorian 'manly love' both for contemporaries and for his construction of figures from the past, see Antonia Ward, '"My Love for Chaucer"'.

[155] Letter to Furnivall, 28 Feb. 1851, FU 232. E.g. also, Johnson thought much in *Politics for the People* 'very *crude*', and noted 'I was disappointed with Ludlow, but I wish he was in the House of Commons'; letter of 5 Aug. 1848, FU 206.

[156] As reported by Hughes, 'Prefatory Memoir', p. xxxiv. Kingsley challenged 'the worthy Eton parson [sic] . . . to vent his whole dislike in the open Council', promising to reply with the utmost mildness and courtesy: 'It will at once be a means of gaining him, and a good example, please God, to the working men.'

[157] Letter to Furnivall, ?Apr. [1852], FU 235.

of your Journal is particularly good . . . There is nothing in it to offend a sensible man.'[158]

The newspaper, the *Christian Socialist* (which later became the *Journal of Association* to avoid the unnecessarily provocative 'socialist'), was distinct from the series of *Tracts by Christian Socialists* which Maurice had urged his senior followers who attended his more select Monday evening Bible classes to write to explain the movement's purposes and general principles, and for which the Society for Promoting Working Men's Associations was directly responsible.[159] The *Tracts* were a riposte to the Oxford Movement's earlier *Tracts for the Times*. The *Christian Socialist* was Ludlow's initiative, the successor to *Politics for the People*. Ludlow felt that, given the chance to express it, the working men showed 'a large amount of talent . . . which was either lying idle, or forcing its way through wrong channels'. Maurice was opposed to a newspaper (though not to a penny journal), and he carried with him Neale, Mansfield, Walsh, and—strangely as it seems—Furnivall. Ludlow was supported only by Lloyd Jones and Lechevalier.[160] The publication was initially undertaken by John Tupling, of 320 the Strand.[161] However, when no other established publisher could be found for it, Bezer was given the job. The first number, as a penny journal, appeared on 2 November 1850, and Ludlow assumed the editorship, though Maurice contributed articles.[162] Circulation reached fifteen hundred copies and doubled the following year, although they had trouble in getting notices of the paper and advertisements for it into the established press. Much of the writing was done by Ludlow, though Furnivall, Hughes, Kingsley, Mansfield, Maurice, and Walsh were regular contributors. Elizabeth Gaskell, known to the Maurices, allowed them to use two short tales.[163] J. A. Froude also contributed,

---

[158] Letter to Furnivall, 23 Jan. 1852, FU 235.

[159] Hughes, *Memoir of a Brother*, 114: 'English Socialists generally have instinctively avoided it ever since and called themselves "co-operators," thereby escaping much abuse.'

[160] For a fuller account of the circumstances, see Ludlow, *Autobiography*, 188–92.

[161] Diary, Wednesday, 5 Mar. 1851, Bodl MS Eng. e. 2316, f. 17ᵛ. See further Raven, *Christian Socialism*, 158–62.

[162] Maurice wrote to Kingsley, 22 Nov. 1851: 'I have not the least dream of becoming editor . . . I have been too often burnt in the periodical fire not to have a reasonable dread of it. I opposed the undertaking at first, but was overruled by Ludlow's strong feeling of its necessity'; *Life of Maurice*, ii. 88.

[163] 'The Sexton's Hero', and 'Christmas Storms and Sunshine', previously printed elsewhere; Furnivall, diary, Tuesday, 4 Mar. 1851: 'Copied out poetry for *Christian Socialist*, & a very fine letter from Mrs Gaskell.' The next day he read her 'Moorland Cottage'; Bodl. MS Eng. e. 2316, f. 17ᵛ. He met her on 7 Feb. 1852; f. 64ʳ. On 4 Mar. he also went to see

as did David Masson. And a number of working men wrote essays and poems, thus fulfilling Ludlow's hopes. Furnivall became 'an excellent sub-editor' and was left in sole charge of the paper in the summer of 1851 while Ludlow was away visiting associations of working men and co-operatives in the north of England. Later Hughes took on the role of editor. Furnivall's diary shows that he spent much of his time every Friday between May and July, often in chambers when presumably he should have been more professionally occupied, correcting proofs and preparing the index.[164] William Johnson gave him his candid opinion of the paper and its style of journalism:

I like the last part of No 2 much less than the first. There is a danger of breaking the 3rd Commandment in such writing. There is careless exaggeration & cant about honesty. What you are really attacking is selfishness—deliberate selfishness on the part of tax-payers, master-tailors, &c thoughtless selfishness on the part of customers. I fancied on Saturday that I could interpret your policy in a style more likely to satisfy kind and sober people than the writers of No I & the latter part of No 2. But the early part of No 2 is modest ingenuous and practical. Nor will I withhold my sympathy because of *style*—now that I feel pretty safe about your theory.[165]

As acting editor, Furnivall received the detailed reports and descriptions of the various co-operative and associative initiatives. It is not surprising in the circumstances that he became immersed in the movement at the expense of the law. And the great national struggle over the winter of 1851–2 between the ironmasters and employers and their workmen aroused bad feeling which long outlasted the dispute. It was, as Hughes said, 'the first of a new class of strikes or lock-outs. It was carried on and fought out with the greatest vehemence and stubbornness, and excited the deepest interest throughout the whole country.'[166] Furnivall was closely involved in the industrial agitation of the period, and, with all his other activities, spoke at public meetings. Independently of the other Christian Socialists he wrote his pamphlet on *Association a Necessary Part of Christianity*. Two entries from his 1851 diary perhaps convey the character of his commitment and activity:

his 'Cousin George' with a copy of Ruskin's *Seven Lamps of Architecture* (first published 1849).

[164] Bodl. MS Eng. e. 2316, from Friday, 9 May, f. 27^r to Friday, 18 July, f. 37^r. There was more proof correction on Friday, 12 Dec., f. 58^r, which occupied him until 2 a.m.
[165] Letter of 23 Apr. 1850, FU 230.
[166] Hughes, *Account of the Lock-Out of Engineers*, 5. The summary given here is based on Hughes, whose account was derived from contemporary documents, reports in the press, and his own recollections; see also Raven, *Christian Socialism*, 242–57.

Mon 17 March
... to chambers, read the Jurist... wrote to Macmillan, Miss Martin, Mr Maurice &c. till 7.15; in a cab to the Central Office, and then drove about to find the place where Walford had put up a Public meeting on Associations—there at 8.30—in a railway arch at Lambeth, 40 or 50 people—took the chair & made a speech. Walford spoke too—home at 11; tea; read Coleridge, Cowper, and Kingsley; wrote till 3.

Wed 9 April
In chambers till 7 . . . Lloyd Jones's lecture on Associations & Co-operative Stores, improving the condition of the people—very interesting—rooms full— a pleasant chat afterwards till 11.20, home; wrote to the editor of the Hampshire Independent on the practical working of Associations till past 4.[167]

Most of the trades' associations sponsored by the promoters were composed of artisans and craftsmen and craftswomen: tailors, needlewomen, shoemakers, pianoforte makers, builders, bakers . . . The Christian Socialist movement was not directly concerned with the emerging trades unions, their key principle being the encouragement of associations of work people to govern themselves and organize their own production. The Trades Societies at this time tended to consist of small amalgamations of the skilled trades and were generally confined to specific trades, rather than alliances of related skills. The first to enlarge their scope was the amalgamation in January 1851 of the trades' societies of engineers and ironworkers to form the Amalgamated Society of Engineers (ASE: in full, Amalgamated Society of Engineers, Machinists, Millwrights, Smiths, and Pattern Makers). Furnivall was enthusiastic in his support for the ASE, which contacted the Society of Promoters as to the best use of their large funds, and to explore the possibility of setting up Associations among the ironworkers.[168]

During 1851, Furnivall was closely involved, as many entries in his diary show, in setting up a block-printing factory affiliated with the Block Printers' Trade Union.[169] In 1851 the woodcutters in Bermondsey went on strike. Furnivall reports a deputation of the men on Thursday, 2 October, and a 'skirmish between Maurice and me about the strike'.[170] Furnivall promised the men £100 in support, to be raised from the sale of his own books, and, on the 20th, the men went out on strike. The

---

[167] Bodl. MS Eng. e. 2316, ff. 19ᵛ, 22ᵛ.
[168] Furnivall, diary, Thursday, 16 Jan. 1851, Bodl. MS Eng. e. 2316, f. 11ʳ: 'to Council of Promoters—deputations from iron traders, 12000 men and £10,000 wanting a scheme of Association.'
[169] See further Christensen, *Origin and History of Christian Socialism 1848–54*, 250.
[170] Bodl. MS Eng. e. 2316, f. 48ʳ.

following day he asked his friend Thomas Badger to arrange the sale, and paid the men on the 25th. He records on the 28th, 'to Badger's at 2.15 executed the Bill of Sale of my books to worthy Haggard for 100£, for the Woodcutters'. Further payments were made on 1 and 8 November.[171] It can certainly be said of Furnivall that he put his money where his mouth was. The sale was necessary because he had little money of his own: Munro tells us that he was costing his father some £180 per year at this time, over and above what he was earning as a conveyancer early in his career.[172]

THE BALLAST-HEAVERS AND THE PRINCE CONSORT

However, the working men with whom Furnivall is particularly associated were the London ballast-heavers. Ships bringing coal to London needed to be unloaded by the coal-whippers, but, before their return journeys, they needed to be laden with ballast to compensate for the load they had brought. This work was done by the related trade of the ballast-heavers. The ballasting of the empty coal-ships was organized by Trinity House, which relied on middlemen—principally publicans—to recruit and pay the gangs of ballast-heavers. It was, of course, hard physical work.[173] Their plight had been described at length by Mayhew. As he noted, matters were made worse by the men's dependence on the riverside publicans, who had secured a monopoly, for work and wages and 'forced' or 'induced' them to spend 'at least one half' of their earnings every week 'on intoxicating drinks'. The consequent 'compulsory and induced drunkenness of the husbands' brought hardship upon

---

[171] Bodl. MS Eng. e. 2316, ff. 51ʳ–52ᵛ, e.g. Friday, 24 Oct. (f. 53ʳ), when Haggard, to whom he sold the books, also appears as 'Haggart'. The woodcutters' representative was one Worsfold, with whom Furnivall first went to visit his brokers. On receipt of the note for £100, it was necessary to visit a bank to change it into smaller denominations, and Worsfold was given £5. It is possible that the woodcutters received more than £100; on Tuesday, 28 Oct. Worsfold visited Furnivall in chambers 'for a long talk, gave him £50' (Bodl. MS Eng. e. 2316, f. 51ᵛ).

[172] 'Biography', p. xix. Furnivall's own accounts give a sense, in 1848, of his frugality, living expenses, and eclectic reading: they include 'pocket-money for Will', £2, for travel (including cab to the station, 2s. 6d.; train to Bury, 15s. 8d.; bus 1s.; coach and driver to Cambridge, 6s.; bus 6d.; train to town 9s., and bus 6d.). Medical expenses included Leeches 3s.; Wilson on Healthy Skin, 2s. 2d.; Ward's Osteology, 4s. and another 4s. on 'medicine'. Books included Cicero's *De Officiis*, 1s. 9d.; Whateley's *Christian Evidences*, Tanner's *Notes on Herodotus*, 7s.; Arnold's *Greek Accidence*, 4s. 6d.; Welchman on 39 Articles 1s. 8d.; Long's *Herodotus*, 3s. 6d., Travels of Homer, 2s., *History of Greece*, 2s. A ticket to Exeter Hall cost 3s. The main expense was 'half quarter's rent £3 17s. 6d. with a new cloth coat, £1 10s. 7d., 'mending old one 3s. 6d.' Bodl. MS Eng. e. 2315, ff. 34ᵛ–36ʳ.

[173] See illustration of ballast-heavers at work in Mayhew, *London Labour*, iii. 279.

their wives and families (Mayhew gave graphic accounts of what the wives told him). Matters had been somewhat improved by the Coal-Whippers' Act (1843), which provided for registration of the men and cut out the middlemen; however, the Act expired in 1851, and the Bill promised by the government to secure the rights of the ballast-heavers had been thrown out. The Whig government under Lord John Russell argued that giving the ballast-heavers job security would be a restriction on trade—Furnivall noted disapprovingly in his diary that 'Lord John Russell & Co. in again' after Lord Stanley had failed to form a government.[174]

In 1851, Thomas Hughes wrote a leading article in the *Christian Socialist* of 8 November, in which he summed up two years of wasted effort in which he had tried to help the ballast-heavers.[175] He had been helped in the writing by two of the ballast-heavers themselves. Thomas Flynn, a remarkable man, gave up two or three days a week to the campaign. Hughes observed: 'He has been at my house at 11 and 12 o'clock at night, with a four-miles' walk home, and a ship to be ballasted at six the next morning; and has canvassed with a patience truly wonderful, careless Members of Parliament, wary City-merchants, crotchety total abstainers, and every one else, gentle or simple, whom he thought could lend a hand.'[176] The other was Flynn's second in command, Henry Barthorp. When hopes of a fresh Bill finally to settle the dispute were dashed in 1851, Flynn left to find another job, and Hughes reported that the trade was now 'inundated with starving competitors, and all the best men . . . are leaving them in despair'.[177] The Christian Socialists were in principle committed to supporting trade associations, which meant in this case supporting the skilled workers, but were also bound to be sympathetic to the starving Irishmen, out-of-work dock-labourers, tailors, and agricultural workers who were taking the work from the skilled men at cheaper rates. Their solution was to persuade the unskilled men of the advantages of registration, so all would compete on equal terms. But who was to undertake the persuasion? Someone from among the Christian Socialists, even though 'I know we have too much work on our hands already'. But, Hughes added, perhaps the publicity might induce 'some friend', who 'may be led to embark on this crusade'.[178]

---

[174] Bodl. MS Eng. e. 2316, f. 17ᵛ.
[175] 'The London Coal-Whippers and Ballast-Heavers', *Christian Socialist*, Saturday, 8 Nov. 1851, II, no. 54, 289–91. [176] Ibid. 289.
[177] Ibid. 291. [178] Ibid. 291.

'Crusade' is a telling word, showing the Christian Socialists' fondness for seeing themselves as knights errant, going about and righting wrongs. Kingsley, in particular, had grown up with Malory's *Morte D'Arthur* and Spenser's *Faerie Queene* as favourite books—it is not by chance that the hero of Kingsley's *Yeast* was called 'Lancelot'.[179] Hughes's appeal seemed almost calculated to galvanize Furnivall, young, energetic, and probably, after the woodcutters, looking for some way in which he could take on a cause to prove himself to the senior members of the movement and use his power and influence as a barrister in some more exciting way than conveyancing. Furnivall became increasingly jealous of Hughes—he was not disposed to be charitable when he met Hughes and his wife at the Maurices' with his '2 ugly little cross puddingy children'.[180] Though Furnivall had 'pooh-poohed' Hughes's admission to the Christian Socialists, considering him a lightweight, Hughes had subsequently proved himself an admirable and highly capable member of the group. He had taken a full part in the ironworkers' lockout, which had been a major test of strength between employers and workers in heavy industry. A 'crusade' to right what Mayhew had called the ballast-heavers' 'deep and atrocious wrongs' would allow Furnivall to earn his own spurs, and prove himself to be 'thoroughly kindly and *serviable;* full of zeal and pluck in everything he undertakes; above all mercenary considerations', as Ludlow described him, before in the next breath calling him 'utterly wrong-headed'.[181]

Furnivall's perversity had yet to appear to the rest of the group, and his chivalry had been aroused by the Tennyson he had copied out for the *Christian Socialist*. Hughes, and Mayhew, had thrown down a challenge: 'The tales I have to tell are such as must rouse every heart not positively indurated by the love of gain.'[182] Accordingly, early in 1852 Furnivall pledged himself to the cause of the ballast-heavers of the Port of London. That their numbers were small—maybe around 500, on nothing like the scale of the ironworkers' lockout—that their work was specialized, deeply unglamorous, and its nature obscure was immaterial, though somehow characteristic of Furnivall. That already much had been done to arouse public awareness gave him a chance to win a name for himself and finish the job after the initial lobbying had already been

---

[179] F. E. Kingsley (ed.), *Kingsley, Letters and Memories*, 10.
[180] Tuesday, 8 July 1851, Bodl. MS Eng. e. 2316, f. 35^v.
[181] Ludlow, *Autobiography*, 131.
[182] Mayhew, *London Labour*, iii. 267–8, 272–88 (pp. 268, 272).

done. Tilting at publicans and the Trinity House Corporation gave him the opportunity to bring together the humblest workpeople and some of the grandest people in the political establishment; indeed he went all the way to the top. And, along the way, Furnivall thoroughly enjoyed the spectacular social incongruities he created.

The ballast-heavers' injustices were already known to be parliamentary unfinished business when Hughes gave up his endeavours. Furnivall's energetic lobbying before the discussion of 'The Ballast Heavers (Port of London) Bill' at the sitting of the House of Commons on 6 April may have done something to bring the matter forward on the agenda. He certainly raised awareness, though the correspondence suggests that he was largely pushing at an open door. Yet the politicians had many other things on their minds to distract them—there was a change of government in 1851, at the early stages of his campaign, which cannot have helped. He lobbied senior politicians on both sides of the House to establish an office, under the aegis of Trinity House, enabling the men to apply directly to ship owners for work.[183]

Whether or not to introduce a bill in favour of the ballast heavers was initially down to Henry Labouchere, President of the Board of Trade until Russell's Whig government fell on 21 February and was succeeded by the Earl of Derby's Conservative ministry.[184] Furnivall first wrote to Lord John Manners, MP for Colchester and Duke of Rutland, on 11 February. Manners was a likely supporter: a member of the 'Young England' group, concerned with social politics and urban conditions. He had toured the industrial areas of Lancashire, investigating child labour, and had supported the Factory Act of 1844. And he was both supportive and confident that, if Labouchere introduced a bill, 'he could carry it through both Houses of Parliament with hardly any opposition'. Labouchere could command the support of the Government, the Tory Protectionists, the liberal Radicals, and Mr Gladstone's friends. He had no other important business which would delay a bill, and Manners pledged his 'best support'. 'Lest I should be too sanguine', he noted, he supplied names of other gentlemen whom Furnivall could also approach. He offered to ask Labouchere his intentions as to pressing the bill in the House.[185] Three days later, Manners also agreed to

---

[183] Ballast-heavers (port of London). A Bill for Establishing an Office for the Benefit of the Ballast-heavers of the Port of London (1852).
[184] William Menzies Tweedie, 'Labouchere, Henry, Baron Taunton (1798–1869)', ODNB.
[185] FU 545; Lord John Manners, letter of 11 Feb. 1852: 'If Mr Labouchere chooses

see a deputation from the ballast heavers.[186] Furnivall also wrote to Labouchere, and received a reply from his private secretary, Sir Louis Mallet, telling him that he was not prepared to answer questions in the House but would be willing to make a statement.[187]

Though Furnivall lobbied senior politicians from both parties, he sensibly concentrated on those who were known to have a concern with the working conditions of the poor. He began with Disraeli, Chancellor of the Exchequer in Lord Derby's government, and Leader of the House, asking him to receive a deputation of the men, which Disraeli agreed to do.[188] This was the occasion which Furnivall later described to Munro, when he recalled the ballast heavers' representatives 'sitting shyly on the delicate white and gold chairs in Dizzy's drawing room'.[189] This was an early triumph for Furnivall's practice, maintained throughout his life, of throwing the most unlikely people together. Disraeli, whose *Sybil, or the Two Nations* (1845) had appeared just a year after Engels's 'Condition of the Working Class in England', had studied the Chartist movement, and was known to be concerned with 'Condition of England' questions.[190] Furnivall then called personally on Gladstone, at this time one of the breakaway Peelite Conservatives, who had previously introduced the bill in 1842 on behalf of the coal whippers. Gladstone was not able to see him, but wrote to him cautiously expressing his individual support:

to introduce such a bill as you describe in favour of the oppressed Ballast heavers, he could carry it through both Houses of Parliament with hardly any opposition.' See further Jonathan Parry, 'Manners, John James Robert, seventh duke of Rutland (1818–1906)', *ODNB*. Also FU 342, letter to Furnivall of 15 Febr. 1852: Robert Grosvenor, First Baron Ebury (one of those recommended by Manners), pledged his support.

[186] FU 546, J. Manners (Rutland), letter of 14 Feb. [1852]: 'I regret that on Tuesday at 11 o'clock I am to see a Deputation from the shipping Interest: from ½ past 11 till 2 o' clock on that day I shall be disengaged and will be glad to receive the Ballast Heavers at any hour most convenient to them.'

[187] FU 544, letter of 5 Feb. 1852: 'I am desired by Mr Labouchere to inform you that the Bill which was prepared last session for this Department with a view of placing them under the Trinity House has not been printed, and that he is therefore unable to send you a copy yet. I am at the same time today in answer to the question contained in the concluding part of your letter that Mr Labouchere does not think it desirable that he should be asked in the House of Commons what course it is the intention of the Government to take in this matter, but he will be ready without delay to state that course to the House.' See also William Donovan, 'Mallet, Sir Louis (1823–1890)', *ODNB*.

[188] FU 167, letter from David Bryce, Disraeli's private secretary, 12 Feb. 1852: 'I am directed by Mr Disraeli to acknowledge the receipt of your note and to state that it will afford him much pleasure to receive the Deputation to which you refer, on the subject of the "Ballast Heavers", at half past 12 o' clock on Tuesday next'; FU 167.

[189] Munro, 'Biography', p. xix.

[190] On Disraeli's concern with social injustice see further Alexander, *Medievalism: The Middle Ages in Modern England*, 81–2, passim.

'any pledged or political judgement as to my view of that cause I cannot give . . . until after having had the opportunity of hearing what the opponents of the contemplated matter may have to urge'.[191] Because of his capacity to maintain opposing points of view, Gladstone was an unpredictable ally to approach: it was said of him that 'He cares even more than trades' unions for the welfare of the working man; more than the manufacturers for the interests of capital.'[192] He havered between the two in his views on the ballast heavers. Subsequently Furnivall wrote again to Gladstone, with fuller information—Gladstone's reply warned of possible objections from those MPs who thought that the men would use the privilege to press for higher wages if they were allowed formal recognition of their trade—though, 'Practically I quite agree with you'.[193] Others were openly noncommittal. The new President of the Board of Trade, J. W. Henley, reserved his judgement until he should himself be able to see '"the bill" said to be about to be brought in he can do nothing as to supporting it'.[194] Furnivall then appealed again to Manners, who spoke to Henley on his behalf, and agreed that another deputation from the ballast heavers themselves would be an appropriate suggestion.[195] Meanwhile, Thomas Flynn, the leading ballast heaver, had written to the Local Marine Board to ask what had become of the petition which they had presented. He was given a polite brush-off.[196]

[191] FU, letter of 20 Feb. 1852: 'I regret that I was unable to see you when you did me the honour to call & I beg you not to suppose my inability in any way betokened indifference. When I introduced the Coalwhippers Bill in 1842, / I felt the objections to such legislation so strongly that I cannot even now have a stronger conviction of them. But a paramount object of humanity and justice induced me to encounter them. Should I, when I have been enabled thoroughly to comprehend the subject, come to the conclusion that the case of the Ballast heavers is a parallel one, I shall be prepared, acting as an individual, to pursue a similar course. Any pledged or political judgment as to my view of that cause I cannot give, until after having had the opportunity of hearing what the opponents of the contemplated matter may have to urge . . . because the state of my engagements would not allow me to devote him the time which would be necessary for the full investigation of a subject which in my view is one of the greatest difficulty.'
[192] By R. H. Hutton, the editor of *The Spectator*, quoted by Hogben, *Richard Holt Hutton*, 53-4.
[193] FU 324, letter to Furnivall, 10 Apr. 1852: 'I thought it right to warn you of the probability that the exercise of that right which rather appertains to their open labour-market, might endanger their Parliamentary privileges.'
[194] FU 374, letter of 24 Feb. [1852]. Richard Hooper, revised by H. C. G. Matthews, 'Henley, Joseph Warner (1793-1884)', *ODNB*.
[195] FU 276, letter of 9 Mar. 1852: 'I spoke to Mr Henley a few days ago in favour of the Ballast Heavers' Bill; he seemed to have an impression that the Trinity House Corporation could now afford the benefit of a registry if they thought fit to do so. A deputation to wait upon him would be, I should imagine, a proper and respectful course to take.'
[196] FU 276, letter of 11 Mar. 1852, from John Domett of the Board to Flynn, copied to

The Ballast Heavers (Port of London) Bill was a private Member's Bill, moved by the local MP, George Thompson (Tower Hamlets), and it was discussed in the House of Commons on 6 April. Its substance was plain enough: to establish an office for the ballast heavers, following the precedent of the coal-whippers, but it was not yet in draft. Henley and some others felt that they were being invited to vote prematurely and could not pledge themselves to the bill's particular provisions, especially since the numbers of men involved were small. As there were no more than 500 involved it was perhaps unreasonable to single them out. This was a cue for some inconclusive discussion about the possibilities of extending registration to some kind of all-embracing employment office which could mediate between operatives and capitalists more widely. Predictably the Whigs and the members of the Board of Trade were concerned that registration of the ballast heavers would create yet another monopoly which would restrict the employers' freedom to choose workers. Gladstone, who had warned Furnivall this might be an objection, noted himself that the coal-whippers had used their privilege to engage in something 'in the nature of a strike'. He dominated the discussion, speaking at length, balancing his concerns about possible strikes by observations that the coal whippers had benefited from and generally not abused their privileges, and there was good reason for the House to place its reliance on the good conduct of these working men. Furnivall's supporters, Disraeli and Manners, spoke briefly, but to good effect, in support of the Bill. The House was divided, not on the principle of remedying a well-publicized abuse, but on whether the Bill should proceed to a second reading before or after a select committee had been appointed to investigate and make recommendations. Caution prevailed: subject to the report of the select committee, leave was given to bring in a Bill.[197]

In the discussion it is striking how much reliance was being expressed, by Gladstone and others, on the fundamental decency of these working men who were petitioning to be trusted not to take advantage of a benefit unfairly. To that extent the Christian Socialists' mission to encourage harmony between the social classes had apparently had some effect. The object of Furnivall's introduction of various depu-

Furnivall: 'I am directed to inform you it is the intention of the Lords of the Committee of Privy Council for Trade to communicate on the subject with the Local Marine Board before anything further is done.'

[197] 'Ballast Heavers (Port of London) Bill', Hansard, 1803–2005, 6 Apr. 1852, Commons Sitting, http://api.parliament.uk, accessed 17 Mar. 2020.

tations of ballast heavers to government offices and polite drawing rooms was to show that they might be rough, but were well behaved, and would not damage Disraeli's delicate gilt furniture. Above all they were sober. The radical, but self-styled liberal, Ralph Bernal Osborne decided to introduce some brass tacks into the debate by observing that of the twenty-nine middlemen employing the ballast heavers, twenty-seven were keepers of public houses.[198] The moral tone was high, not least because the ballast heavers had been so widely reported to be in thrall to the publicans, who were forcing them to spend up to half of their wages in drink. The horror of working class drunkenness, and its deleterious effects on family life, was a dominant theme throughout the entire ballast heavers' affair, and was probably one of the evils which particularly exercised Furnivall.

The continued delay while a select committee deliberated was frustrating both to Furnivall and the men. Manners wrote to reassure him that 'you could not find a more efficient advocate of the Ballast Heavers' claims than Lord Robert Grosvenor, in the House of Commons'.[199] But Furnivall was receiving other letters from Henry Barthorp, who had largely taken over the effective leadership of the men from Flynn. Barthorp was fronting a publicity campaign to display the contents of the proposed Bill, with the ballast heavers' own explanations before a public meeting could be held, significantly in the Temperance halls.[200] 'I think it most important that the Public should thoroughly understand the subject—you will also perceive that it will take some short time to obtain the sanction of the parties for the use of the Temperance Halls so that the place of meeting can be named with the date of the evenings in addition to the Bill containing the whole matter. I would suggest that we had some moderate sized posters.' Things were starting to turn black: the ship-owners and brokers were themselves taking action: 'We are doing no business the small shipping is very scarce—there was only 1 ship sold on the Corn Exchange yesterday—I shall be glad if you will step down as early as possible. The Publicans are using the greatest intimidation and things look far from cheering.'[201]

It was in August, at this grim moment, when nothing seemed to be happening, that an article appeared in the radical and political newspaper *The Leader* on the 'Grievances of Ballast Heavers'. It is a reply

[198] Derek Beales, 'Osborne, Ralph Bernal (1808?–1882), *ODNB*.
[199] FU 548, letter of 6 Nov. 1852, from the Office of Works.
[200] FU 17, letter of 11 Nov. 1852, from 3 Saint John St., White House Lane, Stepney.
[201] FU 18, undated, but probably Nov. 1852.

to the *Morning Chronicle*, which was continuing to campaign on the men's behalf, and an update of the story told by Hughes in the *Christian Socialist*. It is unsigned, but, given the inside knowledge presented here, the author was certainly Furnivall, whose name (albeit misspelled) had earlier appeared in an April issue of *The Leader*. William Johnson commented wryly, and perhaps a touch snobbishly, on Furnivall's new celebrity: 'Your name misspelt appeared in the Leader as a popular speaker. There are tailors in Windsor who take in the Leader'; it is implied that Johnson would not otherwise have seen the paper.[202] 'Grievances of Ballast Heavers' expresses intense frustration at the deadlock caused by lassitude and the Grim Reaper.

At once time the Right Hon. H. Labouchere, the late President of the Board of Trade, pledged himself distinctly to a deputation of the ballast-heavers that he would bring in a bill for the establishment of a public office, from whence the men might be employed. This intention was never carried out, through the resignation of the Whig Government. A bill to remedy this evil was brought in by Mr George Thompson, the late Member for the Tower Hamlets, but for some cause the matter was allowed to drop.[203]

Finally, in November 1852, the ballast heavers, with Furnivall's encouragement and assistance, decided to bypass Parliamentary procedure and go straight to the top. They petitioned Prince Albert, recently appointed the Master of Trinity House, and known to have a lifelong concern with the misfortunes of the labouring poor. Sir Charles Grey, Prince Albert's private secretary and equerry to the queen, wrote to Furnivall:

Sir
I have received the commands of His Royal Highness Prince Albert to acknowledge the receipt of your letter, with the enclosed memorial from the Inhabitants of Shadwell &c. It relates to a subject in which His Royal Highness takes the liveliest interest, & I have forwarded it as well as your letter, & other enclosures, to Mr Shepperd, the Deputy Master of the Trinity 'House' & expressed His Royal Highness' earnest desire that that corporation should take the case of the Ballast Heavers with their serious consideration.

His Royal Highness cannot at this moment give any opinion as to the particular plan suggested by you, but it will give him the greatest pleasure to find that it shall be in the Powers of the Corporation of the Trinity House, in anticipation

---

[202] Letter from William Johnson to Furnivall, 7 Apr. 1852, Furnivall Papers, FU 237; Johnson took a lively interest in Furnivall's part in the ballast heavers' struggle; see letter following, FU 238, undated [Apr. 1852].

[203] *Leader and Saturday Analyst*, 21 Aug. 1852, p. 793.

of any Legislation on the subject, to take such steps as may to tend to give to this deserving class of men the relief of which they stand so much in need.[204]

Prince Albert's representations brought almost instant results. At the Prince's suggestion, the President of the Board of Trade, Edward Cardwell, inserted a clause in the Merchant Shipping Act of 1853 which provided for the establishment of a registry for the ballast heavers, under the direct control of Trinity House. Jacob Herbert, of Trinity House, assured Furnivall that the necessary alterations at the Ballast Office, Ratcliff, to set up a registry, 'will now be proceeded with forthwith'.[205] And Herbert wrote a circular letter to the men themselves:

> Adverting to the Memorial from the Inhabitants of Shadwell, Wapping and adjacent districts which you recently transmitted to His Royal Highness Prince Albert praying the adoption of measures for the abolition of the Truck System to which the Ballast Heavers on the River Thames are subjected I am directed to acquaint you that a Committee of the Elder Brethren will meet at this House for the consideration of the subject.[206]

Good news was needed, as, by early in the new year of 1853, the men were feeling real hardship, and Barthorp was forced reluctantly to approach Furnivall for money: 'I am ... at the present time put to more than my ordinary expenses having an Aged mother residing with me 73 years of age in a bed of sickness whose dissolution is hourly expected and I should be doing myself injustice if I denied that Assistance would not be most acceptable.' But expectation of change was buoying up the men's spirits:

> I hope in a few days things will bear a different aspect from the strong assurances we have received of support we were compelled on Saturday last to give a Ballast Heaving Agent into custody for endeavouring to create a breach of the peace in the Office—Mr Yardley severely admonished him on the impropriety of his conduct and bound him over in his own recognizance to keep the peace for six months.[207]

Another of the men, James Brown, was also seeking publicity, as Barthorp told Furnivall:

> Brown has had an interview with the Editor of the Shipping and Mercantile Gazette who has appointed 3 o Clock on Monday afternoon to come down to

---

[204] FU 341, letter of 15 Nov. 1852, from Windsor Castle.
[205] FU 380, letter of 15 Dec. 1852. Also, 'The Ballast-Heavers at Home', *The Spectator*, 36, 1 Aug. 1863, 2315; Brian Bond, 'Cardwell, Edward, first Viscount Cardwell (1813–1886)', *ODNB*. [206] FU 379, letter of 23 Nov. 1852.
[207] FU 19, letter of 17 Jan. 1853.

the Office and examine the men himself if you can possibly come down I should be glad. You will be glad to hear that we have received an order for 100 Pound from Mr Lindsay—I think if we could but obtain some pecuniary aid we should yet triumph over all opposition. Myself &c. unhappily are very closely pressed and unless things brighten up considerably one of us at least will have to beat a retreat I regret to have to touch upon these matters but the fact is we are desperately poor—be assured I do not mention this to work upon your sympathy but merely that you may understand exactly how we are situated if things do not improve speedily.[208]

This story had a happy ending in several huge tea parties. Flynn and Barthorp were appointed 'ruler and deputy ruler of the Registry', and the men's lives began to improve, though the new conditions took a little while to settle down, and the ship-owners took some advantage of a loophole to get agents to employ men other than those registered at Trinity House, and a 'tremendous uproar ensued' when it was reported that the Trinity House men had enlisted the support of William Newton, who was one of the leaders of the Amalgamated Society of Engineers during the great lockout of 1852.[209] Gladstone's fears that the ballast-heavers could not be entirely trusted not to strike for higher wages seemed to be justified. But on the whole the reforms were beneficial, and the men modestly flourished. Prince Albert died on 14 December 1861, and two years later the ballast heavers presented a memorial tribute to Queen Victoria on her birthday (24 May):

May it please your Majesty—We Hundred and Forty Ballast-Heavers of the Port of London, having this morning had our annual Van Excursion to Epping Forest, and having finished our plentiful dinner after it, cannot but think with heartfelt gratitude, of that good man, your late Royal Consort, to whom we owe, not only this day's enjoyment, but eight years' contented life in our hard labour, after a long time of misery from which he relieved us . . . Your Majesty, we tried hard to get out of this accursed system, we appealed to men of all classes, but got no help till we sent—by our present Chairman—an appeal to your late Royal Consort on his election to the Mastership of the Trinity House. He at once listened to us. Your Majesty, he loved the wife of his own bosom, and he loved the children of his love; he could put himself down from the throne which he shared to the wretched home of us poor men and could feel what we and our wives and children were suffering . . . At once our wrongs were redressed and

[208] FU 20, undated, ?Jan. 1853. 'Perhaps some arrangement might be made for Brown to take the place of one of us. I would say by all means keep the place in existence.'
[209] 'Ballast Heavers at Home', 2315; FU 22, Barthorp to Furnivall, 9 Feb. 1853: 'Having been now six weeks at the Ballast Heavers Office I am enabled now to form a better opinion as to its necessary mode of arrangement.' 'Proceedings of Ballast Heavers', *The Observer*, 23 Sept. 1855, p. 6.

the system that had ruined us swept away... We celebrate our deliverance by an annual treat on your Majesty's Birthday; and your Majesty will not wonder that we then think with special gratitude of our Deliverer. He, year by year, asked after us, and rejoiced to hear of our improvement while he lived on earth, and now that he's in heaven, we trust that he knows of us still.[210]

The 'Chairman' who was the go-between between the men and the Prince was, of course, 'Fredk. J. Furnivall', listed among the signatories of the message sent from The Three Colts Inn, Grove-street, South Hackney, on 6 June. The men respectfully requested two engravings of the Prince which they could display in their waiting and reading rooms. Furnivall could not resist the huge satisfaction of printing the Queen's reply, accompanied by two images of the Prince, one in uniform, one in ordinary dress, with, additionally, one of herself, 'as the Queen would wish, in the remembrance of these grateful men, to be associated with the memory of her great and good husband'. They were sent from Windsor Castle by her private secretary, Sir Charles Phipps (Furnivall could not resist adding his own name to the article as though he were a co-author):

Her Majesty has been deeply touched by this spontaneous testimony to the active benevolence of her beloved husband, and amongst all the tokens of sympathy in her grief, which she has gratefully received from all classes of her people, no one has been more gratifying to the Queen, and no one more in harmony with her feelings, than the simple and unpretending tribute from these honest, hard-working men... Her Majesty rejoices to hear of the happy change in their moral and social condition.[211]

The *Spectator* observed that 'this mark of Royal favour seems to have created a great sensation in the neighbourhood of Wapping and Ratcliff Cross', and the men installed the pictures with yet another celebration. 'As old acquaintances of the men in their hard times', the *Spectator* rejoiced in their change of fortune. 'We had not, indeed, to the best of our belief, set eyes on a ballast-heaver since the passing of their Emancipation Act in 1853 ... Could these be the ragged, dirty sallow-faced, hunger-stricken men who used to crowd the meetings of twelve years

[210] The story went worldwide; the text here is cited from the *South Australian Weekly Chronicle*, Saturday, 22 Aug. 1863, p. 2; see also the record of the memorial in T. Martin, *The Life of H.R.H. The Prince Consort*, iv, ch. 74, pp. 3–4. See also FU 496, undated. The signatories to the letter included James Brown, Henry Barthorp, and Thomas Tighe Flynn.
[211] *The Examiner*, 20 June 1863, p. 13. K. D. Reynolds, 'Phipps, Sir Charles Beaumont (1801–1866)', *ODNB*.

ago?' Barthorp made a speech: 'Thanks to God, and Prince Albert, and the Trinity House, we've done with the publicans!' And he concluded with appropriate exhortations to teetotalism, in which not all those present acquiesced.[212]

The story of the ballast heavers has the quintessential Furnivall characteristics of quixotism—people asked who these grubby men with a strange name were, now tidied up and made respectable? But it also shows his earnest concern for working men, as well as a wish to establish his own name, even somewhat intrusively, as an up and coming campaigner. He was starting to become known in the wider world. It may be said that the 'vanity' of which Ludlow complained was becoming apparent. But also the essential kindliness. He had reasons to be proud of what he had achieved. So far as the EETS and Furnivall's other publishing ventures were concerned, Furnivall's activities as a young man on behalf of the ballast-heavers gave him invaluable experience in approaching great persons, without any introduction, in support of public-spirited enterprises. Self-confidence and tenacity he already had.

[212] 'Ballast-Heavers at Home', *The Spectator*, 36, 1 Aug. 1863, pp. 2315–16.

4

Christian Socialism and Socializing: Prelude to the Working Men's College, 1851–1853

> It was well for their ultimate success that the great majority of intelligent working-men ... concerned themselves little with beatific visions of the promised land of their inheritance.
>
> Beatrice Potter, *The Co-operative Movement in Great Britain* (1895), 32

SOCIALIZING AND SELF-IMPROVEMENT: THE GREAT EXHIBITION

Furnivall's diaries for 1848 and 1851 are rich documents, showing many facets of his life in London at a time when he was taking an active role in the Christian Socialists' campaign of encouraging trade associations and co-operatives. The leaders of the movement were well connected and highly influential men within their wide circle. They were personally impressive, and highly cultivated in literature and music—Ludlow's and Scott's musical knowledge has already been noticed, and their instruction rubbed off on Furnivall. Kingsley saw the value in encouraging working people to go to art galleries, and Furnivall, too, under Ruskin's influence, became able to appreciate visual art in an informed way—his taste moved on from 'Family Devotion' to Raphael, as well as Turner. Maurice's charisma (and, less spectacularly, Kingsley's) drew in many, even if they ultimately disagreed with them; Ludlow and Hughes were highly capable men of business, as well as acute observers. Association with these men was a remarkable experience for Furnivall, and, through them, he was able to move in their wider circles of acquaintances and meet an extraordinary range of London society, from the working poor to sympathetic lords and ladies. As noticed above, an interest in language was widespread in these circles, and Furnivall, thanks to his UCL and Cambridge connections, became involved in the Philological Society of London at this time.

Towards the end of 1851 his diary becomes rushed, and finally peters out in notes—there was no time to keep it fully up to date as Furnivall became engrossed in activities only distantly related to conveyancing and which kept him up very late at night while he sustained himself with scratch vegetarian snacks of buns and apples. The diaries are both frenetic and kaleidoscopic. For purposes of clarity, it has been necessary to separate out different narrative strands of Furnivall's life at this time. But they were interwoven in ever more complicated patterns. Two entries, from June and December, may convey something of their turbulence and variety.

On Friday 13 June, Furnivall went to his chambers, finished a draft, visited his friend Badger, read *The Jurist* '&c.', corrected proofs of the *Christian Socialist* until 5.30, had a Vegetarian dinner at the Whittington, went to the Philological Society at 7.45, where, after a meeting, Thomas Watts read a paper on the Sanskrit alphabet, followed by tea.[1] At 10 in the evening he went on to visit Thomas Hughes at his house, where he found Mr and Mrs Hensleigh Wedgwood, Mrs Ruskin with a Spanish friend, Mr and Mrs Maurice, Vansittart Neale and his wife, and Mrs Judith Merivale, wife of Charles Merivale, '&c'.[2] Furnivall did not know the Merivales well, though they were part of the Wedgwoods' 'set'. Charles Merivale was yet another Cambridge graduate, a former Apostle, a friend of the philologist J. M. Kemble, as well as Trench, and with an interest in Anglo-Saxon and Saint-Simonianism.[3]

On Tuesday, 9 December, Furnivall was again burning the candle at both ends. He did not get up until 1.30 in the afternoon, having been up late the previous night. He went to chambers for breakfast, a chat with Badger, more breakfast, and some legal work. At 6.20 he took a bus to the Clarendon Hotel, where the Pimlico Builders association were having their dinner—'about 50'. Vansittart Neale, Ludlow, Hughes and his wife, Lord Goderich, Lloyd Jones, and others were there. Then 'away at 8.15, by busses to the Bethnal Green Weavers' meeting, 15 or so, pleasant chat till past 11, home with Rice to see a loom work, walked home, had coffee on my way; diary &c. till 2'.[4]

---

[1] Librarian at the British Museum, and formidable polyglot, Watts was familiar with all Western European languages, including Celtic, Slavonic, and Hungarian, as well as being a student of Oriental languages. See further Richard Garnett, revd. P. R. Harris, 'Watts, Thomas (1811–1869)', *ODNB*.   [2] Bodl. MS Eng. e. 2316, f. 32ʳ.

[3] J. M. Rigg, 'Merivale, Charles (1808–1893)', *ODNB*. Also Allen, *Cambridge Apostles*, 97–8, 161, 177, 224. The Comte de Saint-Simon advocated a socialist system of common property ownership. Furnivall also met another Apostle, the Hon. Stephen Spring Rice, a philanthropist, who had experience of the 1847 Great Irish Famine, and his wife, socially, as well as the barrister Henry Bonham Carter, who was a cousin of Florence Nightingale and assisted her in her work. Wednesday, 14 May, Bodl. MS Eng. e. 2316, f. 27ᵛ.

[4] Bodl. MS Eng. e. 2316, f. 57ᵛ. Rice was the weavers' manager. Weavers' Fields in Bethnal Green are named for the weavers' cottages serving the silk industry, which occupied this area in the nineteenth century.

The two entries show how Furnivall's philological and Christian Socialist friends overlapped. The Wedgwoods' circle was especially important. Furnivall visited there frequently and enjoyed a 'romp' with their son Tim, and daughters Dot and Effie. He also kept up with his family connections in town, thanks to his sister Mary, who lived in London with her husband, William Davenant, and their children. These occasions were more purely social, but also offered opportunities for mixing in good society and the chance to meet 'pretty girls' of his own class. With the Davenants he attended Lady Spearman's parties, bringing with them his brother Charles and sister Louisa ('Loo'), if they were visiting. The Spearmans, who lived in 7 Portman Square, but had their family home in Hanwell, are likely to have been family friends, and their social gatherings offered Furnivall at least the prospect of dancing. But, though they had a 'fine large house', there were 'no pretty girls', and a great many men.[5] Other family acquaintances, the Summers, whom Furnivall knew from his UCL days, also held a small party of about forty people where there were 'two pretty girls, no very good dancers', but he enjoyed 'two *famous* Galops' and 'the Sturm March'.[6] On another occasion, 'a Miss Randall fainted away in my arms from waltzing too long—rooms too small and hot'.[7] These purely social events again show Furnivall's fondness for outrageous juxtapositions with his social activism—dancing with Miss Randall had followed hard upon a meeting of the Council of Promoters which had continued until 10.45 in the evening. At this stage in his life Furnivall could not afford, either emotionally or financially, to become involved with 'pretty girls' other than as dancing partners, or if they were safely married, like Henrietta Vyner, who married Lord Goderich in 1851, and for whom Furnivall seems to have sustained an enthusiastic *amour lointain* which was the subject of long-running teasing both from her husband and Hughes.[8] His admiration of Effie Ruskin seems also to have been of this kind. Furnivall's donations

[5] Wednesday, 30 Apr. 1851, when he danced until 2 a.m., having earlier attended a meeting at Lambeth on co-operation, where he spoke for twenty minutes. Bodl. MS Eng. e. 2316, f. 25^v. Also Wednesday, 14 May, f. 27^v. At the top of the page Furnivall noted that their daughter, Augusta, was presented at Court, 15 May; also 'Mrs. Ruskin to Almack's' (f. 28^r). See further J. C. Sainty, 'Spearman, Sir Alexander Young, first baronet (1793–1874)', *ODNB*.
[6] Tuesday, 4 Febr. 1851 (Furnivall's birthday), Bodl. MS Eng. e. 2316, f. 13^v. The Summers family also knew the Spearmans.
[7] Thursday, 12 June 1851, Bodl. MS Eng. e. 2316, f. 32^r.
[8] Colloms, *Victorian Visionaries*, 118. *The Young Man from Home* also warned against 'the rash formation of attachments' (pp. 89–90), reinforcing advice Furnivall was certain to have received at home.

to hard-up workers, together probably with neglect of his career, had left him short of money. He had to ask his sister Mary and brother-in-law William Davenant if he might move in temporarily with them.[9]

Meanwhile the younger members of Furnivall's family had continued to perplex their elders. As the eldest brother in the family, he was still expected to take some responsibility for his younger unmarried siblings. After leaving Eton amidst scandal, Will continued to be a scamp, and Frederick was urgently summoned home to Egham by Charles because Will had been embezzling money.[10] In May, Frederick saw him off at Paddington for Coleford (Somerset).[11] Frederick had been put in charge of Will in 1848, when it was decided to send him to KCL, where he was entered in the chemistry and general literature departments, and it was agreed that while there, he should live with Frederick, who brought him up to London and undertook to give him coaching in the evenings, in Homer and Euclid. He had found Will '*very* backward'.[12] Ted, the only one of the Furnivall sons to follow his father into medicine, but not to be outdone in academic underachievement, 'was plucked at Apothecary's Hall'.[13] Selina, now aged 25, was also giving cause for concern, as she wanted to leave home for reasons that were evidently more substantial than just wishing for a change of scenery, and which provoked a serious family conference. Something which needed to be hushed up had occurred between her and the (married) vicar of the Furnivalls' parish church at Egham.[14] Meanwhile 'Charley drove to Banstead to look at a farm of 600 acres, liked it—but how to raise £4000 to go in?'[15]

The event which above all others brought many, including Furnivall's friends and family, to London in 1851, quite apart from the round

---

[9] Monday, 11 Aug. 1851, Bodl. MS Eng. e. 2316, f. 40^v. He moved in on Sunday, 21 Dec. (f. 59^v).

[10] Saturday, 11 Jan. 1851, 'note from Charley that I am to go home—Will embezzling Kilver's money'. Bodl. MS Eng. e. 2316, f. 10^r. Furnivall went home the next day to talk to his father.

[11] Saturday, 24 May 1851, Bodl. MS Eng. e. 2316, f. 29^r. Later 'Gregg in, about Will, who is going on better', Friday 1 Aug., f. 39^r.

[12] Diary, Tuesday, 26 Sept.; Tuesday, 3 Oct.; Wednesday, 4 Oct., 1848, Bodl. MS Eng d. 2104, ff. 46^v, 47^v.

[13] Wednesday, 22 Oct., Bodl. MS Eng. e. 2316, f. 50^v. That is, he failed his examinations, administered by the Worshipful Society of Apothecaries, to qualify as a medical practitioner.

[14] Saturday, 8 Mar. 1851, Bodl. MS Eng. e. 2316, f. 18^r. 'Selina wants to go away on account of the Biedermann ⟨. . .⟩.' The Revd. William Henry Biedermann was the vicar at Egham parish church. He had married in 1842. On Easter Sunday (20 Apr.), William Davenant joined with 'Papa' and 'Mama' in talking to her (f. 24^r); on 5 May she went to Clevedon (Somerset) (f. 26^v).   [15] Monday 2 Oct. 1851, Bodl. MS Eng. e. 2315, f. 47^v.

THE GREAT EXHIBITION

of visits, business, and shopping, was, of course, the Great Exhibition. It was a must-see, even interspersed as it was for Furnivall with his Christian Socialist activities. On Septuagesima Sunday, the day Maurice began his course of sermons in Lincoln's Inn chapel on the Old Testament, Furnivall walked after the sermon with the architect Frank Penrose, the engineer George Grove, and Ludlow to see the new Great Exhibition building in Hyde Park. Furnivall knew Grove as a sympathizer with the movement, but he is better known to history as the editor of the classic *Dictionary of Music and Musicians* ('Grove's'), of which the first volume appeared in 1878.[16] As Furnivall described, the Exhibition was opened on Thursday, 1 May, by the Queen in state. Effie Ruskin was present, having been sent a ticket, but was unaccompanied by her husband.[17] Furnivall, less well connected, had to make do with calling on the family friend of his UCL days, Mrs Radcliffe, for the gossip—after reading Mayhew's *London Labour and London Poor*.[18]

He got to see the exhibition a couple of weeks later, after the entry price had dropped from £1 to 5s.: 'by bus to the Great Exhibition, & was there from 10.20 to 6.20, walked about all the time—there is nothing very striking, much curious & interesting; a collection of very smart shops, for the finery; the produce of the different countries very interesting; & the engineering things; sculpture good'.[19] He was sufficiently impressed by the sculptures to go and see them again, towards the end of the show, on Tuesday, 7 October: 'to the Exhibition to see Jellishaw's Adam & Eve &c, the Denmark statuettes—Thorvaldsen the most striking of them'.[20] It is probably unworthy, but not perhaps irrelevant, to note that these neoclassical statues' chaste white marble

---

[16] Sunday, 16 Feb. 1851, Bodl. MS Eng. e. 2316, f. 15^r. On Grove, see Percy M. Young, 'Grove, Sir George (1820–1900)', *ODNB*; also Christensen, *Origin and History of Christian Socialism*, 92, and Ludlow, *Autobiography*, 130, 190. The Great Exhibition was the turning point in Grove's career: he became the secretary to the Committee of the Society of Arts, planning the exhibition, and subsequently the secretary to the Crystal Palace after its move to Sydenham, where it was used, with his encouragement, for concerts. On the history of the Exhibition, see Luckhurst, 'The Great Exhibition of 1851'. The price was subsequently reduced to 1s.

[17] Ruskin described his impressions of the Palace in Hyde Park and later Sydenham in a pamphlet, *The Opening of the Crystal Palace*. In 1851 Turner died, and 'while we have been building this colossal receptacle for casts and copies of the art of other nations, these works of our own greatest painter [Turner] have been left to decay', 7.

[18] Thursday, 1 May 1851, Bodl. MS Eng. e. 2316, f. 26^r; Hilton, *John Ruskin*, i. 157.

[19] Monday 19 May 1851, Bodl. MS Eng. e. 2316, f. 28^v.

[20] Bodl. MS Eng. e. 2316, f. 48^v. Furnivall shared his taste for Thorvaldsen with William Johnson, who told him: 'I am rejoicing in the arrival of four of Thorvaldsen's Apostles in plaister from Copenhagen.' FU 242, 26 May 1856.

nudity, barely covered by moral uplift, was one of the most controversial displays—much as Hiram Powers's *The Greek Slave*, wearing nothing but her chain, was one of the most provocative sculptural exhibits, but who lent herself to the abolitionist cause, even though she was a representation of a white girl captured by Ottomans during the Greek War of Independence. It provoked a direct response by the sculptor John Bell: *A Daughter of Eve: A Scene on the Shore of the Atlantic* (*The American Slave*, (1853))—a representation of a Guinean captive destined for the cotton fields.[21] It is surprising, especially in view of his abhorrence of slavery, that Furnivall does not mention Powers's much talked about highlight of the show.[22] He, like others, noted with astonishment the rising numbers of visitors, which eventually reached around six million before the exhibition's closure on 15 October. After visiting the exhibition, Furnivall went home to study Exodus chapter V in the light of Maurice's comments on eternity, the deluge, '&c.'

The Exhibition was meant to be educative, not merely a collection of marvels. As such, it was essential to Furnivall's self-improvement project. There is notably less simple frivolity in the 1848 and 1851 diaries than in the entries dating from Furnivall's time at UCL. Now, instead of the latest novels, he reports himself to be reading, in addition to the Christian Socialists' publications and replies to reviewers, political works relating to both home and abroad. *The Glory and the Shame of England*, by the American abolitionist C. Edwards Lester, had an evident appeal.[23] And Furnivall, like many others, read Gladstone's best-selling and shocking exposé of the judicial system and prison conditions in the Kingdom of Naples, all the more sensational

---

[21] See further Charlotte Ribeyrol. Matthew Winterbottom, and Madeline Hewitson (eds.), *Colour Revolution: Victorian Art, Fashion and Design*(Oxford, 2023), 126–8 (Bell's figure is shown on p. 127).

[22] See the discussion in Smith (ed.), *Exposed: The Victorian Nude*, 38. Also comments by the art critic Anna Jameson, who visited the Great Exhibition of 1851 and wrote the guide to the display of modern sculpture (casts) later shown in the Crystal Palace after its removal to Sydenham: ability to appreciate nudity in art was a mark of education: 'A man whose education and habits of life have never led him to form classical associations in art . . . says very naturally, "I do not like your undraped gods and goddesses".' *Hand-Book to the Courts of Modern Sculpture*. Thorvaldsen's purity of taste is commended (pp. 11–12).

[23] Friday, 29 Aug. 1851, Bodl. MS Eng. e. 2316, f. 43^r. *The Glory and the Shame of England* (1841). Just about the only light reading reported at this time (while Furnivall was at home in Egham during the Easter vacation) is Richard Hort (Lieutenant Colonel)'s novel, *Penelope Wedgebone: The Supposed Heiress* (London, 1850); Monday, 21 Apr. 1851, Bodl. MS Eng. e. 2316, f. 24^v. Wedge*bone* is a glance at the Wedg*wood* family with whom Furnivall socialized.

because of Gladstone's reputation and the scrupulous forensic account he gave.[24]

Early in 1851, the Whig politician R. A. Slaney, MP for Shrewsbury, obtained and chaired a Select Committee to investigate 'Investments for the savings of the middle and working classes'. It enquired into the financing of the working men's co-operative associations, and, among other men in Furnivall's circle, Thomas Hughes, J. M. Ludlow, and Vansittart Neale were called as witnesses, as also was John Stuart Mill, who gave evidence in support of the associations: 'I think there is no way in which the working-classes can make so beneficial a use of their savings . . . as by the formation of associations . . . provided always that experience should show that these associations can keep together.'[25] Furnivall, of course, followed the proceedings with keen interest, which prompted him straightaway to embark on reading Mill's *Principles of Political Economy* (1848).[26] William Johnson had already read it, and had warned him: 'The whole first volume of Mill I have gone through with much alacrity—but the first half of the 2nd is too much for my digestion & I have skipped several chapters, being eager to traverse his two last books which look much the most attractive, being more connected with history and less with mercantile technicality.'[27]

After this Furnivall put himself through a course on economics, moving from Mill to Francis Newman's lectures on the subject, given at Bedford College and published in 1851.[28] Newman, brother of John Henry Newman, was professor of Latin at UCL, and a student of a wide

[24] Wednesday, 3 Sept. 1851, Bodl. MS Eng. e. 2316, f. 43^v. Gladstone, *Two Letters to the Earl of Aberdeen on the State Persecution of the Neapolitan Government*. On the whole episode, see Miller, *Prince of Librarians*, 242–63.
[25] Quoted in *Life of Maurice*, ii. 52. See also Ludlow's account, *Autobiography*, 194–7. Ludlow considered Slaney 'a very worthy, well-meaning man, but hazy-minded'. Nevertheless, Slaney moved for leave to bring in a Bill, which received royal assent on 30 June, by which he, with the Christian Socialists' help, achieved 'a momentous good in the legalising of co-operation' (Ludlow, *Autobiography*, 194). The report was printed on 5 July. The Bill was blocked by Labouchere of the Board of Trade, but the Industrial and Provident Societies Partnership Act became law in 1852.
[26] Wednesday, 22 Jan. 1851, Bodl. MS Eng. e. 2316, f. 11^v. 'Read Hughes's evidence &c. for Christian Socialism . . . home—tea—read Mill's Political Economy and the Biblical Cyclopedia.' Furnivall lent his copy of *Political Economy* to Ludlow, who replied: 'Many thanks for your Mill. I was only waiting for it to set to work upon taxation myself, but as I find my hands quite full enough already, I should be very glad if your friend Johnson would take up the subject', FU 513. The Huntington tentatively assigns the letter to 1848 (the book's date of publication), though 1851 seems a better fit.
[27] Letter of 1 Aug. 1848, FU 208.
[28] Newman, *Lectures on Political Economy*; see further Timothy C. F. Stunt, 'Newman, Francis William (1805–1897)', *ODNB*.

range of ancient languages; Furnivall met him at the Wedgwoods', along with Maurice and Carlyle, and, later, Newman was present, along with Mrs Wedgwood, at a *conversazione* at which Ludlow lectured on Christian Socialism.[29] Newman would go on to join the EETS in 1873.[30] Perhaps because it had been favourably reviewed by J. S. Mill, Furnivall also read Thomas De Quincey's *Logic of Political Economy* (1844).[31] And Carlyle's and De Quincey's interest in Jean Paul Richter may have led him to his novel, *Leben des Quintus Fixlein* (1796), which otherwise seems out of character.[32] But either Ludlow or Kingsley may have been an influence here, and led Furnivall also to John Morell's *Sketch* of the French philosopher and socialist thinker Charles Fourier (1772–1837).[33] Carlyle's *Life of John Sterling* was a must-read: although Sterling had died young, in 1844, he was a leading member of the Cambridge Apostles, a friend of many other rising young men in this group, including Maurice, Trench, Arthur Hallam, Tennyson, and Kemble. Like Furnivall, he had attended Trinity Hall, and he had known Samuel Taylor Coleridge personally.[34] Furnivall also met the German political economist Moritz Mohl (1802–88), visiting London from Württemburg; he talked to him and took him to tea.[35]

S. T. Coleridge's influence both on Sterling himself, and on Maurice, had been profound. It is not surprising that Furnivall, on the edge of this circle, and powerfully influenced by Maurice, should have read not only Coleridge's *Reflections*, but also his *Table Talk*, which Sterling had annotated, as well as *On the Constitution of the Church and State*, and Hartley Coleridge's biography of his father.[36] Because it was published anonymously, Furnivall may have thought that *Guesses at Truth*

---

[29] Wednesday, 12 Feb.; Monday, 9 June; Bodl. MS Eng. e. 2316, ff. 14ᵛ, 31ᵛ; after finishing, Furnivall began a reply to Newman, Saturday, 21 June, f. 33ʳ.

[30] Ninth Report of the Committee, 23. Living at 127 Finsborough Road, West Brompton.

[31] Thursday, 10 Apr. 1851, Bodl. MS Eng. e. 2316, f. 23ʳ.

[32] Tuesday, 15 Apr. 1851, Bodl. MS Eng. e. 2316, f. 23ᵛ. Furnivall began reading the book in chambers, and resumed later, after a 'long chat' with Daniel Macmillan.

[33] Friday, 4 Apr. 1851, Bodl. MS Eng. e. 2316, f. 22ʳ; Morell, *Sketch of the Life of Charles Fourier*. Furnivall on the same evening read 'Haweis's Reformation', perhaps by the evangelical clergyman Thomas Haweis (c.1734–1820).

[34] Sunday, 26–Monday, 27 Oct. 1851, Bodl. MS Eng. e. 2316, f. 51ʳ⁻ᵛ. Allen, *Cambridge Apostles*. On the influence of Carlyle on the Cambridge circle in the first half of the 19th c., see Vidler, *F. D. Maurice and Company*, 205–20.

[35] Tuesday, 29 July 1851, Bodl. MS Eng. e. 2316, f. 38ᵛ; also entries for Wednesday, 23, Friday, 25 July (f. 38ʳ); Wednesday, 10 Sept. (f. 44ᵛ).

[36] Furnivall read Coleridge's 'Talk', Tuesday, 15 July, Bodl. MS Eng. e. 2316, f. 33ᵛ; 'Church and State', Sunday, 15 June 1851 (f. 32ʳ).

(1827), by A. W. and J. C. Hare, was also written by Coleridge.[37] He was also seeking out Coleridge's works in June and July, after he had got to know Herbert Coleridge, his wife, Ellen, Herbert's mother, Sara, widow of Henry Nelson Coleridge, and her daughter, Edith, all of whom Furnivall met at the Wedgwoods.[38] His reading was thus driven by his lifelong enthusiasm for cultivating modern members of a famous family while researching their ancestors. He summed up the modern members of the family as the 'Coleridges of Regent's Park and Eton'.[39] Herbert Coleridge, like Furnivall, was a barrister of Lincoln's Inn, but, unlike Furnivall, 'his private means were adequate to his needs',[40] and enabled him to indulge his philological pursuits. As one would expect of Furnivall, his interest in the famous, senior member of the family had been piqued by these new friendships; he also read Derwent Coleridge's edition of Hartley's *Essays. Marginalia, and Poems* (1851) for its memoir of his brother.[41] He also read Keats, and Shelley's *Alastor*, '&c'.[42]

Furnivall was still a devout young man, who recorded receiving communion on the great festivals of the Church's year. He was also putting himself through a course of serious theological reading prompted by his association with Maurice and Kingsley, whose sermons he attended and made notes on.[43] Maurice was going through a difficult period in his career: his association with the Christian Socialists, and his *Theological Essays*, published in 1853, would lead later that year to his forced resignation as professor of theology at KCL.[44] Maurice's close friend, Kingsley, considered a firebrand after the publication of *Yeast* (republished in 1851) and *Alton Locke*, also caused controversy. Furnivall's presence at discussions of theologically provocative passages of the Old

[37] He read it at the same time as Coleridge's *Table Talk*, on 15 July.
[38] See further Cherry Durrant, 'Coleridge, Henry Nelson (1798–1843)', *ODNB*.
[39] Wednesday, 15 Jan. 1851, Bodl. MS Eng. e. 2316, f. 10^v. The Herbert Coleridges lived at 10 Chester Place, Regent's Park; Herbert had also been educated at Eton.
[40] Edith Coleridge, revd. John D. Haigh, 'Coleridge, Herbert (1830–1861)', *ODNB*.
[41] Monday 31 Mar., Bodl. MS Eng. e. 2316, f. 21^v. He also read 'Coleridge, Cowper, and Kingsley' on Monday, 17 Mar. (f. 19^v).
[42] Furnivall read Keats on Tuesday, 8 Apr., Monday, 26 May 1851. He probably read Keats in the edition by Richard Monckton Milnes, *Life, Letters, and Literary Remains*, 2 vols. (London, 1848). He read his friend Johnson's review in the *Guardian* on Wednesday, 10 Sept. 1851, Bodl. MS Eng. e. 2315, f. 44^v; he had earlier considered either Johnson's review, or, perhaps more probably, Johnson's verdict on Milnes's comments, to be 'very good, sensible and religious'. He read Shelley on Tuesday, 8 Apr., Bodl. MS Eng. e. 2316 (f. 22^v).
[43] Communion, Egham, Easter Sunday (20 Apr.) and in Lincoln's Inn Chapel for Ascension Day (29 May), Bodl. MS Eng. e. 2316, ff. 24^r, 30^r.
[44] Morris, *To Build a Kingdom*, 6.

Testament probably did much to lead him from passive, and perhaps rather unthinking, piety to a taste for exciting religious argument, especially when it was enlivened by the compelling personalities conducting it. Furnivall followed up what he heard with study of the Apocrypha, John Oliver Willyams Hawes's *Sketches of the Reformation* (1844), the *Ecclesiastical History* of Eusebius, George Roberts's *Seculum episcopi: The Mirror of a Bishop* (1848), Trench on Augustine, and on the Parables,[45] B. F. Westcott on the Inspiration of the Bible,[46] and a subject which would prove increasingly contentious, James Gray, *Harmony of Geology and Scripture*.[47]

Public opposition to the Christian Socialists had attracted harsh criticism of Maurice's theological teaching in the religious press. His personal charisma did not entirely compensate for preaching which gave 'the impression as of a man who was immersed in a thick metaphysical fog'.[48] This comment was made by Tom Arnold, son of Dr Arnold of Rugby, who twice heard Maurice preach in 1846, and who came to know Furnivall at about this time, along with Hughes, as indeed is suggested by Furnivall's own comment, that he had discussed 'Tom Arnold's Biblical Criticism, &c.' along with Grisi's singing. Tom Arnold evidently thought Furnivall and Hughes, by contrast with Maurice, to be active and practical men, though he disapproved of their democratic ambitions, Nevertheless, writing in 1899, he still counted Furnivall 'as a very old friend': 'I am sure that both he and Hughes have done immense good, and have perhaps prepared intermediate stages whence something still better will one day be evolved; and yet I cannot applaud and rejoice in their work without reserve.'[49] Maurice's son reflected bitterly that anonymous writers, especially those of the *Quarterly Review*, were using the opportunity 'to denounce a man . . . when you know that he has no chance of having a fair hearing, and when every mis-statement that you make against him will be greedily swallowed'.[50] Furnivall's comment on Saturday, 4 October, 'Read the attack on us in

---

[45] Richard Chevenix Trench, *Exposition of the Sermon on the Mount Drawn from the Rritings of St Augustine, with Observations and an Introductory Essay on his Merits as an Interpreter of Scripture*, 3rd edn., revd. (London, 1869); *Notes on the Parables of Our Lord*, 4th edn. revd. (London, 1850).

[46] *The Elements of the Gospel Harmony: With a Catena on Inspiration, from the Writings of the Ante-Nicene Fathers* (Cambridge, 1851).

[47] 2nd edn. (London, 1851). See further Rupke, *The Great Chain of History*, 168.

[48] Arnold, *Passages in a Wandering Life*, 151; he observed of Maurice 'I felt quite unable to look to him as to one capable of helping other people to find their way into sunshine.'

[49] Ibid. 34: 'It seems to me too democratic, too content with low and commonplace strivings after comfort and recreation.'   [50] *Life of Maurice*, ii. 51.

the *Quarterlys*', probably refers to the most detailed and hurtful of these attacks, by J. Wilson Croker in the September edition of the *Quarterly Review*.⁵¹

In February, Maurice began his series of sermons on the Old Testament, preached at Lincoln's Inn Chapel, the first, in Furnivall's view, 'a very fine one'.⁵² It was followed by the *very striking* sermon on the Fall.⁵³ A couple of years before, Kingsley had been visiting London and was present at one of the discussions in Parker's the publisher's rooms, and, as Furnivall reported, his views on the same topic were provocatively expressed: 'The Fall nowhere so called in Scripture, was a great step in man's spiritual progress, before it, man's will was `passive' not, by it the will called into action. Can take all Genesis literally, except serpent talking. Herding in cities our Babel—Tories can't understand.'⁵⁴

In June, Maurice preached 'a very fine sermon on Joshua and John, justifying the Canaanite slaughter', when, as described in the Book of Joshua the people of Israel massacred the Canaanite tribes, men, women, and children.⁵⁵ Later, Furnivall discussed this troubling topic at some length with his friend William Johnson—who pointed out that it all depended on whose point of view one took.⁵⁶ The subject was (and is) a thorn to theologians, and it continued to trouble the Christian Socialists. Kingsley had also considered the subject in provocative articles on 'Socialism in the Bible' for the *Christian Socialist*; while defending the passage's brutality, even he may have found it 'irksome'.⁵⁷ Furnivall, of course, read the articles, and stayed up until 5 in the morning writing Kingsley a reply on the question of the population

---

⁵¹ Bodl. MS Eng. e. 2316, f. 48ʳ. See further *Life of Maurice*, ii. 71–4.

⁵² Sunday, 16 Feb. 1851, Bodl. MS Eng. e. 2316, f. 15ʳ. Published later that year as *The Old Testament: Nineteen Sermons*, Sermon II, pp. 21–41.

⁵³ Sunday, 23 Feb., Bodl. MS Eng. e. 2316, f. 16ʳ.

⁵⁴ Monday, 18 Sept. 1851. Kingsley had come up to London. In the evening there was a meeting at Parker's, where the discussion ranged over Chartists, Whigs, and Tories. It was remarked that 'Language confused. Babel, a text for our emigration sermon'. Bodl. MS Eng. e. 3215, f. 45ᵛ.

⁵⁵ Sunday, 22 June 1851, Bodl. MS Eng. e. 2316, f. 33ʳ. See also Numbers 21: 2–3, Deut. 20: 17, Joshua 6: 17, 21.

⁵⁶ Letter of 15 Aug. 1851, FU 207. Should a new book be discovered, written by a fugitive Hittite or Perizzite, 'It would be perhaps a pathetic account of the sufferings of the unoffending Canaanites `& the' cruelties of the (Jews) Hebrews. But we should correct it by reference to the known wickedness of the Canaanites—not the less condemning the cruelty of the conquerors.'

⁵⁷ Jan Martin Ivo Klaver's word; see 'Charles Kingsley and the Limits of Humanity', 138. Yet Ludlow suppressed Kingsley's comments on the extermination of the Canaanites, as too savage; Chitty, *Beast and Monk*, 142.

of Judaea.⁵⁸ The articles caused a discussion at the Wedgwoods.⁵⁹ He was also present on the electrifying occasion in June when Kingsley managed to get himself into the national press after he had been a guest preacher at St John's, Charlotte Street, and was denounced at the end of the sermon by the man who had invited him, G. S. Drew, speaking in his surplice from the altar. The drama was only defused by Kingsley's dignified refusal to reply. The subject, 'The Message of the Church to the Labouring Man' (which had been suggested by Maurice) had attracted a crowd of working men: Drew's plan 'succeeded in drawing audiences beyond those of ordinary piety'.⁶⁰

Maurice was also already engaging in the controversial teaching which appeared to doubt the orthodox doctrine of eternal punishment. He found the Church's use of the doctrine as a means to maintain its moral authority over unrepentant sinners obnoxious. In addition to uncertainty about the origins of the idea in the Old Testament, and especially the meaning of 'gehenna', the New Testament's word *aionios* ('everlasting') was a source of paradox. It could mean the indefinite stretching out of periods of time ('aeons'), and, since eternity cannot be measured out in periods, the teaching in the New Testament might be thought to allow for remission of punishment at the end of an 'aion'.⁶¹ When Maurice made this teaching public in 1853, with the publication of his *Theological Essays*, he was forced to resign his professorship in theology at KCL—meanwhile the subject was a source of lively debate among his friends. Furnivall, walking to Hyde Park Corner with Ludlow and another of the Co-operative Promoters, A. H. Louis, spent the time 'fighting about Turner's colouring; then Louis & I came to Gray's Inn talking of ⟨struck through⟩ punishments eternal or for an "aion"; home; looked out passages in the Bible'.⁶²

⁵⁸ Saturday, 22 Mar. 1851, Bodl. MS Eng. e. 2316, f. 20ʳ. He also read Kingsley's *Yeast*.
⁵⁹ Sunday, 30 Mar. Bodl. MS Eng. e. 2316, f. 21ʳ. Kingsley replied: Friday, 28 Mar., f. 21ʳ; Furnivall responded, Friday, 4 Apr., f. 22ʳ.
⁶⁰ Chadwick, *Victorian Church*, i. 358–60 (p. 358). The sermon's text was taken from Luke 4: 16–21: 'The spirit of the Lord is upon me because He hath anointed me to preach the gospel to the poor.' See also Hughes's account of the occasion, *Memoir of Kingsley*, pp. xxxii–xxxiv, and Kingsley's wife's account *Kingsley: Letters and Memories*, 115; also Chitty, *Beast and Monk*, 144. Furnivall's laconic comment was 'to Drew's Church in Charlotte Street, Kingsley preached on the message of the Gospel to the Labouring Classes, Liberty Equality, Brotherhood—after it Drew protested against it'. Sunday, 22 June 1851, Bodl. MS Eng. e. 2316, f. 33ʳ.
⁶¹ Morris, *To Build Christ's Kingdom*, 16–17; Maurice, *Life of Maurice*, ii. 163–94. *OED*, 'aeon', n. sense 2.
⁶² Thursday, 14 Aug. 1851, Bodl. MS Eng. e. 2316, f. 41ʳ. Louis was a shadowy but colourful figure in the movement, a Jew whom Ludlow had converted to Christianity,

FRIENDSHIP WITH JOHN RUSKIN

Mention of Furnivall's growing taste for Turner and theological controversy is the cue for introducing John Ruskin more directly into the narrative. The close friendship Furnivall enjoyed with him was one of the most formative passages of his life (it was less important to Ruskin). However, though they had much in common, Ruskin and the Christian Socialists did not agree, and it was a problem of biblical interpretation which revealed this fundamental lack of sympathy.

Part of the history of the Canaanite slaughters concerns the killing of the Canaanite general, Sisera, by Jael, the wife of an ally, when he sought refuge in her tent, and she showed him hospitality before hammering a nail into his head. The story presents a moral conundrum on several levels, as well as being shocking for the savage manner of Sisera's death. Maurice treated the subject in one of his Old Testament sermons, which were based on the Bible readings which he held at his house, and which Furnivall attended, along with Hughes and Ludlow.[63] Ruskin was also present on this occasion, drawn, as he said, by the magnetism of Maurice's personality: 'I loved Frederick Maurice, as everyone did who came near him.'[64] Maurice took what Ruskin considered an inappropriately 'enlightened modern view' of behaviour belonging to dark biblical ages. Ruskin recalled the incident, which had deeply offended him, many years later, when Maurice had warned, in Ruskin's sarcastic paraphrase, 'that no religious and patriotic Englishwoman ought ever to think of imitating Jael by nailing a Russian or Prussian's head to the ground'.[65] At the time, he challenged Maurice and was so disgusted by the reply that he never went back to hear Maurice again.

Ruskin had himself been hurt in a particularly tender spot, which

though he later returned to Judaism. Masterman, *Ludlow*, 80. Furnivall noted Louis's baptism by Kingsley at Eversley on Saturday, 8 Nov. 1851, when 'Maurice, 'Mansfield', & Ludlow' were present, Bodl. MS Eng. e. 2316, f. 53ʳ. Furnivall saw Louis often. He had recently married (on Sunday, 3 Aug., Furnivall mentions 'Louis & his bride' (f. 39ʳ)). See further Maurice, *The Word 'Eternal'*.

[63] *The Old Testament*, Sermon XVIII, pp. 328–45: 'Here we have the very puzzle to which I have been alluding . . . Deborah is an inspired woman . . . And Deborah, thus speaking praises a woman for persuading a man at peace with her father and the Kenites to take refuge with her, that she may privately and deliberately murder him' (p. 339).

[64] *Praeterita: The Autobiography of John Ruskin*, (text based on the three-volume edition of 1899), 451–3, at 451. See further Hilton, *John Ruskin*, ii. 70–1. Ruskin reverted to the matter in *Praeterita*, 463–4.

[65] *Praeterita*, 452. 'Maurice was by nature puzzle-headed, and though in a beautiful manner, *wrong*-headed; while his clear conscience and keen affections made him egotistic, and in his Bible-reading, as insolent as any infidel of them all' (pp. 541–2).

explains his anger: Jael's deed is lauded in the Song of Deborah (Judges 5), which Ruskin considered as sacred to him as the Magnificat, and it vexed him to be told that it was 'no more to be listened to with edification or faith than the Norman's sword-song at the battle of Hastings'.[66] It is clear that Ruskin's manner in the meeting had been excessively vehement,[67] and that he had caused considerable disturbance to those present, who had included Ludlow, Hughes, and Mansfield.[68] Furnivall is recalling the same incident (though there are differences of details) when he recorded a visit to Maurice's with Ruskin, and after a reading of the first chapter of Exodus, there was a discussion. Furnivall noted sadly, 'R(uskin)'s views and ours so different'. Afterwards he walked back with Ruskin.[69] Ruskin himself later acknowledged that, though 'I loved Mr. Maurice', he did not consider him a great man, 'but only as the centre of a group of students whom his amiable sentimentalism at once exalted and stimulated, while it relieved them from any painful necessities of exact scholarship in divinity'.[70] Maurice may have been personably lovable, but Ruskin had doubts about his political ideas, as well as his Bible teaching, and, at least in hindsight, distanced himself from the Working Men's College, considering that 'the only proper school for workmen is the work their fathers bred them to'.[71] Meanwhile, in the dealings between Ruskin and Maurice concerning the College, Furnivall was perhaps only too willing to act as an intermediary.

Furnivall first met the Ruskins in around April 1850 after Ruskin and his wife had returned to London from Venice.[72] Ruskin's father had leased a house for the couple in Mayfair, 31 Park Street, running

[66] *Praeterita*, 452: 'Maurice, with startled and flashing eyes, burst into partly scornful, partly alarmed, denunciation of Deborah the prophetess, as a mere blazing amazon.'
[67] Ruskin said himself that he sat silent during Maurice's instruction, before challenging him in the discussion afterwards: *Praeterita*, 452.
[68] Ludlow, *Autobiography*, 141–2. Ludlow and Hughes wrote a letter to Ruskin protesting against this published account, to which Ruskin did not reply.
[69] Tuesday, 29 Apr. 1851, Bodl. MS Eng. e. 2316, f. 25^v. The story of Jael and Sisera was not the set reading on this occasion (as Ruskin thought he remembered). The first chapter of Exodus concerns Pharaoh's orders to kill all newborn male children among the Israelites. Ruskin is clear that he only went once to Maurice's Bible class. It is likely that discussion of the one atrocity may have led to others in the Old Testament, especially since the Canaanite massacres had been such a matter of theological concern.
[70] *Fors Clavigera*, Letter 22 (19 Oct. 1872), 888–9. Maurice's character was 'always honest (at least in intention) and unfailingly earnest and kind . . . he was harmless and soothing in error, and vividly helpful when unerring' (p. 889). Ruskin was explaining his decision to decline to contribute to a memorial to Maurice in Westminster Abbey.
[71] *Praeterita*, 453. See further Norman, *The Victorian Christian Socialists*, 121–43.
[72] Note from Effie Ruskin, 13 Apr. 1850, FU 633.

down to Hyde Park, though Ruskin himself spent his working days at the family home on Denmark Hill (hence Furnivall tended to meet him on Sundays or in the evenings). The fashionable address was intended by his father to give Ruskin an opportunity to shine in polite society and make useful contacts.[73] He had become a much-prized literary lion after the success of the first two volumes of *Modern Painters* (1843-6) and *Seven Lamps of Architecture* (1849). The first volume of *Stones of Venice* had just been published in March 1851. Ruskin himself sent Furnivall a copy, which he rightly considered a signal honour.[74] However, Kingsley, an amateur draughtsman with a keen visual sense himself, who rather resented Ruskin's *éclat* achieved by publicizing foreign beauty spots in picturesque prose, would urge Hughes to

> Leave to squeamish Ruskin
> Popish Apennines,
> Dirty Stones of Venice
> And his Gas-Lamps Seven;
> We've the stones of Snowdon
> And the lamps of heaven.
> Where's the mighty credit
> In admiring Alps?
> Any goose sees 'glory'
> In their 'snowy scalps'.[75]

Kingsley was another who decided that Ruskin was deficient in manliness, and declared, after the annulment of Ruskin's marriage, that 'the first day he ever saw him', 'That man and I, unless utterly changed can never be friends'.[76] Yet there was an attempt at a rapprochement: Ruskin reported to D. G. Rossetti that 'I expect Kingsley, the *Alton Locke* man, to come out here [to Denmark Hill] on Monday, in order to be converted to Praeraphaelitism'.[77] However, there would be a further exchange of minor hostilities between the two after Kingsley rather unnecessarily used his guide to the natural history of the seashore, *Glaucus*, to make a passing swipe at Ruskin—Kingsley's observations of seaweeds led him to contradict 'that somewhat hasty assertion of Mr. Ruskin, that nature makes no ribbons, unless with a midrib, and

[73] See letter of 1 Aug. 1848 from Ruskin's father, describing his ambitions for his son, printed in W. James (ed.), *The Order of Release*, 150-2.
[74] 'Chambers, found Ruskin's Stones of Venice, vol. 1 there, which he had sent me on Saturday, read it'. Monday, 10 Mar., Bodl. MS Eng. e. 2316, f. 18ᵛ.
[75] Kingsley, *Letters and Memories*, 184. Letter to Hughes, 1856.
[76] Chitty, *Beast and Monk*, 159.
[77] Letter, ?Mar. 1855, *Works of John* Ruskin, ed. Cook and Wedderburn, 38, xxxvi. 190.

I know not what other limitations, which seem to me to exist only in Mr Ruskin's fertile, but fastidious fancy'.[78] Ruskin vented his fury in a letter to Furnivall—probably in the hope that his response would get back to Kingsley, without the need to dignify a 'side-snarl' with a printed response (Furnivall's indiscretion was fairly dependable):

> I don't know when I have been more provoked than by that fatuous side-snarl of Kingsley's at me, in the Glaucus—Whatever mischief does he mean by shortening my hands, when I am playing into his—and for no purpose too—and in a thing he knows *nothing* about—He ought to have a good sound thrashing with certain seaweeds that I know of—by no means like ribands—but very like cats' o nine tails.[79]

A more serious matter of disagreement with the Christian socialists was Ruskin's published howl of protest against the 'Papal aggression', the name given by anti-Catholic elements to the establishment, on 29 September 1850, of the Catholic Church's hierarchy in England, in which Nicholas Wiseman, acting as an informal diplomatic envoy to Pope Pius IX, had played a leading part, and as a result of which he became Cardinal Archbishop of the newly created see of Westminster.[80] Again Furnivall was Ruskin's confidant, and intermediary between him and Maurice, reporting that he 'called at Ruskin's, Mrs R. with a bad cold—had a fierce argument with R. about Papal Aggression, he wants to *transport* Wiseman &c.'.[81] Ruskin followed this preliminary expression of his feelings with a pamphlet, *Notes on the Construction of Sheepfolds*, issued just three days after *Stones of Venice*, to which it was planned as an appendix—Ruskin's assertion that, in writing it, he had 'no purpose of being drawn, at present, into religious controversy', indicated his taste for a serene life, above such quarrels, but he must have realized that this plea was unlikely to be heeded, and it was not.[82] Ruskin's suggestion that the existing Church of England might be merged with the other Protestant denominations, so that 'priests' should be replaced by 'ministers', as a means of opposing 'the most pestilent of the Romanist theories',[83] seemed calculated to offend most parties: Catholics, Puseyites, Anglicans, and non-conformists.

[78] *Glaucus, or, The Wonders of the Shore*, 57.
[79] FU 776. Letter of 3 June [1855], from Tunbridge Wells. See *OED*, 'shorten', v.1. e for Ruskin's archaic biblical usage, 'to limit the power of'.
[80] See further Chadwick, *Victorian Church*, i. 281–309. The protests led to the passing of the Ecclesiastical Titles Act, 1851, repealed in 1871.
[81] Sunday, 2 Mar., 1851, Bodl. MS Eng. e. 2316, f. 17ʳ
[82] *Notes on the Construction of Sheepfolds*, Preface, p. iii.   [83] Ibid. 38.

Furnivall read it,[84] and ten days later, 'Mr Maurice sent me a long letter on Ruskin's Notes on Sheep-folds, to chambers . . . copied out M's letter'.[85] Maurice was using Furnivall as a postbox: Ruskin, of course, responded, and continued to reissue the pamphlet as late as 1875.[86] Wiseman, as will be seen, was also a member of the Philological Society, of which Furnivall was Secretary. It would not be the only occasion on which Furnivall's reluctance to shun some of his acquaintances would annoy others, and it is ironic that the pamphlet reveals Ruskin's own philological sensitivity to semantic change, as well as his deep familiarity, inculcated in him from childhood, with the Bible. Ruskin, with his wife, apparently attempted to open Furnivall's eyes to what they considered Wiseman's enormities by taking him, after dinner, 'to 'the' Romanists' St George's Southwark, but Cardl. Wiseman did not preach'.[87] St George's was a new church, designed by A. W. N. Pugin, which had been opened by Wiseman in 1848, and became officially the Cathedral Church of the new diocese of Southwark in 1852. Since *Sheepfolds* was in part a riposte to Pugin, Ruskin, though frustrated in his intention to exhibit the Cardinal to his friend, probably used the occasion to instruct Furnivall in his disapproval of Pugin's architecture.

Although enthusiastically participating in paper wars, Ruskin did much to frustrate his father's plans in 1850-1 for his social advancement in London high society. He disliked grand parties, where he could be sulky—his own word to describe himself—and boorish. Ruskin confided to Furnivall: 'People don't know how shy I am, from not having ever gone into Society until I was seventeen. I forget who it is who says that the mixture of hesitation and forced impudence which shy people fall into is the worst of all possible manners. So I find it.'[88] However, his wife, Effie, adored such occasions, and she soon became a hit with people of rank and fashion—it was one of the points of incompatibility between them. She often attended social gatherings without him

---

[84] On Saturday, 15 Mar., Bodl. MS Eng. e. 2316, f. 19ʳ.

[85] Tuesday, 25 Mar., 1851, f. 20ᵛ.

[86] Ruskin's reply was later published as *Two Letters Concerning 'Notes on the Construction of Sheepfolds'*. On the response, see Hilton, *John Ruskin*, i. 149-51.

[87] Sunday, 27 Apr., 1851, Bodl. MS Eng. e. 2316, f. 25ʳ.

[88] Letter of 5 Dec. 1852. Ruskin, *Works*, xxxvi. 144. Ruskin had been inadvertently rude to Bellenden Ker at a meeting of the Arundel Society, and he apologized to Furnivall. Quoted by Hilton, *John Ruskin*, i. 207 (see further i. 129-30). Ruskin, *Works*, xxxvi. 143. See also Effie Ruskin's letters from this period, quoted in James (ed.), *The Order of Release*, 158-70.

at this time, though she was careful not to entertain male visitors if her husband was not present. Even so, Furnivall's fondness for gossip caused her considerable embarrassment and annoyance when he told tales to her brother, George Gray, about her seeing too much of her friend Clare Ford. George was jealous of Effie's reputation and quick to suspect the worst, and he passed on the story to their mother, whom Effie had to reassure: 'although you think me unsuspicious I am quite quick enough to see, observe or hear if any one thought lightly of my conduct'. Ruskin was 'very angry with Mr. Furnivall for putting such ideas into George's head'.

George Gray suspected that, by leaving Effie so much to herself, the Ruskins were hoping that she would compromise her reputation, and so give them an excuse for separation: Furnivall was not yet aware of the secret unhappiness of the Ruskins' marriage, though he clearly took an interest in their unusual domestic arrangements.[89] The Ruskins moved in rather grander London circles than did Furnivall, and Ruskin's time at Christ Church also brought visitors from Oxford, where Furnivall had no other foothold, people like the Dean of Christ Church, Dr Henry Liddell, and his young wife, whom Furnivall considered 'pretty'.[90] The Dean was visiting the Hensleigh Wedgwoods, where Effie also visited, and where the Hughes's were also to be found, and whom she invited to her own entertainments.[91] Furnivall did, however, through his father, know Sir James Alderson, of the Royal College of Physicians, and he also met Effie at one of Lady Alderson's parties at their house in Berkeley Square.[92] He was already on easy visiting terms with the Ruskins by the time his diary begins in January 1851, and he continued to see them frequently during January through the spring and summer until their departure for Geneva and Venice on 28 July.[93]

Furnivall tells us that he met Effie Ruskin at a party—a *conversazione*, in the fashionable language of the mid-nineteenth century—and that he leaped at the chance to wangle an introduction to her husband. He told

---

[89] Lutyens (ed.), *Young Mrs. Ruskin in Venice. Unpublished Letters*, 175. James (ed.), *Order of Release*, 164.   [90] Friday, 14 Mar., Bodl. MS Eng. e. 2316, f. 19^r.

[91] As on Wednesday, 8 Jan., when she was a guest at Mrs Wedgwood's children's party, Bodl. MS Eng. e. 2316, f. 9^v.

[92] Wednesday, 15 Jan., Bodl. MS Eng. e. 2316, f. 10^v. Robert Harrison, revised Michael Beven, 'Alderson, Sir James (1794–1882)', *ODNB*.

[93] Sunday, 5 Jan. was a busy social day, with serous interludes: 'To Johnson . . . with him to Christchurch, Broadway Westminster. Mr Page preached; walked to the Exhibition . . . J(ohnson) to the river; I to Ruskin's, chatted, walked in the Park with them; . . . Johnson . . . read, chatted . . . to Mrs Wedgwood's, tea & chat . . . read St Augustine &c. till 12.20'. Bodl. MS Eng. e. 2316, f. 9^r.

FRIENDSHIP WITH JOHN RUSKIN

this anecdote some forty years later, though he was by then vague about the dates. Munro says she first met him on 31 May 1850:[94]

> It must have been in 1848, 9, or 1850 that I was one Saturday evening, probably in May, at an 'At Home'—Conversazione then, I suppose—in Chester Terrace, Regent's Park, at the house of a friend whom I first met at the Philological Society, when his sweet-natured clever wife came up to her cousin, with whom I was chatting about the London poor, and said 'John, I want you to come and talk to Mrs Ruskin'. 'Not I', said Dobbin-like John, 'I'm much too shy for such a smart body'. As he spoke, I turned and followed his look at a handsome tall young woman with rosy cheeks and wavy black hair, in a charming pink waterd silk dress, prettily ruched from shoulder to foot (I can see her now). Mrs H. W. said to me, 'Will you come, Mr. Furnivall?' 'I should think I would,' answered I, 'only give me the chance'. I talkt eagerly and enthusiastically about Ruskin to his wife, and she askt me to come and see him in Park Street, at the back of Park Lane, and half past three next day. I put her into her brougham; and on Sunday afternoon, be sure, I was in Park Street to the minute.[95]

Effie's full-length portrait, painted in the following year by Thomas Richmond, bears out this description, though she herself thought it 'much prettier than me. I look like a graceful doll.'[96] Her attractiveness was one lure, her value as a passport to Ruskin's acquaintance another, and it is not clear from Furnivall's account which was uppermost in his mind—Effie was unfailingly polite, as well as pretty, and she provided the sought-after introduction to Ruskin, but she had grounds to be piqued by Furnivall's single-minded conversation about her husband and the blatant hope of an introduction. It is not surprising that she thought Furnivall a bit of an ass, though 'amiable'.[97] Ruskin's parents, when he got to meet them, also considered him rather lightweight, if, again, amiable, radical, and foolish.[98] Furnivall's hostess on this occasion, 'Mrs. H.W.', was Mrs Hensleigh Wedgwood—and she had first intended to introduce Effie to her gauche cousin, rather than Furnivall. By the time he imparted this prize reminiscence, he was talking in old age to a collector of literary anecdotes. Furnivall knew the value of such

[94] 'Biography', p. xxiii.
[95] Nicholl and Wise (eds.), *Literary Anecdotes*, ii. 4. Quoted by Benzie, *Dr F. J. Furnivall*, 49.
[96] James (ed.), *Order of Release*, 167. Reproduced, for example, in the *ODNB* entry, Suzanne Fagence Cooper, 'Gray . . . Euphemia . . . Lady Millais (1828–1897)'.
[97] Hilton, *John Ruskin*, i. 151. Letter to her close Venice friend E. C. R. Rawdon Brown, 9 May 1854. Rawdon Brown had himself met Furnivall: Furnivall's diary, Tuesday, 15 July 1851, Bodl. MS Eng. e. 2316, f. 36ᵛ. Events certainly coloured Effie's unflattering description, written when she was seeking an annulment of her marriage.
[98] Hilton, *John Ruskin*, ii. 36.

anecdotes—none better—and his account is coloured by the anecdotists' expectations that Mrs Ruskin would be the prelude to the glory of the first sight of Ruskin himself, delayed only by the necessary politesse of 'a short chat with the wife'. Furnivall gave full measure, and again claimed to remember the details with photographic clarity, and, as by then the author of many books about 'meals and manners', he was alive to the fascination (which he shared) with what people were wearing forty years before. Effie's pink dress was carefully described, and his audience had to be told that Ruskin's trademark blue 'stock' was a 'neckerchief wrapt round a stiffener'. That it was 'Oxford blue' identified both its colour and Ruskin's university.[99]

On Sunday afternoon, be sure, I was in Park Street to the minute. After a short chat with the wife. I saw the door open, and John Ruskin walkt softly in. I sprang up to take the outstretcht hand, and then and there began a friendship which was for many years the chief joy of my life. Ruskin was a tall slight fellow, whose piercing frank blue eye lookt through you and drew you to him. A fair man, with rough light hair and reddish whiskers, in a dark blue frock coat with velvet collar, bright Oxford blue stock, black trousers and patent slippers—how vivid he is to me still! The only blemish in his face was the lower lip, which protruded somewhat: he had been bitten there by a dog in his early youth. But you ceast to notice this as soon as he began to talk. I never met any man whose charm of manner at all approach Ruskin's. Partly feminine it was, no doubt; but the delicacy, the sympathy, the gentleness and affectionateness of his way, the fresh and penetrating things he said, the boyish fun, the earnestness, the interest he showd in all deep matters, combined to make a whole which I have never seen equalld.[100]

Again, Furnivall knew what his listeners expected from him, and no doubt his memory has touched up the vividness of the recall: it is an idealized and sentimental portrait of a 'fair' young man, lower lip notwithstanding. As their acquaintance ripened, Ruskin would himself have explained this blemish, about which he was self-conscious.[101] Furnivall's description may be compared with that of William Richmond, son of George Richmond, for whom Ruskin sat for his portrait ten years earlier, 'a gaunt, delicate-looking young man, with a profusion of reddish hair, shaggy eyebrows like to a Scotch terrier, under them the gleaming eyes which bore within them a strange light, the like of which I

---

[99] *OED*, 'Oxford blue', n. and adj. sense 2 (a), recorded from 1842. (Ruskin attended Christ Church 1837–40 and returned to take his degree in the spring of 1842.)
[100] Benzie, *Dr F. J. Furnivall*, 49. Also 'Notes on the Construction of Sheepfolds', 8, reprinted in Nicholl and Wise (eds.), *Literary Anecdotes*, ii. 4–5.
[101] See *Praeterita*, 58–9.

have never seen except in his'.[102] It was suggested, probably by Furnivall, who certainly put the idea to Ruskin, that a portrait of Ruskin's head should be carved in marble by Alexander Munro, the Pre-Raphaelite sculptor, who taught modelling at the College.[103] Furnivall doubtless was enthused with the idea of preserving a monument of the great man whom he had introduced to the College—and it is significant that he did not propose Maurice as a subject. Ruskin was initially attracted by the idea, but highly sensitive at all times about images of himself, talked himself out of it, not least because at this time, thanks to the scandal surrounding his marriage, his popularity did not stand high with the public:

I shall be delighted to see Munro with French, and he can then tell me what he thinks can be done with this ugly head of mine, which I often look at very carefully . . . If I could paint, I could make something of the front face, but I cannot conceive how Munro could make anything fit to be seen without gross fallacy, out of the side . . . When people know me better, I have no objection to their knowing as much about my nose and cheeks as may in anywise interest them, but I should like neither to be flattered, nor to leave what appear to me to be the facts in my face subjected, at all events for a year or two yet, to public animadversion.[104]

More humbly, Ruskin's photograph was taken in 1856 by William Jeffrey, a student in Ruskin's class at the Working Men's College, later teacher. Ruskin detested 'that frightful photograph with the hanging lip': it revealed aspects of him, especially the savagery, that he was loth to have visible to the wider world. Moreover, 'the total want of wit and imagination lowers the forehead', and he reflected, with self-pity, that the strangeness of his life had left its marks on his physiognomy: 'it is no wonder the photograph tells such a story'.[105] Furnivall's rather

[102] Quoted by Hilton, *John Ruskin*, i. 72.
[103] Katharine Macdonald, 'Munro, Alexander (1825–71)', *ODNB*. Munro was a friend of D. G. Rossetti, and did portraits both of him and Millais. He had shown work at the Great Exhibition of 1851. Munro and Thomas Woolner shared the teaching. After a time, because 'it made so many of the Drawing Class pupils lazy at their drawing', Ruskin told his students 'they must either draw or model—they had shown him they had not time for both'; Furnivall, 'History', *Working Men's College Magazine*, 2. 189.
[104] Letter to Furnivall, from Dover, 17 July 1855, Ruskin, *Works*, xxxvi. 218: 'Whatever of good or strength there is in me comes visibly, as far as I know myself, only sometimes into the grey of my eyes, which Millais ought to have got, but didn't.' Ruskin's concern with monitoring portraits of himself is fully shown by James S. Dearden, *John Ruskin, a Life in Pictures* (Sheffield, 1999).
[105] Hilton, *John Ruskin*, ii. 16–17, quotation from letter to Pauline, Lady Trevelyan. I am grateful to Witold Szczyglowski, Librarian of the Working Men's College, for information

soppy word picture leaves out Ruskin's dyspepsia and ferocity which he would soon experience—though, like William Richmond, but unlike, in Ruskin's opinion, Millais, he caught the arresting quality of Ruskin's gaze. 'Boyish fun' (which cannot have been apparent to all of Ruskin's acquaintance in the early 1850s) of course appealed to Furnivall, and the penetrating quality of Ruskin's use of words and his intellectual range were never in doubt. By 1895–6 when the anecdote was published, Ruskin's reputation had seriously declined; Furnivall's reminiscence in old age of him at the height of his power had the far-off quality of a golden time—as Furnivall doubtless intended it should.[106]

There and then, according to Furnivall, began the friendship which was for many years the chief joy of his life According to Munro, this friendship was 'beautiful in its tenderness'.[107] It was certainly affectionate, though it also had its jars. It brought some notable highlights in 1851, chief among them the 'most happy morning' when, after chatting to Effie, she and John Ruskin, with Furnivall, 'took up Mrs Wedgwood & drove to Denmark Hill; Ruskin showed us his Turners, about 20 of them, finer than the Winduses, lunch; looked at the pictures again; Mrs Ruskin drove Mrs Wedgwood & me back to town; a most happy morning'.[108] Ruskin clearly enjoyed Furnivall's enthusiasm, and this was the first of several visits when Furnivall took friends, including ladies, to see Ruskin's collection of Turners. Ruskin set out the rules: 'I shall be delighted to see you and your lady friends, and their impedimenta in the shape of husbands, either on Wednesday, Friday, or Saturday, between two and five o'clock.'[109] 'The semi-private 'chat' with Effie Ruskin at the Park Street house while Ruskin was at Denmark Hill was also part of this joy, as well as the glittering social occasions when the association with the Ruskins brought Furnivall into the company of other charming, socially confident, pretty women whom he could

about Jeffrey (1826–77). The photograph is reproduced in Colloms, *Victorian Visionaries*, 163.

[106] See e.g. Sir Charles Oman's description of Ruskin's weirdness at his last Oxford lecture when he was 'far gone in eccentricity'; *Memories of Victorian Oxford*, 210–11.

[107] Munro, 'Biography', p. xxii.

[108] Tuesday, 18 Feb. 1851, Bodl. MS Eng. e. 2316, f. 15^v. Furnivall also included the incident among the highlights of the year in his 'Occasional Memoranda' at the end of the diary, f. 64^r. Another was the gift of *Stones of Venice*, vol. i. B. Godfrey Windus was a rival connoisseur of Turner, who possessed some fifty of his paintings, and from whom Ruskin had learned much. Hilton, *John Ruskin*, i. 55–6. For a description of how Ruskin conducted his showings of his Turners on these occasions, see Derek Hudson, *Munby: Man of Two Worlds*, 31–2.

[109] Letter of 12 May, 1853; *Ruskin, Works*, xxxvi. 147.

admire.[110] As one who prized 'manliness', he, too, had to concede that Ruskin's great charm was 'partly feminine'—he represented qualities of delicacy and sympathy, which Furnivall prized in women. But the friendship also brought him into contact with intellectual leaders— Furnivall was particularly anxious to meet Thomas Carlyle, whose writings he had read, and whom he had met once at one of Effie's parties. A sustained conversation was not to be expected in a crush, and Furnivall seems to have done his best to contrive an invitation through the Ruskins. Carlyle, on whom Ruskin modelled himself, was elusive, and was most likely to be found visiting Ruskin's family home on Denmark Hill, where Furnivall could hardly just drop in: John Ruskin sen. formally invited him to dinner, but warned him: 'There is some small chance of Mr Thos. Carlyle the celebrated writer being here on Sunday next 23rd Ins. to Denmark. It is no engagement ... Whether he comes or not it would give my Son and me pleasure to see you at Dinner.'[111] A few years later, Furnivall missed his chance to meet Elizabeth Barrett Browning, to whom he also hoped Ruskin would introduce him when she came to tea. Ruskin forgot, and Furnivall most uncharacteristically was held back by 'delicacy', for which Ruskin chided him: 'I fully appreciated your delicacy in not speaking again of Mrs Browning; and yet, as it happened, both you and I suffered for your politeness.'[112]

Furnivall's tastes, then, were decisively influenced by association with this young man, just six years older than himself, who, in the first volume of *Modern Painters* had, before he had even completed his degree at Oxford, laid down laws of aesthetic taste with such an

---

[110] *Notes on the Construction of Sheepfolds*, 10–11: this was remembered some forty or more years.

[111] J. J. Ruskin, letter of 19 Dec. 1860, *FU 796. Three days after a red-letter day, when Funivall visited the Ruskins and 'the Carlyles, Milmans, Liddells, Capn. Sterling, Boxall, F. Pollock, Sir C. Eastlake &c there' (Friday, 21 Mar. 1851, Bodl. MS Eng. 2315, f. 20ʳ), Furnivall read Carlyle's *Chartism* (Monday, 24 Mar.), along with Byron's *Don Juan*. He also read Carlyle's newly published *Life of Sterling* (1851), and discussed him (along with Sterling) with Harriet Martineau (Monday, 18 Aug., f. 41ᵛ); a note of Carlyle's address at '5 Chene House, Chelsea' (Carlyle lived in Cheyne Row), Bodl. MS Eng. e. 2315, Friday, 21 Jan. 1848 (f. 11ʳ) probably indicates a wish to write to him, not a meeting. Furnivall met Carlyle on a number of occasions in 1848, e.g. Wednesday, 8 Nov. (Bodl. MS Eng. e. 2315, f. 53ʳ (name inserted suprascript) at one of the Wedgwood's *conversaziones* on Wednesday, 8 Nov., f. 52ᵛ); Sunday, 26 Oct., Monday, 18 Aug., Friday, 21 Jan., ff. 20ᵛ, 51ʳ(*passim*). He read Carlyle's *Life of Sterling* over two nights, Sunday, 26–Monday, 27 Oct. (f. 51ʳ⁻ᵛ).

[112] 'In general, with me, do not be delicate. Ask for what you want, and if I have not answered speak to me about it again, for you may be sure I have forgotten it. It is never a form of refusal with me. If I don't want to do the thing, I shall say so at once.' Letter to Furnivall, 25 July, 1855, *Ruskin, Works*, xxxvi. 219.

irresistible mix of rhetorical logic, appeals from his own wide reading, and extended visits to France, Italy, and Switzerland, unyielding dogmatism, and sheer eloquence, which, like his speech, persuaded one to overlook any blemishes. After getting to know Ruskin, Furnivall naturally sought out *Modern Painters* '&c'.[113] Ruskin had earned his right to lay down the law by being more widely travelled, more widely read, and, simply, more brilliant than Furnivall, who slipped easily into the role of disciple as well as admirer. Ruskin's wife, who though reserved, and a little jaded by the London season, and her private anxieties, was by no means so grand as not to appreciate the splendour and the privileges she was enjoying: not only the 'fashionables', but literary and artistic men, including Carlyle, Thackeray, and G. F. Watts, in afternoon parties at Denmark Hill.[114] It has been said that Furnivall worshipped Ruskin 'abjectly', which seems to go too far—as Ludlow detected, Furnivall was not deficient in vanity himself.[115] And some of the worship was for Effie, who radiated reflected glory, but was also a very attractive woman. Furnivall called round to enquire after she had been presented at Court and found her understandably tired. Ruskin, although despising the occasion, was sufficiently inconsistent to be pleased that Prince Albert put 'markedness' into his bow to him.[116] And, being allowed to stay on familiarly until midnight to have tea and chat after the rest of the Ruskins' visitors, who had included the Carlyles and Sir Charles Eastlake, artist and first Director of the National Gallery, had left was a marked compliment.[117] On another occasion he called on Effie in the afternoon, chatted until Ruskin arrived at 6, when there was a soirée and they had some music. Ruskin read some of Shakespeare's *Richard II*, and Furnivall walked home with Maurice.[118] Effie was being careful about her reputation, and giving Furnivall no encouragement, but he seems to have been trying to attach himself to her as a harmless kind of *cavalier servente*. Her notes to him, which he carefully preserved, along with her husband's letters, are appropriately cool formal acknowledgements.[119] At her

[113] Friday, 17 Jan. 1851, Bodl. MS Eng. e. 2316, f. 11ʳ.
[114] James (ed.), *Order of Release*, 159–65.
[115] Hilton, *John Ruskin*, i. 151.
[116] Thursday, 3 Apr., 1851, Bodl. MS Eng. e. 2316, f. 22ʳ. For Effie's own accounts of her attendances at Court ('We stayed in this broiling but amusing condition for two hours'), see *Order of Release*, 159–60.
[117] Friday, 21 Mar. 1851, Bodl. MS Eng. e. 2316, f. 20ʳ.
[118] Thursday, 13 Feb. 1851, Bodl. MS Eng. e. 2316, f. 15ʳ.
[119] FU 633-56, from 13 Apr., 1850 to 23 Mar. [1854].

parties Furnivall met the grand people who, with her family, would later be her staunch supporters when Effie left Ruskin on 25 April 1854 and petitioned for an annulment of her marriage on grounds of non-consummation: Lady Eastlake and her husband, Lady Davy, and Lord Glenelg.[120]

One of the ways in which John Ruskin, as much as the Christian Socialists, decisively influenced Furnivall was in leading him to read books he might not otherwise have read. The two inevitably overlapped to some extent—Furnivall's reading of Plato's *Republic*, for instance, might be attributable to either.[121] But Ruskin's tastes and the Christian Socialists, as said, did not wholly coincide. Other reading was directly attributable to Furnivall's friendship with Ruskin. And it was not just one-way traffic: Furnivall lent books to Ruskin, too—though Ruskin did not always approve: 'I never was thoroughly ashamed of you and your radicalism till you sent me that ineffably villainous thing of Victor Hugo's.'[122] Ruskin's own writings now included his influential pamphlet *Pre-Raphaelitism*, published in August 1851, before that year's summer exhibition at the Royal Academy ended.[123] The excuse for it was that the show included paintings by Millais and Holman Hunt. In actuality, the title is misleading (the lion's share of Ruskin's critique was given to Turner). Furnivall, under Ruskin's tuition, now learned to appreciate Turner (and argue about his colouring). Again Ruskin did him the honour of sending him a copy: he 'read it & liked it much, specially the Turner part', before passing it on to Mrs Wedgwood.[124] And by calling the public's attention to the Pre-Raphaelites, Furnivall would also be led to seek them out, along with other contemporaries, like William Mulready (1786–1863), the Irish genre painter, whom Ruskin considered in *Pre-Raphaelitism* to be equivalent in technique to the Pre-Raphaelites, though let down by inferior choice of subjects. Meanwhile Furnivall now bought Vasari's *Lives of the Painters*.[125] And he read Samuel Rogers's poem *Italy*, which, in the third, illustrated, edition (1830) had itself introduced the young Ruskin to Turner's steel engravings, and in turn, with all that followed, led him with his

[120] See *Order of Release*, 218–31.
[121] Saturday, 10 May, Bodl. MS Eng. e. 2316, f. 27^r. See Hilton, *John Ruskin*, ii. 54.
[122] Letter to Furnivall, 22 May 1855, *Ruskin, Works*, xxxvi. 212, 'Did you ever read *The Hunchback of Notre Dame*? I believe it to be simply the most disgusting book ever written by man ... for pure, dull, virtueless, stupid, deadly poison, read Victor Hugo.'
[123] Hilton, *John Ruskin*, i. 156–7.
[124] Monday, 11, Tuesday, 12 Aug. 1851, Bodl. MS Eng. e. 2316, f. 40^v.
[125] Saturday, 9 Aug. 1851, Bodl. MS Eng. e. 2316, f. 40^r.

family to become tourists of the picturesque and seek out the places depicted.[126]

Thus, as well as introducing him to books, Ruskin also taught Furnivall to look at pictures—though Furnivall did not entirely learn the lessons (but did learn to appreciate Turner, probably a *sine qua non* for their friendship). As well as the Turner paintings in his collection, Ruskin also showed Furnivall his own drawings, extraordinarily good for an amateur, as Furnivall was well able to appreciate, since he had himself, as a young man, made his own drawings, which he had tied up and put away, very much in the spirit of putting away childish things.[127] And, on a visit to Effie, he 'chatted to her & looked over Ruskin's collection of engravings after Turner till 3,20; had some breakfast & lunch'.[128] (Furnivall may have outstayed his welcome on this occasion.) Ruskin also lent him a drawing of a Madonna and Child.[129] And under Ruskin's influence, as well as Kingsley's, Furnivall spent time during the Long Vacation visiting galleries. Thus on one whirlwind day he went to the Sheepshanks' Gallery in South Kensington to see the Turners '& looked at his collection of modern paintings. 5 large oil Turners, 3 fine Venice 1840, St Michael's Mount, Fishing at Hastings; Cowes & Yarmouth not as good; 15 Mulready's good; Redgrave's 'Ophelia'. Cope's 'Almsgiving', Collins's stray kittens . . . 2 of George Smith, humorous & good'. Then he went 'to the Derby Gallery to see 'Lazarus' the Augdiers, & Correggio's Magdalene (which Kingsley thinks so great, I don't)', and after that to the Dudley Gallery, where he saw 'a most beautiful Ghirlandaio, Virgin praying to child & 2 spirited Tiepolo's'.[130] Furnivall's honestly expressed, but unsophisticated, tastes are very much what one would

---

[126] Saturday, 12 Apr. 1851, Bodl. MS Eng. e. 2316, f. 23ʳ; also, Tuesday, 15 Apr., 'read Rogers's Italy &c till near 3' (f. 23ᵛ). See *Praeterita*, 69.

[127] Sunday, 18 May, Bodl. MS Eng. e. 2316, f. 28ʳ: 'sorted my drawings &c. & tied them up'; Saturday, 15 Oct. 1842, Bodl. MS Eng. d. 2104, f. 54ᵛ, and 'looked over all my old drawings', before beginning his life as a lawyer, Wednesday, 2 July 1843 (f. 110ʳ).

[128] Wednesday, 2 July 1851, Bodl. MS Eng. e. 2316, f. 34ᵛ.

[129] Saturday, 2 Aug., f. 39ʳ: 'Ted to Lords, I to chambers . . . to Mr Baldwin's, the Dudley Gallery for a last look, then at 5 to Ruskins, both out, left them 2 Trenches and brought away a drawing of a Madonna & child . . . wh(ich) Mr R. lends me; hung pictures.'

[130] Wednesday, 9 July 1851, Bodl. MS Eng. e. 2316, f. 35ᵛ. John Sheepshanks (1787–1863) was a cloth manufacturer, whose collection forms the earliest part of what is now the Victoria and Albert Museum, where are Richard Redgrave, 'Ophelia Weaving her Garlands' (1842), Charles West Cope, 'Almsgiving' (1839), and William Collins, 'The Stray Kitten' (1835). There are three paintings by George Smith in the Victoria and Albert Museum: 'Spring Flowers' (1851), 'Temptation: A Fruit Stall' (1850), and 'Another Bite' (*c*.1850). Furnivall is likely to have seen the last two, which could both be described as 'humorous'. The 'Magdalen', probably by Correggio, is likely to be National Gallery no. 2512; the Ghirlandaio 'Virgin' is probably 'Virgin and Child with St John', now Natio-

expect from his upbringing: he enjoyed lively, naturalistic scenes of family life, and did not appreciate Correggio's representation of the penitent Magdalene, as near enough topless as to make no difference, and looking up from her book to stare confrontationally at the viewer. The Virgin and Child can also be seen as a fine-art version of the 'Family Devotion', which Furnivall had on his wall in Trinity Hall, as also might be the four 'Holy Families' by Raphael, which Furnivall saw in the Bridgewater collection, especially 'one of the two boys standing & the mother over, with a landscape, so beautiful'.[131] The sentiment is not dissimilar to Furnivall, at home in Egham, assisting his mother by getting the twins Will and Hen bathed and ready for bed.

Furnivall's friendship with Ruskin would be enduring, though it was to be expected that there would be occasional frictions between such irascible egos: Furnivall annoyed Ruskin, for example, by an ill-advised printed comment on Turner, which elicited a three-point response and a chilly 'Ever faithfully yours', instead of their usual 'ever affectionately yours'.[132] Ruskin confided in him, not only about his marriage to Effie, but also his later tragic devotion to Rose La Touche, and his misfortunes, including his periodic insanity. Ruskin signed up for the EETS—though he was in some doubts about whether he was a member of Furnivall's Chaucer Society or not.[133] He even began editing work on the Middle English translation of the *Romance of the Rose* for the Chaucer Society: 'five years ago I had nearly ready for press an edition of the Dream (not as, alas, a fine example of Chaucer, but as one about which I had much to say), with long notes, and breaking down of words', but was deterred from publication by the controversy raging over Chaucer's authorship: 'Had this come out, I should never have got over it

nal Gallery, no. 2502, formerly in the Dudley collection. Several of Tiepolo's paintings in the National Gallery could be described as 'spirited'.

[131] Monday, 11 Aug. 1851, Bodl. MS Eng. e. 2316, f. 40ᵛ. The Bridgewater collection is now assimilated into the National Gallery.

[132] FU 787, Letter to Furnivall, 22 Dec. 1873, from Herne Hill: '1 Turner never "wondered" at anything. 2 ⟨Had⟩ So far from finding me put meanings into his/pictures which he had not—he tried for a quarter of an hour, on two several occasions, to make me quell a meaning which he *had*;—and was greatly vexed and angry because I could not. 3 Learn to understand any one of his mythological pictures yourself, by thinking a little of the pain of life as well as of its crickets and daisies before you speak of him again in the same page with any other painter.'

[133] 'Am I a member of the Chaucer Society or not? If not, it was only because I never supposed such a society could need furtherance of mine—but, if I am not, please now set me there for on your present showing I am too much humiliated in absence from its ranks.' FU 784 [Nov. 1873], written from Corpus Christi College, Oxford. In his letter of 15 Dec., Ruskin expressed his satisfaction with Corpus, 'my adopted college'; see following note.

in literary disreputation. The Oxford business stopped it, fortunately as I find.'[134] Ruskin himself had no doubts as to its genuineness: 'I have never doubted the translation of the Rom(an) de la R(ose)—because it is done with an ease and yet fidelity unexampled to my knowledge in translation.'[135] He resented the common perception that he was a writer on art and architecture: his friendships and interests were wide.[136] He had returned to Oxford to lecture in Michaelmas Term 1873, and 1874 would be riven by emotional torments arising from his passion for Rose, the child who had now grown up, though chronically ill, to whom he had proposed marriage, and who would die early in the following year. Ruskin's fascination with the *Romance of the Rose*—a prolonged courtship with many setbacks and much anguish of an idealized object of devotion—was autobiographical, though even at his bleakest times he said he felt able to keep his work separate: 'The causes of despondency in work are and have always been entirely separated by me from those of my domestic life. I have been ten years waiting for a girl whom her people would not let come to me—and who is now (people say) mad.— That is not a state of things in which one is likely to take the brightest view of the world.'[137] Meanwhile, 'I congratulate you very earnestly on the fine literary work you have done for England'.[138]

It is likely that Furnivall tried to interest Ruskin in the Philological Society, but that Ruskin resisted, though he knew its leading men, and he generously acknowledged his debt:

[134] Letter to Furnivall, 15 Dec. 1873, FU 786, sent from Herne Hill. There is a transcript of this letter in Bodl. MS Eng. Lett. c. 39, where, for 'stopped' read 'snibbed'. This is the *lectio difficilior*, but does not reflect the letter Furnivall received, though he would have been quite capable of understanding it. 'Snybbe' is a Middle English borrowing which Ruskin either found from his reading of Chaucer, or as a Scottish dialect word: see *OED*, 'snib', v1, to rebuke, to check; compare the General Prologue to the *Canterbury Tales*, l. 523 (*The Riverside Chaucer*, 3rd edn., gen. ed. Larry D. Benson (Boston, MA, 1987), 31.

[135] FU 784, letter to Furnivall [Nov. 1873], sent from Corpus Christi College, Oxford. Ruskin turned to the original French text, 'of which I chanced on an entirely first rate contemporary French MS, and that carried me off Chaucer to Jean de Meung, and French work generally, which has its value, though of another sort, meaning always to come back to Chaucer with ⟨thorough⟩ 'the best' knowledge of the elements of him I could get.—I was always vexed at the pre-eminent position given to the Canterbury—(as to Dante's Hell)—and meant to work mainly on the minor poems'; letter to Furnivall, 15 Dec. 1873, FU 786. The Chaucer Society was having any book club's perennial difficulties with subscribers, and Ruskin advised 'Let me beg you as chief editor to issue punitive orders that the books shall never be sent when subs are in arrears', FU 786.

[136] See Hilton's account of Ruskin's life at this time (1873–4), as reflected in his large collection of books, *John Ruskin*, ii. 252–5.

[137] FU 790, letter to Furnivall, 13 Jan. 1874.

[138] FU 784, letter to Furnivall [Nov. 1873]. Dated from Corpus Christi College, Oxford.

You know how you used to find fault with me for speaking ill of philology, and how you in alliance with the Dean of Westminster first showed me the true vital interest of language. While I have not one whit slacked in my old hatred of all science which dwelt or dwells in words *instead* of things, I have been led by you to investigations of words as interpreters of things, which have been very fruitful to me; and so amusing that now a word-hunt is to me as exciting as, I suppose, a fox hunt could be to any body else.[139]

TENNYSON: *THE PRINCESS* AND THE EDUCATION OF WOMEN

Interest in Romantic scenery and Turner had fused in Ruskin's upbringing with an admiration of Byron, especially *Don Juan*, to which, improbably, his father had introduced him as a child. It was regarded as a wicked book—Furnivall 'read Byron's Don Juan' until 2 in the morning under Ruskin's guidance, '& (was) much disgusted with it'.[140] It is a long work to read in an evening, but Furnivall did not need to go further than the first two cantos to find matter for disgust. Ruskin is likely also to have introduced him to Thomas Hood's 'Hero and Leander'.[141] However, no one in particular needed to have suggested to Furnivall that he should read Tennyson: everyone in his circle was raving about his poetry. Furnivall not only read it, including *In Memoriam*, but he also copied bits of it for the *Christian Socialist*, and during the Easter vacation, he read Tennyson's cautious exploration of the theme of women's higher education, 'The Princess', to his sisters.[142]

As his experiences with the Little Ormond Yard school showed, Furnivall would discover that his crusade would be undertaken in the cause of widening education, though, as yet, educating women was not prominent among his concerns. He probably supported women's education as it was construed in the 1850s rather unthinkingly. Yet some of the men around him, particularly Kingsley and Maurice, were taking an interest in women's higher education. *The Princess* does not make it easy to as-

[139] FU 779, Letter to Furnivall, 22 Mar. [1860]. The Dean of Westminster was Richard Chenevix Trench. Letter quoted in full, Munro, 'Biography', p. xxiii. Reference is probably to Trench's *On the Study of Words* (1851), and *A Select Glossary of English Words* (1859).
[140] Saturday, 2 Aug. 1851, Bodl. MS Eng. e. 2316, f. 39^r. See also Ruskin, *Praeterita*, 52, 131–2, 134. James, *Young Man from Home*, 58.
[141] Thursday, 9 Oct. 1851, Bodl. MS Eng. e. 2316, f. 49^r; Ruskin owned Hood's poems: see the account of his poetry shelf in Hilton, *John Ruskin*, i. 214.
[142] Sunday, 23 Mar., Monday, 21 and Tuesday, 22 Apr. 1851, Bodl. MS Eng. e. 2316, ff. 20^r, 24^v. I gratefully acknowledge the help of Dr Michael Sullivan in the ensuing remarks on Tennyson.

certain Tennyson's views, and even his admirers, like Elizabeth Barrett Browning, were doubtful when they heard he was writing a fairy story in blank verse about a university for women.[143] The story takes its starting point from a Victorian girl's wish to be the hero of a story in her own right, and from her jealousy of a group of young men gossiping about their time at college—a conversation in which she could not share. The story which they tell her to appease her figures her as a princess in a romance's unspecified days gone by, who refuses to marry because she and her female companions have set up a women's university. Furnivall did not record what his sisters thought of *The Princess*. Though the story in summary sounds daring, contemporary reviewers did not find it subversive: Furnivall's sisters probably enjoyed the story (influenced by *Love's Labour's Lost*), and the serio-comic, entertaining way in which the romance is told, with its heroism grafted onto a frame narrative set in a summer festival in the grounds of a Victorian gentleman's house, based (with 'what amounted to a fetish about accuracy') on Park House, near Maidstone, belonging to the Lushington family (known to Furnivall), with many genteel contemporary knickknacks.[144] It is very hard to pin the author's views down—as Kingsley put it, 'the idyllic manner alternates with the satiric, the pathetic, even the sublime, by such imperceptible gradations ... the old is interpenetrated with the new—the domestic and scientific with the ideal and sentimental'. Kingsley saw the result as a 'mirror of the nineteenth century',[145] as a fable of modern woman's hubris in 'taking her stand on the false masculine ground of intellect'. On this view, the marriage and prospective motherhood which are the story's conventional end serve Princess Ida right.[146] Tennyson's view was probably more nuanced.

Furnivall probably appreciated the poem's entertainment value for his sisters—he was an attentive brother; moreover, his sisters, particularly Louisa, later socialized with Vernon Lushington's sister,

---

[143] 'Now isn't the world too old & fond of steam, for blank verse poems, in ever so many books, to be written on the fairies?' Quoted by R. B. Martin, *Tennyson, The Unquiet Heart*, 301. See also pp. 311–16, and Ormond, *Alfred Tennyson*, 96–101. The precedents for Tennyson's discussion of higher education for women are discussed by John Killham, *Tennyson and The Princess*. The poem was first published in 1848 and followed by a second, revised, edition in 1850—which is likely to be the version which their brother read to the Furnivall sisters.

[144] Martin, *Tennyson*, 305. See the report of the event in the *Maidstone and Kentish Advertiser* for 12 July 1842, quoted by Killham, *Tennyson and The Princess*, 61–3.

[145] See also Killham, *Tennyson and The Princess*, 275.

[146] 'Tennyson', Review of *In Memoriam*, in Charles Kingsley, *Literary and General Lectures*, 103–24 at 116–17. Reprinted from *Fraser's Magazine*, Sept. 1850.

THE EDUCATION OF WOMEN

Alice, and Park House may already have been known to them. But it is also likely that he relished the opportunity slyly to introduce ideas to Egham which were being discussed among his Christian Socialist friends, and Tennyson's name was a *carte d'entrée*. Furnivall had made the decision to 'come out' as a radical at the end of the Long Vacation, and *The Princess* was probably softening up his sisters to understand ideas which now mattered to their brother, but which were socially startling. Selina, the only one of his sisters not to marry, was perhaps most sympathetic to his growing unconventionality.

The idea of broadening education for women was topical, and the idea of a women's college for university study was canvased as an idea in the first half of the nineteenth century, though without serious expectation that it would come to pass. Indeed, as was remembered, Samuel Johnson had toyed with the notion in a short passage of *Rasselas* describing a princess's intention to found a 'college of learned women in which she would preside'.[147] Furnivall had himself read *Rasselas* back in 1843—it was out of his usual line, and was presumably a recommendation from someone at Cambridge. Theory did not extend to practice until the foundation in 1848 of The Queen's College, Harley Street, created initially, but not exclusively, with the interests of potential governesses in mind. As well as educating young women, it was soon realized that a preparatory class for younger pupils was needed, and the College quickly developed a school for girls alongside, initially in the converted stables. F. D. Maurice was one of the college's founders, and his other foundation, the Little Ormond Yard school, had included a class for the girls whom Furnivall found 'larkish'. The lecturers at Queen's included some of the best scholars in the country, and, although girls were admitted from 12 upwards, the style of teaching by lectures resembled that of a university.[148] Ludlow drew up its Constitution. Maurice was supported by most of the other professors at King's; as Chairman of its Committee of Education, he became, in effect, its first principal, though he was not formally accorded this title, and was afterwards known as 'The Founder'. Charles Kingsley was appointed as Professor of English Literature and Composition and gave weekly lectures, in one of which he reminded his students 'that it is the primary idea of this College to

---

[147] Quoted by Killham, *Tennyson and The Princess*, 197.

[148] See further Billings, *Queen's College*, 35–51. The original curriculum consisted of English Literature and Grammar, Drawing, German, French, Italian, Latin, Geography, History, Mechanics, Method in Teaching, Geology, Arithmetic, Mathematics. The staff and teaching regimen are described on pp. 40–2.

vindicate women's right to an education in all points equal to that of men', though with the important rider 'the difference between them being determined not by any fancied inferiority of mind, but simply by the distinct offices and character of the sexes'.[149] It was the first institution in the world to offer academic qualifications to women. Tennyson's precise relation to these developments is debatable. He was Maurice's friend and likely to have become aware at Cambridge of the debate on the education of women. By writing *The Princess*, he may have been doing his part to prepare the way for the launch of Queen's (though the first plans for the poem were made ten years earlier). Tennyson's sympathy for the idea is suggested when, in 1865-7, Emily Davies, sister of one of the founding members of the Working Men's College, secured his signature to a memorial on the need for a place of education for adult women students.[150]

Maurice's attention had been drawn to the needs of governesses and women teachers by his elder sister, Mary, who ran a school in Southampton, and who made him aware of the desirability of a standard qualification for such women—Furnivall's own sense of the needs of governesses was probably influenced by a weekend reading of *Jane Eyre*, perhaps prompted by Maurice's concern with the subject, and also perhaps influenced by Alexander Macmillan's admiration of the work.[151] He no longer had compunctions about reading novels on a Sunday.

Nervous prostration and overwork soon forced Kingsley to resign from his professorship at Queen's, where he had lectured *inter alia* on the earliest English literature, which he felt was a necessary foundation for understanding the present: 'clever and earnest young women like young men, are beginning to wander up and down in all sorts of eclecticisms and dilettanteisms', from which they needed to be rescued, even though their destiny was to become 'worthy wives and mothers of a mighty nation of workers':

One year they find out that the dark ages were not altogether barbarous... and begin to adore them as a very galaxy of light, beauty, and holiness. They then

---

[149] 'On English Composition': Introductory Lectures given at Queen's College, London, 1848, in *Literary and General Lectures and Essays*, 229-41 at 240.

[150] Addressed to the Schools Inquiry Commission. Killham, *Tennyson and The Princess*, 173, and see pp. 132-3 for discussion of Tennyson's part in the founding of the college.

[151] Saturday, 3 to Sunday, 4 May 1851, Bodl. MS Eng. e. 2316, f. 26^r. Maurice's published interest in the subject of women's education was expressed in his article of Nov. 1825, for the *Metropolitan Quarterly Magazine*, of which he was a co-editor (Killham, *Tennyson and The Princess*, 72-3). See also *Life and Letters of Alexander Macmillan*, 32.

THE EDUCATION OF WOMEN

begin to crave naturally enough for some real understanding of this strange ever-developing nineteenth century, some real sympathy with its new wonders, some real sphere of labour in it; and this drives them to devour the very newest authors—any book whatever which seems to open for them the riddle of the mighty and mysterious present, which is forcing itself on their attention through every sense.[152]

Kingsley was describing clever young men, as well as women. He was not thinking of Furnivall, but the passage admirably describes Furnivall's concerns and his development from the time when he left home— and of others like him. As yet, the 'dark ages' were not high on Furnivall's agenda, and he used their abuses to point morals for his own time, though, in due course, he would become absorbed in medievalism for its own sake. He, too, in his quest to solve the absorbing riddle of what it meant to be Victorian, read the newest publications eclectically and at top speed.

Furnivall's Christian Socialist activities had mostly concerned working men, but another of the books he read in this eventful year, 1851, was Catherine Napier's *Women's Rights and Duties* (1840)—it was an eloquent, shrewdly observed complement to reading *The Princess*. Again, the tenor of the argument was not radical: education should fit women to be wives and mothers.[153] Catherine Napier had originally planned to add a section on the 'principles of female education, on the cultivation of the mind, and on the effects and uses of particular branches of study', but her views emerge in a more general historical and anthropological survey of women's place in society.[154] She acknowledged that 'philosophers of the present day are generally the earnest advocates for improving the education, and increasing the rights of women', but noted that women's own attempts at self-education, as described by Kingsley, were well-meaning, but lacking in objectivity, 'judgement': the women 'generally possess an ardent temperament which makes them conquer impedimenta and avail themselves of every advantage', and their attempts at self-improvement were pursued in defiance of the general prejudice of society.[155] Kingsley's ideas for teaching the girls and young women at The Queen's College, as a

---

[152] 'On English Literature, Introductory Lecture given at Queen's College, London, 1848', *Literary and General Lectures and Essays*, 245–65 (pp. 247, 265).

[153] Originally published anonymously, *Women's Rights and Duties Considered with Relation to her Influence on Society and on her own Condition*, By A Woman [Catherine Napier], 2 vols. (London, 1840). Diary: Saturday, 1 Feb., Monday, 3 Feb., 1851, Bodl. MS Eng. e. 2316, f. 13^{r-v}.   [154] *Women's Rights and Duties*, i, p. x.

[155] *Women's Rights and Duties*, i. 174–5.

professor of English, consisted of advice on English composition to complement the instruction they also received on English grammar, and on English literature, viewed historically from its earliest beginnings to the present. It was not to be expected that they should receive an education in Latin and Greek equivalent to that received by educated boys, but the study of English was intended to have something of the same rigour: thus study of English poetry would be the nearest equivalent to the boys' classical training in writing Latin and Greek verses at school, as a foundation to writing good prose.[156] It was an early expression of the idea that the formal study of English literature was peculiarly suitable for women.[157] Kingsley's ideas of teaching English literature at college level—as yet, of course, not as a university syllabus in the traditional men's universities—was 'that it be a whole course or none': choice morsels should not be taken from anthologies, it should be 'a really entire course of English Literature . . . of every period, from the earliest legends and poetry of the Middle Age, up to the latest of our modern authors'.[158]

Kingsley did not, in practice, get beyond the Norman Conquest. After he resigned his professorship, he explained to his successor, 'I read out some Cædmon—no Ælfric—I think some Beowulf—but I should counsel you to let that be (as I gave them the Athelstan Ballad, and some of Alfred's, &c.)'.[159] Despite his principle of broad coverage, Kingsley's syllabus was idiosyncratic and reflected his unusual views on the need for Saxon introspection to be modified by Norse grandeur, but it did express tentatively what would become the enduring and traditional idea of a chronological university syllabus in English, beginning at the beginning. The union of Saxon and Norse would produce (in Kingsley's interpretation) the Border ballads which he—and Furnivall—so much admired. Yet again, the object of Kingsley's efforts had been to give his students the equipment to read Shakespeare. The means consisted in teaching 'the old legends and ballads, the old chronicles of feudal war and chivalry, the earlier moralities and mysteries, and tragi-comic attempts'.[160] The material in short, which would become the staple of Furnivall's EETS and his Ballad Society. It was a model which—consciously or not—formed Furnivall's own

[156] Kingsley, 'On English Composition', 235.
[157] See also Palmer, *The Rise of English Studies*, 38–9.
[158] 'On English Literature', 246, 248.
[159] Kingsley, *Letters and Memories*, 78–9. The 'Athelstan Ballad' is probably 'The Battle of Brunanburh' (in its bloodthirstiness in a 'righteous' cause not dissimilar in sentiment to the Canaanite slaughters). [160] 'On English Literature', 252.

attempts at teaching working men, who likewise did not have a traditional classical education: the teacher should pick works which, though demanding in themselves, being written in archaic forms of English, should nevertheless bridge the gap of the centuries and address the concerns of the age in a way which (in Kingsley's view) the neoclassical Pope and Johnson could not.

SELF-ASSERTION

Furnivall was beginning to discover that he had a talent for organization, social mixing, and acting as a facilitator. He was not himself a leader—or at least not yet—though he probably would have liked to have been. He was not a philologist, but he could, and did, administer the Philological Society. He had at least been able to nudge the cause of the ballast-heavers. As yet no glamour of heroism surrounded him. Indeed, his associates among the Christian Socialists thought him a freak, and no closet freak, but one who proclaimed his political stance by the ostentatious unconventionality of his outward appearance. Furnivall's fashion and lifestyle preferences were not trivial. They projected a self-conscious and deliberate change of image. His outward appearance in the 1850s became an expression of his determination to go his own way in the Working Men's College, and to declare war on its principal, the conventional F. D. Maurice.

Thus, towards the end of the Long Vacation, 1851, he decided finally to adopt the conspicuous outward badge of what his contemporaries considered weirdness, and show (literally) that he had the face to be a free-thinking spirit. The day before returning to London from home he 'shaved for the last time'. He had probably been experimenting with a beard before he went home, since he previously noted that he had shaved the day before going home at Easter.[161] Evidently, he had not felt able at Easter to brazen out the strong disapproval he would receive from his family. And he had especially not until now felt brave enough to flaunt this sign of independence in front of his father. 'The beard movement', said Hughes, 'was then in its infancy, and any man except a dragoon who wore hair on his face was regarded as a dangerous character, with whom it was compromising to be seen in a public place—a person in sympathy with *sansculottes*, and who would dispense with trousers but for his fear of the police.'[162] It is no wonder that his friend

---

[161] Sunday, 31 Aug., Wednesday, 16 Apr. 1851, Bodl. MS Eng. e. 2316, ff. 43^r, 23^v.
[162] 'Prefatory Memoir', p. xxv.

William Johnson told Furnivall when he next saw him: 'Cut that beard off!'[163] Furnivall himself later acknowledged, as has already been noticed here, that his cultivation of his beard had been a quite deliberate flouting of conventional taste at the time—for which he remained entirely unrepentant.[164] A photograph of Furnivall as a young man, taken for the College by one of the men, shows the deliberately provocative eccentricity of his appearance.[165] As for sympathy with the *sans culottes*, Furnivall rarely dispensed with trousers in public, apart from a couple of notable occasions—but he did jest about the idea.

Hughes admitted that Tories like his brother (but the description also fits George Furnivall—who might otherwise have agreed with much that the Christian Socialists were saying), were repelled by 'a strong vein of fanaticism and eccentricity', which 'ran through our ranks, which the marvellous patience, gentleness, and wisdom of our beloved president [Maurice] were not enough to counteract, or control':

> Several of our most active and devoted members were also strong vegetarians and phonetists. In a generation when beards and wide-awakes were looked upon as insults to decent society, some of us wore both, with a most heroic indifference to public opinion. In the same way, there was often a trenchant, and almost truculent, tone about us.[166]

Hughes said he quite enjoyed this confrontational attitude, but he recognized its unwisdom. The more fastidious Kingsley found the contact with 'bearded men, vegetarians, and other eccentric persons' 'very grievous': '"As if we shall not be abused enough," he used to say, "for what we must say and do without being saddled with mischievous nonsense of this kind."'[167] Beards and vegetarianism became, for Hughes and Kingsley, outward symbols of the truculence which some of their associates displayed in their cause. Furnivall was clearly one of these, and he was joined by Charles Mansfield (Kingsley's friend from Cambridge days) and Archibald Campbell. Ludlow conceded, however, that Furnivall joined them in their vegetarianism 'in great measure for economy's sake, that he might be able to give the more'. One of the reasons Ludlow alleged for the collapse in 1854 of the trade associations they had promoted was the Promoters' lack of funds, at least until Vansittart

[163] Letter to Furnivall, ?Apr. [1852], Furnivall Papers, FU 238.
[164] See Introduction, p. 00.
[165] Reproduced by Colloms, *Victorian Visionaries*, 47.
[166] *Memoir of a Brother*, 114. The 'wide-awake' was a soft felt hat with a low crown, which was regarded as ostentatiously idiosyncratic. See *OED*, 'wide-awake', n. sense 3.
[167] Hughes, 'Prefatory Memoir', p. xxv.

Neale joined them. Furnivall was not alone in practising such self-denial: 'Charles Mansfield found the means of liberally contributing through such rigid economy in food and drink as bordered on starvation.'[168] Furnivall was not far behind Mansfield.

Thus, at this time Furnivall's personality 'appeared suddenly to become transformed' in the eyes of onlookers, and the beard was the unmissable sign of his metamorphosis.[169] But he was not alone in peculiarity, and the vein of oddity (according to the views of their time) ran through other members of the group: Kingsley and Mansfield had experimented with mesmerism at Cambridge, and Mansfield continued to be a convinced practitioner. Furnivall played with the idea to please Harriet Martineau. Ludlow, with Mansfield's encouragement, also became a practitioner. Ludlow and Mansfield were teetotallers, as was Furnivall, who nevertheless read Kingsley's letter against teetotalism, which Ludlow refused to publish in the *Christian Socialist*.[170] Charles Mansfield, out of respect for animals, wore cloth shoes, and his self-reproach for previous unthinking cruelty was manifested in the ghost of a seal which he had shot on holiday, while still an undergraduate.[171]

Furnivall's defiant changes in manner and outward appearance foretold his change of loyalty when he became a teacher at the Working Men's College. He sided with the working men against the College authority embodied by Maurice. While he was about it, he also renounced his conventional religious beliefs and practice. He never did anything by halves.

[168] Ludlow, *Autobiography*, 206.
[169] Benzie, *Dr F. J. Furnivall*, 14, quoting Masterman, *Ludlow*, 80.
[170] Wednesday, 12 Nov., Bodl. MS Eng. e. 2316, f. 53ᵛ; Chitty, *Beast and Monk*, 143.
[171] Norman, *Victorian Christian Socialists*, 9; Chitty, *Beast and Monk*, 101; Ludlow, *Autobiography*, 319–22.

5
Beginnings of the Working Men's College, 1854–1857

> You ought to look for those artificers in various manual trades, who, without possessing the order of genius . . . yet possess wit and humour, and sense of colour, and fancy for form—all commercially valuable as quantities of intellect, and all more or less expressible in the lower arts.
>
> John Ruskin, first lecture in *The Political Economy of Art* (1857)

F. D. MAURICE'S IDEA OF A WORKING MEN'S COLLEGE

The Working Men's College resulted from Maurice's downfall after he was forced to resign his King's College professorship and to stand down from Queen's, by a combination of bad press and misrepresentation of his views on eternal damnation. From 1850 it seemed as though 'a regular crusade' against the Christian Socialists and their leader began. As Maurice's son indignantly said, the best time, especially for journalists hiding behind anonymity, 'when it is most righteous to denounce a man, from whom you differ in opinion, is the moment when you know that he has no chance of having a fair hearing, and when every misstatement that you make against him will be greedily swallowed'.[1] In March 1850, the *Quarterly Review* led the attacks, at first on the lectures by Maurice, Kingsley, and others, published to mark the opening of Queen's, when Maurice and Kingsley were singled out for attack. Ludlow threw himself into the breach with a reply, but 'this time Mr Maurice was not to be stopped'.[2] Maurice wrote to the Bishop of London, accepting full responsibility, as a professor at both Queen's and of King's. Alarmed by *Alton Locke*, as well as the adverse publicity, one of the professors at Queen's, the Revd Charles Grenfell Nicolay, publicly wrote to dissociate the College from Kingsley, and Maurice at once resigned as chairman of the committee.[3] His theological views were inextricable in the minds of his opponents from his Christian Socialism, and the Principal of King's, Richard William Jelf, 'began to take fright'

---
[1] Maurice, *Life of Maurice*, ii. 50–1.
[2] Ludlow, *Autobiography*, 238.
[3] Maurice, *Life of Maurice*, ii. 54; Billings, *Queen's College*, 55–6. Nicolay took over the administration of the College after Maurice's resignation. Kingsley had already resigned, as the duties were incompatible with his parish work in Eversley.

and sent off a string of his perplexities, to which Maurice painstakingly replied.[4]

It was at this time, too, that Slaney's inquiry into the 'Investments for the savings of the middle and working classes' was being held. Its report was moderate, though 'less explicit' than Ludlow wished—and it provoked further assaults on the Christian Socialists in the *Edinburgh Review*, in which a severe review of *Alton Locke* and *Cheap Clothes and Nasty* led to a stinging personal attack on Kingsley, as 'a clergyman of very impatient benevolence' prone to 'hasty conclusions' and 'disreputable rant'. It continued with an overview of the movement's activities as the work of a well-meaning, but unqualified, bunch of do-gooders lacking scientific understanding of political economy. The *Christian Socialist* was 'conducted with great ability as to everything but logic', and workmen's associations were a harking back to medieval trade guilds. 'The mantra of Messrs. Kingsley and Maurice' was that 'competition is a cruel and unchristian system: Association breathes the very spirit of our divine master.'[5] The comments were difficult to ignore, and Furnivall wrote a reply, with Ludlow's assistance.[6] He also celebrated his twenty-sixth birthday in 1851 by writing a second reply in Maurice's defence.

Not all the *Edinburgh*'s writers were so outspokenly Tory; in the following year, another article supported the newly proposed legislation, while protesting vigorously lest the author be suspected of Christian Socialism.[7] And, after the Whigs had 'shilly-shallied with us through two Sessions' the Tories returned to power on 27 February 1852, led by Lord Derby, 'anxious to curry favour with the working class'.[8] 'The Industrial and Provident Societies Bill' was passed on 30 June 1853, and with it passed much of the need for the Christian Socialists' industrial activism: as Maurice's son said, 'Practically the work of the promoters

---

[4] Ludlow, *Autobiography*, 238; Maurice, *Life of Maurice*, i. 521–5. See also Nowell-Smith (ed.) *Letters to Macmillan*, 27–9.

[5] *Edinburgh Review*, 93 (Jan.–Apr. 1851), 7–33 at 7–8, 11, 13.

[6] Ludlow, *Autobiography*, 196–9 at 196; Diary, Saturday, 18, Tuesday, 21 Jan. 1851, Bodl. MS Eng. e. 2316, f. 11ʳ⁻ᵛ. William Johnson read the reply, but did not wholly agree with it: 'I did not value so highly as you would wish your answer to the Edin. Article, some parts of which I quite agree with. Cooperation is a good thing—but not the opposite of competition'; letter of 28 Feb. 1851, FU 232.

[7] Review of the *Report of the Select Committee Appointed to Consider and Suggest Means for Facilitating Safe Investments for the Savings of the Middle and Working Classes*, *Edinburgh Review*, 95 (1852), 405–53 (discussion of the specific case of working men's associations begins on p. 436). Ludlow identified the writer as Mr. Greg (*Autobiography*, 197).

[8] Ludlow, *Autobiography*, 196.

had been already accomplished more completely than they themselves recognised at the time'.[9] The Working Associations which the Society of Promoters had established were struggling; a grand new undertaking in 1851 to bring the co-operative stores throughout the country together under the direction of a Central Co-operative Agency eventually split the movement when this rival refused to recognize the supremacy of the Society of Promoters' Council. There was a showdown at the Promoters' Council meeting on 6 November 1851, when Ludlow, by a letter to Maurice, forced the meeting to choose between him and the four main leaders of the Agency, especially Neale and Lechevalier, whom Ludlow considered the *agent provocateur* in the business. In an attempt to preserve unity Maurice destroyed the letter but revealed its contents at the meeting.

Furnivall, who strongly supported the Agency, was actively involved in these stirring events. His own account perhaps tends understandably to magnify his contribution—yet Maurice seems to have taken some time and trouble to keep him on side. The discussions about the relations between Agency and Promoters began formally at the Thursday meeting on 1 May, and after it, in the interests of harmony, Maurice walked with Furnivall and Louis, another who was dissatisfied.[10] The matter came to a head in late October; at a Conference of the Council of the Promoters with the Central Agency on the 30th, when, as Furnivall reported, 'Walsh's and my resolution [was] carried; . . . it was agreed that the Agency should operate separately from the Council; that the two are independent'. A Committee was formed 'to see how they can work together'.[11] This Committee, which Furnivall may have chaired, since it met in his rooms, consisted of Hughes, Neale, Crease, and Ellison. It met on 3 November, when it prepared a report—Neale stayed on for an hour afterwards talking to Furnivall, and apparently bending his ear in the other direction.[12] This report was discussed at the meeting of Council three days later when, as Furnivall put it, 'Ludlow [was] in a tantrum & sent in his resignation. Maurice put it in the fire.'[13] Again, on this occasion Maurice spent time afterwards walking with Furnivall

---

[9] Maurice, *Life of Maurice*, ii. 156.

[10] Diary, 1 May, Bodl. MS Eng. e. 2316, f. 26^r.

[11] Thursday, 30 Oct. 1851, Bodl. MS Eng. e. 2316, f. 52^r (see also Thursday, 23 Oct., f. 51^r).

[12] Monday, 3 Nov. 1851, Bodl. MS Eng. e. 2316, f. 52^v. The meeting lasted two hours, from 2 p.m. until 4; Neale left at 5. On Cuthbert Ellison see Ludlow, *Autobiography*, 167–9, a lawyer, another resident of Lincoln's Inn, and 'an unmistakeable man about town'.

[13] Thursday, 6 Nov. 1851, Bodl. MS Eng. e. 2316, f. 53^r. Furnivall's account suggests

to keep this firebrand in order and avoid schism, while also persuading Ludlow to stay on. Yet, just a week later, Ludlow's resignation *was* sent in, and Maurice made a statement about the separation of the Society and the Agency.[14] He then stepped in to close down the *Christian Socialist*, with which the movement was identified by the public. Furnivall's diary makes clear at this time just how caught up he had become in the movement's activities at the expense of his 'proper' job. On the day of the Committee meeting, for example, he had evidently been up very late the night before, overslept, got up at 12.30 p.m., dressed and went straight to his chambers, where he breakfasted on bread and apples, after which there can have been little time before the meeting began at 2.

As Ludlow said, the story of Christian Socialism was intricately interwoven with Maurice's troubles at King's.[15] The dissensions between the Promoters coincided with Maurice's defence of his theological views, which had given offence to the Council of King's College and its Principal, Jelf, following the publication of his *Theological Essays* in 1853. It was the last essay especially, 'On Eternal Life and Eternal Death', which caused offence. As Maurice himself recognized, even before the *Theological Essays* appeared, 'I knew when I wrote the sentences about eternal death, that I was writing my own sentence at King's College'.[16] Knowing that his dismissal was a foregone conclusion and considering that a dismissed professor would be of little use to the associations, he also offered to resign from the presidentship of the Society of Promoters. He was given the opportunity to withdraw quietly from King's but preferred to make a stand: 'The only question is now whether I shall resign or wait for dismissal. Jelf, of course, urges the first course as most convenient to him and to the college, and I am well inclined for my own sake to adopt it. But the question is, which is the right thing to do for the sake of the Church and of the great principle which I am certain is at stake.'[17] Jelf has often been portrayed as the enemy in these proceedings, though Maurice was clear that he bore him no ill will.

Maurice was dismissed at a special meeting of the Council of King's

---

that Maurice destroyed the letter publicly at the meeting, not beforehand, as suggested in other tellings of the story, e.g. Colloms, *Victorian Visionaries*, 111.

[14] Thursday, 13 Nov. 1851, Bodl. MS Eng. e. 2316, f. 54ʳ.

[15] Ludlow, *Autobiography*, 241, and see pp. 238–40 for Ludlow's efforts to defend Maurice, which Maurice countermanded.

[16] Maurice, *Life of Maurice*, ii. 168 (letter to Kingsley).

[17] Letter to Ludlow, 24 Aug. 1853, Maurice, *Life of Maurice*, ii. 177.

on 27 October 1853; Jelf bore testimony to his unvarying courtesy and zeal for the college.[18] He sent his final letter to the Council on 7 November. His resignation from Queen's followed (though he would be unanimously re-elected in 1856), and the Benchers of Lincoln's Inn refused his offer to resign their chaplaincy. An outpouring of letters of sympathy for Maurice followed. In a letter to his brother-in-law, Archdeacon Julius Hare, he enclosed as a scrap of light relief a 'curious and interesting' specimen of the public's interest, a letter to himself from Furnivall, in which Furnivall reported the opinions of the head shop man at J. H. Parker's bookshop:

'You may depend upon it, sir, there are thousands taking the deepest interest in it. We don't know what other points the dispute is on, but if it's only about everlasting punishment, I've had it from all the clergy I've seen, from the archdeacon to the curate this day, that it isn't a Church doctrine, and if they dismiss Mr Maurice for this only, it is most unjust . . . if you take the Bible and common sense to judge by, why, sir, it's the most abominable and horrible doctrine ever preached.' The man volunteered all this and a good deal more, to my occasional, 'ah, indeed!' . . . Coming from Jelf's publishing place, I was glad to hear this report.[19]

Furnivall was also writing round on his own initiative to solicit expressions of support for Maurice from eminent persons, already showing his lack of tact in seeking publicity and earning a gentle rebuke from Elizabeth Gaskell: 'I hope also to write to Mr Maurice by this post; but I do not at all agree to your idea of printing that or any other letter to that most beloved friend of many persons, in a newspaper, if they only contain expressions of affectionate and respectful feeling.' For the same reason she asked him not 'to tell about your feelings before many people'.[20] Furnivall also sought the Duke of Argyll's signature for a petition, only to be reminded by him that, much as the duke sympathized with Maurice, he himself was not a member of the Church of England.[21] It is clear that Furnivall thought Maurice was a milksop and should have made a fight of it, as he doubtless would have done himself. He evidently expressed his views forthrightly in private, and his family's friend, the philanthropist and doctor Edward Harman Maul, wrote a gentle rebuke: 'I am more sorry to hear what you thought of his relinquishing this op-

---

[18] Maurice, *Life of Maurice*, ii. 190–1.
[19] Ibid. 203–4.
[20] Letter of 2 Dec. [1853], FU 313. Also FU 312, 6 Dec. [1853]: '*I am as strong as I can be* about Mr Maurice'.
[21] George Douglas Campbell, 8th Duke of Argyll, letter of 12 Dec. 1853, FU 173.

portunity of good than of the doctrinal enquiry.' He reminded Furnivall: 'I am sure to set an example of submission is an excellent proof of the Christian character far above all, & you know that our Lord submitted to every wrong judgement and has left us an example to follow him.'[22] Furnivall's response to what he saw as Maurice's weakness probably contributed to his hostility a few years later when he challenged Maurice's leadership as Principal of the Working Men's College.

The working men of London also sent Maurice an Address, expressing their sympathy, which was presented to him at a meeting in the Hall of Association on 27 December 1853. It was signed by 953 working men, representing ninety-five different trades, and by a committee of the leading members of the Associations, many of whom would sign up as students of the soon-to-be-founded Working Men's College.[23] One of the speakers expressed the hope 'that he might not find it a fall to cease to be a Professor at King's College and to become the Principal of a Working Men's College'. As Ludlow said, 'To a man like Mr. Maurice such words would under the circumstances sound as a call from God. On that 27th December, 1853 the London Working Men's College may be said to have been spiritually founded.'[24] Furnivall was involved with it for the rest of his life.

CO-OPERATION AND EDUCATION

The effects of Maurice's dismissal, the passing of the Industrial and Provident Societies' Act, and the increasing disillusion of the Promoters with the working men in the trade Associations were to focus the group's attention increasingly on education. As Hughes put it forthrightly in retrospect: 'The squabbles and idlings and swindlings and incompetence of the workmen in the London Associations . . . convinced Mr Maurice that they had to be educated before they would be capable of the self-restraint, staunchness and obedience which are absolutely necessary in an Association for production.'[25] Ludlow also observed that 'The connection of Co-operation with Education . . . had never been overlooked'.[26] He was, however, at pains to point out

[22] Letter of 20 Oct. [1853], FU 563.
[23] J. F. C. Harrison, *History of the Working Men's College*, 18. The text of the address is given in Maurice, *Life of Maurice*, ii. 221–3.
[24] 'The Origin of the College', in J. Llewelyn Davies (ed.), *The Working Men's College 1854–1904: Records of its History and its Work for Fifty Years by Members of the College* (London, 1904), 13–21 at 19.   [25] Quoted in Harrison, *History*, 15.
[26] Ludlow, *Autobiography*, 235.

that 'It must not be supposed that the founding of the Working Men's College at once stopped the Christian Socialist Movement'—several Associations survived its foundation and others were created.[27] Yet he admitted that the College withdrew from the co-operative movement 'the greater part of the moral and spiritual influences which had hitherto been brought to bear upon it and thus caused it to die out'. Maurice's withdrawal from the social work of the movement was thus in effect necessary for it to survive as a secular force. Furnivall certainly continued to be active in the cause and to attend meetings of the Agency and Promoters. His work on behalf of the Ballast Heavers of London preoccupied him during much of 1852–3. William Johnson observed that 'You are evidently in a very bad way—not able to get up in the morning'. He expressed his support for the ironworkers' lockout: 'I will change my £25 into £100 ... I am surprised at your not making a bolder stroke to show the insurgents that your sympathy is solid. The little we could raise would surely be much better spent in a loan than in alms-giving in supporting the strikers.'[28] By 1855 Furnivall was still working long into the night on behalf of the Associations. Johnson expressed his regret for the failure of the iconic Tailors' Association, and offered £100 in support, though he feared the cause was lost: 'I have done my duty to the Promoters and to the movement and I regret the failure.'[29]

Several of the founders wrote accounts of the new Working Men's College's early years, including Furnivall, who, six years after its creation, contributed a brief history in three instalments to the College's *Magazine*.[30] By this time, the narrative of events was settled, but Furnivall's disagreements with Maurice were still very much live, and he had to treat matters fairly dispassionately, while still imparting his unmistakable 'spin'. Thus he made use of his characteristic polemic device of paraphrasing the sentiment of whole groups in a pithy piece of direct speech of his own invention: 'The Paris February Revolution of 1848 ... said to a barrister of Lincoln's-Inn, Mr. John Malcolm Ludlow, "Are you

[27] Ibid. 250, 253 (and see his following account, 253–65).
[28] Letter to Furnivall, ?Apr. [1852], FU 238. Johnson had also expressed interest in the formation of a local Glovers' Association: 'Association if we could ensure their custom ... The slavery is mild, but worth easing. I thought it possible that the Central Agency might order gloves & pay for them before they are ordered by themselves, but it does not seem likely.' On a lighter note, he commented that 'The Exhibition of winter artists, or whatever they call it, I could not find ... The other sheet contains questions which I wish you would if you could without impropriety submit to Ruskin.' Letter of 7 Apr. 1852, FU 237.
[29] Letter of 20 Jan. 1855, FU 241.
[30] *Working Men's College Magazine*, 2 (1860), 144–8, 165–70, 188–92.

lawyers doing your duty to the poor in the place where you earn your fees?"'[31] Quite how a Revolution in France speaks to a London barrister is not clear, yet the comment does also show Furnivall's sustained intention to give most of the credit for the College's success to Ludlow, not Maurice. His history largely consists of his transcriptions of essential documents, with brief prefatory remarks, and is interspersed with short narrative comment. It shows the author's unwillingness to write extended prose, combined with his sense of the primacy of original documents, which characterized the whole of Furnivall's writing career, and which were fundamental to his conception of the EETS. And he already displayed his appreciation of the problems of finding material to fill up empty space in periodical publications, which were to dog his editorship of the Philological Society's Transactions, as well as his literary societies, including the EETS: 'A certain interest our history has; and this number of the Magazine must be filled, so here is part at least of what I know or believe about it.'[32]

Maurice himself traced the origins of the new College back to the Bible reading classes at his house.[33] This had, in turn, been followed by the Little Ormond Yard school. The earlier Mechanics' Institutes were a partial precedent, though they had been created to offer scientific instruction, and the Working Men's College was designed to offer a more liberal education suitable to Maurice's idea of what a 'college' ought to be: 'an association of men *as men*—an association not formed for some commercial purpose and not limited by coincidence of opinion'.[34] And,

---

[31] Ibid. 144.
[32] Ibid.
[33] e.g. Maurice, *Life of Maurice*, ii. 236. Following the account of the founding of the Little Ormond Yard School, Furnivall's remarks show that his sense of priorities was not Maurice's (certainly not by 1860): 'Well, we visitors and teachers used to meet at Mr. Maurice's one evening in the week, to have tea and chat, and read the Bible together; and at these meetings the letters on "Labour and the Poor," then coming out in the "Morning Chronicle" . . . were the subjects of frequent and earnest talk'; 'History of the Working Men's College', 144–5. Furnivall emphasized Ludlow's persistence in drawing attention to local poverty and working conditions.
[34] Maurice, *Life of Maurice*, ii. 220–1. See also his comment in the advertisement circulated before the inaugural meeting: 'The name College is an old and venerable one. It implies a Society for fellow work, a Society of which teachers and learners are equally members, a Society in which men are not held together by the bond of buying and selling, a Society in which they meet not as belonging to a class or a caste, but as having a common life which God has given them and which he will cultivate in them'; *Working Men's College Magazine*, 2, p. 166. See also the remarks by G. M. Trevelyan on the relations between the Working Men's College and the older universities, Davies (ed.), *Working Men's College*, 187–98. On the limitations of the Mechanics' Institutes, see the remarks by Litchfield, 'Beginnings', 6–7.

already in 1852, the Promoters had also begun to arrange lectures and evening classes in the Hall of Association, designed by Penrose out of the upper floors of the workshops of the Working Tailors' Association in Castle Street. A Committee of Teaching and Publication was formed, consisting of some fourteen of the Promoters, of whom Furnivall was apparently not one, though the list included Alexander Macmillan and William Johnson.[35] The lectures advertised for November and December 1852 included Maurice on 'The Historical Plays of Shakespeare'; Walter Cooper, the manager of the Working Tailors' Association, on 'The Life and Genius of Burns'; John Hullah, music professor at King's, on vocal music, as the prelude to a singing class; and R. C. Trench on 'Proverbs'. William Johnson initially agreed to lecture on 'Rivers', but, dismayed by the size of the room, backed out, telling Furnivall: 'You must get a stronger man, a heartier moralist': 'I have thought again and again about lecturing as you and the Council do me the honour of proposing I should. I have a good deal to say but from an historical & political point of view only.'[36]

The lectures began at 8.30 p.m.; admission was 2d. (6d. for reserved seats).[37] There were also evening classes, the subjects including English grammar (Hughes and Vansittart Neale), English history (Maurice, assisted by Neale, Louis, and others), and Maurice's Bible classes were transferred to the Hall from his house. Ludlow offered French. The emphasis on what would now be called 'Arts' subjects was intentional, not just a reflection of the available teachers' capacities. As the inspiration for the College came from Maurice, the religious foundation for the course is unsurprising, as also is the tacit assumption of a top-down model of instruction, which would be at the heart of his disagreements with Furnivall. As Maurice expressed it:

We may proceed to what I shall call, in the old language of the schools (which I do not think is in the least degree obsolete or unsuitable to our purpose), the Humanity course . . . I justify the course, which I have proposed . . . because I think that what working men most want is the feeling of an order in God's government, in their relations to each other, in the world around them, a righteous order and one into which they must enter, which they cannot make for themselves.[38]

---

[35] Furnivall, 'History of the London Working Men's College', 146. Furnivall transcribes at this point Maurice's statement of the proposed College's purpose.
[36] Davies (ed.), *Working Men's College*, 16. Johnson to Furnivall, 23 Feb. 1852, FU 236.
[37] See the advertisement reproduced in Harrison, *History*, facing p. 16.
[38] *Working Men's College Magazine*, 2, p. 147. 'The true treatment of history, especially

When it came to teaching history, 'We must not begin from the past, but make them [the students] feel that they need the past for the explanation of the present'—a sentiment which underlaid Furnivall's own later justification for his first editorial task for the Roxburghe Club, Robert of Brunne's *Handlyng Synne*. Kingsley gave occasional lectures, as did Llewelyn Davies, another who had come under Maurice's influence at Trinity College, Cambridge, but who had come to the attention of the London group after writing to the *Spectator* to contradict Kingsley. He would become the Vice-Principal of the Working Men's College.[39]

And it was at this time, too, that Furnivall met others who gave their time to teaching the working men, though they did not subscribe to the Christian Socialists' principles. Though he left soon afterwards for Australia on account of his health, Charles Pearson, Professor of English History at KCL, and an old pupil there of Maurice's, became a lifelong friend, but Furnivall would fall out with Richard Buckley Litchfield, who became the College's Treasurer, and of whom Ludlow had a high opinion.[40] Litchfield, writing an account of the history of the Working Men's College in 1902 for young men who did not remember what difficulties working people faced fifty years before, described a time when educational initiatives reached 'a fraction of the people'. 'It was then a common thing to meet working men, first rate craftsmen and full of intelligence, who could barely write their names . . . It is no wonder that the co-operators cried out for better instruction.'[41] And yet, when the College was founded, the intention to reach working men above the class of uneducated labourers was made plain by the tests administered to would-be students at the time of their enrolment, as well as by the termly fee of 2s. and 6d. The applicant needed to be over 16, able to read and write, and know the first four rules of Arithmetic.[42] Furnivall reported that, at the opening of the College, 'we sat for six matriculation evenings, setting sums (in words) to candidates for admission, to test their acquaintance with Reading Writing, and Arithmetic'.[43] Frederic Harrison, who lectured to the men on history and Latin, would later be forced by Maurice to resign after an attempt to recast the syllabus on of English history, of ethics, of theology, will, I believe, be better preaching in support of association than any other which we could set on foot'.

[39] A. F. Hort, 'Davies, (John) Llewelyn (1826–1916)', *ODNB*; Ludlow, *Autobiography*, 269.
[40] Ludlow, *Autobiography*, 268–9. Furnivall. 'History', 189. For J. F. C. Harrison, Litchfield 'was, without doubt, one of the really great "college men"', *History*, 42.
[41] Litchfield, 'The Beginnings of the Working Men's College', 4.
[42] *Working Men's College Magazine*, 2, p. 166.   [43] Ibid. 168.

positivist lines, and later founded a smaller imitation of the Working Men's College nearby.⁴⁴ It is no accident that so many of the first teachers had a Cambridge education. Maurice naturally relied initially on his circle of friends. But he intended to recruit teachers from newly graduated young men from both of the two older universities, in the idealistic hope that, in time, a bond would be forged between the universities and the people, so that the nonsectarian 'Church', broadly understood, would show the way in national education, would overcome sectarian differences, and would pool these resources for the common good of all.⁴⁵ Maurice's decision to call the new institution a 'college' reflected this aspiration. It has been said of the teachers at the College that 'their paternalism and quixotism did some good, and exemplified the medieval ideals of chivalry, generosity and charity'.⁴⁶ Chivalric ideals influenced Kingsley, who knew medieval literature, and described himself as 'a joyous knight-errant of God',⁴⁷ and Hughes spoke loosely of a crusade, but, though the early years of the College were too early for the influence of Tennyson's *Idylls of the King*, published between 1859 and 1885, they had all read their Walter Scott. The verdict of quixotism seems unduly weighted by Furnivall's later prominence, thanks to his diversion into literary studies, and the growing awkwardness and crankiness which he displayed in his dealings with the College.

These were high-minded, deeply sincere, capable professional men, undoubtedly profoundly generous, both with their time and their money. 'Charity', viewed as a top-down form of giving, smacks of paternalism, and this verdict rings true, but needs to be divested of patronizing—'paternalism' in this dominant and generalizing modern sense of the word would not have been understood in 1854.⁴⁸ The

⁴⁴ Martha S. Vogeler, 'Harrison, Frederic (1831–1923)', *ODNB*; Ludlow, *Autobiography*, 269. 'The Positivists followed the doctrines of Auguste Comte in rejecting all supernatural belief, and substituting "faith in our common humanity."'; Harrison, *History*, 48, and see 39–49 for a summary of the teachers' backgrounds and intellectual affiliations.

⁴⁵ Maurice, *Life of Maurice*, ii. 233. For Maurice's contributions to the debate on the 'education question' before the 1870 Education Act, see 610–13. As Harrison put it, less idealistically: 'The sense of obligation of the Victorian middle classes ... combined with a certain guilt-consciousness and desire to justify themselves, provided a basis for sanguine expectations of middle-class support'; *History of the Working Men's College*, 27.

⁴⁶ Alexander, *Medievalism*, 155; see also, Girouard, *Return to Camelot*, esp. 131–44.

⁴⁷ Quoted by Girouard, *Return to Camelot*, 132.

⁴⁸ See *OED*, 'paternalism', n. The first sense, of restrictive relations towards subordinates in their best interests, is not recorded until 1873; the second, of showing special

authority of God-as-Father—of course the justification for paternal authority within the family (and within the College), and thoroughly familiar (though not always unquestioned) at this time, is not quite the same thing. For Maurice, 'we have never thought that we could make them [the working men] understand what that common humanity means ... unless we could speak to them of a Son of Man in whom they have a common interest ... The Son of Man must be the Son of God ... there is no Brotherhood for human beings if there is not a common Fatherhood.'[49] One cannot have brothers without a father.

Even Furnivall (for all his chumminess), and certainly the other teachers, did not see themselves as on the same social level as the working men, but the Christian Socialists were hypersensitive in their efforts not to appear condescending. The clue is in the name, *socius*: these men hoped to form a society of fellow workers, albeit one with pupils and teachers, and a *society* was fundamental to Maurice's idea of the working men's college: 'We need continually to be reminded that we are a body of workers ... For a Society it is, with all capacities for healthy action, for continual growth and expansion: our pupils, I am sure, think so; they feel that their union, however imperfect and hindered by English reserve and shyness, is a reality and not a fiction'.[50] And the College quickly established the principle of using those of its students who were able to qualify for a certificate as teachers themselves. As a group of clergy, professional laymen, and men of affairs, the leading Christian Socialists constituted a 'clerisy', the word devised by S. T. Coleridge to describe an estate of the realm which had its symbiotic part to play in the body politic.[51] Their efforts to do their bit to create the new Jerusalem by founding trade associations fizzled out, but the co-operative movement, and trade unionism, did not. And the Working Men's College, 'the oldest adult educational institute in the country', still exists, testifying both to the power of

favour to subordinates to whom one feels superior, is first recorded in 1893. See also Benzie, *Dr F. J. Furnivall*, 46–7.

[49] Dedication and Preface [to J. M. Ludlow], in W. E. Styler (ed.), *Learning and Working* (London, 1968), 28. See e.g. J. H. Kemble's remarks on family relations, deeply unsympathetic to women's aspirations to education and legal protection at this time and bolstered by his extensive reading of early English legal and customary precedents, quoted at length by Killham, *Tennyson and The Princess*, 166–7.

[50] Anon., 'Recruiting for a College', *Working Men's College Magazine*, 1, p. 110 (1 July 1859).

[51] See *OED*, clerisy, n. Vidler, *F. D. Maurice and Company*, 213. For an appraisal of the extraordinary quality of the founders and early teachers, see J. F. C. Harrison, *History*, 45–7.

voluntary Victorian social activity, and its capacity to change to suit the times.⁵²

In actuality, the London Working Men's College was not quite the first 'People's College'. The Promoters had heard of something very similar, founded in Sheffield in 1842, which had been shaped by the working men themselves in 1848. The Promoters' Committee of Teaching and Publication met to discuss 'the establishment of a "People's College" in connection with the Metropolitan Associations'.⁵³ By 7 February 1854, Maurice had drawn up a plan and a circular, *Scheme of a College for Working Men*.⁵⁴ It was to be an institution to nurture the nobility that comes with the recognition of common humanity, not competitive prizes or pragmatic skills:

> Let the skilful quill-driver have his reward . . . but if we want to create heroes, or to save them from perishing when we have them, let those who used to boast that they existed to form English gentlemen, show that their occupation is not gone; only that they believe gentleness is not tied to wealth, not even to birth; that God can cultivate it, and would cultivate it, in the collier and the street-sweeper.⁵⁵

Maurice announced and explained the scheme in a series of fortnightly public lectures in Willis's Rooms during June and July which raised £87. 14s. towards the new College.⁵⁶ Because of the failure of the North London Needlewomen's Association, new premises at 31 Red Lion Square became available (Maurice had made himself responsible for the rent). According to Furnivall, arrangements had been allowed to lapse over the Long Vacation, and the Secretary, Thomas Shorter, thought the opening had been deferred for another year. Furnivall and Llewelyn Davies made themselves very busy in the latter's dining room in his rectory of St Mark's Whitechapel, and 'drew up a Trial-programme of Classes, and arranged a Teachers' meeting'.⁵⁷ Furnivall presented himself as a (self-appointed) prime mover and shaker to give pep to the new College. On 30 October, Maurice, as Principal, delivered the inaugural address in St Martin's Hall, and the College began its courses in

---

⁵² See Ludlow's calm assessment in hindsight of the Christian Socialists' achievements, *Autobiography*, 262–5. Also J. F. C. Harrison, *History*, p. vii, written to celebrate its centenary in 1954.
⁵³ Maurice, *Life of Maurice*, ii. 232–3, and see Ludlow, *Autobiography*, 270, for the legal arrangements.   ⁵⁴ See description by J. F. C. Harrison, *History*, 19–27.
⁵⁵ Styler (ed.), *Learning and Working*, 32–3.
⁵⁶ Furnivall, 'History', *Working Men's College Magazine*, 2, p. 168; Maurice, *Life of Maurice*, ii. 233, 239. J. F. C. Harrison, *History*, 30; the lectures were later published as *Learning and Working* (1855).   ⁵⁷ *Working Men's College Magazine*, 2, p. 168.

November. Seven of the original teachers had been Promoters, among them Maurice, Walsh, Neale, Furnivall, and Ludlow.[58] Furnivall threw himself enthusiastically into the life of the new College—as Ludlow said of him, out of fairness, while deprecating his growing cockiness: 'He worked very hard ... and at the same time took a prominent part in all social gatherings, and made himself very popular.'[59] Later the novelist Mary Ward, who knew Furnivall through her father, Tom Arnold, and drew upon her own knowledge of the Christian socialist movement of his generation, and who herself engaged in similar initiatives, seems likely to have taken some hints for one of her characters for her best-selling novel *Robert Elsmere* (1888) from Furnivall as he appeared at this time. He may have been at least a part-model for her portrait of a young assistant at a new teaching institution for working men in a poor district of London, who had thrown himself into social philanthropy 'mainly out of opposition to an orthodox and *bourgeois* family, and who had a grand idea of his own social powers', and who resented the recruitment of a charismatic young clergyman as a leader in their midst. He also had been 'the "bow" of the Cambridge eight, and possessed muscles which men twice his size might have envied'.[60] This certainly sounds like Furnivall.

Resentments would soon surface, but, at the College's beginning, Furnivall thoroughly enjoyed the sociability and the novelty of self-importance: 'It was a new and agreeable experience to find oneself trusted and lookt up to by a set of men, men double one's own age, knowing more of practical life, and having different traditions and opinions to mine.'[61] He was no longer a junior partner in the company of brilliant older men, looking up to the likes of Tom Hughes, also a man with the common touch, but whose failure to draw an audience to hear lectures on Sanitary Legislation probably gave Furnivall a certain *Schadenfreude*. Hughes was himself dejected at the lectures' failure

---

[58] See Ludlow's account in Davies, *Working Men's College*, 20–1. For one of the founding student's point of view, see John Roebuck's 'Reminiscences of an Old Student' in Davies (ed.), *Working Men's College*, 61–99. Maurice's circular inviting applicants to attend is given in full in Furnivall's history, *Working Men's College Magazine*, 2, p. 166.

[59] *Autobiography*, 271.

[60] Mrs Humphry Ward, *Robert Elsmere*, ed. Ashton, 449–50. The novel's titular hero has much in common with Charles Kingsley, whose work she knew. The founder of the school was 'a devoted and orthodox Comtist', and a struggling barrister (p. 451); other volunteers included 'civil servants, a young doctor, a briefless barrister or two' (p. 449). They, like Furnivall, had drifted away from orthodox Christianity.

[61] From Furnivall's own account (in 1904) of 'The Social Life of the College', in Davies (ed.), *Working Men's College*, 54–60 at 54.

but proposed to Maurice instead a class in physical fitness. Maurice imagined this meant gymnastics, and 'the dear prophet was somewhat taken aback', even though Hughes explained he meant boxing—which was gentlemanly—not prize-fighting, which was not.[62] Hughes's boxing class proved an immense success, as Furnivall later had to admit, though without warmth: 'As I wasn't a boxer, I can't speak of Hughes's boxing-class from experience. But I recollect Jim Donovan's advice to a beginner: "Mind you don't hit Hughes on the nose by accident. If you do, you'll catch it".'[63] Hughes was the other notably clubbable man in the College, and Furnivall still saw him as a competitor for popularity. It is easy to understand how the phrase 'muscular Christianity' caught on at this time as a way of describing Hughes and Kingsley, and those who thought like them.[64]

Sanitary Legislation was not the only damp squib. To the Promoters' chagrin, the working men did not want instruction in law or political economy either.[65] When new recruits arrived in the College, Furnivall actively seized on them to fill his class on English grammar.[66] He had some honest doubts himself about his fitness for this role. One of his first students, Standring, remembered:

I entered your class. You came in and said you didn't pretend to be much of a *teacher*, as you'd never taught before, and had all your business to learn, but you'd worked a good deal at English, and were game to help any one who'd worked less, and at any rate you hoped we should be good friends, and get on *together*. This suited me, tho' you had a lot of most curious notions about words and grammar.[67]

[62] J. F. C. Harrison, *History*, 64–5. In 1860 Maurice had to publish a letter addressed to Hughes dissociating the College from prize fighting: 'A Letter to the Teacher of a Boxing Class on Prize Fighting', *Working Men's College Magazine*, 2, pp. 75–8 (1 May 1860). See also Girouard, *Return to Camelot*, 136.

[63] Furnivall, 'Social Life of the College', 60. Furnivall may not have kept it up, but he had had boxing lessons himself during his time at UCL. For Hughes's own account of the boxing club, see R. H. Marks, 'The College Clubs', in Davies (ed.), *Working Men's College*, 200–7.

[64] The phrase appears to have originated in an anonymous notice in the *Saturday Review* of Kingsley's *Two Years Ago* (1857): both Hughes and Kingsley responded to it by distinguishing between physically strenuous practice of Christian principles and mere brawn; see Girouard, *Return to Camelot*, 142–3.

[65] Ludlow, *Autobiography*, 266. See J. F. Harrison, *History*, 58–9 for a summary of the curriculum and attendances; also John Westlake's reminiscences about Hughes in the volume, p. 24.

[66] J. F. C. Harrison, *History*, 30. Furnivall commented: 'Mr. Walter Cooper ... found some strong-shoemakers, I remember, who wanted to learn English Grammar, and them I asked for as pupils', *Working Men's College Magazine*, 2, p. 168.

[67] *Working Men's College Magazine*, 2, p. 169.

CO-OPERATION AND EDUCATION 179

The reported indirect speech certainly sounds like Furnivall, and also suggests that he was trying out ideas on his students which he had picked up at the Philological Society. It also seems that Standring was already sufficiently proficient in formal grammar to be able to make this independent judgement. Another of Furnivall's first students, John Roebuck, recalled that 'from that day to this, his personality has always been a treasured recollection. His geniality and the winning brightness of his smile were at once appreciated by me, as they have been by hundreds, and perhaps thousands since'.[68] Indeed Furnivall's outgoing personality seems to have effloresced at this time, though its full force would only become apparent when he clashed with Maurice. He basked in the students' expressions of their appreciation of him personally, as well as of the College. After being kept in check (and repeatedly beaten at whist and backgammon) by his father, and being viewed as an enthusiastic, but very junior, contributor to the Christian Socialists, his popularity must have been intoxicating. The College's ethos of fellowship in learning suited Furnivall perfectly: 'I well recollect the pleasure I used to feel as I walkt about the College rooms, and saw face after face light up as I greeted its owner.' As the Christian Socialists turned their attention away from social action towards adult education, he had found his place and his people and revelled in them. It is no wonder if his new status as a member of the College's governing council, and a favourite teacher, went to his head.

JOHN RUSKIN, THE PRE-RAPHAELITES, AND THE WORKING MEN'S COLLEGE

Furnivall had a better idea than lectures on drains and politics to attract new students: art classes. He knew just the man and was thrilled when Ruskin apparently volunteered classes without even needing to be asked. Furnivall had merely sent Ruskin a copy of the circular in the hope of getting a subscription.[69] However, Furnivall's success was not quite so artless as he first described it. As he later said: 'When, after the failure of all our Co-operative Associations, we started the Working Men's College in 1854, I askt Ruskin to help us, he agreed at once to organise the Art Classes.'[70] Furnivall sent Ruskin a circular from the College, and Ruskin responded in a letter volunteering his services.[71]

---

[68] Roebuck, 'Reminiscences', 63.   [69] *Working Men's College Magazine*, 2, p. 168.
[70] Nicoll and Wise (eds.), *Literary Anecdotes* , ii. 46.
[71] Maurice, *Life of Maurice*, ii. 250. Maurice reported to Kingsley: 'Ruskin is doing

The result was that, thanks to his friendship with Ruskin, and despite Ruskin's own disenchantment with Maurice, Furnivall bagged this prize lion to give drawing classes. It was a tremendous personal coup. As Litchfield said, Ruskin's support 'not only gave a splendid start to the Art teaching, but helped the enterprise as a whole by letting the world know that one of the greatest Englishmen of the time was in active sympathy with it'.[72] It was an astonishing piece of luck for the College, and Furnivall deserved much of the credit. He also acted as broker between Maurice and Ruskin.

Ruskin had his own private reasons just then for agreeing to teach the Working Men. 1854, the year of the College's foundation, was also the year in which his marriage to Euphemia ('Effie') Gray collapsed in a blaze of publicity. He needed to keep out of the glare of polite society (which he disliked in any case) and concentrate on his work. After his return from travels with his parents to France and Switzerland during the summer, the prospect of teaching working men (to whom his private affairs were relatively indifferent) offered him an opportunity to instruct respectful and appreciative pupils in his ideas, and in a setting which offered him some privacy. The arrangement thus suited Ruskin very well at the time, though he was rude about the College later. Writing from Paris in 1854, a week before his return to London, he announced in grand utopian style:

I want to give short lectures to about 200 at once in turn, of the Sign painters—and shop decorators—and writing masters—and upholsterers—and masons—and brickmakers, and glassblowers, and pottery people—and young artists—and young men in general, and schoolmasters—and young ladies in general—and schoolmistresses . . . I shall have plenty to do when I get home.[73]

The proposed new College gave him the means to implement at least some of these ambitions. Admittedly the references to young ladies and schoolmistresses did not bode well. Ruskin would find the men 'in general' less biddable than the girls at the school in Winnington Hall, Cheshire, with which he became associated in 1859, after he stopped teaching for the Working Men's College.

The citation to Court in Effie's suit of nullity had been served on

capitally in the drawing-class at the College. Our past term was far beyond our hopes, but we must expect a falling off' (ii. 251). Also Litchfield, 'Beginnings', 4.

[72] Litchfield, 'Beginnings of the Working Men's College', 5.

[73] Letter to Pauline, Lady Trevelyan, quoted by Hilton, *John Ruskin*, i. 202–3; also, at greater length, by Leon, *Ruskin the Great Victorian*, 202–3.

Ruskin, without prior warning, by her lawyers at 6.00 in the evening of Tuesday, 25 April, at the Denmark Hill house. She had been put on the train to Perth in the morning by Ruskin, to visit her parents, without telling him that she was leaving him for good. The Decree of Nullity was granted to Effie on 15 July 1855. In between these dates, the Ruskins, the Grays, John Millais, and their intimates were caught up in emotional turmoil (Millais, as is well known, had been thrown much in Effie's company during his stay with the Ruskins at Brig O' Turk, where he was painting John Ruskin's portrait looking down at the waterfall at Glenfinlas).[74] Furnivall was not really one of Ruskin's intimates (though he would no doubt have liked to consider himself one). But he was a loyal friend, and by chance happened to be at the Denmark Hill house on the very day the citation was served (though just missing the lawyers' visit). He was possibly, therefore, the first outsider to be told the news. He was not in Ruskin's full confidence—probably nobody except his parents was that (and perhaps not even they). But Ruskin had to tell him something, and he used Furnivall as a go-between for news, as he had earlier used him as a broker between himself and Maurice in their theological controversies. The sense that he was serving a reclusive genius must have flattered Furnivall's sense of self-importance, though his sympathy was warm, and Ruskin greatly appreciated it.

Ruskin had invited Furnivall and two of Furnivall's friends to Denmark Hill to view his Turners on the afternoon of the 25th.[75] They enjoyed themselves, as did Ruskin, 'heartily'.[76] Furnivall had not been invited to stay for dinner, yet he heard the news straightaway: a later addition to Ruskin's first letter (begun 21 April) seems to describe the abandoned husband's initial reaction: 'This was written three days ago, and not posted. I have not only a good deal to do, but have had a good deal of annoyance lately, into the particulars of which I cannot enter, and I am more confused than usual.'[77] Furnivall promptly wrote

---

[74] Now in the Ashmolean Museum, Oxford. Ruskin had expressed great satisfaction with the portrait, but after his relations with Millais soured, he told him: 'On the whole the thing is right... always excepting the yellow flower and the over large spark in the right eye, which I continue to reprobate—as having the effect of making me slightly squint—which whatever the other faults of my face may be—I believe I don't. My Father and mother say the likeness is perfect—but that I look bored—pale—and a little too yellow'. Letter of 11 Dec. 1854, printed by Lutyens, *Millais and the Ruskins*, 247.

[75] Letter from Ruskin to Furnivall, begun 21 Apr., but completed three days later; Ruskin, *Works*, xxxvi.163. See also Lutyens, *Millais and the Ruskins*, 184.

[76] Letter dated Monday evening, 24 Apr. 1854; Ruskin, *Works*, xxxvi. 165–6. Like his previous letter to Furnivall, dated 21 Apr., it was completed over more than one day.

[77] The chronology of these two letters, written in stages, is confusing: later in the letter,

a letter of sympathy and support, for which Ruskin was grateful, though his reply is—understandably enough in the circumstances—somewhat elliptical:

> Many and sincere thanks for your kind note. You can be of no use to me at present, except by not distrusting me, nor thinking hardly of me yourself. You cannot contradict reports; the world must have its full swing. Do not vex yourself about it, as far as you are sorry, lest such powers as I may have should be shortened. Be assured I shall neither be subdued, nor materially changed, by this matter. If you hear me spoken ill of, ask people to wait a little. If they will not wait, comfort yourself by thinking that time and tide will not wait either.[78]

Effie herself wrote on 9 May to her confidential friend Rawdon Brown, who had been her adviser, and shared her worries about what the Ruskin family might do. She feared her husband's 'eloquent pen', and hoped he would not use it against her. As yet 'he can have written to nobody but Mr Furnivall, who is an amiable weak young man, a vegetarian, Christian Socialist and worshipper of men of genius'. It is implied by this nicely observed list of eccentricities that she did not consider Furnivall too great a danger—or as a friend whose loss she regretted.[79] Yet Furnivall also knew Millais, and he caused him, as well as Ruskin, considerable embarrassment by sending well-meaning bulletins of the latest news of what people were saying (there were rumours that Millais had already married Effie). Millais wrote to Furnivall on 16 May:

> What is the good of telling me what people have already said about myself, and Mrs R that was? If fashionable [folk] will quietly settle matters among themselves, why let them—it is perfectly immaterial to me—I don't see how a report of that kind is to distress or annoy me—I only wish my kind friends would wait until they knew positively that I am married.[80]

Yet he wrote two days later to Effie's mother, Mrs Gray:

> begun 'three days ago' (i.e. Monday or Tuesday) and completed on Thursday, Ruskin issued his invitation to Furnivall and his two friends.

[78] Letter of Monday evening, 24 Apr. 1854. Ruskin had enjoyed the opportunity to display and talk about his art collection, which now included medieval illuminated missals.

[79] Lutyens, *Millais and the Ruskins*, 207. On 9 May John Ruskin left with his parents on their planned Continental holiday. Effie's verdict on Furnivall, often quoted, should be understood in this context. Her reason for deducing that Ruskin had not written to anyone else was that she had received a letter from Lady Trevelyan, Ruskin's 'greatest admirer and friend . . . with whom he maintains a very constant correspondence. She said she had not had a word on the subject from himself or anyone else but me'. Effie's own friendship with Lady Trevelyan did not survive the break-up (p. 212).

[80] Lutyens, *Millais and the Ruskins*, 211. 'Fashionable folk', corrected from 'gents' (FU 657).

As I expected I hear now that my name is mixed up in the affair, and by some in a manner that makes it advisable that I do not for the present see anybody connected with you... Any personal communication with your family just now would certainly forward the scandal, which has reached the extreme limits of invention. There must be a large proportion of vagabonds in the world to set such rumours afloat.[81]

On 23 May, the day before Millais returned to Brig O'Turk to continue work on the portrait, he again wrote to Furnivall, asking him to contradict rumours (which Furnivall himself seems to have been putting about):

You will I know have the kindness to contradict any absurd conjecture about myself and Mrs R—I confess that I am *disgusted* with the way in which Society has been pleased to mix up my name in the affair ... I should indeed be sorry to hear that any friend of mine imagined that I had the *bad taste* to see Mrs R whilst the matter is in lawyers hands—I write this to you as you are often in a position to refute the wretched [sic] untruthful rumours which are now afloat and I beg you will positively state that I shall make a point of avoiding *all persons connected with the business in Scotland*.[82]

Furnivall could set the record straight because he was himself a gossip and knew so many of the people in society who were also gossiping. The letter hints that Furnivall, whom Millais counted a friend, had himself been coming to wrong conclusions about the purpose of Millais's visit to Scotland—and not keeping his conjectures quiet. Yet Furnivall had his uses as a newsmonger: '*You* may tell Ruskin that I have been working hard at the old place and finished within a few days painting, *although I think it better* not to speak about it as he will judge for himself when he sees it how I have behaved myself.'[83] Millais, like everyone else, was in the dark about what Ruskin thought about the affair: 'I have not heard anything from the author of modern painters. Certainly he is the author of one modern painter being considerably maligned—I shall wait most calmly to hear his statement in defence of himself. If you hear anything please let me know of it.'[84]

Meanwhile Ruskin, still away in Switzerland, continued his silence,

[81] Ibid., letter of 18 May. [82] FU 658.
[83] Letter to Furnivall, 16 June [1854], FU 659. Written from Callander.
[84] Lutyens, *Millais and the Ruskins*, 215–16. FU 658, letter of 23 May 1854. Furnivall evidently did pass on the news that Millais had returned to Scotland to work on the painting: Ruskin wrote to him on 9 June 1854 from Vevey ('Vevay'), Switzerland, that he was 'supremely glad that Millais has made up his mind to go into Scotland and finish his work properly'. In return, Ruskin wished to know, 'What did he say to you—and what to other people say—about his reasons for wishing *not* to go into Scotland? I have no personal

though Furnivall was pressing him to defend himself in some public statement. He probably found Ruskin's outward impassivity about his humiliation, so different from his own pugnacity, hard to bear—and, like everyone else, he wanted to know what had been going on in the marriage: he would hardly have been human if he had not. He was rewarded by what was perhaps the clearest written statement Ruskin ever made (apart from the depositions he made to his lawyers) about the incompatibility and dislike which had grown between himself and Effie. A few months after Effie left him, Ruskin still felt that 'I hardly know how much I owe to myself in this matter—and whether—even supposing I owe *everything* to myself—I am likely to gain much by a defence which could be founded only on statements of my own.' Yet he also felt that Furnivall, as 'one of *the three* people who have been perfectly staunch to me',[85] deserved to hear 'the entire history of my married life'. But it would take 'a day's hard work of writing' when 'an hour's talk will set your mind at rest as soon as I return'. Ruskin had not decided what he should disclose to the wider circle of his acquaintance, though he denied the charge that he had thrown Effie in Millais's way, with the idea of ridding himself of her, as Lady Eastlake suspected: 'I should as soon think of simply denying a charge of murder'; he could only deny and leave it to his enemies to prove him guilty.

Ruskin appreciated that most people among their acquaintance, who had seen Effie only at her graceful and beautiful best in public, would be likely to take her part: 'No-one will ever believe that Effie's general character in her domestic life was what it was—what it *must* have been in order to render my conduct explicable.' He had found her bored, sulky, and snappish, as witnessed by a snatch of conversation between them 'which I happened to put down one day'. Effie had stood looking out of the window, and when Ruskin had pressed her to tell him what she was thinking about, had told him: 'I was thinking of operas—and excitement—and—(angrily) a great many things.' This was further evidence in support of the Ruskins' view that Effie was too addicted to socializing, as well as being vain, too fond of fine dresses, extravagant, and unable to be content with their company. Effie's remark, trivial in itself, was symptomatic in her husband's view: 'this appears little—but imagine every question asked in a kind tone—every answer given with

reasons for asking this—but I wish to know for Millais' own sake poor fellow and you need not fear surprising me by telling me—I know the *facts*—but I want to know the *sayings!*' Lutyens, *Millais and the Ruskins*, 213.

[85] The other two were Lady Trevelyan and Mary Russell Mitford.

a snap—and that continuing the whole day'. Ruskin noted it down as 'an example of our usual intercourse'. She was rude to her in-laws, and she offered 'the most obstinate opposition on serious things'. Ruskin rang the changes on her '*utter* ingratitude for *all* that was done for her by myself—my father—and my mother—not merely ingratitude— but ingratitude coarsely and vulgarly manifested'. In sum, 'you may understand—though I do not see how at present I could make the public understand—why I used no persuasion to induce my late wife to change the position which we held towards each other'. That is, Furnivall could not wonder that the marriage remained unconsummated. In sum, 'she hated me as only those hate who have injured'.[86] In actuality, the letter does not add greatly to what was already known from Effie's and Ruskin's father's letters to her parents and others about the salient reasons for their incompatibility. The letter's significance lies in allowing us to hear, for once, Ruskin's own voice on the subject; moreover, this highly confidential breaking of his silence, at a point when he still had not decided to tell others, was made to Furnivall, as a great act of trust in his friendship.

And Furnivall, for all his well-deserved reputation for indiscretion, did not blab, at least not about this confidence, though the letter was later privately printed, after the principals were dead.[87] But, even after the marriage was annulled the following year, and before his marriage to Effie on 3 July 1856, Millais continued to be wary about giving Furnivall grounds for coupling his name with hers: 'In answer to your questions about Ruskin's late-wife I believe she is at Perth or in Scotland, and I imagine he is in Switzerland, all I know for certain is that I am here.'[88] Millais's tone was light, but Ruskin was offended by this chaff between Millais and Furnivall about Millais's forthcoming marriage to Effie. He reproved Furnivall sternly from Tunbridge Wells:

It may perhaps be well that I should mention to you my surprise throughout this matter, at your treating it with Millais as a jest—or at least—a thing to be

[86] All quotations from Ruskin's letter of 18–19 Aug. 1854, written from Chamonix ('Chamouni'), quoted in full by Leon, *Ruskin the Great Victorian*, 198–9; see also Lutyens, *Millais and the Ruskins*, 232–3. For Ruskin's habit of writing down remarks made by his wife of which he disapproved (for his own gratification or for some ulterior self-vindication), see Garnett, *Wives and Stunners*, 101 (quoting observations by William Bell Scott of Ruskin's behaviour during the visit to the Trevelyans), and 104 (observations by the Millais brothers).
[87] *An Ill-Assorted Marriage: An Unpublished Letter by John Ruskin*, Printed by Clement Shorter (London, 1915), 25 copies. See further Dearden, 'Wise and Ruskin, III'. Ruskin perhaps suggests that Effie's (a woman's) ingratitude is worse even than is man's, as averred in *As You Like It*, II. vii. 184.   [88] Lutyens, *Millais and the Ruskins*, 241.

jested upon. Ordinary love—if true, admits not such treatment—Love which has passed the limits of conscience and prudence—still less—and even if any conceivable good could have been effected by light language—I cannot understand how you could bring yourself to use it, of an act which involved so solemn a sealing of fate—for good or evil—of such a mind as his; (wholly irrespective of any results to others).

He expressed forebodings about the new couple's future happiness, descending from his pedestal to end with a vindictive hope that she, at least, would *not* be happy ever after:

> I do not say that Millais does wrong *now*—whatever wrong he may *have* done. I am not sure but that this may indeed have been the only course open to him; that feeling he had been the Temptation to the woman, and the cause of her giving up all her worldly prospects, he may from the moment of our separation—have felt something of a principle of honour enforcing his inclination to become her protector. What the results may be, to him I cannot conjecture;—I only know that if there is anything like visible retribution in the affairs of this life there are assuredly dark hours in the distance, for her to whom he has chosen to bind his life.[89]

This, then, is the background against which Furnivall was able to negotiate arrangements for Ruskin to teach drawing at the Working Men's College, quite apart from Ruskin's own wish to benefit craftsmen and artisans and redeem workmen from the ignominy of being mere 'hands' in a factory. Teaching gave him a space to concentrate on his work, and doing what he best liked to do, and was most gifted at doing—imparting his insights to others.

Nor was this all. As is well known, Furnivall persuaded Ruskin to agree that the sixth chapter of *The Stones of Venice, On the Nature of Gothic Architecture: and herein of the True Functions of the Workman in Art*, might be excerpted from the second volume and be reprinted as a pamphlet to be given out on behalf of the Working Men's College. Ruskin agreed, provided Furnivall would make the arrangements:

> 'I don't want more in the matter of the chapter myself, having been pamphleteering, etc. as much as I care to do lately... Print the chapter as you think best, just as it is—saying, if you like, "by the author's permission for the Workmen's College." If you lose by it, I will stand the loss; if you make anything, give it to the College funds.[90]

[89] Ibid. 257-8. Letter of 3 June [1855]. FU 776.
[90] Ruskin, *Works*, xxxvi. 178. Dr John Brown had already suggested that the *Nature of*

At the packed inaugural meeting on 30 October, free copies were given out to each new arrival and also officially sold at 4d. a copy (6d. when a wrapper and woodcut were later added) for the benefit of the College.[91] Maurice was himself a draw to attract the curiosity of working men, but Furnivall felt that he was an insufficient crowd-puller on his own, and that the pamphlet would boost the men's enthusiasm. He reckoned that working men 'didn't like parsons' (which the Christian Socialists did not need to be told) and considered that Maurice had written nothing to 'fetch' them, whereas Ruskin's 'sympathetic and noble writing' and 'eloquent appreciation of their class' went down well with many of the six hundred or so who received it at the College's opening meeting in Hullah's Hall at the corner of Endell Street and Long Acre.[92] Furnivall, of course, was *parti pris*. Who would not appreciate the presentation of an attractively illustrated pamphlet by Ruskin? When puzzled visitors asked Furnivall why he was dishing out Ruskin's writing at a meeting called to hear Maurice's (not Ruskin's) inaugural lecture, Furnivall replied so they could see for themselves 'what sort of a fellow one of our Teachers was'.[93] Yet in his later account for the College's *Magazine*, he conceded something to Maurice, perhaps aware that his exaltation of Ruskin had been unfair, adding that interested readers could also judge the quality of the teaching 'by the written Address which Mr Maurice, as our Principal, delivered, almost all of which was printed in the *Morning Herald* next day'.[94]

It is not perhaps immediately clear how the pamphlet would 'fetch' the working men. Of course, it is beautifully written, and in places sublime, not least the description of a bird's view across Europe from the Mediterranean to the north. Though Ruskin wrote with the avowed intention of being as clear as possible, its argument is rich and subtle, with some diversions for all its numbered points. Readers need to get to pp. 8–9 before they find the kind of rousing statements about the

Gothic might be published as a cheap pamphlet, but, though Ruskin had asked his father to approach Smith, Elder's, nothing had come of the idea, The pamphlet's subtitle was added for the occasion; see Leon, *Ruskin, the Great Victorian*, 227.

[91] Ruskin, *On the Nature of Gothic Architecture*. Furnivall's memory may have misled him slightly: the price on the cover is stated to be 4d. See J. F. C. Harrison, *History*, 31; Munro, 'Biography', p. xxxii. Harrison does not mention that the pamphlets were sold on this occasion: 'as the visitors came up the stairs each received a copy'.. See also, Hudson, *Munby: Man of Two Worlds*, 26.

[92] From Furnivall's reminiscences, reprinted in Wise (ed.), *John Ruskin and Frederick Denison Maurice*, 52.

[93] Quoted in Colloms, *Victorian Visionaries*, 146.

[94] *Working Men's College Magazine*, 2, p. 168.

necessity of workmen to have freedom and education which Furnivall could describe as 'sympathetic and noble', and there is much about different kinds of Gothic arches. But Ruskin conveys forcefully the inchoate dissatisfaction of a factory worker: the degradation of the operative into a machine, 'which more than any evil of the time, is leading the mass of the nations everywhere into vain, incoherent, destructive struggling for a freedom of which they cannot explain the nature to themselves'. 'Never had the upper classes so much sympathy with the lower, or charity for them as they have at this day, and yet never were they so much hated by them.' But even the rousing comments and expressions of sympathy are patrician and conservative, based in Ruskin's belief that 'the nature of right freedom' would be understood only when 'men will see that to obey another man, to labour for him, yield reverence to him or to his place is not slavery. It is often the best kind of liberty'.[95] Ultimately, too, Furnivall and his gentlemanly associates—certainly not Ruskin—did not want the world turned upside down: 'though there should still be a trenchant distinction of race between nobles and commoners, there should not, among the latter, be a trenchant distinction of employment'.[96]

What is perhaps more important for the EETS's history is that, whatever it did for the working men—who were certainly appreciative—Ruskin's interpretation of 'the nature of Gothic' most certainly 'fetched' Furnivall himself, not least because of the sheer eloquence with which Ruskin articulated ideas which had become Furnivall's core beliefs, and he expressed them with a grandeur and authority which Furnivall could not hope to emulate. Thus, Ruskin commented on the snobbery of those in contemporary society who considered that manual labour need not, and should not, be informed by the intellect, describing this as a 'fatal error':

For it is no less fatal an error to despise it when thus regulated by intellect, than to value it for its own sake. We are always in these days endeavouring to separate the two; we want one man to be always thinking, and another to be always working, and we call one a gentleman, and the other an operative; whereas the workman ought often to be thinking, and the thinker often to be working, and both should be gentlemen in the best sense. As it is, we make both ungentle, the one envying the other despising his brother; and the mass of society is made up of morbid thinkers and miserable workers. Now it is only by labour that thought

[95] *On the Nature of Gothic*, 9 (§15). Paragraph numbers (omitted in the pamphlet) are included here to assist reference to *The Stones of Venice*.
[96] Ibid. 13 (§21).

can be made healthy, and only by thought that labour can be made happy, and the two cannot be separated with impunity. It would be well if all of us were good handicraftsmen in some kind, and the dishonour of manual labour done away with altogether.[97]

As a professional man's son, Furnivall had himself been brought up to 'do' for himself: to mend his own clothes, bind books, help in the dispensary, and to do manual jobs around the farm: mending horse tackle and helping to bring in the hay. But, more than this, Ruskin offered grand descriptions of what he perceived to be the 'heart' of northern European 'Gothic', though he conceded that these abstract characteristics were less immediately to be perceived in architectural design. They certainly reflected values which Furnivall prized.

Indeed, it does not seem to be going too far to suggest that the younger man, already much in thrall to Ruskin's magic, might have considered that, if these already congenial qualities were what Ruskin admired, he should cultivate them in himself. They were certainly components of Furnivall's public persona as it matured: he was, or became, an exaggerated embodiment of Ruskin's notions of the northern Gothic 'mind'. Northern Gothic style was much more rugged, awkward, and intractable than its southern counterpart, and was expressed by 'strength of will, independence of character, resoluteness of purpose, impatience of undue control, and that general tendency to set the individual reason against authority, and the individual deed against destiny'. Though ostensibly describing architecture, Ruskin goes on to describe northern Gothic as vigorous in opposition to the 'languid submission . . . of thought to tradition' exhibited by the southern European tradition, which had abandoned its strength to 'listless repose'. This Gothic is an expression of 'magnificent enthusiasm, which feels as if it never could do enough to reach the fulness of its ideal'. And, perhaps more significant still, northern Gothic, despite the objections one might reasonably advance, expressed a faith and aspiration, which though Catholic in origin, were nevertheless anticipations of 'the Protestant spirit of self-dependence and inquiry'. It expressed the 'moral habits to which England in this age owes the kind of greatness that she has', including 'accurate thought', 'stern self-reliance and sincere upright searching into religious truth', along with 'the uncalculating bestowal of the wealth of its labour'. To this already heady mix might be added Ruskin's insistence that everybody needed access to fresh

[97] Ibid. 12–13 (§21).

air and greenery. When Ruskin noted that the northern Gothic style 'can hardly be too frank in its confession of rudeness', he praised its honesty and lack of false refinement, but it would not be beyond honest Frederick Furnivall to take such a remark as a licence to extend frankness and 'rudeness' well beyond ordinary literary good manners.[98] And Ruskin's remarks on the characteristics of 'Gothic' style, as expressed in architecture, might readily confirm Furnivall in his inclination to seek out similar qualities in its writing. Furnivall's growing interest in medieval English literature reflected his search for these qualities to instruct his own age and create a bridge between the centuries.

More immediately, the event which inaugurated the College already suggests the beginnings of discord with Maurice, and conveys Furnivall's young man's assurance, based sometimes on evidence which did not entirely support him, that he knew better than Maurice what would go down well with working men. Maurice was 59; Furnivall was thirty years younger, and, however great he was agreed to be, Maurice seemed old.[99] For his part, Maurice claimed no superiority over the other members of the College except 'that I am a little older than any of them, and that circumstances have given me a more lengthened, though certainly not a more honourable, acquaintance with Colleges of one class and another, than has fallen to their lot'.[100] On the occasion of the inauguration, Furnivall was probably broadly right, though his methods of getting his own way were unscrupulous. Llewelyn Davies also recognized that Maurice was not good at unbending: 'his mental home was amongst spiritual principles, and he was accustomed to address himself to what he took to be in the minds of his hearers or readers'.[101] Litchfield, who fell under Maurice's spell, though without sharing his beliefs, conceded that 'it was not easy to know him well; he was shy, and had something of constraint in his manner'.[102] But Maurice brought dignity and charisma to the new foundation. Ruskin, however, thought that

[98] All quotations from *The Nature of Gothic*, 33–4 (§§76, 77, 78).
[99] See, for example, Munby's description of an evening at Macmillan's, where he, Daniel Macmillan, and Litchfield confidentially discussed 'old Maurice, his greatness and his doctrines. However obscure these may be to such as only understand, & do not feel, it is quite pleasant to see what an influence they have on men who, with clear heads, have also sound loving hearts: how as in MacM. they build up in a man a living, loving practical creed, all the better if perhaps it is wanting in logical symmetry'. Litchfield, who agreed with Furnivall, and had also lost his Christian faith, 'kicked & remonstrated in vain'; Hudson, *Munby: Man of Two Worlds*, 22. Munby was three years younger than Furnivall; he offers a vignette of the tensions between the teachers at the College.
[100] Styler (ed.), *Learning and Working*, 31.
[101] Davies (ed.), *Working Men's College*, 3.
[102] Litchfield, 'Beginnings', 10.

Maurice's amiable, but in his view woolly, emphasis on the College's function as what Ruskin called a mere 'collection of friendly persons' left it without a proper head.[103] Luckily, thanks to Furnivall's role as intermediary, Ruskin did not need to have much to do directly with Maurice, or others, like Kingsley or Hughes, whom he also found antipathetic, as he did the College committees: 'Maurice must manage the College, and I will teach there, minding my own business.'[104] After the inaugural lecture, he offered the drawing classes and ran them as he saw fit. Maurice may not have thought art classes important enough to interfere—or recognized that Ruskin would brook no interference.[105] He was determined to run the classes in his own way, for example telling Furnivall: 'I am very anxious to get the room left open for the men to practise in during the day. Several of them and especially the best draughtsmen of them have very earnestly pleaded for this . . . Can you tell me, or get it done for me?'[106] Furnivall, for his part, flattered and coaxed Ruskin into lecturing at the College: 'Your delightfully encouraging letter, falling precisely in with some plans I had been thinking of'. And Ruskin also agreed 'with great pleasure' to come to the tea afterwards, 'if you can arrange that I haven't to sit in a draught, I should be much obliged'.[107]

For all they were run on autocratic and idiosyncratic principles, Ruskin's classes and lectures were wildly popular, not least because, as well as his personal qualities, he also brought to the classes such valuable items as a case of tropical birds, a medieval missal, a Dürer woodcut, or his Turner drawings, as well as specially selected natural materials from the countryside. As this suggests, Ruskin's enthusiasm to impart went far beyond the usual expectations of an adult education class: the men would be invited to his house to see his Turner collection or taken in cabs out into the country on sketching expeditions.[108] Furnivall must have basked in reflected glory and self-satisfaction. Ludlow, too, took part in the classes as a pupil, until Ruskin choked him off with a task which Ludlow found 'an absolute waste of time', and suspected

---

[103] Ruskin, *Praeterita*, 453. On Maurice's vision for the College, see Litchfield, 'Beginnings', 8.   [104] Leon, *Ruskin the Great Victorian*, 228.

[105] Hilton, *John Ruskin*, i. 203. J. P. Emslie, a student at the College, gave his lively personal recollections of Ruskin's and Rossetti's art teaching, 'Art Teaching in the College in the Early Days' in Davies (ed.), *The Working Mens' College*, 34–53. See also Hilton, *The Pre-Raphaelites*, 133–6.

[106] Letter to Furnivall, 17 Nov. 1854; Ruskin, *Works*, xxxvi. 181.

[107] Letter to Furnivall, 11 Dec., 1854, ibid. 182–3.

[108] Leon, *Ruskin the Great Victorian*, 229–30.

was intended to get rid of him: 'Ruskin may have felt it inconvenient to have constantly in his class an influential colleague on the Council, though God knows that spying on him was an idea that never entered my head.' Ludlow's account was characteristically shrewd: 'Ruskin in his class was charming. So long as you were towards him in the position of a disciple,—so long as you were in the looking-up attitude, nothing could be more interesting than his conversation, more winning than his whole demeanour towards you. But you must walk on his lines, do as he bid you.' Things changed when one of his pupils ventured to introduce his own fancies into a study of a mossy branch, which Ruskin did not even notice until they were pointed out to him by 'an injudicious admirer'. 'I remember the jobation', said Ludlow; 'It was the only occasion on which I ever saw Ruskin cross in class. Without giving the young fellow the slightest credit for the real delicacy of his fancy, he rated him fiercely for daring to think that he could improve upon nature.' The student gave up the class soon afterwards.[109] Furnivall, however, was well able to maintain 'the looking-up attitude', and Ruskin carried on with the teaching from the autumn of 1854 until May 1858, again in the spring of 1860, and occasionally for a couple of years later.[110] His principles were continued by his assistant, and successor, Lowes Dickinson, a young artist who had enjoyed a Bohemian life in Italy before he was recruited for the College by Charles Mansfield. To begin with, Ruskin and Dante Gabriel Rossetti taught in the same Thursday evening classes, but after a few months Ruskin and Dickinson held a class for elementary landscape, while Rossetti held classes in figure-drawing, without benefit of instruction manuals: as he reported to W. B. Scott: 'The British mind is brought to bear on the British *mug* at once, and with results that would astonish you.'[111]

[109] Ludlow, *Autobiography*, 267. Ludlow compared the quality of the student's work with that of the illustrator, Richard ('Dicky') Doyle, who specialized in the fantastic, and had previously, and with Ruskin's approval, illustrated Ruskin's fairy story *The King of the Golden River* (1850). In *Nature of Gothic*, Ruskin stated that 'to the Gothic workman the living foliage became a subject of intense affection, and he struggled to render all its characteristics with as much accuracy as was compatible with the laws of his design and the nature of his material', but noted he was 'not infrequently tempted in his enthusiasm to transgress the one and disguise the other' (p. 30). He noted without disapproval how renderings of plant forms could be adapted to fantastic beasts like dragons (p. 43).
[110] Hilton, *John Ruskin*, i. 203–4. For another occasion when Ruskin behaved curtly to a student, see Leon, *Ruskin the Great Victorian*, 229. See the detailed account of Ruskin's teaching method at the College by Colloms, *Victorian Visionaries*, 162–4. Also Munby's eyewitness account of Ruskin's farewell address to the College, Hudson, *Munby: Man of Two Worlds*, 141–2.
[111] Colloms, *Victorian Visionaries*, 149, and see Dickinson's own account of the art

As it happens, we have an eyewitness account by a schoolboy, visiting the College with a fellow pupil on 26 October 1857, of an address which Ruskin gave.[112] The young observer candidly described his surprise at the gentlemanly appearance of the working men:

> The first part that struck me was the remarkable quality of the audience. I had expected to find myself surrounded by fustian jackets, unkempt locks, and smudgy faces; what was my surprise upon beholding broadcloth, white linen, and combed hair; in fact there was great difficulty in dividing the gentlemen, (many of whom were present out of interest in the proceedings) from the students; the intelligent character of the faces was another noticeable point; these facts are not to be wondered at, when it is considered that any working man who devotes his hours of leisure when his day's work is over to self improvement, must of necessity be above par.

This witness well conveys the glamour surrounding Ruskin as the prize attraction, who put even Maurice into the shade. And he had nothing to say about the other teachers' speeches, though all were present (and this must have included Furnivall). The substance of Ruskin's address, and his strongly held personal views, which ranged from the unpicturesque qualities of Scottish cottages compared with Swiss, the atrocities of the Indian Mutiny, and the high quality of Indian fabrics compared with its art—too abstract for Ruskin's taste—are persuasively recorded, as is the speaker's characteristically mesmeric rhetoric and dogmatism, including his blunt views on what his prospective students could (and could not) expect from his teaching:

> He would now say a few words to his pupils; he desired to have as many as possible, but he was anxious that no one should come to him under the idea that he would be able by drawing, to make his bread; such he could assure him would never be the case; to make an art a means of livelihood, it is necessary to labour from morning to night, and sometimes from night till morning; but he could hope to be able to open to them a new field of delight,—to make them see beauties which before were unobserved, and trace the finger of God where they least expected it; such was his aim, and with such expectations he hoped his pupils would meet him.

Ruskin also disapproved of the unsuitability of Malory's *Morte Darthur*, then being portrayed on the walls of the Oxford Union by his protégé:

teaching, *Working Men's College*, 34–8. Also Leon, *Ruskin the Great Victorian*, 228: as Rossetti described it, 'my class . . . is for the figure, quite a separate thing from Ruskin's who teaches foliage'.. See also Hilton, *Pre-Raphaelites*, 137–8.

[112] See Appendix 2, where this account is printed in full.

'Such is the fable which Dante Rossetti has thought best to place before the youth at Oxford.'

The whole account is a skilful exercise in *reportatio*. It is included in the young author's school magazine, *The Brucian*, where he signs himself merely 'XYZ' (the magazine's contributors were generally anonymous or wrote under a *nom de plume*). It is at least worth noting that *The Brucian* was the magazine of Henry Sweet's school, Bruce Castle, Tottenham. Sweet was 12 at the time—so could conceivably have been one of the two visitors. At least we can say that there had been an opportunity for him to have seen Furnivall for the first time. Whoever 'XYZ' was, some of his other contributions to the magazine show him to have had a keen interest in the semantic nuances of contemporary English, particularly slang, and, again, a good ear for reporting it:

Many of our young 'swells' and schoolboys interlard and render disgusting their conversation, with words as much in place as an ichthyosaurus in a swimming bath.

... a fashionable lady would not hesitate a moment in graciously informing you that she was 'devoured by ennui,' but, would require unlimited salvolatile and aromatic vinegar, on hearing her schoolboy brother make use of the monosyllable 'bosh'. Reader, point out the marks of distinction between these two words if you can?

I once heard a boy in the course of a short conversation on various topics, call a clap of thunder, a poem, the 'Leviathan,' a young lady, and a favourite dog,—'stunners'. [113]

Although Furnivall himself thought Maurice an unexciting exhibit at a gala occasion in the College, Ruskin also encouraged his disenchantment by grumbling to him about Maurice's lack of leadership: 'Hardly a fortnight has passed without some new plan. I cannot worry myself with this everlasting "What is to be done?" Maurice must manage the College, and I will teach them there, minding my own business.'[114] Ruskin's own later memories of his time at the College were harsh. It had disappointed him.[115] He did not share its principles, and its instruction was not really designed to implement the vision described in his pamphlet of labourers content to use their skill to represent truth, at

[113] *The Brucian*, no. 17, for Nov. 1857, 186–7.
[114] Letter to Furnivall, from Tunbridge Wells, 22 May 1855, Ruskin, *Works*, xxxvi. 211. However, the latest 'plan' was 'very nicely and wisely put, and very nobly felt!'.
[115] 'I am a little provoked at not having been helped in the least by the Working Men's College after I taught there for five years'; *Fors Clavigera*, Letter 37, Jan. 1874, Notes and Correspondence, 25 (*Works of John Ruskin*, xxviii).

least partially, through the naturalistic representation of living forms which was a characteristic of Gothic architecture. (Ruskin's wrath at the student who embellished the mossy branch he was supposed to represent faithfully is to be understood in this context.) He did not feel that the College advanced his aims, and when he left off teaching, he told Maurice that the reason was not lack of continuing interest, but because 'I ascertained beyond all question that the faculty which my own method of teaching chiefly regarded was necessarily absent in men trained to mechanical toil, that my words and thoughts respecting beautiful things were unintelligible when the eye had been accustomed to the frightfulness of modern city life'.[116] This pettish verdict was exaggerated: Ruskin's teaching was a coup for his students—a number of whom were skilled artisans who worked in printing, joinery, and other applied arts. They belonged to the upper working class, and already enjoyed a certain standard of literacy and cultivation.[117] A few did find Ruskin's teaching insufficiently technical for their needs—Ruskin was quite clear that his classes were not intended to produce professional artists but to endow his students with what would now be called life-skills: the capacity to draw and observe accurately.[118] His view is expressed in the quotation which heads this chapter: *The Political Economy of Art* was written in 1857, while Ruskin was still teaching for the College, but had been increasingly disenchanted, not only by the College, but by his experiences with the workmen at the Oxford Museum. It is no wonder that this book alarmed the Christian Socialists.[119]

Ruskin had recently taken up Dante Gabriel Rossetti, and it was

[116] Letter of 2 Nov. 1867, quoted by Leon, *Ruskin the Great Victorian*, 230–1. The only return the College gave him, in his view, was his recruitment of two special students whom he hoped to advance through his work, one of whom was a disappointment. *Praeterita*, 453. The other was his printer and personal publisher, George Allen, whose firm later merged with that of Sir Stanley Unwin. On Allen, and several others whose lives were permanently changed by Ruskin, see Leon, *Ruskin the Great Victorian*, 231 *et passim*; also Hilton, *John Ruskin*, i. 240, *passim*.

[117] Compare Mary Ward's description of the upper working class in the catchment area of her fictional place of adult education in 'Elgood Street', which seems very similar to Camden Town; *Robert Elsmere*, 452.

[118] As stated in his memorandum to his first class: 'The teacher of landscape drawing wishes it to be generally understood by all his pupils that the instruction given . . . is not intended either to fit them for becoming artists, or in any direct manner to advance their skill in the occupations they at present follow'; Leon, *Ruskin the Great Victorian*, 229. See also Colloms, *Victorian Visionaries*, 162, 189. In 1862, the College's *Annual Report* showed that the majority of those taking the drawing class were handicraftsmen (27 out of 41); J. F. C. Harrison, *History*, 61.

[119] See further Hilton, *John Ruskin*, i. 223–4. The work was reissued in 1880 as *A Joy for Ever (and its Price in the Market)*.

thanks to his influence and support that Rossetti, 'the head of the Pre-Raffaelite school, and the greatest living colourist', as Furnivall described him, probably quoting Ruskin's advice, took classes in the College—his students studied colour and figure drawing; Ruskin limited his classes to black and white.[120] At this time Ruskin favoured Rossetti over the other members of the Pre-Raphaelite Brotherhood.[121] Nevertheless, Ruskin's interest in medievalism and his support for the Pre-Raphaelite painters probably encouraged Furnivall to cultivate the other leading members of the group, especially William Holman Hunt and John Millais, while Ford Madox Brown took over Rossetti's figure-drawing classes in 1858.[122] Edward Burne-Jones also taught figure drawing for the College. Brown, with Christina Rossetti and other Pre-Raphaelites, had already held drawing classes for artisans in Camden Town.[123] Brown was at this time planning his picture 'Work', and told Hunt that 'he was wanting the two intellectual workers contemplating their brothers laboring with bodily strength to be Rev. F. D. Maurice and Thomas Carlyle'.[124] However, the juxtaposition of Carlyle and Maurice as the two 'brainworkers' in the picture is a less straightforward compliment than it appears. His benefactor, Thomas Plint, a Leeds businessman who had lent him money for the painting, had asked for Carlyle, and his first choice, in place of Maurice, had been Charles Kingsley.[125]

Furnivall did his best to recruit Holman Hunt as a teacher for the College after Hunt's recent return in 1856 from his expedition to the Middle East.[126] Hunt's close naturalistic attention in his paintings to details of everyday life, the symbolism in which they were suffused, the uplifting

---

[120] *Working Men's College Magazine*, 2, p. 170; Colloms, *Victorian Visionaries*, 164.

[121] 'Instead of claiming for him a sort of equality with Millais and me ... He henceforth spoke of Millais and myself ... as quite secondary in comparison with his newer *protégé*'; Hunt, *Pre-Raphaelitism*, ii. 163.

[122] See further Hilton, *Pre-Raphaelites*, 138.

[123] Colloms, *Victorian Visionaries*, 165; advertisement of classes in *Working Men's College Magazine*, 1 Aug. 1859; see also Litchfield, 'Beginnings', 5; Leon, *Ruskin the Great Victorian*, 227. Alexander has observed that 'if some fine artists taught in Great Ormond Street [the College's address], so did some great owls', apparently alluding to Furnivall (*Medievalism*, 154).

[124] Hunt, *Pre-Raphaelitism*, ii. 156. Brown referred to the two standing figures in the right-hand side of the foreground: *Work* exists in two versions: the larger (now in Manchester) was begun in 1852 and completed in 1865; the smaller (now in Birmingham) was completed in 1863. [125] Wright, 'On Seeing and Being Seen', n. 18.

[126] Letter to Furnivall, 2 May 1859, FU 402. Letter from Hunt to Furnivall, 28 Oct. 1861: 'I cannot come tonight ... I will hope to appear at eight to take the painting class'. FU 410.

subjects, including scenes from Shakespeare, and the strong religious feeling coincided greatly with what we know of Furnivall's artistic tastes and concerns. When Hunt visited the Working Men's College he was embarrassed to be pointed out by Furnivall as a prize exhibit: 'I have to confess that your allusion to me on Wednesday night when I had come as a visitor to the Working Men's College was as disagreeable to me as it was unexpected. If it had been the ghost of Tintorett that had entered, it does not seem to me that he should have provoked any personal remarks, unless he had come framed or glazed.' Furnivall pounced on him to give an address to the men about his time in the Holy Land, and Hunt agreed:

I will not forget the proposed address to the working men. I shall be glad to take an opportunity of proving my interest in the objects of your college and in a desire to aid in so good a work I shall be ready to lay aside some reserve, but I have not yet decided 'on' the best means of converting my experience in the East into an interesting form for teaching.[127]

It is clear that Furnivall was using the visit to interest Hunt, as well as Ruskin and Rossetti, in teaching for the College, as he presented Hunt with a copy of the College's circular. Hunt's initial guardedness thawed on further acquaintance, and as his work became better known, especially after 'The Finding of the Saviour in the Temple' was shown at the Royal Academy in 1859. The paint was barely dry on the canvas when Furnivall grabbed the chance to get visitors to see the painting: Hunt told him, 'it is scarcely necessary for me to say that your seventeen introductions to see my picture on the sending-in-day afforded me nothing but gratification, excepting perhaps something as amusement of an internal nature enough in the continued arrival of the notes bearing your name'.[128] Again in 1862 Hunt was welcoming a party of the Working Men and their families to visit this work. He had invited Furnivall to make up a party with the Working Men, 'with their wives, sisters, sons and daughters—the last two, of course, in moderation', to see the painting in the Bond Street gallery.[129] Arthur Munby, teacher of Latin in the

[127] Quotations from Hunt's letter to Furnivall of 2 May 1859, FU 402.
[128] Ibid. Hunt, *Pre-Raphaelitism*, ii. 192–3.
[129] Letter of 31 Mar. 1862, FU 412: 'I intended to ask you to make a party to come here to see the Finding in the Temple one Sunday but I find now it is here the draftsman is so much driven for time that he cannot even give up that day from work—it will return to Bond St about the end of April. That locality will I dare say be more convenient to you all, so I have less compunction in deferring the invitation for the present'. The painting was being drawn in black and white for the use of the engraver: *Pre-Raphaelitism*, ii. 193. See

College, also 'walked up to Bond Street to see Holman Hunt's "Christ in the Temple." He having reserved today for the Working Men's College, of whom there were many present. As for the picture, I cannot trust myself to speak of it, writing hurriedly; it is unique, and simply wonderful.'[130] Hunt's special invitation to the members of the Working Men's College was a great honour: the show was attracting eight hundred to a thousand visitors daily, and even the Prince Consort was unable to get near the painting. It was removed from the gallery by Royal Command for the Queen to see it.[131]

FURNIVALL'S TEACHING OF ENGLISH LITERATURE

Furnivall's own teaching for the College in English would directly influence the course of his own future literary career. When he was a young man, his experience of English literature had consisted mostly of light reading, with occasional forays into Shakespeare, before his friendship with the men in Maurice's circle led him to read their books and pursue theological and economic questions more systematically. He sought advice from Maurice's close friend Samuel Clark, of the Battersea Training College, an excellent teacher, who held the study of English literature to be as valuable as the classics for imparting cultural values, especially to the working men.[132] Clark recommended Shakespeare:

I have found the great Tragedies more satisfactory than the Historical Plays. With your class of students, I should be inclined to suggest Julius Caesar—but I should not press the point against Hamlet.

My mode of proceeding is to make such students read, in turn, a short passage & then paraphrase it. As far as I can, I then point out the perfections of the Poet's language compared with the paraphrase. I explain obscurities, notice various readings and interpose remarks on syntax and Etymology—You should go on much in the same manner as a class in the University reading Sophocles or Aeschylus.

also letter of 14 July 1862, FU 413. Hunt later relaxed the numbers, telling Furnivall: 'As many as like can go . . . you have nothing to consider but how to accommodate your own people'. Letter of 19 July 1862, FU 414.

[130] Hudson, *Munby: Man of Two Worlds*, 59, diary entry for Sunday, 6 May 1860. It was at the time of the exhibition that Thomas Hughes and his wife became Hunt's 'valued friends'; *Pre-Raphaelitism*, ii. 203.

[131] Diana Holman Hunt, *My Grandfather, His Wives and Loves*, 213.

[132] William Benham, revd. M. C. Curthoys, 'Clark, Samuel (1810–1875)', *ODNB*. Maurice's letters to Clark had been published in 1837 as *The Kingdom of Christ . . . in Letters to a Member of the Society of Friends*.

As regards materials, I read all the notes I can get. I have not the Variorum Shakspere, but I sometimes get access to it. I have Malone, Knight and Singer. The first is by far the most honest, the most copious and the most useful.

If I could have my way, with plenty of time, I should take every student, in the same manner through 2 books of Milton (or about the same bulk from his smaller works) a play of Shakspere's, Sir T. More's Richard III, Chaucer's Prologue or Palamon & Arcite & and introduction of Robert of Gloucester. I think, if I could add to this list, that I would preface some of Chaucer's Prose (e.g. the Parson's Tale) to Sir John Maundeville.[133]

Clark's 'mode of proceeding' and syllabus gave valuable hints in which one can see in outline the essentials of just about all Furnivall's later educational and publishing initiatives, especially in the priority given to 'Shakspere'. Furnivall's job was to be a commentator, focusing on philological details, paraphrasing in a manner that drew attention to the linguistic differences (not least in register) from the originals, explaining the texts' 'obscurities', recommending approved commentators, and above all, making those texts which were an essential part of the literary heritage widely accessible, especially those parts of it which spoke to the reader's own contemporary concerns.

Furnivall was also influenced by William Gaskell's account of his teaching of the subject at the Manchester Working Men's College. As Furnivall reported to Litchfield,

His class on that subject is the most numerously attended one in the Manchester College; and I have long heard of the great success of his ladies' and other classes in English Literature. Our classes at the London College in it have not succeeded... It would be a great help to every teacher of this subject, if Mr. Gaskell would tell us how he teaches it... though we all know how much his time is taken up in his efforts to rid his city of the dirt and smoke and the ignorance and sin that are in it.[134]

Gaskell told him that he spent the first term teaching the history and composition of the language, which 'proved so interesting to the generality of the students that I was induced to go somewhat more minutely in the subject than I at first intended'.[135] The study of literary texts began with the Anglo-Saxon period. Spalding's *History of English Literature* furnished passages for reading, with commentary on the more remarkable words and their derivations.[136] Etymology was also a conspicuous

---

[133] Letter of 1 Dec. 1856, FU 185. See also Vernon Lushington, 'On the Study of Shakspere', *Working Men's College Magazine*, 2, pp. 179-8 (1 Dec. 1860).
[134] Letter printed in the *Working Men's College Magazine*, 2, p. 72 (1 Feb. 1859).
[135] Ibid.   [136] *Working Men's College Magazine*, 1, pp. 89-90 (1 May 1859).

part of Furnivall's grammar teaching: as he responded to a student's question about the examination for the certificate in competence:

> Perhaps one fourth of the questions are etymological,—but these latter never comprise anything which has not been dealt with in the course of the year's lessons ... Mr M(urray) would apparently define Grammar as the art of using words 'with propriety'. Well: then is it not desirable to know what a thing is before you begin to use it? In other words, must not Etymology, which teaches you what words are, come before (or be included in) Grammar, which teaches you what to do with them?[137]

Furnivall's quest for literary texts which would entertain the men, empower them in their own literary heritage, give them a sense of their place in English history, and address their social concerns led him to introduce into his teaching some of the early English writing to which the Philological Society was at the same time introducing him. He taught 'English Literature—to the Reformation', using as a textbook Spalding's *History of English Literature*.[138] Following this, he ran classes on Tennyson, followed on the same morning by his classes on 'Piers Ploughman; Chaucer'.[139] Spalding's *History* made *Piers* sound irresistible for Furnivall's tastes and purposes: the author, while recognizing the perplexities which still surround *Piers Plowman*, and the poem's acknowledged difficulty, awarded it a pre-eminent position as a leading poem of the fourteenth century: 'Highest by far in point of genius, as well as most curious for its illustrations of manners and opinions ... the poetical vigour of many of the passages is extraordinary, not only in the satirical vein which colours most of them, but in bursts of serious feeling and sketches of external nature.'[140]

Genius, social customs, vigour, serious feeling, and representations of the natural world were all qualities to which Furnivall was drawn.

---

[137] Ibid., 106 (1 June 1859). The College's advertisements of its classes show that Furnivall taught English Grammar in two separate sections, 'Section 1, Etymology' and 'Section 2, Elementary' (see e.g. the edition of 1 Apr. 1859). The teaching of etymology was doubtless facilitated by the publication of Hensleigh Wedgwood's *Dictionary* two years earlier. In Feb. and Mar. 1859, the grammar classes consisted of 'Analysis of Sentences' and 'Correction of Mistakes'. 'Mr Murray' was Lindley Murray (1745–1826), author of the immensely influential *An English Grammar* (first published 1895).

[138] As advertised in the *Working Men's College Magazine*, Feb. and Mar. 1859, referring to 'Spaulding's History': Spalding, *The History of English Literature*.

[139] As advertised in the *Working Men's College Magazine*, Apr. and May 1859. Tennyson was taught between 8 and 9 on Friday mornings, followed by Langland and Chaucer between 9 and 10.

[140] Spalding, *History of English Literature*, 74; Chaucer is described on pp. 77–83. Extracts from Chaucer were included, 127–31, but it seems that Spalding considered Langland's language too antiquated and difficult for beginners.

More controversially, he also introduced men of the working classes to contemporary literature, including modern novels which might deal with sensitive subjects: when staying at Denmark Hill, he gave presents of books to the servants, including a gift of Elizabeth Gaskell's *Ruth* (1853)—which dealt with the subject of illegitimacy—to Ruskin's valet, Crawley, who read it aloud to his fellow-servants.[141] Furnivall was not, however, alone in the College in seeking to broaden the men's appreciation of literary and artistic culture. There was also a steady demand for Arthur Munby's classes in Latin, instruction which was perhaps felt to advance the men more towards equality with the gentlemen teachers, though it was not offered for this reason of prestige. Godfrey Lushington (friend of Ludlow, and a teacher at the Working Men's College, as well as Fellow of All Souls College, Oxford), in the course of a wide-ranging series of arguments, defended the teaching of Latin as a means to acquiring an understanding of how language works, with a nod to recent developments in linguistic study: 'It is only lately however that the science of grammar has been acknowledged.' He also commented on other exciting contemporary aspects of language study, in particular its affinities with the geological study which the men at the College were so actively pursuing. 'Philology', said Lushington,

is doing for language what geology is doing for the earth. Geologists, by examining existing strata, seek to reproduce the ancient world as it was, to exhibit the various phases through which it has passed, and to call up again the forms and life of defunct animal creation. So philologists, by the comparison of different languages investigate the birth and growth of language and thought; work out the pedigree of the family of tongues, tracing it through various generations up to one common head; reconstruct the primitive language, not a word of which remains; and penetrating into pre-historic times, show the existence and even the habits and thought of a nation whose very name has perished.[142]

The comparison was an inevitable one. J. B. Mayor, Fellow of St John's College, Cambridge, who would in due course become an editor for the EETS, and who had taught Latin at the Cambridge Working Men's College, developed the theme further, while somewhat deprecating as

---

[141] See Hilton, *John Ruskin*, i. 223. Crawley's letter of thanks was tactful: 'The language is beautiful and deeply interesting and the morals it sets forth are very good and i [*sic*] trust that all who reads it will view it as a lesson and profit by so doing'. Ruskin's mother, at least, is unlikely to have approved of the gift.

[142] 'Shall We Learn Latin?', *Working Men's College Magazine*, 2, pp. 71–5 (1 May 1860), continued in the next issue (1 June, 1860), 93–7. Godfrey Lushington was Vernon Lushington's twin brother: both had been introduced to Christian Socialist ideas by the Macmillans, in Cambridge.

a waste of effort the quest to find the ultimate roots of words, even beyond Indo-European.[143] Munby, like Furnivall, used the opportunity offered by language teaching to introduce more general topics to his students, whom he described as 'all very good & pleasant fellows, and especially the three first, intelligent and apt'. At a tea party, Munby showed them 'photographs & pictures and books, and we talked—of the Mort d'Arthur and the Idylls of the King, or Norse mythology, whereof I told them something, and of general social subjects'.[144] Furnivall was also promoting Tennyson's poems on medieval subjects: the beginnings of the Early English Text Society are not so far away.

In the meanwhile, since the College was meant to offer an education for life, not merely applied knowledge to enable the men to get higher wages, and since it was a place of mutual learning, its social life was a vital part of its *raison d'être*. In the natural order of things, at the start of the College 'the furthering of its social life fell mainly into the hands of the youngest unmarried members of the Council and some of the leading students: Furnivall, Litchfield, Standring and Tansley were at the College five nights a week'.[145] Indeed, the names of the leading students tend to recur in memoirs of the College's early years— it was noted that the College's social life tended to be dominated 'by the formation of a sort of inner circle in the College life to which it was difficult for new-comers to gain access'.[146] The members of this inner circle were also Furnivall's particular friends. Furnivall, ever fond of 'chat', and with his experiences of taking vanloads of working families, including the ballast-heavers, to have picnics in Epping Forest, was the ideal organizer, especially since he lived nearby in lodgings in Hatton Garden, to which he invited his students. He welcomed and advised new students, introducing them to others. Since his first principle was that 'every man was to be treated as an equal and a friend, and to be trusted till he showed himself unworthy of trust'. his popularity with the men was assured.[147]

---

[143] 'What to Learn: A Plea for Latin', *Working Men's College Magazine*, 2, pp. 125–9 at 127 (1 Aug. 1860).

[144] Hudson, *Munby: Man of Two Worlds*, 80, diary entry for Wednesday, 24 Oct. 1860. The three favoured students included George Tansley (draper's assistant), also taught by Furnivall.

[145] 'Social Life of the College', 54. Colloms, *Victorian Visionaries*, 167. J. F. C. Harrison, *History*, 73. John Roebuck, 'Reminiscences of an Old Student', in Davies (ed.), *Working Men's College*, 64–5.

[146] J. A. Forster, 'A Transition Period: R. B. Litchfield', in Davies (ed.), *Working Men's College*, 100–28 at 101.

[147] 'Social Life of the College', 54–5.

PLATE 1. Frederick Denison Maurice
© National Portrait Gallery

PLATE 2. Herbert Coleridge (1863). Murray Papers, MS 31
© Bodleian Libraries, University of Oxford

PLATE 3. William Alexander Dalziel (1862). Murray Papers, MS 31
© Bodleian Libraries, University of Oxford

PLATE 4. Eleanor Nickell Dalziel, with F. J. Furnivall
and Arthur Cattlin (1862). Murray Papers, MS 31
© Bodleian Libraries, University of Oxford

PLATE 5. Captain George Morris Hantler, 19th Middlesex Rifles (1863). Murray Papers, MS 31
© Bodleian Libraries, University of Oxford

PLATE 6. Hensleigh Wedgwood (1863). Murray Papers, MS 31
© Bodleian Libraries, University of Oxford

PLATE 7. Henry Benjamin Wheatley (1864). Murray Papers, MS 31
© Bodleian Libraries, University of Oxford

Plate 8. Edmund Brock (1866). Murray Papers, MS 31
© Bodleian Libraries, University of Oxford

6

Slander and Strife: Disagreements within the Working Men's College

> Many a man desires a reformation of an abuse . . . He may seem to the world to be nothing else than a bold champion for the truth and a martyr to free opinion, when he is just one of those persons whom the competent authority ought to silence.
> John Henry Newman, *Apologia pro Vita Sua*, 'General Answer to Mr. Kingsley', 26 May 1864

FURNIVALL AND THE FOURTH COMMANDMENT: BREAKING THE SABBATH

The beginnings of disharmony between Furnivall and the College's governing body were already apparent in Furnivall's confidence (not altogether misplaced) that he knew better than the College authorities what working men appreciated. He had worked alongside labourers on his father's farm, while Maurice fretted about 'How is the chasm between Priests and People to be filled up?', answering his own question by advising the priests to 'look for the causes of it in themselves and in their unbelief'.[1] This was not a solution to inspire self-confidence in the College's head when dealing with a turbulent teacher, and Furnivall and Maurice clashed on other concerns as well.

Thus there was an obscure disagreement over a Mr Beecher, apparently a student at the College, who may have paid unwanted attention to one of the women students. This necessitated a messy enquiry as to whose word was to be believed, and who was capable of inventing falsehoods, which seems to have grown into a dispute about logic. Furnivall, always ready to side with the students, seems to have flown to Beecher's defence, and chose to take offence when Maurice described him as Beecher's 'procurator', which Furnivall seems to have misunderstood as 'procurer'. Maurice apologized, while putting him straight:

> I am sorry that my manner is so unfortunate & gives so much offence. I said nothing about Mr. Beecher which I would not have said to him. I thought you knew that a Procurator among the Romans was a man who undertook the

[1] Maurice, *Life of Maurice*, ii. 232.

prosecution of a person whom he secretly befriended; so, as you undertook to attack Logic, being its ally, I called you by that name.[2]

One way or another, women were in the background of most of the arguments between Furnivall and Maurice. Although the College's name declared its constituency of working *men*, Maurice's outline plan for the prospective College expressed the hope ultimately to provide teaching also for women and boys. The founders and early teachers, Maurice, Llewelyn Davies, and Furnivall among them, were in sympathy with education of women and girls.[3] Such classes followed reasonably from the addition of a girls' class to the school in Little Ormond Yard, and the first classes for women were begun in January 1855, and, from April 1858, there was also a girls' school from 10 a.m. to 1 p.m. daily. Some in the College also believed that women should be admitted to the ordinary classes. However, the classes were discontinued in 1860, though the question of what to do for women did not go away.[4]

The disagreement between Maurice and Furnivall came to a head in 1857–8. The College needed to move in 1857, after the lease of the premises in Red Lion Square expired. A property was purchased in Great Ormond Street by taking on a mortgage, but Maurice also contributed a very generous gift of £500.[5] By this act of personal commitment, Maurice thus helped to make the College's future more secure at the very time when his own headship of it was to be challenged in a dispute over its religious and social ethos. While Maurice prescribed an awakening conscience to priests and Sunday observance to the working men, Furnivall's answer (for the men at least) was—beer.

The College's Council had not allowed the men to have beer for their supper and did not permit the College's reading party to meet in the College on Sunday evenings. Accordingly, the men, 'some of them the nicest fellows in the College', were 'driven' to a small public house nearby, 'where many jolly evenings were spent'. The grievance caused by this displacement was additionally provocative, since, in the year of

---

[2] Letter to Furnivall, 19 Mar. [1856], FU 569; see also letter of 11 Oct. [c.1856?], and perhaps 15 Dec. [1857?], FU 570, 572.

[3] See Furnivall, 'History', *Working Men's College Magazine*, 2, p. 147; see also Furnivall's description of the provisions for teaching women and girls by Maurice and his associates, ibid. 191.

[4] J. F. C. Harrison, *History*, 107. See also Maurice's letter to Furnivall, 27 Feb. [1857], describing the arrangements for the women's classes at the time of the move to Great Ormond Street, FU 571.

[5] Litchfield, 'Beginnings', 5. This was the College's second address, which it occupied for nearly fifty years before its removal to its present site in Crowndale Road, Camden Town, in 1905; Colloms, *Victorian Visionaries*, 262.

the College's foundation, unpopular government legislation had strictly limited pub opening hours: John Wilson-Patten's 'Sunday Beer Act' had closed drinking places on Sundays between 2.30 p.m. and 6.00 p.m., and after 10.00 p.m.—the four hours in the evening were the only time available to them.[6] And, as Furnivall phrased it, the reading party 'had to take refuge in such coffee-shops and public-houses as would give them tea and the use of a room for a small payment'. Litchfield would give a much more temperate account of these gatherings, but Furnivall thought Maurice was being unreasonable, as well as a spoilsport.[7] When the aptly named John Sherren Brewer (also a parson) became Vice-Principal and took over Maurice's duties he was more accommodating and, as quoted by Furnivall, told him to take a room outside College for the Sunday reading party, 'but don't talk publicly or make a fuss about it'. Furnivall approved of this compromise on the q.t. (which also diminished Maurice's authority as Principal): 'As a Yorkshire farmer's son he liked his glass of beer, and was for our men having their glass of beer in the College too'.[8]

One can see why Maurice found Furnivall increasingly tiresome personally as well as a troublemaker. There is more than a grain of self-exculpation in these brazen anecdotes, written down many years after Maurice's death: others beside himself connived at the flouting of the College's rules by a teacher and member of its Council, they were jolly good fellows, and College stalwarts—and Furnivall is careful to use the passive voice and thus disclaim any personal responsibility. (Yet Furnivall's agency is implied by his seeking of retrospective permission from Brewer.) Others did not recollect these events as quite so creditable to Furnivall, nor did they see him as the leading promoter of the College's jollifications: Furnivall must have been considerably

---

[6] See B. Harrison, 'The Sunday Trading Riots of 1855', 220; Valpy-French, *Nineteen Centuries of Drink in England*, 361-3; The Wilson-Patten Act, more properly 'A Bill for further regulating the sale of beer and other liquors on the Lord's Day', only lasted for a few months before it was superseded by Henry Berkeley's 'New Beer Bill', which extended opening hours until 11 p.m.

[7] See Litchfield, 'Beginnings', 8. After the College's move to Great Ormond Street in 1857 there was a dedicated coffee room in the building for light refreshments and social gathering: Roebuck, 'Reminiscences', 71-2.

[8] 'Social Life of the College', 55 n. The Revd John Sherren Brewer was a lecturer in classics at KCL, and Maurice's friend; Brenda Colloms notes that Brewer's was a 'thankless appointment', though he did his best (*Victorian Visionaries*, 207). Furnivall does not say what was read at the reading party but notes that a prominent student of the College (who stayed with it for forty-seven years), George Tansley, 'was our best reader of poetry'. On Tansley, see C. B. Lucas's account in Davis (ed.), *Working Men's College*, 129-80; also J. F. C. Harrison, *History*, 112-36.

irritated by Litchfield's published memories of Hughes's dominance in the College, not so much as a teacher, but as a genial companion and presence:

> I shall always remember him best as presiding over a weekly gathering of teachers and students in the coffee room, whereat everybody talked to everybody, and songs and recitings of poetry went round the table. It was rather like what used to be called a 'harmonic meeting', save that there was no drink better than tea... it was the solid strength and simple manliness of Hughes's character, and not only the genial temper shown in these convivial meetings that won him the attachment which made him a governing influence.[9]

It may be noted in parenthesis that the recitations included poems by Shakespeare, Tennyson, Milton, and Hood—probably testimony to the way in which Furnivall's own occasional excursions into English literature as recorded in his diaries (which note all four writers) had found their way into his English classes, and thence into the performing repertoire of his two most prominent students, George Tansley and John Roebuck.[10] Hughes compounded his offence in Furnivall's eyes by achieving fame in 1857 as the author of *Tom Brown's Schooldays*. Harrison speculated that probably a large measure of its sweeping success 'was that it retained the gusto of one who, all his life, remained more of a schoolboy than most men'.[11] The same was said of Furnivall: in some ways the two men were too alike really to take to each other. Furnivall's fame as a literary figure came much later, and Litchfield did not acknowledge it even then, merely noting that it would not be of material interest to single out among the teachers those 'who have become eminent in various lines of life'.[12] Furnivall told his version of events two years later than Litchfield, and by this time he as much as Litchfield was a College stalwart, and, in Furnivall's case, a fixture with his own unof-

---

[9] Litchfield, 'Beginnings', 8. Hughes took a full part in the singing. See also the account of these Wednesday 'smoking concerts' by Roebuck, 'Reminiscences', 71–3.

[10] Maurice envisaged from the start that teaching of the English language would incorporate literature: 'We shall have lessons on *Language*, beginning always with our own. We shall speak of the sources from which its words come: and of its Grammar. These lessons can only be profitable if they are illustrated from good books. Hence they will lead to lessons on English *Literature*, and those to lessons on *Reading* and *Elocution*'. Circular, quoted by Furnivall, 'History', *Working Men's College Magazine*, 2, p. 167.

[11] J. F. C. Harrison, *History*, 38. For Hughes's own comments, see Nowell-Smith (ed.), *Letters to Macmillan*, 30–3. Hughes had some problems with 'Mrs Grundy' and 'damns', though he noted that 'boys then swore abominably. I did myself until I was in the Fifth'; letter of 18 Feb. 1857 (p. 31). The success of *Tom Brown's Schooldays* closely followed the popular acclaim for Kingsley's *Westward Ho!* (1855).

[12] Litchfield, 'Beginnings', 9.

ficial personal seat in the common room.[13] He was seeking to reclaim his personal glory as a 'father' of the College. Moreover, there is again some massaging of the story of the beer in his version of events: though Furnivall cast himself as one with the common man who liked his beer, he was himself of an Evangelical background and a teetotaller, known for his vast consumption of tea.[14] The reading party drank tea; he organized nine-penny teas on Fridays, followed by songs and recitations, and he urged all the other teachers to entertain their students with yet more tea. His later devotion to the ABC café and his entertaining there had its origins in these tea parties.

Apparently, Furnivall felt that still more self-justification was needed. He described how a former student, some thirty-five years after he had attended Furnivall's grammar class and now himself a lithographer, as well as a teacher of drawing at the College, approached him in the street in Camden Town to tell him how well he had got on in life. He put his prosperity down to one of Furnivall's tea parties: 'You askt me to tea with some of the others. I'd never been in a gentleman's room before, and when I came out, after seeing your pictures, books, and chairs, I said to myself, "I'll have as good a room as that." And now I've got a better'.[15] Furnivall called this bluff story of social mobility 'cheering', and it was doubtless broadly true (though maybe touched up in the telling to highlight the social moral). He was putting his memories together for the College's Jubilee in 1904, when it was moving to its new building in Camden Town. Though there may have been numerous lithographers in that district of London, comparatively few had taught art at the College, though a surprising number of its art students went on to make successful careers in various capacities, including printing and engraving, the best-known being perhaps George Allen.[16] Another was William Alexander Dalziel, Furnivall's future brother-in-law, an engraver and illustrator, who became a student teacher at the College after

---

[13] Colloms, *Victorian Visionaries*, 263.
[14] Litchfield (who supported the move) noted that 'years passed before we ventured, after immense debate, on what was thought at that time a daring measure in an institution of our sort, allowing a man to have a glass of beer with his supper'. 'Beginnings', 8. Munro describes an occasion when Furnivall, describing himself as 'a scandalized teetotaller', had to stay outside a tavern while the men with him on one of his College Sunday excursions had biscuits and beer inside; 'Biography', p. xxix (from the *People's Paper*, 21 Aug. 1858).
[15] Furnivall, 'Social Life of the College', 56.
[16] See the reminiscences of Lowes Dickinson and J. P. Emslie in Davies (ed.), *Working Men's College*, 34–8, 39–53. As Dickinson noted, 'Many of the Art students became teachers ... there were, I believe, twelve or thirteen students who became assistant teachers, and some of them Visitors'; p. 37.

attending Furnivall's grammar classes and being examined by him for his certificate of competency.[17] Printers and engravers were a significant, if not large, group among the College's students, and it is not to be wondered that Furnivall met one in Camden, especially given the proximity of the Camden Press, created by the Dalziel brothers, George and Edward (not apparently related to William Alexander Dalziel).[18] The acquaintance's apparent boastfulness about having surpassed his teacher in worldly goods is not surprising, if perhaps not the height of good manners, when it is remembered that Furnivall was a poor man by that time, though in the speaker's view, once a gentleman always a gentleman, unlike himself.

Maurice was clear from the start that, though sociability was a necessary part of a College, 'we do not design our College for a place of amusement', though music teaching might permissibly lead to informal concerts.[19] If Sunday tea parties, harmless in themselves, caused an initial skirmish with Maurice, he viewed Sunday excursions with the men as flagrant breaches of the College rules and its ethos as a Christian Socialist foundation. This applied whatever one's views of the fourth commandment, and even though the College was undenominational, with no religious tests. The parties distressed and angered Maurice, and nearly caused his resignation.

Furnivall, in his version of events, does his best to cover himself with airy bravado. By 1904, most of the other founder members were dead, but Ludlow still remembered the College's early years, and himself contributed the account of its origins to the same commemorative volume. Each was anxious not to revive old hostilities in public on this occasion; Furnivall, as Ludlow knew, always retained respect for him, singling him out with another teacher, Eugène Oswald, as 'especially happy' because of their French upbringing, and resulting 'freedom from English class-prejudice'.[20] But Ludlow never forgave Furnivall for his treatment of Maurice, as he admitted in his autobiography (not published until 1981). Yet, 'whilst I have never spared him, I do not recollect that he

[17] *Working Men's College Magazine*, 1, p. 76 (Supplement, 1 Apr. 1859), where Dalziel's occupation is recorded as 'messenger'. He is described as 'an engraver and illustrator' by Brenda Colloms, herself a lecturer in the Working Men's College. See *Victorian Visionaries*, 189.

[18] The College kept records of its students' occupations: thus, in 1858, out of a body of 242, eight were draughtsmen, lithographers, and engravers, and a further five were wood-turners or engravers. *Working Men's College Magazine*, 4 (1 Apr. 1859), 78. On the Camden Press, see below.

[19] Circular, quoted by Furnivall, 'History', *Working Men's College Magazine*, 2, p. 167.

[20] 'Social Life of the College', 56. Colloms, *Victorian Visionaries*, 167–8.

has ever attacked me'. Ludlow also thought Furnivall was an unreliable reporter, and that, in old age, his memory was letting him down: 'he has for many years been incapable of giving a correct account of anything he has been connected with, and latterly a failing memory has rendered his utterances still more untrustworthy'.[21] It has to be admitted that Furnivall's reminiscences about the College are not entirely reliable, and tend to soothe his vanity. But he was not an introspective man, apt to blame himself, like Maurice.

Before plunging with obvious relief into hearty reminiscences about the College's rowing, the accuracy of which there is no reason to doubt, Furnivall did his best to justify himself in his deliberately sketchy account of the Sunday excursions, with their emphasis on camaraderie and mutual understanding arrived at between those who would not otherwise mix. He clearly felt uncomfortable, if defiant:

> I think our Sunday rowing and walks, mixt later with the girls and men of Litchfield's singing-class brought those who took part in them more closely together than anything else. When folk have a whole day in the open, with 'pitches' on the grass, discussing all possible subjects, and hearing about one another's lives, they get really intimate. And when you've had a hard spell against wind and tide, or a 40-mile walk, with men who put their backs and legs into their work, you get to respect them.[22]

All members of the Christian Socialist fellowship, as well as people like Ruskin, were anxious to find ways to allow working people and their families in the cities opportunities to enjoy fresh air and exercise in the countryside, even by proxy if visits outside central London could not be arranged. Thus, Kingsley supported the creation of the National Gallery for the people to enjoy at least pictures of the countryside: 'How many a man who cannot spare time for a daily country walk, may well slip into the National Gallery . . . for ten minutes. That garden, at least, flowers as gaily in winter as in summer.'[23] Ruskin's classes brought bits of the countryside into the room. The remarkable Octavia Hill, the housing reformer and advocate of fresh air, who, like her mother, Caroline Southwood Hill, admired and supported Maurice,

---

[21] *Autobiography*, 132. In his preliminary notes to the autobiography Ludlow reveals that he completed it on the 29 Oct. 1899, in his 79th year (p. xxvii).

[22] 'Social Life of the College', 56-7.

[23] From the first number of *Politics for the People*, 6 May 1848; *Politics for the People*, 5. Kingsley planned a series of contributions on this subject; see also no. 3, for 20 May, pp. 38-41 (on Bellini). See also F. E. Kingsley (ed.), *Charles Kingsley: His Letters and Memories*, 67-9.

taught women's classes at the Working Men's College, and would become a founder of the National Trust.²⁴ While still a teenager she had managed a semi-cooperative, financed by Vansittart Neale, and she was an enthusiastic admirer of both Furnivall and Maurice. Her description of them at a 'conversazione' in the College conveys her sense of how the personalities of the two, contrasting as they were, dominated the scene, the one, shy and habitually withdrawn in company, the other in his element, here, there, and everywhere:

> There stood Mr. Maurice, his grave face lighted by a smile of delight and sweetness in the realization of much that he had worked for. And here and there and everywhere glanced the fire of Mr. Furnivall's intensely joyous eyes, delighting in all things, seeing everyone, utterly unconscious of himself, doing all that was needed, his soul dwelling continually in sympathy as deep as it is strong.²⁵

Undoubtedly both portraits, especially that of Furnivall, are coloured by the observer's ardent religious principles and youthful enthusiasm. The letter was written in 1857 before the breach between the two men later that year. She joined one of Furnivall's Sunday excursions for the College students and thoroughly enjoyed it, though her conscience pricked her, and she was persuaded by Maurice not to go on others.²⁶ Seven years later the 'seraph' had become a fallen angel: 'It was very queer to meet Mr. Furnivall after all these years, and he is not the least changed. Just that seraph brow, and sweetly happy mouth, and the great dark eyes, and just that provoking, self-willed, arbitrary way of behaving.'²⁷

The trouble was, when most men were working a six-day week, finding time and opportunity to go out for long walks in the countryside unless excursions were organized for them on Sundays. The subject was an inflammatory one in the mid-1850s, and the problems in the Working Men's College should be understood in this broader context. The sense of class division was exacerbated by the belief that gentlemen and ladies could enjoy themselves on Sundays in ways not so readily accessible to working people, though Furnivall's diaries show his own Sundays as a young gentleman to have been rather dull. Evangelical writers came down heavily on young working people with a little money after payday, and only Sundays available to spend it on pleasure. *The Young Man from Home* deprecates those 'alluring baits for sabbath-breaking':

²⁴ See Octavia Hill, *Life of Octavia Hill*, ed. Maurice; Gillian Darley, 'Hill, Octavia (1838–1912)', *ODNB*.
²⁵ Octavia Hill, *Octavia Hill: Early Ideals*, ed. Maurice, 37. Letter of 30 May 1857 to Mary Harris. ²⁶ See Colloms, *Victorian Visionaries*, 120 (*passim*); also 181.
²⁷ Hill, *Octavia Hill: Early Ideals*, 78–9, letter [1864] to Mary Harris.

the nocturnal orgies of certain walks and bowers in the vicinity of Lambeth, the tea-gardens, the parks and the steam-boats to Richmond, to Gravesend, or to Greenwich, by which millions . . . are caught in the snares of Satan. 'What harm can there be,' it is said, 'after we have been shut up all the week in a close street, hard at work, to go out on a fine summer day, to enjoy the clear sunshine, the fresh air, and the beauties of creation? Surely our Maker is not such a hard master as to refuse us gratifications so innocent and so healthful.' And thus sabbath-breaking, which is a manifest violation of the laws of God, is defended by an appeal to his goodness.[28]

The preciousness of Sunday as the one day of rest and recreation in the week for working people is pitiably evoked by the opening of one of the popular novels Furnivall read when he had recently left home: Samuel Warren's *Ten Thousand A-Year*. The hero of the story, a young shopworker, lies in one Sunday morning in a dismal back attic. He apostrophizes the church bells: 'Do you think *I'm* going to be mewed up in church on this the only day out of the seven I've got to sweeten myself in, and sniff fresh air?' He rigs himself out in his absurd Sunday finery, like a young swell, hoping to ogle a rich young lady in Hyde Park.[29] There seemed to be one law for the rich and another for the poor: promenading in the Park was seen as an upper-class privilege (and one enjoyed by Furnivall in his social visits to the Ruskins), and it provoked working-class activism in 1855, the year of the Sunday League's establishment. In June, there were public disturbances and rioting on five successive Sundays in Hyde Park after posters advertised a meeting in the Park 'to see how religiously the aristocracy is observing the Sabbath'. The disorder had been inflamed by the passing of the Wilson-Patten Act in the previous year, and the attempt by Lord Robert Grosvenor to bring in his Sunday Trading Bill (1855), which aimed to forbid all Sunday trading in London, but which was withdrawn following the riots.[30] Furnivall's siding with the working men on the Sunday question is a sign of how far his opinions had changed from his days as a student from a middle-class Evangelical background. And many of the men, London artisans, came from a background in which, as Mrs Humphry Ward said, 'the Church has practically no hold whatever . . . Towards religion in general the prevailing attitude is one of indifference tinged with hostility.'[31]

Following the anti-sabbatarian activism of 1855, it is not surprising that the sabbath question should arise in the College in the following

[28] James, *Young Man from Home*, 25–6.
[29] *Ten Thousand A-Year*, 1–9 (p. 3).
[30] B. Harrison, 'Sunday Trading Riots', 220–4.
[31] M. Ward, *Robert Elsmere*, 453–4.

year. Some of the men announced in the course of a meeting 'in a rather aggressive manner, that they preferred taking a walk on Sunday to attending a place of worship, finding that they were the better for making that choice'.[32] (This was also Furnivall's defence: the men's health benefited, and such innocent entertainments promoted an *esprit de corps*.) Open-air events organized by the College could and did take place on other days of the week: there was, for example, a fondly remembered outing in 1856 to Wimbledon, at the invitation of Hughes and Ludlow, at which one of the men sent up to Furnivall an enormous caterpillar on a plate as 'the nearest thing in the way of a compromise between animal and vegetable edibles that could be offered to him as a meal'—the men knew he was a vegetarian. And Roebuck remembered an elaborate game of leapfrog, at which he was 'ridden' like a horse by Lord Goderich. Ostensibly this was, as Roebuck described it, a remarkable instance of social levelling, as Goderich, future Viceroy of India, almost flattened him—Roebuck recalled 'that was the only time in my life when I could claim to have borne the weight of empire on my back'. Yet, given the enduring class tensions in the College which erupted openly a few years later, the symbolism of a viscount vaulting onto a working man's back, tapping him, albeit in a 'friendly' way, on the 'haunches', while exclaiming 'Good horse! good horse!' might be thought ill-considered, though Roebuck seems to have taken the horseplay in good part.[33]

There was, then, an ideological, as well as practical, reason for Furnivall's preference for Sundays. Maurice found himself unenviably caught between the two sides: zealous dissenters and churchmen greeted the announcement 'with a shriek of horror and indignation'. Maurice offered sweet reason and expressed his willingness to walk with them in between services, but the men declared 'that was not what we wanted', and went for their walks regardless. They later defended themselves by pointing out that Maurice never once reproached them, while, as his son said, characteristically blaming himself: 'it was all his fault that they should choose rather the fields than the church'.[34] Maurice had chosen, as he confided to Kingsley, a hard path for himself, delving 'in the dark flowerless caverns and coal mines of our own souls'. It left him personally no space to enjoy 'the treasures of earth and sky and air . . . I feel that the friends on whom they are bestowed, and who understand that they are richly to enjoy, will become less and less able to tolerate

[32] Maurice, *Life of Maurice*, ii. 290–1.
[33] Roebuck, 'Reminiscences', 75–6.
[34] Maurice, *Life of Maurice*, ii. 291.

me.'³⁵ This prophecy was amply fulfilled by Furnivall at least. Maurice became increasingly distressed by the College's growing secularity, and his own sense of being at odds with many of its members. When he offered prayers, 'two or three listen, probably with reluctance. The teachers and students generally are out in the garden or talking in the library. I have no hold upon either.' By this time his Bible classes 'have lost their interest for all or almost all the teachers and most of the students . . . I believe I have more to accuse myself of than them.'³⁶ He did not wish to impose his own views; yet he reproached himself for the ill effects of not giving firm guidance, scruples wasted on Furnivall and the other anti-Sabbatarians in the College.

By 1858 Maurice was at his wits' end: Ludlow was urging him to impose his authority, and he agreed that 'now, if ever, is the time for acting . . . if only I can see how to do it rightly and not so as to produce a direct schism in the College'.³⁷ Maurice's model of governance had been authoritarian from the very beginning, though he already envisaged that he would be able to withdraw as the College became established: 'We who begin the institution must claim authority over it, and not hastily resign our authority, however we may admit others by degrees to share it, and however willing we may be to creep out of it when the institution can stand without us.'³⁸ Though Furnivall is not named in Maurice's letter to Ludlow, it is clear that Maurice felt him to be the principle source of the trouble. He was familiar with Furnivall's readiness to take up the cudgels on behalf of his friends, the working men, and, in June of 1858, there had already been a preliminary skirmish between them after women teachers and students had been subjected to unpleasantness from some 'bold fellows' among the men, resulting from poor timetabling of the women's classes. Maurice, who made alternative arrangements for the women and acknowledged his own responsibility, told Furnivall: 'You might just as well have left the

---

³⁵ Ibid. 295, letter to Kingsley, 29 July 1856. Maurice's view differed, as he knew, from Kingsley's. Some other clergy, like Kingsley, associated with the College and Maurice's circle, also supported Sunday recreation: Septimus Hansard, H. R. Haweis, and Dean Stanley among them, as also did J. S. Mill. See B. Harrison, 'Religion and Recreation in Nineteenth-Century England', 110. Also *The Times*, Friday, 22 Mar. 1867, p. 12 (on Sir Joshua Walmsley and the National Sunday League).

³⁶ Maurice, *Life of Maurice*, ii. 209, letter to Ludlow, 8 July 1857.

³⁷ Ibid., ii. 319, letter to Ludlow, 9 Aug. 1858.

³⁸ From Maurice's statement of the College's purpose, quoted in Furnivall's history, *Working Men's College Magazine*, 2, p. 165. It was for this reason that the teachers were not to be paid, 'all the fees going at first to the procuring of the necessary machinery for the institution'.

Lady teachers out of your witty remarks about disliking contacts with working men . . . It is I who object to the whole transaction as utterly discreditable and dangerous to the College. Therefore please keep your fists for me and not for those whom they do not the least concern.'[39]

Surely enough, Furnivall took up Maurice's invitation to vent his irritation on him personally as the one who, as its head, represented aspects of the College which he disliked, especially what Maurice called its 'tone'. When Maurice had left London for the summer vacation, Furnivall now felt his position to be strong enough to flout the rules with increasing daring. He was writing articles, under the pen-name 'Q', describing the students' Sunday excursions for *The People's Paper*, the newspaper of the National Sunday League, which had been founded in 1855 by a group of London goldsmiths and other craftsmen, led by R. M. Morrell, with the object of securing the Sunday opening of museums, galleries, and libraries, and promoting Sunday excursions, bands in the parks, and general recreation of an improving sort.[40] Maurice noted that 'Q's' account of the students' tea-meetings was 'written in a very vulgar tone'. He had himself written a letter to the students, explaining his views, and 'Q' had alluded to it in a passage which was

so contemptuous, and as an account of the letter so unfair, that I am afraid of seeming to be actuated by some personal motive if I notice the report in a letter to the Editor of the *People*. But I must take some method of declaring that I disapprove of the tone of the whole document, and that I am no party to these expeditions—or resign.

Maurice concluded: 'It reads to me like a declaration of war.'[41]

Furnivall's contributions to *The People* were, indeed, a slap in the face to Maurice—even Munro, Furnivall's friend, admitted that 'All this was hardly the language of loyalty to the Principal'.[42] Indeed, he con-

[39] Letter to Furnivall, 25 June 1858, FU 573. Maurice arranged for the women to be taught out of College in the Hall of Association. Furnivall: 'In this Hall were begun, at Mr Ludlow's suggestion, classes and lectures, to both of which women were admitted . . . The only successful classes were Mr. Ludlow's French one, and the Drawing-class'. *Working Men's College Magazine*, 2, p. 145.

[40] In addition to B. Harrison, 'Religion and Recreation', see also McVeigh, '"Brightening the Lives of the People on Sunday"'. In 1858 Furnivall appealed to the paper 'for a column a-week . . . to let us [the Working Men's Colleges of England] have our friendly chat among ourselves'; Munro, 'Biography', p. xxvi. Munro's view was that 'while so many were steeped in the bookish theoric of co-operation and fellow-work, Furnivall and his fellows were striving to weave these things into their lives' (p. xxv).

[41] Maurice, *Life of Maurice*, ii. 319.

[42] 'Biography', p. xxxi (and see pp. xxix–xxxii for Munro's account of the whole episode).

ducted the attack on a much broader front than the simple Sunday question—in his later very guarded comment on his disagreements with the College authorities, Furnivall skated over the real hurt he had caused: 'The word "together" did and does, I do believe express the spirit in which we desired, and desire to work, notwithstanding all our differences in opinion and the skirmishes proceeding therefrom, however sharp the latter may sometimes have been.'[43]

Maurice wrote to him to ascertain the truth. And, since Maurice's side of the argument tends to be drowned out by Furnivall's boisterous public campaign to let the men enjoy themselves on their one day off, it deserves in fairness to be heard. It is too easy to accept Furnivall's view that the head of the College was a parsonical spoilsport. Maurice's letter gives a rare view of himself as a sensitive man, who wanted to rule the College with kindness and mutual goodwill, but who had been most reluctantly forced into a confrontation with a defiant junior colleague. His emotion and hurt are evident (not least in the letter's occasionally troubled syntax and numerous deletions), as is his idealism. His comments on the brash style which Furnivall had adopted in print are perceptive:

My dear Furnivall,
A paper has been forwarded to me containing what professes to be a Report of the Students Tea Meeting. I thought for a while that it might have been what it assumes to be, the report of a Student. I *hoped* it might be the work of some regular agent of the Paper. But I arrived at last at the conclusion that it was yours. If I am wrong I | shall offer you my hearty apologies, for I have too much of old regard and affection for you not to wish that you may have nothing to do with it.

I have no reason to think that anything I say will have the least weight with you, but I take the privilege of an old acquaintance and of one who has had something to do with the Working College to say that the tone of that article is scarcely what I desire ⟨not⟩ & which I believe the most earnest promoter of Working Men's Colleges | throughout the country would desire *not* to be the tone which ⟨..⟩ pervades them. It is not the natural tone ⟨which⟩ of the students; that I have always found courteous and reverent. It is a tone which we have never imparted to them, and if they ⟨..⟩ do learn it from one who never knew them coarse—and less gentlemanlike—than men, who are coarse to them.[44]

[43] *Working Men's College Magazine*, 2, p. 169.

[44] The sense is somewhat obscure, but the general drift is clear: if the men have learned coarse language, which they do not naturally use themselves, and which the College has never taught them, they have picked it up from someone (it is implied, Furnivall), who is less of a gentleman than they are.

I cannot answer, of course, for the faithfulness of the Report generally. Much may go on at a Tea Meeting which it is | mere idleness to heed and which must convey a false impression of the general character of our Society. The only passages about which I do know anything, that which applies to my own letter, I should say, with submission, are utterly inaccurate. It represents me as saying what I did not say; it suppresses into a sentence and lessens the the substance of what I did say. The letter might be foolish in way; but I continue to think that it was scarcely entitled to this kind of treatment.

With reference to the last long paragraph in which | the College is identified with the Sunday League—you know my opinions. You know that I have expressed ⟨as⟩ distinctly & in print, my dislike of the Sunday excursions. You know that they have gone on in despite of Ludlow as much as of me. Whether therefore it was quite fair and honest to make me responsible for these proceedings I leave you to judge. However little you may value my opinion, you must remember that these | public comments as(?) with the College—that we are, for the present at least, supposed to have some share in the management of it. That may seem to me, as far as I am concerned, a great misfortune; I have felt long and with ⟨pl..⟩ pain that it does seem so to you and perhaps to the students. But so long as my name is on the Council I must solemnly protest against being in the least | degree mixed up with acts & words which I consider wrong and injurious to the interests of the Working Men.

I shall not write to the Editors of the People of this of whom I know nothing and who would probably treat any communication with much insolence. But I am bound in conscience to express my opinion to you. I hope I have done so | without bitterness. Certainly what I feel is towards myself as towards you. Had I the very slightest ⟨in . . .⟩[45] weight with you—if I did not feel that what I say is likely, because I say it, to confirm you in an opposite conclusion, I should address myself to you individually and say what a somewhat older man occasionally thinks himself at liberty to say to one 'who' probably has experienced less and suffered less. But as it is I ⟨must⟩ write only as a College man and as the (nominal) Principal of the College.

Faithfully yours,
F. D. Maurice.[46]

Furnivall's siding with the students against the authorities was, indeed, impossible for Maurice to overlook. His report on 'The Students' Tea to

---

[45] 'influence'?

[46] Letter of 11 Aug. 1858, FU 574, addressed from Tunbridge Wells. Furnivall evidently acknowledged his authorship to Maurice and made a point of sending him copies of his following submissions to *The People*, which Maurice returned: see letters of 14, 16, and 24 Aug., FU 575, 576, 577. Since the mistakes of grammar and syntax appear to result from *ad hoc* changes of mind and imperfectly executed self-corrections, and speak to the haste and trouble of mind, in which Maurice's letter was evidently written, it is reproduced here diplomatically as it stands. The general sense is clear.

their Teachers' lost no opportunity to be provocative, beginning with the opening salvo: 'tea was to be the leading feature of the evening . . . But on arriving at the College, there was no tea to be had'.[47] The working men described to him the formality which had exsisted between the teachers and the men, but now, it is implied, thanks to Furnivall's interventions, they felt they were really speaking to friends 'and not to a lot of swells who condescended to mix with them for a few hours a week'. In view of Maurice's comment about the respectful and polite style used by the men, this is likely to be Furnivall's language, imputed to the men, rather than a literal quotation, or at least it is likely to have been touched up to make a rhetorical point—though the men may well have been more informal in their usage when talking to, and encouraged by, him than they were in speaking to Maurice. By representing himself as the teacher who really understood the men, Furnivall again enhanced his own importance. He it was who organized the College's social life, which (according to him) the men agreed was more important than anything else. One of the men, Mr Standring,[48] the student father of the College—and one of Furnivall's students and close companions on these walks—declared, as reported by Furnivall, that what 'he valued most was the sociality of the place: he wasn't too particular about the learning', indeed, he thought sometimes that the teaching 'wasn't altogether of the right practical sort . . . we must take care we didn't make our minds like those of some college-men he'd seen—just dusty shelves for musty books to lie on'. (The latter part of this reported remark is surely Furnivall's paraphrase.) Furnivall took the opportunity to reduce Maurice's importance as Principal in favour of Ludlow, telling the men that 'as the co-operative associations out of which the College grew were originated solely by Mr. Ludlow, so the College itself was originated by him'. It was Ludlow 'who gathered the small knot of men around Mr. Maurice, to read the Bible together and visit or teach in Little Ormond Yard'. Indeed, Furnivall took every opportunity to proclaim Ludlow's importance as the de facto founder of the College.[49]

Furnivall had not finished: *his* teaching was, he asserted, *relevant* (as

---

[47] Furnivall printed the text of the students' address to the teachers, after the tea at the Hall of Association in his history of the College's early years. It is, as one would expect, respectful in expressing appreciation for the teachers' generosity: 'At the present time, when men generally appear to have more respect for their own peculiar crotchets than concern for the welfare of their fellows'. *Working Men's College Magazine*, 2, p. 189.

[48] Sam Standring joined the College as a founder member in 1854, and entered Furnivall's class on English grammar; J. F. C. Harrison, *History*, 58.

[49] Munro, 'Biography', p. xxix. In response to Furnivall's article of 24 July, Ludlow wrote

by implication others' teaching was not). Furnivall was already teaching *Piers Plowman* to the men 'because of its sketch of working men in the fourteenth century'.[50] And, as we shall see, in other ways, too, Furnivall's instruction was hinted to be directly relevant to mid-nineteenth-century concerns (and more up to date than the fourteenth century): the fossils hunted on Sunday expeditions into the countryside were more interesting than the human fossils to be found back in the College. Meanwhile, there was nothing stuffy about the expedition he had arranged. It was delightful (he was already using rowing parties as a means of giving working people strenuous and companionable exercise, with men literally pulling together): 'We had a famous pull up to Hampton Court and back ... bathing as we went up—then tea and a walk in the Park, and a lie-down on the scented green fern on the hillside.'[51] While the Principal of the College shilly-shallied in Tunbridge Wells, reproaching himself for his 'unmanliness and want of purpose',[52] Furnivall was expressing his solidarity with the men by manly sports and bathing together in the river in a display of democratic manly camaraderie *sans culottes*.

Munro described much of this article as 'perfectly innocent fun, mere merry comment', though in its context it was not as innocent as he alleged, and he admits 'much must have deeply hurt Maurice'.[53] Maurice knew that he probably could never make his position generally understood, and he accepted the hard words of secularists as only what he, like any religious person, must accept and even welcome for his Lord's sake. Ludlow reproved, and Hughes encouraged him, but Maurice recognized that 'Q' had put him, as well as the other senior members of the College, in an intolerable position:

> Whatever Q- may pretend, the College is committed by his articles in the *People*. The tone of them commits us. He makes us all parties to that vulgar habit of thinking and speaking which he believes to be the best for the men, which I think is making them far less of gentlemen than they were before. He cannot be driven from the College. You say so yourself, and if he were, the impression of what he has done would be left, and would be stronger for their feeling of anger and pity for him.

a denial from Lincoln's Inn on 10 Aug., and stated that Furnivall's articles for *The People* were not authorized by the College's Council.

[50] See Benzie, *Dr F. J. Furnivall*, 52.

[51] *The People's Paper*, Saturday, 7 Aug. 1858. See also Furnivall's later account of the strenuous expeditions he organized at this time: 'Social Life of the College', 57. He was justifiably proud of the organization and physical fitness displayed.

[52] Maurice, *Life of Maurice*, ii. 319.   [53] 'Biography', pp. xxx–xxxi.

If Furnivall could not be fired, then resignation as a means of bearing witness, once again, seemed to Maurice to be the only option:

That will be a witness that some of us have arrived at something else. That will be a just punishment on me for not having done anything to reach the men. It will be a lesson to other colleges ... I see no cause to change my resolution, but everything to confirm it. There is no other way out of the difficulty. The pain of it will be great to me, but that is salutary. I should accept, I think, the offer of almost any curacy in the country to be rid of London.[54]

Maurice told Furnivall that he was not bitter, but subsequent exchanges show that he overestimated his own forbearance. He was, indeed, deeply injured. The general sense is plain, though his handwriting deteriorated under stress: 'You 'intimate' with much kindness that you have no objection to my continuing in the College if I keep my place— (that of delivering lectures which no one hears & holding a Bible Class which all the working(?) [word illegible] of the | College are encouraged to desert)—provided you manage the social life of the College as you think best.'[55]

It says something for Furnivall's sense of the historical significance of the letters he received from Maurice that he preserved them, even though they were so uncomplimentary to himself. One can see why Ludlow described Furnivall as 'a terrible thorn in Mr Maurice's side', even while he conceded that 'I believe that there are few men who, meaning so well, have done more mischief'—Furnivall's good intentions cannot be doubted, nor that he felt that he had right on his side.[56] He had, indeed, done more to bolster his position by his next contribution to *The People*, in which he recorded how he had 'taken it upon himself' to give a vote of thanks, ostensibly on behalf of all the teachers at the College to the men 'for not only the fun and brightness, the attention and kindness they always found in them, but also for the lessons they had learned from them'. It quickly becomes apparent that he is really speaking for himself, not the whole teaching body: the students have been 'a delight to him and a source of strength for the work of his life'.[57] The sentiment is compelling for its earnestness, but the opportunity to express it was both tactless and provocative. But—a slight

---

[54] Maurice, *Life of Maurice*, ii. 320–1, letter to Ludlow, 17 Aug. 1858.

[55] Letter to Furnivall, 14 Aug. 1858, FU 575; 'intimate' is substituted for 'say'.

[56] *Autobiography*, 270. 'Furnivall had always been a man greatly devoid of tact ... But the "wisdom in his own conceit" growing upon him more and more, he became a person with whom intimacy was to be altogether avoided' (p. 271; cf. Prov. 25:6).

[57] *The People*, Saturday 14 Aug. 1858.

extenuating circumstance—the skirmishes with Maurice in *The People*, though wounding, were less potent than they might otherwise have been, as they were conducted in the middle of the Long Vacation.

When term resumed in October, Maurice was still considering his position. He distributed a thirty-four-page pamphlet to the members of the Council, *Statement of my reasons for resigning the office of Principal to the Working Men's College*. It reaffirmed his ideal of religion as the basis for all instruction and passed to his views on Sunday observance before getting down to the real substance: the report in *The People* 'of a meeting of the students, at which I was not present, but to which I sent a letter. I have been seldom more pained than by that report.' He condemned the writer's lack of modesty, and quoted a postscript in which the writer announced 'à propos of nothing' that he had 'made a geological excursion with some other students, the previous Sunday, and that they were about to enrol themselves members of the Sunday League'.[58] Maurice made it plain that he interpreted this as deliberate disrespect to himself, inadequately disguised as a generalized act of vulgar defiance, which he described, quoting Shakespeare, as 'We do not bite our thumbs at you, Sir, but we do bite our thumbs'.[59]

At the meeting the College's Council supported Maurice, who retained his position as Principal until he resigned in 1871, the year of his death. Assured of the Council's support, Maurice had now to make his peace with Furnivall, and followed up his statement with a personal letter to him, in which he asserted that he wished to overlook the incidents, and considered it unfitting to 'out' anyone who differed from him:

> I said in my statement that I should never enquire whether any member of the College chose to connect himself with the Lord's Day Observance Society or with the Sunday League any more than I should enquire how he thought it wise to speak the first day of the week or the second or the third. My objection was to his proclaiming his acts in connexion with his position as a Member of the College. The questions of individual & of corporate responsibility are far too nice and delicate for definition.

Considering, as he did, that the College was itself compromised by the

---

[58] Munro, 'Biography', p. xxx (and for a summary of the paper, see pp. xxx–xxxi). Maurice was mistaken about the intention to enrol in the Sunday League—Furnivall had said that it was proposed to join a Sunday League party on another occasion.

[59] Munro, 'Biography', p. xxx; he described the pamphlet as written 'in the clear and resonant English characteristic of Maurice, and is inspired by the most noble principles and ideals' (p. xxix). Quotation from *Romeo and Juliet*, I. i. 47–8. On the insult, see *OED*, 'bite', v., 16, 'to threaten or defie by putting the thumbe naile into the mouth, and with a ierke (from the upper teeth) make it to knack' (Cotgrave); also 'thumb', n. 5(e).

'acts and words of an individual teacher', he had chosen rather to offer his resignation as a means of obtaining the opinion of the Council in this point than to engage in a long and hopeless controversy which could have ended where it began and would have exhibited the Principal of the College as a mere troublesome clerical meddler.

A *laissez faire* course is far more agreeable to my natural disposition; but if I affect to guide the College—if I am called to that work—I must do it honestly and not suffer myself to become a merely ornamental appendage—an ugly ornament moreover—to the institution. Now that the votes of the Council have put an end to this confusion which existed before, I am not in the least afraid of any evil consequences from the proceedings of any particular person, either teacher or student. Even if he decided—which I am confident you do not—to assert his own self will against their judgment . . . of what is desirable. There appeared to me a great peril of our becoming a mere collection of teachers— of our teachings becoming a mere miscellaneous farrago, without any unity or common purpose.[60]

And, as a final gesture towards reconciliation, Maurice withdrew 'the phrase about *biting the thumb*, which gave you pain'.[61] Furnivall had evidently not relished being compared to a mere henchman and troublemaker, like the followers of Montague and Capulet; nor the insinuation that he was not manly enough to be open about his intentions— biting his thumb, but not *at* anyone.

Nicety and delicacy, so essential to Maurice, were not part of Furnivall's arsenal. And Maurice's offer to let bygones be bygones would not be heeded: this was not the end of Furnivall's challenges to his authority. His campaign to run the College's social life in his own way continued at every opportunity. Asked by Litchfield, the editor of the College's *Magazine*, to contribute a write-up of the yearly *conversazione*, his response was deliberately contrary—he was fortunate in that Litchfield shared many of his views. He would much rather describe his latest Sunday walk with the men than an event already a fortnight old, and proceeded to do so, in the lyrical manner he had used for the *People*: 'Would I not have expatiated on the glories of Hampstead and Hendon fields, the sweet smell of the hay on the mown ones, the brilliant yellow-green on the cleared ones, dotted with white shorn sheep and glowing chestnut cows.' He would have waxed lyrical about 'out-of-the-way-lanes' with 'white roses and woodbine' and the view over London from Harrow Hill, 'but with no tea for thirsty walkers'. In fact, after this

---

[60] Letter of 29 Oct. 1858, FU 578. Maurice's self-corrections and alterations have been incorporated silently. [61] Ibid.

extended grumble, Furnivall settled down to a lavish description of the required event, which he had not organized. A description of the students' art works on display gave opportunity to single out a portrait of 'a magnificent sunburnt Navvy', in striped shirt and red neckerchief, 'seated at ease, pipe in mouth, and spade and jacket on knee'. And Furnivall also singled out the 'wonderful copies of Turner's water-colours, and rapid studies of clouds, made by Mr. Bunney, one of our members, for Mr. Ruskin; and which have so pleased our great and much-loved and honoured teacher that he has sent the doer of them out to Switzerland to see and paint the mountains and pines of that artist's home'. He gave much prominence to the performances by the Women's Singing Class, which pleased the conductor, Litchfield, while allowing him to elaborate the general opinion after a successful party that it should happen more often into a polemical demand for change: 'Why are we only to see one another once a year? How much longer are men-students and women-students, men-teachers and women-teachers to be kept so separate from one another? Both sides would be glad to know more of each other, both know they are as worthy of trust as people who have money enough and houses big enough to meet their own friends whenever they want to.' In sum, let the college authorities not be such prigs: 'Let all Members of Working Men's Colleges know, what all unpriggish members of older Colleges (and Schools too) do, that the social life of a College is worth as much as its intellectual training, and that any College which does only the latter part of its work and leaves the former undone, is as yet performing only half its functions.'[62]

It is likely, too, that it was Furnivall who argued against the high principles espoused by the leading men in the College that gaining intellectual prizes in the form of certificates was not enough, and monetary rewards should also be given. A student from the College's beginnings noted that 'one of Council, for whose opinion I have great respect, has suggested that prizes would enable men to buy good books, or go into the country to study geology or art', benefits which the writer thought were being better supplied by simple generosity.[63] Furnivall was already attempting to strengthen his position by getting his two principal sup-

---

[62] F. J. Furnivall, 'Our Conversazione', *Working Men's College Magazine*, 1, no. vii (1 July 1859), 120–2. On John Wharlton Bunney and Ruskin, see Hilton, *John Ruskin*, ii. 162, 343. The descriptive style used to describe the countryside probably owes something to contemporary guide-books' suggested routes for rambles, with the delights to be seen along the way.

[63] 'Ought Prizes to have a Money Value?', *Working Men's College Magazine*, 2, p. 10 (1 Jan. 1860).

porters among the working men, George Tansley and John Roebuck, elected to the Council as Fellows—Maurice responded by telling him that this was a matter for Council to decide.[64]

Yet the principle that the Council should include equal numbers of students and teachers was one Furnivall had shared with Ludlow from the outset,[65] though Maurice resisted it, and it was not until 1863 that the first three student members of Council, Roebuck, Tansley, and William Rossiter, were elected Fellows of the College and members of its Council after they passed the Associate examination. Roebuck, writing for the College's fiftieth anniversary, described the event in the warm glow of hindsight and of battle won long ago.[66] Yet Munby, describing the event as it occurred, revealed plainly the sharp differences, and chronic class antagonism, between the working men and the teachers on the Council which form the background to Furnivall's discontent. It was clearly an electrifying meeting:

> The new student members, elected under our recent resolutions, were present for the first time. They are three in number: and to the great surprise of every one, they signalized their entrance into membership by violently repudiating the terms of their own election, and making use of that very election to propose certain other rules, which would swamp the old council with innumerable students, who were all to be permanent members like the teachers. It was curious to see the lasting antagonism between the gentlemen and the snob, the educated and the half-educated, breaking out among us, of all bodies, & all our liberal 'radical' members suddenly changed to conservatives & aristocrats in spite of themselves.

Worst of all, in Munby's view, was the use which the students made of the occasion to imperil the ethos of the College: 'these men had been caballing; trying to create parties, and set student against teacher, "university men" against their own class: or tending to do this, if they did

---

[64] On Roebuck, see Colloms, *Victorian Visionaries*, 169–70. At the time of his enrolment in the College in 1854, he was 23, married, and expecting his first child: the expenditure on the College's fee (though low) needed serious consideration.

[65] Maurice considered that students might in future be elected to offices in the College, 'But I would not let them have the least voice in determining what we shall teach or not teach or how we shall teach. We may have social meetings with them; we may have conversations with them individually; but no education will go on if we have general tumultuous assemblies to discuss what has been done or what is to be done'. As Furnivall later recorded, 'On this last point of self-government, strong opposition was made by Mr Ludlow, myself, and others, who wished that the governing body of the College should from the first consist of equal numbers of teachers and working men; but it was settled that only teachers should be on it at first, and that gradually working men should be admitted to the extent of one-third of the whole number'; *Working Men's College Magazine*, 2, p. 165.   [66] Roebuck, 'Reminiscences', 69–70; Benzie, *Dr F. J. Furnivall*, 45–6.

not try'. Maurice, as chairman, tried to restore order, but lost 'not indeed his temper but his judgement'. He was emotional, wounded, and was not at his best when leadership needed to be asserted, but 'broke into one of his most fitful, earnest, pathetic harangues. He was no longer Principal, he said; the College was at an end; class had been set against class, the very principle of cooperation and brotherhood on which we—all men—stood, had been violated; let us confess to the world that we were a failure, a sham—that there was no divine centre of unity among us!' Munby recorded 'He sat down, his frame quivering (I was next to him) and his face electrical with noble but unreasonable emotion.'

With the Principal overcome by his feelings, leadership passed to the rest of the teaching body, most of whom were themselves taken by surprise. Hughes was 'manly and blunt' but unclear. Lushington tried to restore calm; Westlake was 'cold and selfpossest'. Ludlow and Furnivall tried to exploit the situation in favour of the students: Ludlow 'vehement & illogical, took the part of the malcontents, Furnivall of course assisting'. Eventually Litchfield, 'whose comprehensiveness and ease of expression I always admire', took control: 'by his aid things were somewhat calmed and cleared'.[67]

During the next few years Maurice's exchanges with Furnivall veered between respect for the younger man's generosity and manliness of spirit (though combined in equal measure with turbulence),[68] and plaintiveness and hurt at Furnivall's continued criticisms of his leadership. Thus Furnivall did not like the pessimistic tone of a sermon which Maurice had preached to the College concerning the Volunteer movement, to which Maurice asserted the duty of his office as a priest to speak what he thought was the truth, whatever his audience, whether civil or military. That his perception of the truth was based 'above all from the knowledge of one's own continual temptations' probably did nothing to mollify Furnivall. His justification that 'I fear—perhaps this is not the word—I shall always say something which will sound personal to those whom I address, and which will be personal because it will be derived chiefly from my own personal struggles', must just have seemed merely pusillanimous.[69] Maurice's wish that the teachers in the College might participate in reading the nightly prayers, and that at least some of the students might attend, had evidently called down a storm on his head: 'So as you say I am not successful in "caging"

---

[67] Hudson, *Munby: Man of Two Worlds*, 163, diary entry for Thursday, 28 May 1863.
[68] See, for example, the letter from Maurice to Furnivall, [21 Oct. 1861], FU 591.
[69] Letter of 11 Dec. [1860?], FU 588.

the students. They have a reasonable fear of clerical intrusion and impertinence.' The intemperance of Furnivall's remarks thus reported is insolent, and was clearly resented, especially as Maurice had no intention of infringing the students' freedom by obliging them to attend ('caging' them in Furnivall's phrase). And he did not wish to subject the College's teachers 'to the humiliation which it is quite proper that I should undergo'.[70] A display of Christian forbearance and abject humility was never likely to be successful in an appeal to Furnivall's goodwill.

On another occasion Maurice offered a Christian martyr's idea of fair play by telling Furnivall that he would absent himself from two meetings of the College's Council 'so that any unfair influence or restraint which you express them [the students] to have asserted will not be felt'.[71] Furnivall had plans to involve members of the College in social work in Ormond Yard, but left Maurice in doubt as to whether his approval was sought, or whether he was merely being notified. Maurice commented: 'You have told me that *you* only intended that I should be apprised of it. I fancy from what you said of the resolution of the *Students* that they took the other view.' He urged that the matter should be put before Litchfield, Hughes, and the other members of the Council:

I believe the students individually and collectively have full confidence in them; some, I hope, they have in me . . . If I think that any of the influences brought to bear . . . are likely to be injurious influences, or if I find those who are speaking about College fellowship and brotherhood are not behaving to other members of the College as fellows and brothers—I will act upon that conviction as an individual and as a Principal.

It becomes clear from Maurice's ill-suppressed but ineffectual anger (he knew his threat did not count for much), and doubt of his own influence with the College members, how very divided and unhappy the community had become in the 1860s.[72] Furnivall must take much of the responsibility, though he was clear in his own mind that he was acting from the best of motives.

As Munro said, the clashes over the College's social life were important because they seemed to mark 'a new epoch' in Furnivall's career,

[70] Letter [c.1860?], FU 589.   [71] Letter of 28 Jan. [1862], FU 593.
[72] Letter of 18 June [1862], FU 595. Subsequently Maurice tacitly conceded defeat by writing in as conciliatory a manner as possible: 'I am anxious not to throw cold water upon any design which our students have conceived'. In pursuing his scheme Furnivall was trying to keep Maurice out of sight of the public, which Maurice interpreted charitably as 'the evident wish to save me the publicity'. His wish to participate was probably not what Furnivall wanted. Letter of 17 June [1862], FU 596.

in which 'he had passed from Maurice's influence'.⁷³ Having achieved some independence from his father's money and political views, Furnivall was probably reluctant to put himself under the authority of yet another father figure. Meanwhile, the articles in *The People* amply demonstrated that he had now found an effective public voice in print. The articles were unsigned, but, even in the third person, were written in what from henceforth would be Furnivall's signature style—as Munro called it, 'the familiar Furnivallesque manner'.⁷⁴ Indeed, Furnivall's unsigned articles in *The People* can easily be recognized as his, but this is a view in retrospect—these are perhaps the earliest versions of the ostentatiously colloquial style in print which was to be his trademark throughout his later career. The writing was calculated to offend Maurice not only by what the writer said, but the manner—the 'tone'. The defiant vulgarity of the style was, indeed, the equivalent of biting one's thumb, or cocking a snook. It was a demonstration of Furnivall's new-found class solidarity with the working men against the authority of 'college-men'.

Yet in reality he was just as much a 'college-man' himself as Maurice and the other founders—the writing was not so *déclassé* as it seemed. As described above, Maurice's response to the 'vulgarity' of the articles in *The People* had been to say that talking down to side with the men compromised their real nobility as nature's gentlemen. He told Furnivall that the style was not one he heard himself from the working men, and in his view, if they learned this kind of coarse style from Furnivall, they would become less 'gentlemanlike' than they really were—and though expressed indirectly, it is implied that Furnivall would show himself to be less of a gentleman than they. Of course, it was not likely that the men would speak to Maurice in such a colloquial manner, and it was to be expected that he would find them reverent and polite towards himself. They are likely to have relaxed in Furnivall's company, and, as Maurice said, 'Much may go on at a Tea Meeting which it is mere idleness to heed'. That was a large part of the problem: Furnivall was fascinated all his life by details which others regarded as commonplace and trivial, and his speech-based style on this occasion was also largely intended to convey, as vividly as possible, the lively and informal nature of the gathering. But Maurice's response, indicating that, in his view, Furnivall, by lowering the public tone of the College, had not shown himself a gentleman, was a stinging rebuke, and Furnivall was not immune to

---

⁷³ 'Biography', p. xxxi.
⁷⁴ Ibid., p. xxviii.

its sharpness. The cheery demotic idiolect which Furnivall invented for himself never allows the reader—or a working man for that matter—to conclude that he was uneducated. Indeed, apart from the register and the reporting of something approximating to the spoken word, it is highly articulate. He may have taken some hints from John Bezer's speech-based autobiography, which Furnivall had prepared for print, but without the slang. Moreover, such adjectives as 'famous' and 'capital' belong to the informal register of Furnivall's class, rather than that of a working man of his time.[75]

'LACK OF FEMALE SOCIETY'

There continued to be frequent disagreements between Furnivall and Maurice. The organization of the College's social life was an ongoing irritant, but there were also others. Another teacher at the College, the fellow-barrister, and man of letters, Arthur J. Munby, described, after attending an evening meeting in 1859 at Macmillan's at which Litchfield, Vernon Lushington, and Furnivall were present, 'one of those College jars which *will* occur'. J. S. Mill's *On Liberty* had recently been published: Munby commented that 'Furnivall wants to read Mill on Liberty with his class, & Maurice objects to it as a contemporary book on an unsettled question.' As Munby went on to observe, 'F(urnivall) will kick, but Maurice will conquer: for all submit to him, not because he is *Principal* but because he is *Maurice*. Inevitable, & quite right too'.[76] Maurice was not alone in having reservations about Mill; in the following year, as a demonstration of the unsettled nature of the subject, Ruskin would publish controversial articles of his own on political economy, taking a different position from Mill's, which he defended in the idiosyncratic and oracular style all of his own in discussion with Litchfield and other teachers.[77] Back in 1854, Furnivall had already been in

[75] See e.g. *OED*, 'capital', adj. 6(f), supported a little incongruously by Benjamin Jowett's translation of Plato's *Dialogues*, I. 97, 'Capital, Socrates, by the gods, that is truly good'.

[76] Hudson, *Munby: Man of Two Worlds*, 26, diary entry for Thursday, 3 Mar. 1859. On the use of the Macmillan's London premises at 23 Henrietta Street for Thursday evening meetings of intellectuals and men of letters (the so-called 'Tobacco Parliaments'), see Morgan, *House of Macmillan*, 50–6: visitors included Hughes, David Masson, Holman Hunt, Tennyson, Charles and Henry Kingsley, Huxley, and Tennyson. As Munby tells us, Furnivall also attended. There was much talk of Darwin.

[77] Hudson, *Munby, Man of Two Worlds*, 81–2, diary entry for Thursday, 8 Nov. 1860. Ruskin described Mill as 'a fine fellow, but whose brain was full of confused fancies (!): which I will show! cried he conclusively, rising up & down on his toes after his manner, with his hands in his tailpockets, and finally jaunting downstairs in the same springy

correspondence with Mill. Inspired by his own reading of the work, Furnivall wished to promote the circulation among the working men of the chapter of *Principles of Political Economy* entitled 'The Probable Futurity of the Labouring Classes', and Mill had consented.[78] Furnivall once again clashed with Maurice when he began, as requested by the men, to organize shilling College dances.

Meanwhile, Furnivall's Sunday excursions grew into long-distance walking parties during the long vacations: to North Wales, geologizing again, before Lynton in North Devon became a favourite resort. Furnivall also accompanied the men on one of the first excursions abroad, the memorable trip to Brittany and Normandy, where he went with the Secretary of the College, Thomas Shorter, and five of the men, who met up at Rouen. As might be expected, Furnivall's attention was attracted to the beauty of the countryside and cities, the loveliness of the sunsets and starry nights, as well as the customs of the local people, their work and pastimes. The group visited the working men's associations, and Furnivall was evidently the life and soul of the party, chatting with the local people, trying to persuade the gendarmes who inspected his passport that England was not without natural beauties of its own, singing, telling jokes, and having fun with soldiers from the Crimean War. The seven members of the College danced barefoot on the sands at Mont St-Michel, 'crossing the river 4 or 5 times, the water above your loins with a soft wind blowing, and the sun out, we were as jolly as we could possibly be, and danced about like wild Indians'. Furnivall concluded wistfully: 'I wish one could always go without trousers and boots', but paddling on the beach was the nearest he could get to being a *sans culotte*.[79]

Furnivall stayed behind, after the rest of the party had left, to look up his supposed ancestors at Fourneville, where he arrived on Saturday, 25 September. After exploring, interrogating the locals, and returning to the inn, the innkeeper's wife attempted to throw him out, and challenged his English passport, until it was pointed out that his credentials had satisfied the police at Le Havre, 'And then we were all good fashion, with the prim smile of Sir Oracle upon his dry lips'. Ruskin's articles appeared in the *Cornhill* between Aug. and Nov. 1860, later collected in *Unto this Last* (1862). For the adverse criticism they attracted, see Leon, *Ruskin the Great Victorian*, 295–6.

[78] Letter of 13 Feb. 1854, quoted by Benzie, *Dr F. J. Furnivall*, 19. 'I am sure that whatever helps to make them connect their hopes with co-operation, and with the moral qualities necessary to make co-operation succeed, rather than with strikes . . . will do for them what they are greatly in need of'. Furnivall had read the work in several sittings between 22 and 29 Jan. 1851, Bodl. MS Eng. e 2316, ff. 11^v–12^v.

[79] Munro, 'Biography', p. xxxiv. Colloms, *Victorian Visionaries*, 182.

friends'.[80] It was to be his first and last journey abroad, and it had been urged on him by Thomas Shorter and encouraged by Ruskin (to whom foreign travel was a customary thing, and who had prepared the travellers for their visit with an evening's talk about 'French manners and customs, telling us where to see and how to look at the grand architectural monuments of the old French towns').[81] It was not Furnivall's initiative—for all his enthusiasm for *Modern Painters* and *The Stones of Venice*, he seems to have been reluctant, or, more probably not rich enough, to travel or to see for himself the glories Ruskin described in his books.

Furnivall's anxiety that the men should have fun as well as an education was not purely disinterested. He had not enjoyed himself so much since his own time as a younger man at UCL and at home. Initially a large part of the delightfulness of the rowing expedition Furnivall had led up river to Hampton Court was the sense of male bonding in the course of pleasurable, but strenuous, physical activity from which women were excluded, much as in his younger days he had rowed with his college chums and bathed with his brothers.

Yet one of the advantages of entertainments away from the College was that it was easier to include women. Perhaps surprisingly, this does not seem to have occurred to Furnivall unprompted, though he was known in later life for his energetic support of women, and his description of the College's 1859 *conversazione* gives much space to his enjoyment of the women singers 'in white and mauve, blue, pink, and green, and black . . . who come to see us once a year, and brighten us up with the sight of their faces and the sound of their voices', so much more enlivening than the exhibition on the same occasion of an 'animalcule' under the microscope, 'kicking about in its drop of water'.[82] After Cambridge, his early career, and his association with the largely masculine band of Christian Socialists, it was probably an aspect of life which Furnivall, as an impecunious young lawyer, had needed to put in abeyance. But, unlike him, the working men had wives, daughters, and girlfriends whom they had left behind on the one day of leisure in the week. It was probably one of the most conspicuous points of difference between him and them. In the course of an excursion into the Surrey

---

[80] A full account of the expedition, based on Furnivall's own account to him, is given by Munro, 'Biography', pp. xxxiii–xxxvi.
[81] Furnivall, 'College Excursions', *Working Men's College Magazine*, 2, pp. 160-2 at 160 (1 Oct. 1860).
[82] Furnivall, 'Our Conversazione', *Working Men's College Magazine*, 1, p. 121 (1 July 1859).

countryside on Sunday, 11 July 1858, the men 'lamented to Furnivall their lack of female society'.[83] As Furnivall put it: 'It was at a geological walk in a chalk-pit at Caterham, by the station, that two of our men told me of their want of women's society, and askt me to get up some dances for them, as casinos were then the only places where they could meet women.'[84] Munby also noticed the acute shortage of places in London where the lower middle classes and upper working classes could meet 'respectable women' and '*not* prostitutes' socially.[85] After this, the trips were joined by the women and girls in the College's singing class, which John Hullah had initiated, and which were taken over in 1859 by Litchfield and became an important part of College life.[86] Munby described another of the Sunday excursions, to Burnham Beeches on 12 July 1863, after Maurice had lost the battle, and after women were allowed to join in. It was, as Munby described it, a thoroughly enjoyable and innocent pastoral tea party *en plein air* on 'snowy' tables, followed by a sing-song, conducted by Litchfield, of madrigals and Mendelssohn's *Elijah*, which attracted an audience of local 'swells', farmers and cottagers and their wives and families:

> They might well wonder: a strangely clad heterogeneous company of young men and young women and children, evidently belonging for the most part, but not altogether, to the working classes, sitting and lying at ease upon the grass on a Sunday evening, singing such music, and singing it so well. Whatever they may have thought, I never saw the blankness of utter astonishment more plainly than in the faces of our motley audience.[87]

Munro remarked that, in 1858, Furnivall already showed himself 'the friend and champion of women'.[88] It is not entirely clear at this point how he did this, apart from supporting the admission of women to classes and agreeing to promote dances where the men could enjoy

[83] Munro, 'Biography', p. xxvii.

[84] Furnivall, 'Social Life of the College', 58. See *OED*, 'casino', n. sense 2, 'A public room used for social meetings; a club house, *esp.* a public music or dancing saloon'. Furnivall does not allude to the later sense of gambling.

[85] Hudson, *Munby: Man of Two Worlds*, 155; he mentions Caldwell's dancing rooms as one of the few: 'the only representative we have, that I know of, of the German middleclass dancing rooms. Lots of young men, clerks & apprentices, dancing with young women of the same class—also respectable, but not very attractive. Things carried on in an easy & unconstrained but virtuous manner: for fast girls & prostitutes think the place "slow"' (p. 22).

[86] J. F. C. Harrison, *History*, 63–4; Furnivall, 'Social Life of the College', 56. See also Litchfield's detailed account of the 'Methods of Teaching Vocal Music', *Working Men's College Magazine*, 1, pp. 110–19 (1 July 1859).

[87] Hudson, *Munby: Man of Two Worlds*, 168–9.   [88] 'Biography', p. xxvii.

female company in a respectable environment. It is evident from his diaries that he enjoyed women's company socially, but, like other young men of his class and time, apart from his sisters his serious friendships were with men. And, in the nature of the events, the excursions in which women participated did not include many who were unattached. Before he went to Cambridge, he had thoroughly enjoyed dancing into the early hours of the morning. It is likely enough that, under the aegis of the College, he privately welcomed the opportunity to organize such entertainments and meet attractive young women on his own account. It seems probable that he met his future wife, Eleanor Dalziel, at one of these dances, or at a College dinner—it is difficult to imagine how otherwise they might have met, apart from on the long College walks, in which we know she also took part. Holman Hunt had met Eleanor at College events in Furnivall's company: 'I am very sorry that I cannot . . . be present at the first of your jolly dinners . . . To some of the later ones I hope to come so please add to your stock of kindness which I am indebted that of asking Miss Dalziel to keep a menu for me in the next.'[89] Hunt recognized Furnivall's propensity to use the dances to get up flirtations and promote gossip when he told him:

I hope to come on Monday perhaps to bring a demoiselle with me for the sake of having a partner for myself or Woolner . . . Last time I found that the men as a rule only brought a lady each and it seemed clear therefore that the men who like myself came without any could not dance without depriving some one else of the pleasure—the party that I had engaged writes now saying that she has a severe cold, so perhaps after all I shall have to sponge on others . . . I may as well say that she is not the future Mrs H., but only a young lady engaged in business of the best possible conduct and ideas but fond of a dance when it can be enjoyed innocently.[90]

The dances were the winter counterpart to Furnivall's summer Sunday excursions. A committee, of which Litchfield and Roebuck, with other students, were members, was formed, and was invited to tea 'at Mr. Furnivall's, 21 Ely Place, Holborn'.[91] As Litchfield described, 'Some of the students . . . have . . . instituted the custom of having periodical dances, to which members and non-members invite their female friends.' In fairness, he went on: 'These have not been held in indirect connection

---

[89] Letter to Furnivall, 25 Oct. 1860, FU406, written from Hastings. 'Menu' here means 'dance card': cf. *OED* menu, n. II. 2 a.
[90] Letter of 26 Nov. 1860, FU 407. Thomas Woolner, who also taught at the College, was the only sculptor among the members of the PRB. Another member, the painter Val Prinsep, declined the invitation.   [91] Munro, 'Biography', p. xxvii.

with the College, or recognized in any way by its authorities, but they have been promoted chiefly, and managed entirely, by one of the Council of Teachers'—Furnivall, of course. As a result, they 'have practically been College parties', though held in the Salter's Hall, off Snow Hill, not the College premises. Four in the year were originally planned, but the first, in October 1859, was such a success that the enthusiasts could not wait until Christmas for the next, and by June the following year, no fewer than nine had been held, and the pattern was repeating itself.[92] Holman Hunt was one who expressed his enthusiasm: 'I shall be delighted to come and dance at the Ball. I will apply also to other men who like dancing if I may . . . altho they like myself may be not a little timid at unusual compositions like the Spanish dance and the Valse Cotillon taking the place of the legitimate round about Valse and Polka. How much is the ticket?'[93]

Litchfield, however, and some other members of the Council, including Ludlow, felt that the dances were getting out of hand. Maurice also cautiously intervened (after his previous experience with Furnivall he was clearly handling him with kid gloves): 'I am very sorry to be an obstruction, but I think, on the whole, a dance would not be desirable on Wednesday night. There are some who would be annoyed by it and who would be alienated', especially 'if the dances should become, as is rather likely, a mere miscellaneous gathering'.[94] Litchfield's editorial 'Work and Play; or Heads and Heels' was more hard-hitting: 'It is worth while to consider whether the net result has been, or is likely to be, good or bad. After balancing all the circumstances of the case, I, for one, am clearly convinced that it has been bad.'[95]

The dances had become such a success that news of them had travelled to the Wolverhampton Working Men's College, which Furnivall had visited to promote his ideas about social life in the colleges, and his views more generally. Some of their student members did not 'think we shall be able to manage the dancing, as there does not seem to exist a wish for it', but they begged to know when the London Working Men's College was having their Christmas party 'as some of us may come up

---

[92] Litchfield, 'Work and Play; or Heads and Heels', 2. Litchfield continued: 'Much objection had been made to the frequency of last year's entertainments, and it was announced that there would be four in the season, and, as was generally understood, four only; but again another was added a few weeks after the first. A grand "Rifle Ball", fixed for December 27th will have been the third within two months'.
[93] Letter of 24 Apr. 1860, FU 404.
[94] Letter of 14 June [1859], FU 582.
[95] Litchfield, 'Work and Play', 2.

to it if convenient'. Meanwhile, 'Be sure to let us know of your next party'.⁹⁶

The Wolverhampton group seem to have copied the London college's 'Social Committee'. Furnivall wrote to them, on dances and other social matters, and, following London's model, they also looked around to find a boxing teacher of their own.⁹⁷ He also used the chance to advertise his own increasingly radical political activities in a way Maurice would have been unlikely to approve, had he known of them. When they received Furnivall's letter, the Wolverhampton student body was avid to hear it.⁹⁸ This further evidence of his popularity even beyond the London Working Men's College must have done much to confirm Furnivall in his stance of defiance towards the London College's authorities, as did a supportive letter from the educationalist Elizabeth Malleson: 'It has given me a great deal of pleasure to see y(ou)r circular of the 'Four Dances'[;] the plan has our most hearty sympathies—it is so right & good that working men and women sh(oul)d have pleasant intercourse together—that the less educated sh(oul)d enjoy with the more | educated & refined.'⁹⁹

Thus much of Furnivall's popularity with the College's students was based in his alliance with more radical elements among them and his agenda of promoting fun, as well as his attractive, welcoming, and ingenuous social manner. It soon became clear that he was not willing to jeopardize this new-found social success, because he was enjoying it too much himself. His refusal to curb the entertainments brought him into conflict with members of the Council who in other ways were his natural allies: Litchfield in particular. As Litchfield himself observed:

I am sorry to find myself directly opposed in this matter to one of the most active members of the Council, with whom till about six months ago I scarcely

⁹⁶ H. Butler's reply, letter to Furnivall, 7 Oct. 1859, FU 171.   ⁹⁷ Ibid.

⁹⁸ Ibid. 'When we came to the part of your letter referring to your speech being too radical, Bradshaw says, "Not a bit of it." Williams, "tell him he's a *stunner*," and some other observations to the same effect'. Butler thought Furnivall 'ought to have had a little pity' on the Prime Minister, Lord Derby, probably referring to the failed Parliamentary Reform Bill, introduced in Mar. 1859. On the Wolverhampton Working Men's College, see the account by J. N. Langley in the *Working Men's College Magazine*, 1, pp. 51–2 (no. III, 1 Mar. 1859).

⁹⁹ Letter of 9 Oct. 1859, FU 543, from 6 Marlborough Hill, St John's Wood: 'We are very anxious to find means of such enjoyment for our household & our work-people & feel much indebted to you for this winter beginning'. Elizabeth Malleson taught at the experimental Portman Hall School, founded on non-sectarian and co-educational (up to the age of 11) principles, and which mixed middle-class children with those of artisans; in 1864, she opened the Working Women's College at Queen Square, Bloomsbury. Owen Stinchcombe (revd.), 'Malleson [née Whitehead], Elizabeth (1828–1916)', *ODNB*.

ever had occasion to differ on a serious question... Mr. Furnivall is here acting in opposition to the convictions of *all* his friends, and of those especially who are most inclined to think with him on all other points.[100]

Litchfield supported the Sunday excursions, and, as we shall see, he also agreed with Furnivall against Maurice in the disputes over how Genesis could be reconciled with recent geological discoveries. But the dances were a step too far: Ludlow joined Litchfield and Maurice in the conviction that the College was a place of education, not amusement, and eventually Furnivall was isolated in a minority of one on the Council.[101] Litchfield pithily summed it up: 'As a rule, *dancing* men are certainly not *working* men.'[102]

Litchfield was anxious to make it plain that the College authorities, himself included, were not killjoys: 'The question is not, are we to have all work and no play?' But amusement should be rational and something useful should come of it—the question should be turned round: 'What sort of work can we find pleasant enough to be made play of?—and to that there are happily a thousand answers.' Among them are suggestions which may well have seemed austere to the College's pleasure addicts at the time: 'Suppose you play a game blindfold,—a fine piece of brain-gymnastics certainly, but would not a tough differential equation be just as amusing?' Litchfield's argument is that 'Amusement pure and simple is never needed by a rational being under any circumstances whatsoever. This may sound a barbarous doctrine, but it is practically true.'[103] Even simple amusement has its occasional place: 'None can enjoy more than myself such a mode of celebrating Twelfth-night or Christmas Eve, with blind man's buff, hunt-the-slipper, and all the rest of it; but to repeat the metamorphosis once a month, and for a period of seven continuous hours... seems to be taking far too large doses of an innocent restorative,—turning, in fact, a useful tonic into a pernicious drug.'[104]

Litchfield's essay is not as 'barbarous' as it seems, though the points are serious and forcefully made. It was written as a contribution to the Christmas edition of the magazine, and its grumpiness was in part playful, as he elaborated just why, in his view, dancing, though undoubtedly fun, must 'rank as among the least useful form of social enjoyment: You have danced with a variety of agreeable partners... you have seen no end of pretty coiffures; you have spun through clouds of tarlatan and crinoline; and you have been immersed for about seven hours

[100] Litchfield, 'Work and Play', 5 n.
[101] Colloms, *Victorian Visionaries*, 205.
[102] Litchfield, 'Work and Play', 4.
[103] Ibid. 1.
[104] Ibid. 3.

(according to our present practice, adopted, no doubt, in imitation of the fashionable world) in a torrent of fizz and excitement.'[105] Dancing might be good physical exercise, equivalent to a fifteen-mile Sunday afternoon walk, but this was, in Litchfield's view, a much more rational amusement: 'Who would exchange the breezy freshness of the Addington hills for the stifling swelter of a city dancing-room?'[106] Moreover, dances give rise to much extravagance of dress and expense: 'I must . . . protest against the reckless display of millinery which these parties have called forth in an ever-increasing ratio of gorgeousness.'[107] In short, the institution was a place of work, not a casino (even in its more benign sense of 'dance-hall') , although these resorts were undoubtedly more generally popular. The advocates of dancing risked changing the College's essential character. They should take warning from the failure of the Mechanics' Institutes: 'We have made a certain thing our business. Let us stick to that.'[108] Finally, work or play; heads or heels? The men must make their choice.[109]

Furnivall certainly rose to this challenge—considering himself to have been directly attacked in Litchfield's editorial, he responded with '"Heads *versus* Heels;" The Defendant's answer': 'Having been named by our Editor, Mr. Litchfield, in his article, or attack, in the last number, on the dances in which I have taken a leading part, it seems incumbent on me to say a few words in defence of them', which Litchfield printed.[110] Furnivall once again told the story, with embellishments harping on *purity*, of how, when he and a party of young men and women, amateur geologists, were in the chalk pit at Riddlesdown,

> A student-friend and I were chipping rhynconellas and terebratulas out of the broken chalk, when the friend announced: 'There is one thing above all others that some of us want which the College hitherto has not helped us to.' 'What is that?' 'Why the society of pure and good women. Some of us who know no families in London can't get it.' As one looked at the stains on the white chalk round one, and then up to the pure blue heaven above, one could not be touched by the words and the scene; they are as present to me now as eighteen months ago; and when I recollected the life of most men round me at College, and how often they had desired the same help, I saw how real the want was.[111]

In this and the following pastoral outbursts, Furnivall shows a weakness for rather strained pathetic fallacies to bolster the rhetoric. He

[105] Ibid. 2. [106] Ibid. 3. [107] Ibid. 4.
[108] Ibid. [109] Ibid. 5.
[110] *Working Men's College Magazine*, 3 (1 Feb. 1861), 20–2.
[111] Ibid. 20.

promised to help, and the wife of one of the College members assisted him. The first mixed party met at the Crystal Palace, 'and thereafter, throughout the summer, young ladies formed part of all our old fortnightly excursions, whether walking or rowing'. But autumn threatened to bring these pleasures to an end. In Epping Forest, 'while we watched and sang to the sunset, "We cannot give up our meetings; as we cannot have them out-of-doors, we must have them in; and we will have some dances." All liked the notion.' Then and there a committee was formed, which included women (married and single), which prepared a circular. Furnivall's influence on it is evident: 'All Working Men and Women find that they have neither the rooms nor the money to get together a party of their friends for a merry Dance of Social Meeting; the pleasant evening "At Homes" of richer people are out of their reach'. Everything was designed to keep the costs down: evening dress would not be expected, and, to assist social intercourse, 'Ladies will dispense with introductions of partners'. Furnivall chronicled the dances that had taken place and noted, with some exasperation: 'And really the people taking part in them were neither boys and girls at school, who needed telling what was reasonable and lawful for them, and what was not, nor were they fools, as has been half suggested; but men and women able to judge for themselves, attending such dances only as suited them, knowing what their purses and occupations could afford.' The peroration developed the innocence of the merriment further: 'bright spots in the year, for all who took part in them were the evenings of our dances, and our tea, I am sure'.[112]

Furnivall threatened further comments on the subject in the next number of the magazine, but the cause was taken up on his behalf by a student member of the dance committee, Thomas Preston, to repudiate the 'uncalled-for insinuations' in Litchfield's original article, though 'Of course Mr. Furnivall will be able to show the fallacy of three-parts of the argumentation'.[113] Preston took exception to the view that the dances had been extravagant. The Committee had declared against evening dress, but two or three ladies flouted the rule, and attended '*en grande toilette*', and were the most courted all evening; 'there was an

[112] Ibid. 20–2.
[113] Preston's reply has the same title as Litchfield's editorial: 'Work and Play, or Heads and Heels', *Working Men's College Magazine*, iii. 36–8 (1 Mar. 1861), 36. It was dated 25 Jan. 1861, but the editor, Litchfield, recorded that it had not been printed in the previous issue, as his and Furnivall's exchange had, in his view, sufficiently presented the two sides of the argument, but Preston's contribution 'now appears in accordance with a special request'.

immense demand for their programmes'. If, on subsequent occasions, the rest appeared buoyed up by 'clouds of tarlatan and crinoline', this was only natural; 'It is all very well to try to appear insensitive, but a man is as pleased to see a lady prettily dressed as ladies are to dress themselves out to advantage.'[114] Moreover, nearly all leisure activities, including those favoured by Litchfield, incur cost, like the white kid gloves, opera tickets, and refreshments required by Litchfield's singers. And even Sunday walkers to the Addington Hills need transport and sustenance at a roadside inn.[115]

Preston's contribution had been intended for publication in January 1859, but had been held over until the March number of the magazine. By this time the dispute had already been settled but continued to cause excitement. At a 'Conference on the Amusement Question' in February, Maurice had appealed for open discussion, and declared himself on Litchfield's side. His invitation to others to speak was met with 'a few minutes' silence', broken, predictably, by Furnivall, who, sensing that the mood of the meeting was against him, was unusually conciliatory. He distanced himself from Preston's rather overheated remarks, and he recognized that Litchfield's comments had been over-egged for humorous effect: as he put it, they were pervaded by 'a certain tone of pleasant exaggeration or editorial glow'. He observed that the criticisms of excessive expenditure had been overstated, and that the Committee had done what it could to 'check over-dressing'. The parties had been 'studiously kept separate from the College'. The sting came in the tail: He 'was not surprised that the proceeding should meet with opposition from some of the Council and at that conference. Dancing was not a thing which he should expect clergymen to take much interest in.'[116] However, Maurice, in the chair, did not rise to the proffered bait, and it was left to another clergyman, Septimus Hansard, to protest against the notion 'that a clergyman, as such, was a foe to dancing or any other innocent amusement'. They had Christmas dances at his own church, which he attended, and where he enjoyed himself very much. The problem was not with dancing in itself, but that as a 'systematic amusement it produced grave incident evils'.[117] For Ludlow, the matter brought into

[114] Preston, 'Work and Play', 37. [115] Ibid. 36–7.
[116] (unsigned), 'Conference on the Amusement Question', *Working Men's College Magazine*, 3, pp. 22–6 (1 Feb. 1861), 22. Here, and in following quotations, Furnivall's contributions to the discussion are reported in the third person, following the conventions of minuting a formal meeting.
[117] Septimus Hansard, quoted in 'Conferences on the Amusement Question', *Working Men's College Magazine*, 3 (1 Feb. 1861), 23.

question the College's entire existence: it must choose between seriousness and frivolity: 'Is it rational, is it decent, for a Working Men's College to be amusing itself with wreaths and white waistcoats?' Litchfield brought the discussion to a close, and at the subsequent meeting, the proposition was agreed that these entertainments 'are likely to be seriously detrimental . . . and that it is the duty of every Member of the Council to abstain from encouraging them'. Only one vote was against it—having said and done what he had, Furnivall could scarcely support the motion.

Even yet, the matter was not settled: 'a wish had been expressed' (it may be supposed by Furnivall) for a second conference, which took place, with more students in attendance, and which was presided over by Furnivall's supporter, Sam Standring, the 'father of the College', who conducted the meeting with 'tact and genial good-humour'. This time Furnivall was less moderate: 'The dances were designedly kept away from the College that it might not be compromised; and he thought it hard that men could not meet their friends for the purpose of dancing, without the interference of the Council, merely because they happened to be members of the College. It was not intended to increase the number of the dances, as seemed to be feared.' A student member of the Committee, W. Sutton, tried to take the heat off Furnivall, but also administered the *coup de grâce* to his scheme: 'I . . . cannot leave Mr. Furnivall to bear the whole weight of defending the course taken by the promoters of the dances. I like the dances, but I like the College very much more; if the two will not work together, and we must make a choice between them, let the dances go by all means.' Litchfield was Sutton's good friend, as well as Furnivall, and reading Litchfield's remarks in the magazine, 'I had a sensation very like that of being skinned'.[118] After even some of the leading students had spoken against him Furnivall had to bow to the inevitable: 'After the next dance, which had been fixed some weeks back, the present organization of them would be at an end; but he hoped that he might be able, in some way quite different and quite disconnected from the College, to have some kind of social meeting with his friends; but this was not a question on which he intended to stake his position as a member of the Council.'[119] Holman Hunt, recognizing the mood of the College, declined to attend this final Christmas dance:

> I should much like a dance with your party on Monday night, but I am afraid of appearing to be indifferent to the feelings of some good men in the Working

[118] Ibid. 23–4. [119] Ibid. 24–5.

Men's College, who I have been told fear that ill effects may result from such gatherings if not conducted with great reserve. As you mixed up with the 'men' in so many projects for their instruct|tion and enjoyment your absence would doubtless be to be regretted but I have no claim of the same kind to attend as you ... the motive might so fairly be regarded as a selfish one.[120]

It is clear that the question of the College entertainments had isolated Furnivall from the Council and that he was beginning to feel alienated, though not yet ready to compromise his position in the College. Yet he was beginning to think, by 1861, what else he might do for working men independently, and away from the College.

THE VOLUNTEER MOVEMENT

In general, Furnivall's promotion of extracurricular activities cannot be said to have helped the students concentrate on their studies, and his grammar classes, though apparently entertaining, were not something for which he was initially well qualified. As seen, they seemed to at least one observer to be an opportunity for the display of his idiosyncrasies. The last straw for Litchfield had been the 'grand "Rifle Ball"' arranged for 27 December 1860, the third College dance within two months.[121]

This party was called a 'Rifle Ball' because in 1859 men of the College had formed a volunteer rifle regiment, the Nineteenth Middlesex, and were proud that it had been one of the earliest volunteer organizations in the country, including London. They wanted to celebrate. The immediate cause of the formation of the volunteer forces had been the attempted assassination of Napoleon III by the Italian nationalist Felice Orsini on the evening of 14 January 1858, when Orsini and his accomplices threw bombs at the Emperor's carriage. Before the attack, Orsini had spent time in England, lecturing, and learning about explosives; indeed the 'Orsini bombs' had been made in Birmingham, and Orsini had returned to France with a false British passport. Furthermore, the expatriate Italian leader Giuseppe Mazzini, much admired among Furnivall's circle, was living and fund-raising, with his associates, in London. Accordingly, from the French perspective, the Orsini plot had been just the latest in a series of assassination attempts by Italian nationalists harboured in Britain, which had no policy of extradition of political exiles and refugees. Orsini had contacts with English

---

[120] Letter to Furnivall, 27 Dec. 1861, FU 422.
[121] Litchfield, 'Work and Play, Or Heads and Heels', 2.

radicals, including George Holyoake of the Co-operative League, editor of the anti-Christian paper *The Reasoner*, in which he fought hard against the Christian Socialists and eulogized Jelf for his dismissal of Maurice.[122] There was anxiety about French reprisals for the Orsini affair, and this was perhaps the most sensational ingredient of the chronic British fear of a French invasion, which came to crisis point in 1859, when, on 12 May, the Secretary of State for War, Lieutenant General Jonathan Peel, sent a circular to the Lords Lieutenant authorizing the formation of volunteer corps for national defence.[123]

As Roebuck recalled, the threat of French invasion had been the sole topic of conversation at the Wednesday social evenings at the Working Men's College in the early part of 1859, and Tom Hughes had put forward the idea that College members should take part in the volunteer movement to supply at least some of the 'million of deadly marksmen that are to line every hedgerow between Kennington Common and Pevensey Bay, before the first thousand of invaders have formed upon the beach', which, according to Litchfield, were being demanded.[124] In May, Hughes wrote to the Lord Lieutenant of Middlesex, the Marquess of Salisbury, offering to form a company. Permission was provisionally granted subject to finding a practice rifle range of not less than 300 yards and a secure store for the armaments. In the meanwhile Hughes was able to get permission for a corps to drill.[125] After Lord Goderich lent his support, approval was finally sent in November, and a company of seventy-two, which increased rapidly, was formed. Drills were held in the College garden, by gaslight.[126] Though the College was undenominational, the Church of England in general supported the militias, and F. D. Maurice was commissioned as the chaplain of the regiment.[127]

At one of these meetings, on 4 May, a student, Philip Read, who had been keeping quiet about his former service as colour-sergeant in the 33rd Regiment of Infantry, the 'Duke of Wellington's Own', offered to drill the men if a corps was formed. As Munro reported, '"Thanks,

[122] Maurice, *Life of Maurice*, ii. 157, 211 (and for Maurice's admiration of Mazzini, see ii. 548); Ludlow, *Autobiography*, 264–5.
[123] On the volunteer movement, see H. Cunningham, *The Volunteer Force*; also, in relation to the Working Men's College, see Girouard, *Return to Camelot*, 141.
[124] Munro, 'Biography', p. xxxix; *Working Men's College Magazine*, 1, pp. 96–7 (1 June 1859).
[125] 'The College Rifle Corps', *Working Men's College Magazine*, 1, pp. 185–7 (1 Dec. 1859).
[126] Munro, 'Biography', p. xxxix. For Ludlow's impressions of the value of drill, in which he participated, see 'Thoughts on Drill', *Working Men's College*, 2, pp. 21–4 (1 Feb. 1860).
[127] H. Cunningham, *Volunteer Force*, 74; Roebuck, 'Reminiscences', 92.

Read," said Furnivall, "but do you know anything about soldiering?" '[128] This hero, as he proved to be (around 28–30 years old), had retired from active service after being wounded in the Crimean War at the battle of the Great Redan, five years earlier, and had distinguished himself at Inkerman.[129] He was now working as a telegraph clerk in Buckingham Palace, and he was also—perhaps predictably—a member of Furnivall's grammar class.[130] After the new regiment was formed, he was presented by Hughes, on behalf of all, with a handsome sword, and, according to Furnivall, everyone 'always cut and butterd his bread at tea, and paid for it, and would any of us have blackt his boots with pleasure'.[131]

Hughes and Read, the drill-master, did much between them to whip up enthusiasm for the corps, and at one of their meetings, on 23 October, they formed a committee to take charge of its business excluding military control, which rested with the major-commandant, Hughes, with three captains serving under him. The first captain to be appointed was John Martineau, a Cambridge graduate, and Roebuck, Tansley, Read, and other senior students served as subordinate officers. Furnivall, later company commandant, was chosen, with others, to serve on the committee. Another of the teachers to volunteer was Holman Hunt, who told Furnivall self-effacingly: 'I am inclined to think that the drill dance might be a success and I should be happy to take a part in it but not the part of an officer in command because for one thing I could scarcely feel certain of getting thro' my duties without some bungle and also because I want on principle to avoid exhibiting any disposition to aspire to the post of honor.'[132] Hunt expressed his willingness to serve on the corps' Committee: 'Put my name down by all means.'[133]

On the face of it, apart from patriotism, there seemed little incentive for working men to join the volunteer movement, not least because it involved some considerable financial outlay—the volunteers had to pay for their own uniforms.[134] Yet the movement was soon dominated by

[128] 'Biography', p. xl.
[129] Munro, 'Biography', p. xl.
[130] Roebuck, 'Reminiscences', 77–8.
[131] As reported by Munro, 'Biography', p. xl; Furnivall, *Working Men's College Magazine*, p. 59.
[132] Letter of 26 Nov. 1860, FU 407.
[133] Letters of 26 and 30 Nov. 1860, FU 407, 408. Despite his fondness for dancing Hunt was anxious not to offend members of the College (principally Litchfield and Maurice), who foresaw the 'ill effects' that 'may result from such gatherings if not conducted with great reserve' (letter of 27 Dec. 1861, FU 422).
[134] See H. Cunningham, *Volunteer Force*, 26–7.

artisans and tradespeople (though not labourers).[135] Moreover, despite the general patriotism, the College's 19th Middlesex corps did rather little to promote general cohesion within the College, apart, again among the inner circle: the corps attracted new members, 'who came not as students but for the purpose of belonging to the corps, while some of the best students were drawn away from their class work'.[136] Perhaps strangely, volunteering also appealed to artists—Holman Hunt among them—and authors.[137] The College's ready association with the Volunteer movement was very natural, at least for its core members. The atmosphere of the meetings, especially in the early days, was club-like and social, and, like the College itself, it was hoped that volunteering would teach young men obedience and discipline and occupy their leisure time in a way beneficial to their health and well-being. As a Captain in the London Scottish said, volunteering made men 'less idle and dissipated, and more respectful to authority'. Indeed, there were places 'where casinos, dancing saloons, skittle alleys, billiard rooms, and similar places have been closed by the absence of the custom of men who once frequented them'.[138] And the field days away on manœuvres 'made an enjoyable outing for us pent-up Londoners'.[139]

Moreover, the training in the use of firearms and the issue of rifles to the men must also have been a draw, and helped corporate solidarity, though the men did not use real, or even dummy, ammunition. The 19th Middlesex was trained in musketry at the Government School at Hythe. It was an exacting course, though learning did not include 'actually firing off powder, either in blank or ball cartridge—we should have learned little from that'. As a result those who attended became 'competent riflemen and good shots without firing a cartridge'.[140] Rifle-shooting was also a sport which appealed equally to middle- as well as working-class participants: the rifle club was 'an even better mode both of class-mixing and manly recreation than cricket'.[141] Because the officers tended to be drawn from the middle classes, who tended to take

[135] On lower working-class hostility to the Volunteers, see ibid. 78–9.
[136] The heads of the College 'while fully alive to the distraction and interruption which it produced, on the whole . . . considered that the attraction of larger numbers to the College would outweigh the injury to the classes'; Forster, 'Transition Period', 102–3.
[137] H. Cunningham, *Volunteer Force*, 83.
[138] Ibid. 29; also pp. 117–18 (testimony of the *Volunteer Service Gazette*).
[139] Roebuck, 'Reminiscences', 91 (describing a Saturday expedition to Epsom Downs).
[140] Roebuck, 'Reminiscences', 84–5, 87–8. It was a proud moment for Roebuck when he was issued with his own rifle (pp. 89–90). For concerns about military discipline among the volunteers, see Cunningham, *Volunteer Force*, 63; and on musketry training, pp. 110–11. [141] Cunningham, *Volunteer Force*, 114, quoting Martin Tupper.

the initiative in forming a corps, the success of the movement was seen as a 'wonderful testimony to the improvement of class relationships since the days of Chartism, and to the maintenance of the physique of the people in an urban civilization'.[142] The rapid growth of the Volunteer movement was such that, by 1860, 21,000 Volunteers could assemble in Hyde Park on 23 June, to be reviewed by 'Her Majesty the Queen, the Prince Consort, and all the notables of the kingdom'.[143]

Because the men paid for their own uniform, the choice of outfit was a collective one, made by the members of each corps. Understandably, the corps of the Middlesex 19th Rifles gave much thought to the image they wanted to project, as well as to how ostentatious (and consequently expensive) the uniforms should be. Given the class and political tensions within the College, this became a lightning-conductor for larger disagreements.[144] Roebuck noted that the Corps Committee decided the matter 'not without considerable discussion and clash of opinion'. One party wished for an 'attractive, ornamental uniform', which cost £2, beyond the means of the working men, for whom this would be an 'absurd tax'; moreover, Litchfield considered the desire not to be seen in cheap clothing as 'detestable flunkeyism'. In his view 'the Volunteers have been the slaves of tradition and the tailors, none more so . . . than the Committee of the Working Men's College corps'.[145] The second party opted for an 'ultra-plain uniform, Garibaldi shirt and belt'; however, the third carried the day, and chose 'a neat, military-cut suit, with little in the way of ornamentation'.[146] This decision in favour of a plain and serviceable dress was probably wise, and helped to defuse superciliousness from the social elite as well as the mockery of street urchins: as Cunningham said, there was no escaping the realization that 'there was something absurd and comic in this serious playing at soldiers by men whose daily avocations were thoroughly civilian'.[147] Furnivall's desires in the matter

[142] Ibid. 1, and see also pp. 34–5, and tables of occupations of men and officers, pp. 56–8.

[143] Ibid. 1; Roebuck, 'Reminiscences', 87, who puts the number present at the lower figure of 18,000. Munro, 'Biography', p. xl, put the figure at 18,500. See photograph of the meeting of the Metropolitan Rifle Corps, with members of the Working Men's, 19th Middlesex Corps, included by Girouard, *Return to Camelot*, 135.

[144] That any perceived slight from a superior officer to his subordinates could readily stir up a grievance may be seen from the letter of 8 Sept. 1860 from Hughes to Roebuck, quoted in 'Reminiscences', 86–7. Jealousy about whom Hughes chose for the privilege of going to Hythe for the musketry course could also arise: letter to Roebuck, 5 Sept. 1860, 'Reminiscences', 85.

[145] 'College Volunteers', *Working Men's College Magazine*, 2, pp. 113–17 at 116–17 (1 July 1860).   [146] 'Reminiscences', 81–2; see also Cunningham, *Volunteer Force*, 95.

[147] Cunningham, *Volunteer Force*, 83.

are unreported, but the most expensive option seems unlikely to have appealed. It is likely to have been Hughes who took the lead in the final choice of uniform: when the officers of the Volunteer regiments were invited to a *levée* at Court, those of the 19th Middlesex, led by Hughes, declined: 'My reason for not wishing to go to Court, and the majority of the corps thought with me, was that I think the business of the Rifle movement a very serious and solemn affair, and that we ought to keep as far aloof as we can from the frivolity and dandyism which is being imported into it.'[148] As the matter of the 'Rifle Ball' showed, Furnivall, for his part, enjoyed the excuse which being in the militia gave for dressing up and having parties, though they could be noisy and disturb the neighbours, as Hughes noted, in ruling a 10 o'clock curfew for these events, after Furnivall had written to him on the matter.[149]

In 1860, Hughes mentioned Lieutenant Furnivall, with others in the corps, for promotion and commissions. Furnivall remained in the Volunteer movement for twelve years.[150] Hughes himself resigned in 1869.[151] However, it cannot have been easy for Hughes to act as Furnivall's superior officer after, in 1862, the simmering resentment which Furnivall bore towards him erupted into the open. Hughes wrote to Furnivall, offering, if without much hope, a reconciliation. It must have been a difficult letter to write: Hughes was well aware of Furnivall's personal dislike of him.

I have been much grieved to hear what has taken place between you and some of our best men—also at all I have heard of late doings and relations between you & other fellow members of the College. You must see that a crisis has come.

For old sakes sake I should rejoice very much if it may be possible to drown and forget everything unpleasant which has happened in the last 14 years & to start with you again in the old place at the old work. It all rests with you, but I feel that after what has taken place between you and me at one time or another I may be a stumbling block in your way—I can quite fancy, putting

[148] Munro, 'Biography', p. xl. Plate NB shows Captain Hantler, one of the Working Men, in the uniform of the 19th Middlesex Volunteers.

[149] 'Furnivall writes to me . . . of the party at headquarters the other day. The man at No. 13 groaned about the singing, but he must get inured to it . . . As a rule, I think the house should be shut at ten'. Letter to Roebuck, 5 Sept. 1860, 'Reminiscences', 85–6.

[150] Roebuck, 'Reminiscences', 80–1; Benzie, *Dr F. J. Furnivall*, 58; Munro, 'Biography', p. xli; letter from Hughes to the Lord Lieutenant, 26 Aug. 1860, FU 397 (copy of original).

[151] Circular letter of 5 May 1869, FU 401: 'It is useless to fight the inevitable. For years I have felt that I could not give time enough to the Corps and have only held on at the urgent request of Read, Bailey, &c &c—I shall still be honorary Colonel and so capable of advising & helping in many ways. I tried all I could for some first rate outsider but no such thing is to be had now I shall announce my intention on Saturday at the drill having only postponed sending in my resignation till I could get you together to tell you of it'.

myself in your place, that I should rebel against saying or doing anything which might look 'amongst other complex aspects' like giving Hughes a triumph. If any thought of this kind is in your mind 'as I believe it would be in mine,' for God's sake my dear Furnivall, kick it out—I can say most truly that in all our differences the feeling of personal antagonism to you has never I will not say entered into—but has certainly never dwelt in my head or heart—I have always felt that I had much to learn from any course of action which you have chosen to take & have learned much by considering the arguments by which you have supported many places of which I disapproved and which I have opposed. But do believe that, if you will shake hands with Litchfield and bring your plan loyally into discussion on Wednesday advocating your views as strongly as you please, but agreeing to be bound by the decision of the Council so far as anything but your own personal liberty of action is concerned, there is no man who will be more truly glad than I shall be, or will try harder to work with you in Ormond Yard.

There is another matter to which I allude with great reluctance but which must be mentioned as I am making a clean breast of it. If we are to be again *quite* on the old footing, that would have to be satisfactorily settled & there are few pieces of news which would give me such hearty pleasure as to hear that it were so. The day which saw us again *quite* on the old footing of friends and fellow-workers would be a white one in my calendar. Don't answer.[152]

There was probably no single reason for this falling out, which seems to have been occasioned by Hughes's dismay at Furnivall's disagreements with Litchfield and Ludlow over the College's social life which had resulted in his isolation in a minority of one on the Council in the 'Heads versus Heels' debate. The Volunteer corps had been another source of tension between Furnivall and Litchfield, who had argued that the College should sever its connection with the Volunteer movement, though Maurice intervened in support of the students' wishes.

The nature of the 'other matter' to which Hughes so delicately alluded almost certainly refers to the scandal caused by Furnivall's open relationship with Eleanor Nickell Dalziel, sister of William Dalziel, student teacher of the College, whom he married in the summer of 1862 after, as Benzie carefully expressed it, 'she had been inseparable from Furnivall for some time before they were married'.[153] Munby, who visited the pair in Furnivall's lodgings before their marriage, noted that it was for her sake that Furnivall 'has behaved so madly to Litchfield & others of his best friends; & her brother, a student of the College'.[154]

---

[152] Letter of 21 June 1862, from 3 Old Square, Lincoln's Inn, FU 398.
[153] Benzie, *Dr F. J. Furnivall*, 24.
[154] Hudson, *Munby: Man of Two Worlds*, 123, diary entry for 19 May 1862.

The circumstances of Furnivall's marriage are considered more fully below, but it may be said here that Hughes is likely to have meant that he will be glad to hear that the relationship between Furnivall and Eleanor Dalziel had been regularized in the eyes of the world. It is worth commenting, however, that, though the College authorities naturally disapproved of one of their teachers cohabiting with a student's sister, the liaison was no more irregular than the flamboyant love affairs of Rossetti, another teacher at the College. Or the not wholly chaste pursuit of 'stunners' by the wider Pre-Raphaelite group. But anyone less sympathetic to Bohemia than Maurice is hard to imagine.

'GENESIS AND GEOLOGY'

Munby's account of an evening spent at Macmillan's, in Henrietta Street, in the company of other teachers at the College hinted at yet another 'jar' between Furnivall and Maurice:

> Then the talk grew towards Genesis & Geology: Macmillan holding that Maurice had fully explained Chap. I—Litchfield & Furnivall laughing to scorn (though with full recognition of Maurice's greatness) his, or any, reconcilement—Vernon mediating in his clear earnest way—I as usual, watching... And hearing such talk of Maurice, one feels most the brute folly of the Evangelicals, who persecute as infidel & traitor a man who is to many their only hope for loyalty and faith, & whose only crime, with others, is that he believes too much, & holds too strongly what he holds.[155]

'Genesis and Geology' was a convenient and much-used, if oversimplified, slogan to summarize the conflicts which had arisen throughout the first half of the nineteenth century, long before the publication of Darwin's *Origin of Species* in 1859, and which resulted from the attempts to reconcile the new discoveries in the fields of geology and palaeontology with literal or fundamentalist readings of the Creation story in Genesis.[156] Many of the leading protagonists, including William Buckland, canon of Christ Church Cathedral in Oxford, who gave an annual lecture series on geology at Oxford from 1814 to 1849, and for whom a readership in the subject was created, were themselves clergymen, as also was James Gray, whose *Harmony of Geology and Scripture* Furnivall had read at Cambridge. As Buck-

---

[155] Ibid. 26, diary entry for Thursday, 3 Mar. 1859.
[156] See further Rupke, *The Great Chain of History*.

land proved, being a good man of the Church was not necessarily incompatible with being a good geologist.

Though the biblical account of the Deluge in Genesis could not literally be harmonized with geological discoveries, the relationship between theology and geology created much fruitful discussion on both sides.[157] Buckland's lectures were enormously popular—Ruskin, then an undergraduate at Buckland's college, Christ Church, prepared diagrams for his lectures, and collected minerals and fossils throughout his life. Ruskin described him as a man of humour and common sense, 'and benevolently cheerful doctrine of Divinity'.[158] And, while still at Oxford, he also met Charles Darwin, whom he buttonholed in conversation.[159] Charles Kingsley was also an articulate and passionate representative of the clergy who pursued scientific enquiries in the confident belief that better understanding of the natural world would only enhance understanding of God's purposes. He divided his time between parish work, the study of science, and correspondence with scientific men, telling Maurice in 1871 that he was 'very busy working out points of Natural Theology by the strange light of Huxley, Darwin, and Lyell'. By then Darwin was 'conquering everywhere, and rushing in like a flood, by the mere force of truth and fact'. Scientists were finding that 'now they have got rid of an interfering God—a master-magician, as I call it—they have to choose between the absolute empire of accident, and a living, immanent, ever-working God', Kingsley doing his bit to assist them to the latter.[160] His friend, Maurice, 'never tired of quoting the spirit of Mr. Darwin's investigations as a lesson and a model for Churchmen'.[161]

But, if there was no automatic hostility between men of science and men of religion, Maurice would find, in his dealings with the Working Men's College, that the pressure on him, as one who, as Munby said, 'believes too much, & holds too strongly what he holds', would become almost intolerable. When preaching at Lincoln's Inn on the Deluge, he had urged his listeners to take the story, simply, at face value, as a moral history which vindicated God's righteous government and ought to inculcate repentance and humble pride. However, 'we ... are not content to dwell upon its moral history ... We must build great

[157] In addition to Rupke, see Bowler, *Evolution: The History of an Idea*, 109–50.
[158] *Praeterita*, 192.
[159] Hilton, *John Ruskin*, i. 49; Leon, *Ruskin the Great Victorian*, 47.
[160] F. E. Kingsley (ed.), *Charles Kingsley: His Letters and Memories*, 253.
[161] Maurice, *Life of Maurice*, ii. 608.

theories upon it relating to the structure of the globe; theories of which the Bible suggests no hint, which interfere with the directness and simplicity of its story, but yet of which it has to bear the disgrace if science confutes them.'[162] The two modes of investigation could coexist if the listener would subdue intellectual pride. This seems likely to have been the '*very striking* sermon on the Fall' which Furnivall heard on Sunday, 23 February 1851.[163]

Just a few years later Furnivall would laugh Maurice's ideas 'to scorn'. In the meantime Maurice was forced to break with his friend and supporter John Colenso, the Bishop of Natal, when in 1862 Colenso expressed in print his difficulties with taking the Pentateuch literally.[164] Maurice was inevitably much distressed by the breach. And his position as Principal of the Working Men's College became increasingly difficult, in a climate where there was outspoken hostility to his religious views from two of his leading members of Council, as well as the men.

Litchfield, Furnivall's ally in agnosticism, as it would soon be called, would marry one of Darwin's daughters, Henrietta Emily ('Etty') in 1871. Geology, as well as being taught in the College, was a popular recreation for gentlemen, and one highly suitable for bringing gentlemen and working men together. As we have seen, Furnivall, who had now moved on from Gray's *Harmony*, was caught up in the general enthusiasm, this time with Litchfield's full approval: 'Geology is not the only science which should have attractions for working men, but it is this one which seems to me to possess the strongest claims to a place in a general system of education.'[165] Geology, Litchfield said, was also a hobby which took the men into fresh air, and which, at least for amateur collectors, did not require specialist knowledge, at least of the theories underlying it. Thus the long Sunday hikes which Furnivall arranged for the men were defensible as educational, like the excursion described by Munro in 1858, when Furnivall took 'some of the geological men' to geologize and hunt for fossils in the chalk pits, just beyond Croydon, at

---

[162] Maurice, *The Old Testament*, Sermon II, 'The Fall and Deluge', 39.

[163] Bodl. MS Eng. e. 2316, f. 16ʳ, entry for Sunday, 23 Feb. 1851.

[164] Maurice, *The Pentateuch and the Book of Joshua Critically Examined* (1862). See also *Life of Maurice*, ii. 421–4.

[165] Litchfield, 'A Plea for Geology', 64 (1 May 1861). It was not one of the curriculum's initial subjects; Furnivall noted that it was taught by W. Slade and Mr. Allbut (of Caius College, Cambridge), 'History of the Working Men's College', *Working Men's College Magazine*, 2, p. 191 (1 Dec. 1860). This was Thomas Clifford Allbutt, admitted to Caius in 1855, who took a first class degree in the Natural Sciences Tripos. He was a medical student at St George's Hospital in London, and became Consulting Physician and lecturer at the Leeds School of Medicine (*Alumni Cantabrigienses*, Part 2).

Caterham Junction, and Riddlesdown Common, Surrey. 'At the first pit some fine ventriculites were got; at the second, the Caterham Junction, what should the foremost man see before his eyes when he entered, but the beak and body of a pterodactyle—that strange bat-reptile of former days. Here, too, were other good fossils dug out.'[166] Furnivall was more taken with the pleasures of the day than the pterodactyl— and, for the time being, he took care in a public forum to thank his Maker: he rounded off his report with a lyrical account of their return to the station 'with the clouds gold and red above us, the hum of insects in our ears, and thanks to God in our hearts'.[167] Similarly, a notice of a forthcoming Sunday geological visit to the Hertford chalk pits concluded with the happy end to a rowing expedition to Isleworth, 'when we all walked home under one of the clearest and grandest starlit skies I ever saw, singing and chatting, happy and thankful, not unmindful of the maker of . . . the glittering worlds above our heads'.[168] The College started its own museum to display, among other materials, its large and growing collection of fossils: 'The close of the fourth year finds it with about 6,500 fossils . . . the bulk of this vast assemblage has been given by students.' Furnivall, Litchfield, Ludlow, Hughes, and Ruskin (who gave 'a noble collection of minerals') were among the museum's donors. The museum's Secretary was Henry Seeley, one of the students, as well as one of the College's success stories, who would shortly migrate to Sidney Sussex College, Cambridge, and establish himself in his distinguished geological and palaeontological career by working initially as an assistant in the Woodwardian Museum under Adam Sedgwick.[169]

As Munro said, Furnivall's adoption in around 1859 of a rampantly expressed unbelief could not be wholly explained, though his confrontational attitude in the late 1850s to anyone claiming paternal authority over him may well have disposed him to contest that of the Father of all. (Yet earlier correspondence suggests his abandonment of faith was already evident from c.1855–6, a year or so before the brouhaha over Sunday excursions.) Over and above the usual suspects, whom Munro identified as Darwin, T. H. Huxley, and Herbert Spencer, the sources of this change of heart resulted from 'doubtless other influences, not to

---

[166] Munro, 'Biography', pp. xxvi–xxvii. Quoted from the *Working Men's College Magazine*; Munro noted that the signature of the article, 'J. G. F.', was a mistake for 'F. J. F.'.

[167] 'Munro, 'Biography', p. xxvii.

[168] *The People*, Saturday, 21 Aug. 1858.

[169] *Working Men's College Magazine*, 1, pp. 170–2 (1 Nov. 1860); also 1, p. 81 (Supplement, 1 Apr. 1859, Fourth Annual Report).

be detected by the divining-rod of research'.[170] In large part, as Munro said, it was an unsurprising, if not inevitable, consequence of Furnivall's friendship with men whose experience of life had been very different from his own conventional Evangelical upbringing. Indeed, a lack of enthusiasm for devotion was common among the working men in the College: as one reported, 'Mr. Hughes, at the last meeting spoke of the students not attending prayers, saying that he could not undertake to lead the social life of a College in which the very bond and tie of social life was wanting'. The writer deplored young men 'who will read the first chapter of Genesis for its geology' and not for its serious content.[171] Hughes was supporting Maurice's standpoint, and his declaration is likely to have prompted Furnivall to consider that he would be willing to take Hughes's place as leader of the College's social life.

Maurice's bitter remark to Furnivall that the students at the College were being encouraged (presumably by some of the teachers, including Furnivall) to stay away from his Bible classes reflected what can fairly be described as a schism in the College which became more severe as time went on. By early 1861 Maurice, the Principal, ever on the defensive, felt obliged by his conscience to offer a 'Personal Explanation' to the College members. It is a striking illustration of his conviction that all in the institution should be treated as equal, and that he was as answerable as any. The 'Explanation' took the form of a frank letter addressed to Litchfield, as the editor of the College magazine, who had told him 'that my position in the College is not understood either by the students or by some of the Council'. Echoing his earlier words to Furnivall in a private letter, he affirmed his view that 'A Principal ought never to be a merely ornamental appendage to a College', and that 'When I say this, I do not shrink from the shame and disgrace which are implied in your statement. If I have not made myself intelligible to the students and teachers of the College, it must have been through some very grievous failure on my part.'[172]

Maurice recapitulated the history of the Bible classes which had begun at his house, back in 1848, when thrones were toppling throughout Europe, when he was known to a 'few friends' who recognized that, for Maurice, the knowledge of God, derived from the Bible, was the 'key

[170] Munro, 'Biography', p. xxxii.

[171] (unsigned), 'Ought Prizes to have a Money Value?', by 'A Student from the Beginning of the London College', dated Dec. 1859, *Working Men's College Magazine*, 2, pp. 10-14 (1 Jan. 1860), 13.

[172] Maurice, 'Personal Explanation', *Working Men's College Magazine*, 3, pp. 13-15 (1 Feb. 1861), 13.

to all other knowledge', and that he 'accepted the Bible as the interpretation of the history of mankind'. These friends were not required to accept his views—he recognized that 'they might think that the Bible was no better than any other book, or that it was a worn-out book', but they were expected to understand that it was the foundation, in his mind, of the distinctive contribution which he felt he could bring to the College. He trusted that a higher power than his own might persuade them of its truth when he refrained from such explanation himself. He admitted 'This may seem to many a most foolish opinion', but offering explanations in a year when the fall of earthly powers was prompting the question 'Was it true . . . that *all* invisible power was falling to pieces?' seemed a hazardous undertaking. Meanwhile, the reflection that Christ was the King of Men, manifest throughout the New Testament, acquired, for Maurice, a new significance, and he felt it his duty to expound the scriptural Christ, purified from extra-scriptural appropriations of his name. 'I should have no right to tell you in the Magazine what convictions I held in 1848, if these had not been the convictions which led my friends to choose me as the Principal of their College.' This theological cast of mind was, indeed, the only character in which they knew him, and 'But for this one redeeming belief, I was the unfittest person in all England for such an office.'[173] At that time 'I had a bad reputation with religious journals and with liberal journals. I had less knowledge of poor men than most of my brethren.' He felt himself, 'as you have all found too well', with little powers of persuasion or influence. He rested his case on his belief 'that the Revelation of God in Christ is the great power for the renovation of society, and especially for the elevation of the working class of Englishmen', as 'the only claim I ever had or ever shall have to take part in such a work as yours'.[174]

The 'Explanation' is a most Maurician compound of highly principled self-abasement and an extraordinary missive from a Principal to his College. Unfortunately for him, the strategy of proclaiming his own weakness in order to redirect attention to the source of his authority, located outside himself, and seeming as though he could hardly help it, was perhaps the one most likely to arouse derision from those who, like Furnivall, no longer recognized that authority, and would see humility in the Head as a form of unmanliness. The one qualification Maurice offered in his defence now seemed as 'worn out' (his own words) as the Bible itself. For his part Maurice had publicly drawn attention by

[173] Ibid. 13-14.   [174] Ibid. 15.

his confession to the distinction between the man and his office, from which he was growing increasingly detached.

As promised, Maurice followed up his apologia with another letter in the next issue, 'The Bible and the College'. This time he clearly recognized that he had been abasing himself too abjectly for the Principal of the College, and that his previous 'explanation' had been too timorous to win over anyone who held his views in contempt. His case is now alleged 'boldly' and as a challenge: 'what I was not afraid to do "at first," I am not afraid to do now'.[175] He summed up the conflicts between theologians, especially himself and 'eminent men': 'My name has been associated, even in penny newspapers which all people read, with the name of very eminent men who think that the English reverence for the Bible is exaggerated'. And he acknowledged the disputes between theologians themselves as to the Bible's authority and the trustworthiness of its text ('how far its words are affected by the human agents through which they come to us') as they must have appeared to members of the College who 'have other work to do in the world than to follow divines into all their intricacies of argument', and determine 'to let the whole subject alone' and abandon 'all interest in it whatever'.[176]

Maurice had built his career believing in the value of honest enquiry, and now found that this fundamental principle was being discarded: 'the negative conclusion is *taken for granted*—by those whose minds are least embarrassed with what are called religious prejudices'. He now challenged such readers to engage in open-minded investigation: 'If I have faith in it, I dare put it to that proof. Those who have not faith in it may be at least willing to learn what it contains.' Those prejudiced by their previous religious education think 'it has a sort of left-handed connection with the history of the world . . . but that the purpose of its writers is to impose a certain religious theory upon us which we are bound to accept under terrible penalties, though it may happen to contradict all history, though it may be especially at variance with the thoughts which most occupy us in our own day'.[177] He accepted the argument (made by Harriet Martineau and Henry Atkinson, among others) that Christians had built up an image of a 'divine Person' out of their own imaginations, as a kind of false god, and, if his readers would join with him, he trusted in the power of *scriptura sola* to correct this idolatry, so they could see for themselves the Bible's worth as

---

[175] Maurice, 'The Bible and the College', *Working Men's College Magazine*, 3, pp. 29–32 (1 Mar. 1861), 29. [176] Ibid. 29–30.
[177] Ibid. 30.

'a book of Ethics and Politics'. As such it ought especially to commend itself to working men, and 'a clergyman is never so likely to read it in this spirit as when he reads it with a class of men who see things from a point of view altogether unlike his'.[178]

And Maurice did not speak merely to the students: 'What I have said has far more to do with the teachers'. Those trained at the universities must bring their learning to 'bear upon the condition of the toiling, suffering classes'. He trusted that their faith would be confirmed if they 'did fairly meet these problems'. The notion that there was one God for the poor and another for the rich was 'damnable'. 'It was only those who were brought to feel that what the poor man wants they want; that they are men and must have all that men need,—it was only these who could ever learn whether there is any revelation of God or not'. It was a risky belief: Furnivall, for his part, had wholeheartedly thrown in his lot with the working men, and had learned from them their view that there was not. Maurice expressed his deep regret that, 'though I have the truest regard and affection for my colleagues', these feelings were not reciprocated: 'I do not feel that I know them, or that they know me. Our connection is cold and professional, not the least what it ought to be. I know what they will suspect that I intend by such words. They will suppose that I want to find out those who agree with me, and to get rid of the rest'.[179]

These remarks were not addressed exclusively to Furnivall, but he was certainly included in them. Maurice had, indeed, been advised by Ludlow to dismiss Furnivall, but had decided against it. He urged those who disagreed with him to speak out, as friends should, and engage in honest debate: 'I say it boldly, the less they agree with me the more I shall be pleased to meet them, and work with them. I shall think they are doing their own work truly and manfully in their own classes'. He was speaking for himself, as well as others, when he affirmed that 'To learn from the Bible, to feel its power of addressing all states of mind, we must be content to meet those whose education, tempers, and opinions are altogether unlike our own, who do not accept us as oracles, who try us with hard questions'.[180] He would state his position on the 'Genesis and Geology' controversy publicly in an extended series of letters addressed to a layman, published in 1863.[181]

While Maurice's defence of his views amply displayed his remarkable qualities as an individual, such arguments were unlikely to win over

[178] Ibid. 31.   [179] Ibid. 32.   [180] Ibid.
[181] Maurice, *The Claims of the Bible and of Science*.

men like Furnivall and Litchfield, whose beliefs had diverged too far from Maurice's convictions. While disagreeing with him thoroughly, Litchfield revered Maurice for being what he was, but the best Maurice could hope for from Furnivall (who was now assured that Maurice was too honourable to fire him for conscientious disagreement) was that he might be persuaded not to belittle his Principal in the eyes of the men by flagrant disobedience, and not to offer provocation which could not be overlooked. It is noticeable, after their falling out, how Maurice refrained from irritating him further by leaving the arguments about the College's social life to others to resolve, and that, when pushed to the brink by the Council, Furnivall drew back, unwilling to prejudice his senior role in the College, and he did not engage in further controversies in the magazine. The unsatisfactory truce seems to have held outwardly until Maurice, having been elected in 1866 to the Knightsbridge Professorship of 'Casuistry, Moral Theology and Moral Philosophy' at Cambridge, finally bade farewell to the Working Men's College in 1871, the year before he died.[182] Furnivall, for his part, without ever formally leaving it, became increasingly absorbed in his own independent literary projects. He became a genial social presence in the place, with his own recognized armchair. Both men may be said to have been adversely affected by their altercation, and to have impaired their association, which they both deeply valued, with the College.

Meanwhile the answer to Maurice's pleas for respect for his beliefs, and for willingness to engage in honest debate, came from Litchfield, who, without engaging in personalities, followed up a plea for a dominant role to be played by physical science in the College's curriculum with 'A Plea for Geology'.[183] Geology 'is the science which professes to tell us the history of the outside crust of our planet; how it came to be such as we find it; what it was in bygone times, before our species made its appearance; and by what changes it has come to its present condition.' 'Fifty years ago, the horizon of the past history of our planet lay close behind us. From the first appearance of our own species on its surface, we dated the beginning of all things. Now we are taught to regard ourselves as but the latest inhabitants.'[184] 'The attempt to compress the history of the world into the one or two thousand years about the epoch of the Noachic deluge, has been seen to be unnecessary and hopeless.'[185] Litchfield showed himself to be well versed in the subject's leading dis-

[182] Maurice, *Life of Maurice*, ii. 542–7; 633–4.
[183] Litchfield, 'Plea for Geology'. [184] Ibid. 64.
[185] Ibid. 65.

coveries and unfolding controversies, though he did not seek to provoke argument, but wished to engage his readers' interest by showing how the geography of parts of familiar parts of southern England and North Wales (which the men had visited in their excursions) had been shaped by geological processes. The very newness of the new science, as it had developed in the nineteenth century, was an attraction in itself: 'There are still worlds to conquer', and 'the youngest worker in the field may add something to the aggregate'.[186] The practitioner needs nothing at starting out but a strong pair of legs, a hammer, and a copy of Sir Charles Lyell's *Principles of Geology*. And the railways made promising sites for discovery easily accessible.[187]

There are other indications which suggest the influences on Furnivall's changing ideas. One was a letter, which Furnivall had requested, from the Quaker John Tindall Harris, whom Furnivall knew from Egham—Harris was the author of a treatise on the Apocalypse, itself coming under scrutiny as it appeared to limit the earth's physical existence to the time-span of human history. If the earth had been subject to a series of long drawn-out progressive successions, as witnessed by the geological record, then it would seem to follow that its future would be equally protracted.[188] Harris was rather nonplussed as to what to write in response to Furnivall, but gave his views on the Calvinist theologian and mystical writer Peter Sterry (1613–73). His comment suggests that this had been prompted, not only by Harris's own interest in eschatology, but by Furnivall's reaction to Maurice's views on the Fall, and desire to know what Harris thought:

I hope I feel at times the earnest longings after Eternal things and a good hope that through the grace of the Lord Jesus and His work . . . Is brought near to me or any one that the dayspring born on high has visited my soul & called me into fellowship with the saints in and through Christ the Lord . . . Sterry, I think, holds that there was an ideal creation of man in the mind of God before the actual creation, and that this ideal state implied in the sort of communion with himself in the words 'Let us make man', &c. is that perfectness 'from which we have fallen &' into which we are to be restored in Christ our Saviour. I only vaguely gather this from careless reading—I only fancy that Maurice has something like it. If you meet with any single sermons of Sterry's buy them for me.[189]

[186] Ibid. 67.   [187] Ibid. 68.
[188] See Rupke, *Great Chain of History*, 209–15.
[189] 'I am disappointed with Bengel. Perhaps having Sterry to read with him has dimmed Bengel . . . but in the "spiritual life" he falls far short of Peter Sternfor . . . I fancy Maurice has put him in one of his books (I think we hit on the 'other' brother (you and I) at

Back in 1851 Furnivall had recorded in his diary that he had been reading the controversial bestseller *Vestiges of the Natural History of Creation*, by the Edinburgh publisher Robert Chambers, first published, anonymously, in 1844, but recently republished in an inexpensive, revised, 'people's' edition to satisfy radicals who were also drawn to the book.[190] Chambers was an amateur *savant* attempting a bold synthesis of current scientific thought in several disciplines. Though his speculations attracted hostile comment from men of science, including Huxley, who, in a savage review, criticized Chambers's 'prodigious ignorance and thoroughly unscientific habit of mind',[191] they were a talking-point among fashionable London society—Prince Albert had even read *Vestiges* to the Queen. Fifteen years before Darwin, Chambers popularized ideas of evolution, though without explaining how it came about, and without forfeiting a divine plan which culminated in humankind at its apogee. Yet the distinction granted to this species was not the product of its inherently divine nature—in common with all other living things, humanity had evolved in accordance with natural laws. This was the point that largely damned the book in the eyes of many of its readers. Furnivall's verdict back in 1848 (which he regrettably did not elaborate) was that it was 'bosh'.[192] His views are likely to have changed since that time. The professor of geology at Cambridge, Adam Sedgwick, described *Vestiges* as a pernicious book, from which it was necessary to protect 'our glorious maidens and matrons', lest they 'poison the springs of joyous thought and modest feeling'.[193] But it was not necessary to protect maidens from Tennyson. It was also in 1851 that Furnivall read Tennyson's *Princess* (1847) to his sisters, while he, along with just about everyone else among the reading public, also read *In Memoriam* on its appearance in 1850. In both poems Tennyson, keenly interested in scientific advances of his

Egham). Sterry I think holds that there was an ideal creation of man in the mind of God before the actual creation and that this ideal state (is) implied in the sort of communion with himself'. Harris, letter of 6 Jan. 1859, from Bournemouth, FU 370. Author of *The Writings of the Apostle John: With Notes by the Late J. T. Harris*, ed. W. F. Brown, 2 vols. (London, 1889)], Harris (1817–87) died 13 May, Windsor. Harris gives his views on the Lutheran theologian Johann Albrecht Bengel (1687–1752), probably referring to his *Exposition on the Apocalypse* rather than his critical edition of the Greek New Testament, with discussion of editorial principles, fascinating though that would be in the light of Furnivall's later career.

[190] Chambers, *Vestiges of the Natural History of Creation*.
[191] Gillispie, *Genesis and Geology*, 162.
[192] Entry for Friday, 15 Aug. 1851, Bodl. MS Eng. e 2315, f. 41ʳ. On *Vestiges*, see further Bowler, *Evolution*, 141–50; Rupke, *Great Chain of History*, 176–9; Gillispie, *Genesis and Geology*, 149–83.   [193] Passage quoted in full by Gillispie, *Genesis and Geology*, 149–50.

'GENESIS AND GEOLOGY'   257

day, fascinates his readers with his accurate and detailed knowledge of the latest theories and geological discoveries while—being Tennyson—leaving his own views sufficiently open to interpretation as not to alarm his audience. The amenities of Park House, for example, include carved stones from its 'Abbey-ruin' which decorate the pavement in a gentleman's jumbled collectanea alongside 'Huge Ammonites, and the first bones of Time'.[194] Princess Ida is well aware of the recent discoveries of fossilized footprints made by extinct reptiles, and she takes her party to a spot where the river has eroded the rock to reveal 'the bones of some vast bulk that lived and roar'd Before man was'.[195]

Then, again in 1851, Harriet Martineau and her friend, the mesmerist and free-thinker Henry George Atkinson, published their extended correspondence *On the Laws of Man's Nature and Development*.[196] Furnivall read it. It was a controversial and radical bestseller, though it did not bring about the social ostracism which the writers feared, largely because the climate of opinion was changing: as Harriet Martineau herself observed: 'If I had known—what I could not know till the reception of our volume revealed it to me,—how small is the proportion of believers to the disbelievers in theology to what I imagined.'[197] The book ranged widely over many matters of lively speculative interest at the time: over the relations between science and theology, mesmerism, spiritualism, a confident account, based on a combination of phrenology and mesmerism, of the brain's geography, and the locations within it of all human faculties and capacities, and much else besides.[198] It was fundamentally a demonstration that physical laws sufficed to account for all natural phenomena without any need to postulate a Creator—as Harriet Martineau said: 'The argument of Compensation, by means of a future life, appears to me as puerile and unphilosophical as the Design argument in regard to "Creation".'[199]

Yet both writers accepted on philosophical grounds the need to postulate a First Cause, however unknowable it was.[200] Thus, though the

[194] *The Princess*, Prologue, in Tennyson, *The Poems of Tennyson*, ed. Ricks, ii. 188–9, ll. 14–15.
[195] *The Princess*, III, ibid. 171. For discussion of Tennyson's use in his poetry of geological knowledge and the current theories about the age of the earth, see Rupke, *Great Chain of History*, 225–30.
[196] Atkinson and Martineau, *Letters on the Laws of Man's Nature and Development*.
[197] Martineau, *Autobiography*, ii. 329–30.
[198] Ibid. 354–5.
[199] Atkinson and Martineau, *Letters on the Laws of Man's Nature and Development*, 164.
[200] After publication of the *Letters* Harriet Martineau explained herself to Charlotte

book was radical, it was not quite the bombshell that the writers' outspokenness made it appear. Henry Atkinson was equally, if not more, forthright: The average young gentleman who goes to college—like Furnivall—is taught 'a confused notion of unintelligible dogmas,—which are called religion'. Adam, 'though he made not himself . . . was punished for being what he was: The designer and creator of this abortion' required satisfaction, though he had predestined the whole mess; he 'makes himself a son—who is himself—to be his own satisfaction for what he has done; and that, in believing this, men shall be saved, and forgiven the sin which is in their nature, and inherited from another'.[201] Atkinson articulated the scorn, which Furnivall increasingly shared, for the inadequacy of a gentleman's education, which taught almost nothing except 'the ability to make a few quotations from the classics, and a smattering of mathematics'. 'The sciences and modern languages are neglected, and he learns but little of general literature and history.'[202] Atkinson was bracing in his advice for those who might mourn their loss of faith: 'They have found that Christianity is not historically true; and they shrink from finding their remnants of supernaturalism unphilosophical.' While 'noble minds', freed from these dogmas, rejoice in the loveliness and wonder of the natural world, those unwilling to shed their religion, and impelled by 'horror of loneliness' and fear of 'annihilation at death', 'create an ideal object and belief to satisfy this longing. As a result, 'their affections are perverted from their proper sphere of action; which is the love and companionship of their fellow-creatures. Men must learn to forget themselves in their love of nature, and the love of their fellow-men.'[203] The unenlightened 'are ridden down by puritanical priestcraft'.[204]

Harriet Martineau enthusiastically agreed: 'There is no theory of a God, of an author of Nature, of an origin of the universe, which is not utterly repugnant to my faculties.'[205] It was ridiculous that 'when men have reached this point under the guidance of science, they should yet cling to the baseless notion of a single, conscious Being, outside of Nature . . . How far happier it is to see—how much wiser to admit—that we know nothing whatever about the matter!'[206] The two writers expressed powerfully the impatience and derision being voiced in more

Bronte: 'I was an atheist in the vulgar sense,—that of rejecting the popular theology,—but not in the philosophical sense, of denying a First Cause'; *Autobiography*, ii. 351.

[201] Atkinson and Martineau, *Letters*, 203–4.   [202] Ibid. 203.
[203] Ibid. 206–7.   [204] Ibid. 210.
[205] Ibid. 217.   [206] Ibid. 218.

down-to-earth fashion by many of the men in the Working Men's College, along with Furnivall and Litchfield. Against such a background, Maurice's increasing sense of isolation within the College and his profound grief at the ill feeling aroused may readily be appreciated. Yet the *Letters* in themselves represented the kind of honest and civil debate he desired. In private conversation, however, as Matthew Arnold noticed, Harriet Martineau 'blasphemes frightfully'.[207]

So what did Harriet Martineau think of Tennyson? Furnivall wanted to know. In around 1855, and prompted by his reading of the *Letters*, he joined with William Johnson to send her *In Memoriam* as a present. He had already urged her (rather against her inclination) to read *The Princess*. She used the opportunity to give Furnivall her views on both poems:

I must beg of you to thank Mr. Johnson very heartily for me for the wonderful present he has sent me in this little volume. Like most people (whom I have met with at least), I shrank from a whole volume of published grief '& the more because I knew Arthur Hallam;' | & like everybody that has read it, I forgo my objection (which I still think natural) during the reading. I began to cut & read last night; & I stopped at last by a virtuous effort from the feeling that I ought not to be able to take in so much at once:—that I ought to spread it out,—though happily, I have the vol. to refer to at all times. I cannot however say that I had anything like so much pleasure from 'The Princess'. There are bits of wisdom & of beauty,—many (but the impression of the whole is more than odd;—it is very disagreeable—to my feeling). It does not follow that I am not glad to know it:—still less that I am not much obliged to you for making me read it as if I had liked it ever so much.[208]

However, Johnson and Furnivall had sent *In Memoriam*, not as a simple gift, but because they wanted to probe her views of Tennyson's reflections on the hot topics of immortality, geology, evolution, and theology. It seems clear that Furnivall, if not Johnson, had seized on the poem as supporting his own changing beliefs, and that there was, in Harriet Martineau's view, an element of finding what he wished to find in Tennyson. The relevant sections of the letter deserve quotation in full, not least because they hint at Furnivall's oversimplification of Martineau and Atkinson's arguments for his own needs, to suit a crude anti-religious propaganda (that 'men are only brain', or 'magnetic mockeries', and that

[207] Letter from Arnold in M. Ward, *A Writer's Recollections*, 24.
[208] Letter to Furnivall, 5 Oct. [c.1855], FU 552. The dating of the letter is probably based on Martineau's references to the imminent appearance of her next book, her autobiography, published later that year. For her acquaintance with Hallam, see *Autobiography*, i. 331.

Francis Bacon—admiringly referenced by both writers throughout the book—was a 'blackguard'):

And now I am wondering how Mr J(ohnson) and you can see any 'answer' in these two poems of T(ennyson)'s to anything Mr. Atkinson and I have said. Who has ever said that men are only brain? Does anyone say that an orange grove is only carbon? &c., or the ◊ 'nightingale' only a chemical and mechanical component;—passing over the product or result,—making no mention of the fragrance & the music? If anyone did say so, & could establish it, would he not be elevating the chemical and mechanical elements & forces, and not observing the blossom or the bird? There they are!—beyond his power to disparage. And so 'we are what we are,—however we come to be', as I said in that book. 'Science' is very far from pretending to say that men are 'magnetic mockeries', or any sort of mockeries but the most real of all things that man may have cognizance of; and therefore proper subjects of science. Science goes to show us that there is far more in them than Tennyson or anyone else has ever dreamed of; & the one very thing that science most strenuously and constantly insists on it that we do not, & cannot know any thing whatever of essences but only of attributes or qualities;—say phenomena. As for the other 'poem'—we should scarcely object to any part of it, & eagerly agree with most of it. You know, we think it nonsense;—a mere jingle of words to profess to disbelieve in a First Cause. It is an inseparable—an essential part of human thought & feeling to suppose a First Cause. (See our book pp. 240, 362.) It is only when men presume to say what are the attributes or qualities,—making it out a magnified human being (which Xenophanes so well saw our tendency to do) that we decline to abet such hardihood, & to attach our awe and reverence to an idol.

As for our making Bacon a 'blackguard' (your word, you know), the question is one of fact—always remembering that the avowal of convictions on speculative subjects be not the same virtue in all times. I do not admit the 'blackguardism' of Moses, for instance, but rather regard his avowal of so much as he did declare as worthy of reverent admiration. Bacon was awfully faulty in that matter; but as you well know, far more criminal in others;—a thorough 'blackguard' as Chancellor,—if timid and assuming as a philosopher. But you can satisfy yourself about this, which is better than taking any body's word for it. *Study* him well, ascertaining his learning, & not forgetting to look into the dates of his various writings, & see how the matter is: & don't blame us for Bacon's weaknesses:—nor yet judge him for the circumstances of your & my station & time. (For that matter, however, do you know no very good people who sanction what they believe to be untrue, for other folks' good 'yet more than' their own peace & quiet?)

As for your question about the grounds of our aspiration after self-sacrifice &c.,—our ground is much the same as yours, I should think. If you were asked why you obey the will of God, you would say that it is because your nature impels you so to do;—because you *feel* it to be best,—because you long & yearn &

love so to do. So we,—if asked *why* we prefer health to sickness, peace to turmoil of mind, benevolence to self-indulgence,—reply simply that we do. Our moral, like our physical faculties, indicate health & happiness as our natural action: & as we incline to temperance as the rule of health, we naturally aspire to a life of self-sacrifice, or say rather, of active good will, because it is inexpressibly desirable in our eyes. This is our ground. But I think it is a higher, & therefore more natural state 'when simply living & not arguing' not to think about the matter expressly at all, but simply to give way to our love of our neighbour, & act from it, without reviewing any 'grounds'.

As for the reviewers,—they have been more fraudulent (in misquotations & the like) than I had supposed possible: but that is their affair, & not ours. As to their wrath,—we must bear in mind that most of them are divines, doctors, or somehow concerned in metaphysics: & that we have attacked the very staple of their thoughts & lives. Thus great allowance is to be made for them, & they really *cannot* do us justice. We do not see that any one of them has touched any one point of our book: & they answer one another so effectually as to save us the trouble of doing it. We have brought a great deal of censure on ourselves through the form of our book,—its mere epistolary form, & its stopping short in the middle. Some day, we shall probably give out our views in a more complete & orderly way. Meantime, we have the pleasure of your hearty sympathy: & where we are most abused, it is a satisfaction to sympathize more with our enemies, the less they are able to do so with us. There is nothing but the sheer dishonesty (of which I am sorry to say there is a terrible deal) that afflicts us at all.[209]

It is a sensible and wise response to a hot-headed young man, urging finer discrimination in argument, charity towards one's opponents, and understanding for their point of view. And, perhaps above all, the letter requires Furnivall to study his subject in a proper and thorough scholarly manner, to pay careful attention to historical context, and to be aware of the dates when books were written, before weighing in with anachronistic accusations against their writers. The advice was needed, though not always heeded, as Furnivall embarked on his literary career.

Around the time of his correspondence with Harriet Martineau, Furnivall was also writing to T. H. Huxley. The letters in the Huntington Library collection begin in late 1856. In the early 1850s, Huxley had been establishing his position in London, becoming celebrated, as George Eliot noted, for his 'brilliant talents' expressed through *'paradox and antagonism'*.[210] Herbert Spencer, who was pursuing an independent literary career after a stint as subeditor of *The Economist*, met

[209] Letter to Furnivall, 5 Oct. [*c*.1855], FU 552.
[210] Quoted by John Collier, 'Huxley, Thomas Henry (1825–1895)', *ODNB*.

Huxley in 1852, and introduced him to the freethinkers of the *Westminster Review*. In an intellectual climate where scientific, theological, and philosophical ideas were in a state of ferment, Furnivall's interest in Spencer was very natural, even inevitable, especially when, after the collapse of Chartism, Spencer developed a concept of a class-free co-operative society with which Furnivall must have had some sympathy. Like Furnivall, Spencer made a point of 'speaking his mind', and was surprised when this caused offence. In articles in *The Leader*, he had argued for an evolutionary model of the natural world, and that the success of human societies would be determined by adaptation to their environment. Spencer, 'the philosopher of evolution',[211] was the author of the phrase 'survival of the fittest'. He would rapidly assimilate Darwin's ideas after the publication of *The Origin of Species* in 1859. *The Principles of Psychology* was published in 1855, and proposed that 'mind' was itself the product of environment and organically generated (a view which at least superficially had points of contact with the more idiosyncratic *Atkinson Letters*). A series of articles on education culminated in 1861 in his best-selling *Education: Intellectual, Moral, and Physical*, which attacked 'cramming' and the dominance of the Latin and Greek classics, and advocated learning from observation and natural science, accompanied by physical exercise. The best-selling first volume of his *Synthetic Philosophy* was published in 1862; like Henry Atkinson and Harriet Martineau, he accepted an unknowable 'Ultimate Cause', which was in no way to be identified with a personalized Creator.[212]

In late 1856 Furnivall encouraged Huxley to apply for a professorial chair at Oxford. Huxley had never heard of the advertisement, but said he was 'very greatly obliged for your kind thought of me'. The prospect was alluring, 'yielding income enough to render other work unnecessary, and allowing plenty of time for the pursuit of original investigation'. However, he told Furnivall that his lack of faith might prove an obstacle: 'Brought up in the Church, I am no churchman—and the meaning of the word "believe" varies so greatly to different men that I am hardly inclined to profess myself one.' He asked: 'Will you ascertain for me whether what I have just said is consistent or inconsistent with the understanding upon which an honest man could become a

---

[211] Mary Ward's description: see Janet Penrose Trevelyan, *The Life of Mrs Humphry Ward* (London, 1923), 181.

[212] See further Jose Harris, 'Spencer, Herbert (1820–1903)', *ODNB*; also D. Wiltshire, *The Social and Political Thought of Herbert Spencer* (Oxford, 1978).

Professor at Oxford?'²¹³ Quite how Furnivall could claim to have any such background knowledge of such a post, in a place where he had few connections, and where his name, as yet, was unknown, is unclear. Huxley thanked him for the trouble he had taken, but had made his own enquiries—if the immediate prospect of remuneration had been adequate, 'I should jump at it. But you see they rather prefer to provide for my old age.'²¹⁴

Huxley satisfied himself with the Professorship of Natural Philosophy at the Jermyn St. School of Mines, to which he had been appointed in 1854, and where he attracted public attention by his addresses to working men.²¹⁵ Hence, no doubt, Furnivall's interest in promoting his cause and seeking his services to lecture in the Working Men's College. Huxley accepted his invitation: 'I am much obliged to you for letting me know of any way in which I *can* aid the Working Men's College. I shall be most happy to lecture on the subject you mention ... I was, I confess, pretty satisfied with the result of my Working Men's lectures here. My audience ... showed an amount of attention and comprehension which I have rarely met with.'²¹⁶ Kingsley, strongly committed to acceptance of the new scientific discoveries, plainly saw the relevance of Huxley's teaching to ideas of society shared by the Christian Socialists, telling J. S. Mill in 1869 that 'My ruling idea has been that which my friend Huxley has lately set forth as common to him and Comte; that "the reconstruction of society on a scientific basis is not only possible, but the only political object worth much striving for"'.²¹⁷ In 1868, in conjunction with a prominent student at the Working Men's College, Huxley set up a South London Working Men's College in Blackfriars Road.²¹⁸ It is not surprising that, as time passed, Huxley became too busy to accept Furnivall's invitations, and, by around 1867, boggled at an invitation to lecture to the young ladies at the Queen's College: 'What on earth should I do . . . in Bedford Square? . . . A bull in a china shop would be nothing to it.' He added: 'depend upon it, I should be turned out in a week', if he strayed into 'some forgetful excursus into the theory of Parthenogenesis or worse'.²¹⁹

As yet, Furnivall could only be described as a lapsed Anglican who

²¹³ Letter of 24 Nov. 1856, FU 429; see also Benzie, *Dr F. J. Furnivall*, 63.
²¹⁴ Letter of 1 Dec. 1856, FU 430.
²¹⁵ Gillispie, *Genesis and Geology*, 199; Leonard Huxley, *Life and Letters of Thomas Henry Huxley*, 2 vols. (New York, 1901), i. 149–50.
²¹⁶ Letter of 23 Feb. [1857], FU 431.
²¹⁷ F. E. Kingsley (ed.), *Charles Kingsley: Letters and Memories*, 294.
²¹⁸ Colloms, *Victorian Visionaries*, 169.   ²¹⁹ FU 433.

had arrived at his scepticism through a blend of exposure to the scientific naturalism represented by Huxley and Spencer and anticlericalism learned in the society of some, perhaps many, of the working men in the College. His abandonment of Christian faith was not primarily in his case an intellectual process, but an expression of his growing impatience with, and defiance of, authority and also his solidarity with the men. Furnivall shared with Huxley an Evangelical background (less strict in Furnivall's case) which valued seriousness and speaking the truth, qualities which readily transferred from religion to scientific enquiry. Both brought their religious values to bear on what they saw as their duty to do what they could to support the working class.[220] Huxley invented the word 'agnostic' in 1869 to describe his own position in his public debates with defenders of the Anglican establishment, though he did not identify himself unambiguously as an agnostic until 1883. Indeed, he did his best in the interim to obscure the fact that the name *was* his own creation, until he finally admitted in 1889 that he was responsible for the neologism. Furnivall was thus not likely to have been able to seize on the name to describe his own religious position until the 1880s. George Bernard Shaw's quip, that Furnivall was 'a muscular Christian agnostic', belongs to the late nineteenth or early twentieth century.[221] Until 1889, while most of the other members of the Metaphysical Society, which included leading intellectual figures (including F. D. Maurice) were '-*ists* of one sort or another', Huxley was 'without a rag or a label to cover himself with'.[222] He first published his coinage in relative obscurity in the meetings of the Society, and the word did not 'catch on' in the 1870s—those who used the word were insiders, familiar with Huxley's views through the Metaphysical Society, until R. H. Hutton drew attention to it in a series of articles in the *Spectator*. It is thanks to Huxley's own creation of confusion about his status as an 'agnostic' that James Murray had to engage in lexicographical detective work to track down his authorship of the word. He credited Huxley with its invention in 1869 in the first edition of the *OED*, but he only discovered this 'after a considerable chase'.[223]

[220] See further Lightman, *The Origins of Agnosticism*, e.g. 28, 96, 118.
[221] White, 'Frederick James Furnivall', 73.
[222] Quoted by Lightman, 'Huxley and Scientific Agnosticism, 274.
[223] On the whole topic, see further Lightman, ibid. (Murray's remark is quoted on p. 280). However, *OED III* (updated Sept. 2012) records 'agnostic' n. from 1870 (*Spectator*, 29 June), and does not mention Huxley; *OED II*, 'agnostic', n. and a., records the word from *Spectator*, 29 June, and also cites *Spectator*, 11 June 1876, in which Huxley's authorship is strongly implied: 'Agnosticism was the name demanded by Professor Huxley

MARRIAGE AND FAMILY

Mention has already been made of the relationship into which Furnivall entered with William Dalziel's sister, Eleanor Nickell Dalziel, in the early 1860s. The pair were living together in Furnivall's lodgings and causing considerable scandal in the College, but not open scandal. Eleanor's circumstances were kept discreetly quiet. We know that her brother, William Alexander Dalziel, attended the College. And we know from the census records after her marriage to Furnivall that she was born in Durham. The 1871 Census informs us that Eleanor N. was born in around 1842. She was baptized at Chester-le-Street in that year. The 1841 Census gives the only other certain information that we have before her marriage. Eleanor Nickle was the daughter of George and Martha Dalziel, living at Lambton Gardens, Chester-le-Street. George was around 40; his occupation, market gardener or otherwise, is not stated. His wife, Martha, Eleanor's mother, was around ten years younger than her husband. Eleanor, who was just a few months old at the time of the census, was the youngest of a family of six children; Will was the third son, born around 1835, and thus around six years older than Eleanor.[224]

The family moved south to London at some point when Eleanor and William were growing up. The 1851 Census records the family living at 4 Brook Green Terrace, Hammersmith, with Martha, aged around 44, the head of the household, with two daughters, Martha Eleanor, aged 14, and Eleanor, the youngest, aged 10, and their brother, Henry, aged 12. The two Marthas, mother and daughter, were earning a living as 'needlewomen'. Thus, at the time when Furnivall came to know the Dalziels, brother and sister, their father, George, seems to have been living away from the family, or perhaps had died; this seems likely to have made the cohabitation between Furnivall and Eleanor easier.[225] She was about seventeen years younger than he and was aged around 20 when they married in 1862 at Hampstead Registry Office. That she was around 18 in 1858, at the time they met, when Furnivall would have been 35, together with the class difference between them, may well explain the

for those who disclaimed atheism and believed with him in an "unknown and unknowable God".

[224] The other sons were John, b. 1830, George, b. 1832, and Henry, b. 1839; there was also an older sister, Martha, b. 1837.

[225] George Dalziel (b. 1801), plausibly the father, died 1861 in Uxbridge, Middlesex, the year before Eleanor's marriage. Eleanor Dalziel, understandably, if she was living with Furnivall, does not appear in the 1861 Census.

subservient and acquiescent role she seems to have played in the early days of their relationship. Apart from Furnivall's personal attractions—the glowing eyes and seraphic brow—and his winning manner, Eleanor was doubtless attracted in worldly terms to a gentleman, qualified as a lawyer, who could offer some security, however ramshackle his circumstances seemed, and who lived in lodgings filled with the books, pictures, and nice furniture which had aroused the envy of at least one of his working-class visitors, who then aspired to have as good himself. Furnivall came from a moneyed background, and, however much his father disapproved of his son's mode of life, George Furnivall by this time was retired, old, suffering from senility, and could not live forever: his eldest son would surely inherit money. On his side, Furnivall, quite apart from being attracted to a pretty girl, may have hoped to mould her education and teach her to become, under his guidance, what Brenda Colloms described as a 'working-class Princess Ida, translating a Tennysonian idyll into real life'.[226] Yet the one vignette we have of their premarital arrangements, by Arthur Munby, does not suggest that Furnivall placed Eleanor on any pedestal; the relationship seems to have been decidedly matter of fact. Though the dinner of potatoes and asparagus, washed down with coffee, was bohemian, it was not romantic.

Dalziel, a Scottish name in origin, is fairly common, and the range of first names limited. It is difficult to separate this family from the thicket of Dalziels who had moved south to London via Durham and Tyneside. It is tempting, but probably incorrect, to connect Eleanor's and William's family with the wood engravers and printers George and Edward Dalziel, two sons of a family of twelve children, who had moved south from Wooler, Northumberland, and established a successful business, 'The Brothers Dalziel', founders of the Camden Press, which served not only the leading Pre-Raphaelite painters, Holman Hunt, Millais, Madox Brown, Burne-Jones, and Rossetti, but also Ruskin, and the leading illustrators of the day. They prepared Tenniel's illustrations for *Alice in Wonderland* and Moxon's edition of Tennyson's *Poems* (about which, with much else, they understandably boasted).[227] Many of the

---

[226] *Victorian Visionaries*, 189. See photograph of Eleanor Dalziel, with Furnivall, and a second man ?Arthur Cattlin, dated 1862 and reproduced here, Plate 4, Bodl. MS Murray 31. Both she and Hantler (see below) were photographed for Furnivall's collection of pictures of readers for the Dictionary assembled in the early 1860s.

[227] From the title of their reminiscences, George and Edward Dalziel, *The Brothers Dalziel: A Record of Fifty Years' Work in Conjunction with Many of the Most Distinguished Artists of the Period 1840–1890* (London, 1901).

twelve brothers and sisters worked for the firm. Furnivall is likely at least to have known this prominent business in the neighbourhood, especially as engravers formed a conspicuous element among the students. The two Dalziel families *may* have been connected but Eleanor and her brother William must be ruled out as a part of the firm. The brothers Dalziel occupied an amphibious space between Camden Town and Bohemia and prided themselves on their connections and the gentility they brought to the business. Given their thirst for respectability and the numbers of their siblings and connections, Furnivall would have had difficulty engaging in a liaison with any sister of theirs. Eleanor's only close male relative, William, though clearly put in a very awkward position by Furnivall's behaviour, was only a student-teacher at the College, and seems, from his willingness to engage in thankless secretarial work for the EETS for many years, to have fallen under Furnivall's spell.

Munby knew Eleanor as 'Lizzy', so far as we can tell, a mistake. During their married life, Furnivall called her 'Nelly'. Though Munby professed himself shocked, Furnivall, setting the College authorities at defiance, would not have given two hoots for what he might have thought of the difference in his and Eleanor's social stations. And Munby, fascinated by working women, and highly self-conscious and uncomfortable about his own secret relationship with a servant whom he would later marry, was probably deeply curious to see how this ménage was being conducted.[228] His description of an evening spent in Furnivall's company with 'Lizzy' at Furnivall's house in Ely Place, a few months before their marriage, paints a highly coloured picture of his home life, and its invasion by the Philological Society's Dictionary, at this time:

Found him in a strange dingy room upstairs, the walls & floor and chairs strewn with books, papers, proofs, clothes, everything—in wondrous confusion; the table spread with a meal of chaotic and incongruous dishes, of which he was partaking, along with 'Lizzy' Dalzell, the pretty lady's maid whom he has educated into such strange relations with himself . . . F., who was pleasant and kindly to me as ever, was enjoying a vegetarian banquet of roast potatoes, asparagus, & coffee! Presently came Hantler, the jovial goodhumoured builder, in his uniform as a Captain of the 19th Middlesex . . . and Willliam Sutton, also of the College. After the meal, which lasted from 7 to 9, all four of them set to work, arranging and writing out words for the Philological Dictionary, of which Furnivall is now Editor, in place of poor Herbert Coleridge. 'Missy', as F. calls the girl, is his amanuensis and transcriber: takes long walks too with him and

[228] Benzie, *Dr F. J. Furnivall*, 24–5, 29–31.

others, of ten and twenty miles a day; which is creditable to her; and indeed she seems a quiet unassuming creature.[229]

Hantler, a fellow Volunteer,[230] and Sutton (who supported Furnivall's campaign for College dances) were, of course, of Furnivall's party in the College, and were now annexed to his dictionary work, like Eleanor herself, who seems 'quiet' and 'unassuming', and acts as his 'amanuensis and transcriber'. She was not, so far as we know, a servant—Munby's description of her as a 'pretty lady's maid' patronizes her and highlights the impropriety of the relationship in his view. That Furnivall called her 'Missy' (at least in company) also hardly suggests a worshipful relationship on his part. The whole passage, indeed, indicates that Furnivall presented her as a kind of handmaid, whom he had educated, not into Princess Ida, but 'into such strange relations with himself'. But he had also educated her into becoming a useful helper in his dictionary work, on the same footing as the two students of the College, Hantler, the builder in Volunteer's uniform, and Sutton.[231]

The year of the Furnivalls' marriage in 1862 was probably also the year of the birth of their first child, their daughter, to whom they gave the unusual name Eena. Civil registration of births had been introduced by Act of Parliament in 1836, and was becoming a regular practice during the mid-nineteenth century, but, before around 1875, the requirement, which was not backed up by penalties for non-compliance, could be evaded, and this was even easier for parents living in large cities.[232] The Furnivalls do not seem to have registered Eena's birth, nor had her baptized (not surprising, given the father's secularism, and the marriage in a registry office) and there is some uncertainty over her age at death.[233] In short, it seems probable that the couple was induced by social pressure, and Furnivall's sense of duty, to regularize their relationship by marriage, for the usual reasons, and that they fudged their daughter's exact age and date of birth.

[229] Hudson, *Munby*, 123–4, diary entry for Monday, 19 May 1862.
[230] See Plate 5, showing Captain Hantler in his Volunteers' uniform: Bodl. MS Murray 31.
[231] On the subject of the contribution made by women in the 19th and early 20th c. to the *NED/OED*, see Russell, *Women and Dictionary-Making*, 132–69 (Eleanor Dalziel's contribution is discussed on p. 160).
[232] Non-compliance may have been around 10% of births, maybe rising to 15% in cities. Information by Peter Turvey, 'The History behind your Birth Certificate', https://www.angliaresearch.co.uk⟩Articles, accessed 21 Mar. 2024.
[233] Her birth is not registered under E(e)na Furnivall or Dalziel; her age at death (registered in the June quarter of 1866) is said to have been 3, but Madden recorded in his diary that she was 'a beautiful girl of four years old'; Benzie, *Dr F. J. Furnivall*, 25.

The wedding photograph shows the pair in conventional pose, with Furnivall standing in patriarchal attitude, leaning protectively over his young wife, seated.[234] His brother-in-law William Dalziel married Susan Trinnick in 1867 and established his own household at 9 Milner Street, Islington, which would be his base as Honorary Secretary of the Chaucer Society and the EETS. Their son, perhaps in compliment to Furnivall, was called Frederick.

[234] Reproduced by Benzie, facing p. 116.

PART II

How a Lincoln's Inn Lawyer Became an 'Editor of Old Books': 1858–1864

7

Furnivall and the Philological Society of London

> His childish idea was, in fact, a pushing to the extremity of mathematical precision what is everywhere known as Grimm's Law—an aggrandizement of rough rules to ideal completeness.
>
> Thomas Hardy, *Jude the Obscure* (1896), ch. 4

'PHILOLOGY', AND THE PHILOLOGICAL SOCIETY

Quite apart from Furnivall's battles with F. D. Maurice, the Working Men's College was in a state of considerable turmoil. This was thanks, in large part, to the controversy over governance and student membership of Council, in which Furnivall's views were in the minority. And there were also financial problems after the College's removal to Great Ormond Street in 1857, which made the need for a legal constitution urgent. The College formed itself into a company, in which the Principal and Council of Teachers had the entire control of the property and management of the College, as Directors of the Company. Ten of the teachers, including Maurice, Ludlow, Furnivall, Hughes, Kingsley, and Litchfield, became shareholders. This showed the courage of their convictions since there was no limited liability, and the shareholders' entire fortunes were at the disposal of the Council—not surprisingly, this financial liability caused anxiety. The shareholders showed themselves to be men of principle, as well as nerve. Furnivall at this point in his life did not have much to lose, but he had a wife and children dependent upon him, and he had future expectations. There was further major upheaval after Maurice's death in 1872, when the College had to address long-term problems of governance.[1] Furnivall's battles in the late 1850s with Maurice and Maurice's supporters in the Working Men's College are likely to have had the effect of turning him increasingly towards his other main interest outside office hours: the Philological Society. He probably felt that he could make better use of his energies by putting them at the Philological Society's disposal, and in turn be more appreciated than he was by the senior men at the Working Men's College.

As has already been said, many influences combined to persuade

---

[1] See further J. F. C. Harrison, *History*, 87–102.

Furnivall to participate in the Philological Society, among them memories of his old Latin teacher at UCL, Thomas Hewitt Key, a founding member of the new university,[2] and of Henry Malden, his professor in Greek.[3] Many of Furnivall's friends and acquaintances also belonged to this wider circle of people interested in philology. As previously described, Maurice, R. C. Trench, Connop Thirlwall, and J. M. Kemble had all been Cambridge Apostles. Furnivall tells us he met Hensleigh Wedgwood at the Philological Society, and, thanks to the Wedgwoods' hospitality, he frequently attended their evening parties, becoming a friend of the family and going to their house to 'romp' with their children, especially their son, Tim. Harriet Martineau was another old friend of theirs.[4]

It was not mere pique, however, which drove Furnivall to spend more of his time on philological pursuits. As already noticed, he was using men from the Working Men's College, as well as his wife-to-be, to assist with the Philological Society's great project, the New English Dictionary after its beginnings in 1858—this initiative in itself was enough to absorb even Furnivall's energies—though never exclusively.[5] Furnivall had a great many projects in hand, and perhaps rather more than Eleanor Furnivall had anticipated: in addition to his work for the College, he had his excursions with the men, Volunteering duties, and in 1860 he began a Working Men's Rowing Club, with himself as President—the club started in earnest in 1865, with forty members.[6] Looking back at this time, Furnivall took the opportunity to reiterate his personal manifesto: 'We studied and took exercise together, we were comrades and friends, and helpt one another to live higher, happier, and healthier lives, free from all stupid and narrow class humbug.'[7] This was also the time during which he first became involved in the editing of early English texts, both for the Philological Society (in 1858) and the Roxburghe Club. And, besides all this, Furnivall became the

---

[2] Key held the post of professor of Roman language, literature, and antiquities from 1828 in London University; Malden resigned the headmastership of University College School in 1842, while continuing to teach Greek in the school; Key continued as headmaster (*ODNB*).

[3] Malden (1800–76), from 1831 Professor of Greek at UCL (then the University of London, renamed University College, London in 1836).

[4] Martineau, *Autobiography*, i. 375. She knew the Wedgwoods 'in their Clapham home first, and then in Regent's Park'.

[5] See further Gilliver, *Making of the Oxford English Dictionary* and Murray, *Caught in the Web of Words*; also Mugglestone, *Lexicography and the Oxford English Dictionary* and the same author's *Lost for Words*.   [6] Colloms, *Victorian Visionaries*, 189

[7] 'Social Life of the College', 60.

father of a young family. He did not compartmentalize these multifarious activities—a biographer's job would be easier if he had. That the account of his domestic life must be squeezed in round everything else, no doubt reflects the actuality.

The Philological Society, now the oldest learned society in Britain devoted to the scholarly study of language, and with which Furnivall was to be so long associated, was founded as a student society in 1830.[8] It was instituted as a national, rather than purely UCL, society on 18 May 1842, and its purpose was 'the Investigation of the Structure, the Affinities, and the History of Languages, and for the Philological Illustration of the Classical writers of Greece and Rome'.[9] After 1842, meetings were held at the London Library, St James's Square. They began at 8.00 p.m. and were held on the second and fourth Fridays in every month between November and June, excepting the Easter and Christmas holidays.[10] Later the venue moved to UCL, which then became proudly associated with the Society. And, thanks to the connection, UCL would subsequently host Furnivall's other societies. The leading members of this first Philological Society had been a group of men from Trinity College, Cambridge, including Malden. Membership was carefully vetted. Prospective members applied, and certificates of their application had to be signed by at least three existing members, 'of whom one must certify from his personal knowledge'. Following the second meeting at which the application was read from the chair, 'he is balloted for, and a majority of the votes in his favour secures his election'. New members paid 3 guineas on admission, and thereafter 1 guinea annually.[11]

The founding members in 1842 had in many cases also been leading members of the slightly older Cambridge Etymological Society, by this time dissolved.[12] The Cambridge connection is likely to have attracted Furnivall as well as the presence of Malden and Key. Furnivall had joined the Philological Society himself in 1847, soon after his return to London. In 1853, the Honorary Secretary (since 1842), Edwin

[8] It was recorded that the manuscript Minute Book of the former Philological Society was presented to its successor by T. H. Key, 'in accordance with the wishes of the Members of that Society', *TPS* 5, issue 108 (1851), 61.

[9] Hume, *The Learned Societies and Printing Clubs*, 117. Hume, a corresponding member of the Society of Antiquaries, Scotland, was a member of the Philological Society.

[10] Ibid. 117. *TPS*, 2, issue 1 (1855), p. iv, a 'Notice' that, after Michaelmas 1856, when the rent expired, the Society would meet in the Rooms of the Royal Astronomical Society at Somerset House, rather than the London Library, 12 St James's Square, as formerly.

[11] Details supplied by Hume, *Learned Societies*, 117.

[12] By the Master of Trinity College, W. Whewell, 'An Account of the Late Cambridge Etymological Society'.

Guest, resigned at the anniversary meeting on 27 May, and Key and Furnivall were elected jointly as the new Secretaries, that is, while Furnivall was still busy with activism on behalf of the trade associations, and just before the beginnings of the Working Men's College. He was then 28, and he did not give up his duties until three weeks before his death in 1910, aged 85.[13] The Treasurer was Darwin's brother-in-law, Hensleigh Wedgwood.

In the early years, Furnivall, with Philip J. Chabot, audited the Society's cash account. He was no philologist himself, but seems to have earned his place on the Council by what might be described as his gentlemanly fizz: his enthusiasm for the subject (probably fired by his teaching of the history of the language in the College), his know-how as a legal man of affairs, as well as by his energy and capacity for getting things done, when not thwarted by others' inaction. And he was also backed by friends who were themselves prominent members of the Society. In its early years the Society had been not only select; it was obscure. But, by 1853, this was changing: 'For some time its members were comparatively few, and its meetings were not extensively known; but it has lately assumed a much more prominent position.'[14] This greater prominence is likely to reflect awareness that the Society was devoting more of its time to enquiries into the English language. And perhaps membership was boosted by Furnivall's energies in promoting awareness of it outside the immediate circle of its members.

The joint secretaryship thus combined Key's knowledge and experience with Furnivall's youth and energy. Already in the previous year, 1852, there had been a long conversation at the end of the reading of Whewell's paper concerning the Cambridge Etymological Society, about the best ways in which the London Philological Society might promote scholarship in the study of the English language. During this discussion, 'it was suggested that an organization of labour, such as was adopted in the Etymological Society of Cambridge, provided advantages that could not be expected from the isolated efforts of individuals'.[15] This suggestion is not attributed, but sounds like Furnivall's attempt to commend the principles of association to the Philological Society, and, in the process, become himself more closely involved. Whether or not Furnivall was the speaker, the principle—an important one—commended itself to the meeting. The members then added a vital new ingredient to the discussion: the Society's members should not

[13] *TPS*, 6, issue 135 (1853), 87. [14] Hume, *Learned Societies*, 117.
[15] *TPS*, 5, issue 117 (1852), 142.

only pool resources; they should be *systematic*: 'The impression seemed very general, that a more systematic investigation of our language might lead to a much more satisfactory knowledge of its peculiarities.'[16] A 'worker's association' which was committed to systematic philological principles was a heady new idea in this congeries of gentlemen. Systematic investigation of English would require the compilation of a large corpus of data. The obvious repository would be a dictionary, one much larger than the traditional one-man compilations of the past. Furnivall must have been struck by the serial contributions to the Society's *Transactions* being made by his friend Hensleigh Wedgwood on 'English Etymology', and which culminated in Wedgwood's own one-man etymological dictionary, whose publication, as he acknowledged, owed much to Furnivall's encouragement.[17] The members were already receptive to ideas that would soon lead to the active pursuit of the grand project of the New English Dictionary. And, as one of the Secretaries, Furnivall could hardly escape involvement, even if he had wished.[18]

'Systematic' was a charged word, which reflected rapidly changing views of how language study should be conducted, largely coming from abroad. Malden and Key's colleague in the University of London was the German scholar and professor of Oriental languages Friedrich August Rosen,[19] who, despite his short life, did much to introduce the English scholars in his circle to the new study of comparative philology: the so-called 'new philology', co-founded by the Danish scholar Rasmus Rask (1797–1832) and Jakob Grimm (1785–1863) with Franz Bopp (1791–1867).[20] Rosen had himself attended Bopp's Sanskrit lectures, and, in turn, Key had attended Rosen's lectures on Sanskrit and held the (non-remunerative) position of professor of comparative grammar at University College School. Rosen had been invited to become the Professor of Oriental languages in the new University of London, a post he occupied 1828–31, when he resigned in protest over the expulsion of the anatomist G. S. Pattison, but was reinstated in 1834.

[16] Ibid.
[17] Letter [1859]: 'I will send you a copy of my dictionary as soon as I get it and you are the first person to whom it is due as it is entirely owing to your activity and perseverance . . . that I ever either set seriously about it or got a publisher.' FU 935.
[18] On the inception of the *NED*, see further Gilliver, *Making of the OED*, 10–13, *passim*.
[19] See further Stanley Lane-Poole, revd. J. B. Katz, 'Rosen, Friedrich August (1807–1837)', *ODNB*.
[20] See further Aarsleff, *The Study of Language in England 1780–1860*, 177–8. Also Momma, *From Philology to English Studies*, 64–5. And see the review of Momma by Lynda Mugglestone: *Historiographica Linguistica*, 41 (2014), 380–6. See also the obituary of Bopp, by his former student, Russell Martineau, *TPS*, 12, no. 1 (1867), 305–14.

UCL and the Philological Society deserve all credit for their vital part in the study of comparative philology in England. UCL's role, especially, in pioneering the 'new philology', red hot from the Continent, more especially the German-speaking states, as well as the College's long association with the Philological Society (both the original and its successor) would much later be celebrated passionately by a future Director of the EETS, R. W. Chambers, at a time when European civilization seemed about to be extinguished by the rise of Nazism. That UCL, to which Chambers was devoted, should be seen as a beacon of the new 'scientific' study of language that had been pioneered in the nineteenth century by 'Germans' (though we should not forget the Danish contribution and that of other north Europeans) was one of several historical ironies in 1939.[21]

But, if the London Philological Society had been founded at an exciting time of major discoveries in the comparative study of languages, it had a broader agenda than this. It owed much to its members' own cultural inheritance, which was derived largely from gentlemanly love of literature in the Classical languages as well as in English, and only in part from their guarded excitement at the new developments on the Continent and the personal contacts which some of them had with the pioneers of the new study of language. This became more prominent when the younger generation of scholars joined it, men like Henry Sweet and Arthur Napier, who had been trained in Germany and embraced many of the values of their German education. Browsing the Philological Society's early *Transactions* shows that most of its papers were contributed by well-informed, widely read empirical observers of aspects of language use, who were particularly interested in charting historical changes. One of them, indeed, was J. M. Ludlow, who is likely to have become involved through Furnivall's influence, and who contributed papers where he felt he had some expertise, notably in French (in which he was fluent), especially legal terms derived from French.[22]

The Philological Society was never wholly 'scientific' in the German sense to which we must shortly turn. Though all languages were germane to the members' interests, it is unsurprising that the Classical

---

[21] R. W. Chambers, 'Philologists at University College, London': 'within a very few years of its foundation, this College first created, and then for many years took the main share in carrying on the Philological Society' (p. 350). See also the Society's own description: it was founded 'to investigate and promote the study and knowledge of the structure, the affinities, and the history of languages'; https://www.philsoc.org.uk/history.asp, accessed 21 Mar. 2024.

[22] e.g. 'Jottings in Legal Etymology', *TPS*, 1, no. 6 (May 1854), 113.

languages, and those spoken in the British Isles, especially English, constituted the greater part of the business. Offcuts from publications in preparation, including Hensleigh Wedgwood's *Etymological Dictionary* and the *NED*, were trialled among the contributions. Thus, thanks to the Philological Society, Furnivall met most of the leading medieval and linguistic scholars of his day. It provided the principal forum for discussion of things that increasingly mattered to him: the history of the English language expressed in its rich collection of 'early English' texts, its dialects, pronunciation, and spelling.

So, what was meant by 'philology' at this time? The Classical scholar F. A. Paley in 1868 described philology as 'the connecting link between ancient and modern languages and science, its study requiring 'a philosophical acquaintance with the science and general principles of language, grammar, etymology, and the laws of inflexion'.[23] It is a term notoriously difficult to define, and in the twentieth century it came to acquire a certain opprobrium. In part this was because it became associated with uncongenial drudgery forced on those who did not wish to study it, and in part because comparative philology had in the nineteenth century been dominated by German scholarship, which rendered it suspect in some circles, especially after the First World War.

The word's meaning changed in the nineteenth century, as one of the stalwarts of the Philological Society, Alexander J. Ellis, observed. Ellis divided its legitimate terrain into no fewer than nine separate areas, while observing: 'It is quite useless to trace the changes of meaning which the word Philology has undergone, from the more grammatical range which it once possessed, to the immense sphere which it now arrogates.'[24] It is, as Chambers (who joined the Philological Society in 1906) acknowledged, a slippery word: 'it was once used in its widest sense, for a love of all polite literature; it included "all humane liberal

[23] *'The Proposed Changes in the Classical Tripos* (privately printed, Cambridge), quoted by John Henderson in *Juvenal's Mayor*, 74.
[24] 'First Annual Address of the President . . . Friday, 17th May, 1872', *TPS*, 15, no. 1 (1873–4), 4. For Ellis, 'philology' comprised study of the vocabulary and grammar of living languages, viewed independently, historically, comparatively (as well as historico-comparatively, 'so that the comparisons relate to the past as well as the present'), ethnologically, and geographically; the 'genesis' of words and syntactic constructions. Literary study, excluded from 'philology' in Ellis's account (he was not himself a literary scholar) was a legacy from the tradition of studying 'dead literary languages and their literature'. Ellis's bias towards English as a 'living language' is revealed by a subsequent comment that 'almost in our own days came the study of Sanscrit, and philology proper began— but alas! at the wrong end' (p. 21). See further Momma, *From Philology to English Studies*, 4–11. For fuller discussion, necessarily compressed here, see Aarsleff, *Study of Language*, ch. vi.

studies"'. It has retained much of this sense, especially in Classical and medieval circles, more so in America than in Britain (where the dry-as-dust senses have tended to prevail). Yet readers have sometimes to be reminded even in the United States of this broader sense.[25] Chambers noted that, even when used in a narrower sense, philology included the study of literature as much as grammar. But 'nowadays' (Chambers was writing in 1939), 'Philology is often limited to comparative grammar, and to the science of linguistics which is based upon it'.[26]

It is worth considering for a moment Chambers's description of the study of language—'linguistics'—as a 'science.[27] By 1939, this could be taken for granted, but the ground had been carefully laid in the nineteenth century. Of course, 'science' needs to be taken in its older and wider sense of systematic study of any scholarly discipline, rather than restricted to the natural and physical sciences which have generally become synonymous with 'science' in modern usage. What nineteenth-century observers meant cannot be better put than by Murray's *OED*, rather than the later revisions: 'A branch of study,' in this case the study of language, 'which is concerned either with a connected body of demonstrated truths or with observed facts systematically classified and more or less colligated by being brought under general laws, and which includes trustworthy methods for the discovery of new truth within its own domain.'[28] The key concepts here are empirical obser-

[25] See, for example, the American scholar Siegfried Wenzel's eloquent apologia, 'Reflections on (New) Philology'. Wenzel, a distinguished classical scholar as well as medievalist, has served philology throughout his working life, as recognized in his Festschrift, Newhauser and Alford (eds.), *Literature and Religion in the Later Middle Ages*.

[26] *Man's Unconquerable Mind*, 342. Compare *OED* 2, 'philology' senses 1 and 3 (where it is noted that the narrow sense has never been current in the US). Now on both sides of the Atlantic, 'Linguistics is now the more usual term for the study of the structure of language, and, with qualifying adjective or adjective phrase, is replacing *philology* even in the restricted sense.' John Lyons, *Introduction to Theoretical Linguistics* (first published 1968), is cited in support: 'The term "comparative philology" . . . though less commonly used these days by linguists themselves (who tend to prefer "comparative and historical linguistics"), is not infrequently met in general books on language, and like many other unsuitable terms, has been perpetuated in the titles of university chairs and departments and of prescribed courses of study.' R. H. Robins (*General Linguistics*, 1964; *OED* 2, 'philology', sense 1) noted that 'in German . . . *Philologie* refers more to the scholarly study of literary texts, and more generally to the study of culture and civilization through literary documents . . . This meaning is matched by the use of *philology* in American learned circles.' However, see also Shippey, *The Road to Middle-Earth*, 5–21. Shippey noted the general unhelpfulness of the 19th-c. *OED* definitions, 'though conceived and created by philologists' (p.7)). See also Burrow, 'The Uses of Philology in Victorian England', 181.

[27] See also Aarsleff, *Study of Language*, 201; Momma, *From Philology to English Studies*, 62.

[28] *OED* 2, 'science', sense 4(a), reiterated in *OED* 3.

vations systematically classified, and explicable by general 'laws'. The knowledge thus accrued is of value in itself, 'wholly irrespective of utilitarian application'.[29] The observer needed to be trained—one can see here the beginnings of the increasing value placed on professionalism by the German scholars who dominated the study of 'philology' in the nineteenth century. George Eliot's usage of 1863 (cited in the *OED*) is telling, not least for her connection between 'scientific' and 'German': she described the French scholar Ernest Renan as one who 'has always seemed to me remarkable as a French mind that is at once "scientific" (in the German sense)'.[30] The Germans were trained in their universities not merely to be proficient in knowledge, but as future professors. The academy bred academics. It also bred schoolmasters: English philology and the editing of medieval English texts owed much to German as well as English schoolteachers. In England, in the less restricted and exclusive 1850s and 1860s, when Furnivall was a young man teaching the history of the English language from Spalding's textbook, while at the same time going on geological expeditions with the men in the Working Men's College, such study was part of a well-rounded general education, pursued seriously.

'Scientific' became a purr word among nineteenth-century savants. It was a value which Furnivall claimed to admire, while he could not emulate it, and he would become increasingly sceptical. The analogies between philological enquiry and the geological quest for chronology, as well as Darwinian ideas of evolution, were thoroughly familiar to the members of the Philological Society as well as topical, though, in hindsight, Ewald Flügel observed that the analogy 'had not to wait for Darwin, as some people seem to think'.[31] Geology was a source of convenient similes: 'The language, like the soil, of England, is compounded of several strata, which have become in the progress of time, confusedly and curiously mingled.'[32] Strata of languages, like those of

[29] Hart, *German Universities*, 250: 'By *Wissenschaft* the Germans mean knowledge in the most exalted sense of that term, namely the ardent methodical, independent search after truth in any and all of its forms.'
[30] *OED* 2, 'scientific', sense 4(b), and see also sense 4(a), 'Based upon or regulated by science, as opposed to mere traditional rules or empirical dexterity. So of a worker or agent.'
[31] Flügel, in 'The History of English Philology', in the *Flügel Memorial Volume*, 9–35 at 34, observed that 'on the contrary, philological sciences may proudly assert that the careful observation of the development of its object was an established working principle with them before it was ever applied to the natural sciences'. See further Alter, *Darwinism and the Linguistic Image*. See also Aarsleff, *Study of Language*, 201.
[32] Fry, 'On Some English Dictionaries', 272.

geology, in theory present an orderly record of historical change, but, as Danby Fry's comment indicates, subsequent events may disturb the evidence and confuse the chronological picture in a way which may compromise the rigorous pursuit of the 'laws' of comparative philology. Furthermore, the discovery of fossils within strata which may have been disturbed is a matter of chance survivals and luck: the same may be said of documentary and other kinds of material evidence for philological, archaeological, and historical study. Moreover, material has been lost or discarded because it has been undervalued and not known to be wanted (and lacked the glamour of fossils):

> The scientific study of history is of so recent a date, that we cannot blame our predecessors for neither recording facts nor preserving documents which seemed to them of no value; but it is somewhat surprising to find persons, otherwise intelligent, unable to comprehend that many of the more obscure human records are deserving of as high a regard as a fossil footprint or the bone of an extinct animal.[33]

Comparison between philology, history, and the natural sciences can too easily become glib, but the analogy did nevertheless form a part of these men's image of themselves as 'scientists', even though this word was a neologism which had grated on some ears. Yet it was recognized that the ugly coinage usefully filled a semantic gap in the language.[34] Henry Sweet disliked the word, but he also disapproved of the unscientific study of English by Englishmen which was characterized by suspicion of conjectures and unwillingness to accept that language, like other phenomena in the natural world studied by scientists, is governed by 'laws': 'What means does the scientific philologist employ to get at the facts underlying all this vagueness and inaccuracy? Simply

---

[33] *English Church Furniture*, ed. Peacock. Peacock edited for the EETS, and 'Furnivall' [sic] is acknowledged, p. 12.

[34] As noted by W. Whewell in the *Quarterly Review* (1834), cited in *OED*, 'scientist', sense 1, which spoke of 'the want of any name by which we can designate the students of the knowledge of the material world collectively. We are informed that this difficulty was felt very oppressively by the members of the British Association for the Advancement of Science, at their meetings . . . in the last three summers . . . *Philosophers* was felt to be too wide and too lofty a term . . .; *savants* was rather assuming . . . some ingenious gentleman proposed that, by analogy with *artist*, they might form *scientist*, and added that there could be no scruple in making free with this termination when we have such words as *sciolist, economist*, and *atheist*—but this was not generally palatable.' Sweet commented: 'There was a great dispute some time ago about the word "scientist", and to what is its legitimate equivalent . . . Nor do I see why we might not by degrees Anglicise a good deal of our scientific nomenclature, which is getting more and more unwieldy every year'; Sixth Annual Address, p. 15.

common-sense guided by the universally received laws of Comparative Philology?'[35]

Sweet would later modify his views of German professors as time went on, after he was disappointed in his efforts to gain an academic position. Meanwhile, as Murray said, he persevered in his 'thankless efforts to hold the mirror of German perfection up to English amateurs'.[36] The view (in a few years to be dubbed 'neogrammarian') that phonetic changes took place according to observable principles without exception was incompatible with the opinion, summed up in the slogan usually attributed to the Franco-Swiss scholar of dialect linguistics, Jules Gilliéron, that 'chaque mot a son histoire' ('each word has its own history').[37] This approach, it must be said, was far more congenial to the members of the Philological Society. Students of language, like A. J. Ellis, who were engrossed by close study of dialect and phonology, and the collection of specimens, were apt to be suspicious of the view that sound change obeys 'laws'. Moreover, the adherents of rigorous comparative philology themselves needed dialectal study when they had to turn to dialectal forms for illustrations of sound change which could not be shown from the standard language.

In pointing these things out, members of the London Philological Society were asserting their independence from the German method, while still considering themselves 'scientific' and 'systematic' in their willingness to modify their views to take account of empirical observations. This was especially important when a commentator had to deal with a living language such as English, when words, like fossils, were apt to appear anomalous when encountered out of context—though they were still governed by general rules. Richard Morris, as President of the Society, when reminding his audience of the debt which the German philological heroes like Bopp owed to the English scholars of the eighteenth and early nineteenth centuries, told them:

> Geologists were doing, as philologists are very apt to do—shutting their eyes to the silent and unceasing alterations going on around them. But Sir Charles Lyell studied these changes as produced by present active forces, and proved that they sufficiently accounted for all that had taken place in the past. Geology took its proper place among the exact sciences.[38]

Thus to be 'scientific', while not being überscientific, when engaged in

[35] Henry Sweet, Seventh Annual Address... 17 May 1878, TPS, 17 (1877–9), 414.
[36] Eighth Annual Address... 16 May 1879, ibid. 571.
[37] Sweet, Seventh Annual Address, p. 413; OED, 'neogrammarian', n., first recorded, 1885.   [38] Fourth Annual Address, 21 May 1875, TPS, 14 (1875–6), 9.

language study and its concomitant, editing texts, was a high compliment in the environs of the Philological Society. To be a 'dilettante' was merely to prod the language's spoil heap with a trowel, like the stones on Riddlesdown Common, to decorate a glass case back in the Working Men's College, regardless of their geological context.

At this point, it is worth giving a brief sketch of the major developments in the subject which had taken place in the late eighteenth and early nineteenth centuries, though readers are referred to more comprehensive studies elsewhere.[39] Grimm's *Deutsche Grammatik*, first published in 1819, marked a watershed. It was a work so 'stupendous', as Ewald Flügel described it, looking back in the early twentieth century over the whole vista of the nineteenth, 'that we must divide the whole history of Germanic philology into a period before the appearance of the grammar and one after'.[40] Hensleigh Wedgwood, reviewing in 1833 the five volumes which had appeared between 1822 and 1831, remarked that, despite its 'dry and naked title', it was 'one of the most interesting and instructive works that ever issued from the German press'. The dauntless Grimm,

> Unappalled either by the inconceivable labour of the task, or by the fear of being thought tedious . . . has here given us, under the modest title of *a German grammar*, a thorough history not only of his own language, but that of every descendant of the Gothic stock throughout Europe, tracing, at the same time, every inflection in every dialect through every intermediate stage up to the earliest period of which any literary monuments remain![41]

The focus of most of these philologists' interest was the comparative study of Germanic languages. After all, as Shippey has pointed out, they were mostly Germans.[42] Grimm's distinctive contribution was to extend the insights drawn from study of Sanskrit to the Germanic and Scandinavian vernacular languages and their antecedents (including Old English). He built upon the observations generally credited to the eighteenth-century orientalist Sir William Jones that there were affinities between Sanskrit and Greek and Latin, as well as the '*Gothick* and

---

[39] For example, Aarsleff, *Study of Language*; Momma, *From Philology to English Studies*; Matthews, *The Invention of Middle English*, 22. Regrettably, this useful book lacks an index.

[40] Flügel, *Flügel Memorial Volume*, 9–35 at 24. On Flügel (who trained in Leipzig and emigrated to Stanford in 1892), see the more extended study of English and German editors in vol. ii (forthcoming).

[41] 'Grimm's Deutsche Grammatik', 169.

[42] *Road to Middle-Earth*, 13.

the *Celtick*' languages, which led him to infer that they all derived from a common ancestor, later called 'Indo-European'.[43]

As is well known, Grimm formulated the systematic pattern of sound changes which differentiate the Germanic languages from others in the Indo-European 'family', and which are known after him as 'Grimm's Law', though they were built on observations first made by Rask (and therefore are also known as Rask's-Grimm's rule).[44] Grimm's Law haunted philological study in the nineteenth century and later, as an aptly named spectre which might nevertheless offer a passport to learning classical languages and social betterment, as the young Jude Fawley had hoped in the late nineteenth century.[45] In the 1870s, the pioneering headmistress Dorothea Beale made unsuccessful efforts to enthral her pupils at Cheltenham Ladies' College with Grimm's Law's consonantal acrobatics. The subject was *avant garde* material for British young ladies of school age, though the 'Law' was a matter talked about among the intellectual circles to which Dorothea Beale herself belonged.[46] It would soon come to be seen as an essential key to learning early English language and literature. By 1884, James Murray was able to praise the University of London's enlightened policy of including the formal study of English in its curriculum, 'which has obliged examiners and examinees alike to learn something of the history of the language, and its connexion with general philology has made "Grimm's Law," and "Latin Elements in English," and "Strong Verbs" familiar expressions'. Additionally, 'it has called forth the appearance of better text-books, such as Dr. Morris's "Historical English Grammar" and "History of English Accidence"'. It 'has sent its candidates for degrees to the actual texts of Chaucer and Piers Plowman, and even to King Alfred himself'.[47]

---

[43] Quoted by Aarsleff, *Study of Language*, 133 (the reader is referred to this study, and to Momma, *From Philology to English Studies*, for a fuller account of the effects of contact with the 'new philology' and English scholarship). Wedgwood gave a digest of the 'rule', 'Deutsche Grammatik', 170–2: 'It is easy to perceive of what importance this rule is to etymology, as a test of the truth of any supposed derivation', 172.

[44] As noted by R. W. Chambers, 'it might just as properly be called Rask's rule', *Man's Unconquerable Mind*, 345. For details of the consonantal changes, see e.g. Momma, *From Philology to English Studies*, 66–7.

[45] Thomas Hardy, *Jude the Obscure*, ed. C. H. Sisson (London, 1978), 71 (first published 1896).   [46] Raikes, *Dorothea Beale of Cheltenham*, 263.

[47] 'Thirteenth Address of the President to the Philological Society, 16th May 1884', TPS, 19, no. 1 (1884), 591–31 at 529; reference to R, Morris, *Elementary Lessons in Historical English Grammar*, and *Historical Outlines of English Accidence*. *Accidence*, the first of the two textbooks to appear, was intended for a more advanced level of instruction (for 'students and by the upper forms in our public schools' (p. vii)), whereas *Elementary*

Grimm himself had concluded his preface to *Deutsche Grammatik* with an optimistic prediction of future progress: 'What was most difficult to us will appear child's play to our posterity, who will then apply themselves to new modes of analysis of which we have no idea, and will meet with difficulties where we thought all smoothed down.'[48] Meanwhile, his 'Law' became a bogey to frighten the young. The obligation to know something of comparative philology was apt to dismay students rather than enlighten them (even those taught by persons who could explain the matter better than Dorothea Beale). The difficulty of the subject was conceded by Chambers, who noted: 'I have been told in an examination paper that "The Early Germanic Tribes decided to shift their consonants at the instigation of a man called Grimm".' Nevertheless even though Grimm's Law, Verner's Law, and the rest rose up before students, as Chambers also put it, 'in successive terraces of horror' in a modern version of Dante's *Inferno*, they became a standard part of the English university curriculum well into the twentieth century.[49] The diffusion of the 'new philology' and its concomitant promotion of study of the older phases of English literature as part of university curricula, and even in the upper forms in schools, had the Philological Society's blessing. It is a salient feature of the history of education in the nineteenth century. Nineteenth-century changes in university education were to be even more radical than in elementary schooling (the fame of the 1870 Education Act notwithstanding). And in these developments the EETS and its personnel, especially the schoolmaster Richard Morris, would play their part. Furnivall's concern to promote the study of 'early English' in schools was explicit. Just two years after the EETS's foundation, he announced the founding of annual prizes to be awarded in eleven universities and colleges 'to the best pupil in an Examination

---

Lessons was meant for teachers engaged in 'the higher education of boys and girls' (p. vi), but both include information on Grimm's Law. Either would have provided Dorothea Beale with the teaching materials she wanted (both very recently published at the time of her experiment). She would later write a preface to a school textbook by Laura Soames, *An Introduction to Phonetics*, in which she claimed that the vagaries of standard English spelling hindered intelligent school study of phonology, 'without which that of philology is almost impossible to the young' (quoted in an unsigned review, *Educational Review*, NS 2, no. 1 (1892), 40–2 at 40). Morris was himself a teacher, at this time appointed as the Winchester lecturer on English language and literature in King's College School (London). A copy of the third edition of Stratmann's Middle English dictionary (1878) (see below) held by the English Faculty Library, Oxford, has the bookplate of Leeds Girls' High School.

[48] Translated and quoted by Wedgwood, 'Deutsche Grammatik', 188–9.
[49] *Man's Unconquerable Mind*, 345, 343.

in English before Chaucer'. The prizes were examined and judged by a professor in the institution 'in such manner as he thinks fit'.[50]

Thus, the Philological Society strongly reflected the deep respect for the work of the 'Germans and Danes' which existed alongside the feeling that it was high time that English scholars themselves began to contribute to the subject.[51] The Society was a high-minded institution, whose president to 1868 was Connop Thirlwall, Bishop of St David's. Church dignitaries, London-based scholars and those affiliated with Oxford and Cambridge (especially the latter), and men in public life formed the core of its early membership.[52] Its list of honorary members in 1854 included the philological stars Franz Bopp and Jakob and Wilhelm Grimm (lifelong honorary members) alongside others from Berlin, Bonn, and Copenhagen.[53] Two of these, Immanuel Bekker and Johan Nikolai Madvig, were best known as scholars of Greek and Latin, and this reflects the Society's interest, especially in its early years, in more traditional Classical study, alongside the 'new' Germanic philology, a combination which Aarsleff traced to the preponderance of the Cambridge-educated men among its key members, in particular those from Trinity College.[54] Later, other Continental luminaries, including the Frenchman Paul Meyer, would be added to the list of honorary members. In addition, thanks to the revolutions of 1848 in the German

[50] Second Annual Report of the Committee (1866). The prize was two years' free subscription, later reduced to one. The initial list comprised Oxford; Trinity College, Dublin; King's College London; University College London; Owen's College, Manchester; Edinburgh; Glasgow; Aberdeen; Belfast; Galway; Cork. The Oxford prize was judged by Joseph Bosworth, professor of Anglo-Saxon (1858–76). However, the previous incumbent had been John Earle, ordained in 1857, and presented by Oriel College to Swanswick, near Bath; accordingly, the final prize was to be judged by 'the Rev. J. Earl [sic], at Bath'. Although the number of institutions withered away, the prizes (which failed to recognize the expansion of higher education after Furnivall's day) were awarded until 2014/15 (Daniel Wakelin, private communication).

[51] As Richard Morris said in 1875, 'For the last sixty years, a period that embraces the beginning as well as the growth and development of linguistic science, we have been content to look to Germany for nearly all our scientific knowledge in this department, but have done little ourselves to advance the study of comparative philology by independent research'; 'Fourth Annual Address of the President to the Philological Society, 21 May, 1875, TPS, 16, no. 1 (1876), 1–138 at 1–2.

[52] Aarsleff, Study of Language, 214–23.

[53] Others were the Greek scholar and textual critic Professor August Immanuel Bekker (University of Berlin); the Old Frisian scholar Montanus de Haan Hettema (Leeuwarden); the Norwegian-born Sanskrit and oriental scholar Professor Christian Lassen (University of Bonn); Johan Nicolai Madvig best known for his work on Latin and Greek syntax (University of Copenhagen and Kultus Minister); and the Danish scholar Christian Molbech (University of Copenhagen).

[54] Aarsleff, Study of Language, 213–15.

states, the Philological Society had acquired a distinguished German philologist residing in London, the Sanskrit scholar Theodor Goldstücker, who had been ordered to leave Berlin on account of his liberal political opinions. He moved to London, taking up the chair of Sanskrit at UCL in 1852. Later described by Furnivall as 'the greatest scholar I ever knew', Goldstücker soon became an ordinary member of the Philological Society's Council, and later its President.[55]

Despite these Continental connections, members of the Philological Society did not immerse themselves in the new philology to the extent that might have been anticipated. They sought an English middle way that was neither a muddle nor *einseitig*. Some of its members considered that those Germans who seemed to them more system-besotted might have strayed beyond the bounds of common sense into wild conjectures which were not founded in the close observation on which they prided themselves. As the German-trained Henry Sweet would put it himself in his 1877 Presidential Address, 'Our Society's work during the last year still shows that healthy preference for special investigations over hazy generalization, which is the surest sign of true progress'.[56] The eccentric Early English scholar Oswald Cockayne expressed his views of unprovable theories of 'German fanatics' with characteristic warmth:

> It may be that some competent and enthusiastic Sanscrit scholar may have agreed to assist in developing the comparative philology (filology), and in shewing that the language of the Brahmins has affinities with our own; it may be, that endowed with a cautious judgement such a Mr. A. may be able to restrain the burning warmth of Sanscrit scholars, and keep his comparisons within some rational limit; but it is not comparative philology (filology) nor Bopp nor Pott nor an army of German fanatics in language that we want in a Saxon Dictionary. We look for a work that shall reassure young students, that shall shew them their way in old English sentences, that shall convince them that our old tongue was grammatical.[57]

So far as English was concerned, the contributors of papers to the Philological Society continued to offer carefully observed studies of etymologies, dialects (Alexander Ellis's absorbing interest), and forms of words, as well as the interesting usage of words by good authors, espe-

---

[55] *Political, Religious and Love Poems*, ed. Furnivall, EETS, OS 15 (1866), p. xviii. He was elected at the meeting of 10 Feb. 1854; *TPS*, 1, no. 2 (1854), 29. See further N. J. Allen, 'Goldstücker, Theodor H. (1821–1872)', *ODNB*. He had studied in Bonn under Lassen, as well as Schlegel.

[56] Sixth Annual Address of the President . . . delivered at the Anniversary Meeting, Friday, the 18th of May, 1877, *TPS*, 17, no. 1 (1879), 1–122 at 1.

[57] Cockayne, 'Dr Bosworth and his Saxon Dictionary', in *The Shrine*, 2.

cially, of course, Shakespeare. (The emphasis on the history of English was expressed in its project par excellence, the *New English Dictionary on Historical Principles*.) Ellis, far from being an advocate of Teutonic neo-grammarians, went to the other extreme, and described his relation to the varied forms of language study encompassed by 'philology' as being like that of a butterfly collecting honey: 'he has not made any, but he has tasted many, and perhaps from not being a bee himself, he has no very marked apiarian prejudices'. And, since close study of dialects, and older varieties of English pronunciation, required some means of recording their sounds, one of the Philological Society's main contributions to language study would be its experiments in phonetic notation.

Familiarity with dialects would be essential for editing medieval English texts. In 1873 W. W. Skeat, himself a member of the Philological Society, founded the English Dialect Society (dissolved in 1896). The Society collected materials which would ultimately be published as Joseph Wright's monumental *English Dialect Dictionary* (begun in 1889), a project to which Skeat personally gave a great deal of money. He would declare: 'My endeavour has been to understand every dialect of every period of English, so as to obtain a complete grasp of the subject.'[58] The Philological Society's interests in dialect study, the history of pronunciation, and etymology were fundamental to its ongoing work on the Society's 'Dictionary'. Thus the Philological Society's practical work was predicated on the assumption that each word has indeed its own history. Nevertheless, this assumption coexisted with a passion, as well as a need, for classification—and this is where the 'system' came in. While Ellis, who had a weakness for quirky extended metaphors (as well as dreadful puns), likened himself to a butterfly, flitting from one flower to another, this was not the whole story. He also had much in common with the taxonomical enthusiasm of an entomologist or ornithologist in his quest to record new specimens of spoken sounds in dialects of English and in cognate Germanic languages. A *rara avis*, an Icelander visiting London, was a great addition to the collection.[59]

---

[58] From his prefatory letter to his 'Testimonials in favour of the Rev. Walter W. Skeat, M.A., A candidate for the Elrington and Bosworth Professorship of Anglo-Saxon in the University of Cambridge' (Cambridge, 1878), 5: 'For three years I was sole Director and Honorary Secretary, and did nearly all the work which this involved. The strain was too great, so that, when the Society was fairly started and successful, I resigned the responsibility. The Society is now managed by a Committee of twenty.' See also *A Student's Pastime, Being a Select Series of Articles Reprinted from 'Notes and Queries'* (Oxford, 1896), pp. xxx–xxxi, lv–lvi.

[59] Letters to J. A. H. Murray, 16, 24 Nov., 17 Dec. 1868, Murray Papers, Box 1.

The Philological Society's Rules stated: 'The Philological Society is formed for the investigation of the Structure, the Affinities and the History of Languages' as well as 'the Philological Illustration of the Classical Writers of Greece and Rome.' Yet, as Sweet said, however wide the Society's sympathies, in practice, interest in the *English* language came to be regarded as its leading specialism, and he for one welcomed this. The leading members of the Society were becoming fed up with the traditional pedagogical emphasis on Greek and Latin: 'Although our Society was originally founded mainly for the "Philological Illustration of the Classical Writers of Greece and Rome," we still refuse to look at classics. Most of us have probably had enough of them at school and college: I know I have.'[60] Furthermore, because the study of comparative philology inevitably courted 'interesting and important investigations' into ethnology and the migration of races there was also an ongoing concern with the study of exotic languages (from an English perspective), especially Oriental languages.[61] Interest in the Oriental languages continued in the Society, though, as time went on, some of this work was diverted to more specialist societies: Sweet noted enviously 'the formidable rivalry of a "Royal Asiatic Society", endowed by Government', unlike the Philological Society, which had to survive on subscriptions, and also 'our vigorous young contemporary, the "Society of Biblical Archaeology".'[62] The reform of English spelling along more or less radical lines was also a preoccupation, especially in the 1870s, under the influence of the phoneticians A. J, Ellis and Henry Sweet. Even the Latinist, Key, contributed a paper on 'Metathesis' (the rearrangement by speakers of the sounds or syllables in a word) which included examples from 'Anglo-Saxon'.[63]

Of course, the Philological Society was dominated by men. The first woman member to be elected (in 1847) was the distinguished independent scholar Anna Gurney. In 1848 she presented a copy of her *Literal Translation of the Saxon Chronicle, by a Lady in the Country* (1819),

---

[60] 'Sixth Annual Address', TPS, p. 3. A. J. Ellis had also been put off the classics by having 'the good or ill fortune to go through one private and two public schools, where of course Latin and Greek were the staple products—where the usual imperfect methods resulted in the usual imperfect fabric'; 'First Annual Address', TPS, 15 (1874), 5. In his 1875 address, Richard Morris noted that 'out of twenty-three papers read during the period under survey [January 1874–May 1875] no less than fifteen had some connection, more or less direct, with our mother tongue', 'Fourth Annual Address of the President', TPS, 16 (1876), 18.

[61] F. A. Paley, quoted in Henderson, *Juvenal's Mayor*, 74.

[62] 'Sixth Annual Address', 3.

[63] TPS, 1 (1854), 206–16 at 209.

the first translation into modern English of the *Anglo-Saxon Chronicle* to be printed, and in 1855 she read her paper on 'Norfolk Words'.[64] Yet, despite this impressive figure to lead the way, women's interest in philology might still be received rather warily by the men, as diminishing the subject by popularizing it. A. J. Ellis, in his 1872 Presidential address, quoted the Scottish man of letters John Stuart Blackie, who had begun 'a recent lecture on modern Greek by defining Philology as "cracking about words"'. Blackie had said that everyone now-a-days, 'ladies and all', understood what it meant, thanks to Archbishop Trench and Professor Max Müller.[65] Ellis, for his part, welcomed ladies' contribution, and enviously noted the success Müller had enjoyed in attracting 'provokingly mixed audiences to his popular philological lectures'.[66] Ellis could only address 'Gentlemen'. But, by 16 May 1873, he could begin his second address with the novel opening vocative, 'Ladies and Gentlemen, Members of the Philological Society'.[67] The ladies' attendance was, however, not guaranteed. In 1881, Ellis recorded that 'There are, I am glad to think, still two ladies who are members of our Society, so that the terms in which I commenced this series of Annual Presidential Addresses nine years ago are still applicable. I would that we had more lady members, and that those we have would more frequently attend our meetings', especially since 'we remember how very apt women are in the use of language, both with tongue and pen, how easily they acquire foreign tongues, and how peculiarly adapted for feminine occupation is all the work of the philologist.'[68] He politely rebuffed the comment of the German philologist, and fellow member of the Society, Wilhelm Wagner, who had poured scorn on '*elegant* scholarship—which is all very nice, but perfectly useless—in fact we do not work like ladies, but like men mindful of a serious purpose'. Ellis responded: 'Our friend, Dr. Wagner, gauges women's work by the old standard . . . superficiality

[64] *TPS*, 2 (1855), 29–39. See further Helen Brookman, 'Gurney, Anna (1795–1857)', *ODNB*, and 'Accessing the Medieval'; Toswell, 'Anna Gurney'. Also, Brookman, 'From the Margins'; Toswell, 'The Lost Victorian Women of Old English Studies'.

[65] 'First Annual Address', delivered 17 May 1872, *TPS*, 15, no. 1 (1874), 'On the Relation of Thought to Sound as the Pivot of Philological Research', 3. Ellis went on to indulge his weakness for word play—he intended, like Blackie, the Scottish (and Irish) sense of 'crack' as convivial conversation. See further E. Kerr Borthwick, 'Blackie, John Stuart, 1809–1895', *ODNB*. Blackie, a classical and Gaelic scholar, was another who had studied in Germany.

[66] 'First Annual Address', 3.

[67] 'Second Annual Address', *TPS*, 15, no. 1 (1874), 201–52 at 201. See also his opening remark in the 'Tenth Annual Address' on 20 May 1881.

[68] 'Tenth Annual Address', 20 May 1881, *TPS*, 18, no. 1 (1881), 252–321 at 252.

does not depend on sex, but on habits of civilization, which may change, and we hope will change for the better.'[69]

Serious philological study by women would, Ellis hoped, increase, thanks to the impetus given to their university education, initially by London, followed by Cambridge. In 1874, he remarked that Merton Hall at Cambridge, and Girton College close by, were insufficient to satisfy the demand by enthusiastic women students:

Like all neophytes, the women enter upon the new career with enthusiasm, and the men who simply go to college because their fathers did so before them, and take a degree because it's the 'proper thing'... will have to look to their laurels. We have long allowed that women are quick. We must now allow that they are anxious to learn. We shall soon have to allow that they are steady workers. And then we shall have to admit that men are no more alone in the field of learning and science than in society, and both sexes, with learning and science to boot, will, let us hope, be the better for this admission.[70]

On the one hand aptitude for patient application to detail, as well as ladies' facility with language, commended philology as a suitable subject for women. On the other, precisely the same requirement of hard slog could be made to sound heroic, rather than ladylike, in the unremitting demands that Lady Philology exacted from her male disciples. Gentlemen, rather than gentlewomen, 'toiled'—that is, laboured with metaphorical sweat on their brows. The emphasis of comparative philology on 'scientific' knowledge of dead languages was a major deterrent to women at this time. But it is to the Philological Society's credit that leading members, including, of course, Furnivall, Ellis, and Sweet, campaigned for wider university access for all, including women. And the Society's own bias towards living languages, especially English, rather than Greek and Latin, helped women who wanted to venture further than those who had had their appetites whetted by Max Müller's fashionable London lectures. Müller, the German-born Sanskrit scholar, and Oxford's first Professor of Comparative Philology (1868–75), had left his homeland for England, where his lectures

---

[69] 'Second Annual Address', 233. W. Wagner, of the Johanneum, Hamburg, had sent in a resumé of work on Latin philology. Ellis instanced Anna Swanwick (translator of Aeschylus) and Mary Somerville as notable women scholars, along with two stellar students at Antioch, CA, Miss Strickland and Miss White (in Greek and mathematics). Women at Cambridge, however, had not excelled academically, though the examination results had been 'sufficiently encouraging', when it was remembered 'that they had not been to classical schools, like the young men' (pp. 234–5).

[70] 'Third Annual Address of the President ... 15th May, 1874', TPS, 15 (1874), 358.

on philological and literary subjects showed him to have a flair for interesting the non-specialist public.[71]

AIDS TO STUDY OF 'EARLY ENGLISH': 'BOSWORTH-TOLLER' AND 'STRATMANN'

The impact of the new philology in England in the early 1830s was initially felt in the study of the classical languages, and also of Old English, which at this time was more commonly called Anglo-Saxon (the names given to the chronological varieties of early English were at this time in flux). Rask had, in 1817, published a grammar of Anglo-Saxon/Old English (*Angelsaksisk Sproglaere*) in his native Danish. It was a philological milestone, but it nevertheless drew upon the seventeenth-century dictionary of William Somner and the eighteenth-century grammar by George Hickes.[72] The second edition of Rask's grammar was, in turn, translated into English in 1830 by Benjamin Thorpe (1781/2–1870),[73] who felt 'impelled' to undertake this task 'by a sense of the humiliating condition into which the study of the noble old language and literature of our forefathers had fallen in its native land'. Thorpe had gone to Copenhagen, attracted by Rask's scholarly reputation, and his translation was published there with the hope that 'Though printed in a foreign land, my volume will, I trust, not be found wanting in typographical accuracy'. He described himself on the title page as a 'Member of the Munich Royal Academy of Sciences' (as well as of the Society of Netherlandish Literature, Leiden), and he acknowledged the help of Moritz Heyne, Germanic scholar, editor of *Beowulf*, and at this time Professor in the University of Halle. Thorpe was in touch, therefore, not only with Rask himself, but with German scholars in the forefront of the new developments in language study (like Rask, Heyne worked with Jakob Grimm).[74] Rask's grammar included extracts from Old English texts for

---

[71] As noted, enviously, by Ellis, First Annual Address, p. 3, who described Müller's lectures 'to those singularly and provokingly mixed audiences which crowd the theatre of the Royal Institution, when a "crack" man has to "crack"—whether about words or anything else'. Müller gave two series of lectures popularizing comparative philology, in 1861 and 1863.

[72] On Hickes, see further Matthews, *Invention of Middle English*, 15–18.

[73] On Thorpe and publication of Anglo-Saxon, see Aarsleff, *Study of Language*, 185–91, 195; Momma, *From Philology to English Studies*, 68–73.

[74] See Thorpe (trans.), *A Grammar of the Anglo-Saxon Tongue, from the Danish of Erasmus Rask*, Preface, pp. iii–vi. Nothing is known of Thorpe's early life and education apart from the few meagre facts given here. In addition, he was a Fellow of the Society of Antiquaries and a member of the Icelandic Literary Society of Copenhagen.

study—called by Thorpe the 'praxis'—taken from the printed material available to him. Thorpe was able to check the texts against manuscripts (Rask 'never having seen an Anglo-Saxon manuscript himself' (p. iv)).

Thorpe followed up this translation not only with a second edition, but his own *Analecta Anglo-Saxonica* (1834), a primer of prose and verse, including extracts from texts which would now be considered to be early Middle English, but which Thorpe, according to the common practice of his time, called 'Semi-Saxon' (when referring to 'The History of King Leir and his Daughters', from Laʒamon's *Brut*), or, inventing a term for himself, 'Dano-Saxon' (when referring to the *Ormulum*). The *Analecta*, reissued in 1846, established itself as the standard elementary reader for the study of Old English, though with American and German rivals, until it was superseded, first by Richard Morris's *Elementary Lessons in Historical English Grammar* (1874), and then by Morris's more famous successor, *Sweet's Anglo-Saxon Reader* (1876), both by leading members of the Philological Society.[75] Thorpe's *Analecta* may, then, be said to have done much to achieve its object, to promote 'the study of the old vernacular tongue of England, so much neglected at home, and so successfully cultivated by foreign philologists' (p. iii). In addition, there was an abridged version of Rask's grammar by Edward Johnston Vernon, published in 1845 with Thorpe's blessing, 'to furnish the learner, if it may be, with a cheaper, easier, more comprehensive, and not less trustworthy guide to this tongue than may hitherto have been within his reach' (p. v). It was dedicated to the other great English Anglo-Saxonist, John Mitchell Kemble, 'who shares with Mr Thorpe the honour of making his countrymen independent of foreigners'.[76] Vernon's grammar taught 'classical' Old English: 'pure Anglo-Saxon only'.

---

[75] Thorpe, *Analecta Anglo-Saxonica*. Like the grammar, it was printed in ordinary type, apart from a chapter of the extract from the Gospels which 'is given in the Saxon character, that the student may have no difficulty when he meets with any work in that character, either printed or manuscript' (p. iv). The grammar was taken from Thorpe's own translation of Rask. See further, review of Sweet's *Reader* by Moritz Trautmann, *Anglia*, 1 (1878), 379–90.

[76] See John D. Haigh, 'Kemble, John Mitchell (1807–1857)', *ODNB*. Kemble, a scion of the theatrical family, acquired his passion for language study at Cambridge before training as a lawyer in the Inner Temple (alongside F. D. Maurice). While studying at Cambridge he travelled to Germany and began a serious study of German philology. He followed this by manuscript study in Cambridge and the British Museum, where he studied Grimm's *Deutsche Grammatik*, before entering into a correspondence with him and visiting him in Göttingen. See further B. Dickins, 'John Mitchell Kemble and Old English Scholarship'; Skeat, *Student's Pastime*, pp. lx–lxi, lxii–lxv. On Kemble, and his views of Thorpe, see Momma, *From Philology to English Studies*, 68–77; Levine, *The Amateur and the Professional*, 25, Aarsleff, *Study of Language*, 191.

He expressed the belief that 'One well grounded in the language in its perfect state, will not find it hard to bring down his knowledge of his native tongue through Semi-Saxon and old and middle English to our own time' (p. vi): in 'scientific' philological study of English, one begins at the beginning, goes on to the end, then stops. Kemble, in his review of Thorpe's *Analecta* for the *Gentleman's Magazine* (1834), used the opportunity to stir up a war of words between those students of Anglo-Saxon who, like himself and Thorpe, had first-hand experience of the new philology abroad, and old-style antiquarians who had not.[77] Furnivall did not learn Old English at this time (and remained content for the most part with Middle English), though Spalding, the author of the textbook he used in the Working Men's College, had asserted that 'It is a fact not to be concealed, that every one who would learn to understand English as thoroughly as an accomplished scholar ought to understand it, must be content to begin by mastering Rask's excellent "Anglo-Saxon Grammar," in Thorpe's translation', while Thorpe's *Analecta*, and other works 'by this same distinguished philologist', along with Kemble's, made specimens accessible. Spalding had also included samples of the Old English Boethius and Exodus.[78]

Not only did the study of 'early English' require grammars and readers; it urgently needed dictionaries of both what would now be called Old and Middle English. Thus there was a need for an Old English dictionary to replace William Somner's *Dictionarium Saxonico-Latino-Anglicum*, first published in 1659, and again in a second edition, augmented by Thomas Benson in 1701 and followed by Edward Lye's *Dictionarium Saxonicum* (1772).[79] In 1838, during that eventful decade for the study of the new philology in England, there appeared Joseph Bosworth's *Dictionary of the Anglo-Saxon Language*.[80] Though Bosworth nodded towards 'the erudite labours of Professor Rask and Grimm, as well as of those who adopt their system' (p. vii), he did not make much use of their ideas, preferring English to the Continental 'system'.[81] Bosworth was appointed in 1858 to the Rawlinson Professorship of Anglo-Saxon at Oxford. He had a Midas touch: unlikely

---

[77] Aarsleff, *Study of Language*, 195–203, 199–201.

[78] *History of English Literature*, 99, 107–11.

[79] *Dictionarium Saxonico-Latino-Anglicum*. Lye, *Dictionarium Saxonico et Gothico-Latinum*.

[80] See further, Aarsleff, *Study of Language in England*, 205–6.

[81] The dictionary included an outline, printed separately in 1848, of Old English grammar, condensed from Rask and Grimm. In 1848 Bosworth also condensed the work into *A Compendious Anglo-Saxon Dictionary*, from which the following quotations are taken.

as it might seem, by his own reckoning his writings earned him the astonishing sum of £18,000, which perhaps makes him in real terms one of the most affluent Anglo-Saxonists ever. In 1867 he gave £10,000 to the University of Cambridge to establish a chair in Anglo-Saxon.[82]

Bosworth undoubtedly knew how to appeal to the emotions of an English audience which felt both resentful and, at the same time, guilty, that the main work on the ancestor of their own language had been done by 'erudite Germans and Danes'. Yet the Germans and Danes did not have the Englishman's advantage of 'easy access to our own rich manuscript stores' (p. v)—this echoes Thorpe's observation that Rask never saw an Anglo-Saxon manuscript in his life. And Bosworth also knew how to make a virtue of English descent from people who were seen as energetic barbarians, free from the shackles of those enervated southern peoples who had their liberty curtailed by Roman rule: 'How tame is the Romanised *liberty*, in comparison with the old Gothic, Germanic and English *Freedom!*' (p. i). The English language, despite the 'ornaments' accrued from other languages in its later history, consequently had 'the strength of iron, with the gleam and sparkling of burnished steel', as befitting descendants of men with 'a robust conformation of the bodily frame, and great energy of mind'. Men, indeed, very like Furnivall. Such comments in an abridged and cheaper version of Bosworth's dictionary ten years later, were the stuff to rouse Englishmen from the sluggish indifference to their German roots inculcated by an unthinking classical education. The same mythology, less floridly expressed, but nonetheless vehement, was, for all their reservations about the unphilological nature of Bosworth's dictionary, the engine that powered the English scholars in the Philological Society. It is at work, too, in their descendants, Chambers and Tolkien, faced with the prospect of German invasion in 1940.

For Bosworth, the 'disciples' in England of 'the celebrated Dr James Grimm' (as he called him), and by whom he principally meant Thorpe and Kemble, had forfeited some of this vaunted English 'freedom' by their servitude to Germans and Danes, however erudite. By contrast Bosworth offered a very English compromise. It is another minor—and regrettable—irony that, despite his snub to Rask, the dictionary, on

[82] Henry Bradley, revd. John D. Haigh, 'Bosworth, Joseph (1787/8–1876)', *ODNB*. According to Skeat, who could 'well recall' his 'tall and upright figure', Bosworth made his money, not from Anglo-Saxon, but by the simple expedient of publishing grammars of Greek written in English 'such as every schoolboy could understand', rather than Latin, 'and he had his reward in an enormous sale'; *Student's Pastime*, pp. lxvi–lxviii. See also Momma, *From Philology to English Studies*, 80, and Aarsleff, *Study of Language*, 205–7.

which Bosworth's reputation principally rests, was compiled while he was living in Leiden, with no access himself to the rich manuscript stores in English libraries.[83] The Anglo-Saxonist Oswald Cockayne thought that the popularity of Bosworth's dictionary was owing to its augmentation and updating of Lye's 'noble and honest and copious work' by the more recent work of Grimm, Rask, Kemble, and Thorpe— not from any originality of Bosworth's own. The result, according to Cockayne, was 'a very great convenience to students', not least because 'in these days of easy chairs a folio is unreadable'. That was about the only kind thing he had to say about Bosworth's dictionary. Most of his review is taken up with detailed and merciless fault-finding.[84] Invited by 'some private representations' to moderate his criticisms, he replied: 'In Dr Bosworth's dictionary I see just the small merit that I admitted, it is no more trusty footing than a Welsh bog.'[85]

Bosworth's Anglo-Saxon dictionary, though an improvement on its predecessors, undoubtedly had its faults. As he told Furnivall in 1864, he continued to revise it:

My great object is to make the new ed[itio]n of my Dictionary as complete as possible. It is almost a new work. I have been correcting it and adding to it ever since 1838. I have been and still am assisted by most of the eminent Teutonic Scholars at home and abroad. Grein's work is the best and most practical book Germany has produced. I have made a legitimate use of it, as far as it is published, as I had previously of Ettmüller's *impracticable* 'Lexicon Anglosaxonicum'. And Dr Loo's small book. I believe I possess every important work published at home and abroad, on the Gothic and Anglo-Saxon language and literature that I might have every means of improving my work. Nor is there scarcely any valuable *Anglo-Saxon* MS which I have not consulted. Instead of 'Anglo-Saxon' I prefer calling Alfred and Aelfric *always* Old *English*.[86]

He was still revising it at the time of his death in 1876. The Delegates of the Oxford University Press, which had purchased the copyright, invited Thomas Northcote Toller, at this time a lecturer at Owens College (from 1880 the Victoria University of Manchester) to undertake a new edition, the first instalment of which appeared in 1882. James Platt, for

---

[83] Kemble had embroiled himself in controversy by his attack on Anglo-Saxon studies at Oxford, to which it is possibly Bosworth who replied from the Netherlands, presenting Kemble more explicitly as a slave of the Danes and Germans.

[84] Cockayne, 'Dr Bosworth and his Saxon Dictionary', *The Shrine*, I. i.

[85] 'Postscript on Bosworth's Dictionary', *The Shrine*, II. 23–4 at 23. Bosworth had himself written a riposte, described by Cockayne as 'the noisy, unsubstantial Bosworthian pamphlet' (pp. 23–4). Cockayne had by no means finished: 'my stock of Bosworthian blunders is not exhausted' (p. 24). [86] Letter of 6 Feb. 1864, FU 45.

the Philological Society, took his full part in the chorus of critical howls with which it was greeted: 'Would it not have been far better for Bosworth's memory to have let the good he did live after him, the evil lie interred with his bones, rather than to have thus raked up all the errors of the infant Anglo-Saxon scholarship of his time and republished them in this year of grace 1882, a confession of Englishmen's ignorance of the philology of their own tongue?'[87] Yet 'Bosworth-Toller', thanks to Toller's extended labours, would go on to become a standard reference work, 'a dictionary', as Scragg said, 'for which no leniency of judgement is required, one that was entirely appropriate to the period in which it was produced, and that has continued to serve the academic community well for a great many years'. Eventually, like Stratmann's dictionary of Middle English, it paled in significance with the arrival of a large North American successor, in this case the *Dictionary of Old English* published by the University of Toronto.[88]

Largely because of Rask's and Grimm's interests in the philology of the older Germanic languages, the material for the study of Old English ('Anglo-Saxon') became available at this time, typically in German, before the equivalent study aids were devised for 'Middle English'. As Flügel noted, Middle English studies 'were profited less directly by Grimm, who had not read many texts other than Tyrwhitt's Chaucer and Walter Scott's *Sir Tristrem*'.[89] The division of English into historical periods was not yet clearly determined, and opinion was divided as to what to call them (Furnivall's own perplexities on the subject will be discussed in a later chapter). This uncertainty embraced the forms of English spoken and written before the Conquest, the language which its users them-

---

[87] 'The Bosworth-Toller Anglo-Saxon Dictionary', *TPS*, 19 (1884), 237–46 at 237. Cockayne's review, referred to above, was prompted by the thought that Oxford University Press would associate its august name on the title page with the unworthy Bosworth's. Toller was at this time young and untrained: 'Since no eminent scholar would link his name with such a work, the carrying of it through has had to be entrusted to an as yet unknown hand.' However, he went on to publish the enlarged Bosworth dictionary in two further parts, and the complete book appeared in 1898, when he embarked on a supplement, consisting of major revision of the early part of the alphabet, and published between 1908 and 1921, *An Anglo-Saxon Dictionary, Based on the Manuscript Collections of Joseph Bosworth*, 2 vols.: see further Donald Scragg, 'Toller, Thomas Northcote (1844–1930)', *ODNB*; P. Baker, 'Toller at School'.

[88] Begun in 1970 under Professor Angus Cameron, and succeeded by Professor Antonette diPaolo Healey. See further Hyer, Momma, and Zacher (eds.), *Old English Lexicology and Lexicography*, in particular the contribution by Toswell, 'Genre and the Dictionary'.

[89] 'History of English Philology', in *Flügel Memorial Volume*, 26; see also extract from the *Deutsche Grammatik*, 2nd edn., in Matthews, *Invention of Middle English*, 22.

AIDS TO STUDY OF 'EARLY ENGLISH'

selves called 'Englisc'. 'Old English' might mean 'Anglo-Saxon'. It was (and is) also used more loosely to signify 'early English' before and after 1066. Dictionaries of Old English (in the strict sense) were available long before Middle English. Thus the earliest texts published by the EETS (initially all Middle English) were prepared without much benefit from historical dictionaries or text books.

The first part of Francis Henry (aka Franz Heinrich) Stratmann's Middle English dictionary (except he called it 'old English') coincided in 1864 with the foundation of the EETS and was done without knowledge of its existence. As he noted, 'When I resolved to print the present dictionary I did not expect that in the next time many more materials would become accessible, but soon after the first part was published, in 1864, I learned that a new Society had been formed for the purpose of printing old English texts'. As his not quite idiomatic English shows, Stratmann was, despite his anglicized forenames, a German, working in Krefeld, Prussia, where he seems to have felt cut off from Anglophone fellow savants, though he visited England in 1867 'to examine our unprinted Manuscripts' for his dictionary, and for his forthcoming edition of *The Owl and the Nightingale*.[90] He wrote his dictionary in English (but a short Middle English grammar in German), in 'hopes of receiving communications from fellow students', hopes which were largely disappointed.[91]

Thus, he sent the first part of his dictionary to Sir Frederic Madden, Keeper of Manuscripts at the British Museum, as a gift in the hopes of getting feedback and publicity, but was disappointed not to get an early reply: 'I am now anxious to hear your opinion of my work, and should be very glad if you would favour me with a few lines to that effect. If at the same time you would be so kind as to introduce this child of mine to the English public by a review in a convenient paper, I should feel much obliged.'[92] Yet 'I was happy enough to find in Frederic [sic] J. Furnivall, Esq. M.A., of London, a friend, who kindly pointed out to me, and readily lent me several rare books which furnished valuable contributions'.[93] The first edition 'was not wholly satisfactory'.[94] Stratmann's

---

[90] See Stratmann, *A Dictionary of the Old English Writing*, Advertisement, p. iii. By 1867, Stratmann had been able to use the EETS editions to enlarge his work. See also 'Our Weekly Gossip', in *The Athenaeum*, 14 Sept. 1867 (no. 2081), 336 (information probably supplied by Furnivall, in view of the detailed knowledge shown and other titbits relating to the EETS). [91] Stratmann, *Mittelenglische Grammatik*.
[92] Letter of 4 June 1864, from Krefeld; BL, MS Egerton 2848, f. 78, 'the publishing of the rest depends on the sale of this part'.
[93] Advertisement, p. iii: 'A great deal of whatever merit my work has is due to him.' The
[*See p. 300 for n. 93 cont. and n. 94*]

'child', which went through three editions in his lifetime, was revised and enlarged by Henry Bradley in 1891; at Furnivall's suggestion, the copyright was bought by the Clarendon Press, Oxford.[95] It had a rival: Eduard Mätzner's *Altenglische Sprachproben*, which, as its list of sources shows, was made possible by the EETS publications, and was described by Ewald Flügel as 'the first real dictionary of Middle English', whereas 'Stratmann gave the earliest Middle English glossary on a large basis'.[96] But, even though Mätzner gained a high reputation as the author of a pioneering descriptive historical grammar of modern English, his dictionary never ousted Stratmann, probably because to an Anglophone readership it had the disadvantage of being written in German, and unlike his grammar, was not translated.[97]

The Stratmann–Bradley dictionary established itself as the standard

---

grammar appeared later, a year after the author's death in 1884. Stratmann also produced the first 'critical edition' (his description) of *An Old English Poem of The Owl and the Nightingale* (1868), in English, and with acknowledgement in the Preface to Furnivall, 'the zealous promoter of old English literature'. Furnivall advertised 'Dr. Stratmann's excellent edition' to the EETS members, recording that it appeared thanks to 'the Society's influence' (Fifth Annual Report, 1869, p. 4). Stratmann also prepared an old-spelling edition of *The Tragicall Historie of Hamlet, Prince of Denmark, by William Shakespeare, edited according to the first Printed Copies, with the Various Readings and Critical Notes* (London and Krefeld, 1869). The interest in Shakespeare, and the use of Trübner as a publisher, again point to Furnivall's support.

[94] Skeat, *Student's Pastime*, pp. xxxii–xxxiii at xxxii.

[95] Ibid., p. xxxii.

[96] 'History of English Philology', *Flügel Memorial Volume*, 30. A. J. Ellis, reviewing the first part of Mätzner's dictionary, described it as 'refreshingly full in vocabulary and quotation, with careful distinctions of the shades of meaning in the uses of every word—a point in which Dr. Stratmann's work is defective. The only fault that I can see in Dr Mätzner's book is that the quotations are not arranged in either strictly chronological or dialectal order, so that the student gets confused as to the history and locality of the forms of a word; and the only drawback I know to an Englishman's use of the book is that the meanings of the early words are given in German only, instead of both German and English'; 'Second Annual Address', *TPS*, 15 (1874), 242. See also Skeat, *Student's Pastime*, pp. xxxii–xxxiii; Matthews, *Invention of Middle English*, 30–2.

[97] Mätzner, *Altenglische Sprachproben nebst einem Wörterbuch*; Mätzner, *Englische Grammatik* (Berlin, 1885), translated as *An English Grammar: Methodical, Analytical, and Historical . . .*, by Clair James Grece, in which there is a valuable biographical sketch of Mätzner, pp. vi–vii. Eduard Adolf Ferdinand Mätzner (1805–1902), in Greifswald in Prussian Pomerania, and at the University of Heidelberg. He became headmaster of 'a collegiate establishment at Berlin for the higher education of girls', a post which left him time for his favourite philological researches. Grece describes him as a 'Fellow' [sic] of the Philological Society, of which Mätzner was elected an honorary member in 1869. Mätzner's grammar was paired by commentators of the day with that of Koch, which preceded it: both being seen as indispensable aids to study (Koch, *Historische Grammatik der englischen Sprache*). On Mätzner and Grece, see further Matthews, *Invention of Middle English*, 30–2; on Mätzner, see Utz, *Chaucer*, 52, *passim*.

lexicon of Middle English until the later twentieth century. It was reprinted photographically from sheets of the 1891 edition by Humphrey Milford for Oxford University Press in 1940 and reprinted again in 1958. It was not finally replaced until 2001, when the University of Michigan's *Middle English Dictionary*, begun under the general editorship of Hans Kurath, with Sherman M. Kuhn as associate editor, was completed. The Michigan project, a team effort, rather than a one- or two-man dictionary, was conceived on a much grander scale, to take account of the vast twentieth-century industry in publishing Middle English texts, in which the EETS again was a leading participant. The scheme was conceived in the 1920s, and the dictionary was published, like the *NED/OED*, in alphabetical fascicles, beginning with the first instalment, the plan of the dictionary and bibliography of works consulted, in 1954. By the time the work was finished, it occupied 15,000 pages; in 2007 it was made freely available online.

Before Stratmann, editors used the glossaries in other editions, especially those prepared by Sir Frederic Madden for Laȝamon's *Brut* and *Havelok*, and they used their own judgement—which was not always trustworthy, as we shall see. The *OED* was a great gain after the appearance of the last fascicule in April 1928, but those in quest of Middle English words had to guess what their modern spelling might be—not always obvious—before they could find them. Furnivall's friend and associate Herbert Coleridge (grandson of the poet), first general editor of the Philological Society's new dictionary, had, as a preliminary to this project, collected vocabulary from the printed editions of thirteenth-century texts for a *Glossarial Index*, which appeared in 1858 (price 6d.), two years before his early death from tuberculosis.[98] The *Glossarial Index*, which Coleridge described as 'the foundation-stone of the Historical and Literary portion of the Philological Society's proposed English Dictionary',[99] was essentially a register of words, though because 'a mere index verborum would but inadequately fulfil its object, a certain amount of explanatory and etymological matter has been added, which it is hoped may render the work more generally interesting and useful' (p. iii). Coleridge followed it with what he called a 'Dictionary of the First, or Oldest Words in the English language', published posthumously, though limited in scope to a period of just some fifty years,

---

[98] *A Glossarial Index*. See Preface, p. iii. Furnivall announced Coleridge's death to the Philological Society on 25 Apr. 1861, *TPS*, 7 (1860–1), 308.

[99] Quoted by Gilliver, *Making of the OED*, 31 (on Coleridge's *Glossarial Index*, see pp. 29–32).

concentrating as it did on material from the middle of the thirteenth century, when 'English literature, as distinguished from Semi-Saxon, is assumed to commence' (p. iii), to c.1300.[100] The fourteenth century was served by J. O. Halliwell's popular *Dictionary of Archaic and Provincial Words, Obsolete Phrases, Proverbs, and Ancient Customs*, which appeared, in two volumes, in 1847, and had reached an eleventh edition by 1889. Its success was not surprising, thanks to its entertaining mix of reference work with antiquarian jottings and miscellanea. It would certainly not be regarded as 'scientific' in any sense that the Philological Society would accept.[101]

HOW LAWYERS BECAME LEXICOGRAPHERS: FURNIVALL, COLERIDGE, AND THE BEGINNINGS OF THE *NEW ENGLISH DICTIONARY*

From the very start Furnivall witnessed and participated in the discussions which led to the Philological Society's decision to commit itself to the new dictionary, beginning with the letter from Whewell concerning the activities of the Cambridge Etymological Society, which had provoked such a long and interesting conversation among the members of the Philological Society back in 1852.[102] The Cambridge group had had its own ambitions to create an etymological dictionary; another Cambridge graduate and founder member of the London Philological Society, Hensleigh Wedgwood, was already reading out extracts of his own Etymological Dictionary as papers for the Society. That the Society should start thinking about a dictionary of its own was probably inevitable, given the ever-increasing space allotted to study of the English language in its proceedings, and its members' interests in etymology and the collection of dialect words, together with their sense

---

[100] Coleridge, *A Dictionary of the First, or Oldest Words in the English Language*. The Preface to this work is identical with that written for the *Glossarial Index*. On the term 'Semi Saxon', see further Matthews, *Invention of Middle English*, 4–5.

[101] Compare R. F. Weymouth's comment on Halliwell's edition of Grosseteste's 'Castle of Love', a text 'greatly modernized and corrupted... printed for private circulation': '"The text of this edition," the reader is told "is chiefly taken from a MS. in private hands;" but unfortunately we are not informed to what extent the editor has allowed himself to depart from the authority or authorities which he "chiefly followed", and I regret to learn from Mr. Halliwell that he has entirely lost sight of the MS. from which this text is in the main derived', *TPS* 8 (1862–3), 49–50.

[102] This is a selective discussion, focusing on Furnivall's involvement in the dictionary and its relation to the EETS in its beginnings. Readers are referred to Gilliver, *Making of the OED*, especially 1–40, for a full and authoritative account of the *OED*'s origins.

that, having digested the principles of the 'new philology', the time was right to supersede previous dictionaries and put English lexicography on a scientific footing. English nationalism also contributed to the desire that the English language should not be left behind by other nations' lexicographers, not least after the beginnings in 1838 of Jakob and Wilhelm Grimm's *Deutsches Wörterbuch*.

As is well known, the event which launched the *NED* project was the paper given in two parts, on 5 and 19 November 1857, by the Revd. Richard Chenevix Trench to the Philological Society, 'On Some Deficiencies in our English Dictionaries'.[103] Trench another of the Trinity College Cambridge alumni, a fellow Apostle, and a friend of F. D. Maurice since their undergraduate days, was elected to the Society at its meeting on 21 May 1857, and clearly wasted no time in making an impression. He had been professor of divinity at KCL before promotion to Dean of Westminster Abbey. Later, in 1856, he was appointed Archbishop of Dublin.[104] Trench shared with Maurice (and, indeed, the President of the Philological Society, and Bishop of St David's, Connop Thirlwall) the conviction that theology and philology were intimately bound up with each other.[105] As author of, among other books, *On the Study of Words* (1851) and *English Past and Present* (1855), both originally written as lectures given to the Winchester Diocesan Training School and King's College, London, Trench had a proven record in writing on the history of languages (especially English and the Greek of the New Testament). When he joined the Philological Society, he was working on a new book, *A Select Glossary of English Words Used formerly in Senses Different from their Present* (1859), an impressive testimony to his sensitivity to fine discriminations of meaning, yet written 'in a popular manner and for general readers'.[106] Both this work and 'Some Deficiencies' give ample testimony to Trench's extraordinarily wide reading in English and retentive memory, making him both an ideal member of the Society and one well suited to encourage its as yet tentative lexicographical ambitions. This subject was discussed at its anniversary meeting in May.

Gilliver suggests that it is likely that Furnivall, always one to seize an opportunity, saw his chance to interest Trench in his vision of a large cohort of suitable people co-operating in the necessary reading and research. Trench told him: 'I shall be very glad to share in so good a work.

[103] On the whole episode, see Gilliver, *Making of the OED*, 12–22.
[104] See Bromley, *The Man of Ten Talents*.   [105] Ibid. 109–10, 228–45.
[106] 'Author's Preface', *Select Glossary*, ed. Smythe Palmer, p. ix.

I will between this & that think over the books which seem to me likely to render up the amplest harvest of words, which have as yet been unregistered. I am sure the incomings may be very large, though doubtless they cannot be gathered in without industry & pains.'[107] In hindsight, when H. B. Wheatley described this time, Furnivall was elevated to the heroic status which was perhaps more clearly visible in 1912 (when Wheatley wrote) than it had been in 1857: he, 'at that time a little over thirty years old', was the one who saw that the creation of a Supplement was requiring 'a great effort . . . for an insufficient result, and grasped the idea that an entirely new Dictionary might be obtained by the machinery set in motion'. As Wheatley put it, 'Furnivall was not . . . afraid of great and far-reaching ideas'. Trench had responded cautiously: 'It is a very fine idea, if you can carry it out; but I don't think you can.'[108]

Furnivall had his own memories of this time. Speaking in 1909 to a meeting of the Authors' Club, he claimed to have been much more reluctant to be involved:

Trench wrote us a paper on the duty of making a supplement to the dictionaries of Johnson and Richardson. Herbert Coleridge, a grandson of the poet, came forward and said, 'I should like to take a part in this'. The question was, who should work with him. I refused absolutely, on which [Thomas] Watts, who was head of the Book Department in the British Museum, reminded me that I was secretary of the Society, and that if I was asked to do a thing it was my duty to do it.[109]

In old age, Furnivall knew how to tell a good story and knew that he was in demand for his memories of over a half century before, which might be enhanced in the telling. And, in his eighties, with many honours to his credit, he had nothing to prove. As Wheatley gently pointed out, the story about Watt's stern injunction should probably be treated with indulgent scepticism.[110]

In the meantime, before Trench delivered his famous paper, the Society had formed a Committee, consisting of Trench, Furnivall, and Herbert Coleridge, 'to collect unregistered words in English'. Trench's paper took the place of the intended first report of this Committee. In this paper, he drew attention to the obvious, but telling point, that previous dictionaries had been unable to make full use of the vast lexical storehouse to be found in older English writings. Trench made it sound so easy: 'Any one who is not merely and altogether a guest and stranger in our earlier literature, has in his power to bring forward

---

[107] Gilliver, *Making of the OED*, 13.
[108] Wheatley, 'The Early English Text Society and F. J. Furnivall', 2. [109] Ibid. 3.
[110] Ibid, footnote: 'This is a strong injunction for an honorary secretary, and few holders of the office would be inclined to acknowledge the obligation, particularly when, as in this case it included the editing of a big dictionary.'

abundant evidence even from his single, and it may be slenderly furnished treasure-house, of the large omissions which it is desirable to supply.'[111]
And he returned to this argument still more explicitly:

> There might well be a general consent among scholars to consider no book of our earlier literature as decently edited, no editor as having tolerably fulfilled the obligations which, as such, he understood, where such a glossary as I speak of is wanting.
>
> It is certain, however, of a vast number of our books, that they will never be reprinted, that the facility of entrance into their philological treasures which good indexes might give will never be afforded . . . we have a mass of English literature, which can only be made available for philological purposes through the combined efforts of many; a dense and serried phalanx of books which the desultory and isolated assaults of one here and there can never hope effectually to penetrate . . . One may read for years in our old literature and light, it may be, during the whole time on some vial which being found, at once testifies for itself, that, however rare in books, it must have been common in speech; so having lighted on it once, we may never encounter it a second time . . . If therefore, we count it worth while to have all words, we can only have them by reading all books; this is the price which we must be content to pay.[112]

Trench demonstrated in passing his own knowledge of such texts as *Piers Plowman*, and tantalized his listeners with the 'much earlier examples of the employment of words', which 'oftentimes exist than any which are cited'.[113] His remarks on the Dictionary's role as a 'historical monument', itself representing 'the history of a nation contemplated from one point of view', gave eloquent expression to what would be Furnivall's strong belief, and the *raison d'être* of the EETS. Trench gave testimony to the power of words to get modern readers (provided they were acquainted with older writers and texts) in some manner to reconstruct the past. His argument goes much further than simply making older texts accessible and read by competent persons to provide the essential materials of the dictionary:

> One of the most effectual means of reducing us to the condition of, of bringing us to live only in the present, is to cut us off from all knowledge of the past. We can only live in the past and draw our ennobling inspiration from it, through acquaintance, and indeed through more or less familiarity, with it . . . In this way I travel back to Shakespeare, to Spenser, to Gascoigne, to Hawes, to Chaucer,

---

[111] 'On Some Deficiencies', 1.
[112] Ibid. 67–9. See also Gilliver's detailed appraisal of the paper, *Making of the OED*, 18–21.
[113] 'On Some Deficiencies', 3.

Wiclif, and at length to Piers Ploughman, Robert of Gloucester, or whatever other work is taken as the earliest in our tongue.[114]

The necessary research, requiring much editing and re-editing of old books, was essential for the Dictionary, but also had further inestimable advantages, of giving access to the people of the past, and even their spoken words. They offered a portrait of Britain (the *NED* was conceived as a national monument). These additional benefits probably meant at least as much to Furnivall as having the lexicon at one's fingertips. His own editions, together with those which were made possible through the EETS and his other societies, promoted this auxiliary agenda for the importance of the study of early English texts in their own right. They did not only provide fuel for the Dictionary.

And, if another lure were needed to tempt Furnivall, the one which he found perhaps most attractive of all was that association with the Dictionary offered him one of the biggest and most important co-operative projects imaginable, one in which he would have a leading part to play and show what he could do among some of the foremost cultural and literary figures of the day. The feel-good factor must have been immense, and the motive was powerful. This new enterprise would surely eclipse the efforts of his former associates among the Christian Socialists, perhaps especially F. D. Maurice, Charles Kingsley, and Tom Hughes. Moreover, it must be remembered that the Philological Society's decision in 1857 to publish its Dictionary, and the subsequent negotiations, coincided *exactly* with Furnivall's quarrels with Maurice over the running of the Working Men's College. He no longer needed Maurice or Hughes (though he surely hoped to impress them), and he could bring his allies among the students of the Working Men's College with him as assistants to work on the Dictionary. And, as a Volunteer and a patriot, he was not likely to be deterred by suggestion that a lexicographical military conquest would be needed to achieve Trench's campaign to bring the English language to order and rule, and administer it, not by haphazard individual 'assaults', but by a concerted and orderly mission to penetrate the 'phalanx' of old books in order to possess their vast stores of treasure, all properly docketed and filed. Trench summed up the ethos of this unabashed invasion of *terra* almost entirely *incognita* by his extraordinary concluding extended metaphor, taken from Herodotus: the army of lexicographers must proceed with the same ruthlessly thorough tactics as the Persians when

[114] Ibid. 8–9.

clearing new territory: they must join hands, encircling the island to be conquered, and gradually move inwards to flush out all the inhabitants. No word, however small, could hope to hide.[115] Of course, this metaphor presupposes that the English lexicon can be so definitely circumscribed in insular terms—Trench acknowledged in his paper the vexed question of what *was* an English word—but, for purposes of arousing enthusiasm among classically educated, patriotic people, within and beyond the Society, its rhetorical force is undeniable.

Even before the announcements were made in Trench's paper the wider public was being invited to come forward as recruits in July 1857 in a circular printed in the leading journals, including the *Athenaeum*.[116] 'Volunteers' (and the word had resonances with the civilian militia which had become such a feature of national—and Furnivall's—life) were invited to take part in this 'truly national work'. At least one of the Working Men's College's rifle corps, the builder G. M. Hantler, did become a reader, and was photographed for the Dictionary's record—in his uniform as a captain of the 19th Middlesex. And he was joined by other College members: W. A. Dalziel, George Tansley and Augustus C. Lawrence.[117] The wider public responded enthusiastically, to such an extent that a revised version of the circular was published in August noting that 'owing to the great amount of friendly cooperation which the Committee have received . . . the scheme has assumed far larger dimensions than was at first anticipated'.[118] As Gilliver observed, the wording, with its stress on *friendly* cooperation, its vast optimism, and its huge ambitions, sounds like Furnivall, who seems already to have been pushing for a grander scheme than that initially envisaged by his colleague on the Committee, Herbert Coleridge.

The co-operation among a wide section of the public, men and women, who all volunteered to act as readers for the Dictionary, was, indeed, celebrated in a commemorative photographic record: the readers sent in signed images of themselves, which Furnivall assembled in albums. It was not seemingly his idea, but that of Jonathan Eastwood, a Derbyshire clergyman, member of the Philological Society, and himself a reader. Eastwood accompanied his photograph with

---

[115] Ibid. 69–70. See also Momma, *From Philology to English Studies*, 112.

[116] See further Marchand, *The Athenaeum*.

[117] For Hantler, see Pl. 5. Dalziel sent in his photograph for the Dictionary's album on 2 Sept. 1862: see Pl. 3; Lawrence's photograph was dated July 1862 (presumably when he became involved with the Dictionary), but was received 2 Jan. 1863: Bodl. MS Murray, 31: 'to' corrected from 'of'.

[118] Gilliver, *Making of the OED*, 15 (and see the whole discussion, pp. 15–18).

a note to Furnivall: 'Thinking it would be rather amusing to have a portrait gallery of the contributors 'to' the Dict[ionar]y. I offer the enclosed as a beginning; it is as like as such things usually are, only that I do *not* squint.'[119] Furnivall took up the suggestion enthusiastically, and carefully collected the growing collection, each image annotated with the sitter's name, address, and the date when it was received. The result is a Furnivallesque, and pointedly democratic, assemblage of landed gentlemen, bishops, Fellows of colleges, wives, sons, daughters, men and women of letters, students of the Working Men's College, army and naval officers. They include among the notables the bishop, Thirlwall, and Dean of Westminster, Trench, the arctic explorer Sir John Richardson and his daughter, Beatrice, and the novelist Charlotte M. Yonge, and all four nations of the United Kingdom are represented. Many of the readers later became subscribers to the EETS: the albums are an invaluable resource to fill in the sparse information in the lists of subscribers and allow us to put faces to many of their names.[120]

Meanwhile Furnivall and Coleridge were busy corresponding with their volunteers and dealing with the mass of paper slips on which they submitted their quotations (Trench, though a member of the Committee, was too busy and too grand to undertake this kind of menial labour). But Trench's paper articulated the magnificence of the Society's final view: 'The horizon of those who had undertaken the scheme enlarging by degrees, it was finally resolved to publish, not a Supplement of existing Dictionaries, which it was felt would only imperfectly meet the necessities of the case ... but an entirely new Dictionary; no patch upon old garments, but a new garment throughout.'[121] This was the stuff to inspire the reading public, and was followed on 3 December by the report of the Unregistered Words Committee, read to the Philological Society by Coleridge, in which the announcement of a scheme for 'a completely new English Dictionary' was made. It is hard to disagree with Gilliver's view that 'the weight of evidence seems to favour giving the credit' for this announcement 'to Furnivall'.[122]

[119] Dated 28 Apr. 1862, from Eckington, Chesterfield. MS Murray, 31, first album.

[120] The three albums together make up Bodl. MS Murray 31, contained in an archival box with some loose photographs. Images from the collection have been reproduced by Murray, in *Caught in the Web of Words*, and by Sarah Ogilvie, in *The Dictionary People*. The first of the albums especially (now in poor condition and held together in a brown envelope) has been much consulted and some of the original photographs are now missing. The photographs were placed in the albums apparently as they were sent in, except that Furnivall separated out the men from the women, who are placed in the second half of each album. [121] 'On Some Deficiencies', 1.

[122] Gilliver, *Making of the OED*, 21.

It had originally been intended that this report by the Unregistered Words Committee, with its great announcement, should have been delivered to the Society before Trench's paper, which thus stole much of its thunder. In particular, Trench's paper had been a proclamation of the Committee's intention to push back the materials collected at least as far as the thirteenth-century chronicler Robert of Gloucester.[123] The Committee's members were becoming increasingly aware of the practical difficulties involved in carrying out the intention to tell words' entire histories, when much of the evidence survived in medieval texts. Here the volunteers' work would be restricted by the printed editions available and by their own lack of expertise in understanding older varieties of English. For the time being, subcommittees were formed to ponder this problem: it was hoped that a sufficiently large cohort of readers could be recruited to leave the members of the Committee 'comparatively free to encounter in propriis personis the greater difficulties of our earlier literature'.[124]

The next step was taken on 7 January 1858, when the Philological Society resolved formally that a new dictionary should be prepared under its aegis. Furnivall, as Secretary, made the announcement:

On the motion of Mr. Furnivall, the Society resolved, 'That a new English Dictionary be prepared under the authority of the Philological Society,'—and 'that the work be placed in the hands of two Committees: the one, Literary and Historical, consisting of the Very Rev. the Dean of Westminster [Trench], F. J. Furnivall, Esq., and Herbert Coleridge, Esq.; the other, Etymological, consisting of H. Wedgwood, Esq., Prof. Malden, and others.'[125]

The 'Literary and Historical Committee' was simply the Unregistered Words Committee under a new name. In August 1858, and, again in September, after Furnivall had returned from his only ever excursion abroad to Normandy with a party of the working men, the Society published its detailed 'Proposal for the Publication of a New English Dictionary', reissued again in December.[126] Among other points, it was decided that the Dictionary's scope should extend back to the middle of the thirteenth century, when 'the definite appearance of an English type of language, distinct from the preceding semi-Saxon' had emerged. Also, that, for the purposes of collecting materials, English should be

---

[123] On the history of editing the *Chronicle*, see A. Hudson, 'Robert of Gloucester and the Antiquaries'. [124] Quoted by Gilliver, *Making of the OED*, 25.
[125] *The Athenaeum*, 13 Feb. 1858, p. 212. There exist two drafts in Furnivall's handwriting, the earlier of the two postmarked 6 Jan.: Gilliver, *Making of the OED*, 26 n. 81.
[126] See ibid. 28–9.

divided into three periods: the beginnings to 1526, when the first English New Testament was published; from 1526 for the death of Milton in 1674; and from 1674 to the present day.[127]

Later on James Murray declared that 'I have heard Furnivall say that he never believed in these divisions, and thought that Coleridge attributed far too much importance to the influence on the language of the Scripture versions; but that no one then knew really how the language could best be divided into periods, and so he accepted this as a provisional order'.[128] For the second period, readers could be issued with Cruden's *Concordance* to the Authorized Version of the Bible and a concordance to Shakespeare, against which to identify new words. And for the third, perhaps rather oddly, they were to use a 'list of Burke's words'—Furnivall's informal description of a work which probably could not perhaps be dignified with the name of a concordance.[129] But no other compendious published wordlist for the period came to mind, and Furnivall recommended Burke because his former student at the Working Men's College, William Rossiter, had already compiled an informal manuscript wordlist for another purpose.[130] Furnivall was no doubt full of satisfaction at being able to supply a literary production by the College for such a significant role in the Dictionary. He also recruited Eleanor Dalziel to read Florence Nightingale's *Notes on Nursing*.[131] Munby's vignette of Furnivall in 1859 at home sorting slips with the assistance of Eleanor and the genial builder, Hantler, both also associated with the College, belongs to this same period, after the work on the Dictionary had begun in earnest.

There remained the problem of what to do with the earliest period. Here, fortunately, Herbert Coleridge, who had a particular interest in this area, was already at work on his own word list, the *Glossarial Index*, covering 1250 to 1300, and published in 1859.[132] Apart from this assistance, any readers of later Middle English were pretty much on their

[127] Ibid. 29. [128] Munro (ed.), *Frederick James Furnivall*, 126.
[129] Gilliver, *Making of the OED*, 29.
[130] Furnivall was in touch with Rossiter in 1857, when Rossiter thanked him 'as a proof that your old protégé still lives in your remembrance', FU 771, dated from Helston, Cornwall; in the following year, he wrote from the School House, in Rumburgh, Suffolk: 'I must appeal to Burke to assist me to carry on the war till the end of the quarter', FU 773, 23 June 1858; this shows both that Rossiter was now a teacher, and that the reading work for the Dictionary was of considerable pecuniary benefit to him. Furnivall also sent Rossiter back numbers of *The People's Paper*, FU 770; see Rossiter's letter of 6 Sept. 1858, FU 770.
[131] 'List of Words, &c', Third Period.
[132] Coleridge's publication, designed as a tool to serve the Dictionary, suffered by comparison with Trench's more accessible *Select Glossary* (Gilliver, *Making of the OED*, 31).

own. Coleridge considered that enough writing from the thirteenth century had been printed to warrant his publication of the *Index*, but he recognized that these texts were difficult for the Dictionary's readers to get hold of. Coleridge was able to draw upon the editions of early Middle English texts by Sir Frederic Madden and others, described below. But, more importantly, for a history of the EETS, it is easy to see that the Dictionary's need for more materials galvanized Furnivall to begin his own transcriptions of significant texts.

Moreover, Furnivall's work on behalf of the Dictionary gave him indispensable familiarity with the wider world of historical scholarship, institutions, book-clubs, and publishing. Getting out the Philological Society's *Transactions* involved its Secretary in extensive dealings with printers and publishers. The Society's English publisher in the early 1850s was Bell and Daldy (which, with Daldy's departure from the firm in 1873, reverted to its original name of George Bell & Sons). Its *Transactions* were also published by A. Asher & Co., of Berlin.[133] Later, in the 1860s, Stephen Austin, of Hertford, took on the printing. Bell was a publisher of educational books; Adolph Asher, another German with an aptitude for languages, was a man with a scholarly interest in bibliography, who had travelled to England and built up a book-selling business in Covent Garden, as well as Berlin, on the strength of his contacts (which included close friendship with Anthony Panizzi, Keeper of Printed Books at the British Museum).[134] However, Furnivall reported at the meeting of the Philological Society on 4 November 1858, that, though Asher & Co. continued to publish the Philological Society's *Transactions*, the firm had withdrawn from its initial undertaking to publish the new Dictionary, and that it would be published instead by another German scholar-publisher, resident in London. This was Nicholas Trübner (1817–84), and, at the Society's meeting of 27 January 1859, Trübner 'was balloted for and duly elected a Member'.[135] Trübner's contribution, as a publisher, to literary and language studies in Britain in the second half of the nineteenth century would be enormous, not

---

[133] As, for example, *TPS*, 3 (1856). George Bell's firm was founded in 1839. On Bell (1814–90), a fellow of the Society of Antiquaries, see further Alexis Weedon, 'Bell family (*per*. 1814–1968)', *ODNB*. Daldy was a partner between 1856 and 1873. The Society's *Transactions* for 1854 included Bell and Daldy's list of publications, featuring, among other items, 'Lectures to Ladies on Practical Subjects, delivered in London during the month of July 1855 by the Rev. F. D. Maurice, Professor Trench *et al*.'.

[134] On A. Asher & Co, see further the website of Asher Rare Books, 'History', https://www.asherbooks.com/about.html (accessed 22 Nov. 2023).

[135] *TPS*, 6 (1859), 292; see also Gilliver, *Making of the OED*, 30.

least by taking on, not only the Philological Society's publications, but also several of Furnivall's subsequent literary societies.[136] Among them was the EETS.

Trübner was the son of a Heidelberg goldsmith, whose parents could not afford a university education for him. Nevertheless, he gained wide scholarly experience through contacts with scholars and from the opportunities for learning offered in the course of his employment by a succession of German booksellers. His introduction to learned circles in London came when he was sent there from Frankfurt by William Longman, of the publishing firm of Longman's (founded in 1724) as a foreign corresponding clerk with 30s. in his pocket. Trübner learned the English trade—and the English language—working as a publisher's assistant for Longman's. After witnessing stirring times, when he was stuck in Vienna during the revolutionary year of 1848, he set up in business for himself in 1851 in Paternoster Row. He had a special interest in Eastern languages, and he gave up much of his spare time to studying Sanskrit with Theodor Goldstücker. His firm established itself as a specialist business, publishing on Oriental literature as well as philology and philosophy, interests which hardly ever brought him into direct competition with existing English publishers. Dinner parties at his house, 29 Upper Hamilton Terrace, Maida Vale, were brilliant cosmopolitan occasions, attended by scholars, diplomats, poets, and explorers, ably presided over by the convivial Trübner and his wife (daughter of the Belgian consul). It was said of him that 'Shrewd as he was in business matters, the cordiality of his friendship, like his enthusiasm for learning, knew no bounds. Nothing could shake his confidence in his friends, when once made; he held loyally by them through good and evil report ... None will know how many of the struggling scholars found in him the best and truest of friends and who owe their success in life to his timely help.'[137]

In short, Trübner had everything to commend him as a publisher and scholar to Furnivall and his friends in the Philological Society, and he was one of the first in the succession of scholarly friendships with affable and erudite Germans which would be such a feature of Furnivall's life. Much later, Trübner would even publish ephemeral pamphlet reprints of Furnivall's abusive public correspondence with Swinburne. Trübner's

---

[136] See further Mumby, *The House of Routledge*, 162–77.
[137] From A. H. Sayce's obituary notice, quoted ibid. 167–8, and see further ch. VII, pp. 162–77. A photograph of Trübner faces p. 162. See further Stanley Lane-Poole, 'Trübner, Nicholas (Nikolaus), (1817–1884)', *ODNB*.

death in 1884, after his long membership of the Philological Society, and his publication of the *Transactions*, along with the publications of the EETS 'and kindred societies', would be marked by James Murray in his President's Address to the Society.[138] However, Trübner did not take on the *Transactions* until 1877, by which time he was already publishing for Furnivall's New Shakspere Society (from its beginning, in 1874) and the Chaucer Society; he would also publish for the Browning Society.

Trübner thus came to the Philological Society's notice around 1858, a year before his election, in connection with its momentous resolution the following year, at its meeting on Thursday, 7 January, to undertake a New English Dictionary, and when Furnivall was looking around for a publisher. Furnivall and Coleridge were empowered to enter into negotiations 'with Messrs. Nutt of London and Asher of Berlin, or such other Publishers as they think fit, to publish the Dictionary on such terms as they see fit'.[139] Asher of Berlin was, of course, the Society's German publisher; Nutt was David Nutt, of the Strand (d. 1863), another specialist in foreign book-selling, and a business associate of Trübner. The name of Nutt's better-known son, Alfred Trübner Nutt, folklorist and Celtic scholar, who would succeed to his father's business, records this close association. Though David Nutt did not take up the offer, Furnivall was able to record at the meeting of 4 November 1858, that 'Messrs Trübner & Co. had agreed to publish the Society's New English Dictionary'.[140]

However, thanks to his determination to get his own way, Furnivall's negotiations with publishers for the Dictionary were at times tortuous, and, some might say, more underhand than would be expected from one who prided himself on manliness and frankness. Even before the Philological Society's resolution of 1859 had authorized him, with Coleridge, to negotiate with publishers, Furnivall had in 1858 approached not only Trübner but John Murray, and matters had gone so far as the devising of a draft agreement before Murray declared: 'I cannot fetter myself by signing it. To bind myself absolutely to publish a work which I have not seen & regarding the contents of which I am to have no control is contrary to any thing of previous occurrence in my literary experience'.[141] Trübner's connection with the Dictionary would also,

[138] 'Thirteenth Address of the President . . . 16th May 1884', *TPS*, 19 (1882–4), 505.

[139] *TPS*, 5 (1858), 'Notice of the Meeting of the Philological Society in 1858', items II and IV, p. 198. Skeat, *Student's Pastime*, pp. xxi–xxii. Gilliver, *Making of the OED*, 30.

[140] A copy of the agreement between Furnivall, Coleridge, and Asher Co. Berlin, dated 9 June 1858, is preserved in the Murray Papers.

[141] 'This Agreement made the — day of 1858 Between John Murray of Albemarle Street London . . . and Frederick James Furnivall and Herbert Coleridge, Members of the

in the end, go no further. Yet the firm did publish Herbert Coleridge's preparatory study for it, the *Glossarial Index*.[142]

Naturally many of the Philological Society's members took a keen interest in the project and took the opportunity to try and solve word puzzles for the Dictionary and exercise their lexicographical hobby horses. The members of the Society did not present an altogether united forum. Thus, the Dictionary provided opportunities for the advocates for spelling reform to express their views. Also, Herbert Coleridge's uncle, Derwent Coleridge (second son of the poet), offered 'Observations on the Plan of the Society's Proposed New English Dictionary', strongly resisting the proposed descriptivist approach, considering that there was a responsibility to arbitrate on usage.[143] Another view was offered by Danby Fry, who would become a leading light in the EETS, as well as a frequent contributor of papers to the Philological Society, of which he was one of the early members. Like Furnivall, Fry was a lawyer (also at Lincoln's Inn). He, too, was not a trained philologist, but an observant and keenly interested amateur, who had caught the philological bug from his father. Fry would now be called a civil servant: his profession was that of a clerk to the Poor Law Board; he was an administrator, who took over the auditing of the Philological Society's accounts from Furnivall, and was for many years its Treasurer.[144] As one lawyer to another, Fry wrote to Furnivall in 1860 on 'a curious question', arising from a recent libel case, 'as to the meaning & libellous character of the word "Truckmaster", which, it was stated, is not to be found in any English Dictionary'. One of the barristers had made 'a startling proposition "that the Jury are bound to know every word in the English language"! If so, I suspect that the Soc[iet]y's Dict[ionar]y is very urgently needed, indeed!'[145] As Treasurer, Fry warned the Society that it

Council of the Philological Society'; letter to Furnivall, 12 May [1858], Murray Papers. See further Gilliver, *Making of the OED*, 47-8.

[142] 'Memorandum of Agreement', dated 19 Jan. 1859, 'between Herbert Coleridge of 10 Chester Place Regents Park ... Barrister at Law ... and Messieurs Trübner and Company of Paternoster Row ... to publish ... "A Glossarial Index of the Printed English Literature of the Thirteenth Century" 1500 copies. The Philological Society to be entitled to receive 160 copies ... copyright to reside with Coleridge and his assigns'; Murray Papers. It was also announced that Trübner would publish Hensleigh Wedgwood's *A Dictionary of English Etymology*, 3 vols. in 4 (London, 1859-65).

[143] *TPS*, 7 (1860-1), 152-68; see also Gilliver, *Making of the OED*, 33.

[144] See further H. B. Wheatley, revd. Catherine Pease-Watkin, 'Fry, Danby Palmer (1818-1903)', *ODNB*.

[145] Letter of 15 Dec. 1860, Murray Papers. The case was that of Homer v. Taunton (1860), and the barrister was William Adam Mundell, of Middle Temple. See further *OED*,

HOW LAWYERS BECAME LEXICOGRAPHERS   315

was spending too much money on its own publications, leaving little in reserve for its future Dictionary.[146] As a loyal son, Fry was also naturally keen to recommend to the Society his father's plans for his own projected dictionary, with which Danby Fry had assisted. The guiding principle was to classify the words of the language 'etymologically in groups or families, according to their natural affinities', rather than alphabetically, as the Society's Dictionary Committee had already agreed to do.[147] The method—roughly that of a thesaurus—had the advantage of attempting a mode of classification which was not merely an arbitrary finding tool, like the alphabet, but 'a more philosophical method'.[148] The Society was happy for him to air his views, but made it plain that it had no intention of adopting them.

'EARLY ENGLISH' TEXTS AND THE DICTIONARY

In 1860 Coleridge wrote an open letter to Trench to report on the new Dictionary's progress. It had been patchy, as was only to be expected from a big project which depended on the goodwill and varying levels of expertise of many volunteer readers (some of whom Coleridge classed as 'hopeless').[149] Progress on the first period, to 1526, was especially hampered by difficulties of access. As Coleridge said, 'Unfortunately...

'truck-master', n., one who engages in small time bartering of goods, originally referring to trade between the settlers and the native Americans in the US. The 'truck' system, whereby workers were paid, not in cash, but only in kind (and consequently lost out financially because middlemen (the truckmasters) took their cut from the men's wages. That Fry discussed such a case with Furnivall might suggest that he shared Furnivall's views on workers' associations and trades unions, but Furnivall was consulted especially because the case turned on lexicographical evidence (or the lack of it). The word was not, of course, purely descriptive: Homer v. Taunton was a case for libel; the defendant had called the plaintiff a 'truckmaster', which the plaintiff resented as defamatory. However, 'truckmaster' was not recorded in any English dictionary then existing (though each of the two parts of the compound was).

[146] See Gilliver, *Making of the OED*, 54.

[147] The Committee, appointed by resolution at the meeting of 8 Dec. 1859, consisted of Trench, Key, Furnivall, Thomas Watts, F. Pulasky, Wedgwood, and Goldstücker. *Roget's Thesaurus* had already appeared, in 1852.

[148] Fry, 'On Some English Dictionaries', 271. The paper included an overview of previous English dictionaries, originally devised by Danby Fry in 1843 as a memorandum for his father. H. B. Wheatley also contributed 'Chronological Notices of the Dictionaries of the English Language,' *TPS*, 10 (1865), 218–93.

[149] 'A Letter to the Very Rev. The Dean of Westminster,' *TPS*, 4 (1857), 71–8 at 73. Coleridge noted that 'Our scheme will bear favourable comparison with that of the Grimms, which is now being carried on in Germany in a manner somewhat similar to our own. In their Preface, these two great philologists ... are constrained to confess that out of eighty-three contributors (and these contributors, be it remarked, Germans) only *six* could be

British Museums and Bodleians are not dotted over the land like circulating libraries, and consequently much of the material which is of primary importance to us is rendered to all intents and purposes inaccessible.'[150] In the Proposal for the Dictionary, a list of works to be read for this first period had been compiled, and at the time when Coleridge wrote 'there have been undertaken ... about 139 of the various works', though only sixty-four had been delivered.[151] Unsurprisingly, Coleridge noted that he was having little success with the thirteenth-century texts listed in his *Glossarial Index*, 'none of which have as yet been transcribed for use', while 'many of the heavier romances' were only available through the select Roxburghe and Abbotsford Clubs. Yet when it came to the other titles on the list:

Nearly all the important works of this period have ... been undertaken, the few exceptions being Syr Gawayne, Barclay's Works, several of Caxton's publications, the two poems entitled Morte d'Arthur, edited by Halliwell, and for the Roxburghe Club respectively; and Trevisa's translation of the Polychronicon, which I am glad to see, is publishing under the auspices of the Master of the Rolls.[152]

Yet the claims of the chronicles of Robert of Gloucester and Robert Mannyng, of Brunne, 'important as philological no less than as historical monuments', had been overlooked.[153] Furnivall's early editorial work was to be closely involved with Mannyng, and he was contemplating the editing of the chronicle to supply this deficiency in the Rolls Series. Finally, Coleridge described the invidiousness of his position: 'as the working member of the Committee' (that is, the committee dealing with literary and historical aspects of the Dictionary), 'I was not unnaturally looked upon and treated by contributors as the editor *de facto* ... I was frequently called upon to decide questions which no one but an

considered as satisfactory.' Only one of these six (the reader of Goethe) 'had entirely come up to their beau ideal of a contributor'. 'Letter', 74.

[150] The letter was dated 30 May 1860, and was intended to complement a new edition of Trench's essay 'On Some Deficiencies'. The publication of the *Transactions* was erratic at this time, as Furnivall noted in 1860: 'The vol. for 1857 is just completed'; *TPS*, 6 (1859), iv (this volume also delayed).

[151] 'Letter to the Dean of Westminster', 74.   [152] Ibid.

[153] Ibid., n., 'A new edition of Robert of Gloucester, based on the Cottonian MS, instead of the later and inferior Harleian MS which Hearne was compelled to use, would form a most attractive volume ... it is to be hoped that these authors will receive the consideration which they most eminently deserve.' Reference to *Morte Arthure: The Alliterative Romance of the Death of King Arthur, Printed from a Ms. in Lincoln Cathedral*, ed. J. O. Halliwell, privately printed (Brixton Hill, 1847), and Thomas Ponton, *Le Morte Arthur: The Adventures of Sir Lancelot du Lake*, Roxburghe Club (London, 1819).

accredited editor ought to have pronounced upon.' Though this may not have been Coleridge's intention, the outcome was inevitable: 'The Society... in the kindest and most flattering manner assigned to myself the editorial superintendence of the literary and historical portions of the work.'[154] This, too, would have repercussions for Furnivall: he was the understudy who would be called upon to take over the editorial responsibilities after Coleridge's early death in 1861.

But, in 1859–60 Furnivall still had a great deal to learn. A good impression is given of the activities of the Literary and Historical Committee at this time in the report which Furnivall made to the Philological Society shortly after Coleridge's death, in which he listed the 143 works and authors from the first period, 1250–1526, which had been assigned to named readers.[155] The list did, indeed, seem to make it clear that there was enthusiasm out there to take on these difficult works, but that few felt confident to undertake very many. Six names dominate the list, among whom Furnivall and Coleridge took the leading roles, each down for fifteen works. Yet this figure is misleading. Coleridge's fifteen included ten in collaboration with Furnivall, and another three in collaboration with two other readers. It is clear that Coleridge was the expert, and that he was training his collaborators, especially Furnivall, in this unfamiliar material. The most prolific of all was E. S. Jackson, who clearly felt confident to take on a wide range of texts, including the alliterative poems in Warton's *History of English Poetry*, Brampton's Penitential Psalms, the romances *Robert of Cysille* ('Sicily') and *Torrent of Portyngale*, a work on freemasonry, the *Visions of Tundale*, *Wyclif's Wicket*, along with the three Wycliffite tracts edited by James Henthorn Todd, and Chaucer's 'Last Age'. Unsurprisingly, clerics with time on their hands were among the volunteers: the Revd. Jonathan Eastwood undertook eleven, including 'Chaucer' (without further specification),[156] and the Revd. W. L. Blackley four (the *Anturs of Arthur at Tarne Wathelyn* in tandem with Jackson).[157] Blackley, who knew and translated from Swedish, was also keenly interested in social questions bearing on the alleviation of poverty, pensions, and working men's

---

[154] 'Letter', 76.
[155] 'List of Books, &c.', TPS, 5 (1858), no. 2, a six-page appendix, with separate pagination, following Furnivall's edition of *Early English Poems*, 1–7.
[156] Marked with an asterisk, indicating that Furnivall had yet to receive this work. Eastwood gave a paper at the meeting of 28 Nov. 1861, based on his reading for the Dictionary, 'Instances of the Use of "Who" as a Relative', TPS, 7, no. 1 (1860), 310.
[157] For which they used the Camden Society edition, and *Syr Gawayne*, ed. Sir Frederic Madden for the Bannatyne Club.

savings, and he would go on to publish extensively on these subjects. In this capacity, he may already have been known to Furnivall, at least by reputation.[158] The Revd. Samuel Cheetham, elected to the Society at its meeting of 31 May 1860, read Capgrave's Chronicle.[159] The Revd. L. W. Jeffray, MA, Rector of Aldford, Cheshire, volunteered 'Piers Plouhman' and the first volume of Andrew Wynton's *Chronicle*, 1420–4.[160] The Revd. George Munford, rector of East Winch, Norfolk, and a keen local historian, topographer, and amateur botanist, essayed 'Political Ballads', as well as extracts from the *Pricke of Love*, also the *Devoute Meditacyon*, both attributed to 'Hampole' (Richard Rolle).[161] Private gentlemen are more difficult to trace, though one who stands out is William Henry Blaauw (1793–1870), a Sussex scholar of independent means, whose reputation as a historian had been established by *The Barons' War*.[162] Joseph Meadows Cowper, an antiquarian with a special interest in Kent, is discussed in a later chapter; he shared Furnivall's fascination with social customs in the past, and would prove a useful ally, both as EETS editor and for enquiries relating to the Chaucer Society.[163] Among others, the especially industrious Mr Gee took on Robert Mannyng of Brunne's chronicle, as well as the chronicles of Fabyan (1494) and Robert of Gloucester (shared with Herbert Coleridge),[164] along with *Floris and Blanchflour* and five other titles for good

---

[158] W. B. Owen, revd. Pat Thane, 'William Lewery Blackley (1830–1902)', *ODNB*. At this time he was in charge of two parishes at Frensham, Surrey. He was also the author of popular essays on English, *Word Gossip* (1869). [159] *TPS*, 7, no. 1 (1860), 305.

[160] *The Vision and Creed of Piers Plowman*, ed. Wright. Jeffray had died by 1867: see record of the marriage in that year of his only daughter, Katherine, to Archibald Hamilton, www.old-merseytimes.co.uk/marriages, accessed 9 Dec. 2020.

[161] 'Political Ballads', from *Archaeologia*, 21, 29; *Devoute Meditacyon*, printed by Wynkyn de Worde, 1507; the extracts from the *Pricke of Love* in *Archaeologia*, 19. Munford (1795?–1871), was author of *An Analysis of the Domesday Book of the County of Norfolk* (London, 1858), and *An Attempt to Ascertain the True Derivation of the Names of Towns . . . of the County of Norfolk* (London, 1870), as well as an account of Norfolk's 'Botanical Productions'.

[162] *The Barons' War, including the Battles of Lewes and Evesham* (Lewes, 1844). See further John H. Farrant, 'Blaauw, William Henry (1793–1870)', *ODNB*. He undertook 'Songs and Carols from a Fifteenth Century MS', part from the Percy Society and part from the Warton Club; also 'Early English Miscellanies (Porkington MS)'.

[163] Cowper undertook work on 'Manners and Household Expenses of England, 13th–15th cent.' (Roxburghe Club), *Selections from the Household Books of the Lord William Howard of Naworth Castle . . .* (published by the Roxburghe Club, 1878), *Gesta Romanorum*, and (first volume published only) *Political Poems and Songs Relating to English History*, ed. Thomas Wright, 2 vols. (London, 1859–61). Only *Gesta Romanorum* had been submitted.

[164] Robert of Brunne, and Robert of Gloucester, ed. Hearne, *Florice and Blanchflour* from the Abbotsford Club edition.

measure. Hearne had printed texts of both the chronicles, and the need for good new editions were, in Coleridge's view, especially pressing.

Soon Furnivall would be able to draw upon this list of volunteer readers to supply editors and supporters to the EETS and Chaucer Society. Prominent among them was Henry Hucks Gibbs, merchant banker, later Governor of the Bank of England, 1875–77, 1st Baron Aldenham, who, as well as being a noted bibliophile, became a member of the Philological Society at this time (1859). In due course, he would subedit the letters C and K for the Dictionary.[165] Gibbs, as might be expected with this background, took on a fairly eclectic selections of texts from the later end of the period, not early Middle English, and with a preference for chronicles, historical materials, and curiosities, rather than what Coleridge called the 'heavier romances'. Living in London, he had access to rare books in the British Museum, as well as his own library.[166] Of course, members of the Philological Society were expected to volunteer; another was Richard Weymouth, who took on the two editions of the *Morte Arthure*, as well as the English version of Robert Grosseteste's *Castel of Love*.[167] Philip Chabot, Furnivall's co-auditor of the Society's accounts, took on George Ripley's *Compound of Alchemie* (1471).

One change to the proposal for the Dictionary was swiftly agreed. As Coleridge told Trench, the title announced to the public, offering an *English* Dictionary, 'is no longer strictly applicable. During last year several offers of assistance came in from the other side of the Atlantic, where our Proposal appears to have created some little sensation, and a wish was expressed that Americans should be allowed to take part in the work.' The 'Hon. George Perkins Marsh, of Burlington, Vermont' (George Perkins Marsh, professor of English literature at Columbia College, New York) became the secretary co-ordinating their efforts.[168] Coleridge 'at once suggested that the Americans should make themselves responsible for the whole of the eighteenth century literature,

---

[165] Martin Daunton, 'Gibbs, Henry Hucks, first Baron Aldenham (1819–1907)', *ODNB*. See also Gilliver, *Making of the OED*, 43 (with photograph of Gibbs as a young man), *et passim*; also Ogilvie, *Dictionary People*, esp. 319–21.

[166] They included an English chronicle of the time of Edward IV, 1465, and the 'Historie of the Arrival of Edward IV' (both available in the Camden Society), Sir Richard Gaylforde's Pilgrimage (1506), William Horman's *Vulgaria*, the *Game of the Chess* (from an 1860 reprint), *Chylde the Wyse*, and *Treatise of a Galaunt*, both printed by Wynkyn de Worde.

[167] *Morte Arthure*, ed. Halliwell, and in the Roxburghe Club; *Castel of Love*, ed. Halliwell and printed by the Caxton Society.

[168] Quotations from the 'Letter to the Dean of Westminster', 72.

which probably would have a less chance of finding as many readers in England.'[169] Yet some of them also volunteered for the first period.[170] One, Mr Norton, undertook Malory's *Morte d'Arthur* (in Southey's edition);[171] G. R. White offered to do Juliana Barnes's [Berners] treatise on hawking and hunting.

The list of works being undertaken by readers fully bears out the difficulties facing Coleridge and Furnivall in taking on the first period. The texts are very patchy, were often available only in partial editions, and many important unprinted works that one might have expected to see are missing from the list. Even with Thomas Tyrwhitt's good edition of the *Canterbury Tales* (1775-8), and Thomas Wright's, prepared (1847-51) for the Percy Society available,[172] it is surprising to see just one volunteer for 'Chaucer'—and if Eastwood was really going to undertake the poet's complete works, it is not surprising that he had not submitted his slips. In the same spirit, C(ornelius) Paine, of Surbiton, was offering 'Gower' (along with other texts). It is evident that most of the readers preferred to offer texts from the later fourteenth century through to the early sixteenth. Coleridge was better placed than Furnivall to deal with the early Middle English material, since he knew Icelandic, and seems to have had some slight acquaintance with Old English (Furnivall, none at all). Yet, even with this advantage, Coleridge was still finding his way, and at times fumbling. Furnivall, with characteristic enthusiasm and a breezy view of obstacles, was getting on fast, though not very accurately.

Furnivall and Coleridge were collaborating on *King Alisaunder*, Robert Mannyng's *Handlyng Synne*, 'Poems and Saints' Lives' (from Furnivall's own edition, just printed, in the Philological Society's Transactions), *Havelok the Dane*, *Kyng Horne*, 'Lonelich's' 'San Graal', *The Owl and the Nightingale*, and a 'Fragment on Popular Science'.[173] Furnivall independently undertook the Kentish *Ayenbite of Inwit*, the *Life of St Margaret (Seinte Marherete)*, along with the Creed of St Athanasius, 'The Parlyament of Devylls', the 'Moral Ode' [*Poema morale*], and 'Land of Cokaygne', and Hoccleve's *De Regimine principum*. A note sent from Coleridge at this time gives a good snapshot of the nature of

---

[169] Ibid.

[170] Ibid.; Gilliver, *Making of the OED*, 32, 35.

[171] Perhaps Charles Eliot Norton, scholar and friend of Ruskin, as well as of other members of the London literary circle, who had travelled widely in England. See further Vanderbilt, *Charles Eliot Norton*.

[172] See Windeatt, 'Thomas Tyrwhitt (1730-1786)'; also, in the same volume, Ross, 'Thomas Wright (1810-1877)'.

[173] From 'Popular Treatises on Science,' c.1300, ed. Wright.

'EARLY ENGLISH' TEXTS AND THE DICTIONARY 321

their collaboration—Coleridge was struggling with the *Poema morale*, and advising on the texts which Furnivall was editing for the one of the two issues of the Society's *Transactions* for 1858. At this time Furnivall was also transcribing William of Waddington's thirteenth-century didactic Anglo-Norman poem *Le Manuel des Péchés* in connection with his reading and transcription work on Robert Mannyng's *Handlyng Synne*—in addition to being inexperienced, he was having trouble with the Anglo-Norman. Coleridge seems to be endorsing an early intention of Furnivall's to print this French text in the Philological Society's *Transactions*, rather than his eventual choices, 'Hickes's Ode' (*Poema morale*), and enough Saints to fill up 100 pages. Eventually Furnivall found a home for this French transcription in his Roxburghe Club edition of *Handlyng Synne*.[174] Coleridge then turned to his collaborator's perplexities with the *Owl and the Nightingale*:

Friday night,
Dear F.,
I should certainly vote for the Manuel des Péchés if it is not too long.[175] Otherwise for Hickes's Ode and enough Saints lives to fill up 100 pages. I wish much some day if you are going to the Museum, you would just look at the two MSS of the Moral Ode to see how they read that extraordinary 2d. line of First Stanza. 'A winter, and ec a *lore*', which I can make nothing of.[176]
'Spele' is I suppose 'spell' or 'turn', but unfortunately this seems to give just the opposite sense to that wanted. 'Let thy tonge have a spell' is=to 'Go on talking' whereas the owl means to say 'Hold your noise'. | 'Hiht' must mean either 'caught' or 'befallen', but I cant find anything in A. S. to lead to either meaning. There is 'haeftan' to catch, but 'hiht' could never come out of 'haeftan'.[177]

[174] M. T. Sullivan describes it as 'execrable': 'The Original and Subsequent Audiences of the Manuel des Péchés', and 'Brief Textual History', 344. Yet, though the manuscript used for the copy text was much removed from the original, the text in the Roxburghe Club volume, under the title *Roberd of Brunnè's Handlynge Synne*, remains the only complete presentation of the whole. Furnivall's subsequent edition of *Handlyng Synne* (the first Middle English translation of the *Manuel*) for the EETS (OS 119, 123 (1901, 1903)) reproduces only those sections of the Manuel adapted by Robert Mannyng of Brunne.
[175] On Furnivall's work on the *Manuel*, see further Sullivan, 'A Brief Textual History'.
[176] 'I am older than I was, both in years and knowledge.' See further Carla M. Thomas, '"Poema Morale": An Edition from Cambridge, Trinity College B. 14. 52', MA diss., University of Florida, College of Arts and Sciences (2008) (Florida State University Libraries, Electronic Theses, Treatises and Dissertations), 11–22 (on Furnivall's and Richard Morris's work on this text).
[177] Compare *The Owl and the Nightingale*, ed. Cartlidge, 8, ll. 258, 272; for 'spell', read *spale* ('a rest', 'a break'). The passage continued to give editors difficulties until this solution, derived from OE *spala*, was proposed in *OED* 1 (1913) as a nonce usage in this poem; entry not yet revised since *OED* 2 (1989). See further *The Owl and the Nightingale*, ed. Stanley, note, p. 111. For 'hiht', read 'hiȝhte', 'hope'.

N B In Madden's note to Warton vol 1 p 55, he says that the Manuel d. P. was *begun* in 1303. In his letter he says '*finished*'.

Yours ever

Herbert Coleridge

If you print a 13th cent piece you render my Glossary incorrect directly it comes out. I would sooner have a 14th cent piece first and then in next volume (when possibly a new Ed[itio]n may be req[uire]d to print the earlier ones, which might then be worked into the body of the book.[178]

Coleridge also solicited the opinions of the members of the Philological Society on the problematic *spele/spale*, which had somehow to mean that the Owl wished to put a stop to the Nightingale's 'apparently interminable harangue', after she 'has already talked more than two pages of small print'.[179]

All these challenging texts were an excellent training for what would be Furnivall's life's work as an 'editor of old books'. The choices of text were a mixture of large philologically and culturally important works which needed urgently to be addressed and writing which frankly just tickled Furnivall's taste for quirky vignettes of the past. He had already edited some of the shorter pieces, was engaged on more ambitious works, and would in the future edit Hoccleve. He was also now feeling sufficiently confident to make his own contributions to the Philological Society, arising out of all this lexicographical and editorial activity. The first shows that his grasp of Middle English was as yet insecure, supported by bravura and ingenious philological muddle, while giving a vivid picture of his activities in the British Museum.[180] He was struggling with a defective line in *Havelok* (1674), 'Hwanne he havede his wille *that*', where the sense appeared to require 'that' to be the past participle of a verb, meaning something like 'done', 'performed', but beginning with initial *th-* (ð).[181] He exercised his utmost ingenuity, without proposing an emendation, to rescue the line by arguing that

---

[178] Letter of 13? Feb. [1857], FU 195. Coleridge's postscript, requesting Furnivall to print texts later than the 13th c. first, so as not to spoil Coleridge's *Select Glossary*, suggests polite disagreement behind the scenes. Furnivall seems to have disregarded the plea.

[179] 'Hints towards the Explanation of some Hard Words and Passages in English Writers', *TPS*, 6 (1859), 68. Coleridge suggested two derivations, one cognate with German *spiel* (play is a time of rest), and the other from OE *spelian, spelung*, a 'spell' of rest. See note above.

[180] 'An Unregistered Sense of the Word *Thing* and its Base *The*', *TPS*, 6 (1859), 125–6.

[181] Compare 'Hwanne [þat] he his wille quath' ('When he had spoken his will'), *The Lay of Havelok the Dane*, ed. Skeat; 2nd edn. revd. Sisam, 55. The Glossary notes *Hwat*, *Wat* among the variant spellings of *quath*.

'that' was, indeed, a form of 'done'. 'A few days afterwards, as I was copying "The Moral Ode" . . . from the Egerton MS. 613', Furnivall found a use of 'de' which, according to the apparent sense, also appeared to be a past tense of 'done', as seemed to be confirmed by a variant reading 'deð'('doth') in another manuscript. The verb occurred again 'in one of the Saints Lives in the Harl-(eian) MS. 2277, but I have lost the reference'. And he found 'þyng', in the sense 'working', in the 'tale of the Witch and her Cow-sucking Bag', which so appealed to him in Mannyng's *Handlyng Synne*, on which he was also at work. When there was no paper available for the Philological Society's meeting of 23 June 1859, Furnivall filled the gap with a reading of extracts from *Handlyng Synne*.[182] He defended his strained connection between 'do' and 'that/the' by claiming that the transfer of sense from an active verb to a noun indicating the result of the action 'is in accordance with a well-known law of language'. And a conjectural, 'if not accepted' derivation of German *ding* ('thing') from *thun* ('to do', *facere*) seemed to offer support.

The passage well illustrates the difficulties facing someone in the mid-nineteenth century who was excited by swashbuckling notions of philology, and who was confronted with early Middle English with little more than his unsupported intelligence and a keen eye for detail to fall back on. It is abundantly clear that Furnivall's later friend, the Austro-German Shakespeare scholar Alois Brandl was justified in saying that Furnivall was not himself, from a German point of view, 'a philologist of thorough linguistic training'.[183] This was true. Furnivall's Dictionary work led him to Middle English (easier to understand for someone self-taught), rather than Old, or early Middle ('Semi-Saxon') English, and it would be some years before his EETS started to publish Old English material.

Yet Furnivall and Coleridge were also aided by observations by members of the Society, who had had their attention drawn by Coleridge at the April 1859 meeting to 'queries respecting etymologies and several difficult passages from Early English books' which were circulated for their comments.[184] Like *The Owl and the Nightingale*, *Havelok* was still

---

[182] *TPS*, 6 (1859), 294 (Key also used the opportunity to comment on Coleridge's *Glossarial Index*).

[183] Munro (ed.), *Frederick James Furnivall*, 10–11. Brandl (1855–1940), born in Innsbruck, gained his doctorate in Vienna, and, with Julius Zupitza, founded the institute of American and English studies in the Humboldt University of Berlin. On Brandl, see further Utz, *Chaucer*, 71, 75–8 *passim*.

[184] Coleridge, 'Hints towards the Explanation of Some Hard Words', *TPS*, 6 (1859), 67–74.

giving trouble: *perne*, l. 298 had to mean something like 'mere girl', but how? The editor, Madden, had dodged the issue; the best guess of most of the correspondents was that it was a metathesized form of *throne*; however, the Revd. Richard Frederick Littledale, Hensleigh Wedgwood, and Mr Metivier came closest by proposing Old Saxon *therna*.[185] *Piers Plowman* perplexed the members of the Society with '*pisseris* longe knyves', which *surely* could not mean what it looked like? Except that, as Skeat later pointed out, it did. One suggestion was that the *pisseris* were bakers (from *pistour*)—a group known for having long knives for cutting bread; another was that they were fishermen, from Old French *pischer*, 'to fish'. Skeat dealt roundly with these absurdities:

> In the Phil. Soc. Trans. For 1859, p. 72, two guesses are made as to the sense of this word. First, that it is a corruption of *pistor*, a baker, which is plainly incredible; and secondly that it means a fisherman... which is equally stupid. William knew perfectly well how to say *bakere* or *fisher* without turning the words into *false* Old French. Surely the word expressed exactly what the sound tells us, and is equivalent to a familiar Biblical expression for "every male"... It was, I suppose, a cant term... I do not think there need be much difficulty here.[186]

It is a small example of the rapid progress that would be made in understanding 'early English' in less than thirty years.

If Coleridge's activity seems frenzied, he was probably trying to make the most of the time left to him. He was ill with consumption and had been advised at around the time he took on the editorship of the Dictionary that recovery was hopeless. As Murray would later write: 'We can sympathize with Herbert Coleridge in his longing to see something accomplished, and we look with loving regard upon the specimen articles on a few early words which he put in type during his last illness, and saw before his eyes closed for ever.'[187] He died, aged only 31, on 23 April 1861. His wife, Ellen Coleridge, wrote a note on the same day to

---

[185] Compare *Havelok*, ed. Skeat, revd. Sisam, who offered 'serving maid', from ON *perna*.

[186] *The Vision of William concerning Piers the Plowman*, ed. Skeat, ii. 281-2, commenting on C Text, XXIII. 218-19:

> Proude preostes cam with hym   passend an hundred;
> In paltokes and pikede shoes   and pissares longe knyues.

As Skeat noted, the context requires '*soldiers* or *armed retainers*, notable in those days for coarse insolence'. The priests' fault was that they were dressing like soldiers, and, as Skeat also pointed out, alleging B Text XV. 121 (likewise describing priests' unsuitable costume), *knyves* might also have a 'cant name'.

[187] Quoted in Munro (ed.), *Frederick James Furnivall*, 128-9; see also Gilliver, *Making of the OED*, 35-8.

tell Furnivall: 'My darling husband is gone—he died this morning while Mr Burrows was administering the sacrament to him.' The deathbed scene prompted several accounts.[188] Hensleigh Wedgwood also shared his information about the event with Furnivall:

> I hear that poor Coleridge was sensible to the last sending for his D(octo)r to thank him for his attention a few minutes before his death, and I should think a person could not have a calmer departure. I should hope he had not much suffering altogether. I am very glad to hear you are able to undertake the dictionary which must otherwise have gone to pot. I was glad to hear from Goldstücker that the commercial prospects of it were good and the first thing that is earned should go to pay you and Coleridge's costs.[189]

As Murray said, 'His death left Furnivall as the only possible successor'; indeed, it was reported in print before the end of the year that 'Before his death he obtained from his friend and colleague, Mr. Furnivall, a promise that he would fill his place as editor, so that the work he so desired to complete might not fall to the ground'.[190] Furnivall himself used this solemn personal commitment as an argument to bind, not just him, but all else involved in the work (including the Philological Society itself) in a common endeavour: 'May our regard for him be an additional pledge to one another that we will not let that for which he cared so greatly, fail.'[191]

Furnivall announced Coleridge's death to the Philological Society two days later, at its April meeting. By the time of its next meeting, on 25 May, he was able to report both the 'present condition of the Collections for the Society's Dictionary' and 'the course he proposed to pursue with regard to the scheme'. It was recognized, albeit not formally, that he was now in charge of the project. Furnivall would serve as the Dictionary's editor for the best part of eighteen years, organizing the reading programme and recruiting and managing the voluntary readers

---

[188] Letter of 23 Apr. 1861, FU 193. See further Considine, 'The Deathbed of Herbert Coleridge' for a discussion of the other various accounts of this event. See also Momma, *From Philology to English Studies*, 119.

[189] Letter to Furnivall [Apr. 1861], FU 938.

[190] By his cousin, John Duke Coleridge, in his memoir, 'The Late Herbert Coleridge', *Macmillan's Magazine*, 5, issue 25, Nov. 1861, 56–60 at 59, here reporting a secondary source. Letter from Ellen Coleridge to Furnivall [late 1861, before November], after, presumably, he had commented to her on seeing the notice: 'I heard some time ago from John that he was going to put some things together about my dear husband, and he intended sending them to Macmillan to publish, but he did not say then in what form it was to come out, but only that he found it a very difficult matter and almost wished he had never undertaken it.' FU 194.

[191] *An Alphabetical List of English Words*, Part II, [p. ii].

and subeditors until he handed over his accumulated materials to Murray in 1879. The full burden fell on him after 1863, when Dean Trench left London to take up his position as Archbishop of Dublin. Furnivall's contribution was not only substantial; it involved him in considerable personal outlay. As he later told James Murray, 'There is 5 times as much of my money in the Dict(ionar)y as of H(erbert) Coleridge)'s'.[192]

[192] Letter to Murray, 21 Jan. 1882, Murray Papers.

8

Furnivall's First Editions: 'Wicked Birds', Handling Sin, and 'Rose-Pink Notions'

> Which Chronicle . . . failed not to be copied . . . and so surviving Henry the Eighth, Putney, Cromwell, the Dissolution of Monasteries, and all accidents of malice and neglect for six centuries or so, it got into the *Harleian Collection*,—and has now therefrom, by Mr. Rokewood of the Camden Society, been deciphered into clear print; and lies before us, a dainty thin quarto, to interest for a few minutes whomsoever it can.
>
> Thomas Carlyle, *Past and Present* (1843), describing the *Chronicle* of Jocelin de Brakelond

THE DICTIONARY, 'WICKED BIRDS', AND SIR FREDERIC MADDEN

When printed editions were either unavailable or unusably inadequate for the Dictionary's purposes, it had sometimes been necessary to go back to the original manuscripts. Just how much Furnivall had copied by 1859 is made clear by Coleridge's acknowledgement in the *Glossarial Index* of the loan of his transcripts of three manuscripts in the British Museum. MS Egerton 613 supplied the *Moral Ode* (*Poema morale*); seven assorted treatises on Christian dogma were taken from MS Egerton 913, including 'A Poem on Miracles', of interest as containing a 'Tale of an Oxford Student'; and eight saints' lives taken from MS Harley 2277. It was valuable material, and, as the transcriptions were required for the Dictionary, the Philological Society had agreed that the texts might be included in a volume of its *Transactions*. In addition, Furnivall was already editing Robert of Brunne's *Handlyng Synne* for the Roxburghe Club, but, Coleridge noted, 'the proof-sheets came into my hands too late to allow of anything like a complete analysis of the language of the poem'.[1] In the long run, the Philological Society's *Transactions* were not a suitable receptacle for extended editorial work, while the elite Roxburghe Club's publications were too expensive and inaccessible for outsiders to consult. Already it was becoming evident that some other venue might be desirable for the printing of early English texts.

---

[1] *Glossarial Index*, pp. vi–vii.

After Coleridge's death, once Furnivall had begun to take stock of his new responsibilities as the Dictionary's editor, he soon began to put his own increasingly distinctive mark on the project. One of his first steps was the preparation and printing of the *Alphabetical List of English Words* for the use of the Dictionary's readers. A striking feature of this compilation is Furnivall's decision to use a new printer, Emily Faithfull and Co., the Victoria Press, for the first part, instead of either of the Philological Society's established printers: Asher and Trübner. The choice clearly demonstrated his wish to harness philology to his social concerns, even though these were not necessarily shared by all members of the Society. Emily Faithfull was a social activist, pressing for legal and educational reforms to benefit women, as well as greater employment opportunities. Like Furnivall, she came from a well-to-do professional middle-class background. She was the daughter of the Rector of Headley, Surrey, and had, moreover, been presented at court in 1857. She enjoyed Queen Victoria's patronage—as shown by the name of her press—though the queen was not noted for her general support of reforms in favour of women. Emily Faithfull was a member of the Langham Place circle, which had, just two years earlier, formed the Society for Promoting the Employment of Women (1859). Her decision to start the Victoria Press reflected the group's wish to open up compositing (a jealously guarded male preserve) as a skilled occupation that women might undertake—Austin Holyoake, brother of George, the firebrand known to Furnivall personally, was employed to instruct them.[2] This new commercial venture was, not surprisingly, an irritant to others in the trade.

Furnivall's choice of printer was thus a strong indication of his political views, as well as a declaration of his determination to exercise his new independence. But, even allowing for the Victoria Press's connection with the Holyoake brothers, it was not as though he had offered the work to John James Bezer, the radical printer whom the Christian Socialists had supported. Emily Faithfull came from a similar background to Furnivall's own and was supported by the Queen. But the Victoria Press did not have the necessary skill or equipment to cope with such specialized material. It is not surprising that the Philological Society seems to have remonstrated: the second and third parts were printed by Stephen Austin, of Hertford, who visited Furnivall regularly when he came to London.[3] Austin's expertise in printing Sanskrit and

---

[2] See Felicity Hunt, 'Faithfull, Emily (1835–1895)', *ODNB*.

[3] This is Stephen Austin (1804–92), the third to bear the family name of the busi-

other Oriental languages commended him to the Philological Society. Thanks to his ingenuity and his investment in new specialist type from London foundries, the firm was able to build on this special knowledge to become printers, not only to the Philological Society, but the British Museum, the Sanskrit and Pali Text Societies, and, in due course, among other philological and literary bodies, the EETS. Stephen Austin's type specimen book would increase to include thirty Oriental languages, Greek, and Russian, and, nearer to home, German, Anglo-Saxon, and Henry Sweet's 'Visible Speech' (a system of phonetic notation). Austin's own personality, which was marked, according to a contemporary, by 'combativeness inspiring a constant craving for change and speculation and a great faith and trust in humanity', doubtless also appealed to Furnivall.[4]

Furnivall continued to draw upon the unusual human resources offered by the Working Men's College. He concluded his preliminary notice to the first part of the *Alphabetical List* with special thanks to William and Eleanor Dalziel, as well as George Tansley, concluding with his gratitude to the Editor of the *Athenaeum* 'for his repeated appeals to the reading public to join our Dictionary Volunteers'—in Furnivall's mind, a lexicographical equivalent to the national Volunteer movement.[5] His interests may also be perceived in the list of contributors.[6] Furnivall himself undertook to read the writing of those of his contemporaries who appealed to him, or were known to him: Elizabeth Barrett Browning, Thomas Hughes, the poet and dramatist Thomas Wade, and the journalist and writer Tom Taylor, editor of *Punch*, noted for his humorous comments on politics, news, and contemporary manners. Furnivall defended Coleridge's use of materials from newspapers, while noting that 'many of the inferior authorities cited ... will, I trust, be displaced by superior ones furnished afterwards'.[7] Meanwhile, he read the *Artists and Craftsmen* magazine, *Macmillan's Magazine*, the *Saturday Review* (with N. W. Senior), *The Times*, and William Howard Russell, the *Times* reporter who had earned international renown for his coverage of the Crimean War and his camaraderie with ordinary soldiers. The reading tastes and interest in military history which

ness which had been founded in 1768. In 1834 Austin's had become the printers to the East India Company, and, thanks to this, and their work for Haileybury College (close to Hertford), the firm had established a name as printers in various Oriental languages. See further Moran, *Stephen Austin's of Hertford*, 23–37.

[4] Ibid. 31.   [5] *Alphabetical List*, Part II, [p. v].
[6] 'List of Contractions, Books, and Contributors', ibid., [p. iii].   [7] Ibid., [p. v].

Furnivall formed as a Cambridge student are apparent here, as well as his own military experience in the Working Men's College. Later he added to his load the anonymous *Our English Home*, which doubtless attracted him thanks to his fascination with the history of social life and manners.[8]

More personally, Furnivall's intention to form, or at least develop, his girlfriend Eleanor Dalziel's tastes and ideas in his own image, but in a softened form, which he is likely to have considered more palatable to a young woman who had not been highly educated, can be seen by his setting her to read Florence Nightingale and Harriet Beecher Stowe's *Uncle Tom's Cabin*, along with Tennyson's *In Memoriam*. Her brother was given Swift.[9] Apart from Eleanor Dalziel, there were only three other women readers listed: Miss Martin, who read Byron, Miss Courtenay, who read Macaulay (later, Johnson as well) and Miss Eisdell, who was confident in taking on a large group of big authors, including Carlyle, De Quincey, Kingsley, Ruskin's *Modern Painters*, and Wordsworth (taking over from Herbert Coleridge). Miss Eisdell was Sophia Louisa Eisdell, living in Colchester, who later became the EETS's first woman member, and who will be introduced more fully in that capacity. When the third part, covering M to Z, was published a year later, Mary Ann Evans (George Eliot) had undertaken to read the *Edinburgh Review*, and Charlotte Yonge the Scottish journalist and historian Gilbert Stuart.[10]

By the time the third part of the *Alphabetical List* was issued in the third week of March 1862, the list of contributors had grown considerably, and the part played by those associated with the Working Men's College is consequently diluted.[11] No fresh work was given to Eleanor Dalziel, who would marry Furnivall later in the year, and may have been expecting their first child. Furnivall mentions her, along with her brother, and Tansley among the friends who have helped him in the preparation of the work; another was Richard Morris, of the Philological Society, who was to play such a large part in the editorial work of the EETS, though, as his interests lay in early English, he did not volun-

---

[8] *Our English Home: Its Early History and Progress*.

[9] 'List of . . . Books, and Contributors', [p. iii]. By the time the third part was issued, W. A. Dalziel was also undertaking the horticulturalist Eugene Sebastian Delamer, author of *The Kitchen and Flower Garden, or the Culture in the Open Ground of Bulbous, Tuberous, Fibrous-rooted, and Shrubby Flowers* (London, 1856).

[10] George Eliot's early novels, beginning with *Adam Bede* (1859), were apparently not yet available, or too recent, for the Dictionary. Henry Hucks Gibbs had volunteered to read G. H. Lewes. Charlotte Yonge may have become involved through Gibbs (a cousin); see Gilliver, *Making of the OED*, 47.   [11] *Alphabetical List*, Part III, [p. ii].

teer his services as one of the Dictionary's readers of the third period. Another notable contributor, who would also play a large part in supporting the EETS, is Henry Hucks Gibbs, whose assistance on the first two periods Furnivall and Coleridge had already acknowledged. As a gentleman *au fait* with the polite literary and political culture of his time, Gibbs clearly felt much more at home with the material of the third period, and his many contributions included Lord Broughton,[12] S. T. Coleridge, Dickens, J. A. Froude, G. H. Lewes, and Charles Reade. Not everyone was happy to be openly acknowledged: some of the work was given to 'A Friend'.

It is probably already evident that Furnivall's conception of the Dictionary's development, as well as his views on the stages of publication, differed from Coleridge's. His first steps had been to attempt to augment substantially the materials being read and made available from the third period, and, in so doing, he inevitably stamped his own views as to what was significant on the list of works, giving a larger place to reference works and the journalism, which he read so widely himself, as a portrait of the age. He was careful to defend himself, at least obliquely, by citing Coleridge, who had responded to the question 'Why have you quoted a newspaper as the authority for a word when you might have quoted Tennyson', by pointing out that he could only work with what the readers sent him.[13] Furnivall subsequently developed this contemporary theme: 'We have set ourselves to form a National Portrait Gallery, not only of the worthies, but of all the members of the race of English words which is to form the dominant speech of the world.'[14] After preparing the work on the third period, he now proposed to concentrate on the earlier periods, where he himself had been working extensively, by compiling 'Two Concise Dictionaries of Early and Middle English, which shall include severally all the materials sent in

[12] Presumably John Cam Hobhouse, first Baron Broughton (1786–1869).

[13] *Alphabetical List*, Part II, title verso. Furnivall's regular practice of submitting quotations from his own daily reading of the papers throughout the 1860s and later far outpaced that of other readers and meant that his contributions from newspapers at this time constituted a large proportion of this class of material available to the later OED editors. Gilliver, *Making of the OED*, 51.

[14] *Alphabetical List*, Part III, [p. iii]. The National Portrait Gallery, London, had been opened just six years before, in Dec. 1856, the first item in its collection being the Chandos portrait of Shakespeare (the gift of Lord Ellesmere). See also Coleridge, 'On the Exclusion of Certain Words from a Dictionary', comments on authorities, p. 42, with Furnivall's notes of the ensuing discussion, pp. 43–4. Additionally, Furnivall may be recalling the remarks on English as a global language by Watts, 'On the Probable Future Position of the English Language'.

for the First and Second Periods, and serve as new Bases of Comparison for those Periods'.[15] This work he reckoned would take four or five years—the delay gave the Philological Society some concern: though it accepted the principles, he was required to submit specimens of his proposed *Concise Dictionary*.[16]

In addition to his undertakings for the Dictionary, Furnivall's role as the Philological Society's Secretary made him responsible for getting out the year's *Transactions*, composed largely of the papers read to the Society by its members. However, it was hard to get the members, keen amateurs as they were, to meet publication deadlines. Furnivall complained: 'The chief grievance of an Honorary Secretary is that certain Members of his Society *will not* send him for press the Papers they have read at the Society's Meetings. Beg for them as he will,—by letter, word of mouth, through mutual friends, by special visits—out of some Members no Papers can be got.' He was already contemplating one obvious solution to this problem, in which the germ of the idea of the EETS may be found: 'What then is left for the unhappy Official, but to write Papers himself, or copy MSS to fill the volume that his refractory friends have left vacant?'[17] But, as we have seen, this is only part of the story: Coleridge had also needed Furnivall's transcriptions of previously unedited or poorly edited early English texts for his *Dictionary of the First, or Oldest Words in the English Language*, published posthumously.[18]

These transcriptions from manuscripts needed to be printed to enable the readers to work with them and qualify them for quotation and reference in the eventual Dictionary. Since the copying work was intended to serve the Philological Society and its Dictionary, rather than a wider public, the Society's *Transactions* made an appropriate *ad hoc* location. Copying and editing were essential to the Philological Society's projects—there had, after all, to be texts as grist for the philological mill to grind. Even so, Furnivall's first edition occupied the whole of an additional volume of the *Transactions* for 1858. Such an expedient could not be repeated often. Meanwhile, Furnivall's remark about

---

[15] *Alphabetical List*, Part II, [p. ii].

[16] *Alphabetical List*, Part III, [pp. ii–iii]; Gilliver, *Making of the OED*, 42–6.

[17] Preface to *Early English Poems and Lives of Saints, with Those of the Wicked Birds Pilate and Judas*, TPS, 5, no. 2 (1858), p. iii. Published for the Philological Society by Asher of Berlin. Later Furnivall would be more specific: 'delay on the part of our late much-lamented President, Prof. Goldstücker, in producing his Sanskrit Affix paper for our *Transactions* of 1858, led to the printing of my *Early English Poems and Lives of Saints* early in 1862', TPS, 15, no. 1 (1874), 236.

[18] Coleridge, *A Dictionary of the First, or Oldest Words in the English Language*.

the difficulty of extracting members' papers for printing is a reminder that his position as the Society's Secretary demanded the steady organization of publications year by year, and this would prove essential training for the future. All of Furnivall's own future societies depended upon a regular annual supply of publications, which had to be contrived, despite all the excuses that editors and contributors could devise.

Furnivall, untrained in philology himself, but wanting to make a scholarly, as well as an administrative, contribution to the Society, could only offer it what he was able to do, and that was to copy manuscripts. As he said, writing papers 'was out of my reach', though this bashfulness did not in fact prevent him from making small contributions, as discussed in the preceding chapter. As he grew in confidence and experience, Furnivall would offer papers based on his manuscript observation, but in 1858 the Philological Society's honorary secretary, man of affairs, and auditor did not care to seem to compete with the learned. He offered his first editorial venture to the Society with becoming modesty. It was a simple 'basket of fruit' for which 'the reader must not blame me' if he thinks it 'a bad substitute for the second course of strong meat that he expected and ought to have had'.[19] Its jocular subtitle, *The Wicked Birds, Pilate and Judas* displayed Furnivall's own humour and tastes.[20] As one of Furnivall's first substantial pieces of editing, the 'Wicked Birds' and their companions deserve some attention: they set the scene for much that followed.

The 'basket', then, offered first a collection of transcriptions of six poems from BM MS Harley 913 (a miscellany of Irish provenance, traditionally known as the 'Kildare Manuscript').[21] BM Egerton 613 provided a text of the *Poema morale* (called here 'A Moral Ode'). To

[19] *Early English Poems*, ed. Furnivall, p. iii.
[20] The second part of *Early English Poem*'s title, 'Wicked Birds', is extrapolated from the opening of 'Judas Iscariot': 'Iudas was a liþer brid', 107. Although the edition was included in the *TPS* for 1858, the real date of publication was 1860, as witnessed by Furnivall's inclusion in his introduction of a letter sent to him by Edwin Guest, dated 30 Jan. 1860. Guest, a founder member of the Philological Society, was like Furnivall, a lawyer from Lincoln's Inn who retired from law to pursue philological and literary interests. The letter concerns 'inverse rhyme': 'I do not remember to have seen so ancient or so elaborate a specimen as the one you have sent me. It is very curious, and to me interesting.' Guest was the author of *A History of English Rhythms* (1838), described by John D. Pickles as 'probably the most important work of the century—for good and ill—on English prosody', to which he brought 'vast reading in medieval literature of which much was still in manuscript or unfamiliar publications'; 'Edwin Guest (1800–1880)', *ODNB*.
[21] The name derives from 'Frere Michel Kyldare', who names himself as author of one of the volume's English poems. The manuscript, a product of the Anglo-Irish Franciscan community, was in Waterford at the Reformation, and may have been written there. See

this Furnivall added excerpts from BM Harley 2277, a copy of the *South English Legendary*, chosen because the 'titles or contents caught my fancy, including those of the two accursed ones, Pilate and Judas Iscariot'.[22] To these texts 'not making a sufficient number of pages in our close print', he added, as a makeweight, material from BM Add. MS 22283, by convention called the 'Simeon MS' (which Furnivall describes as 'the incomplete and later duplicate of the noble Vernon MS in the Bodleian Library').[23] BM MS Cotton Vespasian D. ix ('a Cotton MS. temp. Hen(ry) V') furnished the satirical 'fragment on the Corrupt State of the Nunneries' (pp. 138–48), and this was followed by three further items from the 'Kildare' MS, 'on Old Age, Earth and the Faults of the Monks and People of Kildare (which I had after copying, set aside, as having been printed in the *Reliquiae Antiquae*)'.[24] Almost last, apart from a squib on 'Five Evil Things', also from the Kildare MS, was the twice-printed 'Land of Cokaygne', described by Furnivall as 'the airiest and cleverest piece of satire in the whole range of Early English, if not of English poetry'.[25] The combination of fancy, mild indecency rendered whimsical in early English, and religious satire was just what he liked, and would mark his future contributions for the EETS.

Thus Furnivall's description advertised this first piece of work as a collection of titbits for an intellectual dessert—a fruit basket, chosen by an enthusiastic amateur in part to satisfy his personal tastes from among the vast riches of the British Museum, with occasional forays wider afield. Yet he also saw himself as more than a mere collector of

Poems from BL MS Harley 913, '*The Kildare Manuscript*', ed. Turville-Petre, EETS, OS 345, description of the manuscript, pp. xiii–xxiii at p. xiii.

[22] *Early English Poems*, p. iii.

[23] Ibid. Furnivall copied the first two of the series of short religious poems in the Simeon MS which both manuscripts include (with a few others later in his anthology). By his own admission, a fleeting visit to Oxford did not allow him time to collate more than one item with the Vernon MS. This was 'Mercy Passes All Things'('Bi west, vnder a wilde wode syde'), called here 'A Song of Mercy': see Furnivall's note on Vernon's spellings, 118. See note to the second poem, 'A Songe of Deo Gracias' ('In a chirche þer I con knel'), 124. The poems were later edited by Carl Horstmann, with F. J. Furnivall, for the Society: *The Minor Poems of the Vernon MS*, EETS, OS 98, 117. See further *Religious Lyrics of the XIV Century*, ed. Brown, 2nd edn. revd. Smithers, 125–31, 131–4. *Early English Poems*, 128–30. Furnivall also included 'Deo Gracias II' (from Vernon), and the following two poems in the series ('In a Pistel þat poul wrouȝt' and 'Whon men beoþ muriest at heor mele') from the Simeon MS, *Early English Poems*, 130–8; *Religious Lyrics of the XIV Century*, ed. Brown, 139–48).

[24] *Early English Poems*, 148–56; *Poems from BL MS Harley 913*, 74–6, 87–90, 9–13.

[25] *Early English Poems*, pp. iii–iv, 156–61; *Poems from BL MS Harley 913*, 3–9.

juicy scraps for a philological album: the work was 'copied and edited by Frederick J. Furnivall, M.A. Cambr.'. 'Editing' was higher up the intellectual ladder than copying—after all, many of the edited texts put out by Furnivall's later societies, including those edited by Furnivall himself, were begun by paid copyists, typically skilled clerks, working in manuscript libraries, who needed the money to eke out their salaries. Using copyists made it possible to sustain such a formidable publishing output. The distinction between copying and editing was real, if blurred—Furnivall and his colleagues were not above doing their own copying, and, in the twentieth century, even senior British Museum librarians like A. W. Pollard and J. A. Herbert would be recruited as transcribers. The difference rested in the payment received by the employees (often more experienced than the gentlemen scholars), and the added intellectual value of the editorial aids to the reader provided by the person whose name appeared on the title page. In practice, both paid transcribers and scholars learned on the job: there was no formal instruction in palaeography. For all Furnivall's passionate egalitarianism, there was a social distinction between clerks and the gentlemen with university degrees who employed them. And, as will be seen, Furnivall was not above beating down his assistants' rates in the interests of his impoverished EETS.

Collation of the copy text with other manuscripts might also be undertaken by the librarian copyists, but it was up to the editor's judgement to decide on the correctness of readings and emendations. On this occasion, in the case of texts taken from the Vernon and Simeon manuscripts, Furnivall ingenuously admitted that he had 'time to collate one item only with the earlier copy'.[26] His editing in this early attempt consisted of supplying accompanying translations, or summaries of the texts' content, keyed to the text by line references. There are a few notes concerning points of transcription, or language, at the foot of the page, but there is no explanatory annotation, apart from the addition of a very few endnotes on the last few texts, passing on readers' observations. There was a 'List of Words' not contained in Coleridge's *Glossarial Index*, which sometimes included etymological notes, or longer language notes, as for the word 'goose' and the phrase 'shoe the goose'. A word such as 'queristere' was alphabetically listed under its modern spelling 'chorister', perhaps under the influence of developing lexicographical practice, but did not satisfy readers seeking to find an explanation of

[26] Preface, p. iii. This was 'the fragment on the Corrupt state of the Nunneries' (pp. 138–48).

an unfamiliar-looking word in an early text. In addition, even though the volume was prepared for the Philological Society, Furnivall could not expect that all his readers could read early English, and his list of contents supplies a 'short abstract' of the contents of each item, with page numbers to the relevant part of the text. It is an unwieldy contrivance, but it serves the purpose which would be met in Furnivall's later editions by a précis of the texts in the Introductions and the addition of side notes. The sole exception (probably because it had already been twice printed before) is 'The Land of Cokaygne', described in what was perhaps a 'caveat lector' as 'A Satire on Monks and Nuns, their Abbeys, Nunneries, Ways and Sports', followed by a jocular, if obscure, word to the wise in the form of a quotation from the poem, in the original language, to the effect that anyone who wants to visit that land must expect to do seven years' penance, wading up to his chin in pig shit.[27]

One gets a clear sense of Furnivall's tastes and interests from his selection of texts. he was most drawn to the titbits of everyday life, and to what could frankly be called 'gossip', as he sought to whet his readers' appetites to get past such 'uninteresting titles' as 'Sarmun', 'Moral Ode', or 'Lives of Saints'. They would be rewarded with 'many an other scene of English life', including the 'Old-Englishman's special sin of Envy denounced . . . his Greed and Pride'. They 'will hear Sunday-trading condemned . . . and see the rough mason running from his work to catch and kiss the country-girls coming to market with their eggs, . . . which of course get broken in the struggle' (p. iv). Furnivall revelled in the strange medieval words, as when, for example, St Dunstan 'twengde' ('pinched') the devil's nose. Such vocabulary was, in a word, quaint. He felt bound to deny to an audience of philologists that this rather spurious form of enjoyment strongly appealed to him: 'it is not for the oddities of subject of phrase that one values these poems; it is for their language that the student . . . holds them of worth' (p. v). Amusement was legitimized by its philological value. One is tempted to retort that pigs, as well as monks, can fly. Furnivall's fondness for olde worlde vignettes of bygone England combined with serious scholarship was probably the foundation of his success. He was a popularizer, but his

[27] Whoso wl com þat land to,
Ful grete penance he mot do.
Seue ȝere in swine-is dritte,
He mote wade, wol ȝe i-witte,
Al anon up to þe chynne,
So he schal þe lond i-winne. (p. xxx, ll. 177–82)
Compare the same lines in *Poems from BL MS Harley 913*, 8.

popularizations were securely based in first-hand immersion in manuscript sources. Though it is a style of scholarship which has now long been out of favour, and the writer's unabashed strong personal engagement with it is now considered to be inappropriate, Furnivall should be given his due.

And he was not alone. The ability to popularize serious manuscript research and give interested readers access to primary sources was the leading characteristic of the other 'greats' of the nineteenth century and first half of the twentieth, including even Richard Morris and Walter Skeat. Among historians, one thinks of Hope Emily Allen's Cambridge mentor, G. G. Coulton, or another of Furnivall's friends, the French scholar J. J. Jusserand. Though tempered by finer literary sensibilities and sense of decorum, R. W. Chambers was in the same line of descent. The anti-clerical material, in particular the 'airy' satire, the Anglo-Irish *Land of Cokaygne*, was just the kind of thing to have appealed to Furnivall, and he included it even though he admitted that there were already two previous printed texts. In addition to its social interest, it acted as leaven to the saints' lives in his collection. The ribaldry in *Cokaygne* was suited to the almost exclusively men's club that the Philological Society was in the 1850s: the repeated use of the masculine pronoun to describe the prospective reader ('he will see . . . he will get . . . he will find . . .) is strident. Furnivall, as an aficionado of early English life and manners, could not afford to be prudish, and he also clearly enjoyed the occasional smut himself, for example glossing 'Arsmetrike' ('arithmetic') with the quotation 'a love þat of figours al is', in case of doubt. Nevertheless, he had to be circumspect about what he published and where. In *Cokaygne*, the flying monks who 'þakkeþ' a maiden's 'toute' (l. 142, i.e. smack her bare bum), could only be appreciated in the obscurity of 'early English'.[28]

Thus, this anthology of saints and 'wicked birds' for the Philological Society was prophetic. Many of Furnivall's tastes, and those of his associates, are already apparent. There was a lexicographical interest in recording 'new', or more accurately, newly observed, words. There were the tableaux of early English life and manners. There is a passing reference to the 'deeper feeling' to be found in some of the texts, including the 'self-abasement' in the 'Sarmun', the 'triumphant faith' of

---

[28] The gloss supplied here uses Turville-Petre's word choices supplied in the glossary to *Poems from BL MS Harley 913*. 'Thakke' is glossed in Coleridge's *Glossarial Index* as 'thwack', under the influence of a later dialectal survival (and perhaps public school) and 'toute' as 'rump'. See *OED*, 'thack', v. 1a 3, dialect, 'to thwack, beat, flog'.

the martyrs, and the tender love of 'Christ on the Cross'. Though Furnivall was always susceptible to 'tender love', gentlemanly reticence and the decorum of the Philological Society required that he merely refer to where such things were to be found by the readers privately for themselves. What really excited him intellectually was rhyme, metre, and the related matter of final -*e* on the end of words, vestiges of English's older and more developed system of grammatical word endings. Metre would preoccupy him in his dealings with Shakespeare as a means of establishing the chronology and authenticity of the canon—like Skeat, Furnivall assumed that early English metre was entirely regular. Like most who have transcribed medieval English manuscripts, he was perplexed by scribal flourishes at the ends of words which might, or might not, signify that a final -*e* should be supplied, or might merely be a calligraphic habit. 'Some final *es* in italics, to help out the rhythm, I inserted in the first few pages, as noticed in the note to p.1, but soon gave this up ... In the lines whose rhythm cannot be in any way made good without the insertion of a final *e* at the end of a word, there the reader may insert it (as erroneously omitted by the scribe), but not otherwise.'[29]

As this indicates, Furnivall was a practical man, and no slave to metrical 'rules', such as those devised by the German scholar Reinhold Pauli, whose edition of Gower had appeared just the year before, in 1857. Furnivall observed tartly:

> The doctrine ... of Dr Pauli's edition of Gower's *Confessio Amantis* as to the final *e* in Early English is not strictly borne out by any MS., or any undoctored edition of one, that I have ever read; and far more experienced readers and better judges than I, have condemned the attempt to impose on a language constantly changing in words, inflexions, and spelling, written often by half-lettered men, a rigid rule applicable only to the well settled speech and literature of a cultivated nation.[30]

Pauli's was a topical illustration of what Furnivall called a 'doctored' text, in that the editor regularized the spelling (removing thorns and yoghs, and, with exceptions, emending *y* and *i* and *u* and *v* to accord with modern orthographic values) and he smoothed the metre. The publishers, Bell and Daldy, wanted to make Gower accessible to an educated readership, who could cope with Chaucer and wanted an attrac-

---

[29] *Early English Poems*, p. vi.
[30] Ibid. Later in the texts, final -*e* was supplied at the end of words ending in -*i*. See further on the matter of final -*e*, and the particular case of Skeat, Pearsall, 'Chaucer's Meter'.

tive book, rather than hardcore philology.³¹ What Furnivall meant by a 'doctored' text, and what he felt about 'doctoring', is probably already apparent from this context: one in which the editor, in all likelihood a 'doctor of philosophy', emends manuscript readings to accord with philological rules or principles of recension. Furnivall regarded this—to change the metaphor—as cooking the books, tampering with evidence to make it fit a hypothesis, rather than improvement. 'Doctoring' will in due course claim further attention.

SIR FREDERIC MADDEN

Furnivall's philological capers in *Early English Poems* were likely to seem distasteful to a serious scholar such as Sir Frederic Madden, the Keeper of Manuscripts at the British Museum, knighted in 1833. As a budding, if wayward, student of medieval texts, Furnivall had headed off to his nearest manuscript library, and put himself under Madden's direction—or, more accurately, hoped to pick his brains. Whereupon, as Furnivall said, Madden 'kindly directed me to the earliest unprinted English MSS. under his charge'.³² Herbert Coleridge had already sent Madden the prospectus for the 'New English Dictionary' and consulted him about dates and difficult passages for his *Glossarial Index*. Coleridge's enquiry and his own association with the dictionary gave Furnivall an entrée to the great man. Coleridge testified warmly in print to Madden's generosity to scholars and leadership in editing medieval English texts to a high standard (though Madden would not have seen Coleridge's compliments at the time of Furnivall's approach to him): 'I cannot terminate this brief preface without expressing my deep sense of the obligations I am under to Sir F. Madden, not merely for the help of his invaluable editions of Laȝamon and Havelok . . . but also for much

---

³¹ 'The chief labour, however, consisted in restoring the orthography, and in regulating the metre'; Gower, *The Confessio Amantis of John Gower*, ed. Pauli, p. xliv. For all the parade of collation, Pauli based his text on the Berthelette printed edition of 1532, which he compared with the two best-known Harleian manuscripts in the British Museum, with some use of two other manuscripts in particular passages of difficulty. He relied on H. O. Coxe, Bodley's Librarian, for descriptions of the ten copies in the Bodleian, while F. R. Daldy, BA, provided the Glossary. In case anyone thought this was short measure from a *Herr Doktor*, Pauli commented that 'The text of a work like the Confessio Amantis does not require the same scrupulous attention to every existing MS. as that of an ancient classical author. Everybody who examines the MSS. of Gower will soon be satisfied that the principal differences are merely of an orthographical nature' (p. xliv).

³² Preface to *Early English Poems*, p. iii. On Madden, see further Michael Borrie, 'Sir Frederic Madden (1801–1873)', *ODNB*; Ackerman and Ackerman, *Sir Frederic Madden*; Matthews, *Invention of Middle English*, 196–203.

kind personal advice and assistance, which probably few, if any, living philologists beside himself would have been competent to bestow.'[33]

Madden would find that Coleridge was far less annoying to deal with than Furnivall, who had approached him with the abrupt demand 'Can you tell me of any early English MS. 'in London', before 1300 if possible, which would take up from 100 to 150 octavo pages and which we could print as a Supplement to our Philological Society's Transactions? We shall have about 100 pages to spare this year, and I should like to make them available for some Early English matter.'[34] Furnivall's demands not only lacked finesse; they were immoderate. Coleridge tried to smooth things over, telling Madden, 'I hope that Furnivall will be able to print something interesting in his 100 pages. I should have voted for Robert of Gloucester myself, but I hear that would exceed his space. That clearly ought to form one of the R(oll)'s Series, and I wish I could hear that it was in your hands.'[35] Madden's initial reply to Furnivall was patient, as well as courteous:

> I am not aware that you will find in any of the MSS. in the London libraries a poem of the 13th cent. long enough to fill 100 pages, unless you thought proper to print a selection from the Collection of Saints Lives in Alexandrian verse, in MS Harl. 2277, or the first portion of Robert of Gloucester's Chronicle from MS Cott(on) Calig(ula) A. xi. which Hearne printed from a late MS of the 15th century. Both of these deserve a critical edition.' Other texts of various lengths of the 13th century remain inedited in the Trinity College (Cambr.) MS B. 14. 39. and MS Jesus College Oxford, 29; likewise some in MS Lambeth 487. MS Digby (Oxford) 86, and some, I think still not printed in Harl. 913 and one of the Egerton MSS the number of which I do not recollect. The latter contains two copies of the very curious Moral poem partly printed by Hickes, of which other copies are in MS Digby 4, Coll Jes(us) 29 and a Lambeth MS. If you were not very particular as to date, why not print a portion of that very curious poem, Robert of Brunne's translation of the Manuel des Peches, finished in 1303. A copy is in Harl. 1701, and I only know of one other, in MS Bodl. 245. The French original text is always at hand in case of deficiencies.[36]

In *Early English Poems*, Furnivall gave a candid reply to this list of *desiderata*: 'Of these Robert of Brunne's *Handlyng Synne* was the most important, but it was too long for our Society, and I have therefore

[33] *A Dictionary of the Oldest Words in the English Language*, 3.
[34] Letter of 31 Jan. 1859, BL MS Egerton 2847, f. 32^{r-v} (also cited in part by Matthews, *Making of Middle English*, 147; Benzie, *Dr F. J. Furnivall*, 80). Furnivall later sent a complimentary copy of the finished work, which Madden acknowledged; letter of 16 Sept, 1862, FU 537. [35] Letter of 7 Feb. 1859, MS Egerton 2847, f. 34^{r-v}.
[36] Letter of 2 Feb. 1859, FU 534.

edited it for the Roxburghe Club.'[37] The short poems appearing first in *Early English Poems* had been Madden's second choice. The decision to include in the fruit basket material from Add. MS 22283, the 'Simeon' Manuscript, was driven by crude anxiety to get there first: a fortnight before the purchase was complete, Furnivall had written to Madden to demand: 'Have you bought Sir R. Simeon's duplicate of the Vernon MS. yet?'[38] The purchase, from Sir John Simeon, was completed on 13 February 1858. Both 'Simeon', and the 'Vernon' manuscript in the Bodleian Library, which appears to derive from the same place of production, overlap in content. They resemble each other in their unusually large dimensions, and both date from the late fourteenth century.[39] Furnivall claimed to have collated just one of these items with Vernon, which was all that time permitted on a flying visit to Oxford, though the scholarly obligation to compare Simeon with the earlier and more complete Vernon is tacitly conceded. At this stage in his career, Furnivall stuck to manuscript material in London out of convenience (though Madden noted *desiderata* in Oxford and Cambridge). And the need to get the material out in a hurry to fill the *Transactions* dictated his preference for copying from single manuscripts. Yet, because of Furnivall's connection with the *NED*, Madden had recommended 'critical' editing, for lexicographical, rather than textual, reasons: 'in my viewing of the matter, I think philology gains immensely by the collation of *various copies* because the scribes change one word for another, and thus many obsolete terms find their equivalents.'[40] Furnivall did not take this advice.

Madden's scholarly eminence, and his position as Keeper of Manuscripts in the British Museum, made him vulnerable to tiresome and occasionally impertinent enquiries from scholars seeking to expedite their research at the expense of his time and energies. Whereas Coleridge had been diffident in his approach, Furnivall, once put in sole charge of the Dictionary, and given half a chance, became a pest. Furnivall had waited upon Madden in the Museum in 1861 to consult him on the editions of Robert of Brunne's *Handlyng Synne* and the *Sankgreal*. Now, in 1862, although he could not afford to fall out with Madden,

---

[37] Preface to *Early English Poems*, p. iii.

[38] Letter from Furnivall to Madden of 31 Jan. 1859, MS Egerton 2847, f. 33ᵛ. Furnivall's error of 'R[ichard]' for Sir John Simeon is apparently by confusion with Sir John's father. Madden replied: 'We have bought the duplicate of the Vernon MS but it is unfortunately very imperfect. I shall write to Mr. Coleridge in a day or two, but can promise him but little'; letter of 2 Feb. 1859, FU 534.

[39] See further, Doyle, *The Vernon Manuscript*; Doyle, 'The Shaping of the Vernon and Simeon MSS'. [40] Letter to Furnivall of 2 Feb. 1859.

relations between them became strained. A query as to whether Madden knew of any plans to print the fifteenth-century cookery book the *Liber Cure Cocorum* from MS Sloane 1986, which Furnivall had in mind for the Philological Society—or any other 'short MS on the same or a kindred subject' to fill up a bit more space, was accompanied by a curt demand, unadorned by many of the social niceties, for help in dating a formidable list of some thirty-eight medieval texts, nearly all romances, 'for our Dictionary'. In his reply Madden tried to stem the tide:

> I have some faint recollection of having seen the Liber Cura de Cocorum in print, but I am not at all sure about it. Does it occur in the series of the Percy Society? I should think that Mr. Halliwell could probably tell you better than anybody. Your list of Romances rather alarms me, and I assure you I have not the leisure at present to attend to the subject with the care it requires. I think the late Mr. Coleridge sent me a list of this kind, & I then roughly put down the *centuries* to which I thought the Poems might be assigned. But I am surprized that you have not a Sub-Committee for the preparation of your *Dictionary* whose task it should be to judge of the age of these Poems by the language, as well as by any incidental notices | that might seem to fix the period, as well as 'by'the 'date'of the MS. in which they are found. For some time past I have given up my Romance reading for historical researches, and should have to track over the whole range of those you mention before I committed myself to any opinion as to a fixed date of composition.[41]

Furnivall was impervious to the mild and courteous tone of this remonstrance, though he did apologize—rather too airily—for taking too much of a busy man's time:

> When will the Government give you another Assistant to note up the Catalogue of MSS? Not in these iron-plating-of-ships days, I suppose? As to the long list of dateless books, I do owe you an apology for asking the dates for it. But one never knows what amount of learning is at your fingers ends ready to be jotted down like the dates of the Kings, and for the chance of this I asked.[42]

Just a week later he was demanding to know Madden's opinion of the dates of the two Wycliffite translations of the Bible into English; this request was more reasonable, since not least among Madden's editorial achievements was his massive four-volume text of the Wycliffite Bible, published in 1850, prepared with Josiah Forshall, Secretary of the

[41] Letter of 7 Apr. 1862, FU 536. 'Date' is substituted for 'age'.
[42] Letters of 4 and 8 Apr. 1862, MS Egerton 2847, ff. 262–8. Furnivall is characteristically topical in his reference to iron-clad warships: the Royal Navy began building two iron-hulled frigates in 1859, and by 1861 had decided to fit the entire battle fleet.

British Museum, previously under-keeper of the department of manuscripts.[43] Madden noted privately in his diary that he had doubts of Furnivall's capacity as an editor, though he would later recommend his appointment as a professor of English literature at King's College, London. He recorded that he did not object to speaking well of the man. Yet relations between them would be soured in 1865 when Madden discovered that Furnivall had supported William Stubbs's unsuccessful candidature as the new Principal Librarian of the British Museum. Yet Furnivall continued to write to him from time to time.[44]

As Furnivall and Coleridge acknowledged, Madden, an expert, and meticulously careful, palaeographer, was an inspiration to the next generation of early English scholars.[45] His editions had made him an acknowledged authority on early Middle English, as well as on manuscripts. His 1828 edition of *The Ancient English Romance of Havelok the Dane* marked the beginning of his serious scholarly attention to Middle English, and was very gratifyingly praised by no less a critic than Sir Walter Scott.[46] Other editions which followed, included La3amon's *Brut*, and, as part of an anthology of Gawain stories, the text of *Sir Gawain and the Green Knight*, from the Museum's MS Cotton Nero A. x. Madden was the first to recognize that there were four poems in this manuscript, not one.[47] All these texts were landmarks of early English publishing.[48] Madden was himself aware that his work set out clear guidelines for his successors, announcing in *Syr Gawayne* that the poems 'taken from original manuscripts are printed with a scrupulous regard for accuracy . . . The truth is, that editors of our old poetry have, with few exceptions, paid too little attention to the system of writing used by the early scribes, and the consequence is, that but a small portion of all that have been published will bear collation with the originals.'[49] Yet John Kemble, when he heard that Madden was to undertake La3amon, expressed his doubts of his capacity, as no expert

[43] *The Holy Bible*, ed. Forshall and Madden. See further A. Hudson, 'The Making of a Monumental Edition'. See also Madden's accounts of his researches on the project in Rogers, *Sir Frederic Madden at Cambridge*.
[44] G. P. Ackerman, 'John M. Kemble and Sir Frederic Madden', 27.
[45] See further Matthews, *Making of Middle English*, 113–37.   [46] Ibid. 125.
[47] *Syr Gawayne*. For an account of Madden's engagement with the Gawain narratives, see Edwards, 'Observations on the History of Middle English Editing', 44–45. Also Matthews, *Making of Middle English*, 130–3.
[48] R. W. Ackerman, 'Madden's Gawain Anthology'.
[49] Quoted by Edwards, 'Observations', 45. Madden's transcription of the texts left the abbreviations unexpanded, though he provided a separate list of them 'for the convenience of the reader'. Abbreviated words were expanded in the Glossary and Notes. As

in Anglo-Saxon; Madden's response had been to acquaint himself deliberately with early English philology—he acknowledged his debt to Kemble.[50]

Madden's *editio princeps* of the early fourteenth-century romance of *Havelok*, done for the Roxburghe Club when he was still only 27, and sub-keeper of the manuscripts in the British Museum Library, was a groundbreaking edition of a Middle English text. He observed with pardonable pride that, though it was found 'by accident' among the Bodleian Library's Laudian manuscripts, it afforded him the 'greatest satisfaction' 'to have been the humble means of retrieving from oblivion a poem so long supposed to have perished'.[51] The publication was thus a personal coup, as well as one for the Club. *Havelok* in English survived in one complete text (Bodleian Library, MS Laud. misc. 108), as well as partial texts. In addition, two French versions offered ample opportunity for comparisons which enabled Madden, in the absence of Middle English dictionaries, to reconstruct the meaning of the words and to create the full glossary which later lexicographers and editors could themselves then use in studying other texts. The lexicographical value of collation was uppermost in his mind: his intention was 'to produce what might be considered an additional contribution towards that great desideratum, A DICTIONARY OF THE OLD ENGLISH LANGUAGE'.[52] In the absence of that dictionary, Madden did what he could to supply brief etymologies, leaving those unknown 'to the researches of future Glossographers'.[53]

The circumstances of *Havelok*'s textual survival made it less useful for recension. This may have suited Madden's editorial taste, though he was not averse to conjecture based on comparisons with other versions of the material and his own wide familiarity with the locutions used in

---

Edwards notes, Madden felt confident to introduce emendations in the texts, marked off with square brackets.

[50] See G. P. Ackerman, 'John M. Kemble and Sir Frederic Madden'; Matthews, *Making of Middle English*, 125.

[51] *The Ancient English Romance of Havelok the Dane*, ed. Madden, pp. iii–iv.

[52] Ibid., p. lv. Madden saw himself in preparing his glossary as following the example of his 18th- and early 19th-c. predecessors, Thomas Tyrwhitt and Alexander Chalmers.

[53] Ibid., p. lv: 'The use of a Glossary formed on a grammatical basis, and illustrated by examples, has long been known to the writer, but the difficulties of composing it must be obvious to all who have ever made the attempt.' Inevitably, given the materials available to Madden, there are some misidentifications, such as *caliz*, 'chalice', attributed by him to 'Saxon' (i.e. the OE loan word 'calic', itself derived, as Madden well knew, from Latin 'calix'), though *caliz* is an independent 12th-c. borrowing of calix into Old French (see *OED*, 'chalice', n.).

other Middle English romances.⁵⁴ His glossary and explanatory notes show him to have been formidably widely read in such material, as well as chronicles, and to have had an excellent memory for detail. He included with the text a full introduction and the two twelfth-century Anglo-French versions: that of Geffrei Gaimar and *Le Lai d'Havelok* (both derived from a lost earlier source). Madden's work on *Havelok* still compels admiration. Although the poem has been edited several times since, it is this particularly full editorial apparatus which rendered Madden's volume in Kenneth Sisam's opinion 'still precious' almost ninety years later.⁵⁵ This editorial apparatus goes far to meet the expectations of any standard modern edition of a medieval text, including the EETS, went far beyond what Madden had been commissioned by the Roxburghe Club to do.⁵⁶

Madden's second Roxburghe offering was the edition of the mid-fourteenth-century English romance *William and the Werwolf*, also known as *William of Palerne* (1832), presented to members of the Club by the first Earl Cawdor (1790–1866), who had commissioned it.⁵⁷ The unique manuscript in King's College, Cambridge (MS 13) had only recently become accessible after being kept under lock and key, 'impervious to mortal eyes!', as Madden recorded, for some fifty years.⁵⁸ It had first come to public notice in 1781, when Jacob Bryant, Fellow of the College, used its linguistic evidence to support his case for the authenticity of the Rowley forgeries of Thomas Chatterton. Another Fellow, Dr Robert Glyn, also a Chatterton believer, was responsible for its incarceration, after he had allowed the Shakespearian commentator George

---

⁵⁴ For example, on p. 5/46, Madden incorporates a conjectural reading to satisfy the sense, 'Wel fifty pundes, Y woth, or more' concocted out of similar phrasing elsewhere in the poem and in *Guy of Warwick*. It was retained by Skeat and Sisam. He also ran into difficulty at l. 2289 with MS 'þhes', proposing 'thighs', or 'yhes' ('eyes'), 'or perhaps 'theues' ('thieves'). Later opinion has preferred 'þef' ('thief'), so Skeat and Sisam, supposing confusion between long s and f: 'He dreddes him so þef does clubbe' (doubtless thighs and eyes are both averse to bludgeons, but 'thief' seems more plausible).

⁵⁵ Sisam revised Skeat's text, which was itself, though revised, closely based on Madden's work: *Ancient English Romance . . . Havelok*, p. v.

⁵⁶ On 5 Mar. 1827, 'It was proposed 'that a M.S. of general interest, should be selected and printed at the expense of the Club . . . It was resolved that the Lay of Havelok should be chosen, and eighty copies printed at the Shakespeare Press in crown quarto and in black-letter, of which each member should have two copies, six being given to Frederic Madden, to whom the Club is indebted for the loan of the transcript of the Romance, that each member should pay six guineas for his own copy and two guineas for a second, and that £100 be given to Madden as his fee'; quoted by Nicolas Barker in *The Publications of the Roxburghe Club 1814–1962*, 16–17.

⁵⁷ See further Matthews, *Making of Middle English*, 126–8.

⁵⁸ Rogers, *Sir Frederic Madden at Cambridge*, 2.

Steevens to 'see the Werewolf, and on the latter drawing some inference from it contrary to the sentiments of Dr. G., the Doctor determined that the Poem should not again serve as an argument against himself'. [59] Just a few years after *Havelok* and the *Werewolf had* appeared, the Roxburghe Club, at its meeting on 17 June 1836, resolved that an annual subscription of 5 guineas should be levied and 'that the sum so raised, or a competent portion of it, shall be expended under the direction of a Committee, in printing some inedited Manuscript, or in reprinting some Book of acknowledged rarity and value'; this resolution would not interfere with the previous custom whereby individual members would present works to the Club at their own expense: *Havelok* was the first beneficiary of this decision.[60] By it the Club became one of the literary societies most committed to publishing early English texts and Furnivall's chief template on which he formed the much humbler EETS.

Madden went on to edit the collection of exemplary tales the *Gesta Romanorum* (1838), also for the Roxburghe Club, and his influential text of *Laʒamon's Brut* (1847) for the Society of Antiquaries; his *Sir Gawayne* was prepared for the Bannatyne Club.[61] He also edited the thirteenth-century Latin chronicle of Matthew Paris, the *Historia Minor*, in three volumes, for the Rolls Series, which had been established in 1857 for publishing 'materials for the History of this Country from the Invasion of the Romans to the Reign of Henry VIII'.[62] The preamble by the Master of the Rolls, which prefaced each volume in the series, provided a clear framework within which the editors were required to work: 'each chronicle or historical document to be edited should be treated in the same way as if the editor were engaged on an Editio Princeps'. The 'best' manuscripts should be collated to establish 'the most correct text', that is, to establish which manuscript should serve as the copy-text, to provide an authoritative text but with access to variants at the foot of the page: 'no notes should be added, except such as were illustrative of the various readings'.[63]

[59] *The Ancient English Romance of William and the Werwolf*, ed. Madden; Rogers, *Sir Frederic Madden at Cambridge*, 2.

[60] Barker, *Publications of the Roxburghe Club*, 21.

[61] *The Old English Versions of the Gesta Romanorum*, ed. Madden; *Layamon's Brut, or Chronicle of Britain*, ed. Madden; *Syr Gawayne*, ed. Madden. In addition, he provided a preface to *How the Goode Wif Thaught hir Doughter*.

[62] *Matthaei Parisiensis . . . Historia Minor*, quotation from the prefatory notice recording the Master of the Rolls' submission of his proposal for the series, of 26 Jan. 1857, and its approval by the Lords of the Treasury, minuted on 9 Feb. 1857.

[63] Madden's edition faithfully followed this prospectus, with full description of the manuscripts, notice of the historical value of the chronicle, and biographical informa-

Matthew Paris provided 'materials for the History of this Country'. Yet the medieval writers who offered versions of the alternative, but in its time wildly influential, history provided by Geoffrey of Monmouth and his successors, the *Brut*, did not. Madden claimed for the priest, Laʒamon, that he was the English Ennius, the father, that is, of English poetry, in the form of a historical epic; he was a poet rather than an historian. Laʒamon's *Brut* fell into the category of a Literary Remain, and for this reason came within the purview of the Antiquaries. In February 1831 the Society of Antiquaries had set up a subcommittee, convened by Benjamin Thorpe 'to examine a Proposal for publishing Anglo-Saxon and Early English Literary Remains at the expense of the Society'. Funds were not lavishly available for this work, and the series was suspended in 1844, its resources largely depleted, indeed, by Madden's edition of Laʒamon, and he withdrew from the Society before his final volume appeared.[64] Madden's work on Laʒamon's *Brut* was, in part, an outgrowth from the dedicated labour that he expended over many years supervising the restoration and rescue of the burned fragments left after the disastrous fire of 23 October 1731 in the library of Sir Robert Cotton at Ashburnham House; both manuscripts of the *Brut* belonged to this collection. MS Otho C. xiii had been badly damaged, and subsequent editors are in Madden's debt for readings in the manuscript which are now illegible. In the opinion of the elder Richard Garnett, Madden's colleague at the Museum: 'Our readers do not require to be told that a poem of more than thirty thousand lines, of the transition period of our language—embodying a greater amount of a peculiar form of that language than can be collated from all other reliques of the same century—must be of no small importance for the grammar and history of the vernacular tongue.'[65] Garnett thus echoed Madden's opinion that the main interest of Laʒamon was philological, not historical. Madden apologized for the years it had taken since then before publication in 1847, but the delay is surely forgivable— if forgiveness were needed—given the prodigious labour he described in collating both manuscripts, and comparing the text with Wace in the

tion about the author. For an account of his visits to see manuscripts of the *Historia Anglorum* in Cambridge in 1859 and 1863, see Rogers, *Sir Frederic Madden at Cambridge*, 49–70.

[64] See further Joan Evans, *A History of the Society of Antiquaries*, 236–7, and Madden's own account, p. viii; also Birrell, 'The Society of Antiquaries and the Taste for Old English, 1705–1840'.

[65] 'Antiquarian Club-Books', in [Richard Garnett, jun. (ed.)], *The Philological Essays of the Late Rev. Richard Garnett*, 129. First published in the *Quarterly Review*, Mar. 1848.

printed edition and in manuscript, as well as versions of Geoffrey of Monmouth's *Historia Regum Britanniae* in Latin, French, and Welsh, and Bede's *Ecclesiastical History* in Latin and Anglo-Saxon.

It had been Madden's intention to compile a complete glossary of every instance of every word, 'but after writing near 50,000 slips, it was found impracticable to carry the design into execution, unless a separate volume were allotted to the Glossary' (p. xl). He disdained a 'mere Verbal Index' and the 'grammatical glossary' provided was the only necessary compromise made with an imperfect world. The edition was a formidable achievement for the leisure hours of a busy Museum public servant, and Garnett knew of what he spoke when he noted 'with a full sense how heavily the task must have pressed on a gentleman not a little burdened already with official duties'.[66] As the 'grammatical' glossary indicates, philology dictated the edition's design: Madden provided what would later be called 'diplomatic' transcriptions of both English texts, without expanding manuscript abbreviations, and relegating conjectural readings and notes of scribal correction to the foot of the page; however, the special letters, yogh, thorn, and wynn, were modernized 'as tending to render the English poem more intelligible and less difficult to read' (p. liv).[67]

Yet Garnett, though an admirer of Madden, was no fan of the Roxburghe Club's exclusivity. It differed from the Society of Antiquaries, where 'the great point was to place the entire poem within reach of those who have neither opportunity nor inclination to grapple with the obscurities of MSS.; and this has now been done under a very careful eye, and with a rich accompaniment of elucidation.'[68] Care

---

[66] Ibid. 129.

[67] 'The principal aim of the Editor has been to furnish the reader with as correct a representation of the text of the manuscripts as possible ... As it was thought desirable also to preserve the character of the writing as nearly as letter-type would admit, the abbreviations have been preserved throughout, but they are few in number, and present no particular difficulty' (pp. xxxviii–xxxix). The abbreviations in Latin marginal notes were, however, expanded. Corrections by the first hand of undoubted errors were accepted silently 'except when anything may be learnt by the correction'. The whole point of presenting both English versions was to enable understanding of how the language had changed between the earlier and the later, 'and to note to what extent the diction and forms of the earlier text had become obsolete or unintelligible' (p. vii). For the better understanding of the language, Madden also provided a literal modern English translation, tolerating obsolete words and avoiding paraphrase, for ease of comparison with the original.

[68] 'Antiquarian Club-Books', 146. Madden noted (*Layamon*, pp. xxxvii–xxxviii) that 'the remains of this manuscript ... have since been inlaid and bound, by my direction, and now consist of 145 leaves, more or less imperfect', and in a footnote that 'Many of the

and full editorial matter were the hallmarks of a Madden edition; the speed with which he worked can be gauged from his transcription of the forty folios of *William and the Werwolf* in a packed fortnight in Cambridge, during which he was looking at and transcribing other material, including manuscripts of the Wycliffite Bible, paying visits, walking, and mourning the anniversary of the death of his first wife.[69] Skeat, who later revised his edition for the EETS, was careful to tell him that 'inaccuracies in the former edition are nowhere to be found'.[70] Undoubtedly, he was buttering up the prickly Madden with a lavish hand, to persuade him to accept revisions and additions to his intellectual offspring, but he was not therefore insincere. Skeat noted in his preface to the re-edition (the first title to be included in the EETS's Extra Series) that

> The thorough excellence of both the text and glossary of this edition is known to all who have had the opportunity of access to it, and it has always ranked as a contribution of great importance to our knowledge of Early English literature. Sir F. Madden justly claims to have been one of the first editors who insisted on the necessity of strict and literal accuracy, and it is impossible to say how much we owe to him, directly and indirectly.[71]

Furnivall would go to much trouble to persuade Madden to lend his lustre by letting him include his editions in the more democratic EETS.[72]

Indeed, praising Madden became almost *de rigueur* for his English

leaves are so contracted and blackened, that the only means of reading them was to hold the leaf up to the light of a powerful lamp. From the tender state also of the vellum, many letters, and even words, have perished since the text was printed in the present work.'

[69] Rogers, *Sir Frederic Madden at Cambridge*, 1–5.

[70] Letter to Madden, n.d., BL MS Egerton 2848, ff. 253^r–254^v (f. 254^r).

[71] *The Romance of William of Palerne*, ed. Skeat, EETS, ES 1, p. ii. The same verdict on Madden's significance is passed by Edwards, 'Observations', 45: 'Madden sustained his new editorial standards to produce works that retain their importance to our own day . . . we see the demonstration of a sustained application of editorial method that is valid and ably executed. In an important sense he established a tradition of Middle English editing that continues to our own day in ways that are not very advanced.'

[72] Matthews argues that Madden's editions were superseded 'by the scholarship that emerged from the new philological ascendancy of the 1840s' (*Making of Middle English*, 135). This may be true of Skeat's and Richard Morris's contributions in the 1860s, but, in other cases, perhaps the time lag may have been greater, to allow for the greater impact of German scholarship in the 1870s. Many of the early editions of the EETS are not significantly different from Madden's in their principles, and the editorial matter is often less substantial. Of course new scholars have always wanted to seem to surpass their predecessors, but Furnivall's society was also driven by expediency: the need to publish annually and to get out texts as swiftly as possible.

successors, who were probably anxious to prove that not all competent editing of early English was done by German scholars, and also that some English scholars of the first half of the nineteenth century could put aside their traditional prejudices in favour of Latin and Greek. As Alexander Ellis of the Philological Society would say, 'Perhaps few have contributed so much to forming habits of strict scholarly accuracy as the late Frederic Madden. He clearly regarded our English speech as worthy of the same kind of exact critical study . . . as it has generally been the English habit to reserve for the study of the "classical languages" only.'[73] Moreover, coming to editing as Furnivall did, from the lexicographical needs of using early English records as witnessed by the scribes themselves for the Dictionary, any tendency that he may have felt towards making his own mark by a display of his ingenuity and erudition in a daring emendation of a base text would have seemed inappropriate in the EETS editions (though Shakespeare and Chaucer would offer temptations). Accordingly, the 'conservationist cast' of Madden's editing, expressed in the felt need 'to represent the surviving forms of a text as scrupulously as possible, both in transcription and collation', was very much to his taste.

THE ROXBURGHE CLUB AND OTHER TEXT SOCIETIES

As Furnivall had noted on the title page of *Early English Poems*, he had himself become involved in editing 'Lonelich's' *Seynt Graal*,[74] and Robert Manning of Brunne's *Handlyng Synne*, with its French source. It is time to look briefly at the Roxburghe Club, for which Furnivall prepared his first large editions, as blazoned on the title pages of his subsequent publications.[75]

The Club had been created on 16 June 1812 by a group of wealthy book collectors and bibliophiles who had dined together on the eve of the sale of John Ker, Duke of Roxburghe's great private library, 'during which many of the most valuable books ever offered for public compe-

---

[73] *TPS*, 15, no. 1 (1874), 245.

[74] 'Lonelich' was a mistake for 'Lovelich'. In the beginning, Furnivall was seduced by his source, itself drawing upon Warton's *History of English Poetry*, into perpetuating the mistake, which had arisen by confusion of -*u* and -*n* in handwriting: 'In the English MS. the *u* and *n* are generally so alike' (*Seynt Graal*, i, p. xii). The matter was eventually settled by Henry Bradley and Walter Skeat: see Skeat's 'The Translator of "The Graal"'. For pertinent excerpts from George Ellis's writings, see Matthews, *Invention of Middle English*, 117–37.

[75] On the broader subject, see Steeves, *Learned Societies*. See also the account by Matthews, *Making of Middle English*, 85–109.

tition were purchased at higher prices than had previously or have since been obtained'. They agreed to dine together on the anniversary of the sale of Christopher Valdarfar's 1471 print of Boccaccio's *Decameron*, which had been bought by the Duke of Marlborough for the stupendous sum of 'Two-thousand-two-hundred-and sixty Pounds'.[76] It was, and is, a select group, limited to forty elected members drawn from the world of the nobility and other connoisseurs who could afford to acquire, or at least appreciate, bibliographical rarities. A sense of the exclusive world from which its members are drawn can be gathered from the Society's list, published on its website. It is the oldest society in existence which is dedicated to printing unpublished texts and documents and reprinting old and rare books from all historical periods, but including, in the nineteenth century, much medieval English literature.[77] The EETS largely superseded this function, but Furnivall began his trade as an editor, and at the same time learned about the workings of book clubs, by producing an astonishing amount of material for the Roxburghe, commissioned either by the Club itself or one of its members.

The Club has evolved during its long history, but, at the beginning, its publications began a year after its institution with a resolution that each member should bear the expense of printing a unique or rare printed book or manuscript, typically from his own collection, for presentation to the other members. (There were no women members until the twentieth century, and they are not numerous.) As Nicolas Barker has said, the publications were at the outset 'designed as an amusing present, rather than as a work of scholarship'.[78] There was no editorial apparatus. Thus, the early reprints of books printed by Caxton bore an antique 'black-letter' appearance to please the eye of a gentleman, rather than satisfy the soul of a scholar.[79] The sort of material to be issued

[76] Quotations from Hume, *Learned Societies and Printing Clubs*, 219. See also the list of 'Tostes' given at the first dinner, 17 June 1812, p. 221, concluding with 'The Cause of Bibliomania all over the World'.

[77] See the list of titles in the *Catalogue of the Books Presented to and Printed by the Club*, Roxburghe Club (London, 1884); the publications down to 1846 are also listed by Hume, *Learned Societies and Printing Clubs*, 223-7, the source likely to have been used by Furnivall and Coleridge in allocating readers for the Dictionary's 'first Period'.

[78] Barker, *Publications of the Roxburghe Club*, 2: 'At this stage there was no question of the "scholarly value" which was to preoccupy the Club in later years' (p. 3). There were originally to be only as many copies as members; the copy presented to the Chairman was printed on vellum. See further Husbands, 'The Roxburghe Club'.

[79] Compare Hensleigh Wedgwood's near-contemporary praise of the example set by Grimm 'in abolishing the use of the Gothic characters; there is no more reason for our employing them, than for our using the Roman capitals in pointing Latin; the common type was equally unknown to both nations, and the use of the uncouth Gothic letters

was reported in the *Gentleman's Magazine* for July 1813 as 'a scarce and curious tract', or 'some original manuscript'. The first two books to be printed from manuscripts were Gower's *balades*, presented by his namesake, Lord Gower, and *The Chester Mysteries*, presented by James Markland.[80] The Chester Plays were one of the first collections of medieval English drama to be printed. They were followed in 1822 when the antiquary and collector Francis Douce edited the play of the Judgement from the unique manuscript of the Towneley Plays.[81] The York Plays, however, were more elusive. Richard Garnett described them as 'the most curious and important collection of the kind after the Townley'. But they 'have disappeared for the third time to an unknown "limbus librorum" where they will probably slumber as unprofitably as they did at Strawberry Hill and at Bristol'.[82] It is likely that Garnett got his information from his senior colleague, Sir Frederic Madden, who deserves credit as the one who identified the manuscript in 1844, before it passed into the collection of Lord Ashburnham in 1847.[83] It was bought by the British Museum at the sale of the Ashburnham Library in 1899 (and given its current shelfmark, Additional MS 35290).[84]

In 1825 the Club passed a resolution, quoted above, that, in addition to the members' presentations, the Club itself should select and print

both increases the difficulty to the reader, and adds to the expense of printing, without affording any countervailing advantage', 'Deutsche Grammatik', 169–70.

[80] Barker, *Publications of the Roxburghe Club*, 7. See also David Mills, 'Theories and Practices in the Editing of the Chester Cycle Play-manuscripts', and references there given; Matthews, *Making of Middle English*, 94.

[81] *Judicium, a pageant extr. from the Towneley MS*, ed. Douce. On Douce, see C. Hurst, 'Douce, Francis (1757–1834)', *ODNB*; A. N. L. Munby, *Connoisseurs and Medieval Miniatures*.

[82] Garnett, 'Antiquarian Club-Books', 115. The York Plays 'slumbered' until the *editio princeps* by Lucy Toulmin Smith (1885). Horace Walpole bought the manuscript in 1764 at the sale of Ralph Thoresby's library, and it was sold in 1842, with the rest of the Strawberry Hill library. See *The York Play: A Facsimile*, x; Cawley, 'Thoresby and Later Owners of the Manuscript of the York Plays'. The book's interment at 'Bristol' alludes to its ownership by B. H. Bright.

[83] Madden mentioned this discovery in an entry in his journal in Apr. 1844. Quoted by Cawley, 'Thoresby and Later Owners', 82; see also *The York Plays*, ed. Beadle, EETS, SS 23, 24, i, pp. xxii–xxiii.

[84] As recorded in his journal for Tuesday, 23 Apr. 1844. Madden was afraid of the manuscript falling into the hands of 'a second Mr. Bright, and shut up from the public'. (He referred to B. H. Bright's unwillingness to share his manuscript with others.) The fourth Earl of Ashburnham (1797–1878), who purchased the manuscript, was notorious for denying access to his manuscripts. Madden wrote to Sir Thomas Phillipps on 28 Oct. 1850: 'His Lordship is a dog in the manger, and allows no one to consult them' (Cawley, 'Thoresby and Later Owners', 80 and 89 n. 40, quoting Munby, *The Formation of the Phillipps Library*, 26).

a manuscript of general interest, with additional copies, not more than 100, available for sale, and would pay a reputable editor who was not a member to do the work. Madden's edition of *Havelok* was the first in this class, and aroused some opposition, on the grounds that commissioning an editor made the members look as though they were not able to do the work themselves. These publications would be financed from the 5 guinea subscription; in Barker's view, 'if the Club had not thus guaranteed its future by this annual levy on its members, it would not have survived'.[85] Private grandee collectors, though by no means extinct—Sir Thomas Phillipps, for one, was very much alive until 1872—were not the phenomena they once they had been, and the changes towards more scholarly publications were a response both to the more serious attitude being taken towards publishing early literature, and the formation of other book clubs whose interests overlapped or coincided with those of the Roxburghe. Richard Garnett gave a masterly overview of the whole scene, though he did not flatter the 'Half-learned smatterers, who never swarmed more than they do at this time', and who 'are the very plague and pestilence of our literature' (Thomas Wright and J. O. Halliwell being his chief whipping boys).[86] As his son, Richard Garnett, jun., noted in his memoir of his father, Garnett, sen. had come to the attention of learned circles, both on the Continent and at home, following his publication in the *Quarterly Review* for September, 1835 of 'English Lexicography', which attracted the admiration and friendship of both Madden and Hensleigh Wedgwood.[87] Garnett was, unlike Wright and Halliwell, a member of the Philological Society, whose foundation, by his friend Edwin Guest, he thoroughly approved.[88] His essays reflect his fellow philologists' tastes and prejudices down to citing the discoveries of Georges Cuvier and William Buckland in the fields of palaeontology as analogous to those of philology and lexicography.[89]

[85] Barker, *Publications of the Roxburghe Club*, 22.
[86] Garnett, 'Antiquarian Club-Books', 126; see also Matthews, *Making of Middle English*, 106–7.
[87] 'Memoir of the Late Rev. Richard Garnett', *Philological Essays*, pp. i–xvi at p. xi.
[88] Ibid., p. xiii.
[89] 'English Lexicography', *Philological* Essays, 1–40 at p. 2: 'It would have been equally easy to ask fifty or sixty years ago . . . what can be the use of collecting and comparing unsightly fragments of bone that have been mouldering in the earth for centuries?' See further Richard Garnett, rev. John D. Haigh, 'Garnett, Richard (1789–1850)', and Alan Bell, 'Richard Garnett (1835–1906)', *ODNB*. Both Garnetts worked in the British Museum Library: Garnett sen. became Assistant Keeper of Printed Books in 1838; Garnett jun. became an assistant in the Printed Books Department in 1851 and rose to be Keeper in 1890.

In his account of progress in publishing early English texts, Garnett made the familiar points about the 'number and value of our vernacular literary monuments from the eighth to the fourteenth centuries', with which 'perhaps no nation in Europe... can compete'. He cited 'the code of Anglo-Saxon laws, the poem of Beowulf, various pieces in the Vercelli and Exeter books'.[90] Yet, 'with all our wealth and all our affectation of public spirit, not only the Germans, Danes and Swedes, but even the Bohemians, have surpassed us in their well-directed, systematic, and successful cultivation of these fields'. Something had been done to redeem England's reputation, but 'a great deal remains undone'. Nothing could be done to create a broader understanding of the nation's cultural inheritance 'and particularly the origin and progress of our native language' until more of the materials were made accessible in inexpensive print: Garnett found the snobbery (as he saw it) of the Roxburghe Club antithetical, citing its initial reluctance to sanction the inclusion of Madden's edition *Havelok*, though a new and enlarged edition of the text was greatly wanted. 'This simple request was positively refused! And was only at length conceded with an indifferent grace, on discovering that the execution was likely to get into the hands of another party, little qualified to do justice to the subject.' Garnett commented: 'Surely this is not the way to *diffuse* a taste for our early language and literature!'[91] Since the print run of the Club's publications was so limited, they were not easy of access, and Garnett noted with disgust that 'Some influential members of the Roxburghe were told that more than half their publications were wanting in our great national repository [the British Museum]. The reply was "We are glad to hear it!".'[92] Garnett's comments anticipated the *raison d'être* of the EETS: 'We do not hesitate to say that there are valuable materials for the elucidation of national theology, hagiology, popular opinions, and particularly the origin and progress of our native language, which have not perhaps been seen by ten persons now living, and whose very existence is unknown to the great mass of our literary public.'[93]

Reprinting old books was not a new idea when the Roxburghe Club was founded.[94] Work had been done in the eighteenth century on the texts of Shakespeare and Chaucer. Moreover, there had been the work

[90] Garnett, 'Antiquarian Club-Books', 113; see also the letter from Kemble cited in the 'Memoir', pp. xi–xiii.　　　　　　　　　　　　　　　　　　　　　　　　　[91] Ibid. 115.
[92] Ibid.　　　　　　　　　　　　　　　　　　　　　　　　　　　　　[93] Ibid. 113–14.
[94] For another overview of the growth of the publishing book clubs and societies, see Matthews, *Invention of Middle English*, 10–11.

of the Society of Antiquaries in the early nineteenth century. And in the first half of the nineteenth century other specialized text publication societies were also founded.[95] Notable among them were the Bannatyne Club, founded by Sir Walter Scott in 1823 to publish works of Scottish interest (dissolved 1861); the Maitland Club, founded in 1828, named for the sixteenth-century Scottish poet Sir Richard Maitland, and similarly dedicated to publishing texts illustrative of early Scottish literature and history; the Camden Society (now merged with the Royal Historical Society), founded in 1838, which published editions of sources of British history;[96] and the Surtees Society, founded in 1834 in honour of the Durham historian Robert Smith Surtees, and committed to publishing editions of material relating to the North-East of England. The Maitland Club, as its name perhaps suggests, was modelled on the Roxburghe and Bannatyne Clubs; in this world of learned associations, the 'clubs' dealt more in social cachet than the more democratic 'societies'. The Abbotsford Club (1835–66), named for Sir Walter Scott's residence, and modelled on the Roxburghe and the other Scottish societies, had, as was to be expected, a Scottish bias, but included Middle English texts, among them the romances found in the Auchinleck Manuscript. The very first publication was Thomas Sharp's edition of a group of the Digby plays,[97] while the Scottish editor James Morton also provided the first edition of *Seinte Katerine* from the group of texts associated with *Ancrene Wisse*.[98] Garnett added to this list the prominent new societies founded in the late 1830s and 1840s, the Percy Society (1841), the Welsh

---

[95] On the literary and antiquarian clubs, see further Matthews, *Making of Middle English*, 104–9; Hume, *Learned Societies and Printing Clubs*; and the critical overview by Richard Garnett, 'Antiquarian Book-Clubs'.

[96] Following financial difficulties, the Camden Society amalgamated with the Royal Historical Society in 1897; the Camden name was revived in 1901 by the joint Society for the 'Camden Third Series', though published under the Royal Historical Society's imprint. The name was retained for the ensuing Camden Fourth and Fifth Series.

[97] *Ancient Mysteries from the Digby Manuscipts* ed. Sharp. Sharp, described as 'of Coventry', aimed at a diplomatic text ('No pains have been spared in making a faithful and minutely accurate transcript of the original MS'), facilitated by 'the present improved means of printing ancient MSS, and a greatly extended taste for studying the Religious Mysteries and Moralities which laid the foundation of our National Drama' (pp. i–ii); the text reproduces the manuscript's marks of abbreviation. There is a Glossary, consisting of a simple word list, noting perplexities, one at least of the scribe's or editor's making: 'conctypotent' for 'omnipotent' (*Mary Magdalen*; the scribe had difficulties with the play's aureate vocabulary). The names of speakers are occasionally supplied in square brackets. See also *The Late Medieval Religious Plays of Bodleian MSS Digby 133 and E Museo 160*, ed. Baker, Murphy, and Hall, Jr., EETS, OS 283, pp. lxxii–lxxiv.

[98] *The Legend of St Katherine of Alexandria*, ed. Morton. Morton, as he acknowledged in his preface, was assisted by his friends Benjamin Thorpe and Joseph Stevenson (p. xv). The

Manuscripts Society (1837), the Cambridge Camden Society (1841),[99] the Chetham Society (1843),[100] and the British Archaeological Association (1843).[101] Of these, the Chetham, Percy, and Welsh Manuscript Societies were committed to the publication of texts.

The British Archaeological Association, which at first sight appears to sit rather oddly in this list, was founded in 1843 by a group from the Society of Antiquaries, Thomas Wright and Albert Way among them, who, while not wishing to compete with the Antiquaries, wished to offer outreach to a wider public, away from the capital, because, as public interest in ancient monuments increased, the monuments themselves were under threat from decay, demolition, and damage inflicted through ignorance.[102] As Way noted: 'The general impulse which, of late years, throughout almost all countries of western Europe, has caused an increasing attention to be paid to ancient memorials of a national and medieval character, in place of the exclusive admiration of objects of more remote antiquity, and more pure and classical taste, but of foreign origin, has now attained a great degree of popular favour.'[103] Broader in its interests than its name suggests, the Association provided for the study of archaeology, art, and architecture, 'Roman to post-medieval'.[104] Though it was not a text society, early documents which gave information about the appearance or materials of monuments could be included: under this heading Wright was able to include fourteenth- and fifteenth-century English recipes for painting and gilding, and Halliwell an extract from *Sir Degrevant* (on the grounds that it described a castle's interior decorations).[105] The Antiquaries' journal,

text is printed as verse, with a translation at the foot of the page, and an apparatus supplying variant readings from BL MS Royal 17 A. xxviii below that.

[99] From 1845, after it moved to London, it became the Ecclesiological Society, founded to promote the study of Gothic architecture.

[100] A Manchester-based text society dedicated to publishing material relating to 'the palatine counties of Lancaster and Chester'. See further Levine, *The Amateur and the Professional*, 43.

[101] Evans, *History of the Society of Antiquaries*, 227, 235, 264.

[102] Albert Way, 'Introduction', *Archaeological Journal*, 1 (Mar. 1844), 2. See further Levine, *The Amateur and the Professional*, 48–9.

[103] Way, 'Introduction', 1–2. The rivalry between Way and Wright would later split the British Archaeological Association into two separate bodies; Levine, *The Amateur and the Professional*, 21.

[104] *British Archaeological Association*, 1st series, 1 (1845), no. 1. For further illustration of 'the promiscuous mix of sources, literary and material, used by archaeologists at the time, see Levine, *The Amateur and the Professional*, 71.

[105] 'Early English receipts for Painting, Gilding, &c.', 'Early English Artistical receipts', *Archaeological Journal*, 1, 64–6, 152–5; 'Description of the Interior of a Chamber in a

THE ROXBURGHE CLUB AND OTHER SOCIETIES 357

Archaeologia, had been more accommodating, and had included material of philological (including dialectal), documentary, historical, and literary interest, sometimes even swamping archaeological papers.[106] Thus Madden had published in it a group of six fifteenth-century political poems, five Yorkist and the last Lancastrian.[107] J. J. Conybeare, Professor of Anglo-Saxon at Oxford, 1808-12, published many Anglo-Saxon texts in the journal; Sir Henry Ellis, the official editor of the Antiquaries' publications, was interested in this material, and he persuaded the Society to publish Conybeare's *Illustrations of Anglo-Saxon Poetry* (1826). Indeed, Ellis's extravagance in spending the Antiquaries' funds on this kind of material was a precipitating factor in the creation of the breakaway Association.[108] Joseph Brooks Yates (an original member of the Philological Society) printed extracts for the Society of Antiquaries from his own manuscript of the fourteenth-century pastoral compendium in verse *The Prick of Conscience*, attributed to Richard Rolle de Hampole.[109]

The Percy Society, founded in 1840, and which included John Payne Collier, Wright, and Halliwell among its founding members, collapsed in 1852, but, during its short life, its members were committed to seeking out and publishing rare poems and songs from manuscript materials and printed ephemera, both from the major scholarly libraries and their own collections.[110] It was itself an offshoot of the Roxburghe. Furnivall's

Castle', 243-5. See The Crafte of Lymmyng *and* The Maner of Steynyng', ed. Clarke, EETS, OS 347, 229-31. Clarke notes that these are 'probably the earliest recipes in the corpus', 371; see description by Clarke, p. lxxix. *The Romance of Sir Degrevant*, ed. Casson, EETS, OS 221, 86-9. Halliwell noted that he was preparing an edition for the Camden Society, *Early English Metrical Romances*, ed. Halliwell.

[106] Evans, *History of the Society of Antiquaries*, 235.
[107] 'Political Poems of the reigns of Henry VI and Edward IV', *Archaeologia*, read 10 Mar. 1842, *Archaeologia*, 29 (1842), 318-47. Preceded by Madden's 'Letter containing intelligence of the Proceedings of the Court and Nobility at the commencement of the year 1454..', 305-17.
[108] *Illustrations of Anglo-Saxon Poetry*... By John Josias Conybeare, together with additional notes, introductory notices &c. by his brother William Daniel Conybeare (London, 1826). See further Momma, *From Philology to English Studies*, 83-9.
[109] Evans, *History of the Society of Antiquaries*, 235-6. 'An Account of an Unprinted English Poem, Written in the early part of the Fourteenth Century, by Richard de Hampole, and entitled "Stimulus Conscientiae", or "The Prick of Conscience", *Archaeologia* 19 (Jan. 1821) (read 14 Dec. 1820), 314-35. The essay includes a summary of the poem's contents with interpolated excerpts, and a list of the manuscripts known to Yates. See also Michael Borrie, 'Ellis, Sir Henry (1777-1869)', *ODNB*.
[110] Founded 'for the purpose of bringing to light important but obscure specimens of Ballad Poetry, or works illustrative of that department of Literature... For some years the Society issued a volume each month; its publications are now less frequent though

Ballad Society would be its heir, while Collier, Wright, and Halliwell drew on their own enthusiasm for early drama to found the Shakespeare Society.

As Garnett remarked in 1848, it was the Camden Society which, 'from its numbers, the professed comprehensiveness of its plans and the high literary character of many of its members, bids the fairest to supply a notorious deficiency in our literature, namely in the departments of our early national history and the illustration of the early period of our language'.[111] The Camden published Latin texts, but it did also include early English texts, albeit many under the editorship of Wright and Halliwell, and 'we have our reasons for distrusting everything done under the superintendence of those two gentlemen, if the task demand the smallest possible amount of critical skill or acumen'.[112] Garnett's main criticism of the Camden was that it did not do enough for English philologists like himself: 'What we are most dissatisfied with is the little that has been contributed towards the illustration of the progress of our vernacular language. It was understood at the commencement that this was to form one of the Society's chief objects; and the most rational method of promoting it would seem to be the publication of the remains of our early national writers—if not of the Anglo-Saxon period, yet at all events of those from the twelfth century to the end of the fourteenth.' Garnett proceeded to animadvert against 'societies' which wilfully reneged on this lofty endeavour, preferring instead 'to pander to the corrupt taste of a frivolous and novel-reading generation'—the biblical echo reminds us that he was a parson by training, as well as one with a turn for satire.[113]

---

still numerous and respectable'; Hume, *Learned Societies and Printing Clubs*, 270, and see list of the Society's publications, 270–6.

[111] As described in an early advertisement, 'The Camden Society is instituted to perpetuate, and render accessible, whatever is valuable, but at present little known, among the materials for the Civil, Ecclesiastical, or Literary History of the United Kingdom, and it accomplishes that object by the publication of Historical Documents, Letters, Ancient Poems, and whatever else lies within the compass of its designs, in the most convenient form, and at the least possible expense, consistent with the production of useful volumes', *Notes and Queries*, 7 (177) (19 Mar. 1853), 300.

[112] Garnett, 'Antiquarian Club-Books', 117–18. Wright and Halliwell took on English, French (in which Wright was a specialist), and Latin. Garnett's collation of Latin 'Memorial Verses' (i.e. mnemonic verses) included in *Reliquiae antiquae* (i. 287–91) with the manuscript, 'which is not more difficult to read than the generality of the same period, gave a result of more than thirty gross errors of transcription by Halliwell, with as many false punctuations in the course of two pages—many of them subversive of every shadow of meaning' (p. 119). Illustrations of egregious howlers follow.

[113] Garnett, 'Antiquarian Club-Books', 118: 'Hitherto, however, works of this class have

THE ROXBURGHE CLUB AND OTHER SOCIETIES 359

Among the literary and historical book-printing clubs, the Camden Society, founded on 15 May 1838 'for the publication of Early Historical and Literary Remains', was perhaps the closest model for the EETS. The Society proposed to concentrate on publishing previously unedited manuscripts, though scarce printed books might also be included. It was remarkably successful in its early years: the membership grew rapidly. Even in its first year, its list of members approached five hundred, and it was 'widely representative of Victorian culture'.[114] The appetite for this kind of early historical and literary material thus demonstrated must have been one of the considerations behind Furnivall's decision to create the EETS. The Camden Society also provided an excellent model for the EETS to show how such a society might be successfully administered and maintain its publications list.[115] As we shall see, Furnivall was, not surprisingly, himself a member of the Camden—quite apart from its antiquarian interest, its English language publications were essential material for the Dictionary. In addition to governance and book-keeping, the Camden had to devise ways to communicate with members outside London (pending Rowland Hill's reforms of the postal system in 1839).

The Camden had institutional members as well as individuals. Enough copies of its publications were printed to supply each of its members, and the surplus was offered to the public (a principle still followed by the EETS). As a result, the Camden had to steer the same course (as the EETS still does) between rational calculation and inspired guesswork in deciding how many copies of each work should be printed. Its mistakes offered a salutary lesson.[116] It was resolved that each of its volumes should contain 'separate and distinct works without any necessary connection; so that they may be bound and arranged as most agreable to individual taste'.[117] What is more, the Camden disavowed the exclusivity and social cachet of the aristocratic clubs. Its object was to

hardly constituted one in ten of the Society's publications, and we have reason to believe that proposals to edit very valuable ones have been absolutely discouraged by leading members of the Council, on the ground that they would not suit the generality of readers.'

[114] See C. Johnson, 'The Camden Society, 1838–1938', 26.

[115] Already in 1862 Furnivall had been making enquiries of the Director, Albert Way, concerning back numbers. Way told him: 'I saw Mr John Gough Nichols last night and enquired what are the precise conditions of obtaining the volumes for some of the years past.' Letter of 26 Nov. 1862, FU 930.

[116] After several such miscalculations of the print run and falling membership the Camden Society came to an end on 2 May 1897.   [117] Johnson, 'Camden Society', 25.

perpetuate and *render accessible*, whatever is valuable, but at present little known, amongst the materials for the Civil, Ecclesiastical, or Literary History of the United Kingdom. This it accomplishes by the publication of Historical Documents, Letters, ancient Poems, and whatever else lies within the compass of the designs of the Society—in the most convenient form, and at the least possible expense, consistent with the production of useful volumes.[118]

The annual subscription was one pound, comparable with Furnivall's one guinea. It presented a complete set of each of its titles to Chetham's Library, Manchester, and another to the Marylebone Public Library, following the application of the library's Working Men's Committee.[119] The Camden's achievement was that it 'brought within the reach of scholars a series of texts of the highest historical and literary value which would otherwise have remained unpublished as being commercially unprofitable'.[120]

In its early years, the literary side of the Camden Society's work was at least as important as the historical, though later the Percy Society, the Shakespeare Society, and Furnivall's own initiatives, including the EETS, would take over much of the literary material. Indeed, there would be direct lexicographical links between the work of the EETS and the Camden. In 1865, the Camden published the third and final volume of Albert Way's edition of the fifteenth-century English-Latin bilingual dictionary, the *Promptorium Parvulorum*.[121] Way's work on the *Promptorium* gave the '*impetus* . . . to philological studies, which brought to light the scarcer *Manipulus Vocabulorum*, by Peter Levins', and the EETS would subsequently co-operate with the Camden and also the Philological Society in bringing out this complementary glossary, edited by Henry Wheatley.[122] Considerably later the EETS published

---

[118] Quoted in Hume, *Learned Societies and Printing Clubs*, 256, and see list of works published, 257–61.   [119] Johnson, 'Camden Society', 29–30.

[120] Ibid. 31.

[121] Bernard Nurse, 'Way, Albert (1805–1874)', *ODNB*. *Promptorium Parvulorum sive clericorum: Lexicon anglo-latinum princeps*, Camden Society 25 (1843), 54 (1853); 89 (1865). In addition to his antiquarian interests (he became the Director of the Society of Antiquaries, and responsible for its publications, before becoming joint secretary of the British Archaeological Association); he was a noted philologist, with knowledge of most European languages, in addition to Hebrew. For a note of Furnivall's correspondence with Way concerning the *Promptorium*, see letter from Way, 10 Nov. 1862, FU 929. The EETS later published the *Promptorium parvulorum*, ed. A. L. Mayhew, ES 102 (1908).

[122] 'This present edition . . . has been printed at the joint expense of the Early English Text Society, the Camden Society, and the Philological Society', from the Camden's preface to their edition: *Manipulus Vocabulorum*, ed. Wheatley; *Peter Levin's Manipulus Vocabulorum*, ed. Wheatley, EETS, OS 27. William J. Thoms (Secretary) to Furnivall, 7 Apr. 1866: 'I have great pleasure in acquainting you that the Council of the Camden

the *Catholicon Anglicum*, edited by Herrtage, and to which Wheatley supplied a preface, dedicated to 'Frederick James Furnivall, Esq. M. A., to whose labours in the cause of our national language . . . this volume owes so much of its value, in grateful acknowledgment of innumerable acts of kindness and help'.[123] By 1881, the publication of the *Catholicon* would be seen as a fitting tribute to pay to Furnivall, though, since Murray had by then taken over the editorship of the *OED* from Furnivall, it was probably judicious to pass over Furnivall's lexicographical work and emphasize that his contribution to the cause of the national language had been made through the formation of the EETS and other societies. Wheatley commented that 'it may be interesting to the reader to know how this work has at last got into print'. Albert Way had described the *Catholicon* in the preface to the final volume of the *Promptorium*, and Wheatley had written to Way to discover that the manuscript had been lent to him by Lord Monson. It had then been temporarily lost before it could be lent to Wheatley, who had the work copied by Edmund Brock.[124]

As Wheatley commented, the EETS had announced in its report for 1865 that the Society would be issuing a series of old English dictionaries. Shortly afterwards, Furnivall's relations with the Camden would be marred by a controversy which consolidated an important principle in Furnivall's mind as to how English texts should be edited, and it cemented his determination that the EETS should—unlike the Camden—do things properly, that is, according to his principles. The episode is also an early example of Furnivall's literary polemics, carried on in a letter to *The Athenaeum*, and written in the impromptu and aggressive style which he had developed during his campaigns in the Working Men's College. Indeed, he flouted the ordinary courtesies of gentlemanly disagreement in print to a degree which horrified members of the Camden. In 1867, the Camden published John Bargrave's account of Pope Alexander VII.[125] The Camden had not established clear principles whether original English spellings might be modernized in its editions—in this case a work of the mid- to second half of the seventeenth century. After reproducing a six-page specimen of the original, the editor had partially

---

Society . . . agreed to join the Early English Text Society in printing the Catholicon, on the same terms as the Levins, it being distinctly understood that the Text of the MS. will be strictly followed, any suggested corrections or emendations being confined to the Notes'; KCL, Furnivall Papers, 4/1/3.

[123] *Catholicon Anglicum*, ed. Herrtage and Wheatley, EETS, OS 75.
[124] Ibid., p. viii.   [125] Bargrave, *Pope Alexander the Seventh*, ed. Robertson.

modernized the rest. The result brought a howl of protest from a person signing himself merely 'M.A. Cantab.', whose concerns about the finer points of variation in seventeenth-century spelling were most relevant to a lexicographer, and who alleged the remarks of Danby Fry in the *Transactions of the Philological Society* in support of his argument. If we add to these clues the similarities of style, the hastiness, and the ruderies, there can be no doubt that 'M.A. Cantab.' was Furnivall, who, moreover, used his Cambridge degree prominently after his name in his books. And it was Furnivall who subsequently brought the motion before the Camden Society's general meeting of 2 May that 'in the Society's books the spelling of the original document be preserved, and that contractions be extended in italics'.[126] That the motion was withdrawn must have confirmed Furnivall in a determination to exert his wishes in his own Society, regardless of how things were done by the Camden. The letter deserves quotation in full:

You lately printed a letter about Bishop Percy's 'Reliques', containing the words, 'Editors are in the main a cursed meddling crew; cannot keep their fingers off texts', or some similar phrase. I desire to call your attention to a flagrant instance of this in a book which has just reached me as a member of the Camden Society. Canon Bargrave's 'Pope Alexander the Seventh and the College of Cardinals', edited by James Craigie Robertson, M.A. Canon of Canterbury. This dreadful person, instead of humbly and faithfully copying his author's manuscripts, as he was bound to do when editing a text for a body of antiquaries, has had the audacity to alter the old Canon's spellings almost throughout. He says of Dr. Bargrave's work, 'After having given in the first six pages an exact specimen of his very arbitrary spelling, I have contented myself, in the remainder of the volume, with reproducing the most remarkable of his variations from common usage, instead of copying every caprice of his pen.' I cut the passage out of my copy of the work, as it may be difficult to you to believe that any Camden editor would venture to take, or the Council of the Society allow, such liberties with a book brought out under their sanction. I do trust that when the subject is brought under their notice, the Council will stop any like impertinence for the future. 'Caprices of his pen.' Indeed!—and of a writer of 1650–80, a transition period, when the variations of spelling are very important, as some of our words were settling down into the form which they have now assumed; for instance, the old *then* into *than*, as shown by Mr. Danby P. Fry in *The Philological Society's Transactions*. No editor has any right to falsify orthographic evidence, or any other evidence that his manuscripts afford. If he is ignorant on this point, and cannot appreciate the worth of the evidence, he is bound to preserve it for those who can. If a body of antiquaries like the Camden Society lends its sanction

[126] Johnson, 'Camden Society', 35.

THE ROXBURGHE CLUB AND OTHER SOCIETIES 363

to the modernization and corruption of old forms irreparable mischief will be done. And this is why I desire to protest against the evil precedent the moment it comes under my eyes.[127]

'M.A. Cantab.', of course, had a point: ideally, original documents ought to be published by a learned society in their original spelling, and modernization of forms was especially galling to the editor of the Dictionary, whose readers were busy collecting this evidence. Yet there was real doubt as to the value of preserving the casual minutiae of a later seventeenth-century text, as compared with Old and Middle English. Another member of the Camden, who replied to his letter, also anonymously, acknowledged that the necessity of preserving 'the very form of words' served the purposes of philology, but added in a telling parenthesis 'down to a certain time'. The question which was yet to be determined was when that cut-off point was. To 'M.A. Cantab's' claim that 1650–80 was a 'transition period' (and hence important), he responded 'No doubt of it. Every period is a transition period' (but some transitions are more significant than others). Moreover, the editor had, as he pointed out, supplied a faithful transcription of six pages of the text in his Introduction.[128]

There was nothing in this legitimate difference of opinion that made it prudent for Furnivall to obscure his identity. But what really scandalized 'Another Member of the Camden Society' was not so much the matter as the manner in which a younger man, apparently knowing no better, had insulted a fellow member, a churchman, an established scholar, and a model of respectability:

Is not 'M.A. Cantab.' somewhat hasty? Instead of spoiling his copy of Canon Robertson's Camden publication, and writing off to you in a paroxysm of excitement, would it not have been better to have toned down his vehemence until he had read the book? He might then have been better able to judge of the doings of that 'dreadful person', the Editor? . . . And now a final word as to the treatment of the editor by your correspondent. It is clear that the M.A. never saw him, never before heard of him . . . Upon what literary food the M.A. has been brought up, not to be familiar with the 'History of the Christian Church' and other works of this distinguished writer, I cannot conjecture. It must have been poor windy stuff at the best.[129]

In 1857–8, Furnivall had taken up working men's rights to recreation

[127] 'Privilege of Editors', Letter of 30 Jan. 1867, *The Athenaeum*, 2 Feb. 1867, 156–7.
[128] 'Privilege of Editors', Letter of 4 Feb. 1867, *The Athenaeum*, 9 Feb. 1867, 191.
[129] Ibid. Robertson's *History of the Christian Church from the Apostolic Age to the Reformation* was regarded as a standard work; he would subsequently edit *Materials for*

and caused F. D. Maurice much grief and aggravation by his disrespect for 'parsons' and by his 'windy' rhetoric in support of the Sunday League. From Furnivall's point of view Canon Robertson's status counted for nothing when weighed in the balance with what he saw as the canon's orthographical misdemeanours and he merited a drubbing in print. However, from the Camden's point of view, someone who hid behind his modest academic qualifications did not have the licence to abandon the usual courtesies and pick public quarrels with fellow gentleman scholars. It would not be the last time that Furnivall would rush into print and make a fool of himself. At least 'M.A. Cantab.' would in future conduct his fights in the open, and he would soon be able to add an impressive list of his own editions to his Cambridge degree.

Several of these societies and clubs overlapped not only in their objectives but in their personnel. The pool of editors available was limited. For example, Madden edited for the Roxburghe, Society of Antiquaries, and Bannatyne. Furnivall, in the pre-EETS years, edited for the Roxburghe, Philological Society, and Rolls Series; later he would also edit and transcribe copiously for his own Chaucer Society. Wheatley would edit extensively for the Camden Society, as well as the EETS, initially thanks to the interests of both societies in early dictionaries. In the EETS's early years, to try and spin out the Society's meagre resources, Furnivall pursued the idea of collaborative projects with other societies and institutions.[130] It was a small world. Thomas Wright, the Secretary to the Camden Society, and one of the leading and most prolific of these scholars, was a prominent member of the Society of Antiquaries; he had edited the Chester Plays for the Shakespeare Society in the 1840s. His edition of *The Book of the Knight of La Tour-Landry* would appear in the EETS in 1868, after which his interests turned decisively towards archaeology and antiquities, and away from the philological tastes he had acquired from association with J. M. Kemble in Trinity College Cambridge, of which Wright, too, was an alumnus.[131]

the History of Archbishop Thomas Becket, 6 vols., for the Rolls Series (1875–82). W. H. Fremantle, revd. G. Martin Murphy, 'Robertson, James Craigie (1813–1882)', *ODNB*.

[130] As well as Camden, report was made of 'an arrangement which the Committee hope to make with the Delegates of the Oxford University Press as to the Early Dictionary Series', whereby 'the cost to the Society of these books will be much lessened'; Prospectus, 1864.

[131] *The Book of the Knight of La Tour-Landry*, ed. Wright, EETS, OS 33. His associate, Hallliwell, had edited the N-Town Plays in 1841; the Surtees Society had put out an edition of the Towneley Mysteries, by James Raine and Joseph Stevenson, in 1836. On Wright, see also Skeat, *Student's Pastime*, pp. lx–lxii.

The avalanche of learned societies, which began in the 1830s, and which gained momentum from the 1840s onwards, attested to the developing interest, growing out of a taste for curiosities which was becoming increasingly well informed, among Victorian gentlemen—they were mostly gentlemen—in their national language, history, cultural and literary monuments, and antiquities. And, as the various Scottish and regional societies also showed, this interest was local as well as national. The two could be complementary: Garnett especially commended the Surtees Society, 'both on account of the liberality of its constitution and the general value of its work', though 'we must remember that the society was organized for local purposes and with a restricted sphere of work'. Nevertheless, it had produced a text of the Towneley Plays, which was a northern text, albeit one of undoubted national importance.[132] Local patriotism flourished alongside a broader sense of the importance of material illustrative of early customs, education, and social mores, often epitomized in documents pertaining to early drama. Shakespeare and Shakespeariana were never far away.

The EETS, and Furnivall's other enterprises, were rooted in this culture where colourful personalities abounded: Furnivall copied what he saw as the best features of the existing societies. By virtue of his sheer ebullience and energy, Furnivall came to dominate the scene in the second half of the nineteenth century, but he and his publishing ventures were not essentially new. Yet it is nonetheless clear from Garnett's testimony that the EETS filled a gap, being aimed at a wide audience, editing texts of national significance, and devoted entirely to the English vernacular. What would be new, though again not entirely without precedent, was Furnivall's creation of societies dedicated to the study of a particular author: Chaucer, Shelley, Browning, Wyclif (and there were tentative efforts to set up societies for Hoccleve and Lydgate), which Furnivall intended would come to an end after they had essentially done their work. What is distinctive about Furnivall's creations is summed up by his 'New Shakspere Society'. It was aggressively 'new' and thus

---

[132] 'Antiquarian Club-Books', 116: 'On many accounts therefore we are wellwishers of the "Surtees," and would gladly see it organized on a broad basis, and in the receipt of an income adequate to more extensive operations', 117. See A. W. Pollard's appraisal of the Surtees edition, as 'on the whole, very creditably accurate... though it was not, however, a transcript with which students of the present day could be content in the case of a unique manuscript, the ultimate destination of which is still, unhappily, uncertain'. *The Towneley Plays, Re-edited from the unique MS*, EETS, ES 71, p. ix. The manuscript was owned at this time by Bernard Quaritch, before its sale in 1900 to Sir Robert Eden Coates, who sold it by auction in 1922 to the Huntington Library; *The Towneley Plays*, ed. Stevens and Cawley, EETS, SS 13, pp. xv–xvi. See further Levine, *The Antiquary and the Professional*, 41.

thumbed its metaphorical nose at the old guard of Halliwell, Wright, Collier, *et al.*; its spelling of 'Shakspere' (though recommended also by Madden)[133] was similarly provocative and expressive of the founder's incapacity even when professing to take a back seat to do so, or to refrain from scoring points in what he regarded as a right cause. The EETS, too, though less strident, was to be a kind of 'new' Roxburghe. It was intended to be socially progressive, as was only to be expected of an associate of the Working Men's College.

ADMONISHMENT OF THE UPPER CLASSES: 'HANDLYNG SYNNE'

Furnivall's editing career began with the recommendations of Sir Frederic Madden to edit Robert Mannyng of Brunne's *Handlyng Synne*,[134] while he was simultaneously editing the *Early English Poems* for the Philological Society. Mannyng, whose origins were in Brunne, now Bourne, Lincolnshire, was a Gilbertine canon, writing in the first half of the fourteenth century. *Handlyng Synne* was intended as a practical handbook to assist lay people making confession—like other such penitential compendia, it offered much social commentary, including exemplary stories, and thus it commended itself to antiquarians interested in medieval daily life. Madden pointed out that, because *Handlyng Synne* was a translation of a French treatise, William of Waddington's *Le Manuel des pechiez*, an editor would have the great advantage, as Madden had found for himself when editing *Havelok*, of having a source text to which to refer. The scarcity of authoritative dictionaries and other study aids made it sensible for the pioneer editors of early English to edit texts which were themselves translations. Furnivall, however, was more interested in the French source for what it could reveal about the supposed originality of the English writer, and he ascribed all the merits of social observation to Mannyng, whose 'individualising touches' showed that, in Furnivall's view, 'he had studied from the life'.[135] Furnivall's entrée to the Roxburghe came through the Philological Society. One of the ordinary members of its Council was Beriah Botfield, MP for Ludlow, member of learned

---

[133] Madden, 'Observations on an Autograph of Shakspere, and the Orthography of his Name', *Archaeologia*, 27 (1 Jan. 1838), 113–23.

[134] *Roberd of Brunne's Handlyng Synne*, ed. Furnivall. Later issued by the EETS: *Robert of Brunne's 'Handlyng Synne', A.D. 1303*, re-ed. Furnivall, EETS, OS 119, 123.

[135] *Handlyng Synne*, p. ix, and see pp. xiv–xv.

societies, including the Roxburghe, and, at different times its treasurer and secretary.[136]

When he began work, Furnivall naturally consulted other titles in the Roxburghe series, especially the edition of another, comparable, penitential handbook, this one completed in 1340 by the Kentish monk Dan Michel of Northgate, and known as the *Ayenbite of Inwyt* ('Remorse of Conscience'), edited by Joseph Stevenson.[137] Furnivall began by pointing out that both writers deliberately chose to write in English 'for lewde men'—untaught lay people. The implication, though not stated explicitly, is clear: Robert of Brunne's work appealed to Furnivall because it was an early illustration of the same kind of educational initiative for which the Working Men's College had been founded. The *Ayenbite* and *Handlyng Synne* were also illustrations of the growing importance of the English vernacular amidst what a writer for *The Saturday Review* had called 'the howling wilderness of French and Latin'.[138] The editor describes himself on the title page as 'Frederick J. Furnivall, Esq. M.A., of Trinity Hall, Cambridge, and the Working Men's College, London; Captain 19th Middlesex Rifle Volunteers; One of the Honorary Secretaries of the Philological Society'. The unusual credentials (which are carefully chosen to delineate an educated gentleman democrat, an officer in a largely working-class movement created to defend Britain against the French, and at the same time an officer of a respectable learned society), advertise loudly that this will be no ordinary Roxburghe book.

Madden had told Furnivall that 'this work of R. Brunne's was one of the most, if not the most, valuable Early English Poem in his Department unprinted'. Furnivall wanted to edit a poem—this was the beginning of his interest in metre—and, for the sake of the Dictionary, it should be one in early Middle English. So far, perhaps, so dull. Yet Furnivall was surprised by *Handlyng Synne*'s capacity to entertain him: 'I read the first page or two of it, and was so amused by the Tale of the Witch and her Cow-Sucking Bag, &c., that I copied eleven hundred lines to try whether the interest of the book continued.'[139] Mannyng's achievement was to preach 'in an unboring way'.[140] And Furnivall liked what he inferred about the author: 'Of our Roberd's personal qualities

---

[136] *TPS* 7, no. 1 (1860), 303–11, 'Notices of the Meetings of the Philological Society in 1860–1 (pp. 305, 309). Pettigrew, *Memoir of Beriah Botfield*.

[137] *The Ayenbite of inwyt*, ed. Stevenson.

[138] Quoted by Levine, *The Amateur and the Professional*, 79.

[139] *Handlyng Synne*, p. xxii. [140] Ibid., p. ix.

we must judge from his books.'¹⁴¹ 'Our Robert', as recreated in Furnivall's imagination, helped out by Thomas Hearne's verdict on the man,¹⁴² was, in effect, a fourteenth-century Christian Socialist: 'A man of a beautiful spirit he seems to me; witness his "love of simple men" (p. iv. L. 77), his "luf of þe lewed men" (p. v. l. 126)', and 'his deep sympathy with the poor.'¹⁴³ Though handicapped by his 'monkery', Robert Mannyng was sufficiently manly to praise a good wife: 'Ne no þyng ys to man so dere As wommanys loue yn gode manere.'¹⁴⁴ Furnivall had himself recently married, and the extended quotation also serves as a tacit compliment to his own wife. Despite monastic vows of celibacy, Furnivall's 'Robert' was in many ways a man in his own ideal image: 'an appreciator of good company, and a lover of music . . . hating false pride . . . liking plain speech . . . knowing the difference between a gentleman in deed and a lord in name . . . aware that kings are fools, as well as other people . . . Also a man who will not take shamming excuses . . . Altogether a direct, straightforward, practical man, with many right sympathies, working in a sensible way for the improvement of his fellow countrymen, teaching them Morals and History.'¹⁴⁵ Robert also seemed to Furnivall 'the worthiest forerunner of Chaucer': a 'cheery dear old man, who so loved women, and the "glad light green" of Spring'.¹⁴⁶ This was, indeed, a model on which Furnivall would form his own persona in later life, as his friends, like Alois Brandl, professor of philology at Berlin, remarked: 'With Chaucer he literally lived on terms of personal friendship. Chaucer's character, indeed, was perhaps most closely analogous to his own.'¹⁴⁷

But, as a young man, Furnivall was most drawn to the evidence of Robert Mannyng's social conscience (apart from Robert's admonitions to his readers on the merit of giving gifts to the Church for the good of their souls). On the oppression of the poor by the wealthy and well-born 'he speaks out nobly and well', and his remarks provided Furnivall with the opportunity for a lengthy disquisition on comparable modern evils. It was extended considerably beyond the usual drawing of lessons from the past to become a means to air the grievances of working

---

[141] Ibid., p. viii. [142] Quoted ibid., p. ix.
[143] Ibid., p. viii.
[144] Ibid., p. viii. Furnivall also acknowledged Robert's 'frequent lecturing of and against women' (p. xi). [145] Ibid., pp. ix–x.
[146] Ibid., p. iv.
[147] Munro (ed.), *Frederick James Furnivall*, 11. On Furnivall's ideas of Chaucer's congenial character, extrapolated from the Hoccleve portrait of the poet, see further Matthews, 'Speaking to Chaucer', 6.

ADMONISHMENT OF THE UPPER CLASSES 369

people in the nineteenth century and gain the ear of the Liberal and liberal Conservative political class (he could be confident that some of his readers would be sympathetic, and the rest would, presumably, be none the worse for a bit of plain speaking by honest Frederick Furnivall). It seems clear that he was influenced by, and attempting to imitate, Carlyle's *Past and Present* (first published 1843). Carlyle had powerfully evoked the capacity of historical records in modern editions to offer authentic eyewitness glimpses of medieval events, and redeem them from 'dryasdust' history books, and his character-study of the twelfth-century monk Jocelin of Brakelonde ('a cheery-hearted, innocent, yet withal shrewd, noticing, quick-witted man') anticipates Furnivall's essays in this genre.[148] Needless to say, Furnivall went far beyond the conventions and courtesies of a Roxburghe volume:

> When one thinks of the 'Condition of England' question since, of the causes of the Mining and Factory Acts, the *Morning Chronicle* Letters on 'Labour and the Poor', of the Game-Laws, the Law of Settlement, and what comes of them, there is little wonder that in modern times we can match the old monk's indignation, and produce a clergyman and poet's Curse by a Poacher's Widow, 'A Rough Rhyme on a Rough Matter' in *Yeast*, Mrs Browning's 'Cry of the Children', and many a denunciation from teachers cleric and lay of the special selfishness, neglect, and sin, of our rich and titled men; nor is one surprised that even an anti-democratic Journal should denounce 'the long adherence to all political injustice of our gentry'.[149]

If any of the Roxburghe's members had taken up these suggestions for further reading they would have been in for a surprise. In addition to Charles Kingsley and Elizabeth Barrett Browning, Furnivall drags in mention of three articles in the *Saturday Review*; all three, if the Roxburghe reader is prepared to chase them up, say a great deal about Furnivall himself and his trains of thought. Articles in the *Saturday* were anonymous, and it would not be surprising if, indeed, Furnivall wrote them himself. He had means, motive, and opportunity, and the short form of an article suited him perfectly—he was never comfortable with extended writing. Most of the *Saturday*'s writers were, like him, well-educated young men, to be found among London barristers and graduates of Oxford and Cambridge, especially the latter, who regarded

---

[148] Carlyle, *Past and Present*, ed. Traill, 41: 'Our Jocelin, for the rest, has read his classical manuscripts, his Virgilius, his Flaccus, Ovidius Naso; of course, still more, his Homilies and Breviaries, and if not the Bible, considerable extracts of the Bible. Then also he has a pleasant wit; and loves a timely joke, though in a mild subdued manner.'

[149] *Handlyng Synne*, p. xi.

journalism as an exciting way to influence public opinion. They were not professional journalists, and they knew each other. The newspaper's political stance was, though not radical, supportive of co-operation and trades unions.[150]

The first article to which Furnivall referred his readers was evidently written by a firebrand, as well as staunch democrat, and it is a piece of propaganda to persuade the gentry to come forward as officers in the civilian Volunteer regiments, rather than those of the regular army in which they would traditionally serve: 'The natural defence of a free country ... is its militia, officered by the upper classes', not a standing army. 'Our gentry have now a fair chance of redeeming some portion of that national respect and influence which they must in their cooler moments be aware that they have forfeited by a long adherence to all political injustice, by their selfish resistance and ignominious defeat in the matter of the Corn Laws, and by the degradation into which, as a political party, they have since been dragged.' The expression of his hostility to the Conservative party is arresting in a journal which the writer called 'anti-democratic'. Its core readers were liberal Conservatives, who sought an alternative to *The Times*. The writer of the article, however, offers gentlemen a chance of redemption: 'Here is an occasion on which the people will be rejoiced to see them at its head, and on which it is their bounden duty to put themselves at the head of the people. By doing so they will revive the only Conservatism that has any life left.' And the gentry's passion for hunting, even if joined with fine dining and idleness, is an optimistic sign: 'fortunately ... their pleasures are of the manliest kind, and they are capable of becoming first-rate officers'. If they do not, they should remember that the Roundheads won in the past, and 'the nation will seek its salvation in the fierce energy of a revolutionary government'.

The writer expanded the theme. The Volunteer movement had been created as a response to fear of French invasion. If this happened, and the social classes did not pull together to resist it, 'the ebbing waves of conquest will leave England a Republic, and the peasants Lords of the land'.[151] The salvific rhetoric, with its call to secular repentance, re-

---

[150] See further Bevington, *The Saturday Review 1855–1868*, 1–2, 13, 26–7, 40–2, 60–4; 'It is not unfair to think of their weekly effusions as the resultant opinions of the best informed conversational circles of the time, sharpened into literary form' (p. 53). See also the list of contributors, where these can be established or conjectured, 331–91. They included Furnivall's friend the historian Charles Henry Pearson, who wrote for the paper in 1856–9, and again in 1861.

[151] Quotations from 'Our Natural Defences', *The Saturday Review of Politics, Literature,*

inforced by an echo of the Book of Common Prayer, with the hope of manly self-redemption in a vision of harmonious relations between aristocracy and working men, of course describes Furnivall's credo, and the excitable social analysis is also his. Though Charles Kingsley, especially in his younger days, and Thomas Hughes (himself an officer of the 19th Middlesex) were likely to have approved the general thesis, they were neither of them likely to play the *sans culotte* (Kingsley especially with his aversion to truculent eccentricity). If not by Furnivall, the article was, at the very least, by someone in his circle from a similarly educated background and with identical views. The reference to the article in *Handlyng Synne* is deliberately jarring but was as far as Furnivall could go in that space to let off the political steam which he had stored up in accepting the commission from this book club for wealthy grandees. (One suspects it was also a sop to his conscience.) Its anonymity, like 'M.A. Cantab.'s' attack on the Camden Society two years earlier, shows that Furnivall—if it were he—was not yet brave, or foolhardy, enough for direct confrontation, though in neither case can the writer be mistaken for anything other than a gentleman himself. For all their swaggering, neither the article in the *Saturday* nor the Roxburghe edition is truly revolutionary: both are testimonies to Furnivall's belief that the social divide could be bridged, and that he was a privileged interpreter of the poor to those much richer and more socially secure than he was. And whose bounden duty it was to support him. In the circumstances, his ostentatious description of himself on the title page of the Roxburghe edition as 'Captain 19th Middlesex Rifle Volunteers', takes on an extra meaning, roughly 'Go, and do thou likewise'.

The remaining two references to the *Saturday Review* continue the theme of Napoleon III's aggression and threatened invasion of Britain as a lesson to English readers. And, in the edition, too, Furnivall gets in some other hits. Robert Mannyng remarkably anticipated the 'agitation for the Saturday Half-holiday, of late so wisely revived for other ends'. This was an outrageous sideswipe at clergymen like Maurice, who would have recognized this fourteenth-century priest's wish that his people might keep Saturday afternoons holy, not spend them in worldly amusement. This aside is a preface to Furnivall's comment on Mannyng's iteration of the saying that the leading sin of the French is lechery and that of the English envy, as an 'especially English' observation 'in contrast with foreign customs'. This leads to Furnivall's

Science, and Art, 8, no. 196 (30 July 1859), 121. For the *Saturday's* hostility to Napoleon III, see Bevington, *Saturday Review*, 64.

account of the equivalent vices and virtues of the two countries in the nineteenth century, especially in the garish light of the French Emperor's recent victory over the Austrians at Magenta (4 June 1859), in which the casualties were 'equal perhaps to the whole population of Winchester'.[152] Furnivall stretches 'envy' to include 'invidia vulgi': popular dissatisfaction—expressed in grumbling—'at want of political justice and ability in their Rulers'.[153] But grumbling is a safety valve, contrasted with the notorious volatility of the French, which 'may at least teach us to value as it deserves, that inestimable habit of grumbling which has done more to preserve the English nation from exposing itself than any other quality'. Furnivall shared the philosophy of stoic acceptance and abstention from mere (French) sentimentality said to be English virtues: 'to see things as they are, and to speak of them as we see them, to despise all cant, and to avoid all brag, are some of the most important duties of man'. Indeed, Furnivall approvingly quotes this passage in a footnote.[154] Since the review he cites concerns the political writing and popular novels of 'Madame Dudevant', better known as George Sand, his comments are also covert praise for manly seriousness expressed in rugged plain early English, saying it as it is, reflected in the reading taste of the Roxburghe Club's male membership, rather than popular sentimental fiction.[155]

This seriousness derived, in Furnivall's view, from a landed gentleman's proper education: 'No one is fit to be the owner of a considerable estate who is altogether ignorant of Law, of political economy, or of the rudiments of military discipline', all of them kinds of knowledge which Furnivall had been at pains to acquire himself as a young man.[156] The advice recalls Furnivall's later comments about the education of the gentry in Elizabethan times, previously noted in the present study in connection with his own upbringing. In a strained bit of rhetorical ingenuity, to get across his political agenda, Furnivall notes that if 'envy' in the sense of 'grumbling' can be read as an English virtue, so can absence of envy. The *Saturday* also featured yet another comparison of

[152] Review, 'Madame Dudevant on the War', *Saturday Review*, 7, no. 189 (11 June 1859), 716–17 at 717. The writer is emphatic that lamentation for the tragedies of war is to be kept firmly in check. Furnivall's interest in the article reflects his taste for reading about military campaigns. *Handlyng Synne*, pp. xii–xiii at xii.

[153] Ibid., p. xiii.

[154] 'Madame Dudevant on the War', 717; *Handlyng Synne*, p. xiii.

[155] 'Madame Dudevent on the War', 717: 'She portrays a young man who seduces a woman merely for the sake of having something to be sentimental and melancholy about.'

[156] 'The Revue des deux mondes on French Politics', *Saturday Review*, 8, no. 197 (6 Aug. 1859), 159–60 at 159.

English and French politics which returns Furnivall's readers yet again to the duties of their class, and the potential for class hostility. Furnivall again ventriloquizes, if not himself, someone very like him:

> In some particulars, English country gentlemen are in an invidious position, and if it were not for that noble absence of envy which is a characteristic, equally creditable and peculiar of the English nation, they would probably be exposed to a considerable degree of odium; but they have it in their power to destroy any inclination towards this feeling by making it their occupation and their point of honour to do gratuitously for England what the swarms of préfets, sous-préfets, procureurs de l'empereur, &c. are paid to do for France.[157]

The form of this freely given service for England is predictable: 'If the country gentlemen did their duty, we should have a militia, a yeomanry, and a system of volunteer corps which, without endangering the liberties of the country, would absolutely secure it against invasion.'[158]

Thus, Furnivall found that the élite Club could—with a bit of ingenuity and much self-assurance—give him a space for his inveterate fondness for autobiography, scoring points, preaching social causes, and didacticism in the service of editing. His Roxburghe prefaces mark the origins of his cultivation in print of the unmistakable Furnivall persona. Yet, although the Roxburghe editions had originated as wealthy bibliophiles' *bonnes bouches*, Madden had shown what could be done in the way of serious scholarship within their pages. Furnivall took his task of describing the manuscripts and their contents seriously, as well as giving his readers, most of whom must be presumed to be unfamiliar with Middle English, the help they would need in appreciating this pre-Chaucerian text. *Handlyng Synne* was printed with Waddington's French source in parallel columns. Of course, this was to show that Mannyng was no mere translator, but it is also likely that readers would have found the French a helpful way of tracking the English, in the manner of side notes. Furnivall knew readers could reasonably expect a glossary and explanatory notes. He explained that he had laid the text aside for nearly two years 'in the hope that I might find time', for which 'have the spare hours of my last Long Vacation sufficed . . . I dare not detain this book longer.'[159] A list of words had been 'half made by my late able friend Herbert Coleridge', but did not include the latter part of the text. Instead of notes, Furnivall expended his energy on devising an elaborate summary of contents, with a list of the chapter

[157] Ibid.   [158] Ibid.
[159] *Handlyng Synne*, p. xxv.

headings and an index.[160] It is likely that many readers read the list of contents first, and with more care than the text itself; each part of the text is fully paraphrased, and carefully signposts where the material can be found in the original. The abstract draws attention to Mannyng's *narrationes*, or exemplary stories, which were the main attractions in a penitential text.[161] Furnivall also felt it his duty to describe how the text being edited had been found—the Roxburghe bibliophiles liked stories of literary discoveries, and this was an exciting time, as 'finds' were turning up in the manuscript libraries. He also described how he had pursued these finds, as well as what he thought about them, under the guise of describing their literary merit. Though he was influenced by the precedents established by previous titles, Furnivall was given *carte blanche* in his decisions on what editorial and ancillary matter to include. Because *Handlyng Synne* was printed at the Club's expense, rather than being a presentation copy by one of its members, Furnivall had no single patron to gratify, or who might censor him.

Indeed, Furnivall had insisted from the beginning on having a free hand in editing *Handlyng Synne*. He had intended it for the Philological Society, but, as he told the story, after Mannyng had passed Furnivall's personal test and continued to amuse him for eleven hundred lines, he had approached Beriah Botfield, in charge of the Roxburghe publications, and offered 'to edit the work for the Roxburghe Club gratis, if the Club would let Mr. SEELEY copy the rest of it, for it was too long for the Philological'.[162] Harry Govier Seeley was his protégé from the Working Men's College, where he had studied English and mathematics (and curated its geological collection). He was supporting himself at this time by copying work in the British Museum. On Furnivall's recommendation, he would, soon after 1859, be taken on by Adam Sedgwick, professor of geology at Cambridge, as an assistant in the Woodwardian Museum.[163] Because of Furnivall's characteristic interest in his author's

---

[160] In addition, appendices present information on Mannyng's sources, and comparable extracts from his Chronicle, the *Ayenbite*, and some other items of interest.

[161] Listed, *Handlyng Synne*, pp. xv–xvii.   [162] Ibid., p. xxii.

[163] See J. A. Secord, 'Harry Govier Seeley (1839–1909)', *ODNB*, also letter of Adam Sedgwick to Furnivall of 2 Sept. 1859, FU 799. Iinitially Sedgwick dithered, attracted by the prospect of the services of a 'zealous young naturalist', but not sure he could pay for one out of his salary. However, 'The account you give of him astonishes me; and were I a man of fortune I should probably secure his services for a year or two'. Seeley's father, a goldsmith, had gone bankrupt, and Seeley as a child was sent to learn pianoforte-making; his uncle paid to have him trained for the bar, where he felt himself to be one of the 'great unwashed'. He would progress to become professor of geography and geology, first at Queen Mary's College, and subsequently King's College, London.

originality, he decided that the French must be included for comparison, and Seeley copied that too, 'I helping occasionally'. (Such luxuries could be afforded by the Roxburghe Club.) Seeley's industry prompts the reflection: who was editing these texts? Seeley, or Furnivall? Furnivall anticipates this, and, in doing so, maintains the distance between copyist and gentleman editor: 'Either the copy or the proof I read with both English and French MSS. In the British Museum and at Oxford collated about three-fifths of the English text with the Bodleian copy of it; the rest of it was collated for the Club by Mr. GEORGE PARKER of the Bodleian Library, who took great pains about it.'[164] Both manuscripts of *Handlyng Synne* also contained copies of the early fourteenth-century 'Meditations on the Supper of Our Lord', which Seeley offered to copy for the Club 'without cost to them, as an Appendix to this volume, but Mr. Botfield preferred that the "Handlyng Synne" should appear by itself'.[165] When, much later, Furnivall re-edited *Handlyng Synne* for the EETS, he retained the French text, 'tho' this is against the Early English Text Society's custom—imposed on it by its poverty'. But the cost was met on this occasion by a gift of over £200 from the Furnivall Commemoration Fund, 'raisd for the editor's 75th birthday on Feb. 4, 1899'.[166]

An ongoing anxiety haunted Furnivall in this 'freshman's first performance', as he called it:[167] the problem of whether scribal flourishes at the end of words indicated the abbreviation of a final -e which the editor should accordingly supply, or whether they were just ornamental. Later he would ignore them, but here 'one mistake that I know I made' was supplying final -e after words ending in -d.[168] 'I am sorry that,

---

[164] *Handlyng Synne*, p. xxii. Parker was one of the Bodleian's clerks, whom Furnivall would use extensively in the future for paid transcription work in Oxford.

[165] *Handlyng Synne*, p. xxiii. The *Meditations*'s appearance in the same manuscripts as *Handlyng Synne* gave rise to the view that Mannyng was also the translator of this pseudo-Bonaventuran text, though it is 'probably not by him'. See Raymond G. Biggar, 'Mannyng, Robert [Robert Mannyng of Brunne] (d. in or after 1338)', *ODNB*. The Roxburghe's loss was the EETS's gain: the 'Meditations' would be edited by Furnivall's friend Joseph Meadows Cowper, *Meditations on the Supper of our Lord*, EETS, OS 60. Despite the confident title, Cowper himself claimed more modestly that Mannyng is 'probably the author' (p. xiii). He was persuaded by the verdict of Thomas Laurence Kington Oliphant, who read the proof, and asserted 'I think there is no doubt that the "Soper" must have been compiled by Robert of Brunne' (p. xvii), arguing from similarities of expression (pp. xvii–xviii; see also p. xiii). See also Kington Oliphant, *The Sources of Standard English*, 196.

[166] *Robert of Brunne's 'Handlyng Synne'*, ed. Furnivall, EETS, OS, 119, 123, i. half-title verso. [167] Ibid., p. xxv.

[168] 'This was partly owing to my being misled by a theory of an Editor of many Early

when correcting the copy, I did not know of the sensible plan I have since seen adopted, of printing all expansions of contractions in italics' (pp. xxiii–xiv)—a custom which would haunt the EETS for many decades afterwards. Final -*e* mattered when editing poetry, and Furnivall added a dotted *ë* to make up Mannyng's octosyllabic lines. 'Having been greatly bored myself by the want of these *ë*'s—their absence allowing one so frequently to read a line wrong and thus forcing one to try back and read it over again—I hoped to save readers of this text the like annoyance.'[169] Furnivall's common sense warned him against forcing the text: 'the endeavour to be uniform and get the same eight syllables into every line, has in some cases spoilt the rhythm . . . However, I trust that in most instances the dotting will be a help. When it is not, the reader can at least relieve his mind by such exclamations against me and my dots as he thinks proper.'[170] He reiterated here the caution against adding hypothetical -*es* which the anonymous critic in the *Gentleman's Magazine* had thought Pauli *should* have included in his Gower.[171] But 'the handiest edition of Chaucer . . . has been made symmetrical, or cooked, in accordance with this *e* theory; and we have still to desire a satisfactory edition of the Father of English verse'.[172] This inferior, 'cooked' edition was said to have been 'edited' for J. W. Parker and Son by Robert Bell and an unnamed 'young clergyman', whom though as yet unfamiliar to Furnivall, would soon be better known as W. W. Skeat, at this time in his twenties and ten years younger than Furnivall.[173] By the time the edition was revised in 1878–80, Furnivall had changed his tune: 'If only all professors of English literature and writers of articles on Chaucer

English books, that wherever in Anglo-Saxon there would have been an inflection of a word (and in certain other cases), there in Early-English, before 1400, you will find, or ought to put, a final *e*.' As Furnivall told this editor to his face, 'I undertake to prove it wrong from every Early-English text you have yourself edited' (*Handlyng Synne*, pp. xxiii–xxiv). He seems likely to have been Richard Morris.

[169] *Handlyng Synne*, p. xxiv. [170] Ibid.
[171] Ibid. [172] Ibid., pp. xxiv–xxv.
[173] This was Thomas Wright's text, which, despite poor reviews of Wright's work, Robert Bell published in four volumes, 1854–6, in his popular series of English authors. Skeat's association with the work probably explains his 'curious' later reprinting of it in 1878, prefaced by his 'Preliminary Essay'. See Ross, 'Thomas Wright', 154. Furnivall's praise is directed towards Skeat's 'boldly putting all the spurious poems . . . in an Appendix', as 'an outward and visible sign . . . of the inward conviction that we Chaucerians have for years been working to bring about, and it will, I hope, soon convert that chief sinner in this matter, who, in a well-known London College and many provincial lecture-rooms, still confuses his pupils' minds . . . by giving them "mixtelyn" for the pure flour of Chaucer's brain'. 'Mixtelyn' is 'middling' flour (i.e. of intermediate grade, still containing bran); *OED*, 'middling', n. 2b. Furnivall appears to derive it from 'mixed'.

could be endowed with Mr. Skeat's clear common-sense, critical power, and knowledge of the English language in all its stages, from Beowulf to Shakspere, Chaucer's memory and genius would soon be cleared from all the rubbish which old printers and editors heaped round it.'[174]

Despite its ostentatious idiosyncrasies, Furnivall's edition of *Handlyng Synne* was impressive as a first effort—Munro thought it one of his best texts 'if only he had printed the best manuscript of it'.[175] And it was additionally impressive when one remembers that he was also working on, or contemplating, at least two other Roxburghe editions: Lovelich's Grail romance in two volumes, 'and one of Merlin, (possibly also the hitherto unknown Romance *Syr Generides*)',[176] cramming as much literary work as possible into the Long Vacations.

'ROSE-PINK NOTIONS': FURNIVALL AND KING ARTHUR

Thanks to these other importunities, which overlapped in his mind, and not forgetting the Dictionary, Furnivall was not always fully able to stick to what he was supposed to be doing at any one time. *Handlyng Synne*, for example, included as an appendix the entirely irrelevant 'few Characteristic Bits out of R. Brunne's Account of Arthur, the readers of my edition of the St. Graal will excuse me for extracting'.[177] The readers were given no choice: coming upon 'some bits about Arthur which I chanced to hit on in the Inner Temple MS', he 'could not resist copying' them.[178]

Later in life Furnivall told Alois Brandl that he had been inspired by Tennyson's 'Morte d'Arthur', published in 1842, when Furnivall was an impressionable 17-year-old.[179] Tennyson would revise the 'Morte' as

[174] Review: 'Poetical Works of Geoffrey Chaucer; with Poems formerly Printed with his or Attributed to him', *The Academy*, no. 312 (27 Apr. 1878), 365.

[175] Munro, 'Biography', p. xlvi.

[176] *Handlyng Synne*, p. xxv. See also letter to Bradshaw, 19 May 1866: 'I'm very grateful to you for having found out that Sir Generides has been printed, and so preventing me getting myself and the friend who was going to pay for its printing, into a scrape. Your printed text has all the names of the MS, and tho' I have not been able to find the passage yet, I have no doubt at all that the text and MS are the same Romance. But it's odd that neither Madden, nor any of the learned in such matters to whom I have spoken about the Romance, even heard of it. What is the printed title, and where was the book published?' CUL MS Add. 2591, 213.

[177] *Handlyng Synne*, pp. xxxviii–xli. These were extracts from the chronicle.

[178] Ibid., p. vii.

[179] 'I have it on Furnivall's authority that this beautiful fragment, the true centre of the Arthurian epic, first kindled in him the flame of his enthusiasm for the older literature'; quoted in Munro (ed.), *Frederick James Furnivall*, 11.

'The Passing of Arthur' in *The Idylls of the King*, of which publication began in 1859—exactly when Furnivall was editing the *Holy Graal*. He was to tire of Tennyson's romanticism in favour of Browning, but at this early stage of his career Furnivall was thrilled, even while he was being increasingly drawn to scientific and rational explanations of natural phenomena. Back in 1851, his reading of *The Princess*, coupled with copying out poems for the *Christian Socialist*, had even inspired him to attempt to write poetry himself after a crowded day which summed up his intellectual and social interests at this time. He received 'a very fine letter from Mrs Gaskell; at 4.30 to Cousin George's with the "7 Lamps," (Store meeting at 7.30), to Mrs. Ruskin & had long chat with her; to the Tailors' Association; talked to Cooper, Field, and Ballard (from Southampton) ... at 9 to Mr Maurice's, 'tea'read Genesis &c. ... wrote to Mrs Gaskell; read the Princess, tried to write verses.'[180]

Tennyson's 'Morte' is mystic and wonderful enough on its own account to have turned the young Furnivall's head. And it is likely to have had an additional meaning for him as a young man in his twenties, prefaced as it originally was by the framing poem 'The Epic' (dropped in the later *Idylls*). 'The Epic' contrasts the literary excitements of the past with a modern parson's soporific jeremiad, which takes in 'church commissioners ... geology and schism ... the general decay of faith', before Tennyson's speaker modestly ushers in the 'Morte' as a token effort in a more romantic and soul-stirring direction. He alleges that it is the sole surviving remnant of an Arthurian epic written and subsequently destroyed by a bashful college friend. Tennyson used this fiction as a way of distancing himself from an archaizing heroic style perhaps unfitted to the nineteenth century, much as the tyro, Furnivall, had also found the experiment impossible. Tennyson was more eloquent:

> For nature brings not back the mastodon,
> Nor we those times. (ll. 35–6)[181]

Now, almost ten years later, Furnivall still could not resist the appeal of Excalibur's hilt glittering in the winter moonlight, any more than could the dying Arthur's companion, Sir Bedivere. Throwing it away was a romantic extravagance which the teenage Furnivall could appreciate, though the whole tenor of his later life was to agree with Bedivere that the sword was an antique relic which could have spoken eloquently to later ages if only it had been kept in a museum. In Furnivall's case,

---

[180] Diary entry for Tuesday. 4 Mar. 1851, Bodl. MS Eng e. 2316, f. 17ᵛ.
[181] *Poems of Tennyson*, ii. 1–2.

romantic relics came in the form of Arthuriana in medieval manuscripts, and the museum would be the British Museum. Contemporaries identified Tennyson's Arthur with Prince Albert, and it is probably not merely fortuitous that the first volume of the *Holy Graal* was published in the year of the Prince's death in 1861.[182]

Inevitably Furnivall came to the Grail story having read Malory:

> There can be few readers of "The Most Ancient and Famovs History of the Renowned Prince Arthvr King of Britaine," who have not been deeply affected by the legend of Galahad and the Graal. On the dark background of Arthur's incest, Lancelot and Guenevere's, Tristram and Iseult's, guilty loves, the star of Galahad's chastity shines out pure and clear, and draws one to it with the powers of fascination. In its centre, the focal light whence its beams of glory flow, is the mystic object of the hero's love and search, the source of his purity, the cause of his strength,—the HOLY Grail.[183]

But he did not only read Malory. Furnivall's preface begins with an epigraph from Tennyson's 'Sir Galahad' (1842), so well known that he felt no need to reference it—if Furnivall's soul was stirred by Arthuriana, so was just about everyone else's. His friend Holman Hunt had illustrated 'The Lady of Shalott'.[184] Hunt's second illustration of this subject appeared in the lavish 1857 illustrated edition of Tennyson by Edward Moxon, which also included work by the other principal Pre-Raphaelite artists, including Millais. Between 1857 and 1859, despite Ruskin's reserve about their ambition to paint frescoes, the Pre-Raphaelites had additionally been engaged on the decoration of the Oxford Union with Arthurian scenes: adorning 'a monument to adolescent self-importance', as Hilton has described it.[185] 'Sir Lancelot's Vision of the Holy Grail' was Rossetti's contribution (Rossetti's image of a man being distracted from pursuit of his ideal by an ultimately disappointing romantic attachment has a certain ironic pertinence to Furnivall.)[186]

Once again, being Furnivall, he included mystical titbits of autobiography in the unlikely pages of another of his Roxburghe Society editions. At this stage in his life, romance was inextricably entwined with

---

[182] See further Alexander, *Medievalism*, 106–17.

[183] *Seynt Graal, or the Sank Ryal*, ed.Furnivall, i. 1.

[184] 'The Breaking of the Web', pen drawing (1850). Hunt returned to the subject in later life in the large oil painting of 1886–1905, now in the Wadsworth Atheneum, Hartford, CT, and in the smaller panel in the Manchester City Art Gallery.

[185] *John Ruskin*, i. 224.

[186] As well as Rossetti, they included the others who had taught for the Working Men's College: William Morris, Valentine Prinsep, and Edward Burne-Jones. Rossetti also recruited Arthur Hughes.

philological enquiry, both, after all, forms of quest, except that this romance would be followed by a bumpy descent from the clouds. Indeed, his philological curiosity was the occasion for his fall. Aroused by a famous line from Tennyson's *Morte d'Arthur*, he, like many after him, wanted to know what 'samite' was, *exactly*. He naturally turned to Hensleigh Wedgwood to find out:

'Clothed in white samite,—mystic, wonderful!' The very name of the vesture even stirred one's imagination. What could the wondrous texture be? ... While busy with the sins of our ancestors in the fourteenth century, visions of the Graal would float before me, with its covering of mystic samite—a web not of the earth, earthy, but spun with angel hands, divine. In this mood one day I turned over the pages of my friend, Mr. Hensleigh Wedgwood's 'Etymology of the English Language', and by chance my eye lighted on the word DIMITY:— DIMITY. Originally a stuff woven with two threads ... In the same way the German name for velvet, *samnat*, is contracted from *exhamita*, from having been woven of six threads.

What! My samite allied to dimity—bed-ticking and dusters! Here was a roll in the mud for all my rose-pink notions![187]

There can be no doubt that Furnivall was a sentimentalist through and through, but he preferred his notions in more rational dress. Rose pink was much too girly. Why, indeed, was Furnivall, who at about this time was pooh-poohing Christian belief and causing pain to F. D. Maurice with a geological hammer, being starry-eyed about mystical samite? Furnivall's idealism was social, not Christian. Yet his acknowledgement that he lived in a prosaic age of dimity was compatible with his easy familiarity with St Paul in the Authorized Version.[188]

As he tells us, Furnivall was at this time teaching medieval romances at the Working Men's College,[189] while also enthusiastically going on geological expeditions with the men. He could, and did, accommodate both mysticism and mastodons. He had to. Anyone seriously engaged in editing early English texts must respect the Christian traditions in which they are based. But this did not stop him from ridiculing them as a way of distancing himself. He poked fun in *Handlyng Synne* by pointing out the craziness, as he saw it, of most people's literal belief in the creation of the world in six days: 'the absurdity of it glides off them like water off a duck's back'. Yet the story retained a value for less well-

---

[187] *Holy Graal*, i pp. ii–iii. Furnivall's business with 14th-c. sins refers to his edition of *Handlyng Synne*.   [188] 1 Cor. 15: 47.
[189] He used *Specimens of Early English Metrical Romance*, ed. George Ellis, of which a new and revised edition was prepared by J. O. Halliwell (London, 1848). *Holy Graal*, p. ii.

educated people in reminding them of the Almighty's power: 'Let him who can now trace the records of the majestic march of the Creator's agents over the world's surface, not despise the credulity of his less instructed brother, and let not those who see the folly of the Middle Age miracles, sneer at the faith of the men who once believed in them.'[190] (There is a certain intellectual snobbery here, even while it is rebutted in evangelical style.) And the very title of his edition of Henry Lovelich's version of the Grail legend, as it spins its great length along, has a joke at the expense of credulous literal belief in the claims made in the text for its ultimate source, '... *from the Original Latin, written by Jesus Christ with his own hand* (p. 357), *Being the only Writing made by God since his uprising*'.

This Tennyson-fuelled passion for Arthur would shortly lead Furnivall to declare that one of his prime motives for founding the EETS was his desire to print all the English Arthuriana he could find. The Roxburghe Club, the Philological Society, and later the EETS gave him a means whereby he could serve the cause of the past, and preserve its relics, while retaining the option of all the facilities to study available to a modern forward-thinking Victorian gentleman which, from 1879/80, included electric light by which to examine the medieval manuscripts after the Siemens electric lighting was installed in the Reading Room of the British Museum—with glass plates installed under the lamps to catch 'any sparks of carbon that might fall'.[191]

Sadly, Furnivall's experience with editing the fifteenth-century verse Grail romance by the London writer Henry Lovelich, translated from the French of the late twelfth- and early thirteenth-century Robert de Boron, did not yield the mystical thrills for which he had hoped at the outset of his own personal quest for the Grail in English. His first sight of the treasure, when, after much perseverance, he got his hands on it,

[190] *Handlyng Synne*, pp. xxv–xxvi.
[191] As reported in *The Academy*, 13 Mar. 1880, p. 195: 'We understand that the Trustees of the British Museum have resolved upon permanently adopting the Siemens system of lighting by electricity which has been in temporary use in the Reading Room for some months.' The lamps did not habitually shed flecks of carbon, but the precaution followed an incident in Jan. 1880, when one had set fire to some paper in the Reading Room. The innovation was welcomed because of the increase in the number of hours during which readers could consult the material. Furnivall himself noted that he was able to write his preface to *The Fifty Earliest English Wills* there on a winter evening, 'at 5 p.m. under the Electric Light, Dec. 5, 1882' (p. xv). The Museum was somewhat in advance of other institutions: Siemens lighting was first used in a British theatre (the Savoy, in London) in 1881. The Trustees gave approval in 1884 for electric lighting to be installed in the Manuscripts Students' Room; see further Harris, *A History of the British Museum Library*, 313–15.

was that it was unmistakable late medieval dimity after all. 'Nevertheless, dimity has its uses; and so has fifteenth-century verse—however poor it be—for students of English':

> 'And yf thou do, withowten more
> [Rewarde] deth schal thow suffren therefore.'
> '[My Lor]de, ȝif it be not so as I haue the told,
> Dis-membre thow me, Sire, manifold.'[192]

Undeterred by this specimen of dreadfulness, Furnivall pleaded in extenuation: 'the subject of the Grail would ennoble any covering of words'. 'I still said to Mr. Botfield that the Romance ought to be printed.'[193]

It was the numinous quality of the Grail that had made him persevere in tracking his Jabberwock through the tulgy wood of manuscript libraries. In part to entertain his audience of bibliophiles, but in part also to magnify his own abilities and determination as a literary detective, Furnivall elaborated the account of how he had made his discovery into his own personal Grail quest in miniature, fated to dissolve in bathos composed in jog-trot measure. As romance it could only be mock heroic because the questing knight was Furnivall, who was a London barrister who lived amidst dusters and mattress ticking. Nevertheless, the finding of Lovelich made a good story. He had come across mention of the existence of the elusive Grail story 'while reading one day for my class at the Working Men's College', and finding mention in Halliwell's revised popular edition for Bohn's Antiquarian Library of George Ellis's *Specimens of Early English Romance* of a forty-thousand-line metrical composition translated from the French by 'Henry Lonelich'.[194] Halliwell mentioned, to Furnivall's great excitement, that the unique manuscript, in Cambridge, had never been printed. That it was kept in the Library of Corpus Christi College was perhaps, in view of its subject matter, almost too good to be true, but what caught Furnivall's attention was the magic word 'Unprinted'.

I could not help exclaiming, "Unprinted! What a shame! Please God, I'll get it printed. Why, it's almost as bad as leaving Wycliffe's Bible unprinted so long— Forty thousand lines about the San Graal with possibly, nay certainly, untold glories, and wonders without end, lying hid in Corpus Library! The thing was

---

[192] *Holy Graal*, i, p. iv. Lines selected by Furnivall (i. 106, ll. 493–6).
[193] *Holy Graal*, i, pp. iv, iii.
[194] Ibid., p. ii.

hardly credible; while all our English world too was delighting in "The Idylls of the King".[195]

The trouble was the 'forty thousand lines'—as Halliwell had observed, 'The interminable ballad romances of the middle ages had daunted all but the few initiated.'[196] Descanting on 'the probable treasures of the Louelich Romance' (before he had read it to find out), Furnivall set out to persuade publishers to 'pay for the copying and printing of the MS. if I would edit it gratis'. But, offered 'forty thousand lines of Early English by an unknown poet', on spec, 'One and all said No!' It was matter for a Society or Club.[197] At this point Providence intervened in the form of Beriah Botfield, whose gift to the Philological Society's Dictionary Committee of Roxburghe books 'brought me into correspondence with him'. Botfield jumped at the chance.

But treasure—even fool's gold—is not won without overcoming dragons: Furnivall had still to win over its custodians. He had to go to Cambridge, and, whereas Madden just a few years earlier had to get there by coach, as Furnivall himself, as a freshman, also had to travel from Egham, via London, now the Eastern Counties Railway had opened access to Cambridge in 1845. Incidentally, back in 1841, Madden, who had then been in quest for the 'Werwolf', also—in passing—found the Holy Grail in Corpus.[198] Madden's journeys to Cambridge provide further illustration of how the rapid progress in democratizing Early English texts in the second half of the nineteenth century owed much to the coming of the railways. Rushing off then by steam, rather than steed, to gloat over his discovery, Furnivall was temporarily thwarted by Corpus Christi College's library rules, which required the presence of two Fellows of the College while a visitor examined the manuscripts; 'Archbishop Parker had no notion of his jewels being thus open to the profane gaze and touch of strangers'.[199] However, he found two Fellows willing to give up their time 'in a fireless Library' in vacation time. At last 'the long-wished for "Romaunce of the San Graal" was put into my hands, a stout folio volume bound in vellum'. The battle was not yet won: written 'in a crabbed Henry-the-Sixth hand', pale from damp and age, it was 'awkward at first to read'.[200]

Luckily, Harry Seeley was still able and willing to transcribe this work for Furnivall as soon as he had finished *Handlyng Synne*, though he

[195] Ibid.
[196] *Specimens*, p. iii.
[197] *Holy Graal*, i, p. ii.
[198] Rogers (ed.), *Sir Frederic Madden at Cambridge*, 15.
[199] *Holy Graal*, p. iii.
[200] Ibid.

would shortly leave the Working Men's College to begin his geological career. The Corpus text was deficient at the beginning, and Furnivall headed back to the British Museum to find the beginning of the story in other sources. 'Not being versed in the mysteries of the British-Museum Printed Books Catalogues', he drew a blank, and turned to the more familiar terrain of the Manuscript Room, which, 'through the kindness of its officers, and the quaint tales of the old vellum pages on its shelves, had given me so many pleasant hours before'.[201] Here he located two manuscripts of the French *Histoire du San Graal*. As Seeley was no longer available Furnivall copied the first nineteen pages himself (89 pages of print), 'but as I could not spare further time, Miss Eleanor Dalziel has copied the rest for the Club'.[202] This must have been a demanding assignment: one presumes that she must already have had some knowledge of French, unlike, apparently, the scribe of MS Royal 14. E. iii, though, thrillingly, it 'really is a royal folio', with the autographs of Richard III, the princesses Elizabeth and Cecily, daughters of Edward IV, and most excitingly of all *'Jane Grey'*.[203]

Furnivall's Grail quest at this point was in danger of diverting him from the stars to another Welsh bog. As he worked methodically through his task, 'the next thing was to ascertain the opinion of competent judges on the origin of the legend of the Graal'.[204] Was it Celtic, or not? The Breton philologist and Arthurian scholar Villemarqué, of course, said yes, but could he be trusted?[205] The Arthurian expert, Albert Schulz said no.[206] Furnivall did not know Schulz personally. Instead, perhaps advised by Ludlow (whose help, as well as Hensleigh Wedgwood's, is acknowledged in the volume), he approached 'my friend Professor Huber', the Christian Socialist whom he had met with the rest of the Lincoln's Inn group when Huber visited England in 1854 for the purpose of studying co-operation.[207] It is hardly sur-

---

[201] Ibid., p. iv.

[202] Ibid. Assisted by David Nutt, folklore specialist (father of Alfred), and business partner of Trübner. Furnivall also unsuccessfully approached Francisque Michel, through his publisher, without response, for permission to reprint his text of the earlier version. It is reproduced anyway as an Appendix, 1–46 (separately paginated): *Le roman du Saint-Graal*, ed. Michel. On Michel, see Matthews, *Invention of Middle English*, 214–18.

[203] The italics are Furnivall's. *Holy Graal*, pp. iv–v. However, see the cautious verdict of Sutton and Visser-Fuchs, *Richard III's Books*, 323, and references there given. I am grateful to Professor Beadle for this reference.   [204] *Holy Graal*, p. v.

[205] Théodore Claude Henri, vicomte Hersart de la Villemarqué (1815–95)

[206] Albert Schulz (1802–93) wrote on this subject under the pseudonym San Marte.

[207] Victor Aimé Huber described his own impressions of Maurice and the work of his 'friends' at Lincoln's Inn in *Reisebriefe aus Belgien, Frankreich, und England im Som-*

prising that Furnivall regarded Victor Aimé Huber, social reformer and literary historian, as his 'friend'. He was a man who had given up his professorship in Berlin to devote himself to social questions, who was a forerunner of the German co-operative movement, and who had visited England, where he had inspected factory conditions in Manchester—and a man who could introduce Furnivall to other German scholars. For Huber knew Schulz, who obligingly supplied the prefatory essay, 'On the Saga of the Holy Grail', which Nicholas Trübner and Theodor Goldstücker just as obligingly translated from the German (Furnivall's UCL German was not apparently up to this standard).[208] Furnivall knew Lady Charlotte Guest's translation of the *Mabinogion*, first published in seven volumes between 1838 and 1845, and was emphatic that he did not want to become involved in the wilder aspects of Grail mysteries, folklore, Druidry, and Welsh nationalism: 'I do not believe that any witch's cauldron, or head in a platter was the germ whence the Romance-writer's beautiful conception sprang.'[209] He turned in relief to an Englishman, 'who really knew his subject', and 'whose keen blade of knowledge, wielded by an arm of vigorous common-sense, has pricked so many wind-bags that ignorance and mistaken national vanity had puffed up'.[210] This was David W. Nash, an Egyptologist turned Celticist, who assailed Welsh 'national vanity' from the safety of Cheltenham.[211] Furnivall admired the vigour with which Nash expressed his views; Hutton has called Nash 'shockingly rude' (a description which likewise fits Furnivall on occasion). It is, indeed, possible that Nash's unsparing ridicule of previous writers bolstered Furnivall's own outspokenness in what he considered a right cause.[212] (Yet such brutal candour is the obverse of Furnivall's

mer 1854 (1855). See biographical sketch by Raven, *Christian Socialism*, 382–3; also Christensen, *Origins and History of Christian Socialism*, 356–7.

[208] *Holy Graal*, pp. xiv–xxi, and p. vi. Inevitably Schulz gave an overview of the Continental sources, though the proof-sheets of Lovelich which Furnivall sent him seemed to him 'of the highest interest for the English language and poetry, and the publication of which redounds to the great credit and honour of the Roxburghe Club, and by which the Club is sure to gain the greatest thanks of the learned world' (p. xx).

[209] *Holy* Graal, p. ix: 'The amount of pounding that the head in the platter must require to enable one to identify it with the Graal and its contents, I cannot conceive.'

[210] Ibid., p. ix.

[211] Ibid. Nash, *Taliesin, or The Bards and Druids of Britain*. For an appraisal of the value of Nash's scholarship, see Hutton, *Blood and Mistletoe*, 261–2. H. Gaidoz complained that Nash, 'who played an honourable part in Welsh studies at a time when they were rather neglected', ought to have been included in the first *DNB* (*Notes and Queries*, ix–xi, no. 283 (30 May 1903), 425); he still has not been included.

[212] Hutton, *Blood and Mistletoe*, 262.

conception of manly generosity.) Though Furnivall did not previously know him, Nash kindly furnished a synopsis of his views, which proved to Furnivall's satisfaction at least that, whatever the Grail was, it was not Celtic.[213] Indeed Furnivall expressed the opinion of the motives for grafting the story into the Arthurian cycle which still generally prevails, though expressed with characteristic down-to-earth bluntness:

> I conceive that any religious poet reading the regular Arthur romances, must have said to himself, 'Is this fighting mainly for fighting' sake, this tourneying and feasting, this high-flown devotion to a lady-love, what a Christian knight, the servant of the Lord and his Blessed Mother ought to be doing and professing? Is this court of Arthur ... with its amours and adulteries, to be the highest object of ambition to a follower of our Holy Faith?[214]

Furnivall had his own reasons for preoccupation at this time with rational (not 'high-flown') chivalry towards women. 1862, the year of publication of *Handlyng Synne*, and when the *Holy Graal* was going through the press, was also the year of Furnivall's marriage to Eleanor Dalziel, whom he, as a gentleman, was bound to protect. His comment in the *Graal* about 'the star of Galahad's chastity', which 'shines out pure and clear, and draws one to it with the power of fascination',[215] described an ideal he could not live up to himself. The nearness of the subject also betrays itself in *Handlyng Synne* in Furnivall's hectoring attack on modern cads:

> Who that sees our streets at night, or has any working-man friend whose family has been the prey of the spoiler,—who, I repeat, can say, that the modern rich man's gifts of grace and refinement, education and wealth, are not now too often perverted, as the strength of Lords of old too often was, to the corruption and ruin of the purity and trusting weakness which every man of gentle blood and knightly manliness is bound by every tie to revere and protect?[216]

His indignation on behalf of working men whose wives and daughters had been preyed upon by so-called gentlemen was probably fuelled by a personal sense of having done the right thing himself. And he implies personal knowledge from his own experience of the grief caused to 'any working-man friend' whose family has suffered in this way.

[213] *Holy Graal*, pp. vii–viii.
[214] Ibid., pp. viii–ix.
[215] Ibid., p. i.
[216] *Handlyng Synne*, pp. xi–xii. He adduced Elizabeth Barrett Browning, d. 29 June 1861, 'England's noblest poetess—now, alas, so lately lost to us' in support.

POSTSCRIPT: FURNIVALL'S
LATER ROXBURGHE EDITIONS

Although *Handlyng Synne* and *Holy Graal* were printed by the Roxburghe Club's usual printer (and fellow antiquary), J. B. Nichols, Furnivall's next title for the Club, *Generides*, was printed by Stephen Austin of Hertford and John Russell's *Boke of Nurture* by John Childs of Bungay. Furnivall was already beginning to take advantage of his gift for calling everyone his friend and enrolling them in his causes: his working men, his wife to be, printers and publishers, including the cultivated Nicolas Trübner, along with a widening circle of German scholars.

In whole or in part Furnivall edited three more titles for the Roxburghe Club, but all were published after the foundation of the EETS. *Generides*, another lengthy verse romance, was contemplated while he was working on the Grail, and Mannyng.[217] The text had been unknown until 'Mr. Groome, of Monk Soham, sent up extracts from it for the Philological Society's Dictionary' (p. xiii). Furnivall had never heard of it, nor had Madden or other authorities, including Francisque Michel and Henri Victor Michelant.[218] But then, 'the great Cambridge discoverer of fragments in unthought-of places', Henry Bradshaw, identified an early printed book in Trinity College naming the hero, and W. Aldis Wright copied the pages for Furnivall.[219] The text of *Generides* itself was copied by Eleanor's brother, W. A. Dalziel. Eleanor herself was married by this time, with her first child, and perhaps felt that she

---

[217] A *Royal Historie of the Excellent Knight Generides*, ed. Furnivall. See also W. Aldis Wright's account of his subsequent research, which led to his identification of a second version of the story, which he edited for the EETS: *Generydes: A Romance in Seven-Line Stanzas*, ed. Wright, EETS, OS 71, pp. v–viii.

[218] See Furnivall's letter to Bradshaw, 24 Dec. 1863: 'I'm very grateful to you for having found out that Sir Generides has been printed, and so preventing me getting myself and the friend who was going to pay for its printing, into a scrape. Your printed text has all the names of the MS, and tho' I have not been able to find the passage yet, I have no doubt at all that the text and MS are the same Romance. | But it's odd that neither Madden, nor any of the learned in such matters to whom I have spoken about the Romance, even hear of it. What is the printed title, and where was the book published?' Bradshaw Papers, CUL MS Add 2591 (1), 213.

[219] On 1 Mar. 1866, W. Aldis Wright wrote to Madden: 'I suppose you may have heard from Furnivall that I have found among our Gale MSS. the whole story of Sir Generides in seven-line stanzas, just like the printed fragments which I also discovered. It represents an entirely different version of the story from that edited by him for the Roxburghe, and is in a very fine folio volume which is catalogued as Lidgate's Poems and contains besides the Siege of Troy and the Siege of Thebes. The class mark is O. 5. 2', BL MS Egerton 2848, f. 204.

no longer needed to slave as an amanuensis.[220] Furnivall enjoyed the absurdity of romance conventions, a hero 'endowed with the extraordinary power of swooning on the shortest notice that we have seen in the Graal knights', a heroine who was 'a somewhat hasty-tempered person', but at least, unlike her father—also hot-tempered—not a 'sneak'.[221] Furnivall could not abide sneaks. The Glossary to *Generides*, as he cheerfully acknowledged, 'is not exhaustive', but fifteenth-century texts were not hard to understand. Roxburghe titles required a résumé of the contents for their readers (who were not all proficient in Middle English or enthused enough to wade through the original). These summaries (which take up many pages) were too lavish for the poorer EETS to contemplate; instead Furnivall developed the side-notes which are such a conspicuous feature of the early EETS editions, and which similarly relieved the subscribers from the effort to read the texts.[222] This kind of précis in side-notes, as well as separate abstracts, soon became for both Furnivall and Skeat a kind of minor literary art form in which they took evident delight at times in exercising a certain facetiousness which reflected their own engagement with the texts: 'It is quite refreshing', Furnivall acknowledged, 'to feel how the romancers 'enjoyed a good stand-up fight': 'The author held fighting the true meat for a man, and that it was quite correct for a knight to fall in love, to be susceptible to any extent, to swoon and fall ill on proper occasions, and be recovered by a kiss from his sweetheart, yet his real function in life was—being on the right side—to break the backs of other men'.[223]

Furnivall's parting shot for the Roxburghe (except that he would contribute the text with 'foreword' and an 'afterword' many years later to *The Pilgrimage of the Life of Man*, edited in collaboration with Katharine Locock),[224] was his edition of the fifteenth-century *Boke of Nurture*, by John Russell, usher in chamber and marshall in hall to Humphrey, Duke of Gloucester ('Valet, Butler, Footman, Carver, Taster, Dinner-arranger, Hippocras-maker', as Furnivall expressed it), with other texts relating to

[220] This suggestion that Eleanor's copying work for Furnivall did not last long after their marriage is strengthened by Furnivall's remark, in 1870, referring to work on William Lauder, done around 1864: 'My wife had kindly copied one volume of them in a hurry years ago, when they were to have gone through the press at once'. *Minor Poems of William Lauder*, ed. Furnivall, EETS, OS 41, p. xxv.
[221] *Generides*, pp. xiii–xx.
[222] Furnivall had already used side-notes to render accessible the earlier French text printed as the Appendix to the first volume of the *Holy Graal*. The notes, which are extensive, part paraphrase and part translate the key ideas of the text, allowing readers to follow the story simply, even without consulting the French.
[223] *Generides*, p. xvi.   [224] *The Pilgrimage of the Life of Man*, ed. Furnivall.

meals and manners.[225] Early etiquette, manners and customs, food and dress were staples of antiquarian curiosity. Furnivall had nothing but contempt for that 'deducated Philistinism', as he called it, 'which lately made a literary man say to one of our members on his printing a book of the fifteenth century, "Is it possible that you care how those barbarians, our ancestors, lived?"'[226] For Furnivall this curiosity was a natural development from the social history in Mannyng, as well as from the romances, in which the exemplification of good manners, especially at table, and the menu at feasts is a prominent theme. He would draw upon the information not only for EETS publications but also as background information for understanding 'Shakspere'.

Furnivall came across Russell thanks to 'a chance turning over, for another purpose, of the leaves of the MS. containing it'.[227] However the Philological Society had already published a fifteenth-century cookery book, edited by Richard Morris, not only because of its exemplification of Northern English dialect forms (which commended it to Morris), but because 'Some knowledge of the composition of these dishes is rendered necessary by the constant allusions to them in our early English Metrical Romances, which give the poem an Archaeological as well as a Philological value'.[228] The cookery book duly appeared as the *Liber Cure Cocorum, Copied and Cdited from the Sloane MS. 1986*, by Richard Morris, Author of 'The Etymology of Local Names', Member of the Philological Society (published for the Philological Society by A. Asher & Co., Berlin, 1862). Morris identified the text's Northern dialect as NW Lancashire. He had a particular interest in descendants of the Northumbrian dialect in later English (meaning the Anglo-Saxon kingdom of Northumbria, and hence comprising Yorkshire, as well as the county of Northumberland) and had written in April 1860 to Madden: 'I should feel greatly obliged if you could refer me to any Northumbrian MSS. of the XIII, XIV, or XV centuries among the manuscripts collection of the British Museum ... The late Mr Garnett says that the literary monuments of the Northumbrian dialects are very numerous (from the xiv to xvi (centuries)). I have not found this to be the case.'[229] Morris adopted Garnett's classification of English dialects into five broad areas: Northumbrian being that spoken throughout the Lowlands of Scotland,

---

[225] *The Boke of Nurture, by John Russell*, ed. Furnivall, M.A., p. vi.

[226] Ibid., p. vii. 'Deducated' (i.e. 'de-educated') was Furnivall's coinage, explained at length in *Hymns to the Virgin & Christ*, ed. Furnivall, EETS, OS 24.

[227] *Boke of Nurture*, p. i.   [228] *Liber Cure Cocorum*, ed. Morris, p. iii.

[229] BL MS Egerton 2848, f. 20^{r-v}.

Northumberland, Durham, and nearly the whole of Yorkshire, 'extending at one time from the Humber to the Forth, and from the German Ocean to the Irish Channel'.[230]

Like many who have ever looked at accounts of medieval banquets, Furnivall was impressed that, did a creature but move, whether on earth in sea or air, a nobleman would apparently eat it with enthusiasm, especially if it was accompanied by piquant sauce. He noted, however, that a seventeenth-century menu of tortoise and snails was 'stranger still'.[231] Weirdness aside, this was not a difficult class of material to edit, at least if each manuscript were taken separately: problems came when recipes survived in multiple copies and versions. These were pragmatic texts and overlapping in content. A critical edition, though it would in any case have contradicted Furnivall's inclinations, would have been unrealistic to achieve. As he put it in his own pastiche of 'olde English': '"wherefore I have thus in this boke folowinge," gathered together divers treatises touching the Manners and Meals of Englishmen in former days'—simply printing the treatises one after the other was the easiest solution.[232] Parts of Russell's text were embedded in Wynkyn de Worde's treatise on carving, and two more manuscripts turned up in the British Museum's Sloane collection. In the absence of any master catalogue of manuscripts pertaining to early English literature (Ritson and Warton were the main search tools),[233] finding them on this occasion was down to 'that special Providence which watches over editors as well as children and drunkards'. Another volume with the promising title of 'How to Serve a Lord', 'said to be of the fourteenth century', was *pro tem.* inaccessibly stowed away in Mr Arthur Davenport's hayloft.[234]

After what Furnivall had said to the Roxburghe readers about widen-

---

[230] See 'On the Languages and Dialects of the British Islands', in R. Garnett, *Philological Essays*, 147–95 at 189.

[231] Furnivall found this in Randle Holme, *Academy of Armory* (1688), Bk. III, p. 60, col. 1.   [232] *Boke of Nurture*, p. xxiii.

[233] Ritson, *Bibliographia Poetica*; Warton, *The History of English Poetry*. Furnivall acknowledged his debt to these two earlier scholars 'to whom every lover of Early English Manuscripts is under such deep obligations, and whose guiding hands (however faltering) in Poetry have made us long so often for the like in Prose. Would that one of our many Historians of English Literature had but conceived the idea of cataloguing the materials for his History before sitting down to write it! Would that a wise Government would commission another Hardy to do for English Literature what the Deputy Keeper of the Public Records is now doing for English History—give us a list of the MSS. and early printed books of it! What time and trouble such a Catalogue would save!' Furnivall described the tortuous route by which he found the materials of his edition, with help from H. B. Wheatley, in *Boke of Nurture*, pp. i–ii. See further Matthews, *Invention of Middle English*, 19–21.   [234] *Boke of Nurture*, pp. i, iv.

ing access, the EETS was the evident way forward—indeed, he had already founded it by the time he edited the *Boke of Nurture*. When the Philological Society was too poor, the Roxburghe too élite, and the Camden refused to listen to his insistence on always reproducing the original spellings, Furnivall was bound to consider that, if others would not do the work to his liking, he would have to do it himself.

This, then, is the story of how an energetic Lincoln's Inn lawyer, with antiquarian and philological tastes, and what would now be called a 'can-do' attitude, turned editor of early English in earnest, with all that followed. 'Dimity' had indeed its uses, and suited Furnivall better than white samite ever would in an age of coal and iron. He had found his métier. Furnivall's first two editions for the Roxburghe Club were defining ventures which shaped the EETS as they formed him and reaffirmed his principles. The passion for making Arthurian legends and romances accessible would be one of the new society's founding aspirations, and the antiquarian interest in early English manners and customs is evident in many of its nineteenth-century publications. And a third motive for the choice of texts was the sense, growing out of Herbert Coleridge's *Glossarial Index*, that it was especially important to get Middle English material into print for inspection by philologists. Poetry and its accompanying controversies over metre and final -*e* would be an abiding concern.

It was also clear that Furnivall's increasingly less Christian, but still staunchly socialist, principles ultimately made the Roxburghe an incongruous home for his publications. Yet he made steadfast friends among its members, notably Henry Hucks Gibbs, and he depended on the goodwill of liberal men of the Establishment (as he would in many of his literary adventures) to preach something perilously close to egalitarianism to them in their own books. Nevertheless, he was careful to distinguish between benevolent wealthy men, who were necessary to advance programmes of social reform and widening education, and the exploiters of the poor. Otherwise, Furnivall scorned tact. In *Generides*, he declared that 'No chance owner of a record or the mind and life of our old-English worthies has a right to turn Dog in the Manger, and do what he will with his own. A Chaucer relic, a Percy ballad;—the curse of all true men on him who misers these up in his own strong box, not for love of the writers, but for gratification of vanity and self.'[235] *Generides* was presented to the members of the Club by Gibbs, who, in his championship both of Furnivall and his EETS, showed that he agreed with the

---

[235] *Generides*, p. xxiv.

sentiments. But it was one thing for Madden privately to criticize bibliophiles who were dogs in the manger, and quite another for Furnivall to preach in evangelical style against them in the pages of a publication designed to flatter their good taste and discerning ownership, especially when a large part of the motive for founding the Club had been to satisfy the members' delight in their own treasured possessions.

9

The Philological Society and the Beginnings of the EETS

> He may be a veritable subject of the kingdom of Cockaigne, for aught I know.
> Benjamin Disraeli, *Sybil; or, The Two Nations* (1845), Book IV, ch. 7

THE PHILOLOGICAL SOCIETY'S EDITORS

Furnivall described himself on the title page of the Roxburghe's *Boke of Nurture* as an alumnus of Trinity Hall, Cambridge, a member of the Philological Society's Council, and a member of the recently founded Early English Text Society, as well as a 'Lover of Old Books'. His new society would need a cohort of editors, and his acknowledgements in the *Boke of Nurture*, published in 1867, show where he went to find them. Reasonably enough, he used his friends in the Philological Society in the first place, and contacts he had made through his work for its Dictionary; he also turned increasingly to his alma mater, Cambridge; and then there were also useful friendships which he had made through the London-based book-publishing clubs.

Accordingly, his thanks went to Oswald Cockayne, Henry Bradshaw, Walter Skeat, William Aldis Wright, Henry Hucks Gibbs, Albert Way, Henry Wheatley, and the American G. P. Marsh. Among others mentioned, improbable though it may seem at first sight, a good candidate for 'Dr. Günther' is the German-born Albert Charles Günther, zoologist and assistant keeper at the British Museum, whose eight-volume catalogue of the Museum's fish collection more than qualified him to advise on the names of the fish consumed in the fifteenth century.[1] The transcription of the *Boke of Nurture* had been done by Edmund Brock (1841–1921), a scholar in medieval and Oriental languages, and reader at Cambridge University Press, father of the illustrators C. E. and H. M. Brock, and 'the most careful copier of the MS'. Brock—a scholar, rather than a clerk—would go on to edit early titles for the

---

[1] R. J. Cleevely, 'Günther [Gunther], Albert Charles Lewis Gotthilf [formerly Albert Karl Ludwig Gotthilf] (1830–1914)', *ODNB*. The *Catalogue of Fishes in the British Museum* was being published between 1859 and 1870.

EETS, including the alliterative *Morte Arthure*, and the *Liflade of St. Juliana* with Cockayne. He would also assist with the Chaucer Society.[2] By the time Furnivall made his adieux to the Roxburghe Club his immersion in fifteenth-century English had reached the point where he could command a fair pastiche: he had prepared this volume 'To the end that, to my fellows here and to come, the home life of their forefathers may be somewhat more plain, and their own minds somewhat rejoiced'. And he also trusted that the members of the Club 'accustomed to editions of from sixteen to a hundred copies' would experience no diminution of their pleasure 'by knowing that these treatises here following are three of several intended, in less luxurious form, for a thousand readers'.[3]

Furnivall's ambitions for making access to early English texts more democratic were shared by his friends in the Philological Society, as well as expressed on occasion by others, including J. O. Halliwell, though Halliwell had recognized that there was a linguistic pain barrier to overcome, and he had exhorted his readers to make the effort: 'Our early writers, whose merit is indeed so great that, whoever possesses the industry to conquer their meaning must inevitably be charmed by the truth and vitality of their pictures, the ingenuous frankness of their sentiments, the force and simplicity of their language, and the buoyancy and joyousness of their general character.'[4]

Halliwell had revised George Ellis's three handsome folio volumes of English metrical romances in a cheaper format for the publisher Henry Bohn's Antiquarian Library.[5] Indeed, while under the influence of Tennyson, Furnivall had been using Halliwell's revised popular Bohn's text of the romances to teach the Working Men. And as a result, he had his own moment of editorial revelation that sent him on his personal Grail quest, with all that followed. Bohn was a shrewd businessman, as well as personally committed to the success of his libraries, and his cheap editions, as the *Gentleman's Magazine* observed, 'established the habit in middle-class life, of purchasing books instead of obtaining them from a library'. Ralph Waldo Emerson thought Bohn's contribu-

[2] He is also listed in the Eighth Report of the Working Men's College, for 1863–4.

[3] *Boke of Nurture*, p. xxiii.

[4] *Specimens of Early English Metrical Romances*, p. iii; enjoyment, however, was 'not infrequently impeded, by the thick veil spread over them by learned affectation'. It is likely that there was an element of pleasing the publisher, Bohn, in saying this, since Halliwell had just the year before he wrote these sentiments turned his hand to a volume for private circulation.

[5] The series was created in 1847, to be followed in quick succession by other Bohn's Library series, including the Shilling (1850), the Philological (1852), and the British Classics (1853).

tion had done 'as much for literature as railroads have done for internal intercourse'.[6]

Meanwhile the Philological Society continued to issue early English texts, either within the *Transactions*, or as separate volumes, published on the Society's behalf by A. Asher & Co. of Berlin. Most were short, apart from one large exception, Richard Morris's edition in 1863 of the *Prick of Conscience*.[7] Furnivall's anthology *Early English Poems and Lives of Saints* was followed by *The Play of the Sacrament*, edited from a Trinity College Dublin manuscript by the Irishman and Celtic philologist Whitley Stokes.[8] Morris's *Liber Cure Cocorum* appeared in 1862, conservatively edited, with close attention paid in the preface to the text's north-western dialectal particularities.[9] And members of the Society might also independently issue early English texts with other publishers, as T. O. Cockayne did with his text of *Seinte Marherete*.[10] Those of the Society's members who were actively reading texts from the First Period for the Society's Dictionary were led to reflect upon the editorial practices they saw elsewhere. Thus, R. F. Weymouth, reading Thomas Ponton's edition of the *Morte Arthure*,[11] 'availed' himself 'of a recent visit to London' from his home in Plymouth[12] to compare the printed copy of this poem with the original MS in the British Museum Harley 2252'. The results of this flying visit 'were very cursory', but nevertheless instructive. Weymouth felt that there was a much greater need for editorial intervention than Ponton had supplied—although this went against the grain of Furnivall's insistence on diplomatic editing to serve lexicography. There were many palpable scribal errors.

[6] Quoted by Alexis Weedon, 'Bohn, Henry George (1796–1884)', *ODNB*.

[7] Also *Stimulus conscientiae*.

[8] Separately published for the Philological Society by Asher (Berlin, 1862). See further Nollaig Ó Muraíle, 'Stokes, Whitley (1830–1909)', *ODNB*. At this time, he was practising law in the Inner Temple.

[9] 'No alteration has been made in the text of the MS. without some acknowledgement in a foot-note' (p. iv). These footnotes included some glossing, as well as suggested emendations (e.g. 'ʒit' for MS 'ʒif', p. 5). Occasionally conjectural emendations were added to the text in square brackets, as on p. 7 'and clene', added on metrical grounds. Medial 'u' and 'n', and difficulties in disambiguating 'c' and 't' were discussed, e.g. on p. 20. 'Conyngus in cyne' was retained, by analogy with other printed texts, but Morris reasonably proposed 'cyve' ('chives', or 'onions'). On p. 36 he proposed emending MS 'smiting' to 'snite', as a variant form of 'snipe'.

[10] *Seinte Marherete þe Meiden ant Martyr* (London, 1862), published by Longman, Green, Longmans, and Roberts.

[11] *Le Morte Arthur: The Adventures of Sir Lancelot du Lake*, Roxburghe Club (London, 1819).

[12] His edition of the *Castel of Loue* is dated 8 June 1864, from the Portland Grammar School, Plymouth.

And there were 'very numerous other passages which readily admit of conjectural, and in most cases, certain, emendations'.[13]

The editors of Middle English texts for the Philological Society whom Furnivall also recruited in the 1860s to edit for the EETS (in several cases issuing revised versions of the Philological's editions) deserve closer inspection. The first to be considered, Richard Francis Weymouth, did not edit for the EETS (though he did engage to produce *The Harrowing of Hell* for it, from manuscripts in the Bodleian).[14] Instead he engaged in combative disagreements with the fellow members of the Philological Society, who were Furnivall's friends and allies, about their knowledge of early English and proper editorial method, and he may thus be considered an active influence on the EETS. Weymouth's philological ideas were at odds with the views prevailing in the Philological Society, as represented by Ellis, Skeat, Weymouth's junior colleague James Murray, and Richard Morris. The arguments and discussions continued before and after the founding of the EETS in 1864, and they form the background to the development of Furnivall's ideas for editing and publishing early English texts. They thus contributed to the establishment of a set of opinions, which hardened into received views, about early English among a dominant group within the Philological Society. Furnivall was a leading light in this group, not least as the Secretary responsible for preparing the Society's *Transactions*. Accordingly, to preserve the narrative, the discussion straddles the year 1864 into the EETS's first ten years.

RICHARD FRANCIS WEYMOUTH'S 'CASTLE OF LOVE'

Weymouth, just three years older than Furnivall, and the son of a naval commander, was an alumnus of UCL, where he studied classics, taking his MA in 1849. A zealous Baptist, he never studied at Oxford or Cambridge; he joined the Philological Society in 1851. He was a highly competent schoolteacher and administrator, teaching Greek, Latin, and English. During the 1850s and 1860s he was running his successful private school, Portland Grammar, before moving to the

---

[13] 'Notes on the Roxburghe Club Morte Arthur', *TPS*, 7 (1860), 279–81 at 280–1. Weymouth also noted the confusion in modern type of þ and y. There were not many actual misprints.

[14] EETS, Second Annual Report, p. 5, where it is listed as one of twenty titles, of which it was hoped twelve would be issued in 1866. It would be edited by Hulme, *The Middle English Harrowing of Hell and Gospel of Nicodemus*, EETS, ES 100 (London, 1907). Richard Morris had originally volunteered to undertake the *Nicodemus*.

Mill Hill School in Middlesex, where he served for seventeen years as headmaster, with James Murray as his assistant. He had a reputation as a strict disciplinarian (though he was not an advocate of corporal punishment).[15] Given his interests in early English and the Dictionary, it is initially surprising that Furnivall did not make more use of his expertise—Furnivall was not one to be deterred by a potential editor's pleas, however genuine, of the scant leisure afforded by 'an engrossing and harassing profession'.[16]

Yet the Philological Society largely consisted of opinionated personalities: Weymouth was irascible and difficult to get along with.[17] Most of the time conflict was subordinated to the sense of common purpose in a good cause, but Weymouth's confidence that he was right (though he said he was always open to reasoned argument) and his headmasterly way of pointing out others' failings, as he saw them, led to strongly expressed disagreements with Richard Morris, Walter Skeat, and Alexander Ellis. Thus, Weymouth disagreed with Skeat, as well as Ellis, over the pronunciation of early English, but Ellis was too easy-going and courteous, and Skeat too pacific to be drawn into battle.

Morris, however, was thin-skinned; moreover, there were reasons why he was particularly stung by Weymouth's criticisms and felt the need to hit back. He and Weymouth were, in some ways, too much alike, though by 1864, Morris's editorial record was a tremendous achievement, unmatched by Weymouth. Furnivall probably decided to side with Morris and the others as his friends. Also, Furnivall, as the man responsible for putting together the Philological Society's *Transactions*, and with strong views of his own, may have been deterred by Weymouth's attraction to critical, rather than diplomatic, editing. Yet Weymouth's expressed views sounded far more radical and inflexible than in practice they were. That, in a nutshell, was the problem: his fondness for orderly reasoning carried him too far, though his genuine erudition always made him worth attending to. As Henry Sweet said: 'Even those who are fully convinced of the erroneousness of Dr. Weymouth's views will find . . . much to instruct, and—we may add—to amuse

---

[15] G. Le G. Norgate, revd. John D. Haigh, 'Weymouth, Richard Francis (1822–1902)', *ODNB*. Weymouth was the first to receive the degree of doctor of literature at UCL, 'after a severe examination in Anglo-Saxon, Icelandic, and French and English language and literature'. See further Braithwaite, *Strikingly Alive*, 87–114. See also Gilliver, *Making of the OED*, 82; Murray, *Caught in the Web of Words*, 101–6.

[16] Weymouth, *On Early English Pronunciation*, preface (unpaginated).

[17] As witnessed by his dealings with James Murray at Mill Hill School; Murray, *Caught in the Web of Words*, 108–9, 112.

them.'[18] This parting shot, at the end of a review, was perhaps undeserved. Weymouth, though he fought on to defend views about the development of the language which have not withstood scrutiny, was not dotty. So far as we can tell, he lacked a sense of humour—he certainly did not display lightness of touch.

Even at an early stage when his reading for the Dictionary led him to check printed transcriptions against the manuscripts, Weymouth's robust common sense led him to assert that he could distinguish between transcription errors, scribal errors which were easily corrected, and conjectural emendations, which he was prepared to admit to the text. Weymouth's engagement with an experimental English edition was an offshoot of his long-standing interest in the textual criticism of the Greek New Testament. He put his ideas into practice in a detailed comparative study of the English and French texts of *The Castle of Love*, translated in the fourteenth century from Robert Grosseteste's early thirteenth-century allegory of man's salvation, the *Chasteau d'amour*.[19] It is a cogent study, amply supported by detailed evidence, and he followed this discussion with an edition of the English text, published separately by the Philological Society.[20] Not only did he have two manuscripts of the French source to compare with the English, he also had access to the four extant copies of the English texts, two of them (those contained in the Vernon manuscript and its 'sister', Simeon) very closely related, as he noticed.[21] All this evidence made a good testing site for his editorial ideas. Moreover, Weymouth's was not the *editio princeps*—Halliwell had prepared a text in 1849, albeit in a scarce edition printed for private circulation.[22] Weymouth did not think much of this effort,

[18] Sweet, 'On "Early English Pronunciation, with Especial Reference to Chaucer"', 461: 'he has otherwise shown considerable sagacity and historical knowledge, and in some important cases seems really to have convicted Mr. Ellis of error'. See also Sweet's comment to J. A. H. Murray: 'I have written a protest against Weymouth's style of criticising his reviewer, wherein I have expressed a hope that some impartial third party may give us a clear statement about the *ee* and *oo* rhymes in Chaucer'; letter of 1 Nov. 1874, Murray Papers. Sweet continued: 'It is a pity Appleton was in such a hurry to print his letter. It will only discredit him (W) and widen the breach between him and the rest of us . . . P.S. I learn from Mr Ellis that he too is going to write to the Academy about Weymouth's misstatements.'

[19] R. F. Weymouth, 'Bishop Grosseteste's "Castle of Love"', *TPS*, 8 (1862), 48–66.

[20] *Castel off Loue* (*Chasteau d'amour or Carmen de Creatione Mundi*), ed. Weymouth.

[21] Vernon is given the siglum 'V' and Simeon 'A' (for BM Additional 22283). The Vernon text was later edited by Carl Horstmann in *Minor Poems of the Vernon MS*, EETS, OS 98, where Halliwell's text was also reprinted. (Furnivall's assistance is acknowledged in the title.) Horstmann edited the text; Furnivall prepared it for press.

[22] *The Castle of Love: A Poem by Robert Grosseteste*.

but had to couch his criticisms, at least outwardly, in diplomatic language, since Halliwell had shown him much courtesy four years earlier, as 'I have great pleasure in acknowledging'.[23]

Halliwell's text had been copied, not from Vernon or Simeon, but from another manuscript, which in Weymouth's view was 'greatly modernized and corrupted'. Halliwell reported that his text 'is chiefly taken from a manuscript in private hands'. The identity of this copy was a mystery since 'I regret to learn from Mr. Halliwell that he has entirely lost sight of the MS. from which this text is in the main derived'.[24] 'Chiefly' and 'In the main derived' were not expressions to inspire confidence—especially since Halliwell admitted that 'the first two or three pages of the MS. were in so bad a condition that he had been under the necessity of filling up some lacunae conjecturally'.[25] Since Weymouth refers to this text by the siglum 'H' (for 'Halliwell'), and because 'we are not informed to what extent the editor has allowed himself to depart from the authority or authorities which he has "chiefly" followed', it is sometimes unclear whether Weymouth's strictures refer to the man or the manuscript: 'The writer seems quite to have failed to apprehend the true sense of the words before him, which therefore he had little scruple about changing, sometimes making sad nonsense by doing so.'[26] But 'It is but fair to H . . . to add that there are other passages here and there in which this text has preserved the true reading which A and V have lost.'[27] Yet since, as Weymouth acknowledged, it would have been bold indeed of Halliwell to have wholly invented 'passages' not present in the other witnesses, the lost manuscript must in all likelihood have existed. Halliwell was mistaken, however, if he thought it belonged to the fourteenth century. Weymouth deduced that it had to have been a later copy of 'a much older MS.', made 'by some person of little learning and less taste not before the fifteenth century'.[28] He was to be vindicated when the lost manuscript reappeared in 1885, when it was purchased by Bernard Quaritch, from whom it was bought by the Bodleian Library. It is now Bodl. Add. MS B. 107.[29]

Weymouth's edition two years later seemed more radical than it really was, not least because his 'Foreword' wastes no time in disagreeing with

[23] Weymouth, 'Bishop Grosseteste's "Castle of Love"', 52.
[24] Ibid. 49. Weymouth also reported the existence of M. Cooke's edition for the Caxton Society, done from BL MS Egerton 927.
[25] Weymouth, 'Bishop Grosseteste's "Castle of Love"', 52. [26] Ibid.
[27] Ibid. 62 [28] Ibid. 66.
[29] *The Middle English Translation of Robert Grosseteste's Château d'Amour*, ed. Sajavaara, 102, 130.

another combative—and more colourful—member of the Philological Society, Thomas Oswald Cockayne, about the wisdom of applying principles of textual criticism to early English. Cockayne was yet another schoolmaster, who, unlike Weymouth, did edit for the EETS. He had argued in his 1862 edition of *Seinte Marherete* that, though, 'the critical study of the Greek and Latin authors gives the mind a bias to a like treatment of the English', yet this would be unacceptable 'to the present generation of English scholars', who 'have not advanced to that point. They expect an adherence to the manuscript and will condemn deviations from it.'[30] Weymouth took this idea, that English scholars would reject a critically edited text which the editor had endeavoured to make 'as perfect as possible, whether by collation or emendation', as a challenge: 'I have ventured on the experiment; with what success, my readers will be able to judge.'[31] In the long 'preface', as he called his separate study for the Philological Society's *Transactions*, he had proposed certain emendations, and no one had howled in protest.[32] The next step was to be brave enough to put them into the text itself, and he was encouraged, as Madden had been before, by the existence of a French source available for comparison, as well as the several English copies: 'I trust it will be understood that my object is to ascertain from *all* these sources *the original words of the English version* of the poem.'[33] Yet, after this display of courage, Weymouth conceded that, in practice, 'not many alterations of the text . . . have been needed, and all the readings . . . are given, so that the reader has in all cases the requisite materials for forming his own judgment'. There are emendations in square brackets, but they are mostly few and cautious. Yet, when need required, Weymouth showed himself a judicious and capable editor of Middle English.[34] He noted Cockayne's remark that '"Doubtless it may be urged" that "we do not know enough of the possible changes and

---

[30] *Seinte Marherete* (1862), p. iii. Confusingly, Cockayne revised and reissued this text four years later for the EETS: *Seinte Marherete þe Meiden and Martyr in Old English*, EETS, OS 13, pp. vi–vii.

[31] *Castel off Loue*, p. iii; compare *Seinte Marherete* (1862), p. iii.

[32] *Castel off Loue*, p. iii: 'I have ventured on the experiment, partly as encouraged by the (at least tacit) approval on the part of our Society of certain emendations which I have already proposed.'   [33] Ibid., p. iv (the italics are Weymouth's).

[34] Ibid. E.g. the addition of 'was' (p. 8/173) and 'and' (p. 9/190). 'Dede' (i.e. 'did'), p. 12/248, is bolder: V and A have 'diȝede'/'dyede' ('died'), making no sense in the context, and the French, as Weymouth noted, did not help at this point. In the line above (247) the added 'þewdome' is persuasive, and was a case where the Halliwell text provided the best reading: 'thewdome', corresponding to the French, 'seruage'. Both V and A failed to recognize the word: 'þe dome'.

meanings in Early English to treat one of its texts like a classical one."' A ready reply was that, as in all cases of doubtful usage, to attempt emendation is just the most effectual way of claiming for them the careful consideration by those English scholars as well worth study as those of Greece and Rome.[35]

Weymouth's disagreements with his fellow philologists were prosecuted on several fronts. They began in the years before the founding of the EETS and were not concluded (in print) until the 1870s (and it is unlikely that he changed his mind thereafter). It is hard to know which of his critics to describe next. Unlike him, they all became EETS editors, and were, loosely, on the winning side. Since Weymouth's deliberations on *The Castel off Loue* were a response to Cockayne, it seems best to consider his contribution.

OSWALD COCKAYNE: 'ST MARGARET', 'ST JULIANA', AND 'HOLY VIRGINITY'

Cockayne had himself toyed with the idea of critical editing, only to dismiss it in his 1862 edition of *Seinte Marherete*. Being Cockayne, he went to the opposite extreme: 'I have attempted to give such a facsimile of the original writing as the printers means allowed, and they have resources beyond most others.'[36] Indeed, the printers, Longman, Green, Longmans, and Roberts, replicated manuscript letter forms, including the distinction between long and short *s*, which give the whole an antiquated appearance, taking the reader almost back to when 'Anglo-Saxon' was printed in the simulacrum of the 'monkish' handwriting that Rask had deplored. Despite Cockayne's expressed view, the text is not easy for a non-specialist to read, even though he supplied aid in the form of a highly literal word for word modernized text, which, in the absence of line numbers, is not easy to relate to the original. It is not intended for the use of the faint-hearted or the casual reader.

---

[35] See *Castel off Loue*, p. iv. Furnivall, along with John Earle, is thanked 'for valuable suggestions tending to solve some of the difficulties of the poem' (p. vi). On the matter of final *-e* Weymouth noted: 'I have nowhere either added or cut off a final *-e*; nor even, by any kind of accent, marked such an *e* as necessarily sounded. My theory is that whenever the final *e* represents a final syllable in Anglo-Saxon, it *may*, not *must*—be sounded; and never otherwise' (p. v).

[36] *Seinte Marherete*, p. vii. 'It has been my wish to print everything as I found it as much as might be, and more than in all cases seemed best' (p. vi). Thus, the text was printed as prose, not set out in short lines as verse (p. v). 'The contractions of the bookfell' (i.e. parchment) 'have mostly been interpreted, there was no difficulty, and to leave them in the text would have been irksome to most readers' (p. vii). Abbreviated **pet/pat** remains, as does **qd** (though **quod** appears in the text (e.g. 4/[4]).

If this typographical finesse seems retrograde, this is appropriate. Cockayne did not accept half measures in his attempt to familiarize the reading public with medieval texts in medieval dress, and he was even more robust in the expression of his views than Weymouth—he was also funnier and more outrageous. We have already briefly encountered Cockayne as the pugnacious reviewer who hounded Joseph Bosworth. Like Weymouth, he was a classicist by profession and training. His interests in English texts turned decisively to 'Anglo-Saxon', and, in due course, 'Semi-Saxon' (on the principle that anyone who knew the former would find editing early Middle English easy). Contemporaries deplored Cockayne's crankiness but recognized his real learning and philological ability—he became a member of the Philological Society's Council. In the end he became an outcast and a figure of tragedy.[37]

The Revd. (Thomas) Oswald Cockayne, after graduating from St John's College, Cambridge, and subsequent ordination, became assistant master in 1837 at King's College School, where in due course Richard Morris would also teach, and where Cockayne taught Morris's contemporary Walter Skeat and the younger Henry Sweet, all leading members of the next generation of philologists and editors of early English texts.[38] His name was not originally 'Oswald Cockayne'; he was married under the name of 'Thomas Oswald Cockin'.[39] He apparently preferred his Anglo-Saxon second name, Oswald, to the less interesting 'Thomas'. And he preferred a more polite and stylish form of his surname. He was after all a schoolmaster, as well as a clergyman, and was doubtless aware of the hilarious abuse to which 'Cockin' might be put by the young. Also 'Cockayne' was more medieval and aristocratic. Since he claimed that a parish in Northamptonshire, where he briefly served, was his birthplace, his 'natal parish', the family may also have wished to suggest an association with the well-known family of Cockaygne, or Cockayne, of Rushton Hall and have regarded 'Cockin' as a debased vernacular form akin to Durbeyfield and 'D'Urberville'.[40]

---

[37] For a full account of Cockayne's life and work see Kenneally and Roberts, 'Oswald Cockayne (c. 1808–1873)'. Also Daniel F. Kenneally, 'Cockayne, Thomas Oswald (*bap.* 1809, *d.* 1873)', *ODNB*. And see further Arsdall, *Medieval Herbal Remedies*, 16–34; also Skeat, *A Student's Pastime*, , pp. lxv–lxvi.

[38] FU 187, n.d. from 17 Montagu St., W.C. Skeat, *Student's Pastime*, pp. viii–ix.

[39] On 14 Oct. 1834, to Janetta Edwards, at Keynsham, Somerset. See also Kenneally and Roberts, 'Oswald Cockayne (c. 1808–1873)', 108.

[40] As also did the genealogist and herald G. E. Cockayne, who took his mother's name, in preference to his father's more humble 'Adams'; see G. S. Woods, rev. P. W. Hammond, 'George Edward Cokayne [formerly Adams] (1825–1911)', *ODNB*. G. E. Cokayne, friend of both Frederic Madden and Furnivall, married the sister of Henry Hucks Gibbs. For

The uncertainty about the date and place of his birth might just possibly suggest illegitimacy.

Cockayne was a man of wide interests, who also wrote on Irish, French, and Jewish history. He was not devoid of the mild personal eccentricities attendant upon a passion for philology which characterized other members of the Philological Society, not least Furnivall himself.[41] Cockayne's foibles were fondness for archaic English in his own prose and a campaign to revive the Old English letters thorn and eth to replace *th* in modern usage. Thus, he wrote to Furnivall in around 1863-4 to tell him that, instead of collating manuscripts in Oxford as he had promised, he was going to ruralize as a locum priest in his 'natal parish' in 'Norþhants', where he would edify the 'yrþlings'—farm workers—on the topical controversy surrounding Bishop Colenso's interpretation of the Pentateuch and the Book of Joshua. He challenged Furnivall: 'Dare you print þ for th in the English of today? I am much drawn to it.'[42] Furnivall had his own spelling idiosyncrasies, but this was not one of them. As the reviewer in the *Edinburgh* said, 'as written signs they have had their fall, and all the king's printers cannot set them up again'.[43] It may, however, have been from Cockayne that Furnivall picked up his habit of writing 'forewords', rather than 'prefaces'.[44]

Cockayne is best known for his massive edition in three volumes of Anglo-Saxon scientific texts, done for the Master of the Rolls, with the wonderful title of *Leechdoms, Wort-Cunning, and Star-Craft*.[45] It collected in print almost all the Old English medical texts, and 'everything done since in this field ... has been done in the shadow of Cockayne's achievement'.[46] One of his daughters (unacknowledged) assisted him

---

T. O. Cockayne's letter to Furnivall, see FU 187, n.d., sent from 17 Montague St. W.C. (the reference in the letter to Colenso, deposed from his see in Dec. 1863, makes 1863-4 the likely date). That Cockayne referred to his temporary residence in Northamptonshire as his 'natal' parish suggests that his family might have moved thence to Keynsham, Somerset, where he was baptized in 1809. His exact date of birth is not known.

[41] The reviewer in the *Edinburgh*, more charitable than some others, noted that 'Mr. Cockayne does his work with a hearty and somewhat eccentric enthusiasm ... But we are in no humour for picking holes. Mr. Cockayne has edited genially and as thoroughly as he could' (pp. 237-8).   [42] FU 187.

[43] *Edinburgh Review*, 1 Jan. 1867, p. 237: 'All that Mr. Cockayne can effect he does effect—namely the mystification of his readers.'

[44] Yet a reviewer (Cockayne?) in *The Athenaeum*, 27 June 1868, no. 2122, p. 885, of Furnivall's *Bishop Percy's Folio Manuscript: Ballads and Romances*, observed that what 'he is pleased to call "Forewords"', should more accurately be called '*Fore-speech*, which occurs both in Anglo-Saxon and in the Ayenbite of Inwyt'.

[45] *Leechdoms, Wortcunning and Starcraft of Early England*ed. Cockayne.

[46] M. L. Cameron, quoted by Kenneally and Roberts, 'Oswald Cockayne', 121.

by copying the illustrations of the plants in the volume from the text in the British Museum.[47] He also edited three of the texts associated with *Ancrene Wisse* for Furnivall's EETS—at least he transcribed them: the editorial matter was light. He was working on at least two of them concurrently with the *Leechdoms*. The first, *Seinte Marherete* (foreword dated 1862), is the most temperate.[48] It includes a full essay on the language, and, by early EETS standards, a reasonably full set of glossarial notes. It also has a modernized translation, though this follows the archaisms and word order of the original so closely as not to make easy reading. The saint's prayer in her extremity, 'Glad me with thy glee, God, and hope of heal ['salvation'], that my prayer may through-drill ['pierce'] the welkin ['heaven']', may serve as a random illustration.[49] He collated four versions of the text, presenting three of them in full.[50] As his disagreements with Weymouth showed, and thanks to his classical training, he was acquainted with new ideas of textual criticism, though he considered English scholars of his own time incapable of accepting them.

Cockayne's idiosyncrasies and unremitting pugilism towards his critics grew on him. When he moved on to the treatise on *Holy Virginity*, known as *Hali Meidenhad* or *Hali Meiðhad*, he had yielded to his demon for reviving thorn (þ) and also yogh (ȝ) in modern prose.[51] He even included them in the modernized version of the text being presented in parallel, though this might be thought rather to defeat the object.[52] Many years later the EETS, under Gollancz, republished the 1866 edition, re-edited by Furnivall, now including for the first time the version of the text in Bodl. MS Bodley 34, 'issued, as left by Dr. Furnivall, without any changes or addition. The volume may be regarded as Furnivall's (and Cockayne's) last contribution to the work of the Society...

---

[47] Rogers, *Sir Frederic Madden in Cambridge*, 68. Madden, visiting Cambridge in 1863, met Cockayne on this and other occasions.

[48] *Seinte Marherete þe Meiden ant Martyr*, ed. Oswald Cockayne, first published by Longman, Green, Longmans, and Roberts (London, 1862). As indicated above, it was subsequently reissued by the EETS. Cockayne also intended to edit *Seinte Katerine*, as noted in the *Edinburgh Review*, 1 Jan. 1867, p. 237.

[49] *Seinte Marherete* (1862), 57.

[50] The text in British Museum, MS Royal 17. A. xxvii is presented in full, and carefully compared in a series of textual endnotes with the text in MS Bodley 34.

[51] *Hali Meidenhad*, ed. Cockayne, EETS, OS 18.

[52] The special letters are not used, however, in the translations offered in the glossary or the side-notes. A reviewer noted 'the extreme length of pedantry in printing his preface with the two Saxon aspirates, which has no better effect than to provoke a smile'; *London Review*, 22 Sept. 1866, p. 334.

It was no doubt Dr. Furnivall's intention to write a new introduction, Cockayne's being slight and altogether obsolete.'[53]

Cockayne's treatment of *Hali Meidenhad* was considered to be, even when first published, not only eccentric, but to have short-changed his readers. Its eccentricities could hardly be missed, even without the use of thorn and eth in modern English. The volume was appraised at some length in the *Saturday Review*; it was a thoughtful and well-informed review, but the writer did not spare his criticisms and had considerable fun with its oddities, beginning with the use of the special letters: 'The path of the philological reviewer is literally beset with Thorns.'[54] The effect of their use in the preface and the accompanying parallel translation was, 'we are sorry to say . . . to make Mr. Cockayne's translation look almost as strange as the ancient text'.[55] It is a fair point, as were the comments about the scanty editorial matter: 'Mr. Cockayne does not illustrate the tract as a specimen of language, a philology study, nearly so fully as we should have expected. It strikes us as unusually harsh and difficult.'[56] Again this is fair: the language *is* difficult, especially for anyone coming to it from later Middle English, rather than from first studying Old English, which was Cockayne's expectation. He conceded the deficient and incomplete state of dictionaries and grammars but referred his readers to the translation and explanatory materials in his previous edition, *Seinte Marherete*.[57]

Apparently under a sense of compulsion, Cockayne again supplied a facing-page translation and marginal commentary in *Hali Meidenhad*. However, he had originally not wanted to include a translation because some of the portions of the text's advice to virgins to remain immaculate were so 'coarse and repulsive'. Cockayne intended that the text should be 'laid out for printing wiþout a modernized version; but þe printer complained þat þe explanatory footnotes were a trouble to þe compositors and an encumbrance on the page, and þe translation became a last resource'. Still hoping to defeat the dissemination of filthy medieval

---

[53] (Later reissue of the 1866 edition.) *Hali Meidenhad: An Alliterative Homily*, ed. Furnivall, EETS, 18 (London, 1922 (for 1920)), 'prefatory note' by Gollancz, dated 24 July 1922.

[54] '*Hali Meidenhad*', *Saturday Review*, 22, no. 566 (1 Sept. 1866), 279–80. The reviewer noted the partial precedent set by Kemble: 'We never could quite understand why Mr. Kemble thought it necessary to write Æðelred and Ælfðryð in the middle of a page of modern English printing' (p. 279). The reviewer also noticed the misleading nature of his translations (p. 238). He is likely to have been the historian E. A. Freeman, a regular writer for the *Saturday*, who reviewed several of the early EETS titles.

[55] '*Hali Meidenhad*', 279. [56] Ibid. 280.

[57] Headnote to glossary, *Hali Meidenhad*, ed. Cockayne, 49.

heresy by making it available in modern English, Cockayne noted that 'þe most objectionable portions have been Latinized'.[58] The result, as the reviewer noted, was 'a confused jumble... In the middle of the marginal analysis we stumble on this sort of thing:- "Ita episcopus noster, quasi Montanista haereticus, nuptias sanctissimas vituperat. Scripture interpolated. Mentiris, episcope."'[59] Cockayne was a married priest with two daughters,[60] and used much of his preface to defend the state of matrimony, though, as the reviewers said: 'It would hardly, we should have thought, have come into the head of any mortal man, that an editor, who edits a mediaeval work for philological purposes, was bound to stop and protest against everything that he thinks false in its theology.'[61] Cockayne shared the common dismay among members of the Anglican clergy at the revival of celibate communities for women which had taken place in the 1840s and 1850s:

> In his praise of þe virgin state, þe auþor has given such way to his zeal, as to fall into frequent attacks on wedlock; and against þem þe editor has sometimes entered a lively protest. No age of Christianity has sanctioned any such condemnation of "marriage honourable in all," and, of right, holy. Where any fanatics ventured on such folly, þey were quickly branded, by þe truer sense of þe church, as unsound. None, perhaps, in our days can be so ignorant as to declare in favour of þose notions.[62]

The subject of holy virginity had been a live one[63]—Kingsley's *Yeast* (1848), for example, had addressed the same subject—but it was perhaps beginning to lose a little of its force. As the reviewer remarked, the medieval author's opinions 'are not commonly preached from our pulpits'. And: 'The young curates and young ladies who hit it off so well together in the ball-room and the croquet ground are in no danger of

[58] Ibid., foreword, p. v. The printer was Stephen Austin.
[59] '*Hali Meidenhad*', 279; *Hali Meidenhad*, ed. Cockayne, 8: 'Thus our bishop, like a Montanist heretic, reviles most holy matrimony... Bishop, you lie.' Cockayne's view that the author of *Hali Meidenhad* and *Juliana* was a bishop is discussed below.
[60] Florence Louisa, who died from cancer two months after his dismissal, and Alice Eden, who survived him.
[61] '*Hali Meidenhad*', 279; compare *London Review*, 22 Sept. 1866, p. 334: 'The Bishop carries his argument to an absurd length in his ridicule of the drawbacks of the married state, and the editor ... takes him to task in quaint side-notes, losing his temper at last and calling him a "ranter".'
[62] *Hali Meidenhad*, ed. Cockayne, p. v. On p. 8 an English side-note observes that the content is 'Too gross and false for weak sisters.' The graphic description of the woes of pregnancy, p. 34, is 'a painful description of maternal distresses', and in Latin are noted the prolonged and vile symptoms which mothers endure for ten months, 'matri longa decem tulerunt fastidia menses'.
[63] As noted by Alexander, *Medievalism*, 155.

being led astray by them.' As for the intended readership of Cockayne's book, the reviewer noted: 'We should have thought that the philologists of the Early English Text Society hardly needed such very slender safeguards.' After all, the author's views 'are not very terrible, though certainly they are not exactly in the style of a modern Bishop's address to candidates for confirmation'.[64] The reviewer prophetically identified in these obsessions a troubling instability in Cockayne's mental health:

> The truth is that there is evidently a certain twist in Mr. Cockayne's mind which is undoubtedly growing, and which, if he does not take care, will soon make him quite unfit for any serious work. There was a good deal that was very grotesque about the 'Saxon Leechdoms', and the way in which he deals with the little tract which he has now undertaken to edit is more grotesque still.

Furnivall, predictably, was fascinated by the text: '*Hali Meidenhad* has also brought into bright relief a passage in the life of English girls in 1220–30 A.D., unequalled in interest by any known publication of the time.'[65]

Six years later Cockayne, with Furnivall's Cambridge friend and fellow philologist Edmund Brock, edited another of the thirteenth-century religious texts aimed at professed women religious, *The Liflade of St. Juliana*.[66] The two manuscripts were presented *en face*, each with its own modernized version below; Brock was responsible for the left-hand pages, setting out the text from BM Royal MS 17 A. xxvii, Cockayne for the right-hand pages, presenting the text from MS Bodley 34. After a preface, in which he set out his views on þ and ð, Cockayne's passion for reviving special characters now extended to the Tironian *et* and long *s*, with which the printers, Austin's, again obliged.[67] His former pupil, Henry Sweet, took him to task over the translations, which fell 'into the common error of confounding translation with transliteration'. Sweet continued: 'This style of translation not only makes the old language ridiculous, but also exercises an injurious influence on English scholarship by deadening the modern reader's perception of the changes (often very delicate) of meaning which many

---

[64] '*Hali Meidenhad*', 279–80.
[65] Third Annual Report, p. 3.
[66] *The Liflade of St. Juliana*, ed. Cockayne, EETS, OS 51.
[67] Cockayne's 'cherished idol, the letter Thorn' inevitably came in for mockery: 'Even Mr. Furnivall does not think it his duty to plant a modern sentence with Thorns ... but Mr. Cockayne himself þinks þis and þat, and tells us about the Truð and about an inborn ðeory, about ðeological tenets and about St Caðerine'; *Saturday Review*, 28 Sept. 1872, p. 411.

old words preserved in the present English have undergone.'[68] Thus to describe the saint's tyrannical persecutor as 'þe moody Maximien' is a case in point ('modi' is more properly 'proud', or 'arrogant'); to say that he glorified and praised 'heaðen mammets' ('heathen idols') does not help matters.[69]

The pool of reviewers available to the *Saturday Review* who were able and willing to appraise this text was small; perhaps inevitably it was taken on by the same person (likely to have been E. A. Freeman) who had reviewed *Hali Meidenhad*.[70] Cockayne had attacked the 'Mr. Novice' who had criticized his book so severely, and the reviewer observed: 'it did just flash across our mind that we might, by some ill-luck be Mr. Novice. It is certain that, when Mr. Cockayne's *Hali Meidenhad* appeared in 1866, both Mr. Cockayne and ourselves were six years nearer to the state of novices than either of us is now.'[71] By now the reviewer felt that Cockayne's increasingly strident peculiarities were fair game for ridicule. Cockayne declared he had intended 'to take some vivacious notice of any criticisms on þe last treatise I had undertaken for þe Early English Text Society', noting that 'My critics made some easy and cheap fun out of þ and ð', and adding sourly that 'Much learning arises in reviews out of moþer wit'.[72] Cockayne, however, considered that 'he must, after so many years, be "sobered down into temperance and calm"'. 'It follows', said the reviewer, 'that we have Mr. Cockayne before us in the state of temperance and calm into which he has been brought down by the sobering process.' The promise of a 'vivacious notice' aroused his lively anticipation of entertainment: and, captivated by Cockayne's attack on dedicated virgins, he satirically urged him on to greater efforts: *St Juliana* 'certainly fills us with a strong desire to see Mr. Cockayne in his natural state, to see him as he would have been if a stern sense of duty had not driven him so cruelly to smother his inborn vivacity. Mr. Cockayne . . . can smite hard and give good knocks. What would the vivacious notice have been if we

---

[68] For Sweet's review, see Arsdall, *Medieval Herbal Remedies*, 23. See also the examples of misleading archaisms cited in the *Edinburgh Review*, p. 237.

[69] *The Liflade of St. Juliana*, 5 ('heinde ant heriende heðene maumez'; MS Royal 17 A. xxvii); 'heriende & heiende heaðene maumez'; MS Bodley 34).

[70] 'St. Juliana', *Saturday Review*, 34, no. 883 (28 Sept. 1872), 411–12.

[71] Ibid. 411. The reviewer noted that Cockayne had now changed his mind and had come to agree with him that there was no phonetic difference between thorn and eth. For Cockayne's remarks on thorn and eth, see *The Liflade of St. Juliana*, Preface, pp. iii–iv.

[72] *The Liflade of St. Juliana*, Preface, p. v. See pp. v–vi for Cockayne's responses to some other reviewers.

could only have got it?'⁷³ At least Cockayne no longer intruded his personal opinions into the side-notes, but he 'has given us no account of the manuscripts from which the book is printed, nor any help, historical or philological, of any kind'. Cockayne did not discuss the dialect, and the glossary is 'somewhat meagre'. And, because Brock had assisted with the volume, it presented the oddity that his modernized version of one manuscript was 'thornless', whereas Cockayne's was 'thickset with thorns'. And Brock's modernized text made better sense: the reviewer noticed that Maximian, the persecutor observing Juliana, 'saw her exceptionally fair and noble' (so, Brock) was preferable to 'he had very earnestly beholden her exquisitely fair and lady-like youð'. 'Lady-like', rendering *freoliche*, captured the etymology, but 'certainly sounds not a little ludicrous in modern English' (and, it might be added, 'beholden' could also be misleading).⁷⁴ This reviewer's opinion was crushing: 'It is really unfair that the writings of grave scholars like Dr. Morris and Mr. Skeat, and the merry gambols of Mr. Furnivall and Mr. Cockayne should come under the same guise as members of the same fellowship.'⁷⁵

Though Cockayne may have ignored the philological aspects of both *Hali Meidenhad* and *St. Juliana*, yet his speculations about the texts' authorship were to have a long history. Here he deserves the credit for being the first to notice the similarities in language as well as subject matter between these texts (along with others), and *Ancrene Wisse* (*Ancren Riwle*),⁷⁶ and to posit a common origin (as well as common authorship):

I assume from þe tone of þe tract, its eager advocacy of nunneries and profession, its mixture of advice and authority, þat þe writer was of no less þan þe episcopal order. A probability is visible þat he was also þe auðor of þe Ancren Riwle, of þe life and passion of St Margaret, St. Juliana, St Kaðarine, of þe piece Si Sciret paterfamilias, of þe Oreisun of St. Mary, and of oþer tracts now lost. þese are all in þe same homely, terse, eloquent English of þe former half of þe þirteenþ century, and are all of a devotional character, and almost all addressed to maidens, professed and veiled. þe story of St. Margaret is distinctly named in þe Ancren Riwle as known to þe ladies to whom þe latter piece is addressed,

---

⁷³ 28 Sept. 1872, p. 411.
⁷⁴ All quotations from '*St. Juliana*', 411–12. Cf. *The Liflade of St. Juliana*, 4–7. Brock's paper, 'On the Grammatical Forms of Southern English as Shown in the *Ancren Riwle*, ab. 1220–30', was read at the meeting on 18 Nov. 1864, *TPS*, 10, no. 1 (1865), 2.
⁷⁵ '*St. Juliana*', 411. 'The Liflade of St. Juliana, from two Old English MSS of 1230 A.D.', *The Athenaeum*, 5 Oct. 1872.
⁷⁶ Available to him in James Morton's edition, *The Ancren Riwle*.

and in þe tract now printed (p. 45) þe examples of St Kaðarine, St Margaret, St. Agnes, St. Juliana, St. Lucy, St Cecilia are recommended.[77]

Cockayne was convinced that the author had been a bishop (though he based this view purely on the writer's tone of authority and concern with the governance of nuns). The *Saturday's* reviewer was sceptical: 'To us it reads not at all like the composition of a Bishop, Bishops being commonly in those days practical men and well skilled in temporal affairs. It is much more likely to have been written by some fanatical confessor to a nunnery, whose thoughts were always running on the beauty of virginity and on little else.'[78] If we overlook 'fanatical', this view, too, would have a long future in the arguments that would rage over the authorship of *Ancrene Wisse*.

Cockayne went further: he accepted James Morton's view that the sisters being addressed belonged to the nunnery at Tarrant Kaines, in Dorset, and, based on this, he put a name to the author. He had noticed the attribution in the Latin version of *Ancrene Wisse* in Oxford, Magdalen College MS Latin 67 to Simon of Ghent, Bishop of Salisbury, but, agreeing with Morton's view that the Latin was a translation from the English, Cockayne deduced that Simon of Ghent was not the author of the English, but of that Latin version only. Cockayne accordingly proposed an earlier bishop of Salisbury, Richard Poore (1217–29), as the author of the English.[79] The reviewer pointed out the dubiousness of this attribution: 'He (Cockayne) still, we cannot conceive why, maintains that the author . . . is Bishop Richard le Poor, founder of New Sarum. He assumes, he does not tell us why, that the book was written for the nuns of . . . Tarrant in Dorset, of which house Bishop Richard is said—though it is not very clear on what evidence—to have been a chief benefactor.'[80] As we shall see, scholars would be looking for the sisters of Tarrant Kaines as the original audience of *Ancrene Wisse* and its associated treatises well into the twentieth century.

St. Juliana was delayed in printing. Cockayne conceded: 'From want of subscribers enough to þe Early English Text Society þis Juliana has taken so long to appear in type þat some want of cohesion has crept into my association of ideas about it.'[81] By this time his troubles had

---

[77] *Hali Meidenhad*, pp. vi–vii. [78] '*Hali Meidenhad*', 250.

[79] *Hali Meidenhad*, p. vii. Here he was undecided between Richard Poore and the earlier Herbert Poore (1194–1215), but settled on Richard. See further *Ancrene Wisse: A Corrected Edition*, ed. Millett, EETS 325, 326, i, pp. xvii–xviii.

[80] 'St. Juliana', 411. For Cockayne's full argument, see *St. Juliana*, Preface, pp. vii–viii.

[81] *The Liflade of St. Juliana*, Preface, pp. vi–vii.

caught up with him. Cockayne was evidently a controversial teacher: he was dismissed from his post at King's College School in 1869 on charges of using unsuitable language by 'unnecessarily' discussing with the boys 'subjects which could only tend to corrupt them'. The 'subjects' related to sexual matters, the indecent details connected with questionable allusions in Classical authors. Among them it was alleged that Cockayne's explanation as to 'Why Paris did not want to go to the fight' had been 'Because of course Paris wished to lie all day in bed with Helen'.[82] It seems that the school authorities were determined to get rid of him, despite the protest which Cockayne registered during the proceedings. He did, however, admit to having made at least nine of the fifteen allegations of 'unfit language'.

Cockayne, though perhaps recklessly outspoken, seems to have intended to discuss such matters with the boys honestly and with frankness. Though the investigators accepted that he had no intention to corrupt his pupils, they considered that he had acted 'in direct opposition to the feeling of the age . . . which will tolerate no such teaching in an English School'.[83] The effect was to render Cockayne incapable of future employment as a schoolmaster elsewhere. On the same day that he was dismissed, he issued his own detailed statement of the events, in *Mr Cockaynes* Narrative.[84] This may have helped temporarily to relieve his feelings, but his worldly prospects were bleak. In the circumstances, *Juliana* became an occasion for him to vent some of his accumulated spleen, though he made a perfunctory effort to preach patience to himself: 'Whatever I say, þerefore, must be sobered down into temperance and calm; must be simply þe result of þe toil of þe student and translator.'[85] The mockery he received from the writer in the *Saturday Review*, though within the bounds of the rough and tumble accepted in nineteenth-century reviewing, and not without good humour, is likely to have contributed to Cockayne's sense of alienation; the reviewer had sensed his mental fragility when *Hali Meidenhad* was published, but had not made such allowances the second time round.

Cockayne's end was to be sensational, as well as tragic. In 1873, as

---

[82] Kenneally and Roberts, 'Oswald Cockayne', 114.
[83] For a full account of the process leading to Cockayne's dismissal, see ibid. 112–16. There had been anxieties from 1865 more broadly surrounding the school's future, following a sudden drop in enrolment, and concerns were being expressed about teaching and discipline. The investigation in 1866 also resulted in the resignation of the headmaster, John Major, after 35 years' service, and that of the Principal, Jelf.
[84] Extracts quoted by Kenneally and Roberts, 'Oswald Cockayne', 115–16.
[85] *The Liflade of St. Juliana*, Preface, p. v.

was widely reported in the national as well as local newspapers, unemployed, and suffering from melancholia, he died from a gunshot wound to the head while staying in St Ives, Cornwall. Gruesome accounts of the finding by children of his decomposing body near St Ives and its subsequent identification appeared in *The Cornish Telegraph*.[86] His death was reported as suicide. He had written to his family to tell them that he would never return. But there were odd features in the descriptions of the finding of his body, for example that his discharged pistol was found *inside* his breast pocket. At the inquest, the verdict was 'Found dead, the cause of death being a pistol shot, but by whom fired unknown'. This report, not previously printed in full, deserves to be given at length here because of the interest of the case, the pathos of what it reveals of Cockayne's demeanour beforehand—he was apparently engaging in local 'wort-cunning' enquiries—and the mysteriousness of some of the details:

The inquest relative to the death of the man found at Carthew Point, near St Ives, on Sunday last, has been concluded after repeated adjournments. Deceased was discovered lying on the ground in an unfrequented spot, and on examination it was found that he had been shot through the head. A discharged pistol was also found in his left breast coat pocket. The evidence on the inquest went to show that deceased arrived at Hodge's Western Hotel, St Ives, the 1st instant. He slept at the hotel that night and the boots of the hotel who gave evidence, was called to identify deceased by his boots, which were of a very peculiar make. Deceased was last seen alive on Monday evening the 2nd instant, by Mr. William Bennetts. Deceased asked Mr. Bennetts several unimportant questions, such as the names of the various kinds of herbs growing in the locality; and Mr Bennetts described him as a tall upright, intelligent gentleman. They parted near the village of Ayr, deceased going down towards the cliffs. Mr. Bennetts saw deceased about half an hour afterwards, in a field close to the place where he was discovered. It appears that deceased was observed by some boys on Sunday, the 8th instant, but the boys thinking he was asleep, threw stones at him and ran away. In the deceased's carpet bag at the hotel were found a night shirt, a night cap, pocket handkerchief, scissors, brushes and combs, a lock of hair and pair of black-kid gloves. He appears to have taken great pains to prevent identification, for the handkerchief and his carpet-bag had a piece cut out of it (probably where the name was), and the name was also cut out of the high hat he wore. Having stated at the hotel that his luggage was at St Ives-road station, the inquest was adjourned to one o'clock on Thursday, to ascertain if this was correct, and if so to examine the luggage. The adjourned inquest was held on Friday afternoon. A young man named Monk stated that he had a long conversation

[86] Quoted by Arsdall, *Medieval Herbal Remedies*, 26–8.

with deceased on the 2nd instant. Deceased appeared to talk very rationally for some time, and enquired about the nature of the different kinds of herbs growing in the locality. Witness asked him where he came from, and he replied with a laugh, 'From the moon.' Mrs. Hodge, the landlady of the hotel, also spoke as to the deceased's manner, and described him as being gentlemanly, and showing no signs of insanity. The jury, after deliberating, returned a verdict of 'Found dead, the cause of death being a pistol shot, but by whom fired unknown.' It appears that deceased was the Rev. Thomas Oswald Cockayne, a clergyman of the Church of England, without charge, aged 65 years. He left his home, near Bristol, some weeks ago, with the avowed intention of going to Hastings for the benefit of his health. About a week before the fatal occurrence his relatives were shocked to receive a letter from him, bearing a Western postmark; and stating that he should never return home again. Their suspicions and fears were at once aroused, and they instituted a searching but fruitless search after him. They sent a telegram, however, to St Ives, having seen the report of the occurrence in the papers, and one of the friends of the deceased identified him from his clothes.[87])

As a final irony, the local priest in St Ives, the Revd. John Balmer Jones, who conducted the funeral, could not have realized that he was burying his own former schoolteacher at King's College School: Cockayne's shockingly decaying body had to be buried quickly, before he could be identified from his effects.

The last word on Cockayne may be given to Furnivall, who in 1889 responded to a reviewer in *The Academy* who had complained that Cockayne had omitted a word from the text of *Hali Meidenhad*. Furnivall confirmed the omission but put it down to oversight: 'That it is not in the volume as issued is, I believe, his misfortune, and not his fault. His sad end should save him from needless blame. He was hardly used in life.'[88]

RICHARD MORRIS: 'THE PRICK OF CONSCIENCE' AND DISAGREEMENTS WITH R. F. WEYMOUTH

Morris, born in 1833, and yet another of this pedagogy of schoolmasters, was the youngest of the group, and the most reserved: to know his

---

[87] 'The Mysterious Tragedy at St Ives', *The Royal Cornwall Gazette*, 28 June 1873. The 'boots' was the hotel's servant who cleaned visitors' footwear.

[88] F. J. Furnivall, 'Cokayne's Edition of "Hali Meidenhad"', *The Academy*, 36, no. 908 (28 Sept. 1889), 206. He described 'the late Oswald Cokayne' as 'a man devoted to our earliest literature and the "skin-books" (as he called them)'. The spelling 'Cokayne' is used throughout. The word omitted from p. 21, l. 28 was 'held', corresponding to 'kept' in the translation. In fact, despite his best efforts, Cockayne had been led to misreadings of MS Bodley 34, which, as the later editor, S. R. T. O. d'Ardenne, conceded, was written in a difficult hand, minims and the vowels, **e**, **o**, **a**, being sometimes insufficiently distinguished. *þe Liflade ant te Passiun of Seinte Iuliene*, EETS, OS 248, p. xv.

books is probably the nearest we can get to knowing him.[89] He was also of much humbler origins than Weymouth, and largely self-educated, which makes his achievements still more impressive. He might be called Furnivall's beau ideal: someone of a working-class background who had, by his own efforts, taught himself philology and been elected to the Philological Society. They were lifelong friends. Neither was rich: Morris's wealth at death was £615 19s. 4d., largely earned from his educational writing, and comparable with Furnivall's £796 19s. 2d. Both in later life received modest civil list pensions of £150 from Gladstone in recognition of their financial need and their literary work. Their financial standing at death may be contrasted with Weymouth's estate of £4,586. 17s. 10d.

Morris was born in Bermondsey, the son of a Welsh hatter, David Morris, who, with his wife, Elizabeth, had moved to London from Llanfaglan, Montgomeryshire.[90] As was probably to be expected, his background was non-conformist; he was baptized as a Wesleyan Methodist.[91] He trained as an elementary schoolteacher at St John's College, Battersea, founded in 1839 by the pioneer of teacher training, and promoter of a national system of education, Sir James Phillips Kay-Shuttleworth, who expanded the pupil–teacher system whereby promising boys taught in elementary schools in return for receiving teaching from their heads. In 1856, Morris married Hannah Ary, a coachman's daughter, and they had three daughters.[92] In 1869 he was appointed Winchester lecturer in English at King's College School. He was ordained in the Church of England in 1871 and served for two years as curate of Christ Church, Camberwell, before becoming headmaster of the Royal Masonic Institution for Boys. Afterwards he was for a short time master of the old Elizabethan grammar school at Dedham, Essex. Images of Morris are far to seek; by contrast, Weymouth's formal portrait

---

[89] See further J. S. Cotton, revd. John D. Haigh, 'Morris, Richard (1833–1894)', *ODNB*. It is typical of Morris that much of the information in this biography was derived from the first writer's personal knowledge.

[90] As stated in the 1841 Census, which showed the family living at Cross Street, St Mary Magdalen, Bermondsey. Richard was the eldest of a family of three children: the household was shared with four members of the Owens family and Evan Humphreys. In the 1851 Census, aged 17, he is described as a pupil teacher.

[91] On 29 Sept. 1833, London, Aldersgate Street, formerly St Mary Axe (Wesleyan): Births and Baptisms.

[92] They lived at 4 Cloudesley Place, Jubilee Street, Mile End, Old Town: 1861 Census, in which Morris is described as a schoolmaster, with three daughters: Hannah E, Emily L, and a baby, Ellen.

shows him in full academic dress, looking every inch the headmaster.[93]

To fill out these meagre facts we may turn to Morris's publications before he became one of Furnivall's leading editors for the EETS. His first book was a short etymological study of English place-name elements, published by a short-lived company, Judd and Glass, of New Bridge Street, Blackfriars, in which Morris describes himself simply as 'formerly student of Battersea Training College'.[94] The modest list of reference works cited, drawing heavily on Kemble and Bosworth among others, tells its own story of self-instruction from limited resources. It is a young man's book, small in scale, but big in ambition, which clearly shows that he saw his way to advancement, and personal and intellectual fulfilment, lay in his fascination with the power of the 'new science' of comparative philology to reveal how nations 'now separated by wide regions ... have proceeded from a common seat; it discloses the directions and paths of ancient migrations'.[95] Like several of Morris's later publications, it was written to assist teachers, on this occasion by listing 'the chief *root* or *key* words which are necessary for the explanation of local names in England'. Perhaps strangely, for a young man from a Welsh family, he asserts: 'we have chosen English names . . . because they are more familiar, and, indeed, of more importance than any others'.[96] As a 'science' and the object of 'careful study by eminent scholars', philology attracted him by its logic and order; but Morris was also clearly drawn to the romance of names as a source of intimations about the legends and stories of prehistory, just as Tolkien would be. Morris quoted Emerson in support of his concentration on English names: they evoke for him 'an atmosphere of legendary melody'. More prosaically, they are as intimate and essential as a woolly vest: 'Older than all epics and histories which clothe a nation, this under-shirt sits close to the body. What history, too, and what stores of primitive and savage obsessions it unfolds!' Morris, however, stated the need to keep primitive obsessions under strict control. Fairyland may be admitted, but only as a last resort: 'Perhaps local names are indebted to the fairy mythology. MAB, the elf-queen, occurs in Mab's-Hill, and the merry PUCK in Puck-pool Bay . . . GRIM, a ghost, hag, or witch is found in Grims-by . . . It is the safest plan, however, in tracing names to their origin, to resort to such a

[93] Braithwaite, *Strikingly Alive*, 113, and see the group photograph, p. 86.
[94] *The Etymology of Local Names*.
[95] Ibid. 5.
[96] Preface.

mode for their explanation only when we find ourselves unable to offer a more rational etymology.'[97]

Though this side of Morris's nature was kept so sternly within rational bounds, he would in due course go on to edit *Sir Gawain and the Green Knight* for the EETS. We know from the personal knowledge of his first *ODNB* biographer that he enjoyed a good story. In the light of this, it is unlikely that he did not appreciate the magical toponymy of that poem's real, and yet fictionalized, landscape, though, like Furnivall in dealing with the Grail, he did not wish to discredit himself in the world of scholarship by appearing to sanction sorceresses and magical decapitated heads. Comparative philology was Morris's route to bettering himself as a schoolmaster, pursued with grit and determination—and, unlike Jude Fawley, he succeeded. With this background, when Weymouth assailed him on his philological knowledge, it hit him in a vital spot.

His editorial career began with the *Liber cure cocorum* already mentioned, published for the Philological Society by Asher in 1862, after the Society had also published Whitley Stokes's edition of the fifteenth-century *Play of the Sacrament*.[98] Morris's interest in the cookery book was in its Northern dialect (identified by him as NW Lancashire). He had a particular interest in northern texts whose language showed descent from the Northumbrian dialect (meaning the whole large extent of the Anglo-Saxon kingdom of Northumbria). He had written in April 1860 to Madden: 'I should feel greatly obliged if you could refer me to any Northumbrian MSS. of the XIII, XIV, or XV centuries among the manuscripts collection of the British Museum . . . The late Mr Garnett says that the literary monuments of the Northumbrian dialects are very numerous (from the xiv to xvi [centuries]). I have not found this to be the case.'[99] Morris adopted Garnett's classification of English dialects into five broad areas: Northumbrian being that spoken throughout England north of the Humber and the Lowlands of Scotland, 'extending at one time from the Humber to the Forth, and from the German Ocean to the Irish Channel'.[100]

---

[97] Preface. Morris quotes Kemble as one of his epigraphs: 'It cannot be doubted that *local names*, and those devoted to distinguish the natural features of a country, possess an inherent vitality which even the urgency of conquest is unable to remove.'

[98] *The Play of the Sacrament, a Middle-English Drama*, TPS (1860–1), 101–52, and separately published by Asher (1862). (The Philological Society's Council was apparently persuaded by Furnivall to publish the *Liber Cure Cocorum* on the same terms as the *Play of the Sacrament*: see Gilliver, *Making of the OED*, 45 n., and reference there given.

[99] BL MS Egerton 2848, f. 20^{r-v}.

[100] 'On the Languages and Dialects of the British Islands', in *The Philological Essays*, 147–95 at 189.

Morris's 1860 quest for 'Northumbrian' texts in the British Museum led him three years later to his next volume for the Philological Society, an edition of the fourteenth-century rhyming pastoral treatise *The Prick of Conscience*, in 9,621 lines, and in the nineteenth century attributed to the Yorkshire hermit Richard Rolle of Hampole. Morris's edition was a formidable achievement.[101] The text is now known to have survived in around 116 manuscripts, making it the most popular Middle English text ever, judging simply by number of copies, outstripping by far both Chaucer and Langland. Morris 'carefully examined' the ten copies in the British Museum 'for the purpose of obtaining a good text'; one, Cotton MS Galba E. ix, stood out on philological grounds. Morris made the usual assumption of 'Hampole's' authorship and looked for the British Museum copy which seemed closest to this region of Yorkshire and most 'archaic'. When he was far advanced with the transcription, and large portions were set up in print, he discovered that a quire was missing, which had to be supplied from another copy.[102] Although not by Rolle, the text is nevertheless from Yorkshire, and Morris's choices were particularly apt. After he had chosen his best manuscript as his base text, he made no attempt to use his collations to provide a critical text—Morris's was in the pragmatic traditions of most other mid-nineteenth-century editions of medieval texts, but it has served its purpose well, and the high quality of the editor's work has ensured its continuing long life.[103]

Of course, Morris gave an extensive account of the work's linguistic value but recognized that even readers who were members of the Philological Society might be interested in other things. Like Furnivall he

[101] *The Prick of Conscience (Stimulus Conscientiae)*, ed. Morris. Morris described himself on the title page as 'Author of "The Etymology of Local Names," Editor of "Liber Cure Cocorum," Member of the Council of the Philological Society'.

[102] *Prick of Conscience*, pp. i–iv: 'The Editor of the present volume would remark that he has endeavoured to make the text as correct as possible, the proof sheets in every case having been read *twice* . . . It is hoped that the Glossary will be found useful for lexicographers' (p. xxxiii).

[103] A revision of Morris's text, in a corrected and expanded form, with consultation of the full archive, and with full commentary and glossary, was undertaken by Ralph Hanna and Sarah Wood: *Richard Morris's* Prick of Conscience, EETS, OS 342. Reissue of a mid-Victorian text as the basis of a modern edition was an innovation for the Society in 2013, a testimony both to the need to get out a good working edition of a text that was immensely popular and influential in its day in order to facilitate study despite the huge number of manuscripts, and also to the quality of Morris's work: 'His edition provides an unusually apt, if not always accurate, version of the Northern original from which all other copies of *PC* descend' (p. xv). See further Lewis and McIntosh, *A Descriptive Guide to the Manuscripts of the* Prick of Conscience.

needed to find a means of discussing the writer's theology while, unlike Cockayne, maintaining his distance. Morris's way was to describe these features ironically, in the manner of a guidebook to an exotic land: 'If any Protestant reader should not believe in the existence of Purgatory, our author will give him trustworthy information upon it as if he had travelled through the country and seen its "sights".' In the same vein: 'If any one desires information upon future punishment he will find an interesting question . . . "How may the soul feel pain?"' And 'about Antichrist there is no lack of information . . . And of Gog and Magog . . . the general opinion concerning them is that they live beyond the mountains of the Caspian Sea, and are kept quiet by the queen of the Amazons.'[104] Indeed, when it came to describing non-linguistic features of interest, Morris modelled himself on Furnivall's Roxburghe editions. His comments read like wry remarks addressed to Furnivall, and any other 'reader who is on the lookout for what is curious': 'Valuable as is the *language* of Hampole to the student of our early literature, the matter will be found to be almost as interesting.'[105] After giving his short guide to the poem's religious 'sights', he comments: 'For other points of interest the reader must consult the volume itself.'[106] It could fairly be said of Furnivall's Roxburghe editions that they give readers every facility for finding titbits *without* having to read 'the volume itself'. Morris evidently felt that he had been obliged to be more discursive than he felt to be necessary in 'this somewhat rambling preface'.[107] He provided straightforward, rather than chatty or facetious, side-notes, an index, and glossarial index; his notes largely concern matters of vocabulary.

These important editions (and those he would undertake for the EETS) did not pay the bills. Morris gradually achieved financial security and was able to retire from teaching to devote himself to researches into Pali, the sacred language of Buddhism, after publishing a series of influential and widely used textbooks to promote the teaching of English in schools, including *Elementary Lessons in Historical English Grammar* (London, 1874)[108] and *English Grammar* (London, 1875), by which time he was able to describe himself as the Revd. Richard Morris, M.A. LL.D., President of the Philological Society. One of the most influential of his textbooks was his *Historical Outline of English Accidence*, first published in 1872, which went through twenty editions, and which was the fruit of the conviction which he had announced

---

[104] *Prick of Conscience*, p. xxxi.   [105] Ibid., p. xxx.
[106] Ibid., p. xxxii.   [107] Ibid., p. xxxiii.
[108] Later revised by Henry Bradley (London, 1897).

back in 1857: 'Grammatical analysis and comparison is the only true method for the classification of languages according to their radical affinity.'[109] By 1872 he was able to describe himself on the title page as 'Editor of Hampole's "Pricke of Conscience," "The Story of Genesis and Exodus," "Ayenbite of Inwyt," "Old English Homilies," etc. etc. Member of the Council of the Philological Society, Lecturer on English Language and Literature in King's College School.' This omitted his edition of Chaucer for Bell and Daldy's Aldine Edition of the British Poets series (1866), the first edition of the poet to be based on first-hand study of the manuscripts since Tyrwhitt, before it was overshadowed by Skeat's.[110] It also omitted his standard anthology, *Specimens of Early English*, first published in 1867.[111]

Morris's achievements and distinction were recognized, first, when he was awarded the LLD degree by Archbishop Tait, and subsequently when the University of Oxford conferred an honorary MA on 28 May 1874, the year in which he became President of the Philological Society. The Oxford degree required preliminary soundings and lobbying among members of the University beforehand to ensure that the honour would be acceptable, as support was not unanimous. Max Müller urged Furnivall to be discreet:

I asked Mr Twentyman to keep the matter regarding Dr. Morris quite quiet, because what is meant as a compliment might if refused become almost a slight. I also told him that there is a certain unwillingness on the part of some of the Curators and that Dr. Morris's friends should do what they could to urge his claims particularly on the Rector of Lincoln [and] Professor Stubbs. But it should be done very cautiously and at all costs kept from the papers before it is settled. The Vice Chancellor is very willing and must also be written to. I hope we will succeed.[112]

It was *English Accidence* which caused the angry exchanges in print between Morris and Weymouth, who wrote his own practical text book two years later, 'intended to meet a want which is largely felt by students, especially the numerous class of those who seek to prepare themselves by self-tuition', for the University of London's matriculation

---

[109] *Etymology of Local Names*, 5. *English Accidence* would be later revised by Henry Bradley and L. Kellner in 1895.

[110] See references in Ruggiers (ed.), *Editing Chaucer*; Spencer, 'F. J. Furnivall's Six of the Best', 607-8.   [111] *Specimens of Early English Selected*, ed. Morris.

[112] Letter of 28 Feb. [1874], FU 690. Max Müller was appointed as Oxford's first Professor of Comparative Philology in 1868. The Rector of Lincoln College was Mark Pattison (elected 1861, d. 1884); William Stubbs was elected Regius Professor of Modern History in 1866 and held the post until 1884.

examination.[113] In it Weymouth noted occasional disagreements with Morris, who tactlessly began the public argument by asserting that Weymouth had 'fallen into some very grave blunders in his anxiety to show that I have gone astray'.[114] There were seven of these 'blunders', ruthlessly numbered in the manner of Cardinal Newman exposing Kingsley's schoolboy 'blots' in the *Apologia pro vita sua*. Morris, eleven years his junior, gave Weymouth (the headmaster of a public school), the raking down meted out to an errant pupil, and, what was worse, in print, not in the privacy of the headmaster's study:

> Dr. Weymouth very boldly denies . . . what most Teutonic philologists have made tolerably clear (at least to my dull comprehension), that *did* is a reduplication of *do* . . . Dr. Weymouth commits the grave error . . . mere tyros in philology know, however that this is wrong . . . *Fourthly*. As Dr. Weymouth professes to write for young students he ought not to make their knowledge hazy by the introduction of mere unsupported conjectures . . . *Fifthly*. Dr Weymouth is far too positive and dogmatic in his assertions when, in the face of all philologists, he says . . . *Sixthly*. Dr. Weymouth complains of my non-historical classification of weak contracted verbs. Of his own I cannot see that it is very scientific or historical . . . Lastly. Of Dr. Weymouth's peculiar notions about Early English pronunciation, I will not now say anything, but am content to let them be dealt with by Mr. Ellis.

Morris's fury at having his hard-won philological expertise impugned (even if only in occasional remarks) had led him to stray beyond the expected bounds of gentlemanly disagreement. Weymouth's reply showed his concern to put the argument on a more courteous and conciliatory footing (while conceding very little and rebuking Morris from a superior height for his bad manners):

> I have read with considerable surprise the letter of my friend, Dr. Morris . . . One would scarcely gather from it that of the various useful books to which the student is referred in my *Answers to Questions* . . . Dr Morris's *Accidence* is more frequently commended there than any other; for such is the fact. But high as is my appreciation of that work, and far as I have been from entertaining any 'anxiety to show that' its author has 'gone astray', I do not give him credit for omniscience, nor is it reasonable that my dissenting in a very few instances . . . from the opinions which he has expressed . . . should have evoked such a querulous epistle . . . As for my being 'far too positive and dogmatic' . . . would it not have been more candid to say that these were the closing words after a page

---

[113] Weymouth, *Answers to Questions on the English Language*, p. iii.

[114] Richard Morris, 'Dr. Morris and Dr. Weymouth', *The Academy*, 5, no. 108 (30 May 1874), 607. Morris's letter is dated 25 May.

and a half of what at least professed to be reasoning?... But I must notice some of the 'grave blunders' into which I have fallen ... I am not a professed Sanscrit scholar, for 'non omnia possumus omnes,' but at least to a small extent I have studied the language for myself... I have been 'violating at the very outset Grimm's law.' Are there then no exceptions to Grimm's law?... Any thought of depreciating the book was most remote from my mind. My hope was that those few strictures, by no means unkindly meant, in a truly valuable book, might lead to the correction of errors... in a future edition, which it is sure to reach.[115]

Weymouth concluded with a pacific appeal to the 'brotherhood' of philologists and their common purpose: 'Surely in philology, as in other sciences, men who are honestly seeking truth will recognise the fact that all err here and there; none are infallible. And it is sad if members of the great community and brotherhood of learning cannot co-operate heartily in their common high endeavour, without selfishness and jealousy.' He was clearly hurt. This wording towards the end, where Weymouth descends somewhat from his altitude, may be a rebuke, not only to Morris, but, tacitly, to Furnivall. The public quarrel shows that, now that the history of the English language was coming to dominate the Philological Society's affairs, there were different sides. Weymouth, as a long-standing member 'for nearly a quarter of a century',[116] resented the consensus growing up among members of a party represented by Furnivall and his friends, Morris, Skeat (also mentioned in Weymouth's letter), Ellis, and later Sweet. Weymouth did not care for the role of eccentric lone voice into which he was being cast; he clearly felt that this group was having things too much its own way, and that the expression of alternative views was being discouraged: 'those men are not quite worthless in the world who investigate for themselves instead of taking everything on trust from others, and truth is often found on the side of a small minority, yes, even of a minority of one. And it will be quite soon enough to adopt this contemptuous tone ... when I have been *proved* to be wrong.' It was they who were too dogmatic, not he, and who were having too much their own way.

Weymouth, however, was not quite so moderate as he claimed: just a month before Morris attacked him, he had published a small book written in open disagreement with Ellis's pioneering and vast study of early English pronunciation, then in course of publication between 1869 and 1889. He presented himself as a knight, obliged to joust in the interests of philological truth, who could no longer 'consent to be silent': 'It is

[115] 'Dr. R. Morris and Dr. Weymouth', *The Academy*, 110, 13 June 1874, pp. 663–4.
[116] Weymouth, *On Early English Pronunciation* (1874).

now nearly four years since I first laid lance to rest to tilt at Mr. Ellis's views—expounded in a work of already 996 closely printed pages 8vo, and still growing.'[117] Weymouth knew he was being quixotic: 'it seems futile to attempt to uproot by this short essay those views which his large and learned book has caused to be so generally received in our Society'.[118] And, as usual, in his insistence on logical argument, Weymouth went too far, as he recognized: 'I fear some expressions in the preceding pages may seem to indicate a degree of confidence in the conclusions arrived at which I do not in reality entertain.'[119] Henry Sweet did justice in his review to Weymouth's reasonable reservations about aspects of Ellis's work, but what abides is the sting in the tail: 'If we omit . . . all the expressions of doubt and depreciation, it would be impossible to find a clearer and more satisfactory statement of the views universally accepted by the philological world—with the exception of Dr. Weymouth and the unfortunate schoolboys who have his extraordinary Chaucerian pronunciation drilled into them.'[120]

The disagreement with Weymouth has its interest in showing Morris's sense of insecurity. And it would not be the only time when he was to feel angered because his contribution was being devalued by senior and well-established scholars who had enjoyed a more secure start in life than he had. He was careful to see that his authority and standing as a philologist was unassailable. But in general he was described as a cheerful man who enjoyed a good tale.[121] This humour is only hinted at in his publications, where he occasionally quietly teased his friends.

A SURFEIT OF EARLY ENGLISH

The three texts (*Liber cure cocorum*, *Prick of Conscience*, and *Castel of Loue*) were published together in what was called the Philological Society's Early English Volume in 1865, but by then the Society had had enough. The printing was too great a strain on its resources, and English was taking the lion's share. As Wheatley put it: 'The Council rebelled. Members complained that Philology was not confined to the English language.'[122] The Philological Society's decision was only reasonable in the view of the *Saturday Review*: 'We have sometimes rather wondered at the latter body [the Philological Society] so often publish-

---

[117] Ibid.. 1, and preface. [118] Ibid.. 1.
[119] Ibid. 116. [120] Review, 'On "Early English Pronunciation"', 461.
[121] By J. S. Cotton, in his personal recollections in the *ODNB*.
[122] 'The Early English Text Society and F. J. Furnivall', 5.

ing the whole of long early poems, which seemed to ask for a world of their own and to be rather out of place in the Transactions of a Society.'¹²³ The decision was made to print no more texts. Apparently, Furnivall instantly set about founding a new society exclusively for this purpose: 'delay did not enter into his scheme of things at all'.¹²⁴ Undoubtedly, Furnivall was impetuous, but another factor, perhaps even the immediate cause, was Richard Morris. According to one of Furnivall's accounts written in hindsight, Morris, baulked of publishing texts in the Philological Society's *Transactions*, and lacking other outlets in England, 'was sending extracts from English MSS. abroad to be printed in foreign journals'. Furnivall's national pride was piqued: 'It *did* seem to me a shame, and that if people only knew the fact they would put an end to such a state of things. The result was the getting-up of the Early English Text Society', which, as he remarked with satisfaction, 'to say the least of it, has done some worthy work for our language and literature'.¹²⁵ And, according to Skeat, the foundation of the EETS was an inevitable next step, undertaken largely because Morris begged Furnivall to do it:

There was only one course to be taken. The MSS., especially of the thirteenth and fourteenth centuries, had to be printed at a reasonable price, and such of them as had only been edited in an expensive form, had to be printed over again. With this end in view, and at the urgent request of Dr. Morris, Mr. Furnivall started the Early English Text Society in 1864, with a goodly list of subscribers at a guinea apiece; and he had to look about for patriotic editors, who were willing to do the editing gratis, if the Society would pay for the printing.¹²⁶

Though the broad outlines of the story have been told a number of times, it is difficult to get behind the mythology surrounding the creation of the EETS. Not only did Furnivall have his own point of view to convey to posterity, but we also have two accounts by two of its leading

---

¹²³ 'Early English Texts', *Saturday Review*, 5 Nov. 1864, p. 570: 'The first-fruits of their labours, the two texts now before us, might easily pass for a continuation in the same series of the texts which the Philological Society has already published.'

¹²⁴ Wheatley, 'The Early English Text Society and F. J. Furnivall', 5. Annual Report of the [EETS] Committee, 1875, 'The Society's First Ten Years' Work', 2: 'it may therefore be well to look back over its work since, in February 1864, its Founder's first Circular went out, announcing that "A few of the members of the Philological Society, being anxious to continue the publication of Early English Texts, which that Society lately commenced, but has now for a time resolved to discontinue, have formed a committee for the purpose of collecting subscriptions, and printing therewith Early English MSS."'

¹²⁵ F. J. Furnivall, 'The Early English Text Society', *Gentleman's Magazine*, Aug. 1867, pp. 212–3 at 212. As noted above, Morris's edition of *The Prick of Conscience* was published in Berlin.   ¹²⁶ *A Student's Pastime*, p. xxii.

early members, H. B. Wheatley and Henry Sweet. Sweet's brief version, written in 1871, is closer in time, but, apart from summarizing the main points of the early Annual Reports, Sweet had an axe to grind—he disapproved of the Society's decisions on including modern English translations, a matter to which we shall return. Wheatley's extended account was written in 1912, after Furnivall's death, but, as a founding member, and the EETS's first Treasurer, and Honorary Secretary, he witnessed the events described at first hand.[127]

The EETS was undoubtedly founded in a rush. Eleanor Furnivall told the visiting Austrian scholar Alois Brandl that her husband had come home suddenly one day, called for paper, and spent the entire night writing letters to recruit members for his newly conceived Society. He appeared the next morning with a packet of letters that cost 'pounds in postage', as she ruefully recalled. Brandl remarked that her sighs were understandable, given Furnivall's exiguous private income and lack of proper employment: 'He was an idealist of the purest water.'[128] This was true, but Furnivall evidently also felt that if one wants a thing done, one had better do it oneself.

---

[127] Sweet, 'The Early English Text Society'; Wheatley, 'The Early English Text Society and F. J. Furnivall'.

[128] *Zwischen Inn und Themse*, 136: 'Er war ein Idealist vom reinsten Wasser.'

APPENDICES

APPENDIX 1

Correspondence Relating to the Appearance and History of Great Fosters House

1. 'F. J. F.', 'Mr. Albert Way's Letter on Great Fosters, near Egham and Thorpe, Surrey', *Notes and Queries*, ser. 4–1, no. 22, 30 May 1868, pp. 504–5

This interesting Elizabethan mansion has been passed over with very slight notice by the county historians (Manning & Bray, iii. 353; Brayley, ii. 264), and its history is very obscure. The royal arms are on the Elizabethan porch (which is supposed to be later than the house) with the date of 1578. The date on the drawing-room ceiling is 1602; and that on one of the leaden spouts of the house is 1508. One tradition is, that the princess Elizabeth was confined in the house during Queen Mary's reign; and another, that the place was one of Elizabeth's hunting-lodges; but the first fact about it recorded (so far as we now know) is, that Sir John Doddridge died there in 1628. One of his servants was buried at Egham in 1622, and one of Lady Doddridge's in 1629, the year after the judge's death; so that it was no doubt his family residence near London and Windsor, though he bought estates and built a mansion in Devonshire. Mr. Albert Way was kind enough to visit Forsters last December, to see what its decorations say, and from his interesting letter to the owner, Col. Halkett,[1] we have been allowed to make the following extracts:—

"In the Dining Room the central compartment is decorated by the device that had been used by Anne [p. 505] Boleyn, and was unquestionably retained by her daughter Elizabeth, who had capricious emblems without end. Camden tells us that they would fill a volume, and I am disposed to believe that the Armillary (bracelet-like) sphere, so strangely riven asunder, may be one of Elizabeth's impresses. The falcon on the root of a tree should properly have white and red roses springing up around the root; but this is not material. The rose, the fleur-de-lys, the arched crown, the lion passant, with sprigs of roses (doubtless, if coloured, red and white), the portcullis also—all found on this beautiful ceiling, are all appropriate to Tudor times and the reign of Elizabeth.

---

[1] Purchaser of Great Fosters after the death of Furnivall's father, and the decay in the family's fortunes.

The sprigs or branches of the oak are quite in proper keeping. I have a fine achievement of the royal arms, in which the Tudor rose, on one side, has a sprig of oak as its counterpart on the other. But the great mystery in the present ignorance as to who was the grantee or the builder of the mansion, is presented in your Drawing Room. Here we might expect devices more especially of personal associations with the founder; those complimentary to the sovereign, whose favour he enjoyed, being appropriately displayed in the chamber beneath, where she may have banqueted as his guest. In the 'Withdrawing Room' above we find unquestionably a variety of devices exclusively appropriate to the noble house of Percy; and yet no connection with that family appears amongst the particulars that we can glean regarding Egham, 'Forsters,' or any place in their vicinity.

"We here find the silver boar ducally gorged and chained in gold, and the silver unicorn similarly gorged and chained, the supporters of the coat of Percy. If evidence be desired, I would cite the Garter plate of Henry, fifth Earl of Northumberland, 1489–1527. The boar and the unicorn are found likewise on pennons and other insignia of which drawings are preserved at the Heralds' College. The key erect, crowned, is found on the pennon of Poynings, one of the baronies of the noble lineage of Northumberland; the scymetar is found in like manner on that of Fitzpayn. The silver boar has been ascribed to Bryan, the unicorn to Poynings. Key and scymetar are found, amongst others, as the exclusive and indubitable insignia and badges of the Percys. At the period, 1602, the closing year of Elizabeth's reign, occurring on this interesting ceiling, and, as it should seem, unquestionably the date of its execution, the head of the noble house of Percy was Henry, ninth Earl of Northumberland, who had succeeded his father in 1585, when that nobleman, committed to the Tower under suspicion of conspiracy for the release of Mary Stuart and the invasion of the realm, was found dead in his bed, shot (as alleged) by his own act. The earl speedily made demonstrations of valour and loyalty in Leicester's campaign in the Low Countries, and by chartering ships at his own charges to repel the Invincible Armada in 1588.

"He was elected K(night of the) G(arter) in 1593; engaged warmly in the cause of King James of Scots, and in promoting the union of the two kingdoms. A fatal reverse fell upon the earl and his family in 1605, through suspicion of being associated in the Powder Plot. The earl was heavily fined. He died in 1632. This Earl of Northumberland, you will remember, was distinguished as a promoter of science and literature;

he was himself an able mathematician, and patronised liberally several of the most learned scholars of his day, skilled in recondite science, philosophical and mathematical studies.

"'Henry the Wizard', as the ninth earl was familiarly designated, was perhaps the most highly informed nobleman of his age in all scientific pursuits.

"If we could discover any clue to associate 'Forsters' with the great family of the Northern Marches, whose badges occur amongst its decorations, doubtless the remarkable and hitherto inexplicable device of the Armillary Sphere might appear to be singularly appropriate to the Wizard Earl. It occurs conspicuously on the staircase as well as on the ceiling of the upper chamber. It is neither a globe, as sometimes formed, nor the mound of sovereign power, the orb, as more commonly termed, borne by emperor or king: it is properly an instrument such as may properly be ascribed to the astronomer or the votary of the natural sciences. It is adjusted to a handle for convenient use, and consists of a framework that represents the general structure of the system of which our globe forms part — the sphere traversed diagonally by the zodiac."

In Norden's Map of Windsor Forest, Harl. MS. 3749, a house is marked which is probably meant for "Forsters." It was certainly in the Egham Walks of the forest, where red deer were in Norden's time, and of which Creswell was keeper. In a former part of the letter which we have quoted from, Mr. Way says:—

"The manor of Egham, which had been part of the possessions of Chertsey Abbey, was given up by the abbot and convent in 1588 to Henry VIII. on condition that they should receive in exchange the possessions of Bisham Abbey. The king, having thus become possessed of the manor of Egham, granted it to Sir Andrew Windsore, who resided at Stanwell, near Hounslow, the ancient seat of his family. Some years after the king proposed to visit him at Stanwell, and, to his great mortification, compelled him to resign his estates in Surrey and the adjoining counties in exchange for those of Bordsley Abbey, Worcestershire. This compulsory conveyance to the crown occurred in 1542 (33 Hen. VIII.), and the manor of Egham thus reverting to the king, remained with the crown. It was made part of the jointure of Queen Henrietta Maria by Charles I."

The above details are given, not only to make known to antiquaries the curious problem which this remarkable old mansion, so strangely neglected by prior inquirers, presents, but also in the hope that some reader of "N. & Q." may be able to produce some earlier evidence regarding the history of "Forsters" before the epitaph on Sir John Doddridge's tomb in 1628.

Mr. Albert Way points out that the evidence most to be desired is a grant of "Forsters," either from Henry VIII. to some courtier, or from Elizabeth to Sir John Doddridge. The name of the place I suppose to be derived from the forester or 'forster' (to spell it as Chaucer does), who may have lived there. Creswell, the keeper in Norden's time, was buried at Egham after Sir John Doddridge had Forsters, namely, in 1623.

F. J. F.

2. Extract from a letter from Albert Way to Furnivall, FU 931

Wonham Manor, Reigate
12 August, 1868

My best thanks once again ... sending me the interesting Book of Curtesye[2] ... This curious Book is a valuable complement to your former volume. Your list is very rich[;] you may not welcome suggested additions and doubtless you have a much longer Catalogue of works under consideration. As the Texts are not limited to MSS may I ask whether such curious rarities as Caxton's Book for Travellers have been considered. There are other early *viatoria* of the same class well known to you. I devoured that to which I allude at Althorp ... Pray did you print my crude notes on Great Fosters as you proposed?

3. Extract from a letter from Albert Way to Furnivall, FU 932

25 August, 1868

I am sincerely obliged by your kindness in regard to Little Fosters. I know now which is the house in question and had imagined it to be on the other side of the road.

I have sent the particulars that you have been so good as to give me to the Rev. W. J. Vernon of Leek,[3] whose family procured the place as he believes. He is very desirous to gain any information ... having seen the communication that you sent to N. & Q.

---

[2] *Caxton's Book of Curtesye*, ed. F. J. Furnivall, *EETS*, ES 3 (1868).
[3] William James Vernon, Cantab., curate of Leek (Staffs.).

4. F. J. Furnivall, 'Little Forsters, Egham, Surrey', *Notes and Queries*, ser. 4-II, 5 September 1868, p. 234

I cannot tell Mr. VERNON[4] whether his family sold this estate to the next owner to theirs, whose name I have heard of, Mrs. Blathwaite, but I believe that they did. From Mrs. Blathwaite or her descendants, Little Forsters was bought by a Jamaica merchant, Richard Logan; and after his death it passed to his daughter, Mrs. Dobinson, the wife of Joseph Dobinson, a tea-merchant (I believe) and a magistrate, who or whose family, sold it a few years ago to Mr. Henry Worms, a Jewish merchant, who now inhabits the place. It has been called Egham Lodge ever since I can remember it; and in my time also Mr. Dobinson severed the property still more from Great Forsters, by turning the road to Strood, which formerly ran all round the north boundary of Littler Forsters, making a great curve into a nearly straight road between Little and Great Forsters. This was a decided convenience to the inhabitants of Egham and Strood,[5] but threw both the houses above-named more open to the public view. The road would have been made quite straight had it not been for the objections of my father's partners to bringing the road so close to their asylum. Mr. Dobinson's offer of a corner of the Little Forsters' property on the south of the road, for leave to bring the road close to Great Forsters, was refused; and this corner being of no possible use to the owner of Little Forsters, was planted with trees. It ought to form part of the Great Forsters' property; and general regret was expressed in the neighbourhood lately when it became known that the liberal offer of the owner of Great Forsters for this little corner was not met in the neighbourly spirit that it ought to have been.

F. J. Furnivall

5. 'F'. 'Great Forsters, near Egham.', *Notes and Queries*, ser. 4-II, 14 November 1868, pp. 463–4.

In continuation of the notice of this Elizabethan mansion, by Mr. Albert Way and Mr. Furnivall, in "N. & Q." (4th S. i. 504), I give the following:—

Notes from the Will of Sir John Doddridge (P.C.C. Barrington, 96), &c.,

---

[4] The Vernon family, beginning with John Vernon (1696–1765), holder of an estate in Antigua, had owned Little Forsters in Egham for three generations until it was sold by his grandson, John Joseph Vernon (d. 1825). See further 'John Vernon of Vernons and Little Fosters. Profile and Legacies Summary 1696–1765', https://www.ucl.ac.uk/lbs/person/views/2146644093, accessed 29 June 2024.

[5] Now 'Stroude', near Egham.

who is the earliest occupant of the house yet known. These notes we owe to the kindness of Edward J. Sage, Esq.—'In the Name of God, Amen. This is the last will and testament of me, Sr John Doddridge, Knight, written with mine owne hand.' 1st August, 4th of K. Charles I, in perfect health. Wishes to be buried in the Cathedral Church of Exeter, near his deceased wife Dorothy. To his best beloved wife all the furniture, plate, and chattels, &c., *"in the house or tenement called fforsters, in the parishe of Egham,"* or on the lands belonging. Also to said wife, his estate in the barton and demesnes of Heywood, in the parish of Wemworth, co. Devon, held on lease; with remainder of said lease to his nephew John Doddridge, eldest son of his brother Penticost Doddridge. Other estates devised are Bembridge, South Molton, Ilfercombe, &c., in co. Devon. Mentions his father, Richard Doddridge, deceased. House with furniture, &c., in same, at Mont Radford, near Exeter, to his grandson John Hancock. Mentions books, &c., in his lodgings at Serjeants' Inn, Chancery Lane. To the poor people of Egham, 5*l*. (£5.). To Trinity College, in Cambridge, "to which societie I haue been much beholding, the two greate Gloabes which are in the Gallery of my howse of fforsters." And fforasmuchas in the course of my life, I haue esteemed books as the best of my treasures,' goes on to devise his books, manuscript books, and note books to his nephew John Doddridge. Other bequests; but the estate of Forsters not further named.

Signed, 20 Augt 1628.
Proved in November following by Anne Doddridge, widow.

From there being no devise of Great Forsters in the judge's will, and from Lady Doddridge having resided in the house after her husband's death, Mr. Sage concludes that the Forsters property was either settled on her, or that Sir John, and she after him, were only tenants without a lease. F.[6]

I have sent the particulars that you have been so good as to give me to the Rev W J Vernon of Leek whose family procured the place as he believes. He is very desirous to gain any | information ... having seen the communication that you sent to N & Q.

---

[6] It seems just about certain that 'F.', the signatory of this letter, is again Furnivall, though in it he refers to himself in the third person, perhaps to suggest that the correspondents were more various and that he was not dominating the discussion or riding a hobby horse.

6. Albert Way to Furnivall (extract), FU 933

26 April, 1869

I hasten to return my sincere thanks for your friendly remembrance in sending me a copy of your Preface to Chaucer[7] ... I can no longer participate in the valuable labours by yourself and others who have entered so successfully and so vigorously upon the *Origins* of our Literature and Language ... I am now quite out of the course of learned interests ... I have an occasional glance at the Athenaeum ... I was lately at Thorpe and called on Col. Halkett. The mystery of the Forsters & Dodderidges is not less perplexing still than the undeniable traces of the Percys.

[7] *A Temporary Preface to the Six-Text Edition of Chaucer's Canterbury Tales, Part I, Attempting to Show the True Order of the Tales and the Days and Stages of the Pilgrimage, etc.*, by F. J. Furnivall, Chaucer Society, 2nd series, 3 (London, 1868).

APPENDIX 2

An Account by a Schoolboy of a Visit to the Working Men's College, October 1857, with a Report of the Address Given by John Ruskin

From *The Brucian*, no. 17, November 1857, pp. 174–6, 'The Working Men's College'

On Wednesday, the 28th of October, I had the pleasure, in company with two friends, of being present at a quarterly meeting of the Working Men's College, and as the proceedings may perhaps be interesting to some of the Brucians,[1] I have ventured to describe them here.

The College is established in a stately old mansion in Great Ormond Street, once the favoured abode of fashion, but now a dreary wilderness with an oppressive air of departed greatness. In what used to be the drawing rooms, we found assembled an audience of some two hundred or so, presided over by the Rev. F. D. Maurice, the Principal and chief originator of the College.

The first part that struck me was the remarkable quality of the audience. I had expected to find myself surrounded by fustian jackets, unkempt locks, and smudgy faces; what was my surprise upon beholding broadcloth, white linen, and combed hair; in fact there was great difficulty in dividing the gentlemen (many of whom were present out of interest in the proceedings), from the students; the intelligent character of the faces was another noticeable point; these facts are not to be wondered at, when it is considered that any working man who devotes his hours of leisure when his day's work is over to self improvement, must of necessity be above par.

The meeting commenced with a short general record of the proceedings of the College during the past quarter; which seemed to show that, though but in its infancy, the college was in a very satisfactory state. Then a few certificates of merit were distributed amid great applause; after which each teacher rose to give an account of the well-being of his own class, or address the meeting upon his particular subject.

To attempt a summary of these speeches would both occupy too much space, and weary the readers of the *Brucian*, but one from Mr. Ruskin

---

[1] Members of Bruce Castle School, Tottenham.

SCHOOLBOY ACCOUNT OF THE COLLEGE 435

was so interesting, that perhaps it would not be out of place humbly to endeavour to report it here.

During the recess he had been much perplexed by a question which he would put before them. This year he had passed the summer in the north of Scotland contrary to his usual custom, which led him southwards;[2] and for the first time in his life he had found himself amongst a people which possessed no art whatever. France possessed a noble architecture; Italy both architecture and paintings; and even Switzerland (where English travellers had not penetrated), possessed a picturesque form of dwellings embellished sometimes with beautiful carving; but Scotland's thatched roofs were ornamented only with such devices as a cook scores upon pastry; and her patterns for articles of dress were blue, green, and yellow stripes, intersecting each other at right angles.

It was in the North of Scotland that he heard tidings of the horrors which have long occurred, and perhaps are still occurring in India; and he could not at first comprehend how a nation which had committed outrage unparalleled in history,—a nation, which after having learnt the arts, and experienced the benefits of civilization had turned those very arts against the hand that had taught them, could be capable of producing tissues which for beauty of abstract form, and subtle combinations of color, are still unequalled by all the fabrics of the West.

Scotland could boast of no costly web, no embroidered silk, but she possessed a noble spirit, and it was better to have the heart that beat beneath the fustian, than that covered by the tissue of cashmere.

In Scotland there stands a granite rock whose point is scored by many a tempest, and on whose top the birch tree waves; it is celebrated in history by one of Scotland's noblest deeds of heroism,—the rock of Craigelahie—and whilst gazing on the rock, he thought that perhaps at that very moment some of Scotland's sons upon the plain of India, might be urging each other on to the work of retribution, by the cry of 'Remember Craigelahie!'[3]

[2] Ruskin travelled to Scotland with his parents in July 1857: *Works*, 36. 254; also, *Praeterita*, p. 450, Ruskin's account of 1857: 'My mother wants me to see the Bay of Cromarty and the Falls of Kilmorock. I consent sulkily to be taken to Scotland with that object.' He heard news of the Indian Mutiny, and of Field Marshall Sir Patrick Grant's role in directing operations there, while travelling in the Highlands. See note following. Ruskin was in Aberfeldy, Perthshire, in late August: see letter of 27 August to the aspiring artist, J. J. Laing, Ruskin, *Works*, 36. 265.

[3] 'Remember Craigelachie,' is the war-cry of the Grant clan, referring to the rock of Craigellachie, near Aviemore, their traditional rallying point. Field Marshall Sir Patrick Grant served as acting Commander-in-Chief, India, directing operations during the Indian Mutiny from May until August, 1857.

But to return to Indian art, he found upon examination that no natural forms were introduced, at all were abstract forms. Nature had never been observed from the love of her, and thence it was possible for minds capable of the cruelties that the Hindoos have perpetrated, to produce such works of art.

His fellow teacher, Dante Rossetti, was not there present, he was engaged in painting upon the Debating Hall at Oxford, a series of pictures illustrating the Morte d'Arthur.

The Morte d'Arthur was a beautiful romance; a nation in the height of prosperity is suddenly affected with calamity by the crime of her greatest knight; reverses still attend the country till the crime-stained sword of the king is thrown into the lake; where it is seized by the arm of an unseen figure and dragged away for ever from mortal gaze; and the nation is subsequently saved by one knight, who throughout his prosperity, had kept himself pure, chaste, and undefiled.

Such is the fable which Dante Rossetti has thought best to place before the youth at Oxford; India is the blood-stained sword which is among us, and till it be removed, we shall suffer for our crimes.

He would now say a few words to his pupils; he desired to have as many as possible, but he was anxious that no one should come to him under the idea that he would be able by drawing, to make his bread; such he could assure him would never be the case; to make an art a means of livelihood, it is necessary to labour from morning to night, and sometimes from night till morning; but he could hope to be able to open to them a new field of delight,—to make them see beauties which before were unobserved, and trace the finger of God where they least expected it; such was his aim, and with such expectations he hoped his pupils would meet him.

Mr. Ruskin's new work, 'A Treatise upon Elementary Drawing' is a reprint of the lectures delivered to his class during the past session.[4]

X. Y. Z.

[4] See further Hilton, *John Ruskin*, i. 236–7.

BIBLIOGRAPHY

UNPRINTED PRIMARY TEXTS

Bodl. MS Don. D. 109/2.
Bodl. MS Eng. d. 2104. Furnivall's diary, 9 October 1841–14 January 1844.
Bodl. MS Eng. e. 2315. Furnivall's diary, 1 January 1848–31 December 1848.
Bodl. MS Eng. e 2316. Furnivall's diary, 1 January 1851–17 June 1852.
Bodl. MS Eng. lett. d. 79.
Bodl. MS Eng. lett. d. 187.
Bodl. MS Eng. misc. d. 177.
Bodl. letters and papers of J. A. H. Murray.
CUL MS Add. 6184.
CUL MS Add. 8916/A70/70.
Huntington Library, San Marino CA, Furnivall Papers
KCL, Furnivall Papers.

EDITIONS OF EARLY ENGLISH TEXTS

The Ancient English Romance of Havelok the Dane, Accompanied by the French Text: with an Introduction, Notes, and a Glossary, ed. Frederic Madden, Roxburghe Club (London, 1828).
The Ancient English Romance of William and the Werwolf, Edited from the Unique Copy in King's College, Cambridge, ed. Frederick [sic] Madden, Roxburghe Club (London, 1832). See also *The Romance of William of Palerne*.
Ancient Mysteries from the Digby Manuscripts, Preserved in the Bodleian Library, Oxford, ed. T. Sharp, Abbotsford Club, 1 (Edinburgh, 1835).
Ancrene Wisse: A Corrected Edition of the Text in Cambridge, Corpus Christi College MS. 402, with Variants from Other Manuscripts, ed. Bella Millett, with a Glossary and Additional Notes by Richard Dance. 2 vols. EETS, OS 325, 326 (Oxford, 2005–6).
The Ancren Riwle: A Treatise on the Rules and Duties of Monastic Life . . ., ed. James Morton, Camden Society, 57 (London, 1853).
Arthur; A Short Sketch of His Life and History in English Verse of the First Half of the Fifteenth Century, ed. Frederick J. Furnivall, EETS, OS 2 (London, 1864); 2nd edn. 1869, repr. 1998.
Ayenbite of Inwyt. See *Dan Michel's Ayenbite of Inwyt*; [Michael of Northgate].
The Babees Book, ed. Frederick J. Furnivall, EETS, OS 32 (London, 1868). Subsequently published as *Early English Meals and Manners*.

Bishop Percy's Folio MS. Ballads and Romances, ed. Frederick James Furnivall and John W. Hales (London, 1867).

The Boke of Nurture, by John Russell, ab. 1460–70; The Boke of Keruynge by Wynkyn de Worde, a.d. 1513; The Boke of Nurture by Hugh Rhodes, a.d. 1577, edited from the originals in the British Museum Library, &c. by Frederick J. Furnivall, Roxburghe Club, printed for the Honourable Robert Curzon (Bungay, 1867).

The Book of the Knight of La Tour-Landry, Compiled for the Instruction of His Daughters; Translated from the Original French into English in the Reign of Henry VI, and Edited for the First Time from the Unique Manuscript in the British Museum, with an Introduction and Notes, ed. Thomas Wright, EETS, OS 33 (London, 1868).

Borde, Andrew, *The Fyrst Boke of the Introduction of Knowledge Made by Andrew Borde, ... A Compendyous Regyment or A Dyetary of Helth, ... Barnes in the Defence of the Berde ...*, ed. F. J. Furnivall, EETS, ES 10 (London, 1870).

Castel off Loue (Chasteau d'amour or Carmen de Creatione Mundi), an Early English Translation of an Old French Poem by Robert Grosseteste, Bishop of Lincoln, Copied and Edited from MSS in the British Museum, and in the Bodleian Library, Oxford, with Notes, Critical and Exegetical, and Glossary, ed. Richard Francis Weymouth (London and Berlin, 1864).

The Castle of Love: A Poem by Robert Grosseteste, Bishop of Lincoln. Now First Printed from Inedited Manuscripts of the Fourteenth Century, ed. J. O. Halliwell (Brixton Hill, printed for private circulation, 1849).

Catholicon Anglicum: An English-Latin Wordbook, ed. Sidney J. H. Herrtage and H. B. Wheatley, EETS, OS 75 (London, 1881).

Caxton's Book of Curtesye, ed. Frederick J. Furnivall, EETS, ES 3 (1868).

Charles of Orleans. See *Letters and Poems*.

Coneybeare, J. J., *Illustrations of Anglo-Saxon Poetry*, ed. *together with additional notes, introductory notices, &c. by his brother William Daniel Conybeare* (London, 1826).

The Crafte of Lymmyng and The Maner of Steynyng, ed. Mark Clarke, EETS, OS 347 (Oxford, 2016).

Dan Michel's Ayenbite of Inwyt, vol. 1: *Text*, ed. Richard Morris, revd. Pamela Gradon; vol. 2: *Introduction, Notes and Glossary*, by Pamela Gradon, EETS, OS 23 (1866, reissued 1965); OS 278 (1979).

The Digby Mysteries ..., ed. F. J. Furnivall, New Shakspere Society Series VII, no. 1 (London, 1882).

Digby Plays. See also *Ancient Mysteries* and *The Late Medieval Religious Plays*.

Early English Alliterative Poems in the West-Midland Dialect of the Fourteenth Century, ed. Richard Morris, EETS, OS 1 (London, 1864).

Early English Metrical Romances of Perceval, Isumbras, Eglamour, and Degrevant ..., ed. J. O. Halliwell, Camden Society (London, 1844).

Early English Poems and Lives of Saints, with Those of the Wicked Birds Pilate and Judas, ed. F. J. Furnivall, TPS 5 (1858).
The Ellesmere MS. of Chaucer's Canterbury Tales, ed. Frederick J. Furnivall, Part 2, Chaucer Society (London, 1869), First Series, 2.
Emblemes and Epigrames . . ., ed. Frederick J. Furnivall, EETS, OS 64 (London, 1876).
English Gilds: The Original Ordinances of More than One Hundred Early English Gilds . . ., ed. J. Toulmin Smith, with an Introduction and glossary by Lucy Toulmin Smith, and a Preliminary Essay on the History and Development of Gilds by Lujo Brentano, EETS, OS 40 (London, 1870).
Generydes: A Romance in Seven-Line Stanzas, ed. W. A. Wright, EETS, OS 71 (London, 1878). See also *Royal Historie*.
Gesta Romanorum, see *Old English Versions*.
Gower, John, *The Confessio Amantis of John Gower, Edited and Collated with the Best Manuscripts*, ed. Reinhold Pauli, 3 vols. (London, 1857).
Hali Meidenhad, from MS. Cott. Titus D XVIII, fol. 112c: An Alliterative Homily of the Thirteenth Century, ed. Oswald Cockayne, EETS, OS 18 (London, 1866).
Hali Meidenhad: An Alliterative Homily of the Thirteenth Century from MS Bodley 34, Oxford, and Cotton MS. Titus D. 18, British Museum, ed. F. J. Furnivall, EETS 18 (London, 1922 (for 1920)).
Hali Meiðhad, ed. Bella Millett, EETS, OS 284 (London, 1982).
Handlyng Synne. See *Robert of Brunne*.
The Harley Lyrics: The Middle English Lyrics of M.S. Harley 2253, ed. G. L. Brook (Manchester, 1956).
Havelok. See *Lay of Havelok the Dane*.
The Holy Bible, Containing the Old and New Testaments, with the Apocryphal Books: In the Earliest English Versions Made from the Latin Vulgate by John Wycliffe and his Followers, ed. J. Forshall and F. Madden, 4 vols. (Oxford, 1850).
How the Goode Wif Thaught hir Daughter, ed. F. Madden (London, 1838).
Hymns to the Virgin & Christ, The Parliament of Devils, and Other Religious Poems, ed. Frederick J. Furnivall, EETS, OS 24 (London, 1867).
Judicium, a Pageant Extr. from the Towneley MS. of Ancient Mysteries, ed. Francis Douce, Roxburghe Club (London, 1822).
Juliana, St. See *þe Liflade ant te Passiun of Seinte Iuliene* and *The Liflade of St. Juliana*.
Katherine, St. See *The Legend of St Katherine of Alexandria*.
Langland, William. See *The Vision and the Creed of Pier Ploughman*; *The Vision of William Concerning Piers the Plowman*; *William Langland: Parallel Extracts*.
The Late Medieval Religious Plays of Bodleian MSS Digby 133 and E Museo 160,

ed. Donald C. Baker, John L. Murphy, and Louis B. Hall, Jr., EETS, OS 283 (Oxford, 1982).

The Lay of Havelok the Dane: Re-edited from MS. Laud misc. 108 in the Bodleian Library, Oxford, by the Rev. Walter W. Skeat; 2nd edn. revised by K. Sisam (Oxford, 1915).

Layamon's Brut, or Chronicle of Britain: A Poetical Semi-Saxon Paraphrase of the Brut of Wace . . . Accompanied by a Literal Translation, Notes and a Grammatical Glossary, ed. Frederic Madden, 3 vols., Society of Antiquaries of London (London, 1847).

The Legend of St Katherine of Alexandria, Edited from a Manuscript in the Cottonian Library, ed. James Morton, Abbotsford Club, 41 (London, 1841). [*Seinte Katerine*]

Leechdoms, Wortcunning and Starcraft of Early England, Being a Collection of Documents, for the Most Part Never before Printed, Illustrating the History of Science in This Country before the Norman Conquest, ed. T. Oswald Cockayne, 3 vols., Rolls Series (London, 1864-6).

The Letters and Poems of Charles of Orleans, ed. Robert Steele and Mabel Day, EETS OS 215, 220 (London, 1941, 1946, repr. with bibliographical supplement 1970).

Liber Cure Cocorum, Copied and Edited from the Sloane MS. 1986, ed. Richard Morris, Philological Society (Berlin, 1862).

þe Liflade ant te Passiun of Seinte Iuliene, ed. S. R. T. O. d'Ardenne, EETS, OS 248 (London, 1961 (for 1960)).

The Liflade of St. Juliana from Two Old English Manuscripts of 1250 A.D., ed. Revd. Oswald Cockayne [with the assistance of Edmund Brock], EETS, OS 51 (London, 1872).

Ludus Coventriae: A Collection of Mysteries, formerly Represented at Coventry on the Feast of Corpus Christi, ed. J. O. Halliwell, Shakespeare Society (London, 1841).

Manipulus Vocabulorum: A Dictionary of English and Latin Words . . ., ed. Henry B. Wheatley, Camden Society, 95 (London, 1867).

Margaret, St. *See Seinte Marherete þe Meiden ant Martyr.*

Manners and Household Expenses of England in the Thirteenth and the Fifteenth Centuries, Illustrated by Original Records, ed. Beriah Botfield, Roxburghe Club (London, 1841).

Matthaei Parisiensis, monachi Sancti Albani, sive ut vulgo dicitur, Historia Minor. Item, ejusdem Abbreviatio Chronicorum Chronicorum Angliae, ed. Frederic Madden, 3 vols., Rolls Series (London, 1866-9).

Meditations on the Supper of Our Lord and the Hours of the Passion, by Cardinal John Bonaventura, the Seraphic Doctor, Drawn into English Verse by Robert Manning of Brunne . . ., ed. Joseph Meadows Cowper, EETS, OS 60 (London, 1875).

BIBLIOGRAPHY 441

The Middle English Harrowing of Hell and Gospel of Nicodemus, ed. W. H. Hulme, EETS, ES 100 (London, 1908).

The Middle English Translation of Robert Grosseteste's Château d'Amour, ed. Kari Sajavaara, Société néophilogique (Helsinki, 1967).

[Michael of Northgate], *The Ayenbite of inwyt written (or rather tr. from Laurent's La somme des vertues et des vices) by dan. Michel*, ed. J. Stevenson, Roxburghe Club (London, 1855). See also Dan Michel's Ayenbite.

The Minor Poems of the Vernon MS, ed. Carl Horstmann and F. J. Furnivall, 2 vols. EETS, OS 98, 117 (London, 1892–1901).

Minor Poems of William Lauder, ed. Frederick J. Furnivall, EETS, OS 41 (London, 1870).

Le Morte Arthur: The Adventures of Sir Launcelot du Lake, ed. Thomas Ponton, Roxburghe Club (London, 1819).

Morte Arthure: The Alliterative Romance of the Death of King Arthur, Printed from a Ms. in Lincoln Cathedral, ed. J. O. Halliwell (Brixton Hill, privately printed, 1847).

Old English Homilies and Homiletic Treatises (Sawles Warde, and þe Wohunge of Ure Lauerd: Ureisons of Ure Louerd and of Ure Lefdi, &c) of the Twelfth and Thirteenth Centuries, First Series, ed. Richard Morris, EETS, OS 29 (London, 1868).

An Old English Miscellany: A Bestiary, Kentish Sermons, Proverbs of Alfred and Religious Poems of the Thirteenth Century, ed. Richard Morris, EETS, OS 49 (1872, repr. 1997).

An Old English Poem of The Owl and the Nightingale, ed. Franz Heinrich Stratmann (Krefeld, 1868).

The Old English Versions of the Gesta Romanorum, Edited for the First Time from Manuscripts in the British Museum and University Libraries, Cambridge, ed. Frederic Madden, Roxburghe Club (London, 1838).

The Owl and the Nightingale, ed. J. H. G. Grattan and G. F. H. Sykes, EETS, ES 119 (1935).

The Owl and the Nightingale, ed. E. G. Stanley (Manchester, 1960).

The Owl and the Nightingale: Text and Translation, ed. Neil Cartlidge, Exeter Medieval English Texts and Studies (Exeter, 2001).

Pearl, Cleanness, Patience and Sir Gawain: Reproduced in Facsimile from the Unique MS. Cotton Nero A. x in the British Museum, with Introduction by I. Gollancz, EETS OS 162 (London, 1923 (for 1922); repr. 1931, 1955, 1971).

Peter Levin's Manipulus Vocabulorum, ed. Henry B. Wheatley, EETS, OS 27 (London, 1867).

Piers Plowman. See *The Vision and the Creed of Pier Ploughman*; *The Vision of Piers Plowman I*; *The Vision of William Concerning Piers the Plowman*; *William Langland: Parallel Extracts*.

The Pilgrimage of the Life of Man, Englished by John Lydgate, A.D. 1426, from the French of Guillaume de Deguileville, A.D. 1330, 1355, Introduction, Notes,

Glossary and Indexes by Katharine B. Locock, Roxburghe Club (London, 1905).

The Play of the Sacrament, ed. Whitley Stokes, Philological Society (Berlin, 1862).

The Play of the Sacrament, a Middle-English Drama, Edited from a Manuscript in the Library of Trinity College, Dublin, ed. Whitley Stokes, TPS (1860–1).

Poema Morale: Carla M. Thomas, '"Poema Morale": An Edition from Cambridge, Trinity College B. 14. 52', MA diss., University of Florida, College of Arts and Sciences (2008).

Poems from BL MS Harley 913: 'The Kildare Manuscript', ed. Thorlac Turville-Petre, EETS, OS 345 (Oxford, 2015).

Political, Religious, and Love Poems, ed. Frederick J. Furnivall, EETS, OS 15 (London, 1866).

Popular Treatises on Science Written during the Middle Ages: In Anglo-Saxon, Anglo-Norman and English, ed. Thomas Wright (London, 1841).

The Prick of Conscience (Stimulus Conscientiae), a Northumbrian Poem by Richard Rolle of Hampole, Copied and Edited from Manuscripts in the Library of the British Museum, with an Introduction, Notes, and Glossarial Index, ed. Richard Morris (Berlin, 1863).

Promptorium Parvulorum sive clericorum: Lexicon anglo-latinum princeps, ed. Albert Way, Camden Society, 25 (London, 1843), 54 (1853); 89 (1865).

Promptorium Parvulorum: The First Latin Dictionary, ed. A. L. Mayhew, EETS, ES 102 (1908).

Queene Elizabethes Achademy (By Sir Humphrey Gilbert), A Book of Precedence, The Ordering of a Funerall..., ed. F. J. Furnivall, EETS, ES 8 (London, 1869).

Religious Lyrics of the XIV Century, ed. Carleton Brown, 2nd edn., revd. G. V. Smithers (Oxford, 1924).

Reliquiae Antiquae: Scraps from Ancient Manuscripts, Illustrating Chiefly Early English Literature and the English Language, ed. Thomas Wright and James Orchard Halliwell (Berlin, 1841).

Richard Morris's Prick of Conscience: *A Corrected and Amplified Reading Text*, ed. Ralph Hanna and Sarah Wood, EETS, OS 342 (Oxford, 2013).

Roberd of Brunnè's Handlyng Synne (Written A.D. 1303), with the French Treatise on which it is Founded, Le Manuel des Pechiez by William of Wadington, Now First Printed from MSS. in the British-Museum and Bodleian Libraries, ed. Frederick J. Furnivall, Roxburghe Club (London, 1862).

Robert of Brunne's 'Handlyng Synne', A.D. 1303, with Those Parts of the Anglo-French Treatise on which it was Founded, William of Waddington's 'Manuel des Pechiez', re-edited from MSS. in the British Museum and Bodleian Libraries, ed. Frederick J. Furnivall, EETS OS 119, 123 (London, 1901).

Le Roman du Saint-Graal; publié pour la première fois d'après un manuscrit de la Bibliothèque royale, ed. Francisque Michel (Bordeaux, 1841).

The Romance of Sir Degrevant, ed. L. F. Casson, EETS, OS 221(London, 1949).

The Romance of William of Palerne . . ., ed. Walter W. Skeat, EETS, ES 1 (1867). See also *Ancient English Romance of William and the Werwolf.*

A Royal Historie of the Excellent Knight Generides, Edited from the Unique MS of John Tollemache, Esq. M.P., of Peckforton Castle, South Cheshire, and Helmingham Hall, Suffolk, ed. Frederick J. Furnivall, Roxburghe Club, printed for Henry Hucks Gibbs, Esq. (Hertford, 1865).

Seinte Marherete þe Meiden ant Martyr, in Old English, now First Edited from the Skin Books, ed. Oswald Cockayne (London, 1862).

Seinte Marherete þe Meiden ant Martyr, in Old English, now First Edited from the Skin Books in 1862, ed. Oswald Cockayne, EETS, OS 13 (London, 1866).

Seinte Marherete, þe Meiden and Martyr, re-edited from MS. Bodley 34, Oxford and MS. Royal 17A xxvii, British Museum, ed. Frances M. Mack, EETS OS 193 (London, 1934).

Seynt Graal, or the Sank Ryal: The History of the Holy Graal, Partly in English Verse, by Henry Lonelich, Skynner (temp. Hen. V. A.D. 1422–1461) and Wholly in French Prose, by Sires Robiers de Borron, from the Original Latin, Written by Jesus Christ with his Own Hand, Being the Only Writing Made by God since His Uprising . . ., edited from MSS in the Library of Corpus Christi College, Cambridge, and the British Museum, by Frederick J. Furnivall. Printed for the Roxburghe Club (London and Krefeld, 1861).

Shakespeare, William, *The Tragicall Historie of Hamlet, Prince of Denmarke, by William Shakespeare. Edited According to the First Printed Copies, with the Various Readings and Critical Notes*, ed. F. H. Stratmann (London, 1869).

Shakspere's England: William Stafford's Compendious or Briefe Examination of Certeyne Ordinary Complaints of Diuers These Our Countrymen in These Our Dayes, A. D. 1581 (Otherwise Called "A Briefe Conceipt of English Pollicy"), introduction by Frederic D. Matthew, New Shakspere Society, Series 6, no. 3 (London, 1876).

Sir Gawayne and The Green Knight, an Alliterative Romance-Poem (Ab. 1320–30 A.D.) by the Author of Early English Alliterative Poems, Re-edited from Cotton MS Nero A. x. in the British Museum, ed. Richard Morris, EETS OS 4 (London, 1864); repr. 1869, 1893; revd. Israel Gollancz, 1897, 1905, 1910.

Specimens of Early English Metrical Romances: To Which is Prefixed an Historical Introduction on the Rise and Progress of Romantic Composition in France and England, ed. George Ellis, 3 vols. (London, 1805); revd. edn. prepared by J. O. Halliwell (London, 1848).

Specimens of Early English, ed. Richard Morris with W. W. Skeat (Oxford, 1872); 2nd edn. ed. W. W. Skeat and A. L. Mayhew (1898).

Specimens of Early English Selected from the Chief English Authors A.D. 1250–A.D. 1400, with Grammatical Introduction, Notes, and Glossary, ed. Richard Morris (Oxford, 1867).

Syr Gawayne: A Collection of Ancient Romance-Poems by Scotish and English

Authors; Relating to that Celebrated Knight of the Round Table, ed. Frederic Madden, Bannatyne Club Publications, 61 (London, 1839).

The Towneley Mysteries, ed. James Raine and Joseph Stevenson, Surtees Society (London, [1836]).

The Towneley Plays, ed. Martin Stevens and A. C. Cawley, EETS, SS 13 (Oxford, 1994).

The Towneley Plays, Re-edited from the Unique MS by George England with Sidenotes and Introduction by Alfred W. Pollard, EETS, ES 71 (London, 1897).

The Vision and Creed of Piers Ploughman, Edited from a Contemporary Manuscript, with a Historical Introduction, Notes, and a Glossary, ed. Thomas Wright, 2nd revd. edn. (London, 1856).

The Vision of Piers Plowman I, Text A, EETS, OS 28 (London, 1867).

The Vision of William Concerning Piers the Plowman, in Three Parallel Texts, Together with Richard the Redeless, by William Langland, ed. Walter W. Skeat, 2 vols. (Oxford, 1886).

William and the Werwolf (William of Palerne). See *Ancient English Romance* and *Romance of William of Palerne*.

William Langland: The Vision of Piers Plowman II, Text B, EETS, OS 38 (London, 1869).

William Langland: The Vision of Piers Plowman III, Text C, EETS, OS 54 (London, 1873).

William Langland: The Vision of Piers Plowman IV, IV(ii), EETS, OS 67, 81 (London, 1877, 1884).

The Wright's Chaste Wife, ed. Frederick J. Furnivall, EETS, OS 12 (London, 1865).

The York Play: A Facsimile of British Library MS Additional 35290, Together with a Facsimile of the Ordo Paginarum *Section of the A/Y Memorandum Book*, ed. with an introduction by Richard Beadle and Peter Meredith, and a note on the music by Richard Rastall (Leeds, 1983).

The York Plays: A Critical Edition of the York Corpus Christi Play as Recorded in British Library Additional MS 35290, ed. Richard Beadle, 2 vols., EETS, SS 23, 24 (Oxford, 2009, 2013).

The York Plays: The Plays Performed by the Crafts or Mysteries of York on the Day of Corpus Christi in the 14th, 15th, and 16th Centuries. Now First Printed from the Unique Manuscript in the Library of Lord Ashburnham, ed. with Introduction and Glossary by Lucy Toulmin Smith (Oxford, 1885).

William Langland: Parallel Extracts from 45 MSS of Piers Plowman, ed. Walter W. Skeat, EETS, OS 17 (London, 1866).

SECONDARY SOURCES

Aarsleff, Hans, *The Study of Language in England 1780-1860* (Minneapolis, 1983).
Ackerman, Gretchen P., 'John M. Kemble and Sir Frederic Madden: "Conceit and too much Germanism"?', in Carl T. Berkhout and Milton McC. Gatch (eds.), *Anglo-Saxon Scholarship, the First Three Centuries*(Boston, MA, 1982), 167-81.
Ackerman, Robert W., 'Madden's Gawain Anthology', in Jess B. Bessinger and Robert R. Raymo (eds.), *Medieval Studies in Honor of Lillian Herlands Hornstein* (New York, 1976), 5-18.
—— and Ackerman, Gretchen P., *Sir Frederic Madden: A Biographical Sketch and Bibliography*, Garland Reference Library of the Humanities, 126 (New York and London, 1979).
Acland, Arthur H. D., and B. Jones, *Working Men Co-operators* (London, 1884).
Alexander, Michael, *Medievalism: The Middle Ages in Modern England* (New Haven and London, 2017).
Allen, Peter, *The Cambridge Apostles: The Early Years* (Cambridge, 1978).
Altenglische Sprachproben nebst einem Wörterbuch, ed. Eduard Mätzner, 4 vols. (Berlin, 1867-1900).
Alter, Stephen G., *Darwinism and the Linguistic Image: Language, Race, and Natural Theology in the Nineteenth Century*, New Studies in American Intellectual and Cultural History (Baltimore, MD and London, 1999).
Altick, R. D., *The Scholar Adventurers* (1950; New York, 1966).
Alumni Cantabrigienses, see Venn, J. A.
An American in Victorian Cambridge: Charles Astor Bristed's 'Five Years in an English University', ed. Christopher Stray (Exeter, 2008).
Ambrose, Mary E., '"La donna del lago": The First Italian Translations of Scott', *Modern Language Review*, 67 (1972), 74-82.
Anon., 'Be Domes Dæge', *Saturday Review*, 14 Apr. 1877.
Anon., 'Bodily Vigor of Aged Men', *New York Times*, 21 Oct. 1884.
Anon., 'New Books and New Editions', *The Scotsman*, 27 Apr. 1877.
Anon., *Our English Home: Its Early History and Progress. With Notes on the Introduction of Domestic Inventions* (Oxford, 1860).
Arnold, Thomas, *Passages in a Wandering Life* (London, 1900).
Arsdall, Anne van, *Medieval Herbal Remedies: The Old English Herbarium and Anglo-Saxon Medicine* (New York, 2002).
Atkinson, Henry George, and Harriet Martineau, *Letters on the Laws of Man's Nature and Development* (London, 1851; facs. repr., Cambridge, 2009).
Axon, William E. A. , 'F.J.F', *The Bookman*, 41 (Oct. 1911), 42-3.
Bailey, Richard W., 'The Early Modern English Dictionary', in Peter H. Fries and Nancy M. Fries (eds.), *Towards an Understanding of Languages: Charles*

Carpenter Fries in Perspective, , Amsterdam Studies in the Theory and History of Linguistic Science, Series IV, vol. 40 (Amsterdam, 1985), 173–203.

Baker, Donald C., 'Frederick James Furnivall', in Ruggiers, *Editing Chaucer*, 157–69.

Baker, Peter, 'Toller at School: Joseph Bosworth, T. Northcote Toller and the Progress of Old English Lexicography in the Nineteenth Century', in D. Scragg (ed.), *Textual and Material Culture in Anglo-Saxon England: Thomas Northcote Toller and the Toller Memorial Lectures* (Woodbridge, 2003).

Bargrave, John, *Pope Alexander the Seventh and the College of Cardinals, by John Bargrave, D.D., Canon of Canterbury (1662–1680). With a Catalogue of Dr. Bargrave's Museum*, ed. James Craigie Robertson, Camden Society, 92 (London, 1867).

Barker, Nicolas, *The Publications of the Roxburghe Club 1814–1962: An Essay*, printed for presentation to members of the Roxburghe Club (Cambridge, 1964).

Bell, H. I., 'Robin Ernest William Flower, 1881–1946', *PBA* 32 (1946), 353–79.

Bellot, H. Hale, *University College London, 1826–1926* (London, 1929).

Benzie, William, *Dr F. J. Furnivall: A Victorian Scholar Adventurer* (Norman, OK, 1983).

Bevington, Merle Mowbray, *The Saturday Review 1855–1868: Representative Educated Opinion in Victorian England* (New York, 1966).

Bickersteth, Edward, *A Companion to the Holy Communion . . .*, 2nd edn. (London, 1823).

Billings, Malcolm, *Queen's College: 150 Years and a New Century* (London, 2000).

Birrell, T. A., 'The Society of Antiquaries and the Taste for Old English, 1705–1840', *Neophilologus*, 50 (1965), 107–17.

Black, M. H., *Cambridge University Press, 1584–1984* (Cambridge, 1984).

Black's Guide to the History, Antiquities, and Topography of the County of Surrey (Edinburgh, 1861).

Blanchard, E. L., *Bradshaw's Guide through London and its Environs . . .*, revd. H. Kains Jackson (London, 1861, facs. repr., 2015).

Bloch, Howard R., 'New Philology and Old French', *Speculum*, 65 (1990), 38–58.

Bond Head, Francis, *Rough Notes Taken during Some Rapid Journeys across the Pampas and among the Andes* (London, 1836).

Booth, Charles, *Booth's Maps of London Poverty, East and West* (1889; repr. Oxford, 2013).

—— (ed.), *Life and Labour of the People in London*, 10 vols. (London, 1892–7).

Bosworth, Joseph, *A Compendious Anglo-Saxon Dictionary* (London, 1848).

Bowlby, A. L., *Wages and Income in the United Kingdom since 1860* (Cambridge, 1937).

Bowler, Peter J., *Evolution: The History of an Idea*, revd. edn. (Berkeley, CA, 1983).
Braithwaite, Roderick, *Strikingly Alive: The History of the Mill Hill School Foundation 1807–2007* (Chichester, 2006).
Brandl, Alois, *Zwischen Inn und Themse, Lebensbeobachtungen eines Anglisten* (Berlin, 1936).
Brewer, Charlotte, *Editing* Piers Plowman: *The Evolution of the Text* (Cambridge, 1996).
Briggs, Asa, *Chartism* (Stroud, 1998).
—— *Saxons, Normans and Victorians*, Hastings and Bexhill Branch of The Historical Association, 5 (St Leonards-on-Sea, 1966).
Bristed, Charles Astor, *An American in Victorian Cambridge; Charles Astor Bristed's 'Five Years in an English University'*, ed. Christopher Stray (Exeter, 2008).
Bromley, J., *The Man of Ten Talents: A Portrait of Richard Chenevix Trench 1807–86, Philologist, Poet, Theologian, Archbishop* (London, 1959).
Brookman, Helen, 'Accessing the Medieval: Disability and Distance in Anna Gurney's Search for St Edmund', *Postmedieval*, 10 (2019), 357–75.
—— 'From the Margins: Scholarly Women and the Translation and Editing of Medieval English Literature in the Nineteenth Century', Ph.D. thesis, University of Cambridge (2010).
Brown, Graham S., *see Lincoln's Inn Commonplace Book*.
Burrow, J. W., 'The Uses of Philology in Victorian England', in Robert Robson (ed.), *Ideas and Institutions of Victorian Britain: Essays in Honour of George Kitson Clark* (London, 1967), 180–204.
Carlyle, Thomas, *Chartism* (London, 1840).
—— *On Heroes, Hero-Worship, and the Heroic in History*, repr. of the 'Sterling Edition' of Carlyle's Complete Works, in 20 volumes (Teddington, 2007).
—— *Past and Present*, ed. Henry Duff Traill, *The Works of Thomas Carlyle*, x (Cambridge, 2011).
Carswell, Robert, *Pathological Anatomy: Illustrations of the Elementary Forms of Disease* (London, 1838).
Cawley, A. C., 'Thoresby and Later Owners of the Manuscript of the York Plays (BL Additional MS 35290)', *Leeds Studies in English*, NS 11 (1980 for 1979), 74–89.
Chadwick, Owen, *The Victorian Church*, 2 vols. (London, 1972).
Chambers, R. W., 'Philologists at University College, London', in *Man's Unconquerable Mind: Studies of English Writers, from Bede to A. E. Housman and W. P. Ker* (London, 1939), 342–58.
Chambers, Robert, *Vestiges of the Natural History of Creation*, 8th edn. (London, July, 1850); 9th edn. (London, July, 1859).
Chance, Jane, *Women Medievalists and the Academy* (Madison, WI, 2005).
Chase, Malcolm, *Chartism, a New History* (Manchester, 2007).

Chibnall, Marjorie, *The Debate on the Norman Conquest*, Issues in Historiography (Manchester, 1999).
Chitty, Susan, *The Beast and the Monk: A Life of Charles Kingsley* (London, 1974).
Christensen, Torben, *Origin and History of Christian Socialism 1848-54* (Aarhus, 1962).
Cockayne, T. O., *The Shrine: A Collection of Occasional Papers on Dry Subjects* (London, 1864-70).
Coleridge, Herbert, *A Dictionary of the First, or Oldest Words in the English Language from the Semi-Saxon Period of A.D. 1250 to 1300, Consisting of an Alphabetical Inventory of Every Word Found in the Printed English Literature of the 13th Century* (London, 1862).
—— *A Glossarial Index to the Printed English Literature of the Thirteenth Century* (London, 1859).
—— 'On the word "Gallow" as Used by Shakspere', *TPS* (1856), 123-4.
—— 'On the Exclusion of Certain Words from a Dictionary', *TPS*, 7 (1860), 37-55
Coleridge, S. T., *Aids to Reflection*, 6th edn. (enlarged) (London 1848).
Colloms, Brenda, *Victorian Visionaries* (London, 1982).
Considine, John, 'The Deathbed of Herbert Coleridge', *Notes & Queries*, 61 (March 2014), 90-2.
Cooke, Edward Tyas, *The Life of John Ruskin*, 2 vols. (London, 1911).
Crawley, Charles, *Trinity Hall: The History of a Cambridge College 1350-1975* (Cambridge, 1976).
Crombie, Alexander, *The Etymology and Syntax of the English Language Explained*, 3rd edn. (London, 1830).
Cunningham, A., *Anecdotes of Napoleon Bonaparte, his Ministers, his Generals, his Soldiers, and his Times. With an Interesting Account of his Disinterment on St Helena* (Manchester, 1843).
Cunningham, Hugh, *The Volunteer Force: A Social and Political History, 1859-1908* (Hamden, CT, 1975).
Dalziel, George, *The Brothers Dalziel: A Record of Fifty Years' Work, in Conjunction with Many of the Most Distinguished Artists of the Period 1840-1890* (London, 1901).
Damico, Helen (ed.), *Medieval Scholarship: Biographical Studies on the Formation of a Discipline*, 3 vols. (New York and London, 1995-2000).
Davies, J. Llewelyn (ed.), *The Working Men's College 1854-1904: Records of its History and its Work for Fifty Years by Members of the College* (London, 1904).
Dearden, James S. *John Ruskin: A Life in Pictures* (Sheffield, 1999).
—— 'Wise and Ruskin, III: Wise's Editions of Letters from John Ruskin', *The Book Collector*, 18 (1969), 318-39.
Dickens, Charles, Jr, *Dickens's Dictionary of London* (London, 1879).

Dickins, Bruce, 'John Mitchell Kemble and Old English Scholarship', *PBA* 25 (1939), 51–84.

Dinshaw, Carolyn, *How Soon is Now? Medieval Texts, Amateur Readers, and the Queerness of Time* (Durham and London, 2012).

Doyle, A. I., 'The Shaping of the Vernon and Simeon MSS', in B. Rowland (ed.), *Chaucer and Middle English Studies in Honour of Rossell Hope Robins* (London, 1974), 328–41.

—— *The Vernon Manuscript: A Facsimile of Bodleian Library, Oxford, MS Eng. Poet. a. 1. With an Introduction by A. I. Doyle* (Cambridge, 1987).

Edwards, A. S. G., 'Observations on the History of Middle English Editing', in Derek Pearsall (ed.), *Manuscripts and Texts: Editorial Problems in Later Middle English Literature. Essays from the 1985 Conference at the University of York* (Cambridge, 1987), 34–48.

Egan, Pierce, the Younger, *Wat Tyler*, 3 vols. (London, 1841).

Ellis, Alexander J., *On Early English Pronunciation, with Especial Reference to Shakspere and Chaucer* . . . , 5 vols. (London: published for the Philological Society by Asher & Co., and for the EETS and Chaucer Society by N. Trübner, 1869–89).

Eliot, Simon (gen. ed.), *The History of Oxford University Press*, 4 vols. (Oxford, 2013–17).

Evans, Joan, *A History of the Society of Antiquaries*, The Society of Antiquaries (Oxford, 1956).

Evans, R. J. W., and Hartmut Pogge von Strandman (eds.), *The Revolutions in Europe, 1848–1849* (Oxford, 2002).

Faulkner, Peter, '"The Paths of Virtue and Early English": F. J. Furnivall and Victorian Medievalism', in John Simons (ed.), *From Medieval to Medievalism* (Basingstoke, 1992), 144–57.

Flügel, Ewald, in *Flügel Memorial Volume: Containing an Unpublished Paper by Professor Ewald Flügel, and Contributions in his Memory by his Colleagues and Students*, Leland Stanford Junior University Publications, University Series (Stanford, CA, 1916).

Forster, J. A., 'A Transition Period: R. B. Litchfield', in Davies (ed.), *Working Men's College*, 100–28.

Foster, Joseph, *Register of Admissions to Gray's Inn, 1521–1889* . . . (London, 1889).

Froude, J. A., 'England's Forgotten Worthies', *Westminster Review*, 58, no. 113 (1 July 1852), 18–36.

—— *History of England from the Fall of Wolsey to the Death of Elizabeth*, 12 vols. (London, 1856–70).

—— *Short Studies on Great Subjects* (London, 1867).

Fry, Danby P., 'On Some English Dictionaries, Especially One Proposed by the Late Alfred Augustus Fry', *TPS*, 6 (1859), 257–72.

Furnivall, F. J., *An Alphabetical List of English Words in the Literature of the*

Eighteenth and Nineteenth Centuries; and forming a Basis of Comparison for the Use of Contributors to the New Dictionary of the Philological Society, Part I. A to D (London, 1861); Part II. E to L (Hertford, 1861); Part III. M to Z (London, 1862).

—— Bibliography of Robert Browning, from 1833 to 1881, compiled by Frederick J. Furnivall, 3rd edn., Browning Society Papers, 1 (1881).

—— 'The Early English Text Society', Gentleman's Magazine, Aug. 1867, pp. 212–13.

—— 'History of the Working Men's College', Working Men's College Magazine, II. xxi (1 Sept. 1860), 144–8; xxiii (1 Nov. 1860), 166–70; xxiv (1 Dec. 1860), 188–9.

—— [F.J.F.], 'Mr. Albert Way's letter on Great Forsters, near Egham and Thorp, Surrey', Notes and Queries, 4-1, issue 22, 30 May 1868, pp. 504–5.

—— Review of Hughes, Memoir of Macmillan, The Academy (1882), 112.

—— Shakespeare Tales for Boys and Girls, and When Shakespeare was a Boy, by Dr F. J. Furnivall, M.A. (London, [1932]).

—— 'The Social Life of the College', in Davies (ed.), Working Men's College, 54–60.

—— and Munro, John, Shakespeare: Life and Work (London, 1908).

Garmonsway, G. N., 'Anna Gurney: Learned Saxonist', Essays and Studies, NS 8 (1955), 40–57.

Garnett, Henrietta, Wives and Stunners: The Pre-Raphaelites and their Muses (London, 2012).

Garnett, Richard, jun., The Philological Essays of the Late Rev. Richard Garnett of the British Museum, Edited by his Son (London and Edinburgh, 1859).

Garnett, Richard, sen., 'Antiquarian Club-Books', in [Richard Garnett, jun. (ed.)], The Philological Essays of the Late Rev. Richard Garnett, 111–46.

Gillispie, Charles Coulston, Genesis and Geology: The Impact of Scientific Discoveries upon Religious Beliefs in the Decades before Darwin (New York, 1951).

Gilliver, Peter, The Making of the Oxford English Dictionary (Oxford, 2016).

—— 'OED Personalia', in Mugglestone (ed.), Lexicography, 232–52.

Girouard, Mark, The Return to Camelot: Chivalry and the English Gentleman (New Haven and London, 1981).

Gladstone, W. E., Two Letters to the Earl of Aberdeen on the State Persecution of the Neapolitan Government (London, 1851).

Graham, Thomas J., Modern Domestic Medicine, 2nd edn. (London, 1827, first published 1827).

—— Outlines of Botany, for the Use of Families and Schools (London, 1841).

Graves, Charles L., Life and Letters of Alexander Macmillan (London, 1910).

Great Foster House Lunatic Asylum, Egham: Inmates 1774–1851, transcribed and published by The Eureka Partnership (Stoke Mandeville, 2008).

Green, Peter, Kenneth Grahame, 1859–1932: A New Study of His Life, Work, and Times (London, 1959).

Gregory, James, *Of Victorians and Vegetarians: The Vegetarian Movement in Nineteenth-Century Britain* (London, 2007).
Grimm, Jacob, *Deutsche Grammatik* (Göttingen, 1819; 2nd edn., 1822-40).
Groh, John E., *Nineteenth-Century German Protestantism: The Church as Social Model* (Washington, DC, 1982).
Guest, Edwin, *A History of English Rhythms*, 2 vols. (London, 1838). New edition by Walter W. Skeat (London, 1882).
Gurney, Anna, 'Norfolk Words', *TPS* 2 (1855), 29-39.
Haas, Renate, 'The Social Functions of F. J. Furnivall's Medievalism', in Uwe Böker, Manfred Markus, and Rainer Schöwerling (eds.), *The Living Middle Ages* (Stuttgart, 1989), 319-32.
Halliwell, J. O., *Dictionary of Archaic and Provincial Words, Obsolete Phrases, Proverbs, and Ancient Customs*, 2 vols. (London, 1847).
Hare, Julius Charles, *The Victory of Faith*, 2nd edn. (Cambridge, 1847).
—— and Augustus William Hare, *Guesses at Truth*, 1st ser., 2nd edn. (London, 1848).
Harris, P. R., *A History of the British Museum Library, 1753-1973* (London, 1998).
Harrison, Brian, 'Religion and Recreation in Nineteenth-Century England', *Past and Present*, 38 (1967), 98-125.
—— 'The Sunday Trading Riots of 1855', *Historical Journal*, 8 (1965), 219-45.
Harrison, J. F. C., *A History of the Working Men's College, 1854-1954* (London, 1954).
Hart, James Morgan, *German Universities: A Narrative of Personal Experience* (New York, 1874).
Harte, N. B. *The Admission of Women to University College London: A Centenary Lecture* (London, 1979).
Harte, Negley, and John North, *The World of University College, London 1828-1978* (London, 1978).
Havercan, Peter, 'The Furnivalls of Sandbach', http://roots.havercan.net/furnivall.
Henderson, John, *Juvenal's Mayor: The Professor who Lived on 2d. a Day*, Cambridge Philological Society, Supplementary vol. 20 (Cambridge, 1998).
Hill, Octavia, *Life of Octavia Hill, as Told in Her Letters*, ed. C. Edmund Maurice (London, 1914).
—— *Octavia Hill: Early Ideals*, ed. Emily S. Maurice (London, 1928).
Hilton, Timothy, *John Ruskin*, 2 vols. (New Haven and London, 1985, 2000).
—— *The Pre-Raphaelites* (London, 1970).
Hogben, John, *Richard Holt Hutton of 'The Spectator'* (Edinburgh, 1899).
Horner, Leonard, 'On the Employment of Children in Factories and Other Works in the United Kingdom and Some Foreign Countries', *Quarterly Review*, 67 (Dec. 1840), 171-81.
Howitt, Mary, *An Autobiography*, ed. Margaret Howitt (London, 1889).

Howitt, William, *The Student Life of Germany, from the Unpublished MS. of Dr. Cornelius; Containing nearly Forty of the Most Famous Drinking Songs, with the Original Music, Adapted to the Piano Forte, by the Herr Winkelmeyer* (London, 1841).

Hudson, Anne, 'The Making of a Monumental Edition: The Holy Bible... The Earliest English Versions Made from the Latin Vulgate by John Wyclif and His Followers', in S. M. Rowley (ed.), *Writers, Editors and Exemplars in Medieval English Texts* (Cham, 2021), 127–50.

—— 'Robert of Gloucester and the Antiquaries', *Notes and Queries*, 214 (1969), 323–36.

Hudson, Derek, *Munby: Man of Two Worlds, The Life and Diaries of Arthur J. Munby 1828–1910* (London, 1972).

Huelin, Gordon, *King's College London: 1838–1978* (London, 1978).

Hughes, Thomas, *Account of the Lock-Out of Engineers &c., 1851–2* (Cambridge, 1860).

—— *Memoir of a Brother* (London, 1871).

—— *Memoir of Daniel Macmillan* (London, 1882).

Hume, A., *The Learned Societies and Printing Clubs of the United Kingdom... Compiled from Official Documents*, with supplement by A. I. Evans (London, 1853).

Hunt, Diana Holman, *My Grandfather, His Wives and Loves* (London, 1969).

Hunt, William Holman, *Pre-Raphaelitism and the Pre-Raphaelite Brotherhood*, 2 vols. (London, 1905, repr. Cambridge, 2013)

Husbands, Shane, 'The Roxburghe Club: Consumption, Obsession and the Passion for Print', in Emma Cayley and Susan Powell (eds.), *Manuscripts and Printed Books in Europe 1350–1550: Packaging, Presentation and Consumption*, Exeter Studies in Medieval Europe: History, Society and the Arts (Liverpool, 2013), 120–32.

Hutton, Ronald, *Blood and Mistletoe: The History of the Druids in Britain* (New Haven, 2009).

Huxley, Leonard, *Life and Letters of Thomas Henry Huxley*, 2 vols. (New York, 1901).

Hyer, Maran Clegg, Haruko Momma, and Samantha Zacher (eds.), *Old English Lexicology and Lexicography: Essays in Honour of Antonette DiPaolo Healey* (Cambridge, 2020).

Igoldsby, Thomas [R. H. Barham], *The Ingoldsby Legends, or Mirth and Marvels* (London, 1840 and 1842); 2nd edn. London, 1843.

James, John Angell, *The Young Man from Home*, American Tract Society, 3rd edn. (London, ?1850).

James, William (ed.), *The Order of Release: The Story of John Ruskin, Effie Gray, and John Everett Millais. Told for the First Time in Their Unpublished Letters* (London, 1948).

Jameson, Anna, *Hand-Book to the Courts of Modern Sculpture* (London, 1854).

Johnson, Charles, 'The Camden Society, 1838–1938', *Transactions of the Royal Historical Society*, 22 (1940), 23–38.
[Johnson, William], *Hints for Eton Masters* by W. J. (London, 1898).
Kenneally, Daniel F., and Jane Roberts, 'Oswald Cockayne (c. 1808–1873): Clerk in Holy Orders, Schoolmaster, Scholar'. in Haruko Momma and M. J. Toswell (eds.), *The Study of Old English in Nineteenth-Century Europe*, Poetica 86 (2016), 107–37.
Kent, Christopher, 'The Whittington Club: A Bohemian Experiment in Middle Class Social Reform', *Victorian Studies*, 18 (1974), 31–55.
Ker, W. P., *Epic and Romance: Essays on Medieval Literature* (London, 1897).
Killham, John, *Tennyson and The Princess: Reflections of an Age* (London, 1958).
Kingsley, Charles, *Alton Locke, Tailor and Poet: An Autobiography*. With a prefatory memoir, by Thomas Hughes (London, 1881).
―― *Glaucus, or, The Wonders of the Shore* (Cambridge, 1855).
―― *Literary and General Lectures and Essays* (London, 1898).
―― *Twenty-five Village Sermons* (London, 1849).
―― *Yeast: A Problem*, repr., with corrections and additions from *Fraser's Magazine* (London, 1851).
Kingsley, Frances Eliza (ed.), *Charles Kingsley: His Letters and Memories of his Life* (London, 1890).
Kington Oliphant, T. L., *The Sources of Standard English* (London, 1872).
Klaver, Jan Martin Ivo, 'Charles Kingsley and the Limits of Humanity', *Dutch Review of Church History*, 81 (2001), 115–41.
Koch, Carl Friedrich, *Historische Grammatik der englischen Sprache*, 3 vols. (Weimar, 1863–9).
Leigh, Samuel, *Leigh's New Picture of London: Or a View of the Political, Religious, Medical, Literary, Municipal, Commercial, and Moral State of the British Metropolis*, [ed. S. C. J. Leigh], 9th edn. (London, 1839).
Leon, Derrick, *Ruskin the Great Victorian* (London, 1949).
Lester, C. Edwards, *The Glory and the Shame of England*, 2 vols. (New York, 1841).
Levine, Philippa, *The Amateur and the Professional: Antiquarians, Historians and Archaeologists in Victorian England, 1838–1886* (Cambridge, 1986).
Lewis, Robert E., and Angus McIntosh, *A Descriptive Guide to the Manuscripts of the* Prick of Conscience, *Medium AEvum Monographs*, NS 12 (Oxford, 1982).
Lightman, Bernard, 'Huxley and Scientific Agnosticism: The Strange History of a Failed Rhetorical Strategy', *British Journal for the History of Science*, 35 (2002), 271–89.
―― *The Origins of Agnosticism* (Baltimore, MD, 1987).
A Lincoln's Inn Commonplace Book: The Buildings and Grounds of an Inn of Court, its Dependencies and Neighbourhood over Eight Centuries: in Art, Literature, Reportage and Music, ed. Graham S. Brown (London, 2016).

Litchfield, Richard Buckley, 'The Beginnings of the Working Men's College', pamphlet, published by the Working Men's College (London, 1902).
—— 'A Plea for Geology', *Working Men's College Magazine*, 3, pp. 64-9 (1 May 1861).
—— 'Work and Play; or Heads and Heels', *Working Men's College Magazine*, no. 25 (1 Jan. 1861), 1-5.
Luckhurst, K. W., 'The Great Exhibition of 1851', *Journal of the Royal Society of Arts*, 99 (1951), 413-56.
[Ludlow, J. M.] *John Ludlow: The Autobiography of a Christian Socialist*, ed. A. D. Murray (London, 1981).
Lutyens, Mary, *Millais and the Ruskins* (London, 1967).
—— (ed.), *Young Mrs. Ruskin in Venice: Unpublished Letters of Mrs. John Ruskin Written from Venice between 1849-1852* (New York, 1965).
Lye, Edward, *Dictionarium Saxonico et Gothico-Latinum*, 2 vols. (London, 1772).
Macaulay, Thomas Babington, *Lays of Ancient Rome* (London, 1842).
—— 'Thoughts on the Advancement of Academical Education in England. 1826', *The Edinburgh Review*, 43 (Feb. 1826), 315-41.
Mackenzie, Faith Compton, *William Cory: A Biography with a Selection of Poems* (London, 1950).
Macmillan, Alexander, *Life and Letters of Alexander Macmillan* (London, 1910).
Madden, Frederic, 'Observations on an Autograph of Shakspere and the Orthography of his Name', *Archæologia*, 27 (1 Jan. 1838), 113-23.
Malden, Henry, *On the Origin of Universities and Academical Degrees* (London, 1835).
Marchand, Leslie A., *The Athenaeum: A Mirror of Victorian Culture* (Chapel Hill, NC, 1941).
Marsh, George P., *A Dictionary of English Etymology, with Introduction on the Origin of Language, with Notes and Additions*, 3 vols. (London, 1859-65).
Martin, Robert Bernard, *Tennyson, the Unquiet Heart* (London and Oxford, 1983).
Martin, Theodore, *The Life of H.R.H. The Prince Consort*, 5 vols. (London, 1875-80).
Martineau, Harriet, *Autobiography*, with introduction by Gaby Weiner, 2 vols. (London, 1983).
Masson, Flora, *Victorians All* (London, 1931).
Masterman, N. C., *John Malcolm Ludlow: The Builder of Christian Socialism* (Cambridge, 1963).
Matthews, David O., 'Chaucer's American Accent', in *American Literary History*, 22, no. 4 (1 Dec. 2010), 758-72.
—— *The Invention of Middle English: An Anthology of Primary Sources* (Pennsylvania, 2000).

—— *The Making of Middle English, 1765–1910*, Medieval Cultures, 18 (Minneapolis, 1999).
—— 'Speaking to Chaucer: The Poet and the Nineteenth-Century Academy', in Leslie J. Workman, Kathleen Verduin, David D. Metzger (eds.), *Medievalism and the Academy*, Studies in Medievalism, 9 (Cambridge, 1997), 5–25.
Mätzner, Eduard, *Altenglische Sprachproben nebst einem Wörterbuch*, 2 vols. (Berlin, 1867–1900).
—— *Englische Grammatik* (Berlin, 1885).
—— *An English Grammar: Methodical, Analytical, and Historical . . .*, trans. Clair James Grece, 3 vols. (London, 1874) [translation of *Englische Grammatik*].
Maurice, Emily S. (ed.), *Octavia Hill: Early Ideals* (London, 1928).
Maurice, Frederick Denison, *The Claims of the Bible and of Science: Correspondence between a Layman and the Rev. F. D. Maurice on Some Questions Arising out of the Controversy Respecting the Pentateuch* (London, 1863).
—— *The Old Testament: Nineteen Sermons on the First Lessons for the Sundays from Septuagesima Sunday to the Third Sunday after Trinity: Preached in the Chapel of Lincoln's Inn* (London, 1851).
—— *The Pentateuch and the Book of Joshua Critically Examined* (London, 1862).
—— *The Word 'Eternal', The Punishment of the Wicked: A Letter* (Cambridge, 1854).
—— *The Life of Frederick Denison Maurice, Chiefly Told in His Own Letters*, ed. Frederick Maurice, 2 vols. (London, 1884).
Mayhew, Henry, *London Labour and the London Poor*, 4 vols. (London, 1861–2).
McVeigh, Simon, '"Brightening the Lives of the People on Sunday": The National Sunday League and Liberal Attitudes towards Concert Promotion in Victorian Britain', in Sarah Collins (ed.), *Music and Victorian Liberalism: Composing the Liberal Subject* (Cambridge, 2019), 37–59.
Middleton, Jacob, 'Bearded Patriarchs', *History Today*, 56 (Feb. 2006), 26–7.
Mill, John Stuart, *Dissertations and Discussions: Political, Philosophical, and Historical, Reprinted Chiefly from the Edinburgh and Westminster Reviews*, 2 vols. (New York, 1973).
Miller, Edward, *Prince of Librarians: The Life and Times of Antonio Panizzi of the British Museum* (London, 1967).
Mills, David, 'Theories and Practices in the Editing of the Chester Cycle Play-manuscripts', in Pearsall (ed.), *Manuscripts and Texts*, 110–21.
Mitford, William and John, *The History of Greece*, 8 vols. (London, 1829).
[Mogridge, George], *Old Humphrey's Addresses* (London, 1839).
Momma, Haruko, *From Philology to English Studies: Language and Culture in the Nineteenth Century*, Cambridge Studies in English Language (Cambridge, 2013).

Moran, James, *Stephen Austins of Hertford: A Bi-Centenary History* (Hertford, 1968).
Morgan, Charles, *The House of Macmillan (1843–1943)* (London, 1943).
Morell, John, *Sketch of the Life of Charles Fourier, Introductory to his Treatise on the Human Soul* (London, 1849).
Morris, Jeremy, *F. D. Maurice and the Crisis of Christian Authority*, Christian Theology in Context Series (New York, 2005).
—— (ed.), *To Build Christ's Kingdom: F. D. Maurice and his Writings*, Canterbury Studies in Spiritual Theology (London, 2007).
Morris, Richard, *Elementary Lessons in Historical English Grammar, Containing Accidence and Word-Formation* (London, 1874).
—— *The Etymology of Local Names. With a Short Introduction to the Relationship of Languages. Teutonic Names* (London, 1857).
—— *Historical Outlines of English Accidence, Comprising Chapters on the History and Development of the Language, and on Word-formation* (London, 1872).
'Dr. Morris and Dr. Weymouth', *The Academy*, 108 (30 May 1874), 607.
Mugglestone, Lynda, *Lexicography and the Oxford English Dictionary: Pioneers in the Untrodden Forest* (Oxford, 2000).
—— *Lost for Words: The Hidden History of the OED* (New Haven, 2005).
Mumby, F. A., *The House of Routledge 1834–1934 with a History of Kegan Paul, Trench, Trübner and other Associated Firms* (London, 1834).
Munby, A. N. L., *Connoisseurs and Miniatures, 1750–1850* (Oxford, 1972).
—— *The Formation of the Phillipps Library from 1841 to 1872, with an Account of the Phillips Art Collection by A. E. Popham*, Phillipps Studies, 4 (Cambridge, 1956).
—— 'Sir Frederic Madden at Cambridge', *The Book Collector*, 10, no. 2 (1961), 156–63.
Munro, John J., 'Biography', in Munro (ed.), *Frederick James Furnivall*, pp. vii–lxxxii.
—— (ed.), *Frederick James Furnivall: A Volume of Personal Record* (London, 1911).
Murray, K. M. Elisabeth, *Caught in the Web of Words: James A. H. Murray and the Oxford English Dictionary* (Oxford, 1979).
Nairn, Ian, and Nikolaus Pevsner, *The Buildings of England, Surrey*, revd. Bridget Cherry, 2nd edn. (New Haven and London, 1971).
[Napier, Catherine], *Women's Rights and Duties Considered with Relation to her Influence on Society and on Her Own Condition*, By A Woman, 2 vols. (London, 1840).
Nash, D. W., *Taliesin, or The Bards and Druids of Britain: A Translation of the Remains of the Earliest Welsh Bards, and an Examination of the Bardic Mysteries* (London, 1858).
Nesbit, Edith, *Children's Stories from Shakespeare* (London, n.d. [1910–24]).

New Shakspere Society's Transactions, 1874–92.

Newhauser, Richard G., and John A. Alford (eds.), *Philological Studies in Honor of Siegfried Wenzel*, Medieval & Renaissance Texts and Studies, 118, Center for Medieval and Early Renaissance Studies, State University of New York (Binghamton, NY, 1995).

Newman, F. W., *Lectures on Political Economy* (London, 1851).

Nicoll, W. Robertson, and Thomas James Wise (eds.), *Literary Anecdotes of the Nineteenth Century: Contributions towards a Literary History of the Period*, 2 vols. (London, 1895–6).

Norman, Edward, *The Victorian Christian Socialists* (Cambridge, 1987).

Nowell-Smith, Simon (ed.), *Letters to Macmillan* (London, 1967).

Ogilvie, Sarah, *The Dictionary People: The Unsung Heroes who Created the Oxford English Dictionary* (London, 2023).

Oman, Sir Charles, *Memories of Victorian Oxford* (London, 1941).

Ormond, Leonée, *Alfred Tennyson: A Literary Life* (Basingstoke, 1983).

Our English Home: Its Early History and Progress. With Notes on the Introduction of Domestic Inventions (Oxford, 1860).

Paley, William, *Evidences of Christianity Epitomized . . .* (London, 1835).

—— *A View of the Evidences of Christianity* (London, 1794).

Palmer, D. J., *The Rise of English Studies: An Account of the Study of English Language and Literature from its Origins to the Making of the Oxford English School* (Oxford, 1965).

Parker, Joanne, 'Anglo-Saxonism and the Victorian Novel', in Joanne Parker and Corinna Wagner (eds.), *The Oxford Handbook of Victorian Medievalism* (Oxford, 2020), 632–53.

Partington, Wilfred, *Thomas J. Wise in the Original Cloth: The Life and Record of the Forger of the Nineteenth-Century Pamphlets, with an Appendix by George Bernard Shaw* (London, 1946).

Peacock, Edward (ed.), *English Church Furniture, Ornaments and Decorations, at the Period of the Reformation, as Exhibited in a List of the Goods Destroyed in Certain Lincolnshire Churches, A.D. 1566* (London, 1866).

Pearsall, Derek, 'Chaucer's Meter: The Evidence of the Manuscripts', in Tim William Machan (ed.), *Medieval Literature: Texts and Interpretations*, Medieval & Renaissance Texts and Studies, 79 (Binghamton, NY, 1991), 41–57.

—— 'Frederick James Furnivall (1825, 1910)', in Damico (ed.), *Medieval Scholarship*, ii. 125–38.

—— (ed.), *Manuscripts and Texts: Editorial Problems in Later Middle English Literature. Essays from the 1985 Conference at the University of York* (Cambridge, 1987).

Penny Cyclopaedia, ed. George Long, 27 vols. (London, 1833–43).

Peterson, William S. (ed.), *Browning's Trumpeter: The Correspondence of Robert Browning and Frederick J. Furnivall 1872–1889* (Washington, DC, 1979).

Pettigrew, T. J., *Memoir of Beriah Botfield, Esq., M.P.* (London, 1863).

Phillips, Noelle, '"Texts with Trowsers": Editing and the Elite Chaucer', *RES*, NS 61 (2009), 331–59.
Politics for the People, facs. repr. (New York, 1971).
Polson, Archer, *Law and Lawyers, Sketches of Legal History and Biography*, 2 vols. (London, 1840).
Porter, Anna Maria, *The Hungarian Brothers* Ilondon, 1839).
Postgate, Raymond, *The Story of a Year, 1848* (London, 1955).
Potter, Beatrice, *The Co-operative Movement in Great Britain* (London, 1892).
Prince, Alison, *Kenneth Grahame: An Innocent in the Wild Wood* (London, 1994).
Quirk, Randolph, *The Linguist and the English Language* (London, 1974).
Raikes, Elizabeth, *Dorothea Beale of Cheltenham* (London, 1908).
Rask, Rasmus, *Deutsche Grammatik* (Göttingen, 1819; 2nd edn., 1822–40).
Raven, Charles E., *Christian Socialism, 1848–1854* (London, 1920).
[Rawston, George], *My Life by an Ex-Dissenter* (London, 1841).
Reynolds, G. W. M., *Pickwick Abroad* (London, 1839).
Ribeyrol, Charlotte, Matthew Winterbottom, and Madeline Hewitson (eds.), *Colour Revolution: Victorian Art, Fashion and Design* (Oxford, 2023).
Ritson, Joseph, *Bibliographia Poetica: A Catalogue of English Poets of the Twelfth, Thirteenth, Fourteenth, Fifteenth, and Sixteenth Centurys* (London, 1802).
Roberts, Andrew, 'The Lunacy Commission: A Study of its Origin, Emergence and Character', Part of the Asylums Index, 'Egham, Surrey', http://studymore.org.uk/4asylums.htm.
Robertson, James Craigie, *History of the Christian Church from the Apostolic Age to the Reformation*, 4 vols. (London, 1852–73).
Roebuck, J., 'Reminiscences of an Old Student', in *The Working Men's College, 1854–1904*, ed. J. Llewelyn Davies (London, 1904), 61–99.
Rogers, T. D. (ed.), *Sir Frederic Madden at Cambridge: Extracts from Madden's Diaries 1831, 1838, 1841–2, 1859 and 1863*, Cambridge Bibliographical Society, 4 (Cambridge, 1980).
Ross, Thomas W., 'Thomas Wright (1810–1877)', in Ruggiers (ed.), *Editing Chaucer*, 145–56.
Rossetti, William Michael, *Memoir of Shelley (with a fresh preface)*, 2nd edn., Shelley Society, Series IV, Miscellaneous no. 2 (London, 1886).
—— *Selected Letters of William Michael Rossetti*, ed. Roger W. Peattie (University Park, PA, 1990).
[Roxburghe Club], *Catalogue of the Books Presented to and Printed by the Club*, Roxburghe Club (London, 1884).
Ruggiers, Paul G. (ed.), *Editing Chaucer: The Great Tradition* (Norman, OK, 1984).
Rupke, Nicolaas A., *The Great Chain of History: William Buckland and the English School of Geology 1814–1849* (Oxford, 1983).

Ruskin, John, *Fors Clavigera, Works of John Ruskin*, ed. Edward Tyas Cook and Alexander Wedderburn, xxvii (Cambridge, 1910).

—— *The Genius of John Ruskin: Selection from his Writings*, ed. John D. Rosenberg (Charlottesville, VA, and London, 1964).

—— *An Ill-Assorted Marriage: An Unpublished Letter by John Ruskin* (London, 1915).

—— *Modern Painters*, revd. edn., 5 vols. (London, 1873).

—— *Notes on the Construction of Sheepfolds* (London, 1851).

—— *On the Nature of Gothic Architecture and Herein of the True Functions of the Workman in Art. Being the Greater Part of the 6th Chapter of the 2nd Vol. of 'Stones of Venice'* (London, 1854).

—— *The Opening of the Crystal Palace, Considered in Some of its Relations to the Prospects of Art* (London, 1854).

—— *Praeterita: The Autobiography of John Ruskin*, with an introduction by Sir Kenneth Clark (London, 1949).

—— *Two Letters Concerning 'Notes on the Construction of Sheepfolds', Addressed to the Rev. F. D. Maurice, M.A. in 1851, with Forewords by F. J. Furnivall*, ed. Thomas J. Wise, privately printed (London, 1890).

—— *The Works of John Ruskin*, ed. Edward Tyas Cook and Alexander Wedderburn, 38 vols. (London, 1903–12; reissued Cambridge, 2010).

—— and Maurice, F. D., *John Ruskin and Frederick Denison Maurice on 'Notes on the Construction of Sheepfolds'*, ed. Thomas J. Wise (London, privately printed, 1896).

Russell, Lindsay Rose, *Women and Dictionary-Making, Gender, Genre, and English Language Lexicography* (Cambridge, 2018).

Sandras, E. G., *Étude sur G. Chaucer, considéré comme imitateur des trouvères* (Paris, 1859).

Sherman, James, *A Plea for the Lord's Day* (London, 1830).

Shippey, T. A., *The Road to Middle-Earth: How J. R. R. Tolkien Created a New Mythology*, 2nd edn. (London, 1992).

Sidgwick, F., 'Frederick James Furnivall', *English Illustrated Magazine*, Feb. 1904, pp. 556–9.

Sigmond, G. G., *Tea: Its Effects, Medicinal and Moral* (London, 1839).

Singleton, Antony, 'The Early English Text Society in the Nineteenth Century: A Chapter in the History of the Editing of Middle English Texts' (D.Phil. thesis, Oxford University, 2001).

—— 'The Early English Text Society in the Nineteenth Century: An Organizational History', *RES*, NS 56 (2005), 90–118.

Skeat, Walter William, *A Student's Pastime; Being a Select Series of Articles Reprinted from 'Notes and Queries'* (Oxford, 1896).

—— *Testimonials in Favour of the Rev. Walter W. Skeat, M.A., A candidate for the Elrington and Bosworth Professorship of Anglo-Saxon in the University of Cambridge* (Cambridge, 1878).

—— 'The Translator of "The Graal"', *The Athenaeum*, 3971 (22 Nov. 1902), 684.
Smith, Alison (ed.), *Exposed: The Victorian Nude* (London, 2001).
Soames, Laura, *An Introduction to Phonetics (English, French and German), with Reading Lessons and Exercises* (London, 1891).
Somner, William, *Dictionarium Saxonico-Latino-Anglicum: Voces, phrasesque praecipuas Anglo-Saxonicas, e libris, sive manuscriptis, sive typis excusis aliisque monumentis tam publicis tam privatis, magna diligentia collectas, cum Latina et Anglica vocum interpretatione complectens...* (Oxford, 1659).
Spalding, William, *The History of English Literature: With an Outline of the Origin and Growth of the English Language. Illustrated by Extracts. For the Use of Schools and of Private Students* (Edinburgh, 1853).
Spencer, H. L., 'F. J. Furnivall's Last Fling: The Wyclif Society and Anglo-German Scholarly Relations, 1882–1922', *RES*, NS 65 (2014), 790–811.
—— 'F. J. Furnivall's Six of the Best: The *Six-Text Canterbury Tales* and the Chaucer Societ'y, *RES*, NS 66 (2015), 601–23.
Stanford, Edward, *Stanford's Library Map of London and its Suburbs* (London, 1862).
Stanley, A. P., *Life and Correspondence of Thomas Arnold, Late Head Master of Rugby School...* (London, 1844).
Steeves, H. R., *Learned Societies and English Literary Scholarship in Great Britain and the United States* (New York, 1913).
Steuart, Hilary, 'Catholic Tradition and English Literature', *Downside Review*, 55 (n.s. 36).
Stone, Lawrence, *The Road to Divorce, England 1530–1987* (Oxford, 1990).
Stratmann, Francis Henry [Franz Heinrich], *A Dictionary of the Old English Writing Compiled from Writings of the XIII, XIV and XV Centuries* (Krefeld, 1867).
—— *Mittelenglische Grammatik* (Cologne and Krefeld, 1885).
Styler, W. E. (ed.), *Learning and Working* (London, 1968).
Sullivan, Matthew T., 'A Brief Textual History of the "Manuel des Pêchés"', *Neuphilologische Mitteilungen*, 93 (1992), 337–46.
—— 'The Original and Subsequent Audiences of the Manuel des Péchés and its Middle English Descendants' (D.Phil. thesis, University of Oxford, 1990).
Sullivan, Michael J., 'Tennyson at Trinity', *The Fountain*, 19 (2014), 12–13.
Sutcliffe, Peter, *The Oxford University Press: An Informal History* (Oxford, 1978).
Sutton, Anne F., and Livia Visser-Fuchs, *Richard III's Books: Ideals and Reality in the Life and Library of a Medieval Prince* (Cheltenham, 2024).
Sweet, Henry, 'The Early English Text Society', *The Academy*, 2, no. 21 (Apr. 1871), 210.
—— 'On "Early English Pronunciation, with Especial Reference to Chaucer"', *The Academy*, no. 129 (24 Oct. 1874), 460–1.
Tales of Chivalry and Romance (Edinburgh, 1826).
Tennyson, Alfred, *The Poems of Tennyson in Three Volumes*, ed. Christopher

Ricks, 2nd edn., *Incorporating the Trinity College Manuscripts*, 3 vols. (Harlow, 1987).

Thirlwall, Connop, *A History of Greece*, 8 vols. (London, 1835–44).

Thirlwall, John Connop, Jr., *Connop Thirlwall: Historian and Theologian* (London, 1936).

Thomas, Carla M., '"Poema Morale": An Edition from Cambridge, Trinity College B. 14. 52', MA diss., University of Florida, College of Arts and Sciences (2008) (Florida State University Libraries Electronic Theses, Treatises and Dissertations).

Thompson, Dorothy, *The Chartists: Popular Politics in the Industrial Revolution* (London, 1984).

Thorpe, Benjamin, *Analecta Anglo-Saxonica: A Selection in Prose and Verse from Anglo-Saxon Authors of Various Ages, with a Glossary, Designed Chiefly as a First Book for Students* (London, 1834).

—— (trans.), *A Grammar of the Anglo-Saxon Tongue, from the Danish of Erasmus Rask . . .* , 2nd edn. (London, 1865).

Toller, Thomas Northcote, *An Anglo-Saxon Dictionary, Based on the Manuscript Collections of Joseph Bosworth*, 2 vols. (Oxford, 1908–21).

Toswell, M. J., 'Anna Gurney: The Unknown Victorian Medievalist', in Haruko Momma and M. J. Toswell (eds.), *The Study of Old English in Nineteenth-Century Europe*, Poetica 86 (2016), 69–86.

—— 'Genre and the Dictionary', in Hyer et al. (eds.), *Old English Lexicology*, 229–41.

—— 'The Lost Victorian Women of Old English Studies', in Robin Norris, Rebecca Stephenson, and Renée R. Trilling (eds.), *Feminist Approaches to Early Medieval English Studies* (Amsterdam, 2023), 27–52.

Tredgold, Thomas, *The Steam Engine*, revd. and enl. (London, 1838, first published 1827).

Trench, Richard Chenevix, 'On Some Deficiencies in Our Engllish Dictionaries', *TPS* 4, no. 2 (Nov. 1857), 1–7.

—— *On the Study of Words: Lectures Addressed (Originally) to the Pupils at the Diocesan Training School* (London, 1851).

—— *A Select Glossary of English Words Used Formerly in Senses Different from Their Present* (London, 1859); ed. with additional notes by A. Smythe Palmer (London, 1906).

Trevelyan, Janet Penrose, *The Life of Mrs Humphry Ward* (London, 1923).

Utz, Richard, *Chaucer and the Discourse of German Philology: A History of Reception, and an Annotated Bibliography of Studies, 1793–1948*, The Centre for Medieval Studies, University of Sydney, Australia, Making the Middle Ages, 3 (Turnhout, 2002).

Valpy-French, Richard, *Nineteen Centuries of Drink in England: A History* (London, 1884).

Vanderbilt, Kermit, *Charles Eliot Norton, Apostle of Culture in a Democracy* (Cambridge, MA, 1959).
Venn, J. A., *Alumni Cantabrigienses: a biographical list of all known students, graduates and holders of office at the University of Cambridge*, Part 2, 1752-1900, 6 vols. (Cambridge, 1940-54).
Vidler, Alec R., *F. D. Maurice and Company: Nineteenth-Century Studies* (s.l., 1966).
Vincent, David (ed.), *Testaments of Radicalism: Memoirs of Working Class Politicians, 1790-1855* (London, 1977).
Wakeman, Geoffrey, *Victorian Book Illustration: The Technical Revolution* (Newton Abbot, 1973).
Ward, Antonia, '"My Love for Chaucer": F. J. Furnivall and Homosociality in the Chaucer Society', in Leslie J. Workman, Kathleen Verduin, and David D. Metzger (eds.), *Medievalism and the Academy*, Studies in Medievalism, 9 (Cambridge, 1997), 44-57.
Ward, Mary (Mrs Humphry), *Robert Elsmere*, ed. Rosemary Ashton (Oxford, 1987).
—— *A Writer's Recollections* (London, 1918).
Warren, John, 'Harriet Martineau and the Concept of Community, Deerbrook and Ambleside', *Journal of Victorian Culture*, 13 (2008), 223-46.
Warren, Samuel, *Ten Thousand A-Year*, 3 vols. (London, 1841).
The Wars of Europe: or Annals of Military and Naval Warfare, ed. By a Distinguished Officer, 3 vols. (London, 1838-[40]).
Warton, Thomas, *The History of English Poetry from the Close of the Eleventh to the Commencement of the Eighteenth Century*, 4 vols. (London, 1774-1806).
Watts, T., 'On the Probable Future Position of the English Language', *TPS* 4 (1850), 207-14.
Way, Albert, 'Introduction', *Archaeological Journal*, 1 (Mar. 1844).
Wedgwood, Hensleigh, *A Dictionary of English Etymology* (London, 1857).
—— 'Grimm's Deutsche Grammatik', *Quarterly Review*, 50, no. 99 (Oct. 1833), Art VII, 169-8.
Wenzel, Siegfried, 'Reflections on (New) Philology, *Speculum* 65 (1990), 11-18.
Weymouth, Richard Francis, *On Early English Pronunciation, with Especial Reference to Chaucer, in Opposition to the Views Maintained by Mr. A. J. Ellis, F.R.S. . . .* (London, 1874).
—— *Answers to Questions on the English Language Set at the Matriculation Examination of the University of London, June 1873* (London, 1874).
Wheatley, H. B., 'The Early English Text Society and F. J. Furnivall', *The Library*, 3rd ser., no. 9, vol. iii (Jan. 1912), 1-21.
Whewell, W., 'An Account of the Late Cambridge Etymological Society, and its Plans; with some Specimens of its Labours', *TPS* 5, no. 117 (1852), 133-42.
White, Beatrice, 'Frederick James Furnivall', *Essays and Studies*, NS 5 (1952), 64-76.

Whytehead, Thomas, *Poems* (London, 1842).
Wiltshire, D., *The Social and Political Thought of Herbert Spencer* (Oxford, 1978).
Windeatt, Barry, 'Thomas Tyrwhitt (1730-1786)', in Ruggiers (ed.), *Editing Chaucer*, 117-43.
Wise, Thomas J. (ed.), *John Ruskin and Frederick Denison Maurice on 'Notes on the Construction of Sheepfolds'* (London: privately printed [by Richard Clay & Sons], 1896).
Wittich, Wilhelm, *A German Grammar* (London, 1842).
Woodworth, Arthur V., *Christian Socialism in England* (London, 1903).
The Working Men's College Magazine (1859-60), modern reprint on demand, undated.
Wright, Alastair Ian, 'On Seeing and Being Seen: Beholding Class in Ford Madox Brown's "Work"', *Oxford Art Journal*, 40 (2017), 419-47.
Yates, Joseph Brooks, 'An Account of an Unprinted English Poem, Written in the Early Part of the Fourteenth Century, by Richard de Hampole, and Entitled "Stimulus Conscientiae", or "The Prick of Conscience", *Archaeologia* 19, Jan. 1821 (read 14th Dec. 1820), 314-35.

INDEX

A

Abbotsford Club 316, 355
'ABC' Café, London 207
Abdy, Albert Channing 60, 61, 63
Aberdeen, University 287n.
Abernethy, John 28
The Academy 398n.
Addington, Surrey 235, 237
Ælfric 160, 297
Aeschylus 198, 292n.
Albert, Prince 38n., 40, 122-4, 126, 150, 256, 379
Alderson, Sir James 144
Aldford, Cheshire 318
Alford, Henry (Hulsean Lecturer, Cambridge) 61
Alfred, King 27, 160, 285, 297
Allbutt, Thomas Clifford 248n.
Allen, George 195n., 207
Allen, Hope Emily 337
All Souls' College, Oxford 201
Alphabetical List of English Words 328-32
Amalgamated Society of Engineers (ASE) 113, 124
Ancrene Wisse (*Riwle*) 355, 404, 409-10
Antiquaries, Society of 19n., 275n., 293n., 311n., 346-7, 348, 355, 356-7, 360, 362, 364
Apothecaries' Hall, London 130
Archaeologia 357
Arnold, Mary: see Ward
Arnold, Matthew 89n., 259
Arnold, Thomas, *sen.* 86, 136
Arnold, Thomas, *jun.* 86n., 136, 177
Arthur, King, legends 12-13, 377-81, 384, 386, 391, 436
Artists and Craftsmen Magazine 329
Ash, Surrey 26n.
Ashburnham House 347, 352
(Adolf) Asher & Co. 311, 313, 328, 389, 395, 416
Athanasius: *see* Creed of St Athanasius
'Athelstan Ballad': *see Battle of Brunanburh*
Athenaeum 307, 329, 361

Atkinson, Henry George: *see* Martineau, Harriet
'Auchinleck Manuscript' 355
Austin, Stephen, printer (Austin's) 4, 311, 328-9, 387, 406n., 407
Austin, Thomas 33n.
Ayenbite of Inwyt 320, 367, 374n., 403n.

B

Bacon, Francis 260
Badcock, Jonathan Neale 33n.
Badger, Thomas Smith (Badger-Eastwood) 60-3, 65, 114, 128
Ballad Society 3, 160, 358
Ballast-Heavers of the Port of London 114-26, 161, 170, 202
Bannatyne Club 346, 355, 364
Banstead, Surrey 130
Barclay, Alexander 316
Bargrave, John, *Pope Alexander VII* 361-2
Barham, Richard Harris (Thomas Ingoldsby), *Ingoldsby Legends* 67
Barthorp, Henry 115, 121, 123-4, 125n., 126
Battersea Training College 198, 414-15
Battle of Brunanburh 160
Beale, Dorothea 285-6
Bedford College, London 84n., 108n., 133
Bedivere 378
Beecher (student at the Working Men's College) 203
Beethoven, Ludwig van 84-5
Bekker, Immanuel 287
Belfast, Queen's College 287n.
Bell, John, *A Daughter of Eve* 132
Bell, Robert 376
Bell and Daldy (George Bell and Sons) 311, 338, 419
Bellini, Vincenzo 87, 209n.
Bengel, Johann Albrecht 256
Beowulf 160, 293, 354, 377
Berkeley, Henry 205
Berkeley Square, London 144

INDEX

Berlin 99, 287-8, 300n., 311, 313, 423n.
  University of 6, 96n., 287n., 323n., 368, 385
Bermondsey 99-100, 113, 414
Berners, Juliana 320
Bethnal Green Weavers 128
Bezer, John James 105, 111, 227, 328
Biedermann, Revd Henry (vicar of Egham) 130n.
Birmingham 196n., 239
Blaauw, William Henry 318
Blackie, John Stuart 291
Blackley, W. L. 317-18
Block-Printers' Trade Union 113
Boccaccio, Giovanni, *Decameron* 351
Bodleian Library, Oxford 39, 316, 334, 339n., 341, 344, 375, 396, 399
Boethius (OE) 295
Bohn, Henry 107, 394-5
  Bohn's Antiquarian Library 382, 394
Bonham Carter, Henry 128n.
Bonn, University of 287, 288n.
Booth, Charles 82
Bopp, Franz 48, 277, 283, 287-8
Boron, Robert de 381
Bosworth, Joseph 287n., 295-8, 402, 415
  A Compendious Anglo-Saxon Dictionary 295n.
  Dictionary of the Anglo-Saxon Language 295, 296-7, 298
Botfield, Beriah 366-7, 374-5, 382-3
Boyce, William 52n.
Bradley, Henry 34, 300, 350n., 418n., 419n.
Bradshaw, Henry 6, 15n., 25n., 233n., 377n., 387, 393
Brandl, Alois 80, 323, 368, 377, 424
Brentano, Lujo 61
Brewer, John Sherren 205
Bridgewater art collection 153
Bright, B. H. 352n.
Brig O'Turk, Perthshire 181, 183
Brink, Bernhard ten 61
British Archaeological Association 356, 360n.
British Museum 32, 90, 294n, 299, 304, 311, 319, 322, 327, 334, 339, 352, 354, 374, 381, 384, 389-95, 404, 416-17
Brock, Charles Edmund 393
Brock, Edmund 361, 393, 407, 409
  (ed.) *Morte Arthure* 394

(ed., with T. O. Cockayne) *Liflade of St. Juliana* 394, 407-10
'On the Grammatical Forms of Southern English, as Shown in the *Ancren Riwle*' 409n.
Brock, Henry Matthew 393
Brontë, Charlotte 258n.
  Jane Eyre 158
Brown, Ford Madox 166, 196, 266
Brown, James (ballast-heaver) 123, 125n.
Brown, Rawdon 145, 182
Browning, Elizabeth Barrett 149, 156, 329, 369, 386n.
Browning, Robert 9-10, 12, 14n., 29n., 378
Browning Society 2, 4, 11-12, 16-17, 29n., 313
Bruce Castle School, Tottenham: schoolboy's report in *The Brucian* of Ruskin's address to the Working Men's College 193-4, 434-6
Bryant, Jacob 345
Bryce, David 118n.
Buckingham Palace 241
Buckland, William 246-7, 553
Bunney, John 222
Burke, Edmund 310
Burlington, Vermont 319
Burne-Jones, Edward Coley 196, 266, 379n.
Burnham Beeches 230
Burns, Robert 92n., 172
Byron, George Gordon, Lord 55, 69, 92n., 149n., 155, 330

C

Cædmon 160
Caldwell's dancing rooms 230n.
Cambridge (city) 16, 383
Cambridge and Oxford Railway Committee 67
Cambridge Apostles (Conversazione Society) 74-5, 134, 274
Cambridge Etymological Society 276, 302
Cambridge University 8, 26, 37-9, 41-3, 46, 50, 53-4, 57-76, 106, 158, 163, 174, 177, 217-31, 249, 287, 292, 296, 302, 349, 383, 404n.
Cambridge University Library 6, 7, 29
Cambridge University Press 393

466 INDEX

Woodwardian Museum 249, 374
see also individual colleges and named graduates
Cambridge Working Men's College 201
Camden Press 208, 266
Camden Society (Royal Historical Society) 319n., 327, 359–64, 371
Camden Town, London 109n., 195, 204n., 207, 267
Campbell, Archibald Mansfield 85n., 98, 162
Campbell, George Douglas, 8th Duke of Argyll 168
Canaanite slaughters 137, 139–40, 160n.
Canterbury 362
Capgrave, John, *Chronicle of England* 318
Cardwell, Edward 123
Carlyle, Thomas 13–14, 18–19, 75, 83, 91n., 92, 109, 134, 149–50, 196, 330
  Life of John Sterling 83, 149n., 134
  Past and Present 369
Carne, John 64
'Carroll, Lewis', *Alice in Wonderland* 266
Caterham, Surrey 230, 249
Catholicon Anglicum 361
Caxton, William 316, 351, 430
Caxton Society 319n., 399n.
Central Co-operative Agency 166, 170
Chabot, Philip J. 276, 319
Chalmers, Alexander 344n.
Chambers, Raymond Wilson 8, 17–18, 278–80, 285n., 286, 296, 337
Chambers, Robert, *Vestiges of the Natural History of Creation* 256
Chartists, Chartism 76, 89–91, 93, 99–101, 104–5, 118, 137n., 243, 262
Chatterton, Thomas 345
Chaucer, Geoffrey 20, 32, 35, 59, 153–4, 200, 285, 287, 296, 298, 303, 305, 317, 320, 338, 350, 354, 368, 376–7, 391, 398n., 417, 419, 422, 430, 433
  Canterbury Tales 154n., 199, 368, 376–7, 419, 422
  Romance of the Rose (attrib.) 153
Chaucer Society 2, 3–5, 153, 154n., 269, 313, 318–19, 364, 394
Cheetham, Samuel 318
Cheltenham 385
Cheltenham Ladies' College 285
Cheshunt (Herts.) 83
Chester Plays (*mysteries*) 352, 364
Chester-le-Street, Co. Durham 265

Chetham's Library, Manchester 360
Chetham Society 356
Childs, Charles (printer) 4
Childs, John (printer) 387
Chopin, Frédéric 16, 84–6
Christ Church, Albany St., London 52
Christ Church, Camberwell 414
Christ Church, Oxford 144, 146n., 246–7
Christian Socialism 27, 45, 62, 76, 89, 91–105, *et passim*
Christian Socialist (*Journal of Association*) 81, 92, 105, 110–11
Church Missionary Society 64
Clarendon Press: *see* Oxford University
Clark, Samuel 198–9
Clevedon, Somerset 130n.
Coal-whippers 114, 120
Coates, Sir Edward 365n.
Cockayne, Alice Eden 406n.
Cockayne, Florence Louisa 406n.
Cockayne, Thomas Oswald 288, 297–8, 393–5, 400–13
  theories about the authorship of *Ancrene Wisse* (*Riwle*) and its associated texts 409–10
  (ed.) *Hali Meidenhad* (*Hali Meiðhad*) 404–7
  (ed.) *Leechdoms, Wort-Cunning and Star-Craft* 403–4, 407
  (ed.) *Liflade of St. Juliana* 407–10
  (ed.) *Seinte Marherete* 395, 400, 404–5
Cokayne, George Edward 402n.
Colchester 117
Colenso, John, Bishop of Natal 248, 403
Coleridge, Derwent 135, 314
  (ed.) Hartley Coleridge, *Essays, Marginalia, and Poems* 135, 314
Coleridge, Edith 135
Coleridge, Ellen 324–5
Coleridge, Hartley 134–5
Coleridge, Henry Nelson 135
Coleridge, Herbert 19n., 135, 267, 301, 304, 307–11, 315–26
  'A Dictionary of the First, or Oldest Words in the English language' 301–2, 332
  Glossarial Index 301, 302n., 310, 313–14, 316, 323n., 327, 335, 337n.
Coleridge, Samuel Taylor 113, 134, 175, 339, 391
  Aids to Reflection 71, 134

INDEX

On the Constitution of the Church and State 134
Table Talk 134
Coleridge, Sara 135
Collier, John Payne 261n., 357–8, 366
Collins, William 152
Columbia College, New York 319
Communism 93
Communist Manifesto 89, 93
Connor family 97
Conybeare, John Josias (ed.) *Illustrations of Anglo-Saxon Poetry* 357
Cooper, James Fenimore 55, 63n.
Cooper, Walter 100–2, 172, 178n., 378
co-operation 93, 101–2, 104, 129n., 133n., 224, 228n.
Cope, Charles West 152
Copenhagen 131n., 287, 293
Cork, University College 287n.
Corn Laws 76, 89, 370
'Corncrake' 40
Cornish Telegraph 412–13
Corpus Christi College, Cambridge 64, 382–3
Corpus Christi College, Oxford 153n., 154n.
Correggio, Antonio da 152
Cotton, Sir Robert 347
Coulton, George Gordon 337
Council (Society) of Promoters 104, 106, 113, 129, 138, 162, 165–7, 169–70, 172, 176–8
Courtenay, Miss 330
Covent Garden 311
Cowper, Joseph Meadows 318
(ed.) *Meditations on the Supper of Our Lord* 375n.
Cowper, William 108, 113, 135n.
Coxe, Henry Octavius 339n.
Cranbourne Tavern, London 100
Crawley (Ruskin's valet) 201
Crease 166
Creed of St Athanasius 320
Crimean War 228, 241, 329
Croker, John Wilson 137
Crombie, Alexander, *The Etymology and Syntax of the English Language Explained* 44
Cromwell, Oliver 67
Croydon, Surrey 248
Cruden, Alexander, *Complete Concordance to the Old and New Testaments* 310

Crystal Palace, London 131–2, 236
Cuvier, Georges 353

D

Dale, Thomas 44n., 61
Dalziel, Eleanor Nickell (Furnivall) 231, 245–6, 265–8, 310, 329–30, 384, 386–8
Dalziel, George 265
Dalziel, Martha 265
Dalziel, William Alexander 2, 9, 208, 245, 265–7, 269, 307, 329, 330n., 387
'Brothers Dalziel': see Camden Press
Darwin, Charles 247–8, 276
Origin of Species 227n., 246–7, 249, 256, 262, 281
Darwin, Erasmus 83
Darwin, Henrietta Emily 248
Davenant, Mary: see Furnivall, Mary
Davenant, William 129–30
Davenport, Arthur 390
Davies, Benjamin 15
Davies, Emily 158
Davies, J. Llewelyn 173, 190, 204
Davies, Ruth 39
Davis, Norman 6
Davy, Lady Jane 151
Dedham, Essex 414
Delius, Nicolaus 4
Denmark Hill, London 141, 148–50, 181, 201
Derby, Lord (Edward Smith-Stanley 14th Earl of Derby) 117, 165, 233n.
Derby Gallery, London 152
Dickens, Charles 64, 79–82, 99–100, 331
Dickinson, Lowes 207
Dictionary of Arts and Sciences 66
Dictionary of Old English 298
Disraeli, Benjamin, 1st Earl of Beaconsfield 118, 120–1
Sybil, Or, the Two Nations 92
Dodderidge, Sir John 32, 433
Dodsworth, William 52
Domett, John 119n.
Donizetti, Gaetano 87
Douce, Francis 352
Drew, George Smith 138
Dryden, John 108
Dunbar, Sir William, 7th Baronet 52
Dürer, Albrecht 191

468 INDEX

Durham 265-6, 355, 390

E

Earle, John 287n., 401n.
Early English Drama Society 35
EARLY ENGLISH TEXT SOCIETY
  (EETS) 1-12, 22, 59, 77, 126, 134,
  160, 171, 299, 323, 332, 365, 423-4
  assistants 335, 375
  and Camden Society 339-5, 359-61,
    391
  commemorates Furnivall 12-13, 16-
    19
  editorial practice 332, 375-6, 388
  editors 3, 4 318-9, 330-1
  and lexicography 300-1, 305-8, 311-
    12, 319, 350
  and medievalism 22, 160, 381, 389,
    391
  and Philological Society 286, 313,
    332-4, 393-6, 401
  printers 312-3, 329; *see also* Austin,
    Stephen; Trübner, Nicholas
  relation to Furnivall's other societies
    3-5, 171
  and Roxburghe Society 360-1, 364,
    366, 375, 387, 391
  and Ruskin 153, 188
  *see also titles of individual publications
    and names of editors*
Eastern Counties Railway 383
Eastlake, Sir Charles 149n., 150
Eastlake, Lady Elizabeth 151, 184
Eastwood, Jonathan 307, 317, 320
Ecclesiological Society 356n.
Edinburgh, University 287n.
Edinburgh Review 90, 165, 403-4, 408
Egan, Pierce, *Wat Tyler* 67
Egham, Surrey 16, 25, 28-32, 39, 43,
  53-4, 69, 80, 106, 130, 132n., 135n.,
  153, 157, 255, 256n., 383, 427-33
Eisdell, Sophia Louisa 330
Eliot, George (Mary Ann Evans) 35,
  261, 281, 330
Elizabeth I, Queen, 32, 427-8, 430
Ellis, Alexander John, 3, 4n., 15, 279,
  288-92, 293n., 300n., 350, 396-7,
  398n., 420-2
  On Early English Pronunciation 15,
    397n., 421

Ellis, George 350n.
  Specimens of Early English Romance
    380n., 382, 394
Ellis, Havelock 20
Ellis, Sir Henry 357
Ellison, Cuthbert 166
Elrington and Bosworth Professorship
  289n.
Emerson, Ralph Waldo 394
Emerton, J. A. 36
Engels, Friedrich, *Condition of the Work-
  ing Class in England* 93, 118
Englefield Green, Surrey 35
English Dialect Society 289
Epping Forest 99, 124, 202, 236
Eton College 26, 36, 40-1, 74, 104, 106-
  9, 130, 135
Ettmüller, Ernst Moritz Ludwig, *Lexicon
  Anglosaxonicum* 297
Eusebius, *Ecclesiastical History* 136
Eversley, Hants. 91, 139n., 164n.
'Exeter Book' 354
Exeter College, Oxford 76
Exeter Hall, London 49, 76, 87-88,
  114n.
Exodus (OE) 295

F

Faithfull, Emily 328
Farmer, John Stephen 35
Fielding, Henry, *Tom Jones* 109
Floris and Blanchflour 318
Flügel, Ewald 281, 284, 298, 300
Flynn, Thomas 115, 119, 121, 124, 125n.
Forshall, Josiah 342
Foster House: *see* Great Fosters
Fourneville, Normandy 28, 228
Frankfurt am Main 61n., 312
Freeman, Edward Augustus 32, 405n.,
  408
Frensham, Surrey 318n.
Froude, James Anthony 38, 111, 331
Fry, Danby 15, 282, 314-15, 362
Furnivall, Charles 15, 25-6, 36, 39-40,
  48-9, 51n., 53, 59, 62n., 129, 130
Furnivall, Edward Thomas ('Ted',
  'Teddy') 26, 53n., 106-7, 130, 152n.
Furnivall, Eena 268
Furnivall, Eleanor: *see* Dalziel, Eleanor
  Nickell
Furnivall, Frances Ann ('Fanny') 25

INDEX

FURNIVALL, FREDERICK JAMES
GENERAL
antiquarian interest in social life, manners, and customs 39, 200, 330, 337, 389–90
'Forewords' 10, 403
founder of literary societies 2–5
informal training in medicine 29, 44–7
interest in metre 338–9, 391
loss of faith 247–50, 255–64
religious observance 44, 52–4, 64, 73, 95–6, 135–8
style of dress and personal appearance 14–16, 88, 161–3
support for women 156–7, 386
teetotalism 106, 128, 162, 212, 267n.
use of copyists 335, 375
vegetarianism 106, 128, 162 212, 267n.
views on editing 6–7
views on education of women and girls 157–9
writing style 8, 10, 22, 215–7, 222n., 226–7, 361–2
BIOGRAPHY
assists the Ballast-Heavers of the Port of London 114–26
attends divorce case 56
attends University College London 40–2, 44–9
begins editorial work 332–6 ff.
birth and childhood 16, 25–9, 39
Christian Socialism 93–6, 99–105, 110–26, 136, 139, 165–6, 170
creation of the EETS 423–4
death 12, 16, 18
defends Maurice and Kingsley against attacks in the *Edinburgh Review* 165
dental problems 46
editions for the Roxburghe Club 173, 274, 321, 328, 350–1, 364, 366–77, 379, 381–91
expenses 114n.
friendship with Effie Ruskin 144–6, 148, 150
friendship with John Ruskin 109, 139–55, 180–5, 188–91 (*see also* Ruskin, John)
friendship with William Johnson 104, 106–10, 133 (*see also* Johnson)
indentures of apprenticeship 44

involvement with industrial action 104, 110–26
involvement with the New English Dictionary 9, 34, 267–8, 274, 277, 302, 304, 306–20, 322–32, 341–2, 351n., 363, 367, 387, 397
legal training 56–7, 76–82
marriage and family 245–6, 268
membership of the Camden Society 361–4
promoter of co-operation and trades associations 120–2, 165–7
relationship with Teena Rochfort Smith 11
response to Maurice's resignation from KCL 167–9
schooling 36–7
Secretary of the Philological Society 143, 276, 304, 309, 311, 332–3, 396
seeks partnership with the Macmillan brothers 76–7
social life in London 43–5, 47, 49, 69, 127–9, 131–2
studies at Cambridge 59–77
teaches at Little Ormond Yard school 97–9, 104, 155, 157
visiting the poor 89–90, 97
INTERESTS
drawing 152
music 84–8
reading 54–5, 65–9, 75n., 78, 132–5, 151, 155–7, 159
sculling (rowing) 11, 62–3, 69–70, 218, 229
visits art galleries 49–50, 148, 152–3
WORKING MEN'S COLLEGE
contributes to *The People's Paper* as 'Q.' 214–15, 218–19, 226
disagreement with Tom Hughes 244–6
disputes with F. D. Maurice 190, 194, 203–5, 208, 212–21, 224–5, 227–8, 246, 250–4
gains Ruskin as a teacher for the College 179–80, 186–8, 191
invites T. H. Huxley to teach at the College 261–4
involvement with the 19th Middlesex Volunteer Regiment 239–44
promoter of social life in the College 202–12, 217, 228–39, *et passim*
recruits Holman Hunt as an art teacher for the College 196–8
shareholder of the College 273

teaching for the College 198-201, 218
visit to Normandy 28, 228-9
HONOURS
elected to an honorary fellowship by Trinity Hall, Cambridge 63
memorial volume 17
receives civil list pension from Gladstone 414
EDITIONS AND OTHER WRITINGS
Association a Necessary Part of Christianity 112
contributes to *The Pilgrimage of the Life of Man* 388
diaries 38-9, 44, 54, 60-3, 83-8, 91, 107, 112-13, 115, 117-19, 127-9
(ed.) *Early English Poems and Lives of Saints (Wicked Birds, Pilate and Judas)* 333-8
Emblemes and Epigrames 28
(ed.) *Fifty Earliest English Wills* 381n.
(ed.) *Sir Generides* 377, 387-91
'Heads Versus Heels' 235-6
'History of the Working Men's College' 170-1
(ed.) Henry Lovelich ('Lonelich'), *Seynt Graal* 320, 350, 377-86
(ed.) *Hymns to the Virgin* 389 n.
(ed.) *John Russell's Boke of Nurture* 387-91
(ed.) *Minor Poems of William Lauder* 388
(ed.) *Queene Elizabethes Achademy* (Humphrey Gilbert) 28-9, 37-8
(ed.) Robert Mannyng of Brunne, *Handlyng Synne* 173, 316, 320-3, 327, 340-1, 350, 366-77, 380, 383, 386
Shakspere's England 3n.
Shakespeare: Life and Work (with John Munro) 20, 26
Shakespeare Tales for Boys and Girls 26, 35n.
When Shakespeare was a Boy 26, 49
Furnivall, George Frederick 25, 28, 30-1, 32n., 33, 36, 41, 43-5, 56, 59, 68, 77, 97, 162, 266
Furnivall, Henry ('Hen') 26, 153
Furnivall, Louisa Elizabeth ('Loo') 25, 129, 156
Furnivall, Mary Sophia (Davenant) 25-6, 43, 46, 129-30
Furnivall, Percy 14, 28

Furnivall, Selina 25-6, 51n., 53, 63, 87, 130
Furnivall, Sophia Hughes, née Barwell 25, 26n.
Furnivall, William Douglas 33
Furnivall, William George ('Will', 'Willie') 26, 130, 153
Furnivall, origin of the name 1-27
Furnivall Commemoration Fund 375
Furnival's Inn 81

G

Gaimar, Geffrei 345
Galahad 379, 386
Galway, Queen's College 287n.
Garnett, Richard, *sen.* 347-8, 352-5, 358, 365, 389-90, 416
Garnett, Richard, *jun.* 353
Gascoigne, George 305
Gaskell, Elizabeth 9, 111, 168, 201, 378
Gaskell, William 199-200
Gawain Manuscript 12, 343, 416
(Syr) Generides 377, 387-8, 391
Genesis and geology 137, 234, 246-50
Gentleman's Magazine 19n., 295, 352, 376, 394
Geoffrey of Monmouth, *Historia Regum Britanniae* 347-8
George III, King 31
Ghirlandaio, Domenico 152
Gibbs, Henry Hucks, Baron Aldenham 33n., 34n., 319, 330n., 331, 391, 393, 402n.
Gilbert, Humphrey 37-8 (see also *Queene Elizabethes Achademy*)
Gilliéron, Jules 283
Girton College, Cambridge 292
Gladstone, William Ewart 9, 11, 117-19, 120, 124, 414
Two Letters to the Earl of Aberdeen on the State Persecution of the Neapolitan Government 132-3
Glasgow, University 287n.
Glenelg, Charles Grant, 1st Baron 151
Glyn, Robert 345
Goderich, Lord (Viscount), Frederick John Robinson, 1st Earl of Ripon 104, 128-9, 212, 240
Goderich, Lady Henrietta, née Vyner 128-9
Goldstücker, Theodor 288, 312, 315n., 325, 332n., 385

INDEX 471

Gollancz, Professor Sir Israel 12, 18, 404, 405n.
  (ed.) *Pearl, Cleanness, Patience, and Sir Gawain* 13n. Gonville and Caius College, Cambridge 64, 248n.
Gordon, Jean 39
Göttingen, University 294n.
Gower, John 352
  Confessio Amantis 9, 320, 338–9, 376
Graham, Sir James 65
Graham, Thomas 45, 46
  Modern Domestic Medicine 46n.
  Outlines of Botany 55
Grahame, Kenneth 11–12, 61
Grail legend 22, 377, 379, 381–7, 394, 416
Gray, Euphemia (Effie): see Ruskin
Gray, George, *jun.* 144
Gray, James, *Harmony of Geology and Scripture* 136, 246
Gray's Inn 78, 81, 138
Great Exhibition, The 16, 131, 132n., 147n.
Great Fosters House, Egham ('Fosters House') 30–1, 427–33
Grey, Sir Charles, 122
Grimm, Jakob 48, 248, 277, 284–7, 293, 295–7, 421
  Deutsche Grammatik 284, 286, 294n., 351n.
  Deutsches Wörterbuch (with Wilhelm Grimm) 303, 315n.
  'Grimm's Law' 286, 421
Grimm, Wilhelm 303
Grisi, Giulia 84–5, 87, 136
Groome, Mr., of Monk Soham 387
Grosseteste, Robert, *Castel of Love* (*Chasteau d'amour*) 302n., 318, 398–9
Grosvenor, Lord Robert, 1st Baron Ebury 118n.
Grove, George 131
  Dictionary of Music and Musicians 131
Guenevere 379
Guest, Lady Charlotte, *Mabinogion* 385
Guest, Edwin 275–6, 353
  A History of English Rhythms 333n.
Günther, Albert Charles 393
  Catalogue of Fishes in the British Museum 393

Gurney, Anna 290–1
  Literal Translation of the Saxon Chronicle 290–1
Gwillim, Mary Ann, matron at Great Fosters 32–3

H

Haddon Hall, Derbyshire 31n.
Hali Meidenhad (*Hali Meiđhad*) 404–11, 413n.
Halkett, Col. 31, 427, 433
Hall, Fitzedward 33n.
Hallam, Arthur 134, 259
Halliwell, James Orchard 342, 353, 356–8, 366, 394
  Dictionary of Archaic and Provincial Words 302
  (ed.) *Castle of Love* 302n., 319n., 398–9, 400n.
  (ed.) *Early English Metrical Romances* 357n., 380n., 382–3, 394
  (ed.) *Morte d'Arthur* 316, 319n.
  see also Wright, Thomas
Hammersmith, London 265
Hampstead 61n., 221, 265
Hampton Court 218, 229
Hanna, Ralph 417n.
Hansard, Septimus 213n., 237
Hantler, G. M., Captain 244n., 266n., 267–8, 307, 310
Hanwell (College), Middlesex 36, 38, 40–1, 48, 50, 59, 129
Hare, Julius Charles 74–5, 76n., 168
  and Augustus William, *Guesses at Truth* 71–2, 134–5
  Victory of Faith 71
Hare-Naylor, Georgina 76n.
Harris, John Tindall 255
Harrison, Frederic 173–4
Harrowing of Hell and Gospel of Nicodemus 396
Harrow on the Hill, Middlesex 221
Hastings, Battle of 140
Hastings, Sussex 140, 152, 231n., 413
Havelok the Dane 301, 320, 322–4, 339, 343–6, 353–4, 366
Le Lai d'Havelok 345
Haweis, H. R. 213n.
Haweis, Thomas 134n.
Head, Francis Bond 66
Headley, Surrey 328

Hearne, Thomas 316n., 340, 368
Heidelberg 300n., 312
Hemel Hempstead, Herts. 27n.
Hendon, Middlesex 221
Henley, Joseph Warner 119–20
Henson, Francis. 64
Herbert, Jacob, Secretary to Trinity House 123
Herbert, John Alexander 335
Herodotus 114, 306
Herrtage, Sidney J. H. 34–5, 361
Hertford 249
Hettema, Montanus de Haan 287n.
Heyne, Moritz 293
Hickes, George 293, 321, 340
'Hickes's Ode': see Poema morale
Hill, Caroline Southwood 209
Hill, Octavia 209–10
Hill, Sir Rowland 359
Hobhouse, John Cam, 1st Baron Broughton 331n.
Hoccleve, Thomas 368n., *De Regimine principum* 320, 322, 367n.
Hoccleve and Lydgate Society (Occleve and Lidgate Society) 365
Hoets, John William van Rees 61–2, 74
Holloway Prison 35
Holyoake, Austin 328
Holyoake, George Jacob 240, 328
Holy Virginity: see Hali Meidenhad/ Meidhad)
Homer v. Taunton 314
Hood, Thomas 155, 206
Horstmann, Carl 334n., 398n.
Hort, Fenton 74n.
Hort, Richard, *Penelope Wedgbone* 132n.
Hounslow, Middlesex 28, 429
Housman, A. E. 8
Howitt, Mary 36
Howitt, William, *Student Life of Germany* 67–8
How the Goode Wif Thaught hir Daughter 346n.
Huber, Victor Aimé 96, 384–5
Huckle, Blanche 11, 12
Hughes, Arthur 379n.
Hughes, Thomas 27, 72, 76, 91n., 92–3, 99, 101, 102n., 105, 111–12, 115–17, 122, 127–9, 133, 136, 139–41, 144, 166, 191, 199n., 227n., 329
WORKING MEN'S COLLEGE
  boxing classes at the College 178
  captain of the 19th Middlesex Rifles 240–1, 244–6, 371
  contributes to social life at the College 206–7, 212, 249–50
  support for F. D. Maurice 215, 224–5
  teaching at the College 169, 172, 174, 177, 273
WRITINGS
  Account of the Lock-Out of Engineers 122
  Alfred the Great 27
  Memoir of a Brother 92–3, 97, 111, 162
  Memoir of Daniel Macmillan 65, 72–6
  Prefatory Memoir (of Kingsley) 91n., 92, 99, 101, 110, 138n., 161–2
  Tom Brown's Schooldays 27, 86n., 206
Hugo, Victor 151
Hullah, John Pyke 49, 172, 230
Hullah's Hall 187
Humphrey, Duke of Gloucester 388
Hunt, Leigh 30
Hunt, William Holman, 151, 196–8, 227n., 231–2, 238, 241–2, 266, 379
  The Finding of the Saviour in the Temple 197–8
Hutton, Richard Holt 119, 264
Huxley, T. H. 227n., 247, 249, 256, 261–4
Hyde Park, London 131, 138, 141, 211, 243
Hythe, Kent 242

I

Industrial and Provident Societies Bill (Act) (1852) 133n., 165, 169
Innsbruck 323n.
Iseult 379
Islington, London 269

J

Jackson, E. S. 317
Jackson, William, editor of *The Medical Review* 56
Jacob's Island, Bermondsey, London 99–100.
James, John Angell, *The Young Man from Home* 43–4, 51, 53–4, 64, 69, 88, 93, 97n., 155n., 210–11

Jameson, Anna, *Handbook to the Courts of Modern Sculpture* 132n.
Jeffray, L. W. 318
Jeffrey, William 147
Jelf, Richard William 164, 167–8, 240, 411n.
Jocelin of Brakelonde 369
Johnson, Samuel 18, 161, 330
  Dictionary 304
  Rasselas 157
Johnson, William 26, 74, 101n., 104–10, 112, 122, 131n., 133, 135n., 137, 144n., 162, 165n., 170, 172, 259
  Hints for Eton Schoolmasters 108–9
Jones, John Balmer 413
Jones, Lloyd 101, 111, 113, 128
Jones, Sir William 284
Judd and Glass, New Bridge St., Blackfriars, London 415
Juliana (Liflade of St. Juliana) 394, 406n., 407–11
Jusserand, Jean Jules 337

K

Katherine: *see Seinte Katerine*
Kay-Shuttleworth, Sir James Phillips 414
Keats, John 135
Kemble, John Mitchell 74–5, 128, 134, 175n., 274, 294–7, 343–4, 354n., 364, 405n., 415, 416n.
Kennington Common, London 90–1, 240
Ker, Bellenden 57–9, 61, 66, 78–9, 81–3, 104, 143n.
Ker, John, Duke of Roxburghe 350
Ker, William Paton 8, 17
Key, Thomas Hewitt 48, 49n., 99n., 108, 198, 274–7, 290, 315n., 323n.
Keynsham, Somerset 402n., 403n.
'Kildare Manuscript' (B. M. Harley 913) 333–4
King Alisaunder 320
King's College, Cambridge 65, 345
King's College London (KCL) 41, 75, 82, 130, 135, 138, 164, 167, 169, 173, 205n., 287n., 303, 343, 374n.
King's College School, London 286n., 402, 411, 413–14, 419
KINGSLEY, CHARLES 68–9, 74, 79–80, 89, 133–4, 139n., 152, 178, 191, 196, 209, 232, 213n., 227n., 232, 247, 263, 306, 330, 369, 371, 420
  attacked in the press 164–5
  and Christian socialism 76, 79, 91–2, 94–5, 99–102, 104, 110–11, 127, 135, 137–8, 162–3, 177n.
  disapproval of John Ruskin 141–2
  lectures at the Working Men's College 173–4, 273
  on Tennyson 156
  professor of English literature, Queen's College, London 155–9, 160–1
  WRITINGS
  Alton Locke 101, 135, 141, 164–5
  Cheap Clothes and Nasty 101, 165
  Glaucus 141–2
  Hereward the Wake 27
  'On English Literature' 159–60
  'Socialism in the Bible' 137
  'The Message of the Church to the Labouring Man' 138
  The Saint's Tragedy 71
  Twenty-Five Village Sermons 71
  Two Years Ago 178n.
  Westward Ho! 206n.
  Yeast 45, 116, 406
  see also 'Parson Lot'
Koch, Carl Friedrich, *Historische Grammatik der englischen Sprache* 300n.
Krefeld 299
Kyng Horne 320

L

Labouchere, Henry 117–18, 122, 133n.
Laȝamon's *Brut* 294, 301, 343, 346–7; *see also* Madden, Frederic
Lancelot 316n., 279, 395n.
Land of Cockayne (Cockaigne) 320, 334, 336–7
Langham Place circle 328
Langland, William: *see Piers Plowman*
Lassen, Christian 287n., 288n.
La Touche, Rose 153
Lauder, William 388n.
Lawrence, Augustus C. 307
Lawrence, Effingham 58
Le Blanc, Thomas, Master of Trinity Hall 58, 61
Lechevalier, Jules 104, 111, 166
Lee, Sidney 35
Leeuwarden, University of 287n.
Le Havre 228

INDEX

Leiden 293, 297
Leopold, Prince 10, 20n.
Lester, Charles Edwards, *The Glory and the Shame of England* 132
Lever, Charles 55, 66, 68n.
Levins, Peter, *Manipulus Vocabulorum* 360, 361n.
Lewes, George Henry 330n., 331
Lewes, Sussex 74
Liddell, Dr Henry, Dean of Christ Church, Oxford 144, 149n.
Lincoln College, Oxford 9, 26
Lincoln's Inn and Chapel 2, 57, 61, 69, 72, 76, 78–82, 89–90, 95–6, 106, 131, 135, 137, 168, 170, 247, 314, 333n., 384
Lind, Jenny 16, 84–8
Litchfield, Richard Buckley 173, 180, 190, 199, 202, 205–6, 209, 221–2, 224–5, 227, 230–40, 243, 245–50, 254, 259, 273
  'Work and Play; or Heads and Heels' 232, 234, 237, 239
Littledale, Richard Frederick 324
Little Ormond Yard 97
  school 98, 199, 103n., 104, 107, 135, 157, 171, 204, 217, 225, 245
Llanfaglan, Montgomeryshire 414
Llewelyn: *see* Davies
London University 37, 57n., 274n.
Longman, William 312
  Longman, Green, Longmans, and Roberts 395n., 401, 404n.
Lord's Day Observance Society 220
Louis, A. H. 138–9, 166, 172
Lovelich ('Lonelich'), Henry, *San Graal* 350n., 377, 381–2, 385n.
Lovett, William 89
LUDLOW, JOHN MALCOLM 78–9, 81–3, 127, 131, 163
  and Christian socialism 76, 89–90, 92–8, 100–5, 128, 133–4, 137n., 138, 159, 165–7, 169–70
  and the Philological Society 278, 384
  and the Working Men's College 170–3, 191, 208, 212, 217, 223–4, 232–8, 245, 249, 273
  discusses Maurice's views on eternal punishment with Furnivall 138
  draws up Constitution for Queen's College, London 157
  offers teaching at the Working Men's College 172

  on Chartism 89, 90–1
  on music 84–7
  on Ruskin 109–10, 191–3
  opinion of Furnivall 8, 28, 88–9, 116, 126, 150, 156, 162, 177, 208–9, 219
  resigns from Council of Promoters 166–7
  supporter of F. D. Maurice 8–9, 95–6, 139–40, 164, 169, 189, 213, 218, 253
Lushington family 156
  Alice 157
  Godfrey 201
  Stephen 56
  Vernon 156, 199n., 201n., 224, 227
Lydgate, John 365
Lye, Edward, *Dictionarium Saxonicum* 295
Lyell, Charles 247, 283
  Principles of Geology 255
Lynton, Devon 228

M

Mabinogion 385
Macaulay, Thomas Babington, 41, 43–4, 330
  Lays of Ancient Rome 66
Macmillan, Alexander 62n., 70–4, 76–7, 158, 172
Macmillan, Daniel 70–7, 134n., 190n.
Macmillan, George 70
Macmillan's (publisher), 16, 62, 71n., 113, 201n., 227, 246, 325n.
Macmillan's Magazine 339
Madden, Sir Frederic 8, 19n., 30n., 268n., 299, 311, 322, 339–44, 349–50, 352–3, 364, 366–7, 373, 377n., 383, 387, 389, 392, 400, 404n., 416
  (ed.) *Gesta Romanorum* 346
  (ed.) *Havelok* 301, 324, 339, 344–5, 353–4
  (ed.) *Laȝamon's Brut* 301, 339, 343, 346–8
  (ed.) Matthew Paris, *Historia Minor* 346
  (ed.) 'Political Poems of the reigns of Henry VI and Edward IV' 357
  (ed.) *Syr Gawayne* 317n., 343
  (ed.) *William and the Werwolf* (*William of Palerne*) 345–6, 349
  (ed.) Wycliffite Bible (with Josiah Forshall) 342, 349

INDEX

Madvig, Johan Nikolai 287
Magdalene College, Cambridge 74
Magenta (battle) 372
Maida Vale, London 312
Maitland Club 355
Major, John, headmaster of KCL School 411n.
Malden, Henry 41-2, 48, 58, 274-5, 277, 309
  On the Origin of Universities 41-2, 54, 67, 69, 73
Malleson, Elizabeth 233
Mallet, Sir Louis 118
Malone, Edmond 199
Malory, Sir Thomas, *Morte D'Arthur* 116, 193, 320, 379
Manchester 3, 93, 102, 356n., 379n., 385
Manchester Working Men's College 199
Manners, Lord John, Duke of Rutland 117-19, 120-1
Mannyng, Robert, of Brunne, 316, 318
  Handlyng Synne 320-1, 323, 366-8, 371, 373-6, 387, 389, 320-1
Mansfield, Charles Blanchford 85n., 100, 111, 139n., 140, 162-3, 192
March, Anne 102
Margaret: see St Margaret (*Seinte Marherete*)
Markland, James 352
Marlow, Bucks. 29
Marsh, George Perkins 319, 393
Marsh, William 60-1, 67
Martin, Miss 330
Martineau, Harriet, 51n., 83, 105, 107, 108n., 149n., 163, 252, 257-62, 274
  On the Laws of Man's Nature and Development (with Henry Atkinson) 252-3, 257-8
Martineau, John 241
Martineau, Russell 278n.
Marx, Eleanor 3
Marx, Karl 3, 89, 93
Mary, Queen 32, 427
Marylebone 52, 360
Marylebone Public Library 360
Masson, David 47n., 100, 112, 227n.
Masson, Flora 47
Matthew, F. D. 3
Mätzner, Eduard Adolf Ferdinand (*Altenglische Sprachproben, An English Grammar*) 300
Maul, Dr Edward Harman 29, 168
Maul, Richard Graham 101n.

Maurice, Esther 76n.
MAURICE, FREDERICK DENISON 74-6, 127-8, 147, 162, 196, *et passim*
  appointed to the Knightsbridge Professorship at Cambridge 254
  death 273
  CHRISTIAN SOCIALISM 88-8, 92-7, 99-104, 110-11, 136, 165-7, 169-70
  LINCOLN'S INN
    Bible classes 96, 111, 139-40, 171
    offer of resignation of the Chaplaincy rejected 168
    preaching in the chapel 76, 100, 131-2, 137
    sermon on Joshua, justifying the Canaanite slaughters 139-40, 160n.
    views on eternal punishment 138-9
  KING'S COLLEGE LONDON
    dismissed from professorship at KCL 135, 164-5, 167-9, 240
  QUEEN'S COLLEGE LONDON—WOMEN'S EDUCATION 76, 155-8, 168
  WORKING MEN'S COLLEGE
    arguments with Furnivall over the College's social life and governance, 161, 163, 170, 179, 190, 203-5, 208, 214-28, 230, 233-4, 237, 245-6, 255
    assists move to Great Ormond Street 204
    beginnings 171-7
    chaplain to the 19th Middlesex Volunteers 240
    inaugural address 176, 187
    lectures on Shakespeare 172
    relations with Ruskin 139-40, 142-3, 180, 190-1, 194-5
    resignation as Principal of the College 208, 219, 221, 244n.
    views on the teaching in the College 177-8
  WRITINGS
    'A Letter to the Teacher of a Boxing Class on Prize Fighting' 178n.
    'Personal Explanation' to members of the Working Men's College 250-2
    Scheme of a College for Working Men 176
    Statement of the reasons for resigning the office of Principal to the Working Men's College 220
    Theological Essays 167
Mayfair, London 52

INDEX

Mayhew, Henry, articles in the *Morning Chronicle* on 'Labour and the Poor' and *London Labour and London Poor* 99–100, 114–16, 131
Mayor, Joseph Bickersteth 201
Mazzini, Giuseppe 239, 240n.
Mechanics' Institutes 171, 235
Meditations on the Supper of Our Lord 375
Melbourne, Lord 49n.
Mendelssohn, Felix 87–8, 230
Meredith, George 9
Merivale, Charles 128
Merivale, Judith 128
Merlin 377
Merton Hall, Cambridge 292
mesmerism 83, 163, 257
Meun, Jean de 154n.
Meyer, Paul 287
Meyerbeer, Giacomo, *Les Huguenots* 86
Michel, Francisque 384n., 387
Michelant, Henri Victor 387
Michigan, University of, *Middle English Dictionary* (*MED*) 301
Milford, Humphrey 301
Mill, John Stuart 90, 134, 213n., 263
   On Liberty 227
   Principles of Political Economy 133, 228
Millais, John Everett 9, 38n., 147n., 148, 151, 181–6, 196, 266, 319, 379
Mill Hill School 397
Milton, John 35, 108, 199, 206, 310
Mitford, Mary Russell 184n.
Mitford, William *History of Greece* 73
Mohl, Moritz 134
Molbech, Christian 287n.
Monk Soham, Suffolk 387
Monmouth, Geoffrey of: *see* Geoffrey of Monmouth
Mont Saint-Michel 228
'Moral Ode': *see* 'Poema morale'
More, Sir Thomas, *Richard III* 199
Morell, John Reynell, *Sketch of the life of Charles Fourier, introductory to his treatise on the human soul* 134
Morgan, Augustus de 46
Morning Chronicle: *see* Mayhew, Henry
Morrell, R. M. 214
Morris, David 414
Morris, Elizabeth 414
Morris, Ellen 414n.
Morris, Emily L. 414n.
Morris, Hannah (née Ary) 414
Morris, Hannah E., jun. 414n.
Morris, Richard 1, 4n., 6–7, 283, 285, 286n., 290n., 321n., 330, 337, 349n., 376n., 395–7, 402, 409, 413–23
   (ed.) *Ayenbite of Inwyt* 419
   Elementary Lessons in Historical English Grammar 285n., 294, 418
   English Grammar 285
   Etymology of Local Names 389, 415–16
   (ed.) *Genesis and Exodus* 419
   Historical Outlines of English Accidence 285, 418–21
   (ed.) *Liber Cure Cocorum* 389, 395, 416
   (ed.) *Old English Homilies* 419
   (ed.) *Poetical Works of Geoffrey Chaucer* 419
   (ed.) *Prick of Conscience* 395, 417–18, 422, 423n.
   (ed.) *Sir Gawayne and The Green Knight* 416
   (ed.) *Specimens of Early English* 380n., 419
Morris, William 379n.
Morte Arthure 316n., 319, 395
Morton, James 410
   (ed.) *Seinte Katerine* 355
   (ed.) *Ancren Riwle* 409n.
Moxon, Edward 266, 379
Mozart, Wolfgang Amadeus 84–5
Mulready, William 107, 151–2
Müller, Max 291–3, 419
Munby, Arthur J. 190n., 192, 197–8, 201–2, 223–4, 227, 230, 245–7, 266–8, 310
Munford, George 318
Munro, Alexander 147
Munro, John 2, 10, 12, 16, 20–1, 27, 31, 36, 38–9, 42, 44, 57, 59, 62, 69, 77, 87–9, 114, 118, 145, 148, 214, 218, 225–6, 230, 240, 248–50, 377
Murray, Sir James Augustus Henry, 3, 6 9, 12, 15, 18, 32, 34, 264, 280, 283, 285, 310, 313, 324–6, 361, 396–7
Murray, John 313
Murray, Lindley 200n.

N

N-Town Plays 364n.

INDEX 477

Napier, Arthur Sampson 3, 34, 278
Napier, Catherine, *Women's Rights and Duties* 159
Napoleon Bonaparte 64
Napoleon III, Emperor 239, 371
Nash, David W. 385–6
National Gallery, London 150, 152n., 153n., 209
National Portrait Gallery 331
National Trust 210
Neale, Edward Vansittart 91n., 104, 111, 128, 133, 163, 166, 172, 177, 210
Nesbit, Edith 26n.
New English Dictionary (NED) 9, 274, 277, 289, 308–9, 313–14, 339
Newman, Francis William 133–4
   Lectures on Political Economy 133–4
Newman, John Henry (Cardinal) 52, 71n., 1333, 420
New Shakspere Society 2–5, 10, 12, 17, 20n., 313, 365
Newton, William 124
New York Tribune 11, 104
Nichols, John Bowyer 387
Nichols, John Gough 359n.
Nicolay, Charles Grenfell 164
Nightingale, Florence 128n., 310, 330
Norden, John, *Description of the Honour of Windesour* 32, 429–30
Normandy 27, 28, 228, 309
Northgate, Dan Michel of: *see Ayenbite of Inwyt*
North London Needlewomens' Association 101, 176
Norton, Charles Eliot 320n.
Nutt, Alfred Trübner 313
Nutt, David 313, 384n.

O

O'Connor, Feargus 90
Oliphant, Thomas Laurence Kington 375n.
Onions, Charles Talbut 10, 18–19, 21
'Oreisun of St. Mary' (*Hymn to Our Lady*) 409
Oriel College, Oxford 287n.
Ormulum 294
Orsini, Felice 239–40
Osborne, I. O. W. 87
Osborne, Ralph Bernal 121
Oswald, Eugene 208

Oswin, Fred 46
Our English Home 330
Owen, Robert 93n.
Owens College, Manchester (Victoria University of Manchester) 84n., 287n., 297
Owl and the Nightingale 299, 300n., 320–1, 323
Oxford University 18, 32, 34, 41–2, 50, 72, 76, 111, 144, 146, 148n., 149, 154, 195, 246–7, 262–3, 292, 327, 334, 341, 403, 419
   Oxford University Press (OUP), Clarendon Press 9, 297, 300–1, 364n.
   Rawlinson Professorship of Anglo-Saxon 295, 357
   see also individual colleges
   Union 193, 379, 436

P

Paine, Cornelius 320
Paley, Frederick Apthorp 279
Paley, William, *Evidences of Christianity* 54, 64
Pali 329, 418
Panizzi, Anthony 311
'Papal Aggression' 142
Parker, George 375
Parker, John Henry (Oxford publisher) 168
Parker, John William (Cambridge and London publisher) 84, 93n., 98, 107, 137, 376
Park House, nr. Maidstone, Kent 156–7, 257
'Parlyament of Devylls' 320
'Parson Lot' (Kingsley's pen-name) 91n., 101n., 102
Pattison, Granville Sharp 277
Pattison, Mark, Rector of Lincoln College, Oxford 419n.
Pauli, Reinhold 338–9, 376
Peacock, Edward 33n., 282n.
Pearson, Charles Henry 173, 370n.
Peel, Jonathan 240
Peel, Sir Robert 65
Penny Cyclopaedia 54, 66
Penrose, Francis Cranmer 98, 131, 172
People's Charter 90
People's Paper 207n., 214, 310n.
Percy Society 318n., 320, 342, 357

Percy's Ballads 4
Percy's Reliques 362
Perth 181, 185
Pevensey Bay, Kent 240
Phillips, Thomas, resident physician, Great Fosters 31
Phillipps, Sir Thomas 352n., 353
PHILOLOGICAL SOCIETY OF LONDON 4, 15, 18, 278–9, 281–4, 285–92, 414, 419, 421, *et passim*
  and Early English 274, 320–5, 336–9, 342–3, 360, 393–7, 398, 416, 422–3; *see also individual texts*
  and Furnivall 17, 127–8, 145, 154, 161, 171, 179, 200, 273–7, 303–13, 325–6, 329–30, 366–7, *et passim*
  lexicography and the *NED* 34, 267, 302–20, 387
  members 143, 274–5, 279, 283, 287–9, 290–1, 294, 300n., 302–3, 307, 313–14, 319; *see also named individuals*
  Transactions 171, 277–8, 311, 313, 316n., 320–1, 327, 332, 340–1, 362, 395–7, 400, 423
  women members 291–2
Phipps, Sir Charles 125
Piers Plowman 7, 200, 218, 285, 305–6, 318, 324
Piers the Plowman's Crede 7
Pimlico Builders' Association 128
Pius IX, Pope 142
Plato, *Republic* 151
Platt, James 297–8
Plint, Thomas 196
Plymouth 395
Poema morale ('Moral Ode', 'Hickes's Ode') 320–1, 327, 333
Political Ballads 318
Politics for the People 89, 92–3, 96, 100, 110–11, 209
Pollard, Alfred William 335, 365n.
Ponton, Thomas, (ed.) *Morte Arthure* 316n., 395
Poor Law Board 314
Poore, Richard, Bishop of Salisbury 410
Porter, Anna Maria, *Hungarian Brothers* 67
Portland Grammar School 395n., 396
Portman Hill School 233n.
Potter, Richard 46
Power, Mr. (mathematics tutor) 60, 67
Powers, Hiram, *The Greek Slave* 132

Pre-Raphaelites 147, 151, 196, 246, 266, 379
Preston, Thomas 236–7
Prick of Conscience 357, 395, 417–18, 422, 423n.
Prinsep, Valentine 231n., 379n.
Promptorium Parvulorum 360–1
Pugin, Augustus Welby Northmore 143
Pulasky, F. 315n.
Punch 54, 329
Pusey, E. B. 52, 54, 142

Q

Quaritch, Bernard 365n., 399
Quarterly Review 136–7, 164, 282n., 353
Queene Elizabethes Achademy 29, 37, 38n.
Queen's College, Harley Street, London 157, 159–60, 263
Quincey, Thomas De 330
  Logic of Political Economy 134

R

Radcliffe, Ann 33
railways 25, 59, 67, 131, 255, 383
Raine, James 364n.
Raleigh, Walter 38
Raphael (Raffaello Sanzio da Urbino) 85, 127, 153
Rask, Rasmus 48, 277, 285, 293–8, 401
Read, Philip 240–1
Reade, Charles 331
Redgrave, Richard 152
Red Lion Square, London 101, 176, 204
Regent's Park, London 135, 145, 274n.
Renan, Ernest 281
Revell, Thomas Backhouse, patient at Great Fosters 33
Reynolds, G. W. M., *Pickwick Abroad* 64
Rice, manager of the Bethnal Green Weavers 128
Richard I ('Coeur de lion') 28
Richardson, Beatrice 308
Richardson, Charles, *A New Dictionary of the English Language* 304
Richardson, Sir John 308
Richmond, George 146
Richmond, Thomas 145
Richmond, William 146, 148
Richter, Jean Paul 133–4

INDEX

Riddlesdown, Surrey 235, 249, 284
Ripley, George, *Compound of Alchemie* 319
Robert of Cysille 317
Robert of Gloucester, *Chronicle* 199, 306, 309, 316, 318, 340
Robertson, James Craigie 362–4
Rochdale, Toad Lane 89
Rochester Cathedral Grammar School 37n.
Roebuck, John 179, 206, 212, 223, 231, 240–3, 417–19
Rogers, Samuel 151
Rolle, Richard ('Hampole') 318, 357, 417–19
Rolls Series 316, 346, 364, 403
Romance of the Rose 153–4
Rosen, Friedrich August 48, 277
Rossetti, Christina 9, 196
Rossetti, Dante Gabriel 9, 141, 147n., 191n., 192, 193n., 194–7, 246, 266, 379, 436
Rossetti, William Michael 9, 30n.
Rossiter, William 223, 233, 310
Rouen 228
Roxburghe Club 173, 274, 316, 321, 327, 341, 344–6, 348, 350–5, 357, 364, 366–7, 369, 371–5, 377, 379, 381, 383, 385n., 387–93, 313–14, 418; *see also individual titles*
Royal Academy 38n., 49, 107, 151, 197
Royal Asiatic Society 290
Royal College of Physicians 46n., 144
Royal Masonic Institution for Boys 414
Royal Navy 342n.
Royal Polytechnic Institute 46–7
Rumburgh, Suffolk 310n.
Rushton Hall, Northants. 402
Ruskin, Euphemia (Effie), née Gray 129, 131, 143–6, 148–51, 180–6, 378
RUSKIN, JOHN
and Furnivall 9, 22, 59, 109–10, 127, 139–55, 179, 181, 188–97
appearance 146–8
art appreciation 50, 148, 151–3, 170n.
failure of his marriage 144, 180–6
joins EETS 153
on Deborah (Book of Judges) 139–40
on 'Papal Aggression' 142–3
opinion of F. D. Maurice 139–40, 180, 191, 194

teaching at the London Working Men's College 179–80, 186–96, 209, 222, 249, 266, 379, 434–6
WRITINGS
Modern Painters 110, 141, 150, 229, 330
Notes on the Construction of Sheepfolds 142–3
The Opening of the Crystal Palace 131n.
Political Economy of Art 195, 227–8
Praeterita 139–40, 190–1, 247
Pre-Raphaelitism 151
Seven Lamps of Architecture 112n., 141
Stones of Venice 141, 229; excerpt, 'On the Nature of Gothic' 186–90
Unto this Last 228n.
Ruskin, John James 140, 143, 149, 185
Ruskin, Margaret 201n.
Russell, Lord John 49, 115, 117
Russell, John, *Boke of Nurture* 387–91
Russell, William Howard 329

S

St Bartholomew's Hospital, London 28
St George's Church, Southwark 143
St Ives, Cornwall 412–13
St John's College, Battersea 414
St John's College, Cambridge 201, 402
St Katherine (Seinte Katerine) 355, 404n.
St Margaret (Seinte Marherete) 320, 395, 400–1, 404–5
Saint-Simon, Claude Henri de Rouvroy, comte de 128
Salter's Hall, London 232
Sand, George (Mme Dudevant) 85, 372
Sandbach, Cheshire 27
Saturday Review 32, 178n., 329, 369, 371, 405, 408, 411, 422
Sawles Warde (Si Sciret paterfamilias) 409
Schlegel, Friedrich 288n.
Scholefield, Mr 61
Schultz, Albert 384
Scott, Alexander 84–6, 108, 127
Scott, Sir Walter 27, 55, 63n., 174, 298, 343, 355
Scott, William Bell 155, 192
Sedgwick, Adam 249, 256, 374
Seeley, Henry ('Harry') Govier 2, 249, 374–5, 383–4

Seeley, John Robert 37
Self, John 100
Selwyn, George Augustus 52, 54
Shakespeare, William 2, 4–5, 10, 19–22, 26, 31, 38, 40, 54, 66, 160, 172, 197–8, 206, 289, 300n., 310, 331n., 328
  Hamlet 198, 300n.
  Henry V 107
  Julius Caesar 198
  Love's Labour's Lost 156
  Othello 109
  Richard II 150
  Romeo and Juliet 220–1
  spelling of his name 19, 107–8
Shakespeare Society 358, 360, 364
Shakspere's England: see under Furnivall, Frederick James
Sharp, Thomas (ed.) *Digby Plays* 355
Shaw, George Bernard 14n., 16, 264
Sheepshanks' Gallery, South Kensington 152
Sheffield 176
Shelley, Mary 16, 29–30
Shelley, Percy Bysshe 16, 29–30
  Alastor 135
Shelley Society 2, 17, 21, 30, 365
Shippey, T. 280n., 284
Short, William 97
Shorter, Thomas 176, 228–9
Si Sciret paterfamilias (Sawles Warde) 409
Sidney Sussex College, Cambridge 249
Sigmond, G. G. 67
'Simeon Manuscript' 334–5, 341, 398–9
Simon of Ghent, Bishop of Salisbury 410
Sir Degrevant 356, 357n.
Sir Gawain and the Green Knight 12, 343, 416
Sisam, Kenneth 345
Skeat, Walter William 1, 4n., 6, 7 289, 296n., 324, 337–8, 338, 345n., 349, 350n., 376–8, 393, 396–7, 402, 409, 419, 421, 423; *see also* Piers Plowman; William of Palerne
Slade, W. 248n.
Slaney, Robert Aglionby 133, 165
Slough, Berks. 40
Smith, George 152
Smith, Joshua Toulmin, *English Gilds* (with Lucy Toulmin Smith) 62
Smith, Lucy Toulmin 3, 62, 352n.
Smith, Teena Rochfort 11

Snelgrove, Arthur 3
Socialism 83n., 93–5, 98, 103, 137; *see also* Christian socialism
Society of Biblical Archaeology 290
Society of Painters in Watercolours 49
Society for Promoting the Employment of Women 328
Society for Promoting Working Men's Associations 104, 106, 111
Somerset House 57, 82, 275n.
Somerville, Mary 292n.
Somner, William, *Dictionarium Saxonico-Latino-Anglicum* 293, 295
Sophocles 198
Southampton 29, 71n., 158, 378
South English Legendary 334
Southey, Robert:
  Life of Nelson 109
  (ed.) Malory, *Morte D'Arthur* 320
South London Working Men's College 263
Southwark 143
Spalding, William, *History of English Literature* 21, 199, 200, 281, 295
Spearman, Lady Maria Louisa 129
Spencer, Herbert 249, 261–2, 264
  Education: Intellectual, Moral, and Physical 262
  Principles of Psychology, 262
  Synthetic Philosophy 262
Spenser, Edmund 108, 116, 305
Spring Rice, The Hon. Stephen 128n.
Standring, Samuel 178–9, 202, 217, 238
Stanley, Arthur Penrhyn 86
Stebbing, Henry 47n.
Steevens, George 346
Sterling, John 83, 134, 149n.
Sterry, Peter 255–6
Stevenson, Joseph 355n., 364n.
  (ed.) *Ayenbite of Inwyt* 367
Stevenson's Mathematical & Circulating Library, Cambridge 61, 70, 76
Stimulus amoris (Pricke of Love) 318
Stimulus conscientiae: see Prick of Conscience
Stokes, Whitley (ed.) *The Play of the Sacrament* 395, 416
Stowe, Harriet Beecher, *Uncle Tom's Cabin* 330
Stratmann, Franz Heinrich (Francis Henry) 299
  Middle English Dictionary 286n., 298–301

INDEX 481

(ed.) *The Owl and the Nightingale*, 299, 300n.
(ed.) *The Tragicall Historie of Hamlet, Prince of Denmark* 300n.
Strickland, Miss 292n.
Stuart, Gilbert 330
Stubbs, William 343, 419
Sully, Charles 104
'Sunday Beer Act' 205
Sunday League 211, 213n., 214, 216, 220, 364
Sunday Trading Bill 211
Surbiton, Surrey 320
Surtees Society 355, 364n., 365
Sutton, John, medical friend of G. F. Furnivall 46n.
Sutton, William 238, 267–8
Swanswick, Somerset 287n.
Swanwick, Anna 292n.
Sweet, Henry 6, 194, 278, 282–3, 288, 290, 292, 294, 329, 397, 398n., 402, 407–8, 421–2, 424
  'Dr. R. Morris and Dr. Weymouth' 420–1
  'On Early English Pronunciation, with Especial Reference to Chaucer' 397–8
  Sweet's Anglo-Saxon Primer 6
  Sweet's Anglo-Saxon Reader 6, 294
Swinburne, Algernon 9, 312
Sydenham, Kent 131n., 132n.

T

Tait, Archibald Campbell, Archbishop of Canterbury 419
Tansley, George 202, 205n., 206, 223, 241, 307, 329–30
Tarrant Kaines, Dorset 410
Taylor, Isaac 34
Taylor, Thomas 329
Tennyson, Alfred 9, 22, 74–5, 116, 134, 155–8, 200, 202, 206, 227n., 260, 331, 394
  Idylls of the King 174, 202, 378, 383
  In Memoriam 155, 256, 259, 330
  'Morte d'Arthur' 260, 377, 380, 426
  'Sir Galahad' 379
  'The Epic' 378
  'The Lady of Shalott' 379
  The Princess 155–9, 256–7, 266, 268, 378

Thackeray, William 150
Thalberg, Sigismond 86
Thirlwall, John Connop, Bishop of St David's 73n., 75, 274, 287, 303
Thompson, George 120, 122
Thoms, William, J. 360n.
Thorpe, Benjamin 293, 347, 355n.
  A Grammar of the Anglo-Saxon Tongue 293n.
  Analecta Anglo-Saxonica 294–5
Thorvaldsen, Bertel 131, 132n.
Thynne, Francis, *Emblemes and Epigrames* 28
Tiepolo, Giovanni Battista 152–3
(The) Times 329
Tintoretto, Jacopo (Tintorett) 197
Todd, James Henthorn, *Three Treatises* 317
Tolkien, John Ronald Reuel 296, 415
Toller, Thomas Northcote 297–8
Toronto, University of 298
Torrent of Portyngale 317
Towneley Plays 352, 364n., 365
Tozer, John 64
Tracts by Christian Socialists 101n., 111
Tracts for the Times 111
Trades Associations 104 (see also under Furnivall, Frederick James)
Trench, Richard Chenevix, Dean of Westminster, Archbishop of Dublin 71, 74–5, 128, 134, 136, 155n., 172, 274, 291, 303–9, 310n., 311n., 315, 319, 326
  A Select Glossary of English Words 155n., 303, 310n.
  English Past and Present 303
  'On Some Deficiencies in Our English Dictionaries' 303–6, 308, 316n.
  On the Study of Words 106n., 155n.
Trevelyan, George Macaulay 171n.
Trevelyan, Lady Pauline 147n., 180n., 182n., 184n., 185n.
Trevisa, John (trans.), *Polychronicon* 316
Trinity College, Cambridge 42, 65n., 75, 173, 275n., 287, 303, 321n., 340, 364, 387
Trinity College, Dublin 66n., 395
Trinity Hall, Cambridge 58, 60–1, 62n., 63n., 65, 67, 75, 134, 153, 367, 393
Trinity House Corporation 114, 117, 118n., 119n., 122–4, 126
Tristram 379
Troubridge, Mrs. 97

Trübner, Nicholas, publisher 4, 300n., 311–14, 328, 384n., 385, 387
Tuck, Raphael, and Sons Ltd 26n.
Tunbridge Wells, Kent 142n., 185, 194n., 216n., 218
Turner, Joseph Mallord William 50, 127, 131n., 138–9, 148, 151–3, 155, 181, 191, 222
Turnham Green, Middlesex 36
Tyrwhitt, Thomas (ed.) *Canterbury Tales* 298, 320, 344n., 419

U

University College, London (UCL) 5, 8 17, 36, 38, 40–6, 48–50, 56, 78, 82, 84n., 127–9, 131–3, 178n., 229, 274–5, 278, 288, 385, 396, 397n.
  school 49, 277

V

Vasari, Giorgio, *Lives of the Painters* 151
'Vercelli Manuscript' 354
Vernon, Edward Johnston 294
Vernon family 430–2
'Vernon Manuscript' 334–5, 341, 398–9
Vevey, Switzerland 183n.
Victoria, Queen 10, 21, 40, 87, 122, 124–5, 131, 198, 243, 256, 328
Victoria and Albert Museum 152n.
Victoria Press 328
Vienna 99, 312, 323n.
Villemarqué, Theodore Claude, Henri, vicomte Hersart de la 384
Virgil 35, 64, 68, 369n.
Visions of Tundale 317
Volunteer movement 224, 239–45, 268, 274, 306–7, 329, 370

W

Wace, *Roman de Brut* 347
Waddington, William of, *Le Manuel des pechiez* 321, 366, 373
Wade, Thomas 329
Wagner, Wilhelm 291–2
Walpole, Horace 352n.
Walsh, Charles Robert 100, 111, 166, 177
Walshe, Walter Hayle 43

Ward, Mary (Mrs Humphry Ward) 89n., 211, 262
  Robert Elsmere 177, 195n., 211n.
Warren, Samuel, *Ten Thousand A-Year* 66, 211
Wars of Europe (anon.) 66
Warton, Thomas, *History of English Poetry* 317, 322, 350n., 390
Waterford 333n.
Waterhouse, Charles James 25
Waterhouse, Sir Herbert Furnivall 34
Watson, John 25
Watts, George Frederic 150
Watts, Thomas 128, 304, 315n., 331n.
Way, Albert 32n., 356, 359n., 360–1, 393, 427, 430–3
  (ed.) *Promptorium Parvulorum* 360
Wedgwood, Frances 145, 148, 151
Wedgwood, Hensleigh 108, 151, 274, 276–7, 284, 285n., 286n., 302, 309, 315n., 324–5, 351n., 353, 380, 384
  Etymological Dictionary 108n., 200n., 277, 279, 314n.
Wedgwood family 87, 128–9, 132n., 134–5, 138, 144, 149n., 274
Wellington, Duke of 16, 49, 65, 90, 240
Welsh Manuscripts Society 356
Wenzel, Siegfried 280n.
West, Benjamin 53
Westcott, Brooke Foss 136
Westlake, John 178n., 224
Westminster Review 68, 262
Wethersfield, Essex 60n.
Weymouth, Richard Francis 302n., 319, 395–402, 404, 414, 416, 419–22
  Answers to Questions on the English Language 420
  'Bishop Grosseteste's "Castle of Love"' 302n., 398–9
  'Castel off Loue Chasteau d'amour or Carmen de Creatione Mundi' 398, 400–1
  'Notes on the Roxburghe Club Morte Arthur' 396
  On Early English Pronunciation 397, 420–2
Wharncliffe, Lord 49n.
Wheatley, Henry B 3, 304, 315n., 360–1, 364, 390n., 393, 422–4
  (ed.) *Peter Levin's* Manipulus Vocabulorum 360
  'The Early English Text Society and F. J. Furnivall' 422–4

INDEX

Whewell, William 275n., 276, 282n., 302
Whiston, Robert 37n.
White, Miss 292n.
Whitechapel, London, St Mark's 176
Whitelock, Dorothy 6
Whittington Club 105–6, 128
Whytehead, Thomas 54
William the Conqueror 27–8
Willis family 31
Wimbledon, London 212
Winchester, Hants. 372
Winchester Diocesan Training School 106n., 303
Windsor, Berks. 25n., 26, 30n., 31–2, 40, 52, 54, 80, 122, 123n., 125, 256n., 427–9
Windus, William Lindsay 148
Winnington Hall, Cheshire 180
Wiseman, Nicholas (Cardinal Archbishop of Westminster) 142–3
Wittich, Wilhelm 48, 60
  A German Grammar 48n.
Wolverhampton Working Men's College 232–3
women's education 155–60, 175n.
Wood, Sarah 417n.
Woodwardian Museum, Cambridge 249, 374
Woodworth, Arthur 94
Wooler, Northumberland 266
Woolner, Thomas 147n., 231
Worde, Wynkyn de 318n., 319n., 390
Wordsworth, William 16, 107, 330
Working Men's College, London 1, 16, 92, 104, 140, *et passim*
  admissions and fees 172–3, 230
  college dances 228–38
  disagreements over refreshments 204–7
  evening classes 172
  foundation 96, 99, 164, 169–76, 187
  governance 213–73
  premises 176, 204, 205n., 273
  singing classes 172, 222, 230
  social life 202, 207–10, 217, 222
  student prizes 222
  students' art-work 222
  students' occupations 208
  Sunday observance and excursions 28, 204–5, 208–21, 228, 234, 237, 248–9
  teaching 21, 177–8, 180, 186, 196, 199–21, 210, *et passim*
  women's classes 204
  see also Furnivall, Frederick James; Maurice, Frederick Denison; *and other individuals*; Genesis and geology; Volunteer movement
Working Men's Rowing Club 274
Working Tailors' Association 101, 170, 172, 378
Working Women's College 233n.
Worsfold, representative of the Woodcutters' Association 113–14
Wren, Christopher 53
Wright, Joseph, *English Dialect Dictionary* 289
Wright, Thomas 7n., 320, 353, 356–8, 364, 366, 376n.
  Political Poems and Songs 318n.
  (ed.) *Reliquiae antiquae* (with J. O. Halliwell) 334, 358n.
  (ed.) *The Book of the Knight of La Tour-Landry* 364n.
  (ed.) *The Vision and Creed of Piers Plowman* 318n.
Wright, William Aldis 387, 393
Württemburg 134
Wycliffite Bible translations 342, 349
Wyclif Society 2–5, 11, 365
Wyclif's Wicket 317
Wyntoun, Andrew, *Chronicle* 318

X

Xenophon, *Hellenica* 68

Y

Yates, Joseph Brooks 357
Yonge, Charlotte M. 9, 308, 330
York Plays 352

Z

Zupitza, Julius 323n.